**PEARSON**
ALWAYS LEARNING

Dr. Ritsuko Hirai

# First Year Japanese

Fifth Edition

Cover image of a beautiful Japanese garden in Kyoto (Rakusui Teien) courtesy of Ritsuko Hirai.

Pearson Learning Solutions, 501 Boylston Street, Suite 900, Boston, MA 02116
A Pearson Education Company
www.pearsoned.com

Printed in the United States of America

3 4 5 6 7 8 9 10 V0CR 17 16 15

000200010271909933

EEB/KD

ISBN 10: 1-269-92551-2
ISBN 13: 978-1-269-92551-8

From the Author:

This is a story of Monica, a college student from Pasadena, studying Japanese in Kyoto, Japan. As chapters progress, you will experience daily life with her: shopping, ordering food at restaurants, finding an apartment, cooking with friends, going out for movies and to Kabuki theatres, flower-viewing, writing letters and diary entries to the family, and so much more. I hope you will enjoy learning the Japanese language and culture with Monica.

I am grateful to my students who have been a source of my inspiration and who continue to work with me to improve my teaching. Many thanks go to my illustrator, Emily Solichin, for her excellent artwork. She patiently worked with me to draw the most accurate illustrations that depict varieties of human emotions and actions, which to me was very important to elucidate the meaning of words and concepts in the textbook. It was not an easy task and was a painstaking process, but thanks to her patience, she drew the illustrations most suitable to each situation in each chapter. Most of illustrations in the textbook are her work with a few exceptions: I retained some of my original illustrations from previous editions and some are the work by Steve Robbins, my former student. I also thank many voice actors and actresses who helped in the CD creation process. Lastly but not least, I am grateful to my family who has been always supportive and helped me in any way I needed.

To the Instructors:

The textbook, workbook, and CDs—all three elements complement each other. Along with the grammar lessons presented in the textbook—as well as many activities and exercises—the workbook enhances the newly learned material for students, and the audio CDs recreate situations for students to experience the expressions presented in the textbook. The Workbook is mainly designed for students to master the reading and writing of Hiragana, Katakana, and Kanji. Many exercises are contained in the workbook in the spirit of decreasing the burden for teachers to make extra practice handouts. There are two sets of audio CDs that are used with the textbook: the Dialogue and Vocabulary, and Student CDs. The first set is for the dialogue and vocabulary sections of each chapter; and the Student CD is for "Dictation and Conversation" (called "Dict-A-Conversation") where students listen and verbally perform required tasks, and also write down answers. They can either be done in the classroom or as homework, or both. The Instructor's Manual contains the written narratives of the Student CDs, so that if you decide to give a copy of the Dict-A-Conversation narrative, you may do so for your students to check and learn what they practiced aurally/orally. The manual also includes ideas of activities teachers can use in classroom.

## ABOUT THE AUTHOR

Dr. Hirai has been teaching Japanese language and literature at several universities and colleges over the past two decades. During that period she has been honored several times for teaching excellence, including winning the 2003 Teacher's Award at the California Institute of Technology. In addition to teaching at Caltech, Dr. Hirai is a professor of Japanese at Pasadena City College where she heads the Japanese section, which teaches Japanese to nearly 1000 students annually. The teaching methods that she has developed during her years of teaching form the foundation of this textbook.
Dr. Hirai received her Ph.D. in Comparative Literature at the University of Southern California.

This textbook is a life story of Monica, a Pasadena girl who goes to Kyoto, Japan, and studies Japanese. Each chapter is her learning experiences and students can identify themselves with her.

# CHARACTERS INTRODUCTION:

**MIWA:** girl student who also became Monica's friend. Her major is Physics.

**AIKO:** girl student who became close friends with Monica. They cooked and went shopping together.

**SENSEI** (professor): she is a professor at Kyoto University where Monica studies. She often gives her guidance.

**A mysterious boy:** boy who gave Monica an umbrella at the train station on a rainy day.

**KEN:** boy student in the same college, and a good friend of Monica.

**TETSUYA:** boy student in Monica's class. He invited her for Kabuki-viewing.

**MONICA:** the main character of the textbook story. She is from California, studying Japanese in Kyoto, Japan, as a college student.

# TABLE OF CONTENTS

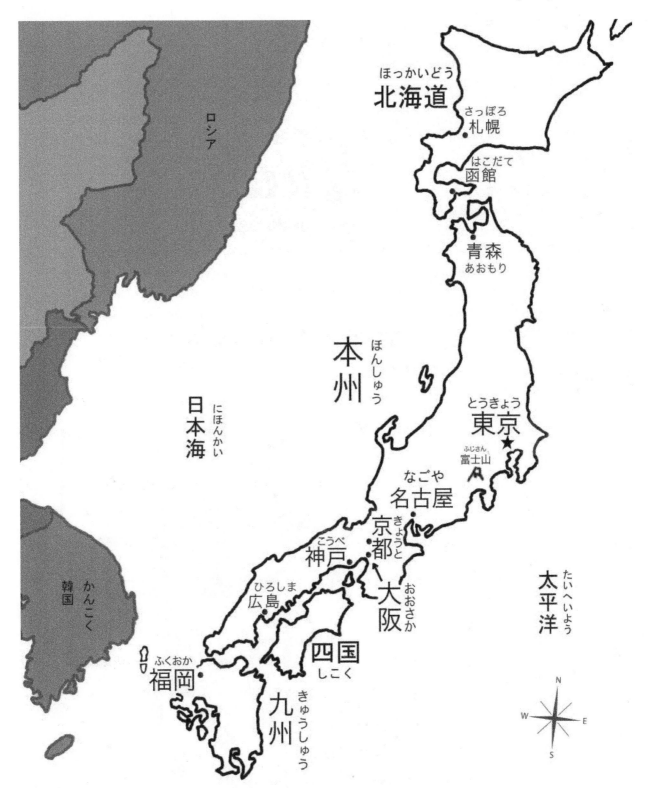

# The Origin of Hiragana and Katakana

Both hiragana and katakana are derived from Kanji (Chinese characters), which came from China with Buddhist sutras during the sixth century. Through them, portions of Chinese characters were taken to shape katakana and entire characters were used to inspire hiragana. During the Heian period (8th Century to 12th Century when Kyoto was the capital), male intellectuals, including Buddhist monks and aristocrats, used katakana to decipher books and documents written in Chinese. They inscribed "yomigana" or "furigana" next to Chinese characters. Women primarily used hiragana to write personal matters including diaries and waka-poems. That being said, not all hiragana and katakana are derived from the same Chinese characters. Please see the charts that show their origins. The hiragana "a" あ came from 安, while katakana "a" ア came from 阿. While katakana "i" イ was taken from the left hand side of the kanji 伊, hiragana い was made from the entire image of a different kanji 以. However, most kana share the same origins. If you look at hiragana "ka" and katakana "ka," their similarities are obvious: while katakana カ derived from the left portion of the kanji 加, hiragana か shows the image of the same kanji as a whole.

阿 →        →ア
安 →        →あ

伊 →        →イ
以 →        →い

宇 →        →ウ
　　　　　　う

加 →        →カ
　　　　　　か

## Hiragana & Katakana Chart (Horizontal)

### **Hiragana**

1. 46 Basic Hiragana Syllables

| a<br>あ | i<br>い | u<br>う | e<br>え | o<br>お |
|---|---|---|---|---|
| ka<br>か | ki<br>き | ku<br>く | ke<br>け | ko<br>こ |
| sa<br>さ | *shi<br>し | su<br>す | se<br>せ | so<br>そ |
| ta<br>た | *chi<br>ち | *tsu<br>つ | te<br>て | to<br>と |
| na<br>な | ni<br>に | nu<br>ぬ | ne<br>ね | no<br>の |
| ha<br>は | hi<br>ひ | *fu<br>ふ | he<br>へ | ho<br>ほ |
| ma<br>ま | mi<br>み | mu<br>む | me<br>め | mo<br>も |
| ya<br>や |  | yu<br>ゆ |  | yo<br>よ |
| ra<br>ら | ri<br>り | ru<br>る | re<br>れ | ro<br>ろ |
| wa<br>わ |  |  |  | **wo<br>を |
| n<br>ん |  |  |  |  |

*The syllables し、ち、つ、and ふ are Romanized as "shi, chi, tsu, and fu" to closely resemble English pronunciation.  **を is sometimes pronounced as "wo."

2. Hiragana with "two dots" (voiced sounds) and "small circle" (p-sounds)

| ga<br>が | gi<br>ぎ | gu<br>ぐ | ge<br>げ | go<br>ご |
|---|---|---|---|---|
| za<br>ざ | ji<br>じ | zu<br>ず | ze<br>ぜ | zo<br>ぞ |
| da<br>だ | *ji<br>ぢ | *zu<br>づ | de<br>で | do<br>ど |
| ba<br>ば | bi<br>び | bu<br>ぶ | be<br>べ | bo<br>ぼ |

| pa<br>ぱ | pi<br>ぴ | pu<br>ぷ | pe<br>ぺ | po<br>ぽ |
|---|---|---|---|---|

*ぢ ji and づ zu are pronounced the same as じ ji and ず zu, respectively, but they have limited use.

3. Hiragana for contraction sounds.

Small や、ゆ and よ follow after letters in the second column (in the line of 'i'-vowel in the hiragana chart, except い). They represent the sounds "kya, kyu, kyo," "sha, shu, sho," and the like. They are considered single syllables.

| kya きゃ | kyu きゅ | kyo きょ |
|---|---|---|
| sha しゃ | shu しゅ | sho しょ |
| cha ちゃ | chu ちゅ | cho ちょ |
| nya にゃ | nyu にゅ | nyo にょ |
| hya ひゃ | hyu ひゅ | hyo ひょ |
| mya みゃ | myu みゅ | myo みょ |
| rya りゃ | ryu りゅ | ryo りょ |

| gya ぎゃ | gyu ぎゅ | gyo ぎょ |
|---|---|---|
| jya じゃ | jyu じゅ | jyo じょ |

| bya びゃ | byu びゅ | byo びょ |
|---|---|---|
| pya ぴゃ | pyu ぴゅ | pyo ぴょ |

## _Katakana_
1. Basic 46 Katakana Syllables

| a ア | i イ | u ウ | e エ | o オ |
|---|---|---|---|---|
| ka カ | ki キ | ku ク | ke ケ | ko コ |
| sa サ | *shi シ | su ス | se セ | so ソ |
| ta タ | *chi チ | *tsu ツ | te テ | to ト |
| na ナ | ni ニ | nu ヌ | ne ネ | no ノ |
| ha ハ | hi ヒ | *fu フ | he ヘ | ho ホ |
| ma マ | mi ミ | mu ム | me メ | mo モ |
| ya ヤ | | yu ユ | | yo ヨ |
| ra ラ | ri リ | ru ル | re レ | ro ロ |
| wa ワ | | | | **wo ヲ |
| n ン | | | | |

2. Katakana with "two dots" (voiced sounds) and "small circle" (p-sounds)

| ga ガ | gi ギ | gu グ | ge ゲ | go ゴ |
|---|---|---|---|---|
| za ザ | ji ジ | zu ズ | ze ゼ | zo ゾ |
| da ダ | *ji ヂ | *zu ヅ | de デ | do ド |
| ba バ | bi ビ | bu ブ | be ベ | bo ボ |

| pa パ | pi ピ | pu プ | pe ペ | po ポ |
|---|---|---|---|---|

*ヂ ji and ヅ zu are pronounced the same as ジ ji and ズ zu, respectively, but they have limited use.

3. Katakana for contracted sounds.

| kya キャ | kyu キュ | kyo キョ |
|---|---|---|
| sha シャ | shu シュ | sho ショ |
| cha チャ | chu チュ | cho チョ |
| nya ニャ | nyu ニュ | nyo ニョ |
| hya ヒャ | hyu ヒュ | hyo ヒョ |
| mya ミャ | myu ミュ | myo ミョ |
| rya リャ | ryu リュ | ryo リョ |

| gya ギャ | gyu ギュ | gyo ギョ |
|---|---|---|
| jya ジャ | jyu ジュ | jyo ジョ |

| bya ビャ | byu ビュ | byo ビョ |
|---|---|---|
| pya ピャ | pyu ピュ | pyo ピョ |

# Kanji List

*Kanji from chapter 1 to 3D should be introduced after Chapter 3D when hiragana and katakana are mastered.  At the completion of Chapter 3, one or two weeks will be spent to introduce kanji from the first three chapters (Chapters 1 ~ 3) with vocabulary review.

*Katakana is being introduced after Chapters 3B.

*Beginning from chapter 4A, the kanji listed below shall be learned with each corresponding chapter.

## Kanji List for Japanese 1　日本語 1 の漢字リスト

| Chapters | Introduced Kanji |
| --- | --- |
| | Introduction of hiragana |
| Chapter 1 | 一、二、三、四、五、六、七、八、九、十、月、日、本，円 |
| Chapter 2A | 大、学、生、何、白、私、犬 |
| Chapter 2B | 年、語、田、山、来 |
| Chapter 3B | 百、小、中、 |
| | Introduction of katakana |
| Chapter 3C | 千、万、水、 女、色、入 |
| Chapter 3D | Ch3D has no kanji. |
| | Introduction of kanji (Chapters 1 ~ 3C) |
| Chapter 4A | 先、人、今、上、下 |
| Chapter 4B | 回、分、言、口、同 |
| Chapter 4C | 食、気、好、方、校 |
| Chapter 4D | 父、母、近、子、兄、妹、目 |
| Chapter 4E | 毎、時、半、行、知 |

## Kanji List for Japanese 2　　日本語 2 の漢字リスト

| Chapters | Introduced Kanji |
| --- | --- |
| Chapter 5 | 土、曜、午、前、後、古、川、会、男、火、木、金 |
| Chapter 6A | 家、遠、新、車、自 |
| Chapter 6B | 見、歩、買、広、明、南、東、朝、光、西、北 |
| Chapter 6C | 井、多、寺、有、名、持、内、外、少 |
| Chapter 6D | 池、魚、英、苦、手、赤、黒、才、若、足 |
| Chapter 7 | 住、和、洋、甘、間、事、戸、所 |
| Chapter 8 | 力、薬、虫、助、強、楽 |
| Chapter 9ABC | 雨、困、駅、帰、記、晴、返、海 |

| Chapter 10A | 玉、肉、米、友 |
|---|---|
| Chapter 10B | 物、牛、初、辛 |

## Kanji List for Japanese 3 　　日本語 3 の漢字リスト

| Chapter 10C | 切、油、煮、止、炊、作 |
|---|---|
| Chapter 10D has no kanji. | |
| Chapter 10E | 文、毛、茶、変、晩、飲、石、度 |
| Chapter 11A | 道、通、信、号、左、右、曲 |
| Chapter 11B | 合、安、高、夜、社 |
| Chapter 11C | 雪、立、札、押、用 |
| Chapter 11D | 書、昨、美、暗、思、出、神、秘、音、読 |
| Chapter 12 | 弟、姉、背、丈、太、青、黄、着 |
| Chapter 13 | 屋、聞、話、化、昔、侍 |
| Chapter 14 | 花、動、鼻、低、怒、天、耳、形、週、番 |

Continue to <u>Beyond the First Year Japanese.</u>

Chapter Organization:  Expressions in Each Chapter

Introduction:  Hiragana  ひらがな
Ch.1  Greetings  あいさつ
    1.  Various greetings
    2.  Vocabulary for the twelve months  （<ruby>一月<rt>いちがつ</rt></ruby>〜<ruby>十二月<rt>じゅうにがつ</rt></ruby>）
    3.  Adjectives (the affirmative non-past tense) for weather （あつい、さむい、
       すずしい、あたたかい）
    4.  Particle "no" modifying a noun  （にほん　の　ふゆ）
    5.  The A is B pattern  （A は B です）
    6.  Sentence-Final Particles "ne" and "yo"  （ね、よ）
    7.  Sentence-Final Particle "ka"  （か）
    8.  Additional Grammar on sentence ending with a noun: Negative （soo jya
       arimasen そうじゃありません), Past tense affirmative （そうでした soo deshita),
       and Past tense negative （そうじゃありませんでした soo jya arimasen deshita)

Ch.2  Asking simple questions  たずねる
   2A.  Asking for directions, the way
    1.  Asking for location with the Interrogative Pronoun "doko" (where)
       （〜は、どこですか。）
    2.  Showing location with the Demonstrative Pronouns: "koko," "soko,"
       "asoko," and "doko."  （ここ、そこ、あそこ、どこ）
    3.  Asking what something is, using the Interrogative Pronoun "nan" (what)
       （なんですか。) or "nani" (what)
    4.  Demonstrative Pronouns showing things:  "kore," "sore," "are," and "dore."
       （これ、それ、あれ、どれ）
    5.  Possessive case of Demonstrative Pronouns:  "kono," "sono," "ano," and
       "dono."  （この、その、あの、どの）
    6.  Asking which one it is, using the Interrogative Pronoun "dore" (which one)
       （どれですか。）
    7.  Particle "mo" to mean "also"  （も）
    8.  Suggestion/offer form "~mashoo ka"  （〜ましょうか。）

   2B.  Simple introduction of yourself  アメリカから　きました。
    1.  Motion verbs (go いきます come きます, return かえります) and particle "e へ"
    2.  Action verbs (all the actions except motion verbs and static verbs [verb of
       existence]) and particle "de で" to show where the action takes place.
    3.  Particle "wo を" to mark a direct object and SOV pattern （おちゃをのみます。）
    4.  Asking who it is, using the Interrogative Pronoun "dare だれ" (who) （だれです
       か。）
    5.  Japanese numerals; the counter for school years:  ~nensei （〜ねんせい）
    6.  Particle "kara" (from)  （〜から）
    7.  Particle "made" (till, up to, as far as)  （〜まで）
    8.  Particle "ga" precedes the statement that expresses "personal" opinions/ideas.
       （が for expressing "personal" ideas） （にほんごが　じょうずですね）

9. Copula Noun (or "Na" Adjective) （じょうず）
10. Particle "de" to show "means" and "instruments" (by means of)
   （おはしで　たべます）

2C. Thank you and Good-by
1. Particle "wa は" and "ga が" with Interrogative Pronouns.
2. Particle "wa は" to show the old information and "ga が" to show the new information.
3. Telephone numbers　でんわばんごう

Ch.3　Ordering food & drinks, and shopping at a store ちゅうもんする／かいものをする
3A. Ordering at a coffee shop.　きっさてんで　ちゅうもんする
1. Expression of "I have decided on~" （～にします。）
2. Alternating interrogative: Is it A or B? （A ですか、B ですか。）
3. Particle "to と" to connect two nouns　（A　と　B）
4. Please give me this one, too.（これも　ください。）

Read the Japanese story: "An Old Man with a Lump on the Cheek"

3B. Ordering at McDonald's マクドナルドで　ちゅうもんします。
1. Numbers and numeral counters　（ひとつ～とお）
2. Japanese currency　（～えん）
3. Simple request form: "Please give me ~"(~ をください，おねがいします)
4. Honorific Prefix "o" & "go"　（おのみもの、ごちゅうもん）
5. Particle "de" to end choices （これで　いいです）
6. Verb "become ~"　（～に　なります）

Read the Japanese story: "Rabbit in the Moon"

Introduction to Katakana

3C. How to shop at a department store　デパートで　かいものをします。
1. Interrogative Pronoun "don'na" (what kind of) (どんな)
2. Japanese numeral classifiers (counters)
3. Verb of existence for the inanimate: "arimasu"（あります）and the animate: "imasu" (います)
4. Particle "ni に" to show the location of existence　（～に［あります］）
5. Particle "ni に" to show the destination of movement　（～に［いれます］）
6. Location words "kochira こちら, "sochira そちら," "achira あちら," "dochira どちら"
7. I want it (～が　ほしいです).

3D. Ordering at a restaurant.　ちゅうもんする
1. Honorific verb "nasaimasu"　（なんに　なさいますか。）
2. "sama" addressing someone politely.（たなかさま）
3. Particle "dake" to mean "only"（だけ）

Introduction to Kanji from Chapter 1 through Chapter 3

Ch. 4   At a campus cafeteria: conversation with another student

    4A. Inviting others to join　さそう

      1.  Invitation/suggestion form: ~masen ka?　（～ませんか。）

      2.  Numeral classifier for counting people: ~nin　（～にん）

      3.  Particle "de" to indicate location of "actions":　（～で + Verb of Actions）

      4.  Particle "to と" to mean "(together) with"　（someone + と）

      5.  Particle "no の" or "n ん" to enhance a sense of reasoning, explanation, inquiry, or surprise: ~n desu (ka)　（いいんですか。）

      6.  Question word "itsu いつ": When?

      7.   Days of the Week: "yoobi ようび"

Sing a Japanese song: "Under a Big Chestnut Tree"　おおきな くりの きのしたで

    4B. Introducing yourself　はじめまして、どうぞよろしく。

      1.  Particle "to と" to quote: "~to iimasu" (It's said ~ぼくは てつやといいます)

      2.  "…tte":  A quotation (What is it that is called ~?…って　なんですか。)

      3.  Particle "to と" indicating similarities and differences:  "~ to onaji" (the same as ~)　（あいこさんと　おなじですね。）

      4.  Particle "koso こそ" for emphasis　（こちらこそ、どうぞよろしく。）

      5.  Negative form of Adjectives and Past tense affirmative and negative.
        "-ku arimasen" (むずかしく　ありません。It is not difficult.)
        "-katta" (むずかしかったです。It was difficult.)
        "-ku arimasen deshita" (むずかしくありませんでした。It was not difficult.)

      6.  "~ no koto のこと" It's about ~.

    4C. Comparison:　にほんの　たべもの　の　ほうが　すきなんです。

      1.  I like A better than B:  A yori B no hoo ga, suki desu.

      2.  Completion form: "-mashita" (もうたべましたか。Have you eaten already?)

      3.  Noun/Copula noun + "na n desu" demonstrating one's attempt to explain something ～なんです。

      4.  Superlative:  A to B to C (no naka) de, A ga ichiban suki desu.
        （～のなか）で、～が　いちばん　すきです。

    4D. Introducing family and hometown　かぞくとじぶんのまちのしょうかい

      1.  Vocabulary for family members and their ages (~ sai さい).

      2.  Conjunctive Particle "kara から" showing reason: （クラスがありますから、しつれいします。Because I have class, I'll excuse myself.)

      3.  Sentence-final Particle "naa～なあ" showing "exclamation" or "personal sentiment"　（犬はいいなあ、しゅくだいがないから。Oh, how envious I am for dogs, since they have no homework.)

      4.  Particle "shika ~nai しか~ない (only)" to show negativity.
        （一ドルしかない。I have only one dollar.)

6D. There is a carp! こい　が　いる
   1. Particle "no" that replaces a noun （あかいの a red one、ちいさいの a small one）
   2. Polite request form "Please do~": "te kudasai" （〜てください。）
   3. Particle "ni に that marks an indirect object （わたしに　おしえてください。）

Ch. 7 Monica's Dormitory life りょうのせいかつ：なんじごろ　おきるの？
   1. Interrogative Pronoun "itsu" (when?)　（いつ？）
   2. Plain form Verbs: Dictionary forms　（なんじに　おきる？）
   3. Conjunctive Particles "node ので" & "kara から" showing reason
         （ねぼうなので〜、にんきがあるから〜）
   4. The expression "become ~": "Noun ni naru に なる"　（じょうずに　なる）
   5. The expression "become ~": "Adj-ku naru く なる"　（あかく　なる）
   6. Sentence Final Particle "no の" to add softness.（おきるの？）
   7. Between & While (aida あいだ & aida ni あいだに)

Ch. 8 Ouch!　あっ、いたい！
   1. Plain/casual form
   2. Reading and writing a diary in plain form Japanese.
   3. Sentence Final Particle "kana かな" to express speaker's conjecture (I wonder).

Ch. 9 At the Station　えきで
   9A. It's raining! あめだわ！
      1. Verbs of "giving" and "receiving": "ageru" （あげる、もらう、くれる）
      2. Male and Female Speech: Sentence Final Particle "wa わ" used by female
         speakers and "zo ぞ" by male speakers in casual situations.
      3. Sentence Final Particle "na (a) な（あ）" to express sentiment.
      4. Casual form of "desu" (copula verb) after a noun: "da だ" and its past tense,
         "datta だった"（ほんとうだ。It's true.）

   9B. It's all right!　だいじょうぶよ。
      1. Te-form Verb + "shimau" demonstrating "completion" （〜て　しまう）
         (行ってしまった。He's gone afar.　かぜをひいてしまった。I've caught a cold.)
         Also the contracted sound of てしまう：ちゃった　じゃった
      2. Verb + "koto こと" changing the verb into a noun.
         (食べることがすきです。I like to eat.)
      3. "Ta" form + koto ga aru たことがある to show past experience.
         (日本に行ったことがあります。I have been to Japan.)
      4. Plain form negative predicate after nouns "jya nai じゃない"
         (かれじゃない。It's not him.)
      5. A tag question （"~ jya nai じゃない? " [Isn't it?]）
         (それって、うそじゃない？ Isn't it a lie?)
      6. Repetition: そうそう、だめだめ、まあまあ、どうもどうも、おやおや、etc.

   9C. Writing a diary　にっきを　かく。
      1. Verb + "tsumori (desu/da)" to show one's intention

（かさを　かえすつもりだ。I intend to return the umbrella.）

2. Verb + "hazu (desu/da)" to show one's expectation
（あめに　ぬれたはずだ。He must have gotten wet in the rain.）

3. Sentence + "daroo ka" as a speaker's conjecture (I wonder ~?)
（できるだろうか。I wonder if I can.）

4. Verb (dict.) + "koto ga dekiru" to show one's ability/potentiality:
（かえすことが　できる I can return [it].）

Ch.10  Inviting a Friend ともだちを　さそう

10A. Why don't you come and see?  （来<sup>き</sup>てみてください。）

1. "Tai form" to show one's desire for actions: たべたい (I want to eat)、いきたい (I want to go), ねたい (I want to sleep).  Add "tai" to the "masu" form verb.

2. "Kamoshirenai" to show one's conjecture.
（できるかもしれない。I might be able to do it.）（雨かもしれない。It may rain.）

3. Particle "no の" that changes a verb into a noun. （そこへ行くのは大変<sup>たいへん</sup>です。It's hard to get there.）

4. Sentence Final Particle "no の" indicating explanation or an emotive emphasis
（いいの？）

5. "Noun + ga dekiru" to show ability  （りょうりが　できる I can cook. ）

6. Te-form verb + miru: try and see    （〜てみる）

7. Te-form verb showing reason
（まどが二<sup>ふた</sup>つもあって、とてもいい。It's nice to have two windows.。）

8. A mo B mo: both A and B, neither A nor B  （野菜<sup>やさい</sup>も肉<sup>にく</sup>もある/ない）
（I have both vegetables and meat/I have neither vegetables nor meat.）

10B. At a Market マーケットで

1. Simile "mitai"  （〜みたい: "It looks like~"（チョコレートみたい It looks like chocolate.みたい)

2. Onomatopoeia and mimesis  （ドロドロ muddy / thick, トロトロ melted ）

3. Adj. "ku" + suru (making things a certain state)  （あまくしてね。Please make it sweet. ）

10C. Recipe レシピ

1. Sequential action expressed by the Te-form Verb  （かえって　ねます I will go home and sleep. ）

2. How to do it: "masu" form verb + kata （たべかた，つくりかた）

10D. Too Spicy!  いただきま〜す！からすぎる！

1. Adj. [stem] + soo (desu): It looks/seems. （おいしそう looks delicious）

2. Adj. [stem] + sugiru: "exceeding"  （からすぎる too spicy）

3. Te-form Verb + aru: "things have been done for future use / for a future purpose"  （かいてある It's been written）

4. "Please don't do it.": request negative action: "~ nai de kudasai"

（からくしないで。Please don't make it spicy. いかないで Please don't go.）

5. "Without doing it" ～ ないで ＋ Main Clause. (あさごはんを食べないで、学校に来ました。I came to school without eating breakfast.)

10E. Composition さくぶん：A Recent Event さいきんのできごと

1. Comparative: Verb (dict.) yori Verb (dict.) hoo ga ～ （I prefer eating to sleeping. ねるより たべるほうが いい）

2. Ta-form Verb + ato de: After having done ～ （たべたあとで、おちゃをのみました。After I ate, I had tea.）

3. Adverbs connecting sentences and paragraphs（そして、はじめに、そこで、まず、それから、そのあと、さいごに、それに、とくに）

Ch.11 Flower-viewing with a Friend ともだちと はなみを する

11A. Asking for Directions みちをきく

1. Verb (dict.) + "to": Conditional. "If you do so…"（そうすると、～。）

2. Vocabulary for giving directions

11B. Meeting with a Friend まちあわせ

1. "After ～ing" （～てから）: Te-form Verb + "kara"
（ばんごはんを食べてからべんきょうします I'll study after eating supper.）

2. "～te morau" （～てもらう）to show receiving of a favor (in action)
（日本語を おしえて もらう）

3. Showing "purpose" in action: Verb (masu form) + Particle "ni" + "iku/kuru/kaeru" to show "purpose" of going/coming/returning（たべに いく [くる], [かえる]）

4. A style of question "n deshoo?" （～んでしょう？）asking for affirmation. Plain form + "n deshoo"? Isn't it right? (行くんでしょう？You're going, right?)

11C. Flower-viewing at night よざくらをみる

1. Expressing permission: Te-form Verb + mo + ii
（さわっても いい。You may touch it.）

2. Expressing "prohibition: Te-form Verb + (wa) ikenai
（さわっては いけない。）You should not touch it.）

3. Emphatic expression "kon'na ni": "this much" following the "ko-so-a-do" pattern こんなに、そんなに、あんなに、どんなに

11D. Writing a diary entry にっきに かく

1. Plain past tense: Ta-form of Nouns, Adjectives and Verbs
（ふしぎなかんじだった、いなかった、さくらがみえた）

2. Expressing "before that action": Verb (dict.) + "mae ni"
（さくらが ちるまえに、いきたい。I want to go before the season of cherry blossoms end.）

3. Particle "wo" + verbs of motion: covering the space taken by a motion
（こうえんのなかを あるいた。I walked through the park.）

4. Sentence + "toki": When S$_1$, S$_2$～.

（しろいさくらがみえたとき、そのことばを おもいだした When I saw white cherry blossoms, I remembered that word.）

5. Simile: "yoo ni" expressing likelihood

（ゆきのように うつくしかった。It was as beautiful as snow.）

Ch. 12    Looking for people ひとをさがす

1. Te-form Verb + "iru" for description of wearing clothing

（あおいズボンを はいている wearing blue pants）

2. Te-form Verb + "iru" to show on-going action

（きょろきょろしている looking around anxiously.）

3. Te-form Verb + "ageru" to show giving a favor

（みせてあげる。I will show it to you.）

4. Te-form Verb + "agetai" to mean "wanting to do that favor"

（みせてあげたい。I want to show it to you.）

5. "naru" to mean "become, " showing change from one stage to another.

（あかくなった。It turned red.）（いなくなった。He disappeared.）

6. "Aida ni": While ~, Sentence. (The event/action stated in the main clause takes place at a certain period during the time described in the "aida ni" phrase or clause)

（アイスクリームを買いに行っているあいだに、いなくなった。He disappeared <u>while</u> I was away buying an ice cream.）

Ch. 13 Writing a Letter てがみを かく: A Letter to My Teacher: 日本のえいが

1. "Soo + na" (Na-Adjective) expressing a speaker's subjective conjecture based on what s/he sees or how s/he feels. "It seems to be~"

（かなしそうな め sad-looking eyes）

2. Quotation Particle "to と" followed by verbs "yobu," "iu," etc.

(He called it a "samurai movie." 「ちゃんばらえいが」と よびました。「～」と いいました。）

3. "After ~": "Noun + no ato (de)" （しょくじのあと [で] after meal）

4. "No matter what": Te-form Verb + Particle "mo" meaning "even if,"

(Even if I have doubts, I won't state them. ぎもんがあっても くちにしません。）

5. "See/hear ~ ing": Verb + "no" Particle followed by the Verbs of five senses (see, hear, taste, smell, feel)： （食べるのを見ました。I saw her eat it. あるいているのを、みました。I saw him walking）

Ch. 14 Diary on Sketching:  Description of people じんぶつびょうしゃ

1. Expressing the speaker's idea (I think that…): Quotation Particle "to と" + "omou" （むずかしいと おもう。I think it is difficult.）

2. Expressing hearsay "I heard that ~" Quotation Particle "to と" + "kiku"

（そうすると きいた I heard that ~.）

3. "It looks like: Stem of Adj. + soo ni + mieru （うれしそうに みえる。S/he looks happy）

4. Easy to do: "masu"V + Aux. Adj. "yasui" （かきやすい easy to write）

5. Difficult to do: "masu"V + Aux. Adj. "nikui" （かきにくい difficult to write）

## Japanese Sounds and Writing System

There are three types of characters in Japanese: Hiragana, Katakana, and Kanji. The fist two are alphabets that represent sounds, while Kanji is Chinese characters, which not only express sounds but also express meanings. All three can appear in the sentence:

私は、今日、大きい　ハンバーガーを　食べました。

watashi wa, kyoo, ookii  hanbaagaa  wo  tabemashita.

(I ate a big hamburger today.)

In this sentence, the word "hamburger" is written in katakana, which is used for foreign words. Kanji is used for nouns and the stems of verbs and adjectives. Hiragana is the most basic alphabet. Children can express everything in hiragana, but gradually they learn and master about one thousand kanji by the end of the sixth grade. The average educated person in Japan learns about two thousand kanji throughout their education.

### *Hiragana*

1. 46 Basic Hiragana Syllables

There are forty-six basic hiragana syllables, which allow you to transcribe all of the Japanese sounds.

| a | i | u | e | o |
|---|---|---|---|---|
| あ | い | う | え | お |
| ka | ki | ku | ke | ko |
| か | き | く | け | こ |
| sa | *shi | su | se | so |
| さ | し | す | せ | そ |
| ta | *chi | *tsu | te | to |
| た | ち | つ | て | と |
| na | ni | nu | ne | no |
| な | に | ぬ | ね | の |
| ha | hi | *fu | he | ho |
| は | ひ | ふ | へ | ほ |
| ma | mi | mu | me | mo |
| ま | み | む | め | も |
| ya | | yu | | yo |
| や | | ゆ | | よ |
| ra | ri | ru | re | ro |
| ら | り | る | れ | ろ |
| wa | | | | **wo |
| わ | | | | を |
| n | | | | |
| ん | | | | |

*The syllables し、ち、つ、and ふ are Romanized as "shi, chi, tsu, and fu" to closely resemble English pronunciation. **を is sometimes pronounced as "wo."

2. Hiragana with "two dots" (voiced sounds) and "small circle" (p-sounds)

| ga が | gi ぎ | gu ぐ | ge げ | go ご |
|---|---|---|---|---|
| za ざ | ji じ | zu ず | ze ぜ | zo ぞ |
| da だ | *ji ぢ | *zu づ | de で | do ど |
| ba ば | bi び | bu ぶ | be べ | bo ぼ |

| pa ぱ | pi ぴ | pu ぶ | pe べ | po ぼ |
|---|---|---|---|---|

*ぢ ji and づ zu are pronounced the same as じ ji and ず zu, respectively, but they have limited use.

3. Hiragana for contraction sounds.

Small や、ゆ and よ follow after letters in the second column (in the line of 'i'-vowel in the hiragana chart, except い). They represent the sounds "kya, kyu, kyo," "sha, shu, sho," and the like. They are considered single syllables.

| kya きゃ | kyu きゅ | kyo きょ |
|---|---|---|
| sha しゃ | shu しゅ | sho しょ |
| cha ちゃ | chu ちゅ | cho ちょ |
| nya にゃ | nyu にゅ | nyo にょ |
| hya ひゃ | hyu ひゅ | hyo ひょ |
| mya みゃ | myu みゅ | myo みょ |
| rya りゃ | ryu りゅ | ryo りょ |

| gya ぎゃ | gyu ぎゅ | gyo ぎょ |
|---|---|---|
| jya じゃ | jyu じゅ | jyo じょ |

| bya びゃ | byu びゅ | byo びょ |
|---|---|---|
| pya ぴゃ | pyu ぴゅ | pyo ぴょ |

4. Long and short vowels.
Some vowels are twice as long as single vowels. Make sure you hold the sound long enough when it occurs since the length of the vowel can literally change the meaning.

aa   おばあさん ob**aa**san (grandmother)      compare to おばさん obasan (aunt)

ii   おじいさん oj**ii**san (grandfather)      compare to おじさん ojisan (uncle)

uu   くうき k**uu**ki (air)   すうじ s**uu**ji (number)   ふうせん f**uu**sen (balloon)

ee   The long "ee" sound is usually transcribed by adding an 'i' to an e-vowel hiragana.

　　めいし m**ei**shi (business card)、せんせい sens**ei** (teacher)、とけい tok**ei**、
　　ゆうめい yuum**ei** (famous)

　　However, in some cases such as おねえさん on**ee**san (big sister), 'e え' is used
　　instead of 'i い."

oo   The second "o" is transcribed by hiragana "u う," as you see in the following:
　　とうふ t**oo**fu (soy bean cake)、むこう muk**oo** (beyond)、
　　こうじ k**oo**ji (construction)

　　But, there are few words in which the second "o" is transcribed with an 'o お' for
　　historical reason. Such words are:とお too (ten)、とおい tooi (far)、とおり toori
　　(street)、こおり koori (ice), and a few more.

5. Double consonants.
Beside the three small letters, や、ゆ、よ, there is another small hiragana letter, つ,
which is used for double consonants such as *cc, kk, pp, ss, tt*, etc.

Examples:
いっち　icchi   (agreement)      compare to いち ichi (one)
ざっし　zasshi (magazine)
りっぱ　rippa   (splendid)

Caution: The consonant 'n' is an exempt from this rule when it is a double consonant.
Therefore, you write 'onna' (woman), 'annai' (guidance), and 'sannen' (three years) as
follows, respectively: おんな、あんない、さんねん.

Hiragana Writing Practice
A. Practice "a, i, u, e, o" あ、い、う、え、お

### a あ
Imagine a crooked "antenna" within a circle.

pen style "a"

あ is similar to [ah] in "father," but is shorter.

### i い
Imagine the last two alphabets in "Hawaii." The shape around it is a square.

pen style "i"

い is similar to [ih] in "eat," but is much shorter.

### u う
Imagine a poor old woman walking with a stoop has been struck on her back by a rock.
The shape around it is an oblong shape, vertically longer than the horizontal line.

pen style "u"

う is similar to [ooh] in "shoe," but is shorter and the lips are not as rounded.

### e え
Imagine the letter "h" with an extra dot and line. The shape around it is slightly oblong, being longer vertically.

pen style "e"

え is similar to [e] in "X."

### o お
Imagine a picture of a flag over the 18th hole, with the golf ball on the green. The shape around it is a square.

pen style "o"

お is similar to [o] in "ocean," but is shorter without [u].

B. "ka, ki, ku, ke, ko," and "ga, gi, gu, ge, go."
か、き、く、け、こ、が、ぎ、ぐ、げ、ご

### ka か
Imagine someone bending over, getting cut.

pen style "ka"

か is similar to [ka] in "cut."

**ki き**

Imagine a <u>ki</u>y and a lock. The shape around it is oblong, being vertically long.

pen style "ki"

き is similar to [ki] in "key," but is shorter.

**ku く**

Imagine the beak of a <u>koo</u>kaburra bird in Australia. The shape around it is oblong, being vertically long.

pen style "ku"

く is similar to [ku] in "coupe," but is shorter without [u].

**ke け**

Imagine a <u>keg</u> of beer. The shape around it is a square.

pen style "ke"

け is similar to [ke] in "keg" of beer.

**ko こ**

Imagine a <u>co</u>in. The shape around it is a square.

pen style "ko"

こ is similar to [co] in "coin."

C. Practice "sa, shi, su, se, so," and "za, ji, zu, ze, zo"

さ し す せ そ　　ざ じ ず ぜ ぞ

**sa さ**

Imagine a <u>sa</u>murai sword and the cut it has made. The shape around it is a square.

pen style "sa"

さ is similar to [sa] in "such," except it's softer.

**shi し**

Imagine the way <u>she</u> puts down her hair in a flip. The shape around it is oblong, being longer vertically.

pen style "shi"

し is similar to [shi] in "she," except it's shorter and lips are spread wider.

**su**  す

Imagine the earth, with a plant growing, and the roots and seed below.  <u>Soon</u> there'll be a flower.  The shape around it is oblong, being longer vertically.

pen style "su"

す is similar to [su] in "soon."

**se**  せ

Imagine a nice <u>setting</u> for a boy and a girl.  The shape around it is oblong, being longer horizontally.

pen style "se"

せ is similar to [se] in "setting."

**so**  そ

Imagine a zigzag through a <u>sewing</u> machine. The shape around it is an oblong, being longer vertically.

pen style "so"

そ is similar to [so] in "sewing."

D.  Practice "ta, chi, tsu, te, to" and "da, (ji), (zu), de, do."
     た ち つ て と     だ ぢ づ で ど
Remember to use じ ji or ず zu usually, unless original sounds are ち chi, or つ tsu.

**ta**  た

た looks like "<u>ta</u>" in English.

pen style "ta"

た is similar to [ta] in "touch," except it's softer.

**chi** ち

Imagine a <u>chee</u>se ball with a toothpick.

pen style "chi"

ち is similar to [chi] in "chicken."

**tsu** つ

Imagine a big sneeze, "<u>tsu</u> ~."

pen style "tsu"

つ is similar to [ts] in "pants."

**te て**
Imagine a <u>te</u>nnis racquet.

  pen style "te"

て is similar to [te] in "tenis."

**to と**
Imagine a profile view of a foot, with a thorn protruding out of the big <u>toe</u>.

pen style "to"

と is similar to [to] in "toe" without final [u]

**E. Practice "na, ni, nu, ne, no"**
          **な に ぬ ね の**

**na な**
Imagine a <u>nun</u> kneeling by a cross.

pen style "na"

な is similar to [na] in "nun" without final [n].

**ni に**
Imagine your <u>knee</u>. Make it a "fat knee."

pen style "ni"

に is similar to [ni] in "knee."

**nu ぬ**
Imagine a bowl of egg <u>noo</u>dles and a pair of chopsticks.

pen style "nu"

ぬ is similar to [nu] in "noon."

**ne ね**
Imagine a tear in the basketball <u>net</u>.

pen style "ne"

ね is similar to [ne] in "net."

no　の
This has caused <u>no</u> trouble to students.

pen style "no"

の is similar to [no ] in "No," but shorter vowel sound and lips are not as rounded.

F. Practice "ha, hi, fu, he, ho," and "ba, bi, bu, be, bo."
　　はひふへほ　　　ばびぶべぼ

ha　は
Imagine a hole in the beer keg.  You rush to the keg with a hole, breathing "<u>haa</u>~, <u>haa</u>~!"

pen style "ha"

は is similar to [ha] in "house."

hi　ひ
Imagine a huge smile, "<u>hee</u>-<u>hee</u>."

pen style "hi"

ひ is similar to [hi] in "he," but is shorter.

fu　ふ
Imagine Mt. <u>Fuji</u>.

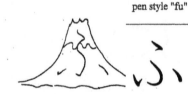

pen style "fu"

ふ is similar to [fu] in "phu~" when you blow a candle, but is shorter.

he　へ
This points in the direction of <u>heaven</u>.

pen style "he"

へ is similar to [he] in "hen" without [n].

ho　ほ
An additional stroke to ha は because it's "<u>hot</u>."

pen style "ho"

ほ is similar to [ho] in "horse" without [r].

G. Practice "ma, mi, mu, me, mo."
まみ むめ も

**ma** ま
Imagine a picture of a telephone pole used to call your "ma."

pen style "ma"

ま is similar to [ma] in "mom," but is softer.

**mi** み
Who is twenty-one years old? "Me." み looks like "21."

pen style "mi"

み is similar to [mi] in "me," but is shorter.

**mu** む
Imagine a picture of a "moo-moo" cow.

pen style "mu"

む is similar to [mu] in "moo," but is shorter.

**me** め
Imagine a "messy" bowl, when you drop an egg into the egg noodles.

pen style "me"

め is similar to [me] in "melon."

**mo** も
You can catch "more" fish with more worms.

pen style "mo"

も is similar to [mo] in "more."

H. Practice "ya, yu, yo."
や ゆ よ

**ya** や
Imagine a hairy yak in the yard.

pen style "ya"

や is similar to [ya] in "yacht"

**yu** ゆ
No "U" turn is allowed.

pen style "yu

ゆ is similar to [yu] in "you" without long [u].

yo よ
Imagine a "yo-yo" for you.

pen style "yo"

よ is similar to [yo] in "yo-yo," but with shorter [o].

I. Practice "ra, ri, ru, re, ro."
らりるれろ

ra ら
Imagine a "rabbit."

pen style "ra"

ら is similar to [ra] in "rabbit," except your tongue is not as curled.

ri り
Imagine "reeds" in the river.

pen style "ri"

り is similar to [ri] in "ribbon," but your tongue must once touch behind the front teeth.

ru る
Imagine a broach with a ruby

pen style "ru"

る is similar to [ru] in "ruby."

re れ
Imagine a man resting against a pole.

pen style "re"

れ is similar to [re] in "record."

ro ろ
A ruby is stolen by a "robber."

pen style "ro"

ろ is similar to [ro] in "rock," but your tongue must once touch behind the front teeth.

J. Practice "wa, wo, no"
わをん

**wa** わ
Imagine a magic <u>wa</u>nd, waved by a magician.

pen style "wa"

わ is similar to [wa] in "Wow," but the lips are not as rounded or pointed.

**wo** を
Imagine an Olympic discus thrower.

pen style "wo"

を is the same as お, but occasionally pronounced as [wo] as in "water."

**n** ん
This looks like an English "n."

pen style "n"

ん is similar to [n] in "Ann."

Can you tell where the voiced sounds are?  Where do you place the two dots?

1)
A.

cliff

B.

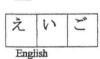

English

C.

bur; (chestnut) case

D.

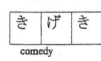

comedy

Where do you put the diacritical mark ( ﾟ ) for "pa, pi, pu, pe, po"?

A.

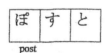

pie

B.

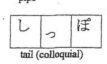

post

C.

pipe

D.

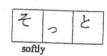

tail (colloquial)

Can you tell the differences between A and B?

1)
A.

outside

B.

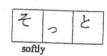

softly

2)
A.

sword

B.

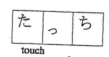

touch

# GREETINGS

*Introduction to Japanese Culture*
Greetings
Climate and Seasons
Dates and Months
Cultural Events

*Expressions*
"Good morning. It's cold, isn't it?"
"Winter in Japan is cold."
"What date is it today?"
"It's Monica. It's not Monica. It was Monica. It wasn't Monica"

*Cultural Notes with Illustrations*
Four seasons of Japan
"Anata (= you) is a dangerous word!"
"Kon'nichiwa (= Hello) is not always suitable for your in-group people"
Japanese customs and seasonal celebrations

*Crossword Puzzles*

*Introduction to Hiragana*
Mastering the lines "a-i-u-e-o" and "ka-ki-ku-ke-ko (including 'ga-gi-gu-ge-go')"

日本のきせつ：はる、なつ、あき、ふゆ
Nihon no kisetsu: haru, natsu, aki, fuyu (Four seasons of Japan)

Chapter 1                    Greetings      あいさつ
                                            a-i-sa-tsu

モニカ：              おはよう　ございます。
Mo-ni-ka:             o-ha-yo-o  go-za-i-ma-su

きんじょのひと：あ、おはよう　　ございます。さむいですね。
ki-n-jyo no hi-to  :  a,     o-ha-yo-o go-za-i-ma-su. sa-mu-i de-su-ne

モニカ：              きょうは、ほんと（う）に　さむい　ですね。
Mo-ni-ka:             kyo-o wa,  ho-n-to (o) ni        sa-mu-i de-su-ne

                     にほん　の　ふゆ　は、さむい　ですね。
                     ni-ho-n  no  fu-yu wa,  sa-mu-i  de-su ne

きんじょのひと：にがつ　は、もっと　さむい　ですよ。
ki-n-jyo no hi-to  :  ni-ga-tsu wa, mo-t-to  sa-mu-i  de-su yo

モニカ：              そう　ですか。じゃ、また。
Mo-ni-ka:             so-o de-su ka.    jya, ma-ta

きんじょのひと：　いってらっしゃい。
ki-n-jyo no hi-to  :  i-t-te ra-s-sha-i

[English translation]:  Greeting

Monica:     Good morning.

Neighbor:  Oh, good morning.  It is cold, isn't it?

Monica:     Today is really cold.  Winter in Japan is
                cold, isn't it?

Neighbor:  It's even colder in February.

Monica:     Is it?  See you later.

Neighbor:  Good bye.

Chapter 1                                Vocabulary List

1. Greetings
   Ohayoo おはよう                                    Good morning. (Casual)
   Ohayoo gozaimasu おはようございます                  Good morning. (Formal)
   Itte (i)rasshai いって（い）らっしゃい                Greeting to see someone off.
   Jya mata じゃ　また                                See you later.

   (Additional greetings)
   Kon'nichiwa こんにちは                             Good afternoon.  Hello.
   Konbanwa こんばんは                                Good evening.
   Sayoonara さようなら                               Good bye. (to your equal)
   Shitsurei shimasu しつれいします                    Good bye. (to your social superior)
   Itte kimasu いってきます                            I'm leaving.
   Oyasumi (nasai)おやすみ（なさい）                    Good night.

2. Nouns
   aisatsu あいさつ                                   greetings
   kyoo きょう                                        today
   Nihon にほん                                       Japan
   soo そう                                          so
   kinjyo no hito きんじょのひと                        neighbor
   nigatsu にがつ（二月）                              February
   fuyu ふゆ                                          winter

   (Additional vocabulary for seasons)
   haru はる                                          spring
   natsu なつ                                         summer
   aki あき                                          fall, autumn

   (Additional vocabulary for twelve months)
   Ichi-gatsu いちがつ（一月）                          January
   (Ni-gatsu)（にがつ）（二月）                         February
   San-gatsu さんがつ（三月）                           March
   Shi-gatsu しがつ（四月）                            April
   Go-gatsu ごがつ（五月）                             May
   Roku-gatsu ろくがつ（六月）                          June
   Shichi-gatsu しちがつ（七月）                         July
   Hachi-gatsu はちがつ（八月）                         August
   Ku-gatsu くがつ（九月）                             September
   Jyuu-gatsu じゅうがつ（十月）                         October
   Jyuu-ichi-gatsu じゅういちがつ（十一月）              November

Jyuu-ni-gatsu じゅうにがつ（十二月）       December

3. Adjectives
   samui さむい                          cold

   (Additional adjectives)
   atsui あつい                          hot
   atatakai あたたかい                    nice and warm
   suzushii すずしい                      nice and cool

4. Adverbs
   honto(o) ni ほんと（う）に             truly
   motto もっと                          more
   jya じゃ                              in that case, then

5. Verbs
   desu　です                           to be (copula verb)
   ~desu ka　ですか                      Is it?
   ~desu ne　ですね                      Isn't it?

6. Others
   a　あ                                Oh.

7. Particles
   ne　ね                               a sentence final, tag question;
                                        used when both speaker and listener
                                        share the information and to get an
                                        affirmation from the other

   yo　よ                               a sentence final; used when a
                                        speaker tells the listener something
                                        the latter doesn't know

   ka　か                               a question marker

   no　の                               modifier; connect two nouns

   wa　は                               topic marker

8. Responses
   Hai はい                             yes
   Iie ( or Ie) いいえ（いえ）            no

......................................................................................

Additional Vocabulary from Grammar Notes, Exercises Section, Dict-A-Conversation

......................................................................................

[Nouns]

| | |
|---|---|
| watashi わたし | I |
| anata あなた | you |
| gakusei がくせい | student |
| daigakusei だいがくせい | college student |
| sensei せんせい | teacher, professor, doctor |
| hon ほん | book |
| kisetsu きせつ | season |

[Adjectives]

| | |
|---|---|
| hayai はやい | early |

[Greetings]

| | |
|---|---|
| Itte (i) rasshai. いって（い）らっしゃい | Said to someone who's leaving. A response to Itte kimasu. |
| Tadaima. ただいま | I'm home. |
| Okaeri (nasai) おかえり（なさい） | Welcome home. |
| Itadakimasu. いただきます | I humbly receive this food/item. |
| Gochisoo sama (deshita). ごちそうさま（でした） | Thank you for the meal (feast). |
| Gomen'nasai. ごめんなさい | I'm sorry. |
| Sumimasen. すみません | I'm sorry (more formal). |
| Sumimasenga,... すみませんが、 | Excuse me, but... |
| Arigatoo (gozaimasu). ありがとう（ございます） | Thank you (very much) (formal). |
| Doo itashi mashite. どういたしまして | You're welcome. |
| Or, Iie. いいえ | (Don't mention it.) Not at all. |
| Yaa, genki? やあ、げんき？ | Hey, how are you? (Casual) |
| Okage sama de. おかげさまで | Thank you for your concern. |

[Questions]

| | |
|---|---|
| Nan desu ka. なんですか | What is it? |
| Itsu desu ka. いつですか | When is it? |
| Nan-gatsu nan-nichi desu ka. なんがつなんにちですか | What day and month is it? |
| Nan-yoobi desu ka. なんようびですか | What day of the week is it? |

The Rules of "Anata (you)": What is right and what is wrong.

It's alright to address someone who is younger than you "anata."

It's wrong of you to address someone older than you "anata."

It's very wrong of you to address your boss "anata," unless you want him/her to fire you.

"Anata" is used affectionately by a wife to address her husband.  It's equivalent of "honey, my dear."

Chapter 1 Grammar

## 1. **X wa Y desu** **X = Y**

DESU

"Desu" is, in English, "is, "am," or "are." "X wa Y desu" means "X is Y" or "As for X, it is Y." "X wa" is often omitted when it is understood from context and simply "Y desu" is said. The final "u" in "desu" is not pronounced.

> SVC → X wa Y desu. (SCV)
> (in English) (in Japanese)
> S = Subject, V = Verb, C = Complement

Unlike in English, the verb comes at the end of a sentence in Japanese!

Examples:

1. Watashi wa Monica desu. (I am Monica.)
   (I) (Monica) (am)

2. Watashi wa, gakusei desu. (I am a student.)
   (I) (student) (am)

3. Kore wa, hon desu. (This is a book.)
   (This) (a book) (is)

## 2. **Particles**

WA

"Wa" is a particle to signal the listener what the speaker is going to talk about. It is a "Topic" of the sentence. One may translate "wa" as "speaking of which," "as for," or "with regard to."

1. わたしは　だいがくせい　です。
   Watashi wa daigakusei desu. (I am a college student.)

2. スパゲティは、おいしい　です。
   Spaghetti wa oishii desu. (Spaghetti is delicious.)

Ka

"Ka" is the same as a question mark. It indicate the sentence is a question.

Questions in Japanese are formulated simply by adding "ka" at the end of a sentence. While the word order changes in English when forming a question, it does not in Japanese

Compare:    Kore wa hon desu.     (This is a book.)
Question:    Kore wa hon desu ka.  (Is this a book?)

1. Q:  Anata wa Keiko san desu ka. (Are you Keiko?)

   A:  Hai, (watashi wa) Keiko desu.  /Hai, soo desu.
                              (Yes, I am [Keiko].)

2. Q:  Kore wa hon desu ka.  (Is this a book?)
   A:  Hai, soo desu.

| No |

The particle "no" is "of" or "in" in English possessive case.

nihon + no + fuyu = Japan's winter / winter in Japan
(Japan)        (winter)

watashi + no + hon = my book
(I)             (book)

anata + no + gakkoo = your school
(you)          (school)

3. **X wa Y jya arimasen**          **X ≠ Y**

| .......JYA ARIMASEN |

"....jya arimasen" is a negative form of "....desu."
It is used after nouns.  Saying only "jya arimasen"
part is ungrammatical. It has to be preceded by a  noun, such as "soo jya arimasen," or
"watashi jya arimasen."  Note:  More formal way to say is "Watakushi dewa arimasen."

| X isn't Y.    X wa Y jya arimasen. |
| (in English)    (in Japanese) |

4. **X wa Y deshita**          **X was Y**

| DESHITA |

"Deshita" is the same as "was" in English, and it's a past tense of
"desu."

Kinoo wa kugatsu yooka **deshita**.  (Yesterday **was** September 8th.)

Watashi wa mae pilot **deshita**.   (I was a pilot before.)

5. **X wa Y jya arimasen deshita**          **X was not Y**

| JYA ARIMASEN DESHITA |
|---|

"-----jya arimasen deshita" is the same as "wasn't"
in English, and it's a past tense of  "jya arimasen."

Note:  More formal way to say "jya" is "dewa."

Kinoo wa ame **jya arimsen deshita**.  (Yesterday wasn't rain.)

Watashi wa mae pilot **jya arimasen deshita**.  (I wasn't a pilot before.)

6. Summary of a **predicate pattern of nouns**.

|  | Affirmative | Negative |
|---|---|---|
| Non-past tense | **desu** | **jya arimasen** |
| Past tense | **deshita** | **jya arimasen deshita** |

7. **Adjectives**

Japanese adjectives have the same word order as English.  It precedes a noun that
modifies.  ("Adj + Noun" order)

Examples:
1. atsui   hi    = hot day
   (hot) (day)

2. samui  hi    = cold day
   (cold) (day)

3. ii      hon  = good book
   (good) (book)

4. Kyoo wa atsui desu. = Today is hot.
   (today)   (hot)

5. Fuyu wa samui desu. = Winter is cold.
   (winter)   (cold)

| SUBJECT |
|---|

WA

| ADJECTIVE + NOUN |
|---|

DESU

6. Kore          wa        ii        hon        desu.
   (This)                  (good)   (book)      (is)

7. Kotoshi      wa        samui      fuyu       desu.
   (This year)            (cold)

Note:  The predicate pattern of Adjectives will be introduced later.  It's different from nouns.

## 8. <u>Adverbs</u>

Just as English adverbs do, Japanese adverbs also modify adjectives, adverbs, and verbs.  Following words appear in Chapter 1.

    1. "Jya" (formal equivalent is "dewa") means "in that case," or "then," often used instead of "good bye."
        (after a conversation)
        A:  Jya, mata.
        B:  Mata ne.

        (when coming to a conclusion)
        A:  Jya, soo shimashoo. (Then, let's do that.)
        B:  Ee, soo desu ne. (Yes, that's right.  "Ee" means "yes, " but it is not as formal as  "hai."

    [Variations of farewell]
        A:  Jya, sayonara.
        B:  Sayoonara. (Additional "o" in "sayoonara" is more formal.)

    [Formal farewell greeting]
        Student:  [sensei], shitsurei shimasu. (Literally: Excuse me.)
        Professor:  hai, sayoonara.

    2. "Mata" means "again," often used with "jya," adding casualness to the farewell greeting.

    3. "Motto" means "more" to modify an adjective, such as "motto samui" (colder).

    4.  "Honto(o) ni" means "truly."  "Honto" is more casual than "hontoo."

## Cultural Note on Greetings ("aisatsu")

Now we know how to say "Good morning," "Hello/Good afternoon," and "Good-bye" in Japanese: "Ohayoo," "Kon'nichiwa" and "Sayoonara." Please note, however, that two of the above greetings are not used to greet your own family members. Which ones are they? Yes, the lattermost two. We do not say "Kon'nichiwa" to our family members when we greet each other in the afternoon, unless we haven't seen each other for many years. We don't say "Sayoonara," to our parting family members, unless we are at our "final" parting in life. Japanese people are keenly aware of the "in-group" and "out-group" distinction, and that is often reflected in the language. Imagine you showed up at work in the afternoon and you wanted to greet your colleagues in Japanese. What would you say? Not "Kon'nichiwa." If you do so, your colleagues will probably think you are joking. "Kon'nichiwa" is a greeting used towards outsiders. Under such circumstances, no greeting would take place. Certain gestures, including bowing or other forms of verbal communication, can often suffice instead.

Chapter 1 Exercises　（renshuu-mondai れんしゅうもんだい）

A. Pair-work:  Respond to your partner who said to you the following greetings.

| | |
|---|---|
| 1. Ohayoo. | 1.　おはよう。 |
| 2. Ogenki desu ka? | 2.　おげんきですか。 |
| 3. Kon'nichi wa. | 3.　こんにちは。 |
| 4. Konban wa | 4.　こんばんは。 |
| 5. Arigatoo. | 5.　ありがとう。 |
| 6. Sumimasen. | 6.　すみません。 |
| 7. Itte kimasu. | 7.　いってきます。 |
| 8. Tadaima. | 8.　ただいま。 |
| 9. Oyasumi nasai. | 9.　おやすみなさい。 |
| 10. Sayoonara. | 10.　さようなら。 |

B. Circle the correct sounds for each month and add "gatsu" to them.
　Example:  "ichi" + "gatsu" = "ichi gatsu" (January)

| | |
|---|---|
| 1. ichi, icchi | 1.　いち、いっち |
| 2. ni, nii | 2.　に、　にい |
| 3. san, mi | 3.　さん、み |
| 4. shi, yo, yon | 4.　し、よ、よん |
| 5. go, goo | 5.　ご、ごう |
| 6. roku, rokku | 6.　ろく、ろっく |
| 7. shichi, nana | 7.　しち、なな |
| 8. hachi, hacchi | 8.　はち、はっち |
| 9. ku, kyuu | 9.　く、きゅう |
| 10. jyuu, jyu | 10.　じゅう、じゅ |
| 11. jyuu-ichi, jyu-ichi | 11.　じゅういち、じゅいち |
| 12. jyuu-ni, jyu-ni | 12.　じゅうに、じゅに |

C. Pair-work: Match-up the right months.

| | | |
|---|---|---|
| 1. January | a. san-gatsu | さんがつ |
| 2. March | b. ku-gatsu | くがつ |
| 3. December | c. hachi-gatsu | はちがつ |
| 4. September | d. jyuu-ni-gatsu | じゅうにがつ |
| 5. February | e. ichi-gatsu | いちがつ |
| 6. November | f. ni-gatsu | にがつ |
| 7. July | g. shi-gatsu | しがつ |
| 8. October | h. go-gatsu | ごがつ |
| 9. April | i. roku-gatsu | ろくがつ |

10. June              j. shichi-gatsu       しちがつ
11. May               k. jyuu-ichi-gatsu    じゅういちがつ
12. August            l. jyuu-gatsu         じゅうがつ

D. Pair-work: Match-up the dates.

1. tsuitachi    ついたち      a. third
2. kokonoka    ここのか      b. first
3. itsuka      いつか        c. ninth
4. yooka       ようか        d. second
5. tooka       とおか        e. fifth
6. futsuka     ふつか        f. seventh
7. yokka       よっか        g. tenth
8. mikka       みっか        h. eighth
9. muika       むいか        i. fourth
10. nanoka     なのか        j. sixth

E.  Pair-work:
  (1) Which dates of the month have "-nichi" endings?  Write their numbers.


  (2) Which dates of the month have "-ka" endings?  Write their numbers.


F.  Pair-work:  With your partner, figure out which months fit best for the following
    descriptions.

  1.  summer vacation (          ) 2.  the coldest month (          )
  3.  the hottest month (        ) 4.  spring (          )
  5.  the busiest month (        ) 6.  the month of your birthday (          )
  7.  when cherry bloom (        ) 8.  when leaves turn red (          )

G. Find someone in class who has the same birthday as you!

  (1) Go around the class to find a person whose birthday month is the same as
      yours.  Use "Nan-gatsu umare desu ka?" (Which month were you born?)
          なんがつうまれですか。
  (2) When you found someone whose birthday month is the same as yours, then ask
      "Tanjyoobi wa nan-nichi desu ka." (What date is your birthday?)
          たんじょうびは、なんにちですか。
  (3) If that date is the same day as you, say "Watashi to onaji desu!" (the same
          わたしとおなじです。
      as mine) and, ask his/her name, "O-namae wa nan desuka?"
          おなまえは、なんですか。

Then write down his/her name below in (2).  Even if the birthday is different, ask his/her name to write down below in (1)

Report to class:

(1)
............................ san wa  ----gatsu-umare desu.  Watashi to onaji desu.
_____さんは、____がつうまれです。わたしとおなじです。

Or,

(2)
........................ san no tanjyoobi wa  .........gatsu...... nichi(or ...ka) desu.
_____さんのたんじょうびは、____がつ____にちです。

Watashi to onaji desu.   わたしと　おなじです。

H.  Mind-reading game:  With your pair, guess the date your partner has in mind.  Each time you play, the choices of dates must be within the range given below.
Examples:
(1) Your partner asks the date, "Tsuitachi desu ka?" ついたちですか。
(from the range of tsuitachi,futsuka,mikka)  （ついたち、ふつか、みっか）

(2) You answer "Hai, soo desu. " if that's the date you had in mind, or "Iie,
はい、そうです。　　　　　　　　　　　　　　　いいえ、
chigaimasu, or "Iie, soo jya arimasen," if that wasn't the date you had in mind.
ちがいます。　いいえ、そうじゃありません。

"Tsuitachi desu ka"          ----------   "Iie, chigaimasu."
"Futsuka desu ka"           ----------   "Iie, "soo jya arimasen.""
"jya, mikka desu ka."        ----------   "Hai, soo desu."

1.  (tsuitachi, futsuka, mikka, yokka)   ついたち、ふつか、みっか、よっか

2.  (itsuka, muika, nanoka)          いつか、むいか、なのか

3.  (yooka, kokonoka, tooka)         ようか、ここのか、とおか

4.  (jyuu ichi nichi, jyuu ni nichi, jyuu san nichi, jyuu yokka, jyuu go nichi,
じゅういちにち、じゅうににち、じゅうさんにち、じゅうよっか、
jyuu go nichi, jyuu roku nichi)
じゅうごにち、じゅうろくにち

5.  (jyuu shichi nichi, jyuu hachi nichi, jyuu ku nichi, hatsuka)
じゅうしちにち、じゅうはちにち、じゅうくにち、はつか

6. (nijyuu ichi nichi, nijyuu ni nichi, nijyuu san nichi, nijyuu yokka, nijyuu go nichi)
にじゅういちにち、にじゅうににち、にじゅうさんにち、にじゅうよっか
nijyuu go nichi)
にじゅうごにち

7. (nijyuu roku nichi, nijyuu shichi nichi, nijyuu hachi nichi, nijyuu ku nichi,
にじゅうろくにち、にじゅうしちにち、にじゅうはちにち、にじゅうくにち

san jyuu nichi, san jyuu ichi nichi)
さんじゅうにち、さんじゅういちにち

I. What date and month of the following?

1.  The New Years' Day     2.  Valentine's Day      3.  April Fool
4.  Christmas Eve          5.  your birthday        6.  Columbus Day
7.  Thanksgiving Day       8.  Black Friday

J. What would you say in Japanese under the following situations?  にほんごで　なん
と　いいますか。

1.  When you are leaving home, you say this to your family.

2.  When your family member is leaving home, you say this to him/her.

3.  When you returned home, you say this to your family.

4.  When you welcome your family member's returning home, you say this.

5.  Before your meal, you say this.

6.  After your meal, you say this.

7.  When class is over, you tell this to your classmates.

8.  When you are ready to go to bed, you say this.

9.  When you want to express your appreciation, you say this.

10. When you want to apologize, you say this.

11. When you want to apologize in a formal manner, you say this.

12. When you met your neighbor/acquaintance in the morning, you say this to
    him/her.

13. When you met your neighbor/acquaintance in the afternoon, you say this to him/her.

14. When you met your neighbor/acquaintance in the evening, you say this to him/her.

Also, what will you say the followings in Japanese?

1. "You're welcome."

2. "That's all right." in response to "I'm sorry."

3. When you come in classroom in the middle of lecture, what would you say? (Literally: "Sorry to be rude.")

4. You want to say "good bye" to your teacher in a most formal way to replace "Sayoonara," a casual "good bye."

K.  Translate into Japanese using "no."
Example:  my book →   わたし の ほん
　　　　　　　　　　　　watashi no hon

1. Japanese language teacher

2. Ken's mother

3. my name

4. my friend

5. college professor

6. winter in Japan (Japan's winter)

L. Pair-work: Connect nouns from each of the columns with the particle "no", making sentences that make sense.

| Noun | particle | Noun |
|---|---|---|
| nihon (Japan) | | tenki (weather) |
| Pasadena | | hon (book) |
| Los Angeles | | haru (spring) |
| America | | natsu (summer) |
| nihongo (Japanese language) | no | aki (autumn) |
| watashi (I) | | fuyu (winter) |
| Monica | | pen (pen) |
| kyoo (today) | | sensei (teacher) |
| daigaku (college) | | gakusei (student) |

M. Rearrange the words so they become coherent. Write the rearrangement on the dotted lines.

    a.  ne, desu, samui            .........................................
        ね、です、さむい

    b.  gozaimasu, ohayoo        .........................................
        ございます、おはよう

    c.  mata, jya                  .........................................
        また、じゃ

    d.  ka, desu, soo             .........................................
        か、です、そう

    e.  kyoo, samui, ne, wa, desu    .........................................
        きょう、さむい、ね、は、です

    f.  fuyu, no, nihon, desu, yo, wa, samui .........................................
        ふゆ、の、にほん、です、よ、は、さむい

    g.  desu, motto, nigatsu, yo, samui, wa .........................................
        です、もっと、にがつ、よ、さむい、は

    h.  ka, desu, no, hito, kinjyo     .........................................
        か、です、の、ひと、きんじょ

    i.  wa, desu, gakusei, watashi    .........................................
        は、です、がくせい、わたし

    j.  hon, kore, wa, desu        .........................................
        ほん、これ、は、です

    k.  Caltech, daigaku, desu, wa    .........................................
        かるてっく、だいがく、です、は

    l.  kyoo, desu, atsui, wa       .........................................
        きょう、です、あつい、は

    m.  wa, daigakusei, watashi, desu  .........................................
        は、だいがくせい、わたし、です

    n.  desu, kyoo, kugatsu, wa, tooka  .........................................
        です、きょう、くがつ、は、とおか

**N-1.** Past tense affirmative でした Exercises
                      deshita

Change きょう to きのう, and change the verb to its past tense form.
        kyoo        kinoo

Examples:

（１）きょうは　ふつか<u>です</u>。きのうは、ついたち<u>でした</u>。
     kyoo   wa    futsuka desu.   kinoo  wa,  tsuitachi  deshita.

（２）きょうは　テスト<u>です</u>。きのうも、テスト<u>でした</u>。
     kyoo   wa    tesuto desu.   kinoo  mo,  tesuto  deshita.

1. きょうは、みっかです。きのうは、（                                              ）

    kyoo   wa,   mikka   desu.   kinoo   wa,

2. きょうは、あめ (rain)です。きのうも(                                              ）

    kyoo   wa,   ame desu.   kinoo   mo

3. きょうは、おてんき (good weather)です。きのうも （                              ）

    kyoo   wa,   otenki desu.              kinoo   mo,

4. きょうは、べんきょう (studying)です。きのうも （                              ）

    kyoo   wa,   benkyoo desu.              kinoo   mo,

5. きょうは、おやすみです。きのうも （                                              ）

                   (holiday; absence)

    kyoo   wa,   oyasumi   desu.   kinoo   mo

6. きょう、シカゴは、くもり (cloudy)です。きのうも （                          ）

    kyoo,   Shikago wa,   kumori desu.              kinoo   mo

Add まえは(before) to the following sentences and change their tenses to that of the past.
Example:

    わたしは、どくしん(single, unmarried)です。

    watashi wa,   dokushin desu.

    わたしは、まえは　どくしんでした。

    watashi wa,   mae wa   dokushin   deshita.

7. たなかさんは、エンジニア (engineer)です。

    Tanaka san   wa,   enginia   desu.

8. かとうさんは、しゅふ(housewife; homemaker)です。

    Katoo san   wa,   shufu desu.

9. いしださんは、かいしゃいん(company employee)です。

    Ishida san   wa,   kaishain desu.

## N-2.  Negative non-past tense じゃありません Exercises

Change the original sentences (on its left) in section N1 to its corresponding negative
form, using じゃありません。 (jya arimasen).

Example:

    きょうは、みっかです。                kyoo wa mikka desu.

        ↓

    きょうは、みっかじゃありません。       kyoo wa mikka jya arimasen.

N-3.  Negative past tense じゃありませんでした Exercises

Change the negative non-past sentences you made in section N2 to its past tense form, using じゃありませんでした。 (jya arimasen deshita)

Example:

      きょうは、みっかじゃありません。       kyoo wa mikka jya arimasen.

               ↓

      きょうは、みっかじゃありませんでした。   kyoo wa mikka jya arimasen deshita.


O.  Pair-work: Ask the following questions and get the answers from your partner.  Then, later, write down the answers in Japanese.

1 ．きのうは、なんにちでしたか。
    kinoo wa    nan-nichi deshita ka.

2 ．きのうは、にがつよっかでしたか。
    kinoo wa    nigatsu yokka deshita ka.

3 ．きょうは、くがつとおかですか。
    kyoo wa    kugatsu tooka desu ka.

4 ．あなたは、せんせいですか。
    anata wa    sensei   desu ka.

5 ．いま、はるですか。
    ima    haru  desu ka.

6 ．いま、ふゆですか。
    ima    fuyu desu ka.

7 ．あなたは、だいがくいんせいですか。
    anata wa    daigaku-in-sei (graduate student) desu ka.

8 ．いま、あさですか。
    ima    asa  desu ka.

9 ．あなたの　たんじょうびは、きのうでしたか。
    anata no    tanjyoobi wa    kinoo deshita ka.

10．あなたは、パイロットですか。
    anata wa   pairotto (pilot) desu ka.

P. Distinguish long and short vowels. Listen to your instructor and circle the one you hear.

1. kite,       kiite        きて、きって
2. shite,      shiite       して、しって
3. oki,        ooki         おき、おおき
4. kuki,       kuuki        くき、くうき
5. sato,       satoo        さと、さとう
6. rubi,       rubii        るび、るびい
7. iso,        isoo         いそ、いそう
8. idesu,      iidesu       いです。いいです。
9. shujin,     shuujin      しゅじん、しゅうじん
10. obasan,    obaasan      おばさん、おばあさん

Q. Distinguish double consonants. Circle the one you hear.

1. saka,       sakka        さか、さっか
2. iki,        ikki         いき、いっき
3. kite,       kitte        きて、きって
4. saki,       sakki        さき、さっき
5. ichi,       icchi        いち、いっち
6. hachi,      hacchi       はち、はっち
7. machi,      macchi       まち、まっち
8. gaki,       gakki        がき、がっき
9. shiki,      shikki       しき、しっき
10. koki       kokki        こき、こっき

R. Distinguish voiceless and voiced sounds. Circle the one you hear.

1. kochi-kochi,    gochi-gochi    こちこち、ごちごち
2. saku-saku,      zaku-zaku      さくさく、ざくざく
3. shoo-shoo,      shoo-jyoo      しょうしょう、しょうじょう
4. kaki,           gaki           かき、がき
5. kake,           gake           かけ、がけ
6. senmai,         zenmai         せんまい、ぜんまい
7. ootaka,         oodaka         おおたか、おおだか
8. takata,         takada         たかた、たかだ
9. mato,           mado           まと、まど
10. karasu,        garasu         からす、がらす

Dict-A-Conversation

This conversation activity can be found on your CD. Play the role of Monica unless otherwise instructed. You will hear one side of a conversation based on a topic covered in the chapter. Write down what you hear (in Romanization, but very soon only in Hiragana), and complete the conversation. You may listen to your CD as many times as you wish for homework unless otherwise instructed.

Chapter 1 A:  Greeting

(1)
Kinjyo no hito:  _____

Monica:          _____

Kinjyo no hito:  _____

Monica:          _____

(2)
Monica: _____

Tanaka: _____        _____

Monica: _____

Tanaka: _____

Monica: _____

(3)
Station master:  _____

Monica:          _____

Station master:  _____

Monica:          _____

Station master:  _____

Monica: _____

(4)
Katoo  : _____

Monica: _____

Katoo  : _____

Monica: _____

Katoo  : _____

Monica: _____

(5)
Sensei  : _____

Monica: _____

Sensei  : _____

Monica: _____

Sensei : _____

Monica: _____


Chapter 1 B:  What date and month is it today?
(1)
Tanaka: _____

Monica: _____

Tanaka: _____

Monica: _____

(2)
Monica: _____

Tanaka: _____          _____

Monica: _____

Tanaka: _____

## Chapter 1:  Crossword Puzzle #1 (Four seasons and Climate)

Across
1. cold
2. winter
3. nice and warm

Down
4. hot
5. summer
6. fall
7. spring

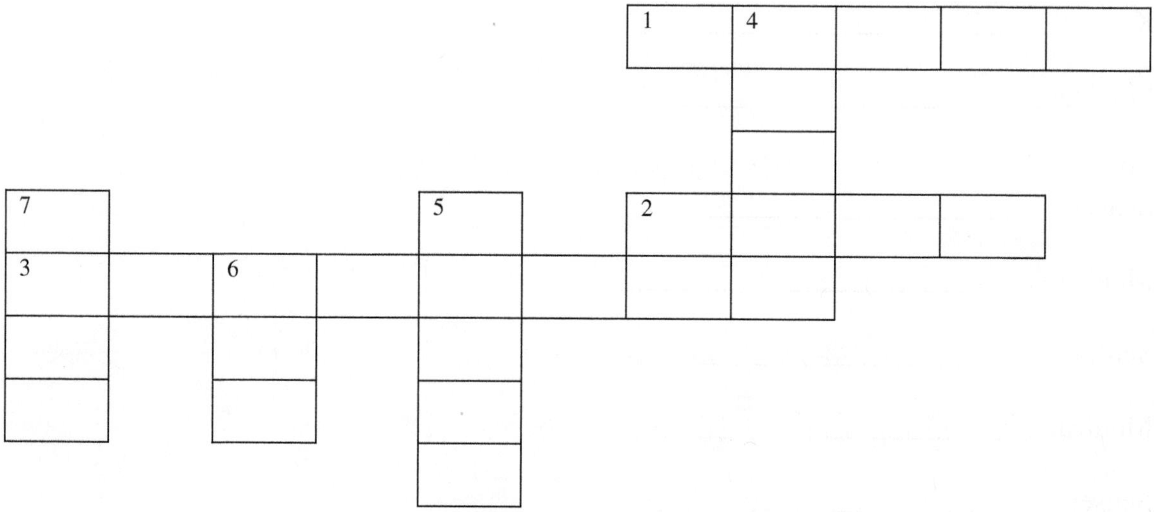

Chapter 1:  Crossword Puzzle #2 (Greetings # 1)

Across
1. Good evening
2. You're welcome.
3. I'm sorry (casual).

Down
4. Excuse me.  I'm sorry (formal).
5. Hello. Good afternoon.
6. Thank you for the feast
   (It was delicious!)
7.  Good morning.

Chapter 1:  Crossword Puzzle #3 (Greetings #2 and Months)

Across
1. What do you say before you eat?
   (I humbly eat.)
2. Japanese word for The New Year's Day
3. Japanese word for "Please"
4. Japanese word for "Thank you"

Down
1. January
2. Welcome home.
5. Good morning.
6. I'm home.

Chapter 1:  Hiragana (a ~ ko) Puzzle    （あいうえお、かきくけこ）

Find the following words in the box and circle/color them.  The words can go horizontally, diagonally, and backward.

あかい red     あおい blue   あい love     いえ house    えいが movie  うえ above
いいえ No    おおい more   かき persimmon     いけ pond    くい stick
おい nephew  かげ shadow  げいこ geisha        がき kids   あいこ& あきこ girl's
names

| え | う | い | お | お |
|---|---|---|---|---|
| い | い | え | く | い |
| い | お | あ | い | こ |
| け | き | か | き | が |
| こ | げ | い | こ | き |

## Japanese customs and seasonal celebrations

1. Kagami-mochi
(New Year's celebration)

2. Kotatsu (an electric heater
under a table covered w/futon)

3. Hina-Matsuri
Doll Festivals,
March 3$^{rd}$

4. Sakura (cherry blossoms)
symbolizes spring.

5. Spring in Japan is described as
"poka-poka" (nice & warm).

6. Koi-nobori (carp-banners)
May 5$^{th}$ is the Children's day.

7. Tsuyu (rainy season)
(mid-June to mid-July)

8. The scorching sun in
mid-summer is described
as "kan-kan."

9. The Taiko drum is often used
during "matsuri" (festivals),
which are many in summer.

10. A girl wearing
yukata (cotton kimono)
is a typical summer scene.

w/uchiwa (fan) & katori-senko
(mosquito repellent coil).

11. Kuri (chestnuts) represents the fall
season.  Many sweets are made
from chestnuts during autumn.

12. Yuki-daruma (snow Dharma)

# **Meeting People On Campus**

Chapter 2A: Asking for Guidance
*Expressions*
"Where is it?"  "What is it?"  "Which one is it?"
"Is this a book, too?"
"This red book is a good book."

*Cultural Note with Illustration*
"Okagesamade" (Thanks to you, shadow)

*Crossword Puzzles*

*Introduction to Hiragana*
Mastering the lines "sa-shi-su-se-so (including 'za-ji-zu-ze-zo')" and "ta-chi-tsu-te-to"
(including "da-ji-zu-de-do)

Chapter 2B: I came from America
*Expressions*
"What year are you?"
"Where are you from?"
"I'll go by bus."
"I speak Japanese."
"Who is he?"  "Whose bag is this?"
Daily life activities: I eat, drink, sleep, study, read, write, listen, watch, get up & talk.

*Crossword Puzzles*

*Introduction to Hiragana*
Mastering the lines "na-ni-nu-ne-no" and "ha-hi-fu-he-ho" (including "ba-bi-bu-be-bo &
pa-pi-pu-pe-po)

Chapter 2C: Thank you and Good-bye
*Expressions*
"What's good?"  "Which one is red?"  "Who is your teacher?"
Count up to one hundred

*Cultural Note*
Numbers and Japanese life

*Introduction to Hiragana*
Mastering the lines "ma-mi-mu-me-mo" and "ya-yu-yo"

Japanese expression:  Okagesamade おかげさまで

お蔭様で

---

Okage sama de (Literally:  Thanks to you, shadow)

It expresses thankfulness for another's concern.  Although the term originates from Buddhism, it has customary been used in greetings where one's well being is questioned: whether concerning health, business, human relations, school, or anything else in life.  Buddhist belief sees that nothing in this universe stands alone; everything is interrelated beyond time and space. And so the shadow of a tree, granting one temporary relief from heat, is not merely an accident.  As such, you would thank the shadow, a work of Nature. Japanese Buddhism – as a result of syncretism – interweaves with indigenous ancestor worship and animistic aspect of Shinto as well. Nature that gives you the sustenance of life, and the people who miraculously live on earth the same time as you, equally deserve an intention of gratitude.

A:  いかがですか。おげんきですか。　　Ikaga desu ka.  O-genki desu ka.

B:  おかげさまで。げんきです。　　　　Okagesamade.  Genki desu.
　　おげんきですか。　　　　　　　　Ogenki desu ka.

A:  ありがとうございます。おかげさまで。Arigatoo gozaimasu. Okagesama de.

Chapter 2          On Campus          大学で
da-i-ga-ku de

(A) Asking the way: Where is it? What is it?

| | |
|---|---|
| モニカ：　ちょっと　すみません。 | 1 |
| Monika:　cho-tto　　su-mi-ma-se-n. | |

| | |
|---|---|
| せんせい：はい、何ですか。 | 2 |
| Sensei:　ha-i,　na-n de-su ka. | |

| | |
|---|---|
| モニカ：　学生かは、どこですか。 | 3 |
| Monika:　ga-ku-see-ka wa,　do-ko de-su ka. | |

| | |
|---|---|
| せんせい：ああ、学生かは、あそこです。あの　白いたてものです。 | 4 |
| Sensei:　ah,　ga-ku-se-e-ka wa,　a-so-ko de-su.　a-no shi-ro-i ta-te-mo-no desu. | |

*white.*　*Building.*

| | |
|---|---|
| 私も　いっしょに、いきましょうか。 | 5 |
| wa-ta-shi mo　i-ssho-ni,　i-ki-ma-sho-o ka. | |

*I*

| | |
|---|---|
| モニカ：　ありがとうございます。たすかります。 | 6 |
| Monika:　a-ri-ga-to-o go-za-i-ma-su. ta-su-ka-ri-ma-su. | |

[English translation]: Asking the way

Monica:　　Excuse me.
Professor: Yes. Is there anything?  (Literally: What is it?)
Monica:　　Where is the Student Office?
Professor: Oh, the Student Office is over there.  That white building.  Shall I come with
　　　　　　you?
Monica:　　Thank you so much.  It will really help.

Chapter 2(A)                    Vocabulary List

1. Expressions

| | | |
|---|---|---|
| chotto | ちょっと | a little |
| Sumimasen | すみません | Excuse me. |
| Hai | はい | Yes |
| Aa(Ah) | ああ | Oh |
| Arigatoo | ありがとう | Thank you. |
| Arigatoo gozaimasu | ありがとうございます | Thank you (polite form). |
| Tasukarimasu | たすかります | It really helps. |

2. Nouns

| | | |
|---|---|---|
| daigaku | だいがく | college, university |
| gakusei | がくせい | student |
| gakusei-ka | がくせいか | student office |
| asoko | あそこ | over there |
| ano | あの | that (noun modifier) |
| tatemono | たてもの | building |
| watashi | わたし | I |

(Additional Vocabulary)

| | | |
|---|---|---|
| koko | ここ | here |
| kore | これ | this one |
| kono | この | this (noun modifier) |
| soko | そこ | there (near the listener) |
| sore | それ | that one (near the listener) |
| sono | その | that (noun modifier) |
| are | あれ | that one over there (far for both listener and speaker) |

3. Adjectives

| | | |
|---|---|---|
| shiroi | しろい | white |

4. Adverbs

| | | |
|---|---|---|
| issho ni | いっしょに | together |

5. Verbs

| | | |
|---|---|---|
| Ikimashoo | いきましょう | Let's go. |
| Ikimashoo ka | いきましょうか | Shall we go? |
| ikimasu | いきます | to go (polite form) |
| iku | いく | to go (informal, dictionary form) |

(Additional verb)

jya (or "dewa") arimasen じゃありません   It isn't.  Negative form of non-past copula verb used after noun.

6.  Interrogative pronoun

| | | |
|---|---|---|
| nan (= nani) | なん（なに） | what |
| Nan desu ka. | なんですか | What is it? |
| doko | どこ | where |
| Doko desu ka. | どこですか | Where is it? |

7.  Particle

| | | |
|---|---|---|
| mo | も | also |

---------------------------------------------------------------------------------------

Additional Vocabulary from Grammar Notes, Exercises, and Dict-A-Conversation

...........................................................................................

[Nouns]

| | | |
|---|---|---|
| kafeteria | カフェテリア (かふぇてりあ) | cafeteria |
| manga | まんが | comic books |
| hon | ほん | books |
| boku | ぼく | male "I" |
| anata | あなた | you |
| kookoo | こうこう | high school |
| Nihongo | にほんご | Japanese language |
| supeingo | すぺいんご | Spanish language |
| otoosan | おとうさん | father (polite form) |
| o-namae | おなまえ | name (polite form) |
| Nihon no kata | にほんのかた | Japanese person (polite form) |
| eki | えき | train station |
| uchi | うち | home; house |
| otearai | おてあらい | bathroom |
| tonari | となり | next to; neighbor |
| haha | はは | mother (humble form) |
| iro | いろ | color |
| nani-iro | なにいろ | what color |
| inu | いぬ | dog |
| kuruma | くるま | car |
| kasa | かさ | umbrella |
| kaban | かばん | bag; briefcase |
| suki na iro | すきないろ | favorite color |
| daigakusei | だいがくせい | college student |
| shakai-jin | しゃかいじん | adult who is a working force in a society |
| shufu | しゅふ | home-maker; housewife |

(vocabulary from Exercise A)

| | | |
|---|---|---|
| enpitsu | えんぴつ | pencil |
| kyookasho | きょうかしょ | textbook |
| nooto | ノート | notebook |
| keshigomu | けしごむ | eraser |
| jisho | じしょ | dictionary |
| tokei | とけい | watch/clock |
| kokuban | こくばん | blackboard |
| hata | はた | flag |
| mado | まど | window |
| to/doa | と/ドア | door |
| tsukue | つくえ | desk |
| isu | いす | chair |
| e | え | picture; drawing |
| hikidashi | ひきだし | drawer |
| kami | かみ | paper |
| chooku | チョーク | chalk |
| kokuban-keshi | こくばんけし | blackboard eraser |

[Adjectives]

| | | |
|---|---|---|
| ii | いい | good |

**(colors)**

| | | |
|---|---|---|
| akai | あかい | red |
| kuroi | くろい | black |
| kiiroi | きいろい | yellow |
| chairoi | ちゃいろい | brown |

[Verbs]

| | | |
|---|---|---|
| kaerimasu | かえります | go home, return |
| tabemasu | たべます | eat |
| hanashimasu | はなします | talk; speak |
| shimasu | します | do |

[Expressions]

| | | |
|---|---|---|
| Hai. /Ee. | はい。/ええ。 | Yes. |
| Chotto sumimasen. | ちょっとすみません。 | |
| Daijyoobu (desu) | だいじょうぶ。 | It's all right. Don't worry. |
| Soo shimashoo. | そうしましょう。 | Let's do that. |
| Dare no desuka. | だれのですか。 | Whose is it? |

Chapter 2 (A)                    Grammar and Culture Notes

## 1. <u>Asking questions:  "What," "Which one," "Where"</u>

Observe the conversation between A and B.

A:  Sore wa <u>nan</u> desu ka.           A: それは　なんですか。

B:  <u>Dore</u> desu ka.  Kore wa pen desu.    B: どれですか。これはペンです。

   Enpitsu mo arimasu yo.              えんぴつも　ありますよ。

A:  <u>Doko</u> desu ka.               A: どこですか。

B:  Koko desu.                    B: ここです。

> A: What is it?    (pointing at a pen of B)
> B: Which one?  This is a pen.  I have also a pencil.
> A:  Where is it?
> B: (showing a pencil) It's (right) here.

A asked B what that was near A.  B asked which one? and said it's a pen.  B said he also has a pencil.  A asked where it was and B replied it's right here.

In this short dialogue, you see three question words: what, which one, and where; namely nan, dore, and doko.  These are the question words you are going to practice in this chapter.

(1)

| Nan desu ka.  (What is it?)<br>なんですか。 | → | (pen) desu.<br>(ペン )です。 |
|---|---|---|

(2)

| Dore desu ka.  (Which one is it?)<br>どれですか。 | → | Kore desu.<br>これです。 |
|---|---|---|

(3)

| Doko desu ka. (Where is it?)<br>どこですか。 | → | Koko desu.<br>ここです。 |
|---|---|---|

## 2. <u>Pointing at things and places:</u> <u>Demonstrative Pronouns</u>

   Japanese demonstrative pronouns are represented by the "ko-so-a-do" pattern.  The "ko" group indicates the object is closer to the speaker than the listener. Conversely for the "so" group, the object is closer to the listener than the speaker. For the "a" group, the object is distant from both. And lastly, the "do" group signifies inquiry.

| | こ ko | そ so | あ a | ど do |
|---|---|---|---|---|
| things | これ<br>kore | それ<br>sore | あれ<br>are | どれ<br>dore |
| Noun Modifiers | この<br>kono | その<br>sono | あの<br>ano | どの<br>dono |
| locations | ここ<br>koko | そこ<br>soko | あそこ<br>asoko | どこ<br>doko |

**(1).** <u>**What is it?** "それは、なんですか。**Sore wa nan desu ka"**</u>

Interrogative pronoun: "nan" or "nani"

While pointing at something you don't know, ask "なんですか。Nan desu ka?"

**(2).** <u>**Which one?** "どれですか。**Dore desu ka"**</u>

Interrogative pronoun: "dore"

| kore これ | sore それ | are あれ | dore どれ |
|---|---|---|---|

When the Nouns follow, you use "kono," "sono," and "ano" before the nouns.
この、その、あの

| kono hon<br>このほん | sono hon<br>そのほん | ano hon<br>あのほん | dono hon<br>どのほん |
|---|---|---|---|

**(3). <u>Where is it?　〜は、どこですか。~wa doko desu ka.</u>**

Example:　**<u>Otearai wa doko desu ka</u>**

| | | |
|---|---|---|
| A: | おてあらいは　どこですか。 | Otearai wa doko desu ka. |
| | | (Where is the bathroom?) |
| B: | そこです。 | Soko desu.  (It's there, near you.) |
| A: | ここですか。 | Koko desu ka.  (Is it here?) |
| B: | いいえ、そこじゃありません。 | Iie, soko jya arimasen.  (No, it's not there.) |
| | そのとなりです。 | Sono tonari desu.    (It's next to it.) |

　　* If the topic that is followed by particle "は wa" is obvious to both the speaker and the listener, you may omit the topic, and simply ask "どこですか。Doko desu ka"

Observe the following story from old Japan.

---

[うらしまたろうのおはなし Old legend of Urashima Taro]　　U: Urashima, S: stranger

うらしまたろう Urashima Taro returned from the Sea King's palace to the sea shore after three days (but in real life, it was 300 years).  He asked a stranger on the beach:

U: すみません、ここは　どこですか。Sumimasen, koko wa doko desu ka. (Excuse me.  Where is this?)
S: "みずのえです。　　　　　　　Mizu no E" desu.     (It's a village called "Mizunoe")
U: え？(Puzzled)　うらしまたろうのうちは、どこですか。
　　　　　　　　　　　　　　Urashima Taro no uchi wa doko desu ka. (Where is Urashima's house?)
S: うらしまたろう？　　　　　　Urashima Taro?
　　それ、　だれですか。　　　Sore, dare desu ka.  (Who is it?)
U: しくしく、、、　　　　　　　(sob….)

---

|  | こ ko | そ so | あ a | ど do |
|---|---|---|---|---|
| locations | ここ<br>koko | そこ<br>soko | あそこ<br>asoko | どこ<br>doko |

Koko: the vicinity of the speaker
Soko:　the vicinity of the listener
Asoko: the area far for both the speaker and the listener

### 3. Particle "も mo" to mean "also"

Particle "も mo" indicates similarity.  In an affirmative sentence, it means "also," and in a negative sentence, it means "either."  In dialogue (A), the professor offers to join Monica, saying "わたしも　いきましょうか。watashi **mo** ikimashoo ka?"  In Japanese, the particle "も mo" is always preceded by the word it being modified and is never placed anywhere else.  Examine the following examples:

A: このほんは、いいほんですよ。　　Kono hon wa, ii hon desu yo.
　　　　　　　　　　　　　　　　　　　　(This book is a good book.)
B: このほんも、いいほんですよ。　　Kono hon **mo**, ii hon desu yo.
　　　　　　　　　　　　　　　　　　　　(This book is also a good book.)
A: じゃ、あのほんも　いいほんですか。Jya, ano hon **mo**, ii hon desu ka.
　　　　　　　　　　　　　　　　　　　　(Then, is that book a good book, too?
B: はい、あのほんも　いいほんです。　Hai, ano hon **mo**, ii hon desu.
　　　　　　　　　　　　　　　　　　　　(Yes, that book is also a good book.)

Notes:
*1 When "も mo" is used in the subject or direct object position, it replaces "は wa," "が ga," or "を wo."

*2  However, as you learn more particles, it will become clear to you that particles "に ni," "で de", "へ e," "から kara," and "まで made" would complement "も mo," not replace.  So, the particle "も mo" follows other particles, resulting in combinations including "にも ni mo," "へも e mo," "でも de mo," "からも kara mo" and "までも made mo."

Summary of particle relationships with "mo":

| |
|---|
| が ga → も mo |
| は wa → も mo |
| を wo → も mo |
| |
| に ni  → にも ni mo |
| へ e  → へも e mo |
| で de → でも de mo |
| から kara → からも kara mo |
| まで made → までも made mo |

Observe the following dialogue:

| | |
|---|---|
| (Pointing at Hiragana) | |
| A: これは　にほんごですか。 | kore wa nihongo desu ka. |
| B: はい、にほんごです。 | hai, nihongo desu. |
| (Pointing at Spanish) | |
| A: これも　にほんごですか。 | kore mo nihongo desu ka. |
| B: いいえ、それは　すぺいんごです。 | iie, sore wa, supeingo desu. |
| A: ああ、そうですか。 | aa, soo desu ka. |

### 4. Colors いろ

Some color words in Japanese only exist as nouns and others have both adjective and noun equivalents.  For example, "orange," "pink," and "green" are nouns, while "white," "black," "blue," "red," "yellow," and "brown" have both adjectival and nominative forms.  It is simple to distinguish nouns from adjectives as "true" adjectives end with "i."  See the examples below.

| Colors | Nouns | Adjectives |
|---|---|---|
| white | しろ shiro | しろい shiroi |
| black | くろ kuro | くろい kuroi |
| red | あか aka | あかい akai |
| blue | あお ao | あおい aoi |
| yellow | きいろ kiiro | きいろい kiiroi |
| brown | ちゃいろ chairo | ちゃいろい chairoi |

What colors are the traffic signals in Japan?  Are they the same colors as in the U.S.?
Yes, but they are "あか aka," "あお ao," "きいろ kiiro," namely "red," "blue," and
"yellow."  The color range of "あお ao" in Japanese culture is much wider, and the word
"あお ao" encompasses various shades of blue and green.

Caution:

Ask your classmates what colors they like, asking "なにいろが　すきですか。nani-iro
ga suki desuka?" When asked the question, answer using a noun form, such as "あか
aka," "あお ao," "しろ shiro," "くろ kuro" with the copula verb "です。desu."
Example:

    Q: なにいろが　すきですか。nani iro ga suki desu ka?
              (What color do you like?)
    A: あおが　すきです。      ao ga suki desu. (I like blue.)

## 5. <u>Adjectives as modifiers</u>

Japanese adjectives are similar to English adjectives: they are placed before nouns to give
description to the nouns that follow.  See the examples below.
Please note also that no "article" is used in Japanese.

    (a) [a] white building
         しろい　たてもの　shiroi tatemono

    (b) [a] big dog
         おおきい　いぬ　　ookii inu

    (c) [a] blue car
         あおい　くるま　　aoi  kuruma

## 6. <u>Word order</u>

When you have two modifiers to a noun, such as with the phrase, "this red book," the
"demonstrative pronoun" comes first, then the "adjective."  The Japanese equivalent of
"this red book" would be "このあかいほん kono akai hon."

| Demonstrative pronoun | Adjective | Noun |
|---|---|---|
| この kono<br>(this) | あかい akai<br>(red) | ほん hon<br>(book) |
| その sono<br>(that) | しろい shiroi<br>(white) | たてもの tatemono<br>(building) |
| あの ano<br>(that over there) | あおい aoi<br>(blue) | うみ umi<br>(sea) |

*Asking "which one?": "どれですか。Dore desuka" or "どの Dono + noun ですか。
desuka"

Chapter 2 (A) Exercises

A. Learn the vocabulary of items in the classroom: Pair-work.  Make a list of what you see around you and write down their names below.  Reference the dictionary listing on the following page and write down the Japanese word equivalents.

    [English]          [Japanese]

(1) pen          ----------------------------

(1) pencil       ----------------------------

(2) textbook     ----------------------------

(3) notebook     ----------------------------

(4) eraser       ----------------------------

(5) dictionary    ----------------------------

(6) watch/clock   ----------------------------

(7) blackboard    ----------------------------

(8) flag         ----------------------------

(9) television     ----------------------------

(10) window      ----------------------------

(11) door        ----------------------------

(12) desk        ----------------------------

(13) chair       ----------------------------

(14) bag         ----------------------------

(15) map         ----------------------------

(16) picture/photo ----------------------------

(17) drawing     ----------------------------

(18) paper       ----------------------------

(19) marker      ----------------------------

(20) blackboard eraser----------------------------

English-Japanese Dictionary

pen; pen, pencil; enpitsu, textbook; tekisuto or kyookasho, notebook; nooto,
eraser; keshigomu, dictionary; jisho or jibiki, watch/clock; tokei, blackboard; kokuban,
flag; hata, television; terebi, window; mado, door; to or doa, desk; tsukue, chair; isu,
bag; kaban, map; chizu, picture/photo; shashin, drawing; e, paper; kami, marker; maakaa,
blackboard eraser; kokuban-keshi

B. Pair-work: Ask your partner what the item is, by pointing at different things in the
classroom. Take turns.
Examples:

        A: あれはなんですか。
           Are wa nan desu ka (by pointing at a blackboard).
        B: あれはこくばんです。
           Are wa "kokuban" desu.


        B: それはなんですか。
           Sore wa nan desu ka (by pointing at A's textbook).
        A: それはきょうかしょです。
           Kore wa "kyookasho" desu.


        A: これはなんですか。
           Kore wa nan desu ka (by pointing at A's watch).
        B: それはとけいです。
           Sore wa "tokei" desu.


C-1. Fill in the blanks with appropriate words/particles.
Examples:

        A: これ（        ）ほんですか。   Kore …………hon desu ka.
        B: はい、ほんです。           Hai, hon desu.

        A: あれは（        ）ですか。   Are wa …………desu ka.
        B: あれは「どあ」です。       Are wa "doa" desu.

    1. A: それ（      ）じしょですか。       Sore ………jisho desu ka.
       B: いいえ、じしょ（      ）ありません。Iie, jisho …………arimasen.

    2. A: これは（        ）ですか。   Kore wa …………...desu ka.
       B: はい、ぺんです。           Hai, pen desu.

    3. A: そのほんは（        ）ですか。  Sono hon wa …………desu ka.
       B: わたしのです。             Watashi no desu.

    4. A: せんせいは（        ）ですか。  Sensei wa …………desu ka.
       B: せんせいは　あそこです。      Sensei wa asoko desu.

5.　A: これはノートです。それもノートですか。　Kore wa nooto desu.  Sore mo
　　　　　　　　　　　　　　　　　　　　　　　nooto desu ka.

　　B: いいえ、これ（　　）ノートじゃありません。Iie, kore ..........nooto jya
　　　　　　　　　　　　　　　　　　　　　　　arimasen.

6.　A: このじしょは（　　　　）のですか。　Kono jisho wa ........... no desu ka.
　　B: いいえ、わたしの（　　　　）ありません。せんせい（　　　）です。
　　　　Iie, watashi no ..........arimasen.  Sensei ...............desu.

7.　A: あなた（　　　）えんぴつ（　　　）どれですか。
　　　　　　　　　　　　　　　　Anata ...........enpitsu.............dore desu ka.
　　B: これです。　　　　　　　Kore desu.

8.　A: がくせいか（　　　　　）どのたてものですか。
　　　　Gakusei-ka ..............dono tatemono desu ka.
　　B: あのたてものです。　Ano tatemono desu.

9.　A: がくせいかは（　　　　）ですか。Gakusei-ka wa.............desu ka.
　　B: あれです。　　　　　　　　　Are desu.

10. A: あれ（　　　）なんですか。　Are ........nan desu ka.
　　B: どれですか。　　　　　　　Dore desu ka.
　　A: （　　　）しろいたてものです。...........shiroi tatemono desu.
　　B: あれは、がくせいかです。　Are wa gakusei-ka desu.

C-2.  Choose the right words.
Example:
　　　わたし（は、の）がくせいです。
　　　Watashi {wa, no} gakusei desu.  [I am a student.]

1.　（それ、その）は、ほんです。{sore, sono} wa, hon desu.

2.　（あれ、あの）かばんは、（たなかさん、たなかさんの）です。
　　{are, ano} kaban wa {Tanaka-san, Tanaka-san no} desu.

3.　（これ、この）ほんは、わたし（は、の）じゃありません。
　　{kore, kono}hon wa, watashi {wa, no} jya arimasen.

4.　（わたしは、わたしの）えんぴつは（これ、この）です。
　　{watashi wa, watashi no} enpitsu wa {kore, kono} desu.

5.　がくせいかは　（どれ、どの）ですか。
　　Gakusei-ka wa {dore, dono} desu ka.

D.  Fill in the blanks with appropriate words.
Example:

    A: これは　ほんですか。　　　　　　Kore wa hon desu ka.
    B: はい、ほんです。　　　　　　　　Hai, <u>hon desu</u>.

1.  A: このじしょは、あなたのですか。　Kono jisho wa anata no desu ka.
    B: はい、（　　　　　　　　　）。　Hai, ………………………………

2.  A: いっしょに　いきましょうか。　　Isshoni ikimashoo ka.
    B: はい、（　　　　　　　　　）。　Hai, ………………………………

3.  A: ありがとうございます。　　　　　Arigatoo gozaimasu.
    B: いいえ、（　　　　　　　　　）。　Iie, ………………………………

4.  A: ちょっとすみません。　　　　　　Chotto sumimasen.
    B: はい、（　　　　　　　　　）。　Hai, ………………………………

E.  Pair-work:  Ask each other where things are.  Ask at least five items.
Example:  A:  （～さんの）ペンは、どこですか。( ~ san no) pen wa doko desu ka.
        B:  （わたしの）ペンは、ここです。(watashi no) pen wa koko desu.

    (Suggested items: kyookasho, kaban, keshi-gomu, enpitsu, uchi (home),
    okaasan (mother), nihongo no sensei)

F.  Pair-work:  Gather information from you partner and give a report to class.  The information must include the following: his/her name, the city s/he lives in, his/her favorite color, the color of his/her car or house, his/her occupation.  One of the sentences must be structured to bring forth the response "jya arimasen."

[Vocabulary help]:
    1.  おなまえは、なんですか。
        o-namae (your "honorable"name) wa nan desu ka. (Answer with "namae")
    2.  うちは、どこですか。
        uchi (home) wa doko desu ka. (Where is your home?)
    3.  すきないろは、なにいろですか。
        suki-na-iro wa nani-iro desu ka. (What color do you like?)
    4.  くるまは、なにいろですか。
        kuruma (= car, or uchi=house) wa nani-iro desu ka. (What color is your car?)
    5.  （～さんは）かいしゃいんですか。
        (~ san wa) kaisha-in desu ka. (Are you a company employee?)
Use also: がくせい gakusei (undergraduate student), だいがくいんせい daigaku-in-sei (graduate student), しゃかいじん shakaijin (a person who works and earns salary), しゅふ shufu (home-maker)

Chapter 2(A)'s Dict-A-Conversation
Listen to the CD and write down the missing part below. At this stage, you may write in Roma-ji, but later, write everything in hiragana.

A：ちょっと　すみません。
　　chotto sumimasen.

B：_____

A：カフェテリアは、どこですか。
　　Cafeteria　　wa　doko desu ka.

B：_____

A：あの　あかい　たてもの　ですか。
　　ano　akai　tatemono　desuka.

B：_____

A：ありがとうございます。たすかります。
　　arigatoo gozaimasu.　　　tasukarimasu.

B：_____

Chapter 2(A):  Crossword Puzzle #1 (vocabulary from Chapter 2A)

Across
6. Thank you.
7. college; university

Down
1. building
2. to go (verb)
3. here
4. student
5. over there

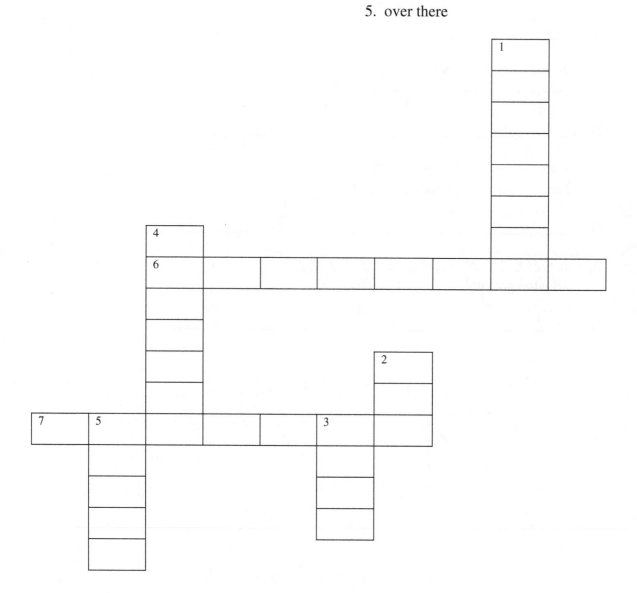

Chapter 2(A):  Crossword Puzzle # 2 (vocabulary from Chapter 2A)

Across
1. Shall we go?
2. It really helps.

Down
3. What is it?
4. white
5. together
6. Where is it?

## Chapter 2(A): Crossword Puzzle # 3 (items in classroom)

Across
1. blackboard
2. eraser
3. flag
4. character/writing
5. pencil
6. map
7. chair

Down
8. window
9. dictionary
10. clock/watch
11. pen
12. picture/photo
13. textbook
14. notebook
15. television
16. desk
17. door
1. paper

Chapter 2 (A):  Hiragana (a ~ to) Puzzle
（あいうえお、かきくけこ、さしすせそ、たちつてと）

Find the following words in the box and circle/color them.  The words can go
horizontally, vertically, diagonally, or backward.

たかい high; expensive   かたい firm   あした tomorrow   ちち father (humble form)
ちかい near   ちいさい small   おと sound   とけい watch; clock   だいがく college
ちず map   うで arms   せいと student/pupil   こい love; infatuation   つくえ desk
せつこ girl's name   くつ shoes   かいこ silkworm   うた song   いとこ cousin
あおいくつ blue shoes

| せ | あ | し | た | た | で | う |
|---|---|---|---|---|---|---|
| と | お | ち | ず | か | だ | た |
| こ | い | か | た | い | ち | ち |
| い | く | せ | が | さ | か | い |
| と | つ | く | え | い | く | さ |
| こ | せ | い | と | け | い | い |

Hiragana Puzzle 1 (Hiragana あ～と)　　なまえ　Name (　　　　　　　　　　)

Find the listed words from the following page in the crossword puzzle and circle them. Words may appear horizontally, vertically, backward, and may also overlap.

| | | | | | | | | | |
|---|---|---|---|---|---|---|---|---|---|
| い | ど | い | と | う | い | ち | ご | た | き |
| す | あ | い | お | つ | そ | う | い | く | す |
| す | い | か | こ | く | が | え | つ | あ | し |
| す | が | お | い | し | し | き | づ | お | い |
| し | い | き | し | い | い | す | く | い | か |
| け | が | し | い | ち | い | あ | き | お | く |
| い | け | あ | と | ど | き | し | ず | か | い |
| こ | う | い | け | う | い | あ | あ | し | か |
| け | し | き | い | き | き | と | と | い | た |

List of words:

| | | | | | |
|---|---|---|---|---|---|
| いか | squid | ごい | vocabulary | きおく | memory |
| かき | persimmon, oyster | けしき | scenery | こい | love, carp |
| たかい | high | どうき | pulse | あい | love |
| おい | nephew | こうい | favorable feeling | いど | well |
| かお | face | いい | good | きく | chrysanthemum |
| しあい | game | とお | ten | きす | kiss |
| すあし | naked foot | いそがしい | busy | すし | vinegar-ed rice |
| えき | station | おかしい | funny, strange | かい | sea shells |
| あおい | blue | いちど | once | たき | waterfall |
| あかい | red | いきいき | lively, vivid | しずか | quiet |
| つき | the moon | うえ | above | うつくしい | beautiful |
| いす | chair | いえ | house | いきがい | hope reason to live |
| こいし | pebble | こいしい | miss someone | あしあと | footstep |
| がけ | cliff | けが | injury | いけ | pond |
| きし | seashore | すがお | makeup-less face | すいか | watermelon |
| あき | autumn | とけい | watch, clock | しきいし | stone laid on the ground |
| けいこ | practice, Keiko (girl's name) | つづく | continue | いと thread きずあと scar |

Chapter 2(B)       I came from America. アメリカから　きました。
                           a-me-ri-ka kara  ki-ma-shi-ta.


せんせい： りゅうがく生　　　の　かた　ですか。
Sensei:   ryu-u-ga-ku-se-i　no　kata　desu ka.

モニカ：　はい、アメリカ　　から　きました。
Monika:   ha-i,　a-me-ri-ka　ka-ra　ki-ma-shi-ta.

せんせい：そうですか。　日本語が、　　　おじょうずですね。
Sensei:   so-o de-su ka. Ni-ho-n-go ga,　o-jyo-o-zu de-su ne.

モニカ：　いいえ、　　まだまだです。
Monika:   i-i-e,　　ma-da ma-da de-su.

せんせい：　何年生　　ですか。
Sensei:   na-n-ne-n-se-i  de-su ka.

モニカ：　二年生　　です。
Monika:   ni-ne-n-se-i　de-su.

[English translation]:

Professor: Are you a foreign student?

Monica:    Yes, I came from America.

Professor: Is that right (= so)?
           Your Japanese is good.

Monica:    No, not yet.

Professor: What year are you?

Monica:    (I am) sophomore.

Chapter 2(B)                    Vocabulary List

1. Expressions

mada mada desu. まだまだです。          I am still no good.

2. Nouns

| | | |
|---|---|---|
| ryuu-gakusei | りゅうがくせい | foreign exchange students |
| kata | かた | a person; politer than "hito" |
| ryuu-gakusei no kata りゅうがくせいのかた | | a polite form of "foreign students" |
| amerika | アメリカ（あめりか） | America |
| nihon-go | にほんご | Japanese language |
| nan-nen-sei | なんねんせい | what year (in school) student |
| ni-nen-sei | にねんせい | sophomore, second-year student |

3. な Adjectives (Copula Nouns)

| | | |
|---|---|---|
| jyoozu | じょうず | skillful, skilled |
| o-jyoozu | おじょうず | polite form of "jyoozu" |

4. Verbs

| | | |
|---|---|---|
| kimasu | きます | come/will come (polite form) |
| kimashita | きました | came, past tense of "kimasu" |

5. Adverbs

| | | |
|---|---|---|
| hai | はい | yes |
| iie | いいえ | no |
| mada | まだ | yet, still |

6. Particles

| | | |
|---|---|---|
| kara | から | from |

..................................................................................
Additional Vocabulary from Grammar Notes, Exercises, and Dict-A-Conversation
..................................................................................

[School years]

| | | |
|---|---|---|
| ichi-nen-sei | いちねんせい | freshman, first-year student |
| san-nen-sei | さんねんせい | junior, third-year student |
| yo-nen-sei | よねんせい | senior, fourth-year student |
| go-nen-sei | ごねんせい | fifth-year student |
| roku-nen-sei | ろくねんせい | sixth-year student |

[Nouns]

| | | |
|---|---|---|
| gakkoo | がっこう | school |
| neko | ねこ | cat |
| gohan | ごはん | meal; cooked rice |

| | | |
|---|---|---|
| atama | あたま | head |
| me | め | eyes |
| ji | じ | letters; characters; handwriting |
| ame | あめ | rain |
| shinbun | しんぶん | newspapers |
| kimochi | きもち | feelings |
| denwa bangoo | でんわばんごう | telephone number |
| nan-ban | なんばん | what number? |
| (o) hashi | （お）はし | chopsticks |
| (o) sushi | （お）すし | cooked rice flavored with vinegar, served often with raw fish or vegetables, fish roe, seaweed, etc. |

**(Transportations)**

| | | |
|---|---|---|
| jitensha | じてんしゃ | bicycle |
| densha | でんしゃ | train; street car |
| basu | バス | bus |
| hikooki | ひこうき | airplane |
| chikatetsu | ちかてつ | subway |
| fune | ふね | ship, boat |
| takushii | タクシー | taxi |
| herikoputaa | ヘリコプター | helicopter |
| toho | とほ | walking |
| toho de, aruite | とほで、あるいて | via walking |

**(Languages)**

| | | |
|---|---|---|
| nani-go | なにご | what language? |
| ei-go | えいご | English |
| furansu-go | フランスご | French |
| Çava? | | How are you? (in French) |
| supein-go | スペインご | Spanish |
| roshi(y)a-go | ロシアご | Russian |
| itari(y)a-go | イタリアご | Italian |
| chuugoku-go | ちゅうごくご | Chinese |
| kankoku-go | かんこくご | Korean |
| tai-go | タイご | Thai |
| betonamu-go | ベトナムご | Vietnamese |

**(People)**

| | | |
|---|---|---|
| otoosan | おとうさん | father (polite form) |

| | | |
|---|---|---|
| okaasan | おかあさん | mother (polite form) |
| otona | おとな | adults |
| kodomo | こども | children |
| tomodachi | ともだち | friends |

(Means of eating)

| | | |
|---|---|---|
| te | て | hand(s) |
| supuun | スプーン | spoon |
| sutoroo | ストロー | straw |
| sashimi | さしみ | raw fish |
| fooku | フォーク | folk |
| naifu | ナイフ | knife |

(food and drinks)

| | | |
|---|---|---|
| miruku sheeku | ミルクシェーク | milk shake |
| suteeki | ステーキ | steak |
| keeki | ケーキ | cake |
| raamen | ラーメン | Chinese noodles in soup |
| aisukuriimu | アイスクリーム | ice cream |

[な Adjectives/Copula Nouns]

| | | |
|---|---|---|
| daijyoobu | だいじょうぶ | all right |
| jyoobu | じょうぶ | healthy |
| genki | げんき | healthy; energetic |
| kirei | きれい | pretty |
| yuumei | ゆうめい | famous |
| shizuka | しずか | quiet |
| heta | へた | unskillful (↔jyoozu じょうず skillful) |
| ookina | おおきな | large |
| chiisana | ちいさな | small |
| rippa | りっぱ | magnificent; great |
| suki | すき | favorite; likable |

[Adjectives]

| | | |
|---|---|---|
| amai | あまい | sweet |
| oishii | おいしい | delicious |
| tooi | とおい | far |
| ii | いい | good |

| | | |
|---|---|---|
| osoi | おそい | late |
| itai | いたい | painful |
| hoshii | ほしい | is wanted; desirable |

[Verbs]

| | | |
|---|---|---|
| nomimasu | のみます | drink |
| kakimasu | かきます | write |
| yomimasu | よみます | read |
| kikimasu | ききます | listen; ask |
| shimasu | します | do |
| benkyooshimasu | べんきょうします | study |
| nemasu | ねます | sleep; go to bed |
| okimasu | おきます | get up |
| asobimasu | あそびます | play |
| arukimasu | あるきます | walk |
| furimasu | ふります | rain: Ame ga furimasu (It rains) |
| (tabemasu) | たべます | eat (Chapter 2[A]) |
| (hanashimasu) | はなします | speak; talk  (Chapter 2[A]) |

[Adverbs]

| | | |
|---|---|---|
| taitei | たいてい | usually |
| mada | まだ | yet; still |

[Particles]

| | | |
|---|---|---|
| made | まで | till; up to; as far as~ |
| de | で | by means of |

[Question words]

| | | |
|---|---|---|
| itsu | いつ | when |

[Expressions]

| | | |
|---|---|---|
| Ie. | いえ | No: short form of "Iie" |
| Nan de? | なんで | in what way?  How? |
| Nan de ikimasu ka? | なんでいきますか。 | How do you get there? |

| | | |
|---|---|---|
| Doo yatte ? | どうやって | how? |
| yaru | やる | casual form of "suru" (do) |
| yatte | やって | the "te" form of "yaru" (do) |
| Doo yatte ikimasu ka? | どうやって　いきますか。 | How do you get there? |

Chapter 2 (B)                    Grammar and Cultural Notes

## 1. Action Verbs

Unlike "desu," which shows "is, am, are," the verb that ends with "-masu" shows actions
such as eating, drinking, studying, reading, writing, etc.

     Ex.

たべます、のみます、はなします、よみます、かきます、ききます、
tabemasu,  nomimasu,  hanashimasu,  yomimasu,  kakimasu,   kikimasu,
(eat)         (drink)      (speak)          (read)        (write)        (listen)

します、べんきょうします、みます、ねます、おきます
shimasu, benkyoo shimasu,       mimasu, nemasu,  okimasu
(do)        (study)                (see; look; watch) (sleep) (get up)

SVO group

| tabemasu たべます | nomimasu のみます | hanashimasu はなします |
|---|---|---|

| yomimasu よみます | kakimasu かきます | kikimasu ききます |
|---|---|---|

| benkyoo shimasu べんきょうします | mimasu みます |
|---|---|

SV group

| nemasu ねます | okimasu おきます | asobimasu あそびます |
|---|---|---|

Among the verbs listed above, there are two types of verbs: SVO and SV.

## 1) SVO group
This is the group of verbs that have Direct Objects (O) and the verbs are Transitive Verbs, such as "eat," "drink," "see," "read," "write," "study," "speak," "hear," etc.

In English, you may say "I eat hamburger," or "I drink milk," and these "hamburger" and "milk" are the Objects of the Verbs "eat" and "drink."  Let's compare the word order of this kind between English and Japanese.

S: Subject, V: Verb, O: Object

| English | Japanese |
|---|---|
| I    eat    hamburger.         → <br> (S)   (V)      (O) | watashi wa   hamburger **wo**   tabemasu. <br> (S)            (O)            (V) <br><br> わたしは　ハンバーガーを　たべます。 |

As you have observed in this comparison, the English word order becomes SOV in Japanese.  Not only that, a particle "を wo" is used after the direct object (hamburger).

## 2)  SV group
Another group of verbs are the last two in the above list: "wake up" and "sleep."  They do not take objects, and the verbs are Intransitive Verbs.

| English | Japanese |
|---|---|
| I  get up  early.         → <br> (S)  (V) | watashi wa   hayaku   okimasu <br> (S)                      (V) <br><br> わたしは　はやく　おきます。 |

**Predicate pattern**

|  | Non-past/incomplete | Past/complete |
|---|---|---|
| **Affirmative** | -masu | -mashita |
| **Negative** | -masen | -masen deshita |

[Examples of non-past tense affirmative to negative]:

| Affirmative | → | Negative | Affirmative→Negative |
|---|---|---|---|
| たべます | → | たべません | tabemasu →tabemasen |
| のみます | → | のみません | nomimasu →nomimasen |
| はなします | → | はなしません | hanashimasu →hanashimasen |
| よみます | → | よみません | yomimasu→ yomimasen |
| かきます | → | かきません | kakimasu→ kakimasen |

[Examples of non-past affirmative to past tense affirmative]:

| Non-past | → | Past | Non-past→Past |
|---|---|---|---|
| たべます | → | たべました | tabemasu →tabemashita |
| のみます | → | のみました | nomimasu →nomimashita |
| はなします | → | はなしました | hanashimasu →hanashimashita |
| よみます | → | よみました | yomimasu→ yomimashita |
| かきます | → | かきました | kakimasu→ kakimashita |

[Examples of past tense affirmative to past tense negative]:

| Past-tense Affirmative | → | Past-tense Negative | Past-tense Affirmative→Past-tense Negative |
|---|---|---|---|
| たべました | →たべませんでした | | tabemashita →tabemasendeshita |
| のみました | →のみませんでした | | nomimashita →nomimasendeshita |
| はなしました | →はなしませんでした | | hanashimashita →hanashimasendeshita |
| よみました | →よみませんでした | | yomimashita → yomimasendeshita |
| かきました | →かきませんでした | | kakimashita → kakimasendeshita |

## 2. Verbs of Motions: come, go, return, walk

Among the SV pattern of "Action verbs," there is a group of verbs that require special attention. They express the motions such as "going, coming, returning, walking, etc." Since they express the motion of moving, the particle that are used with them indicate the directions you are moving to and from. See examples:

| どこへ　いきますか。 | Doko e ikimasuka. (Where are you going to?) |
|---|---|
| がっこうへ　いきます。 | Gakkoo e ikimasu. (I'm going to school.) |
| うちへ　かえります。 | Uchi e kaerimasu. (I'm going home.) |

## Particle "へ e" : "to"

The particle "e" indicates the direction of motion verbs.  It corresponds to "to" or "toward" in English and is usually interchangeable with the particle "に ni."

| To a place | go/come/return | |
|---|---|---|
| | ikimasu | いきます |
| ~ e | kimasu | きます |
| へ | kaerimasu | かえります |

## Particle "から kara":"from"

The particle "kara" means "from," and "Amerika kara" means "from America."
> Ex.
> 1. にほんから　　　　　Nihon kara  (from Japan)
> 2. ちゅうごくから　　Chuugoku kara (from China)
> 3. かんこくから　　　　Kankoku kara (from Korea)
> 4. ドイツから　　　　　Doitsu kara (from Germany)
> 5. ロサンジェルスから Rosanjerusu kara (from Los Angeles)

When you first met someone, you converse as follows:
**A:** どこから　きましたか。　　　Doko kara kimashitaka. (Where are you from?)
**B:** ミネソタから　きました。　　Minesota kara kimashita. (I'm from Minnesota.)

## Particle "まで made" : "as far as ~" "up to ~ "

> 1. がっこうまで　あるきました。gakkoo made arukimashita.
> (I walked to school.)
> 2. どこまで　いきますか。　　doko made ikimasu ka.
> (How far are you going?)

**from A to B =  A から B まで**
**A kara B made**

A & B can be any noun, as well as any place and time.

Examples:
1. from home to school　　　 : うちからがっこうまで uchi kara gakkoo made
2. from 1 o'clock to 3 o'clock: いちじからさんじまで ichi-ji kara san-ji made
3. from adults to children　 : おとなからこどもまで otona kara kodomo made
4. うちから　えきまで　あるきました。Uchi kara eki made arukimashita.
　　　　　　　　　　　　　　　　　(I walked from home to train station.)

## 3. Particle "de": by means of

Particle "de" shows a "means"
    でんしゃで いきます。
    de-n-sha de i-ki-ma-su. ( I [will] go by train.)

(1) Examples with transportations:

by train:     でんしゃで  densha de
by bus:       バスで      basu de
by airplane:  ひこうきで  hikooki de
by subway:    ちかてつで  chikatetsu de
by ship:      ふねで      fune de
by car:       くるまで    kuruma de
by walking:   あるいて    aruite、or とほで toho de

うちから がっこうまで バスで いきます。(From home I go to school by bus.)
uchi kara  gakkoo  made  basu de  ikimasu
うちから しんじゅくまで、 でんしゃで いきました。
u-chi ka-ra Shi-n-jyu-ku ma-de,  de-n-sha de i-ki-ma-shi-ta.
                                    (From home I went to Shinjyuku by train.)

(2) Examples with languages: **Suffix "go" -language**

How does one say "Japanese language" in Japanese?  Simply add the suffix "go" to "Nihon":
    "にほんご Nihongo."
    Add the suffix "go" to the country name to achieve its corresponding language.

Examples:

| Country | Country name | Language |
|---|---|---|
| Japan | にほん  Nihon | にほんご  Nihon-go |
| France | フランス Furansu | フランスご Furansu-go |
| Spain | スペイン Supein | スペインご Supein-go |
| Italy | イタリア Itari(y)a | イタリアご Itari(y)a-go |
| Russia | ロシア  Roshi(y)a | ロシアご  Roshi(y)a-go |
| Germany | ドイツ  Doitsu | ドイツご  Doitsu-go |
| China | ちゅうごく Chuugoku | ちゅうごくご Chuugoku-go |
| Korea | かんこく Kankoku | かんこくご Kankoku-go |
| Thai | タイ  Tai | タイご  Tai-go |
| Vietnam | ベトナム Betonamu | ベトナムご Betonamu-go |
| US, England, Canada, Australia | アメリカ Amerika, イギリス Igirisu, カナダ Kanada,オーストラリア Oosutorari(y)a | えいご Eigo |

| | | |
|---|---|---|
| in English: | えいごで | eigo de |
| in Japanese: | にほんごで | nihongo de |
| in Spanish: | スペインごで | supeingo de |
| in French: | フランスごで | furansugo de |
| in German: | ドイツごで | doitsugo de |
| in Italian: | イタリアご | itari(y)ago de |
| in Russian: | ロシアごで | roshi(y)ago de |
| in Chinese | ちゅうごくごで | chuugokugo de |
| in Korean | かんこくごで | kankokugo de |

たなかさんは、にほんごで　はなします。
Tanaka san wa,  nihongo de    hanashimasu. (Tanaka-san speaks in Japanese.)

**Attention**:

How is "を wo" different in this context from "で de"?

If you say "Tanaka san wa Nihongo wo hanashimasu たなかさんは　にほんごを　はなします。" it is talking about his ability, but he may speak Japanese at home, and may not speak it at school, or he may speak to his mother in Japanese, and not in English. In that case, "にほんごで nihongo de" is appropriate since it's talking about the "means" of communication.

(3) Examples with utensils:

| | | |
|---|---|---|
| with chopsticks: | おはしで | ohashi de |
| with knife and folk: | ナイフとフォークで | naifu to fooku de |
| with spoon: | スプーンで | supuun de |

おはしで　たべます。 (I eat with chopsticks.)
ohashi de　　tabemasu.

| | | |
|---|---|---|
| with chalk: | チョークで | chooku de |
| with pen: | ペンで | pen de |
| with pencil: | えんぴつで | enpitsu de |

ペンで、かきます。 (I write with a pen.)
pen de kakimasu.

## 4. "な na" adjectives (or Copula Nouns)

にほんごが　おじょうずですね。
"Nihongo ga o-jyoozu desu ne." (Your Japanese is good.)
 　　　(じょうず jyoozu = skillful; copula noun)

There are two types of adjectives in Japanese. One is the "i" adjective because it ends in "i" before a noun, as in "しろいたてもの shiroi tatemono (white building)," and "おおきいいぬ ookii inu (big dog)." The other type is the "な na" adjective because it is followed by a "な na" before the noun, as in "げんきないぬ genki-na inu (healthy dog)," "じょうずなひと jyoozu na hito (skilled person)" and "たいへんなクラスtaihen-na kurasu (difficult class)." "な Na" adjective usually express abstract concepts.

## [Three Basic Modifiers]

There are three types of modifiers in Japanese (aside from the sentence modifier [relative clause] that will be learned later). They are the following:

(1) particle "no" (when the preceding noun describes the other)
e.g., English book
えいごのほん eigo + no+ hon

(2) i-adjective
e.g., large book
おおきいほん ookii hon

(3) na-adjective
e.g., favorite book
すきなほん suki-na hon

How are the "na-adjectives" and regular adjectives (sometimes called "i-adjectives" distinguished when the former end with "i"? A small number of "na-adjectives" end with 'i.' They include "きれい kirei (pretty or clean), "ゆうめい yuumei (famous)," "ていねい teinei (polite or wholehearted)," and such. When in doubt, look at the spelling of the word, not only the last 'i,' but also the second from the last letter. If an 'e,' then it is a "na-adjective." The "i-adjectives" end with 'ai,' 'ii,' 'ui,' and 'oi,' with a few exceptions, and all else belongs to the "na-adjective" group.

Endings of 'i-adjectives'
.....ai
.....ii
.....ui
.....oi

Ending of 'na-adjectives'
.....ei  & **everything else**

Now can you tell to which group the following words belong?
1. あまい       amai (sweet)
2. おいしい       oishii (tasty)

3.  さむい　　　samui (cold)
4.  とおい　　　tooi (far)
5.  きれい　　　kirei (pretty, clean)
6.  ゆうめい　　yuumei (famous)
7.  しずか　　　shizuka (quiet)
8.  じょうず　　jyoozu (skillful)
9.  へた　　　　heta (unskilled)
10. だいじょうぶ daijyoobu (all right)

Yes, the first four belongs to 'i-adjective' and, the last six belongs to the 'な na-adjective' group.

Exceptions:  The adjectives "おおきい ookii (big) and "ちいさい chiisai (small)" are only adjectives that can also be used as copula nouns in the form of "おおきな ookina" and "ちいさな chiisana."

## How to negate the "な na" adjective?

Since the 'な na-adjective' (or it is also called the "copula noun") belongs to a 'noun' group, its negative predicate is the same as a noun: (~ じゃありません jya arimasen).

> じょうずです　　↔　　　じょうずじゃありません
> Jyoozu desu (It's skillful.)   Jyoozu jya arimasen (It's not skillful.

Examples:
1.  A:  にほんごが　じょうずですね。
       Nihongo  ga　　jyoozu  desu ne. (Your Japanese is good.)

    B:  いいえ、まだ　じょうずじゃありません。
        Iie,　　　mada　jyoozu  jya  arimasen.  (No, I'm not that good yet.)

2.  A:  そこは、しずかですか。
        Soko wa   shizuka desu ka.  (Is that place quiet?)

    B:  いえ、しずかじゃありません。
        Ie,　　shizuka jya arimasen.  (No, it's not quiet.)

In later chapter, we will learn how to negate the "true" adjectives (or "i" adjectives). A list of な na-adjectives often used:

> すき　な　　　　　suki na (favorite)
> きれい　な　　　　kirei na (pretty; clean)
> ゆうめい　な　　　yuumei na(famous)
> げんき　な　　　　genki na (healthy)

| | |
|---|---|
| しずか　な | shizuka na (quiet) |
| へた　　　な | heta na (unskillful) |
| じょうず　な | jyoozu na (skillful) |
| じょうぶな | jyoobu na (healthy; sturdy) |
| おおきな | ookina (large) |
| ちいさな | chiisana (small) |
| りっぱ　な | rippa na (great; magnificent) |
| ていねい　な | teinei na (polite; thorough) |

## 5. Question word: Who? = Dare だれ "Ano hito wa dare desu ka."

A person or people in Japanese is "hito ひと" and the question word "who" is "dare だれ," but there are politer expressions of them: "kata かた" and "donata どなた," respectively.  Therefore, a much politer expression of "Who is s/he?" is "Ano kata wa donata desu ka.あのかたは、どなたですか。"

Observe the next conversation:

A:  Ano kata wa donata desu ka.

B:  Do no hito desu ka.  Ah,
     ano hito wa Tom san desu.

A:  Tom san wa Amerika no hito desu ka.

B:  Iie, Igirisu  no hito desu.
     Demo, nihongo ga jyoozu desu yo.

A:　あのかたは、どなたですか。

B:　どのひとですか。ああ、
　　　あのひとは、トムさんです。

A:　トムさんは、アメリカのひとですか。

B:　いいえ、イギリスのひとです。
　　　でも、にほんごが　じょうずです。

[English translation]:
A: Who is he?
B: Which person?  Oh, he is Tom.
A: Is Tom an American?
B: No, he is an English man.  But, he is
    good at Japanese.

### だれの ? "dare no": Possessive case of "dare"

A:  Kono hon wa dare no hon desu ka.

B:  Sono hon wa watashi  no desu.

A:　このほんは、だれのほんですか。

B:　そのほんは、わたしのです。

Answer the questions based on the illustration below. えをみて、しつもんにこたえなさい。

1. これは、だれのかばんですか。
   kore wa   dare no kaban desu ka.

2. これは、だれのかさですか。
   kore wa   dare no kasa desu ka.

3. このかさも、はなこさんのですか。
   kono kasa mo Hanako san no desu ka.

4. このかばんは、だれのかばんですか。
   kono kaban wa   dare no kaban desu ka.

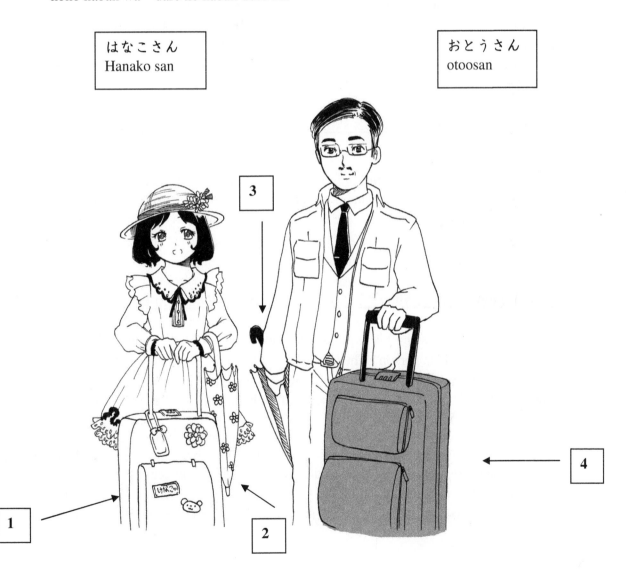

はなこさん
Hanako san

おとうさん
otoosan

# Cultural Notes

**Greeting for the First Time**: はじめまして、どうぞよろしく。

The Japanese greeting for meeting the first time is "はじめまして Ha-ji-me-ma-shi-te," literally saying "This is the first time to meet you," and is equivalent to the English expression "How do you do?" It is often accompanied by theresponse, "どうぞよろしく Do-o-zo yo-ro-shi-ku," literally meaning "Please befavorable with me."

**こちらこそ Kochira koso** (**It is me who should say so**)

Rather than repeating the same said expression, you may also say: "こちらこそ Kochira koso," literally meaning "It's my side (rather than you) that has to say so." So, after someone says "I'm sorry ("ごめんなさい gomen'nasai" or "すみません sumimasen"), the other may say, "こちらこそ Kochira koso" or "こちらこそごめんなさい。Kochira koso gomen'nasai." Likewise, "Thank you" can be followed by "こちらこそ Kochira koso."

**Expression that humbles one's skill set: "いいえ、まだまだです。Iie, mada mada desu."**

When someone makes a flattering remark about you or the skills you possess, it is common to deny the compliment in Japanese culture to socially demonstrate your humility. A common expression to say upon receiving a compliment is "いいえ、まだまだえす。Iie, mada mada desu." "いいえ iie" is "no," and "まだ mada" is "not yet." By repeating the word "まだ mada," meaning is enhanced.

**What school year are you? "なんねんせいですか。Nan-nen-sei desu ka."**

One's grade level at school is expressed by the suffix "-ねんせい nen-sei." "ねん Nen" is "year(s)" and "sei" is person. Thus, first (year) grade is "いちねんせい ichi-nen-sei," second (year) grade is "にねんせい ni-nen-sei," and third (year) grade is "さんねんせい san-nen-sei." The Japanese educational system is more rigid than that of the U.S., and skipping grades is extremely rare. The so-called 6-3-3-4 year system is used throughout Japan: six years of elementary school, three years junior high school, another three years of high school, and lastly, four years of college. The English terms "freshman," "sophomore," "junior," and "senior" are not used to describe grade levels in schools and colleges. Instead, "いちねんせい ichi-nen-sei," "にねんせい ni-nen-sei," "さんねんせい san-nen-sei," and "よねんせい yo-nen-sei," apply to elementary, junior and high schools, as well as colleges.

Chapter 2 (B) Exercises

A. Pair or group work: Introduce yourself to your classmates. Make sure to ask the following information about each other: name, affiliation (school, company, or organization), year in school, and hometown/country.
Practice the following sample pattern:

(A): はじめまして。わたしは、（　　　　　）の（　　　　　）です。
　　　hajimemashite.　watashi wa,　(affiliation)　no　(name)　　desu.
　　　どうぞ　よろしく。
　　　doozo　yoroshiku.

(B): こちらこそ、どうぞよろしく。わたしは、（　　）の（　　　）です。
　　　kochira koso, doozo　yoroshiku. watashi wa,　(affliation)　no　(name)　　　desu.

　　　Ａさんは、なんねんせいですか。
　　　A-san wa,　nan nen sei desu ka.

(A): （　）ねんせいです。Ｂさんは？
　　　(1, 2, 3 or 4) nen sei desu.　B-san wa?

(B): わたしは、（　）ねんせいです。
　　　watashi <u>wa,</u>　(1, 2, 3 or 4) nen sei desu.
　　　[Or, if you happen to be the same year in school,]
　　　わたしも、（　）ねんせいです。
　　　Watashi <u>mo,</u> (1, 2, 3 or 4) nen sei desu.

　　　Ａさんは、どちらから、いらっしゃいましたか。
　　　A-san wa,　dochira　kara,　irasshai mashita ka.

(A): （　　　　）から、きました。Ｂさんは？
　　　(town, country name) kara, kimashita.　B-san wa?

(B): わたしは、（　　　　）から、きました。
　　　watashi wa. (town, country name) kara kimashita.

B. Pair-work: Get the information from each other.
　　1.　　うちからがっこうまで　なんで（どうやって）いきますか。
　　　　uchi kara　　gakkoo　　made　　nan de　(doo yatte)　　ikimasu ka.

　　　　(How do you get to school from home? )

　　　　A. くるまで B. バスで C. タクシーで D. でんしゃで E. あるいて
　　　　kuruma de　　basu de　　takushii de　　　densha de　　　aruite

2. にほんまで　なんで（どうやって）いきますか。
   Nihon made　　nan de　(doo yatte)　　　ikimasu ka. (How do you get to Japan?)

   A. ふねで　B. ちかてつで　C. ひこうきで　D. ヘリコプターで
   　fune de　　　chikatetsu de　　hikooki de　　　herikoputaa de

3. さしみは　どうやって（なんで）　たべますか。
   sashimi wa　dooyatte (nan de)　　　　tabemasu ka. (How do you eat "sashimi"?)
   Or. use a particle ' を wo" for a direct object (in this case "sashimi").
   　　さしみを　なんでたべますか。
   　　sashimi wo　nan de tabemasu ka.

   A. てで　B. おはしで　C. フォークで　D. スプーンで
   　te de　　ohashi de　　　fooku de　　　supuun de

4. おすしは　なんでたべますか。
   　（or を)
   o-sushi wa (or wo)　nan de tabemasu ka.　　　(How do you eat "o-sushi"?)

   A. てで　B. おはしで　C. フォークで　D. スプーンで
   　te de　　ohashi de　　　fooku de　　　supuun de

5. ステーキは、なんでたべますか。
   　　（or を)
   suteeki wa (or wo)　nan de tabemasu ka.　　　(How do you eat steak?)

   A. てで　B. おはしで　C. ナイフとフォークで　D. ストローで
   　te de　　ohashi de　　　naifu to fooku de　　　sutoroo de
   　　　　　　　　　　　　　　　　　　　　　　　(a straw)

6. アイスクリームは　なんで　たべますか.
   　　　　（or を)
   aisukuriimu　wa (or wo)　nan de　　tabemasu ka. (How do you eat ice cream?)

   A.おはしで　B.スプーンで　C.フォークで　D.ストローで
   　ohashi de　　supuun de　　　fooku de　　　sutoroo de

7. ミルクシェークは　なんで　のみますか.
   　　　　（or を)
   mirukusheeku wa (or wo) nan de　nomimasu ka. (How do you drink milk shake?)

   A.ストローで　B.スプーンで
   　sutoroo de　　　supuun de

C. Group-work: Take turns suggesting different "foods" or "drinks," and have the rest of your group identify the means they are consumed. For example, if someone says "milk shake," everyone can reply "ストローで　のみます straw de nomimasu." If someone says, "o-sushi," everyone can answer "て でたべます te de tabemasu," or "おはしでたべます o-hashi de tabemasu."

D. Pair-work: Take turns asking the following expressions, repeating "〜は、なにごですか。……wa, nani-go desu ka?" and answer from what languages they are derived.

1. Xie xie ………………………………..
2. Muchas gracias ………………………………..
3. Guten Morgen ………………………………..
4. An young ha sea yo………………………………
5. Arigatoo gozaimasu………………………………
6. Thank you ………………………………..
7. Bon jour ………………………………..
8. Ciao ………………………………

E. Pair-work: Ask the following questions to each other.

1. あなたは、だいがくせいですか。 anata wa daigakusei desu ka.

2. りゅうがくせいですか。 ryuugakusei desu ka.

3. なんねんせいですか。 nan-nen-sei desu ka.

4. にほんごが　じょうずですか。 nihongo ga　jyoozu desu ka.

5. どこから　きましたか。 doko kara　kimashita ka.　　Or in polite form,

　　どちらから　いらっしゃいましたか。 dochira kara irasshai mashita ka.

6. たいてい (usually)　なにごで　はなしますか。 taitei nani-go de hanashi masu ka.

7. おかあさん(mother) は、なにごで　はなしますか。 okaasan wa nani-go de hanashi masu ka.

8. おとうさん (father) は、なにごで　はなしますか。 otoosan wa nani-go de hanashi masu ka.

9. きょう　うちから　がっこうまで　なんで　きましたか。
　　kyoo　　uchi kara gakkoo made　　nan de kimashita ka.
　　(today)

F. Verb practice as a pair or a group work: (1) Test your classmates on the following verbs whether s/he knows their meanings, past tense, negative form, and past negative form, then (2) ask the following questions.

(1)

たべます、 のみます、 はなします、 よみます、 かきます、 ききます、
tabemasu, nomimasu, hanashimasu, yomimasu, kakimasu, kikimasu,
(eat)　　　(drink)　　(speak)　　(read)　　(write)　　(listen)
します、 べんきょうします、 ねます、 おきます、 あそびます
shimasu, benkyoo shimasu, nemasu, okimasu asobimasu
(do)　　(study)　　　　　(sleep; go to bed) (get up) (play: have a good time)

(2)

1. きょうは、なにを　たべましたか。 kyoo wa nani wo tabemashita ka.
(What did you eat today?)

2. うちで　なにごを　はなしますか。 uchide nanigo wo hanashimasu ka.
(What language do you speak at home?)

3. まいにち　ほんを　よみますか。　 mainichi hon wo yomimasu ka.
everyday (Do you read books everyday?)

4. まいにち　にっきを　かきますか。 mainichi nikki wo kakimasu ka.
diary (Do you write a diary everyday?)

5. どんなおんがくを　ききますか。　 don'na ongaku wo kikimasu ka.
what kind of music (What kind of music do you listen?)

6. しゅうまつ　なにを　しますか。　 shuumatsu nani wo shimasu ka.
weekend (What do you do over the weekend?)

7. きのう、にほんごを　べんきょうしましたか。 kinoo nihongo wo
benkyoo shimashita ka.
(Did you study Japanese yesterday?)

8. きのう、よく　ねましたか。　　　 kinoo yoku nemashita ka.
(Did you sleep well yesterday?)

9. きょう、あさ　はやく　おきましたか。 kyoo asa hayaku okimashita ka.
(Did you wake up early today?)

10. たいてい　だれと　あそびますか。 taitei dare to asobimasu ka.
(Who do you usually play with?)

G.  Pair-work: Obtain the following information from your partner and report to class.
   (1) the language(s) s/he and his/her parents speak
   (2) how s/he comes to school
   (3) her/his major
   (4) the school year
   (5) if s/he likes books and if s/he reads often

   Attention:  When you present the information about your interviewee, start your
   sentence with 〜さんは(so-and-so san wa), then, omit 〜さんは(~ san wa) all
   together till its end.

Sample presentation:
ボブさんは、おとうさんとえいごで　はなします。そして(And)、おかあさんと
スペインごで　はなします。がっこうへ、くるまできます。せんこうは、こう
がくです。いま(Now; currently)、にねんせいです。よく　ほんを　よみます。ほ
んが　すきです。

H.  Pair-work:  Look at the information chart on the next page and locate identical
information (nationality, language, year in school, and how they come to school) between
featured profiles.  Tell your partner something about one of the profiles.  Your partner
should tell you about another profile that shares similarities.

Examples:
(1)
A：きむさんは、かんこくじんです。
     Kimu san wa,    kankokujin desu.

B：ちょうさんも、かんこくじんです。
     Choo san mo,    kankokujin desu.

(2)
A：リーさんは、バスで　きます。
     Rii san wa,    basu de   kimasu.

B：スミスさんも、バスで　きます。
     Sumisu san mo, basu de    kimasu.

(3)
A：ペリネールさんは、ふらんすごを　はなします。
     Perineeru san wa,    furansugo wo    hanashimasu.

B : モネさん<u>も</u>、ふらんすごを　はなします。
　　 Mone san <u>mo,</u> furansugo wo　　 hanashimasu.

[Caution]
Unlike "bus," "car," "train," and "taxi," "あるいて aruite" is a verb.  So, don't use "de" after "あるいて aruite."  It already means "by walking."  Aside from "あるいて aruite," you can use "とほで toho de," since "とほ toho (on foot)" is a noun.

| Name | Nationality | Language spoken at home | Year in School | Means of Transportation to school |
|---|---|---|---|---|
| リー<br>Rii | ちゅうごくじん<br>chuugoku jin | ちゅうごくご<br>chuugoku go | いちねんせい<br>ichinensei | ばす<br>basu |
| キム<br>Kim | かんこくじん<br>kankoku jin | かんこくご<br>kankoku go | にねんせい<br>ninen sei | くるま<br>kuruma |
| ペリネール<br>Perineeru | ふらんすじん<br>furansu jin | フランスご<br>furansu go | *だいがくいんせい<br>daigaku in sei | でんしゃ<br>densha |
| チョウ<br>Chou | かんこくじん<br>kankoku jin | かんこくご<br>kankoku go | さんねんせい<br>san'nen sei | あるいて<br>aruite |
| スミス<br>Sumisu | あめりかじん<br>amerika jin | えいご<br>eigo | よねんせい<br>yonen sei | ばす<br>basu |
| シャン<br>Shan | ちゅうごくじん<br>chuugoku jin | ちゅうごくご<br>chuugoku go | いちねんせい<br>ichinen sei | くるま<br>kuruma |
| ホワイト<br>Howaito | あめりかじん<br>amerika jin | えいご<br>eigo | にねんせい<br>ninen sei | あるいて<br>aruite |
| アラ<br>Ara | すぺいんじん<br>supein jin | スペインご<br>supein go | さんねんせい<br>san'nen sei | タクシー<br>takushii |
| モネ<br>Mone | ふらんすじん<br>furansu jin | フランスご<br>furansu go | よねんせい<br>yonen sei | でんしゃ<br>densha |
| ゴンザレス<br>Gonzaresu | すぺいんじん<br>supein jin | スペインご<br>supein go | だいがくいんせい<br>daigaku in sei | タクシー<br>takushii |

*だいがくいん せい = graduate students
　daigaku in sei

Chapter 2(B)'s Dict-A-Conversation (1)
Respond to questions/comments in a complete Japanese sentence.  At this stage, you may write your answers in Roma-ji, but later, write everything in hiragana.  You listen to A's comments/questions and write in your answers in the line B.  Then, listen to the CD again and this time, write A's comments/questions in Roma-ji on the line A.

A : .................................................................................

B : _____

A : .................................................................................

B : _____

A : .................................................................................

B : _____

A : .................................................................................

B : _____

A : .................................................................................

B : _____

Chapter 2(B)'s Dict-A-Conversation (2):  Follow the instruction in DAC (1)

A : .................................................................................

B : _____

A : .................................................................................

B : _____

A : .................................................................................

B : _____

A : .................................................................................

B : _____

A : .................................................................................

B : _____

Chapter 2(B): Crossword Puzzle # 1 (Country names and telephone number)

Across

1. Vietnam
2. telephone number
3. Spain
4. Korea
5. China
6. England
7. Canada

Down

8. Italy
9. France
10. United States (America)
11. Japan
2. Germany

Chapter 2(B): Crossword Puzzle # 2 (Transportations)

<u>Across</u>

1. ship/boat
2. bicycle
3. subway
4. airplane
5. bus

<u>Down</u>

6. car
7. taxi
8. street car/train
9. on foot/walking
4. helicopter

Chapter 2(B): Crossword Puzzle # 3 (Vocabulary from the Dialogue)

Across

1. school
2. what number
3. foreign student
4. usually (adv.)

Down

5. what year student
6. skillful; skilled
7. home; house

Chapter 2(B):  Crossword Puzzle # 4 (Verbs)
Roma-ji version in the "masu" form

<u>Across</u>
1. speak
2. listen
3. eat
4. walk
5. come

<u>Down</u>
6. drink
7. go
8. write

Chapter 2 (C)　　Thank you and Good-bye

せんせい：ここが　　学生か　　　です。　　　　　　　　　　　　　　1
　　　　　　　　　　　がくせい
Sensei:　　　ko-ko ga　ga-ku-se-i-ka　de-su.

モニカ：　どうも　ありがとうございました。たすかりました。　　2
Monika:　　do-o-mo　a-ri-ga-to-o　go-za-i-ma-shi-ta.　ta-su-ka-ri-ma-shi-ta.

せんせい：いいえ、どういたしまして。じゃ、またね。　　　　　　3
Sensei:　　i-i-e,　　do-o-i-ta-shi-ma-shi-te.　jya,　ma-ta-ne.

モニカ：　はい、しつれいします。　　　　　　　　　　　　　　　4
Monika:　　ha-i,　shi-tsu-re-i-shi-ma-su.

[English translation]:

Professor:　Here is the Student Office.
Monika:　　Thank you so much.　It was of great help.
Professor:　Not at all (= you're welcome).　Then, see you later.
Monika:　　Yes, good bye (= Excuse me.　Literally:　Please allow me to be rude.)

[Vocabulary List]:

1.  Expressions

Doomo arigatoo gozaimashita.　　　　　Thank you so much (for what you have done).
どうも　ありがとう　ございました。　　　(polite form)

Tasukarimashita.
たすかりました。　　　　　　　　　It was of great help.
　　　　　　　　　　　　　　　　　Past tense of "tasukaru" (is saved) in a polite form.

Doo itashimashite.
どういたしまして。　　　　　　　　You're welcome.

Shitsurei shimasu.　　　　　　　　Excuse me.　(Literally:　Please allow me to be
しつれいします。　　　　　　　　　rude.)　In this dialogue, it means "Good bye."
　　　　　　　　　　　　　　　　　An expression to be used toward your social
　　　　　　　　　　　　　　　　　superiors.

.....................................................................................................................
Additional Vocabulary from Grammar Notes, Exercises, and Dict-A-Conversation
.....................................................................................................................
[Nouns]
nihon　　　　にほん　　　　　　　Japan
mukashi　　　むかし　　　　　　　long time ago

| aru tokoro | あるところ | somewhere |
| ojiisan | おじいさん | old man, grandpa |
| obaasan | おばあさん | old woman, grandma |
| yama | やま | mountains |
| kawa | かわ | rivers |
| takigi | たきぎ | firewood |
| sentaku | せんたく | laundry |
| tori | とり | bird |
| kuni | くに | country |
| keshiki | けしき | scenery |
| hito | ひと | people; person |
| mimi | みみ | ears |
| chichi | ちち | father (humble form, my father) |
| hana | はな | flowers |
| umi | うみ | sea; ocean |
| machi | まち | town |
| shiki | しき | four seasons |
| tera | てら | (Buddhist) temples |
| hanzai | はんざい | crime |
| mono | もの | things (concrete things) |
| (me) | め | eyes |
| (atama) | あたま | head |

(Drinks)

| koocha | こうちゃ | black tea |
| koohii | コーヒー | coffee |
| kooku | コーク | coke |

[Food from Exercise A]

| gyooza | ぎょうざ | dumpling |
| tenpura | てんぷら | deep-fried vegetables and seafood |
| chirashi-zushi | ちらしずし | rice dressed with vinegar and topped with egg and seafood |
| chaahan | チャーハン | fried rice |
| sandoicchi | サンドイッチ | sandwich |
| miso-shiru | みそしる | miso soup |
| hotate sarada | ほたてサラダ | scallop salad |
| karee raisu | カレーライス | curried rice |
| teishoku | ていしょく | assorted meal |
| o-bentoo | おべんとう | boxed lunch |

[Cities from Exercise B]

| | | |
|---|---|---|
| pasadena | パサデナ | Pasadena |
| rosu | ロス | Los Angeles |
| nyuuyooku | ニューヨーク | New York |
| tookyoo | とうきょう | Tokyo |
| kyooto | きょうと | Kyoto |
| ankarejji | アンカレッジ | Anchorage |
| rondon | ロンドン | London |
| shikago | シカゴ | Chicago |
| rooma | ローマ | Rome |
| pari | パリ | Paris |
| shishirii | シシリー | Sicily |
| sapporo | さっぽろ | Sapporo |
| amusuterudamu | アムステルダム | Amsterdam |

[Ages and School Years]

| | | |
|---|---|---|
| ~ sai | | counter for a person's age; ~ year old |
| nan-nen sei | なんねんせい | what grade |
| shoogakkoo | しょうがっこう | elementary school |
| chuugakkoo | ちゅうがっこう | junior high school |
| kookoo | こうこう | high school |
| daigaku | だいがく | college; university |

[な Adjectives/Copula Nouns]

| | | |
|---|---|---|
| (shizuka) | しずか | quiet |
| (yuumei) | ゆうめい | famous |
| (kirei) | きれい | pretty |
| (suki) | すき | likable, pleasing, favorable |

[Adjectives]

| | | |
|---|---|---|
| ooi | おおい | more |
| furui | ふるい | old |
| yokunai | よくない | no good (negative form of "ii) |
| oishii | おいしい | tasty |
| yasui | やすい | reasonable, cheap |
| takai | たかい | expensive |
| (itai) | いたい | painful |
| (chiisai) | ちいさい | small |

| | | |
|---|---|---|
| (ookii) | おおきい | big |

[Verbs]

| | | |
|---|---|---|
| nakimasu | なきます | sing, chirp (birds) ("masu" form of "naku") |
| arimasu | あります | exist ("masu" form of "aru") |

[Question words]

| | | |
|---|---|---|
| dare | だれ | who |

--------------------------------------------------------------------------------

## Two dots make a world of difference!

You may change the meaning if you forget to write the two dots or put them at the wrong place. See the examples below.

1.
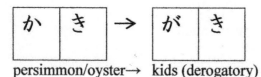

persimmon/oyster→ kids (derogatory)

2.
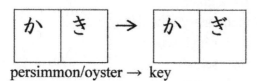

persimmon/oyster → key

3.
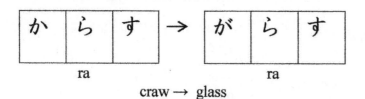

ra                         ra

craw → glass

4.
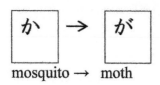

mosquito → moth

Chapter 2 (C)          Grammar and Cultural Notes

1. **Particle "ga"**: "ここが　がくせいかです。 **koko ga gakusei-ka desu**"

In this sentence, "ここ koko" is used as a "subject," and is marked by a particle "が ga." Though the question sentence was never verbalized, it is the answer for "どこが　がくせいかですか。 Doko ga gakusei-ka desuka," where is the Student Office?

In a question sentence, it is a particle "が ga," and not "は wa," which is used **after** the interrogative pronouns (question words, such as who, when, where, which, what). Note that when you are asked with "が ga," you answer with "が ga."

| Rule (1)  I.P always precede particle "が ga" |
|---|

I.P. stands for "Interrogative Pronouns."

I.P. + ga    <u>なにが</u>　いいですか。 (What's good?)
　　　　　　　nani ga　　iidesu ka.

　　　　　　<u>どこが</u>　いいですか。 (Where's good?)
　　　　　　doko ga　　ii desu ka.

　　　　　　<u>だれが</u>　いいですか。 (Who's good?)
　　　　　　dare ga　　ii desu ka.

2. **Particle "wa"**: "がくせいかは　ここです。 **gakusei-ka wa koko desu**"

On the other hand, it is a particle "は wa," and not "が ga," which is used **before** the interrogative pronouns

Question:　がくせいか<u>は</u>　<u>どこ</u>ですか。 Where is the Student Office?
Answer:　がくせいか<u>は</u>、ここです。　　It's here.

Note that when you are asked with "は wa," you answer with "は wa." Or else, you can omit the topic, "~ は wa," and simply say "**..........**です。 desu."

| Rule (2)  I.P are always preceded by "は wa" |
|---|

wa + I.P.    いいの　<u>は、どれ</u>　ですか。 (Which one is good?)
　　　　　　ii no wa　　dore desu ka.

　　　　　　いいの　<u>は、どこ</u>　ですか。 (Where's good?)
　　　　　　ii no wa　　doko desu ka.

　　　　　　いいの　<u>は、だれ</u>　ですか。 (Who's good?)
　　　　　　ii no wa　　dare　desu ka.

You may say either pattern for a question. For example, "Who is the teacher?" can be said in either pattern:

だれが　せんせいですか。　　Dare ga sensei desu ka.
せんせいは、だれですか。　　Sensei wa dare desu ka.

## 3. <u>Sentences which have both particles "は wa" and "が ga"</u>

So far, we have observed the two sentence patters as follows:
(1). A wa B desu.

> | Topic wa Predicate. |

"Sensei wa doko desu ka. "せんせいは　どこですか。
"Sensei wa koko desu."　　せんせいは　ここです。
Or,
"I am Japanese." [わたしは　にほんじんです。watashi wa nihonjin desu.]

(2). A ga B desu.

> | Subject ga Predicate. |

"Dare ga sensei desu ka."　だれが　せんせいですか。
"Watashi ga sensei desu."　わたしが　せんせいです。
Or,
"(Your) Japanese is good." [にほんごが　じょうずですね。Nihongo ga ojyoozu
desu (ne).]

And, there is another pattern: the sentences that have both "wa" and "ga."

(3). A wa B ga ...... desu.

> | Topic wa Subject ga Predicate. |

あなたは、　にほんごが　じょうずです（ね）。
Anata wa　　nihongo ga　jyoozu desu (ne).
　　(Speaking of you, Japanese is good.)

**In this pattern, a big picture (Topic) is first presented by "~は wa," and next, its details are presented by "~が ga" (Subject).**

For example, you may want to talk about your mother (= Topic of the sentence). Then you may say about her physical appearance, her personality, hobbies, and anything to describe her (= Subject + Predicate).
　　1. My mom has big eyes.
　　2. My mom has a small mouth.
　　3. My mom is smart.
　　4. My mom is kind-hearted.

| Topic | particle | Subject | particle | Predicate |
|---|---|---|---|---|
| 1. はは<br>Haha | | め<br>me | | おおきいです。<br>ookii desu. |
| 2. | は<br>wa | くち<br>kuchi | が<br>ga | ちいさいです。<br>chiisai desu. |
| 3. | | あたま<br>atama | | いいです。<br>ii desu. |
| 4. | | こころ<br>kokoro | | やさしいです。<br>yasashii desu. |

This sentence pattern of "Topic wa Subject ga predicate" is very popular in Japanese language especially to describe Natural phenomena, one's body features, characteristics of the topic, etc. Observe:

1. Today is a nice weather.
2. Today is pleasant. (Can be referring to either weather or personal feelings.)
3. Today, my friend will come.
4. Today, the newspaper is late.

| Topic | particle | Subject | particle | Predicate |
|---|---|---|---|---|
| 1. きょう<br>Kyoo | | おてんき<br>otenki | | いいです。<br>ii desu. |
| 2. | は<br>wa | きもち<br>kimochi | が<br>ga | いいです。<br>ii desu. |
| 3. | | ともだち<br>tomodachi | | きます。<br>kimasu. |
| 4. | | しんぶん<br>shinbun | | おそいです。<br>osoi desu. |

More examples of "Topic wa Subject ga Predicate" pattern:

(1) It will rain today (Literally: Speaking of today, rain will fall.)
　きょうは　あめが　ふります。Kyoo wa, ame ga furimasu.

(2) Bob is smart (Literally: Speaking of Bob, [his] head is good.)
　ボブは　あたまが　いいです。Bob wa, atama ga ii desu.

(3) My eyes hurt (Literally: Speaking of I, [my] eyes are in pain.)
　わたしは、めが　いたい（ん）です。Watashi wa, me ga itai (n) desu.

(4) Tom's handwriting is good (skilled) (Literally: Speaking of Tom, [his] words/characters are skillfully written.)
　トムは　じが　じょうずです。Tom wa, ji ga jyoozu desu.

(5) I want a car (Literally: Speaking of I, a car is desirable. ["hoshii" is adjective])
　わたしは　くるまが　ほしいです。Watashi wa, kuruma ga hoshii desu.

| Cultural Notes |
| --- |

## Numbers and Japanese Life

### 3、5、7 ♥ 2 0

Japanese children start elementary school at the age of six and complete their compulsory years of education (gimu-kyooiku 義務教育) at fifteen.  At the ages of three, five and seven, they celebrate "shichi go san" on November 15th (which now takes place the second Sunday of November).  They visit nearby shrines to receive blessings from the priests.  The parents buy them long pieces of candy symbolizing long life.  When they reach twenty years of age, they become legally recognized as adults.  Adult Day (seijin-shiki 成人式) is January 15th (now recognized as the second Sunday of January), and is one of the national holidays of Japan.

Asking Age and Grade  なんさいですか。

It may come of surprise when the Japanese frankly asks for your age without reservation. Their linguistic mindset, connected with formal and casual speech patterns, compels them to find out your age and base their style of speech accordingly.  The degree of linguistic formality is very much determined by age hierarchy. However, there are those who are more tactful about asking for your college graduation year or Chinese zodiac on your birth year instead.  The reasoning behind this: Most Japanese born the same year normally graduates together and would share the same age.

Educational Systems      きょういくせいど
"6-3-3-4" represents the Japanese educational system after World War II.  Six years of elementary school, three years of junior high school, three years of high school, and four years of college.  Compulsory education applies to the first nine years, but most children go to high school and many attend college.

なんさいですか。  (How old are you?)

| 1 | いっさい | (一才) |
| 2 | にさい | (二才) |
| 3 | さんさい | (三才) |
| 4 | よんさい | (四才) |
| 5 | ごさい | (五才) |

6　　ろくさい　（六才）

7　　ななさい　（七才）

8　　はっさい　（八才）

9　　きゅうさい（九才）

10　じゅっさい（十才）

11　じゅういっさい　（十一才）

12　じゅうにさい　　（十二才）

しょうがくせい（小学生）↓
elementary school student

↑

13　じゅうさんさい　（十三才）

14　じゅうよんさい　（十四才）

15　じゅうごさい　　（十五才）

ちゅうがくせい（中学生）↓
junior high school student

↑

16　じゅうろくさい　（十六才）

17　じゅうななさい　　（十七才）

18　じゅうはっさい　　（十八才）

こうこうせい（高校生）↓
high school student

↑

19　じゅうきゅうさい　　（十九才）

20　にじゅっさい（はたち）（二十才）

おとな〔大人〕　Adult

## なんねんせいですか。What Grade Are You In?

| Grade | Japanese School | |
|---|---|---|
| 1 | 1 しょうがく　いちねんせい | しょうがっこう<br>（小学校）<br>Elementary School |
| 2 | 2 しょうがく　にねんせい | |
| 3 | 3 しょうがく　さんねんせい | |
| 4 | 4 しょうがく　よねんせい | |
| 5 | 5 しょうがく　ごねんせい | |
| 6 | 6 しょうがく　ろくねんせい | |
| 7 | 1 ちゅうがく　いちねんせい | ちゅうがっこう<br>（中学校）<br>Junior High School |
| 8 | 2 ちゅうがく　にねんせい | |
| 9 | 3 ちゅうがく　さんねんせい | |
| 10 | 1 こうこう　いちねんせい | こうこう<br>（高校）<br>High School |
| 11 | 2 こうこう　にねんせい | |
| 12 | 3 こうこう　さんねんせい | |
| Freshman | 1 だいがく　いちねんせい | だいがく<br>（大学）<br>College |
| Sophomore | 2 だいがく　にねんせい | |
| Junior | 3 だいがく　さんねんせい | |
| Senior | 4 だいがく　よねんせい | |

Learn numbers from 10 to 100.

| | Japanese numerals | hiragana | kanji |
|---|---|---|---|
| 10 | jyuu | じゅう | 十 |
| 11 | jyuu-ichi | じゅういち | 十一 |
| 12 | jyuu-ni | じゅうに | 十二 |
| 13 | jyuu-san | じゅうさん | 十三 |
| 14 | jyuu-shi, jyuu-yon | じゅうし、じゅうよん | 十四 |
| 15 | jyuu-go | じゅうご | 十五 |
| 16 | jyuu-roku | じゅうろく | 十六 |
| 17 | jyuu-shichi, jyuu-nana | じゅうしち、じゅうなな | 十七 |
| 18 | jyuu-hachi | じゅうはち | 十八 |
| 19 | jyuu-ku, jyuu-kyuu | じゅうく、じゅうきゅう | 十九 |
| 20 | ni jyuu | にじゅう | 二十 |
| 30 | san jyuu | さんじゅう | 三十 |
| 40 | yon jyuu, shi jyuu | よんじゅう、しじゅう | 四十 |
| 50 | go jyuu | ごじゅう | 五十 |
| 60 | roku jyuu | ろくじゅう | 六十 |
| 70 | nana jyuu, or shichi jyuu | ななじゅう、しちじゅう | 七十 |
| 80 | hachi jyuu | はちじゅう | 八十 |
| 90 | kyuu jyuu, or kujyuu | きゅうじゅう、くじゅう | 九十 |
| 100 | hyaku | ひゃく | 百 |

How do numbers work in Japanese?  Simple math does the trick:

$2 \times 10 = 20$          $2 \times 10 + 1 = 21$          $2 \times 10 + 2 = 22$
ni    jyuu $=$ ni jyuu          ni   jyuu   ichi          ni   jyuu   ni
   にじゅう          にじゅういち          にじゅうに

And similarly,

$23 =$ ni jyuu san,   $24 =$ ni jyuu shi or ni jyuu yon,   $25 =$ ni jyuu go,   $26 =$ ni jyuu roku
  にじゅうさん        にじゅうし、にじゅうよん        にじゅうご   にじゅうろく

$27 =$ ni jyuu shichi or ni jyuu nana,   $28 =$ ni jyuu hachi,   $29 =$ ni jyuu ku, or ni jyuu kyuu
にじゅうしち or にじゅうなな   にじゅうはち   にじゅうく or にじゅうきゅう

$3 \times 10 = 30$,  $4 \times 10 = 40$,  $5 \times 10 = 50$,  $6 \times 10 = 60$,  $7 \times 10 = 70$,  $8 \times 10 = 80$
san jyuu         yon jyuu         go jyuu         roku jyuu       nana jyuu       hachi jyuu
さんじゅう         よんじゅう   ごじゅう   ろくじゅう   ななじゅう   はちじゅう

$9 \times 10 = 90$          And lastly, 100
kyuu jyuu                hyaku
きゅうじゅう                ひゃく

Japanese numerals:  Telephone Numbers

| Numbers | Pronunciation |
|---------|---------------|
| 0 | zero, rei |
| 1 | ichi |
| 2 | ni |
| 3 | san |
| 4 | yon |
| 5 | go |
| 6 | roku |
| 7 | nana |
| 8 | hachi |
| 9 | kyuu |

Notes:

1) There are various pronunciations for the numbers 4, 7 and 9.  Telephone numbers are stated with their strongest sounds.  For example, 4 is "yon" instead of "shi," 7 is "nana" instead of "shichi," and 9 is "kyuu" instead of "ku."

2) Particle "no" is used between units/clusters of numbers.
Example:

   Tel: (123) 456-7890
        (123) no (456) no (7890)

3) Note the tendency to prolong vowel sounds at the end of numbers 2 and 5.  Thus, they sound like "nii" for 2 and "goo" for 5.  Not only are they prolonged, their pitches also rise. The rising pitch occurs also with number 9.
Examples:

   Tel: (123) 456-7890 is pronounced as follows.  The underlined sounds are higher in pitch than the rest.

              ichi-nii-san no yon-goo-roku no nana-hachi-kyuu-ree

                                              (or zero)

Important vocabulary for telephone numbers:

   telephone              denwa
   number                 bangoo
   telephone number       denwa bangoo
   what number            nan-ban

Conversation:

A:  Anata no denwa-bangoo wa nan-ban desuka.
B:  (Watashi no denwa-bangoo wa) 622-314-7908 desu.
                     roku-nii-nii no san-ichi-yon no nana-kyuu-zero-hachi desu

Chapter 2C Exercises

A: Find your partner: Find the common factors between you and the classmates. If you find more than seven common factors, then s/he is your partner for the next exercise.

Add "ka か" at the end of each sentence and raise the tone to make a question sentence.

1. (　　　) Iro wa shiro ga suki desu. (Speaking of "color," "white" is pleasing.)
　　　いろは　しろが　すきです。

2. (　　　) Asa, pan wo tabemashita. (In the morning, I ate bread.)
　　　あさ、ぱんを　たべました。

3. (　　　) Uchi de, eigo wo hanashimasu. (At home, I speak English.)
　　　うちで　えいごを　はなします。

4. (　　　) Uchi de, Chuugokugo wo hanashimasu. (At home, I speak Chinese.)
　　　うちで、ちゅうごくごを　はなします。

5. (　　　) Uchi de, Kankokugo wo hanashimasu. (At home, I speak Korean.)
　　　うちで、かんこくごを　はなします。

6. (　　　) Ocha ga suki desu. (I like green tea.)
　　　おちゃが　すきです。

7. (　　　) Koohii ga suki desu. (I like coffee.)
　　　こーひーが　すきです。

8. (　　　) Gakkoo made aruite kimashita. (I come to school by walking.)
　　　がっこうまで　あるいて　きました。

9. (　　　) Se ga hikui desu. (I am short.)
　　　せが　ひくいです。

10. (　　　) Se ga takai desu. (I am tall.)
　　　せが　たかいです

11. (　　　) Me ga kuroi desu.。 (My eyes are black.)
　　　めが　くろいです。

12. (　　　) Me ga aoi desu. (My eyes are blue.)
　　　めが　あおいです。

13. (　　　) Karutekku no gakusei desu. (I'm a Caltech student.)
　　　かるてっくのがくせいです。

14. (　　　) Mimi ga ookii desu. (My ears are big.)
　　　みみが　おおきいです。

15. (　　　) Hana ga hikui desu. (My nose is small [literally "low"].)
　　　はなが　ひくいです。

16. (　　　) Ashi ga nagai desu. (I have long legs.)
　　　あしが　ながいです。

17. (　　　) Ryoori ga jyoozu desu. (I'm a good cook.)
　　　りょうりが　じょうずです。

18. (　　　) Sooji ga heta desu. (I'm not good at clean-ups.)
　　　そうじが　へたです。

B: Obtain the following information from your partner and report it to class. Make sure you ask/answer questions in Japanese.

1) Where s/he is from (originally)
2) When her/his birthday is
3) What language s/he speaks at home
4) What school/company s/he attends/works
5) What color s/he likes
6) What s/he ate this morning
7) How s/he got to school today

C.  Based on the information provided in the chart below, converse a dialogue between you and your partner.

The following chart shows information on the food served at each restaurant. "こうらく Kooraku" is a Chinese restaurant, ワールドカフェ World Café is a coffee shop, まつり Matsuri is a Japanese restaurant, and すしげん Sushigen is a sushi-restaurant.  Make a dialogue, using the "~wa …ga" pattern.

| | こうらく Kooraku | ワールド カフェ World Cafe | まつり Matsuri | すしげん Sushigen |
|---|---|---|---|---|
| おいしい oishii (delicious thing) | ぎょうざ gyooza | コーヒー coffee | てんぷら tenpura | ちらしずし chirashi zushi |
| やすい yasui (reasonable thing) | チャーハン chaahan | サンドイッチ sandoicchi | みそしる misoshiru | ほたてサラダ hotate sarada |
| たかい takai (expensive thing) | ラーメン raamen | カレーライス Karee raisu | ていしょく teishoku | おべんとう obentoo |

Example:
A:  こうらくは、なにが　おいしいですか。
     Kooraku <u>wa</u>    nani <u>ga</u>    oishii desu ka.

B:    （こうらくは）チャーハンが　おいしいですよ。
        (Kooraku wa)  chaahan  <u>ga</u>     oishii desu yo.
[Vocabulary help]:
おいしい(oishii) = tasty, やすい(yasui) = reasonable, cheap, たかい(takai) = expensive, ていしょく (teishoku) = assorted meal

D. Guessing game: Work in groups of three or four.  One person picks a city out of the choices in the box without telling the rest of the group which one it is.  The others will take turns asking questions about various characteristics of the city selected to discover which city has been selected.

Topics (~ wa): Choices of Cities

| パサデナ、 | ロス、 | ニューヨーク、 | とうきょう、 | きょうと、 | アンカレッジ、 |
|---|---|---|---|---|---|
| pasadena | rosu | nyuuyooku | tookyoo | kyooto | ankarejji |
| (Pasaden) | (Los Angeles) | (New York) | (Tokyo) | (Kyoto) | (Anchorage) |

| ロンドン、 | シカゴ、 | ローマ、 | パリ、 | シシリー、 | さっぽろ、 | アムステルダム |
|---|---|---|---|---|---|---|
| rondon | shikago | rooma | pari | shishirii | Sapporo | amusuterudamu |
| (London) | (Chicago) | (Rome) | (Paris) | (Sicily) | (Sapporo) | (Amsterdam) |

Subjects (~ ga):

まち machi = town,
くるま kuruma = cars
たてもの tatemono = buildings
しき shiki = four seasons (はる haru, なつ natsu, あき aki, ふゆ fuyu),
はんざい hanzai = crimes
（お）てら (o) tera = temples
ひと hito = people

Predicates:

おおい ooi = having more,
ふるい furui = old,
おおきい ookii = large, ちいさい chiisai = small,
ゆうめい yuumei = famous, きれい kirei = pretty,
しずか shizuka = quiet,
あつい atsui = hot, さむい samui = cold, あたたかい atatakai = nice and warm,
すずしい suzushii = nice and cool

Example:

A:　その　まちは、はんざいが　おおいですか。
　　　sono  machi wa,  hanzai ga　　ooi desu ka.

B:　いいえ。
　　　iie.

C:　しずかですか。
　　　shizuka desu ka.

B:　はい、ほんとうに　しずかです。
　　　hai,　hontoo ni　　shizuka desu.
　　　= truly

D:　そのまちは、にほんですか。
　　　sono machi wa, nihon desu ka.

B:　はい。
　　　hai.

A:　おてらが　ゆうめいですか。
　　　o-tera ga　　yuumei　desu ka.

B:　はい。
　　　hai.
C:　きょうとですか。
　　　kyooto desu ka.
B:　はい、そうです。
　　　hai, soo desu.

E. Pair-work: Work with your partner to choose the right particles. Discuss the reason
for your choice.

1.　なに（は、が）いいですか。　　　Nani {wa, ga} ii desu ka.
2.　どれ（は、が）いいですか。　　　Dore {wa, ga} ii desu ka.
3.　あれ（は、が）なんですか。　　　Are {wa, ga} nan desu ka.
4.　にほん（は、が）、けしき（は、が）きれいですか。
　　　Nihon {wa, ga}, keshiki {wa, ga} kirei desu ka. (keshiki; scenery)
5.　どのひと（は、が）ホワイトさんですか。
　　　　　　　　　　　　　Dono hito {wa, ga} White-san desu ka.
6.　あのたてもの（は、が）なんですか。Ano tatemono {wa, ga} nan desu ka.
7.　だれ（は、が）いいですか。　　　Dare {wa, ga} ii desu ka. (dare; who)
8.　いいの（は、が）どこですか。　Ii no {wa, ga} doko desu ka.
9.　トムさん（は、が）あたま（は、が）いいです。
　　　　　　　　　　　　　Tom-san {wa, ga} atama {wa, ga} ii desu.
10.　なつ（は、が）、うみ（は、が）いいです。
　　　　　　　　　　　Natsu {wa, ga}, umi {wa, ga} ii desu. (umi; ocean)

F. Change the structure of the sentence to "A wa B ga predicate."

| Noun no Noun wa predicate | → | Noun wa Noun ga predicate |

Example: とうきょうのひとは、おおいです。 →
　　　　Tokyo no hito wa ooi desu. (hito; people, ooi; more, many)
　→　とうきょうは、ひとが　おおいです。
　　　　Tokyo wa hito ga ooi desu.

1.　はるのはなは、きれいです。
　　Haru no hana wa kirei desu. → *Haru wa. hana ga kirei desu.*
　　　　(flowers) (pretty)

2.　キャシーのめは、きれいです。
　　Cathy no me wa kirei desu. → *Cathy wa me ga kirei desu.*
　　　　(eyes)

3.　トムのめは、おおきいです。
　　Tom no me wa ookii desu. → *Tom wa me ga ookii desu.*
　　　　(big)

4. ボブのあたまは、いいです。
   Bob no <u>atama</u> wa ii desu. → *Bob wa atama ga ii desu*
         (head is good= smart)

5. にほんのふゆは、さむいです。
   Nihon no fuyu wa samui desu. → *Nihon wa fuyu ga samui desu.*

6. きょうとのふゆは、しずかです。
   Kyoto no fuyu wa <u>shizuka</u> desu. → *kyoto wa fuyu ga shizuka desu.*
         (quiet)

7. きょうこさんのかみは、ながいです。
   Kyoko-san no <u>kami</u> wa <u>nagai</u> desu. → *kyoko wa kami ga nagai desu.*
      (hair)    (long)

G. Work in groups of three:  Comment on some topics of your choice.  For example,
   if you have decided to talk about "this college," begin you sentence
   with    このだいがくは、
         kono daigaku wa,                 .

   then the second person completes the sentence by commenting :
                  がくせいが　いいです。
                  gausei ga ii desu.

   And, the third person can also comment about this college:
                  おとこのがくせいが　おおいです。
                  otoko no gakusei ga ooi desu.

   Suggested vocabulary:
   おいしい、やすい、たかい、きれい、ゆうめい、
   oishii(tasty), yasui(cheap), takai(expensive), kirei(famous), yuumei(famous),
   おおい、いい、おもしろい、あつい、さむい、むずかしい、やさしい、etc.
   ooi(more), ii(good), omoshiroi(fun), atsui, samui, muzukashii(difficult), yasashii(easy),

   Use the "…wa …ga " pattern.

   Examples:
      (o-sushi)        "Sushi Ichiban" wa <u>anago</u> ga oishii desu yo.  (anago:sea-water eel)
      (supermarket) "Ralphs" wa................ga <u>yasui</u> desu yo.
      (coffee shop)
      (hamburger shop)
      (beach)
      (movie)
      (Japanese class: nihongo no kurasu)

H.  Fill in the blanks with particles.

1.  カフェテリア (      ) どこですか。 kafeteria ( wa ) doko desu ka.

2.  きょう (      ) あついですか。     kyoo( wa ) atsui desu ka.

3.  それ (      ) なんですか。     sore ( wa ) nan desu ka.

4.  なに (      ) いいですか。     nani ( ga ) ii desu ka.

5.  どこ (      ) いいですか。     doko ( ga ) ii desu ka.

6.  さしみは、おはし (      ) たべます。 sashimi wa, ohashi ( de ) tabemasu.

7.  うち (      ) えき (      ) あるきました。 uchi ( kara ) eki ( made ) arukimashita.

8.  にほんご (      ) おじょうずですね。 nihongo ( ga ) ojyoozu desu ne.

9.  わたし (      ) アメリカ (      ) きました。 watashi ( wa ) amerika ( kara )
              from              kimashita.

10.  これから　がっこう (      ) いきます。     korekara gakko ( ne ) ikimasu.
              will go

I.  Translate into Japanese.
1.  Winter is cold.
2.  Summer is hot.
3.  Mountains are tall.   ("Mountains" in Japanese is "やま yama," and "tall" is the same as "expensive.")
4.  Tokyo has many people. (Use " Topic wa Subject ga Predicate pattern.  "People" is"ひと hito" in Japanese.  Use the adjective "おおい ooi (more than usual)."
5.  Mariko has pretty eyes. (Use "wa+ga" pattern. Eyes are "め me," in Japanese.)
6.  Ken has long legs. (Use "wa+ga" pattern. "Legs" in Japanese is "あし ashi," and "long" is "ながい nagai."

J. Pair-work: でんわばんごうを　ききましょう。 You are missing the information. Ask your partner the missing telephone numbers and fill in the blanks. Remember two important hints:

(1) Use strong sounding numbers over the soft sounding numbers (4: "yon" is stronger than "shi,"7: nana is stronger than "shichi," 9: "kyuu" is stronger than "ku.")

(2) Make each number pronounced with equal duration of time so that every number becomes the same length (in this case, two syllables): 2 is "ni-i" and 5 is "go-o."

**Ask:** 〜さんのでんわばんごうは、なんばんですか。

.......san no denwa-bangoo wa nan-ban desu ka.

[A-san has the following information and needs to ask B-san]:

| | |
|---|---|
| やまださん　　Yamada-san | |
| おおぬきさん　Oonuki-san | |
| こたにさん　　Kotani-san | |
| さのさん　　　Sano-san | 323-590-2286 |
| おおたけさん　Ootake-san | 213-990-7488 |
| ブラウンさん　(buraun-san) Mr. Brown | 714-065-8920 |
| スミスさん　　(sumisu-san) Mrs. Smith | 626-585-3309 |
| ホワイトさん　(howaito-san) Ms. White | |
| たなかさん　　Tanaka-san | 626-395-6082 |
| かきうちさん　Kakiuchi-san | |

[B-san has the following information and needs to ask A-san.]:

| | |
|---|---|
| やまださん　　Yamada-san | 052-581-4997 |
| おおぬきさん　Oonuki-san | 626-585-7995 |
| こたにさん　　Kotani-san | 310-814-6863 |
| さのさん　　　Sano-san | |
| おおたけさん　Ootake-san | |
| ブラウンさん　(buraun-san) Mr. Brown | |
| スミスさん　　(sumisu-san) Mrs. Smith | |
| ホワイトさん　(howaito-san) Ms. White | 714-501-3846 |
| たなかさん　　Tanaka-san | |
| かきうちさん　Kakiuchi-san | 626-794-0041 |

Chapter 2 (C) Dict-A-Conversation:  Listening comprehension practice.
(1)  Choose the numbers you heard.

1.  21, 27

2.  34, 43

3.  52, 50

4.  61, 81

5.  99, 79

6.  46, 49

7.  71, 78

8.  88, 87

9.  49, 46

10. 38, 37

(2)  Choose the hiragana you heard.

1.　　　きゆう、きゅう

2.　　　きゅうさい、しゅうさい

3.　　　ゆめ、ゆうめい

4.　　　ここ、こうこう

5.　　　はち、はっち

6.　　　ごこ、ごこう

7.　　　かんこく、かんごく

8.　　　ちょうちょ、ちゅうちょ

9.　　　しゅうそく、しゅっそく

10.　　　いき、いっき

Chapter 2(C): Crossword Puzzle # 1 (Verbs)
Hiragana version in the "masu" form　（あいうえお、かきくけこ、さしすせそ、たちつてと、なにぬねの、はひふへほ、まみむめも）

Find the following words in the box and circle/color them.  The words can go horizontally, vertically, diagonally, or backward.

1. はなします speak
2. ききます listen
3. たべます eat
4. あるきます walk
5. きます come

6. のみます drink
7. いきます go
8. かきます write

| さ | あ | る | き | ま | す |
|---|---|---|---|---|---|
| へ | ほ | た | き | み | む |
| ふ | す | べ | ま | ひ | と |
| の | み | ます | す | か | て |
| さ | え | す | き | ま | す |
| う | あ | ま | ち | い | つ |
| お | す | ま | し | な | は |

Chapter 2(C):  Crossword Puzzle # 2 (Adjectives and な Adjectives [=Copula Nouns])

Hiragana (あいうえお、かきくけこ、さしすせそ、たちつてと、なにぬねの、 はひふへほ、まみむめも)

Find the following words in the box and circle/color them.  The words can go horizontally, vertically, diagonally, or backward.

[Adjectives]

1. ちいさい small
2. おおきい large
3. おおい more
4. いい　good
5. いたい painful
6. おいしい delicious

7. やすい reasonable; cheap
8. たかい expensive

[Copula Nouns]

9. しずか quiet
10. ゆうめい famous
11. すき likable; pleasing

| | | | | | | |
|---|---|---|---|---|---|---|
| さ | あ | ゆ | き | ま | す | づ |
| へ | ほ | う | き | み | む | だ |
| ふ | す | め | い | ひ | と | や |
| や | す | い | お | か | て | よ |
| さ | き | す | お | ま | い | し |
| う | も | ま | き | た | ず | つ |
| ち | い | さ | い | か | た | け |
| な | お | い | し | い | あ | せ |

これまでのまとめ：Review Exercise (Chapters 1, 2ABC)

[A]. Fill in the blanks with appropriate particles.

Example: Anata <u>wa</u> Smith san desu <u>ka</u>. あなた（は）、すみすさんです（か）。
       Hai, soo desu.                はい、そうです。

1. Watashi _____ Bob desu.          わたし（　　）ぼぶです。

2. A: Anata ____ gakusei desu _____. A: あなた（　　）がくせいです（　　）。
    B: Hai, gakusei desu.         B: はい、がくせいです。

3. Watashi _____ gakusei desu.      わたし（　　）がくせいです。
    Bob san _____ gakusei desu.     ぼぶさん（　　）がくせいですか。
           also
    Watashi _____ Bob san wa gakusei desu. わたし（　　）ぼぶさんは、
                          がくせいです。

4. Tanaka-sensei _____ Nihon _____ kata desu. Yamada-sensei _____
    Nihon _____ kata desu.                 also
    たなかせんせい（　　）にほん（　　）かたです。
    やまだせんせい（　　）にほん（　　）かたです。

5. A: Tom san mo Amerika no kata desu ka. A: とむさんも　あめりかのかたですか。
    B: Iie, Tom san _____ Doitsu _____ kata desu. B: いいえ、とむさん（　　）
                               どいつ（　　）かたです。

6. Smith san wa Doitsugo _____ sensei desu ka. すみすさんは、どいつご
                                   （　　）せんせいです。

7. A: Kankoku _____ kata desu ka.    A: かんこく（　　）かたですか。
    B: Hai, Kankoku _____ desu.      B: はい、かんこく（　　）です。

8. A: Smith _____ desu ka.         A: すみす（　　）ですか。
    B: Iie, Brown desu.           B: いいえ、ぶらうんです。

[B]. Answer the questions.
Example: Yamada: Taylor san desu ka.    ていらーさんですか。
         Taylor   : Hai, <u>Taylor desu</u>.     はい、<u>ていらーです</u>。

1. Yamada: Lee san desu ka.        りーさんですか。
    Lee     : Hai, _____.      はい、_____。

2. Sensei　: Gakusei desu ka.　　　　　　がくせいですか。

   Gakusei: Hai, _____.　　　　　はい、_____。

3. Sensei　: Anata mo gakusei desu ka.　　あなたも　がくせいですか。

   Gakusei:　Hai, _____.　　　　はい、_____。

4. Gakusei: Sensei desu ka.　　　　　　　せんせいですか。

   Gakusei: Iie, _____.　　　　　いいえ、_____。

5. Clark　:　Amerika no kata desu ka.　　あめりかのかたですか。

   Meyer:　Iie, _____.　　いいえ、_____。

6. Yamada: Doitsu no kata desu ka.　　　どいつのかたですか。

   Meyer　: Hai, _____.　　はい、_____。

7. Clark　: Yamada-sensei wa Eigo no sensei　　やまだせんせいは、えいごの

           desu ka.　　　　　　　　　　　　せんせいですか。

   Meyer: Iie, _____.　　いいえ、_____。

[C].  Fill in the blanks with appropriate sentences.

1. Meyer: Clark san, kochira wa Lee san desu. M：くらーくさん、

    (kochira; this person [polite form])　　　　こちらは、りーさんです。

   Lee　:　_____.　　L：_____.

   Clark　: Clark desu. _____C：くらーくです。

                          _____。

2. A: Doomo arigatoo gozaimasu.　　　A：どうもありがとうございます。

   B: _____.　　　　B：_____。

3. A: Itte rasshai.　　　　　　　　　　A：いってらっしゃい。

   B: _____.　　　　B：_____。

4. A: Itadakimasu.　　　　　　　　　　A：いただきます。

   B: _____.　　　　　　　　B：_____。

5. A: Tadaima.　　　　　　　　　　　　A：ただいま。

   B: _____.　　　　B：_____。

6. A: Ogenki desuka.　　　　　　　　　A：おげんきですか。

   B: _____.　　　　B：_____。

[D].  Questions with Interrogative Pronouns. (doko [where], nan/nani[what], donata/dare [who])

Example:  A:  Ano kata wa (          ) desu ka.   A:あのかたは、**(どなた)**ですか。
        B:  Clark san desu.                         B:くらーくさんです。

1.  A:  Donata _____Wang san desu ka.      A: どなた （    ） わんさんですか。
    B:  Ano kata desu.                       B: あのかたです。

2.  A:  Ano kata wa _____ desu ka.       A: あのかたは、（      ）ですか。
    B:  Meyer san desu.                      B: めいやーさんです。

3.  A:  Gakusei-ka wa_____ desu ka.         A: がくせいかは、（     ）ですか。
    B:  Asoko desu.                          B: あそこです。

4.  A:  Are wa _____ desu ka.               A: あれは、（   ）ですか。
    B:  Are wa tokei desu.                   B: あれは、とけいです。

5.  A:  Nani ____ ii desu ka.               A: なに （   ）いいですか。
    B:  Ice cream ga ii desu.                B: あいすくりーむ （    ）いいです。

6.  A:  Kyoo wa_____ desu ka.            A: きょうは （          ）ですか。
    B:  Kyoo wa Ichi-gatsu tuitachi desu.    B: きょうは　いちがつついたちです。

7.  A:  Party wa doko _____ ii desu ka.     A:ぱあてぃは　どこ （    ）いいですか。
    B:  Old Town ga ii desu.                 B: おーるどたうんが　いいです。

8.  A:  Osushi _____ nani _____ suki desu ka.  A: おすし （    ）なに （    ）
                   すきですか。
    B:  Osushi wa Hirame (flounder)_____ suki desu.
                    B: おすしは、ひらめ （    ）すき
                    です。

[E].  Change to the negative form.

Example:  Sensei desu. → Sensei jya arimasen. せんせいです。
                →せんせいじゃありません。

1. Lee san wa Kankoku no kata desu. →りーさんは、かんこくのかたです。 →

2. Meyer san wa Mekishiko-jin desu. →めいやーさんは、めきしこじんです。 →

3. Wang san wa gakusei desu. →わんさんは、がくせいです。 →

4. Ayatora san wa Indoneshia-jin desu. →あやとらさんは、いんどねしあじんです。
→

5. Simpson wa handsome desu. →しんぷそんさんは、はんさむです。→

6. Koko wa kirei desu. →ここは、きれいです。→


[F].  Choose the right ones.

Example:  (<u>Kono</u>, kore) jisho wa (watashi, <u>watashi no</u>) desu.
(この、これ) じしょは (わたし、わたしの) です。


1. (Sore, sono) wa, booru-pen (jya, wa) arimasen.
(それ、その) は、ぼーるぺん (じゃ、は) ありません。

2. (Are, ano) zasshi wa (Clark san, Clark san no) desu.
(あれ、あの) ざっしは、(くらーくさん、くらーくさんの) です。

3. (Kore, kono) hon wa watsahi (wa, no) jya arimasen.
(これ、この) ほんは、わたし (は、の) じゃありません。

4. (Are, ano) wa, (nan, nani) desu ka.
(あれ、あの) は、(なん、なに) ですか。

5. (Kore, kono) jisho wa (donata, donata no) desu ka.
(これ、この) じしょは、(どなた、どなたの) ですか。

6. (Watashi wa, watashi no) enpitsu wa, (kore, kono) desu.
(わたしは、わたしの) えんぴつは、(これ、この) です。

# <u>Ordering and Shopping</u>

Chapter 3A: Ordering at a Coffee Shop
*Expressions*
"Please give me water." "Please give me this and that."
Learn the names of animals and write them in hiragana.
Hiragana Rules
Reading a story in hiragana: "An Old Man with a Lump on the Cheek"

*Cultural Note with Illustration*
The Pillow Book by Sei-sho-nagon

*Crossword Puzzles*

*Completion of Hiragana*
Mastering the lines "ra-ri-ru-re-ro" and "wa, wo, n"

Chapter 3B: Ordering at McDonald's
*Expressions*
"We have "large, medium, and small"
"I'm fine with it"

*Crossword Puzzles*
Reading a story in hiragana: "Rabbit in the Moon"

# Introduction to Katakana

Chapter 3C: Shopping at a Department Store
*Expressions*
"What kind of shoes do you like?" "How would you like the black shoes over there?"
"What's in the box?" "There's a dog under the tree." "How many cars are there?"

Chapter 3D: Ordering at a Restaurant
*Expressions*
"How much is it?" "No, thank you"

Particles Summary (Chapter 1 to Chapter 3)

Coffee break: ちょっと　きゅうけい

A thousand years ago, a court lady named Sei Shoonagon 清少納言 wrote an essay titled Makura no Sooshi 枕草子 that contains around three hundred chapters. The famous essay that has been loved by the Japanese for over a thousand years begins with a chapter of four seasons. She lists the best time of each season as follows:

> "Spring is daybreak.
> Summer is night.
> Autumn is twilight.
> Winter is early morning."

"Haru wa akebono　　　　　　はるは　あけぼの
 Natsu wa yoru.　　　　　　　　なつは　よる
 Aki wa yuugure　　　　　　　あきは　ゆうぐれ
 Fuyu wa tsutomete."　　　　　ふゆは　つとめて

Her crisp and rhythmical Japanese can be translated into modern Japanese as follows:
"Haru wa akegata ga ii　　　　はるは　あけがたが　いい
 Natsu wa yoru ga ii　　　　　なつは　よるが　いい
 Aki wa yuugata ga ii　　　　　あきは　ゆうがたが　いい
 Fuyu wa soochoo ga ii."　　　ふゆは　そうちょうが　いい

It falls into a pattern of "A wa B ga ii" (Topic wa Subject ga Predicate).

## Chapter 3 (A)   Ordering at a Coffee Shop   きっさてんで　ちゅうもんする
### ki-s-sa-te-n de   chu-u-mo-n su-ru

ウェイトレス：いらっしゃいませ。何に　なさいますか。　　　　　　　1
u-e-i-to-re-su  : i-ra-s-sha-i ma-se.    na-n ni  na-sa-i ma-su ka.

モニカ：　　　　コーヒーに　します。　　　　　　　　　　　　　　2
Mo-ni-ka:       ko-o-hi-i ni   shi-ma-su

ウェイトレス：ホットですか、アイスですか。　　　　　　　　　　　3
u-e-i-to-re-su  : ho-t-to de-su ka, a-i-su  de-su ka.

モニカ：　　　　ホット（を）おねがいします。　　　　　　　　　　4
Mo-ni-ka:       ho-t-to  (wo)  o-ne-ga-i shi-ma-su

ウェイトレス：はい、しょうしょう　おまちください。　　　　　　　5
u-e-i-to-re-su  : ha-i,    sho-u-sho-u        o-ma-chi ku-da-sa-i.

(After a short while)

　　　　　　　おまたせしました。　　　　　　　　　　　　　　　6
　　　　　　　o-ma-ta-se shi-ma-shi-ta.

(Looking at the menu)

モニカ：　　　　あのう、すみません。これは、何ですか。　　　　　7
Mo-ni-ka:       a-no-u,  su-mi-ma-se-n. ko-re-wa  na-n de-su ka.

ウェイトレス：どれですか。あ、それは、ミックスサンドです。　　　8
u-e-i-to-re-su:    do-re-de-su-ka. a, so-re-wa  mi-k-ku-su sa-n-do de-su.

　　　　　　　きゅうりと　ハムと　たまごの　サンドイッチです。　9
　　　　　　　kyu-u-ri to  ha-mu to  ta-ma-go no  sa-n-do-i-c-chi de-su.
　　　　　　　cucumber      ham          eggs.

モニカ：　　　　これも、ください。　　　　　　　　　　　　　　　10
Mo-ni-ka:       ko-re mo, ku-da-sa-i.

ウェイトレス：かしこまりました。　　　　　　　　　　　　　　　11
u-e-i-to-re-su:    ka-shi-ko-ma-ri-ma-shi-ta.

[English translation:]  Ordering at a Coffee Shop

Waitress: Welcome.  What would you like? (Lit:  What did you decide on?)
Monica:   I'll have coffee.  (Lit:  I decided on coffee)
Waitress: Hot or ice?  (Lit: Hot coffee or iced coffee?)
Monica:   Hot, please.
Waitress: Yes, please wait a moment.
          (After a little while)
Waitress: Thank you for waiting.
          (Monica, pointing at a menu, asks the waitress)
Monica:   Well, excuse me (but), what is this?
Waitress: Which one?  Oh, that is a mixed sandwich.
          It's a sandwich with cucumber, ham, and (cooked) eggs.
Monica:   Please give me this one too.
Waitress: Certainly.  (Lit:  Understood [humble form])

Learn hundred digit numbers.

| hundreds | In Japanese numerals | |
|----------|----------|----------|
| 100 | hyaku | ひゃく |
| 200 | ni-hyaku | にひゃく |
| 300 | san-byaku | さんびゃく |
| 400 | yon-hyaku | よんひゃく |
| 500 | go-hyaku | ごひゃく |
| 600 | ro-p-pyaku | ろっぴゃく |
| 700 | nana-hyaku | ななひゃく |
| 800 | ha-p-pyaku | はっぴゃく |
| 900 | kyuu-hyaku | きゅうひゃく |

Chapter 3A: Ordering at a Coffee Shop  **109**

Chapter 3(A)                    Vocabulary List

1. Expressions

| | |
|---|---|
| Irasshai mase いらっしゃいませ | May I help you? |
| Nan ni nasaimasu ka. なんになさいますか | What would you like to order? |
| Onegai shimasu おねがいします | Please do me a favor. |
| shoo shoo しょうしょう | a little |
| Omachi kudasai. おまちください | Please wait. |
| Omatase shimashita. おまたせしました | Thank you for waiting. |
| Anoo~ あのう | Well (showing hesitance) |
| Ah あ | Oh |
| Kudasai ください | Please give me. |
| Kashikomari mashita. かしこまりました | Understood. (humble form) |

2. Nouns

| | |
|---|---|
| Kissaten きっさてん | coffee shop |
| chuumon (suru) ちゅうもん（する） | an order (to order) |
| ueitoresu ウエートレス | waitress |
| koohii コーヒー | coffee |
| hotto ホット | hot coffee |
| aisu アイス | iced coffee |
| mikkusu sando ミックスサンド | mixed sandwich |
| kyuuri きゅうり | cucumber |
| hamu ハム | ham |
| tamago たまご | egg |
| sando icchi サンドイッチ | sandwich |

3. Interrogative pronouns

| | |
|---|---|
| dore どれ | which one (among numerous items) |
| kore これ | this one (near the speaker) |
| sore それ | that one (near the listener) |

(Additional Vocabulary)

| | |
|---|---|
| are あれ | that one over there (far from both speaker and listener) |

4. Particle

| | |
|---|---|
| to と | and (to connect two nouns) (There are other usages for particle "to," but in this dialogue, it means "and.") |
| wo を | case marker after a direct object |

----------------------------------------------------------------------

## Additional Vocabulary from Grammar Notes, Exercises, and Dict-A-Conversation

----------------------------------------------------------------------

[Nouns]
(drinks)

| mizu | みず | water |
|---|---|---|
| o-mizu | おみず | polite form of "mizu" |
| o-cha | おちゃ | green tea |
| miruku | ミルク | milk |
| remon skasshu | レモンスカッシュ | lemonade |
| orenji jyuusu | オレンジジュース | orange juice |
| wain | ワイン | wine |

(food)

| [wa-shoku] | わしょく | Japanese cuisine |
|---|---|---|
| gohan | ごはん | cooked rice; meal |
| soba | そば | buckwheat noodle |
| udon | うどん | white round-shaped noodle made of wheat-flour |
| sukiyaki | すきやき | thin-sliced beef and vegetables cooked in a shallow pan |
| yasai | やさい | vegetables |
| [yoo-shoku] | ようしょく | Western cuisine |
| supageti | スパゲティ | spaghetti |
| naporitan | ナポリタン | spaghetti with tomato sauce |
| miito soosu | ミートソース | spaghetti with meat sauce |
| hanbaagaa | ハンバーガー | hamburger |
| chiizu baagaa | チーズバーガー | cheese burger |
| bifuteki | ビフテキ | beef stake |
| omuraisu | オムライス | fried rice covered by omelet |
| omuretsu | オムレツ | omelet |
| furaido poteto | フライドポテト | French fries |
| sarada | サラダ | salad |
| pan | パン | bread |
| shiriaru | シリアル | cereal |

(animals & insects)

| ari | あり | ant |
|---|---|---|

| ookami | おおかみ | wolf |
| usagi | うさぎ | rabbit |
| ushi | うし | cow |
| uma | うま | horse |
| kame | かめ | turtle |
| kangaruu | カンガルー | kangaroo |
| kaeru | かえる | frog |
| kitsune | きつね | fox |
| kirin | きりん | giraffe |
| kujira | くじら | whale |
| koara | コアラ | koala |
| sakana | さかな | fish |
| saru | さる | monkey |
| shika | しか | deer |
| zou | ぞう | elephant |
| tanuki | たぬき | raccoon |
| tora | とら | tiger |
| tori | とり | bird |
| nezumi | ねずみ | mouse |
| panda | パンダ | Giant Panda |
| hitsuji | ひつじ | sheep |
| hiyoko | ひよこ | chick |
| buta | ぶた | pig |
| hebi | へび | snake |
| pengin | ペンギン | penguin |
| rakuda | らくだ | camel |
| raion | ライオン | lion |
| wani | わに | crocodile |

(general terms)

| ikimono | いきもの | living things |
| doobutsu | どうぶつ | animals |
| mushi | むし | insects |

[Expressions]
(from Dict-A-Conversation)

Nani wo sashi-age-mashoo?                    What shall I give (=serve) you?
なにを　さしあげましょう？

Chapter 3(A)                    Grammar and Cultural Notes

## 1. と "to": the particle connecting two nouns

The particle "と to" is used only to connect two nouns. It cannot be used to connect two or more sentences or verb phrases. Unlike the case where the particle "の no" connects two nouns, there is no such relationship between the two nouns connected by "と to". In a situation using "の no," the first noun would modify the second noun. (For example, "えいごのほん eigo no hon" means "English book," where the first noun explains the second noun.)   例(examples)：あなたとわたし、これとそれ、えいごとにほんご.

## 2. を "wo": the particle followed by a direct object

The particle "を wo" is used after a direct object. It is used with transitive verbs such as "eat," "drink," "watch," "study," "write," "read," and many others. In the dialogue, it is used with the verb that means "please give (me)," ~ をください。 wo kudasai.

Examples:
(1) おみずを　ください。
　　 O-mizu wo kudasai.  (Please give me water.)

(2) こうちゃを　おねがいします。
　　 Koocha wo onegaishimasu. (Please give me tea.)

Note: When you use another particle, "も mo" (also), usually "を wo" is dropped, though it's not ungrammatical to use them both, such as "をも wo mo." It is, however, not colloquial.
Example:
　　　すみません、おみずをください。あ、それから、おちゃもください。
　　　"Sumimasen, o-mizu wo kudsasai. Ah, sorekara, o-cha mo kudasai."
　　　Excuse me.  Please give me water.  Oh, then, please give me tea, too.

## 3. Alternate question: Is it A or B? (A desuka, B desuka)

The alternate question, "Is it A or B," is expressed in Japanese as follows:
　　　A ですか、B ですか。
　　　A desu ka, B desu ka.

The predicate may vary.
Examples:
(1)　がくせいですか、せんせいですか。 (Is he a student or a teacher?)
　　 gakusei desu ka, sensei desu ka.

(2) こうちゃにしますか、コーヒーにしますか。

koohii ni shimasuka, koocha ni shimasu ka. (Are you going to have coffee or tea?)

(3) とうきょうへ いきますか、おおさかへ いきますか。
    Tokyoo e ikimasu ka, Oosaka e ikimasu ka. (Are you going to Tokyo or Osaka?)

## 4. Polite expressions

It is very common to use the polite form in business situations, like in a store or a restaurant.  The expressions appear in this chapter are commonly used in both a coffee shop and a restaurant.  Understand the following expressions when they are used:

なさいます (nasaimasu): a polite form of "します shimasu" (to do)
ございます (gozaimasu): a polite form of "です desu" (to be) or "あります arimasu" (to exist; have)
しょうしょう　おまちください (shooshoo omachi kudasai): (It means "Please wait for a moment.")
おまたせいたしました (omatase itashimashita) It means "Thank you for waiting."
かしこまりました (kashikomari mashita) : a polite form of "wakarimashita" (Understood.)

## 5.  Typical lunch/drinks served at a coffee shop or a restaurant

Coffee shops are abundant in Japan; and not only do they serve coffee, tea and other types of cold drinks, they serve light meals such as sandwiches, spaghetti, fried rice covered by omelet called "omuraisu オムライス," and curried rice (called カレーライス "karee raisu").  They also serve assorted meals called "ていしょく teishoku (a fixed meal)," with ingredients varying from one store to another.  Vocabulary you may also want to know includes わしょく ("washoku," meaning "the Japanese food) and ようしょく ("yooshoku," meaning "the Western food").  Please also note the following.  The word "hot" means "hot coffee," and simply "ice" sometimes means "iced coffee."  What is called "remon sukasshu" is actually lemonade.  "Spaghetti Napolitan" means spaghetti with tomato sauce, and "Spaghetti Meat Sauce" is what you would think of it in the United States.  "Karee raisu (curry rice)" is different from Indian curry.  It is much thicker in sauce and usually comes with potatoes, onions and carrots, and you can also choose from vegetables, meat (chicken, pork, or beef) or seafood.  Sandwiches come in varieties, but usually it comes with thin-sliced cucumber, boiled eggs, ham, cheese, or "mixed," a combination of the above listed.

This is a menu at a coffee shop. これは　きっさてんのメ<sup>め に ゅ</sup>ニューです。

What would you like to order? 何<sup>なに</sup>をちゅうもんしますか。

---

メ<sup>め に ゅ</sup>ニュー

| Menu | ねだん（円<sup>えん</sup>） |
|---|---|
| コーヒー koohii (hot) | 300 |
| こうちゃ koocha (black tea) | 300 |
| アイスコーヒー aisu koohii (iced coffee) | 350 |
| オレンジジュース orenji jyuusu (orange juice) | 400 |
| ミルク miruku (milk) | 300 |
| レモン・スカッシュ remon sukasshu (lemonade) | 400 |
| | |
| サンドイッチ sandoicchi (sandwich) | |
| 　ミックス mikkusu (mixed) | 700 |
| 　やさい yasai (vegetables) | 600 |
| 　ハム hamu (ham) | 600 |
| スパゲティ supageti (spaghetti) | |
| 　ナポリタン naporitan (tomato sauce) | 700 |
| 　ミートソース miito soosu (meat sauce) | 700 |
| カレーライス karee raisu (curry rice) | 800 |

---

Role play:  Work with a partner.  Order drinks or food at a "kissaten" (coffee shop)
Example:

　　Ａ：いらっしゃいませ。なんに　なさいますか。
　　　　Irasshaimase.　　　　　Nan ni　nasaimasu ka.
　　Ｂ：ホット　ください。それと、おみずも　おねがいします。
　　　　Hotto　kudasai. *Please*　Sore to,　omizu mo　onegai shimasu.
　　Ａ：ホットとおみずですね。
　　　　Hotto to omizu desu ne.
　　Ｂ：それから、スパゲティを　ください。
　　　　Sorekara,　supageti wo　kudasai.
　　Ａ：ナポリタンとミートソースがありますが、、、
　　　　Naporitan to miito soosu ga　arimasu ga....
　　Ｂ：ナポリタンを　おねがいします。
　　　　Naporitan　wo　onegai shimasu.
　　Ａ：ホットとナポリタンですね、しょうしょう　おまちください。
　　　　Hotto to naporitan　desu ne.　　　shoo-shoo　　　o-machi kudasai.

Fill in the blanks with what you would like to order at a coffee shop.

**[Pattern A]**

ウェイトレス：いらっしゃいませ。何に　なさいますか。
Waitress　　：i-ra-s-sha-i- ma-se.　na-n ni na-sai ma-su ka.
　　　　　　　　　May I help you.　　What would you like to order

あなた
You　　　　：_____.

ウェイトレス：ホットですか、アイスですか。
Waitress　　：ho-t-to de-su ka,　a-i-su　de-su ka.

あなた
You　　　　：_____.

ウェイトレス：はい、しょうしょう　おまちください。
Waitress　　：ha-i,　sho-u-sho-u　　o-ma-chi ku-da-sa-i.


**[Pattern B]**

ウェイトレス：いらっしゃいませ。
Waitress　　：i-ra-s-sha-i- ma-se.

あなた　　　　　　　　　　　　　　　　　　　を　ください。
You　　　　：___Supageti_____.
　　　　　　　（　　　　　　　　） wo kudasai.

ウェイトレス：ミートソースですか、ナポリタンですか。
Waitress　　：mi-i-to-so-o-su de-su ka,　na-po-ri-ta-n　de-su ka.

あなた
You　　　　：___miito soosu___kudasai___.

ウェイトレス：はい、かしこまりました。
Waitress　　：ha-i,　ka-shi-ko-ma-ri-ma-shi-ta.

Chapter 3(A) Exercises

A.  Pair-work: Look at the chart below.  The information in the chart outlines what each person has ordered, ate and drunk.  Tell your partner something about one of them: a choice they made, something they ate, or something they drank.  Your partner should exchange information about another person.  Then, rephrase the statements using "to と."  Follow the examples below.

(1)

A：モニカさん<u>は</u>、サンドイッチに　しました。
　　Monika san <u>wa</u> sandoicchi ni shimashita.

B：みわさん<u>も</u>、サンドイッチに　しました。
　　Miwa san <u>mo</u> sandoicchi ni shimashita.

A：モニカさん<u>と</u>みわさんは、サンドイッチに　しました。
　　Monika san <u>to</u> Miwa san wa, sandoicchi ni shimashita.

(2)

A：モニカさん<u>は</u>、みずを　のみました。Monika san <u>wa</u> mizu wo nomimashita.

B：みのるさん<u>も</u>、みずを　のみました。Minoru san <u>mo</u> mizu wo nomimashita.

A：モニカさん<u>と</u>みのるさんは、みずを　のみました。
　　Monika san <u>to</u> Minoru san wa mizu wo nomimashita.

| Name | decided on ~<br>～に　しました<br>~ ni   shimashita | ate ~<br>～を　たべました<br>~ wo tabemashita | drank ~<br>～を　のみました<br>~ wo nomimashita |
|---|---|---|---|
| モニカ<br>Monika | サンドイッチ<br>sandoicchi | ミックス・サンド<br>mikkusu   sando | みず<br>mizu |
| せんせい<br>sensei | スパゲティ<br>supagetti | スパゲティ・ナポリタン<br>supagetti naporitan | ワイン<br>wain |
| みわ<br>Miwa | サンドイッチ<br>sandoicchi | やさいサンド<br>yasai sando | コーラ<br>koora |
| てつや<br>Tetsuya | ようしょく<br>yooshoku | ビフテキ<br>bifuteki | コーヒー<br>koohii |
| あいこ<br>Aiko | わしょく<br>washoku | うどん<br>udon | おちゃ<br>ocha |
| けんじ<br>Kenji | ていしょく<br>teishoku | オムライス<br>omuraisu | コーラ<br>koora |
| みのる<br>Minoru | ようしょく<br>yooshoku | サラダ<br>sarada | みず<br>mizu |
| おとうさん<br>otoosan | ていしょく<br>teishoku | カレーライス<br>karee raisu | ワイン<br>wain |
| こうじ<br>Kooji | わしょく<br>washoku | そば<br>soba | おちゃ<br>ocha |
| ひでき<br>Hideki | スパゲティ<br>supagetti | スパゲティ・ミートソース<br>supagetti miitosoosu | コーヒー<br>koohii |

B. Fill in the blanks with the appropriate words or particles.

1. A: Irasshai mase. Nan ( _ni_ ) nasai masu ka.
   B: Watashi ( _wa_ ) supagetti ( _ni_ ) shimasu.
      Sumimasen ( _ga_ ), pan ( _mo_ ) kudasai. (pan; bread)
      Watashi=                           also
   C: Boku ( _wa_ ), biiru ( _to_ ) hanbaagaa wo kudsasai. (biiru; beer)
   A: Hai, supagetti ( _to_ ) pan ( _to_ ) biiru ( _to_ ) hanbaagaa desune.

2. A: Hotto desu ( _ka_ ), aisu desu ( _ka_ ).
      (hot coffee)          (iced-coffee)
   B: Hotto ( を _wo_ ) onegai shimasu.

3. A: Nani ( を ) tabemashita ka.
   B: Karee-raisu desu.

4. A: ( _Nani_ ) wo nomimashita ka.
   B: Jyuusu desu.

5. A: Supagetti wo kudasai.
   B: Naporitan ( _desu_ ) ka, Miito-soosu ( _desu_ ) ka.
   A: Miito-soosu ( を ) onegaishimasu.

6. A: Mikkusu-sando wo kudasai.
   B: Watashi ( _mo_ ).
   C: Mikkusu-sando o-futatsu desu ne. Kashikomarimashita.
                     二份.

C. Work with a partner: Cross out the word that doesn't belong in the group.

1. たまご、きゅうり、ハム、ジュース、オムレツ
   tamago,  kyuuri,  hamu,  jyuusu,  omuretsu

2. ビフテキ、カレーライス、ワイン、サラダ、スパゲティ
   bifuteki,  karee-raisu,  wain,  sarada,  supagetti

3. うどん、そば、てんぷら、すきやき、コーヒー
   udon,  soba,  tempura,  sukiyaki,  koohii

4. ハンバーガー、フライドポテト、ミルクシェイク、おちゃ
   hanbaagaa,  furaido-poteto,  miruku-sheiku,  ocha

5. パン、ごはん、シリアル、ミルク、アイスクリーム
   pan,  gohan,  shiriaru,  miruku,  aisukuriimu

Chapter 3(A)'s Dict-A-Conversation (1)
Listen to the CD and complete the dialogue by filling in the blanks. Write your answers in complete sentences. For now, you may write answers in Roma-ji; but later when you are instructed, write in hiragana.

1．Ordering a drink.
A : ...............................................................................

B : _____

A : ...............................................................................

B : _____
    You also ask for water.

2．Ordering a sandwich.
A : ...............................................................................

B : _____

A : ...............................................................................

B : _____

A : ...............................................................................

3．More advanced conversation.
A : ...............................................................................

B : _____

A : ...............................................................................

B : じゃ、 _____。

A : ...............................................................................

<u>Review on Particles "wa" & "ga" (Chapter 1~ 3A)</u>
(Correct answers are blocked & underlined for your self-study)

**A.** Sentences with Interrogative Pronouns (=question words, e.g., when, what, who, where).

Model 1:  Kore *wa* nan desu ka. ("wa" precedes IP) これは　なんですか。

Exercise:  Choose the correct particles.
1.  Are (**wa**, ga) nan desu ka. (What is it over there?)　　あれは　なんですか。
2.  Kyoo (**wa**, ga) nan-nichi desu ka. (What date is it today?)きょうは、なんにちですか。
3.  Otearai (**wa**, ga) doko desu ka. (Where is the bathroom?)おてあらいは　どこですか。
4.  Tanaka san (**wa**, ga) dochira desu ka. (Where is Mr. T? Or, Which one is Mr. T?)
　　　　　　　　　　　　　　　　　　たなかさんは　どちらですか。


Model 2:  Nani *ga* ii desu ka. ("ga" is preceded by IP)　なにが　いいでか。

Exercise:  Chooses the correct particles.
1.  Dare (wa, **ga**) sensei desu ka. (Who is the teacher?)　　だれが　せんせいですか。
2.  Doko (wa, **ga**) oishii desu ka. ([As to restaurants] where is good?)どこがおいしいですか。
3.  Dochira (wa, **ga**) Tanaka san desu ka. (Which one is Tanaka san?) どちらが
　　　　　　　　　　　　　　　　　　　　たなかさんですか。
4.  Nani (wa, **ga**) jyoozu desu ka. (What are you good at?)　なにが　じょうずですか。


**B.** Statements to describe characteristics/features of a topic.
*Topic "wa" Subject "ga" Predicate* pattern is often used to convey this information.

| Topic | | Subject | | Predicate |
|---|---|---|---|---|
| Noun | wa | Noun | ga | Predicate |
| Tokyo | wa | hito | ga | ooi desu. |

Tokyo has many people → Speaking of Tokyo, people are many. →Tokyo *wa* hito *ga* ooi desu.  Let's speak more of Tokyo's characteristics:とうきょうは　ひとがおおいです。

*Tokyo wa* kuruma ga ooi desu. (Tokyo has many cars.)とうきょうは くるまがおおいです。
　　　　michi ga semai desu. (the streets are narrow)　　　みちがせまいです。
　　　　Ginza ga kirei desu. (Ginza is pretty)　　　　　　ぎんざがきれいです。
　　　　coffee ga takai desu. (coffee is expensive)　　　コーヒーがたかいです。

| Topic | | Subject | | Predicate |
|---|---|---|---|---|
| Noun | wa | Noun | ga | Predicate |
| Kyoo | wa | (o) tenki | ga | ii desu. |

It's a nice weather today. → Speaking of today, weather is nice. → Kyoo wa (o) tenki ga ii desu.  Let's talk more about "today."    きょうは、おてんきが　いいです。

*Kyoo wa* kion (air temperature) ga takai desu. (Today's temperature is high.)
きょうは、きおんが　たかいです。

        kuuki (air) ga kirei desu. (the air is clean)　くうきが　きれいです。
        sora (sky) ga aoi desu. (the sky is blue)　　そらが　あおいです。

C. Exercise:  Choose the correct particles.

1. Kyoo (**wa**, ga) tenpura (wa, **ga**) oishii desu. (Featuring today's special, tenpura is delicious.)
    きょうは、てんぷらが　おいしいです。
2. Tanaka san (**wa**, ga) me (wa, **ga**) kirei desu. (Tanaka san has beautiful eyes.)
    たなかさんは、めが　きれいです。
3. Katoo san (**wa**, ga) kuchi (wa, **ga**) jyoozu desu. (Katoo san is a smooth talker [to flatter others])
    かとうさんは、くちが　じょうずです。
4. Kyoto (**wa**, ga) otera (wa, **ga**) ooi desu. (Kyoto has many temples.)
    きょうとは、おてらが　おおいです。
5. Nihongo no kurasu (**wa**, ga) gakusei (wa, **ga**) ooi desu. ("ooi" = more. There are many students in Japanese class.)
    にほんごのクラスは、がくせいが　おおいです。
6. Kooen (**wa**, ga) hito (wa, **ga**) sukunai desu. ("sukunai"=fewer; less. There aren't many people in the park.)
    こうえんは、ひとが　すくないです。
7. Osushi (**wa**, ga) "Kimagure Restaurant" (wa, **ga**) oishii desu. ("oishii" =delicious. Speaking of "sushi," "Kimagure Restaurant" is good.)
    おすしは、「きまぐれレストラン」が　おいしいです。
8. Tenpura (**wa**, ga) "Thousand Cranes Restaurant" (wa, **ga**) ii desu. (Speaking of "tenpura," "Thousand Cranes Restaurant" is good.)
    てんぷらは、「せんばづる」レストランが　いいです。
9. Pasadena (**wa**, ga) Rose Bowl (wa, **ga**) yuumei desu. (Speaking of Pasadena, Rose Bowl is famous.)
    パサデナは、ローズボールが　ゆうめいです。
10. Kono daigaku (**wa**, ga) tuition (wa, **ga**) takai desu. (This college's tuition is high.)
    このだいがくは、じゅぎょうりょうが　たかいです。
               (tuition)

生き物（鳥、魚、動物）　　いきもの　の　なまえを　おぼえましょう。

| | | | |
|---|---|---|---|
| 1. | 2. | 3. | 4. |
| 5. | 6. | 7. | 8. |
| 9. | 10. | 11. | 12. |
| 13. | 14. | 15. | 16. |
| 17. | 18. | 19. | 20. |
| 21. | 22. | 23. | 24. |
| 25. | 26. | 27. | 28. |
| 29. | 30. | 31. | 32. |

いきもの（とり、さかな、むし、どうぶつ）

| | | | |
|---|---|---|---|
| いぬ | ねこ | さかな | とり |
| むし | ひよこ | しか | かんがるう |
| ひつじ | うさぎ | きりん | へび |
| きつね | さる | かめ | うま |
| ぱんだ | こあら | あり | ねずみ |
| わに | うし | らいおん | ぺんぎん |
| たぬき | ぶた | ぞう | くじら |
| とら | らくだ | おおかみ | かえる |

Group Activity: Collect animals that share the same hiragana. Fill in the boxes to complete a list of animals that has the hiragana in each column. You may write the same word in more than one box as long as it shares the hiragana. For example, you can put あり in the boxes of both あ and り.

| あ | い | う | え | お |
|---|---|---|---|---|
| あり | | | | |
| か、が | き、ぎ | く | け | こ |
| | | | | |
| さ | し・じ | す | せ | そ・ぞ |
| | | | | |
| た、だ | ち | つ | て | と |
| | | | | |
| な | に | ぬ | ね | の |
| | | | | |
| は, ぱ | ひ、び | ふ、ぶ | へ、ぺ | ほ |
| | | | | |
| ま | み | む | め | も |
| | | | | |
| や | | ゆ | | よ |
| | | | | |
| ら | り | る | れ | ろ |
| | あり | | | |
| わ | ん | | | |
| | | | | |

Hiragana recognition exercise

なまえ（                                    ）

Find the correct hiragana that matches each Romanized syllable on the left.

とくてん(scores, points)

| 2 5 |
| --- |

| | | | | | | | | | |
|---|---|---|---|---|---|---|---|---|---|
| hi | ち | し | き | ひ | ら | て | み | そ | や |
| mi | し | ま | も | む | い | み | そ | き | ち |
| yu | や | せ | し | ね | れ | ろ | ゆ | り | た |
| ru | ら | り | れ | ろ | る | ま | さ | か | の |
| wo | お | を | の | あ | う | ほ | の | と | か |
| jyo | ぎょ | じゃ | じゅ | びょ | じょ | ぢょ | ひゅ | しょ | ちょ |
| gya | じゃ | ぎゃ | ぎゅ | じゅ | ちょ | ひゅ | しょ | ぢゃ | びゃ |
| ho | は | わ | し | れ | ま | な | け | ほ | ゆ |
| wa | れ | ぬ | は | め | わ | け | あ | に | た |
| chi | す | し | き | ぎ | ち | ぢ | じ | す | と |
| n | な | と | を | へ | け | ち | り | さ | ん |
| nya | にゃ | にゅ | にょ | ゆ | にや | みゃ | りゃ | ちゃ | しゃ |
| nu | ね | わ | れ | は | ぬ | の | よ | ま | にゅ |
| i | け | し | う | こ | ち | に | い | て | と |
| u | つ | く | え | お | う | さ | ち | に | へ |
| re | わ | り | ぬ | は | め | ね | れ | ろ | あ |
| so | し | す | そ | ぞ | そう | さ | り | わ | ち |
| shu | す | ちゅ | しゃ | しょ | じゅ | しゅ | ちょ | ちゃ | し |
| jyo | ぎょ | じょ | じゅ | ちゅ | しょ | ぢょ | ぎゅ | びょ | みゃ |
| pyo | ぴょ | ぶ | びょ | じゅ | ぴよ | しょ | ちょ | きょ | ぴゅ |
| ge | ぜ | け | じぇ | ぢぇ | げ | で | しぇ | ぐ | ぐぇ |
| ra | り | ろ | れ | や | ゆ | せ | て | ら | ち |
| o | あ | を | う | え | ほ | け | こ | れ | お |
| ya | お | う | や | あ | ら | せ | け | ご | ぼ |
| ma | み | む | し | ま | め | も | き | て | あ |

Hiragana Puzzle 2 (Hiragana 〜ん)      なまえ  Name (                    )

Find the listed words from the following page in the crossword puzzle and circle them.  Words may go horizontally, vertically, diagonally, backward, and overlap.

| し | ま | い | き | る | れ | す | う | が | く |
|---|---|---|---|---|---|---|---|---|---|
| り | ま | き | れ | り | き | も | う | ふ | や |
| ん | ご | じ | ん | は | し | わ | た | か | み |
| ご | と | び | が | な | か | ま | り | い | ん |
| じ | び | き | し | い | が | ち | め | げ | ぬ |
| な | あ | む | わ | ふ | め | が | ん | く | の |
| み | ま | し | ほ | ち | ね | に | く | ふ | も |
| だ | い | じ | な | ひ | と | げ | ゆ | う | き |
| べ | ん | き　よ | う | す | る | ふ | よ | し | |

List of words:

| | | | | |
|---|---|---|---|---|
| ままごと | doll play | ほし | stars | しまい sisters |
| わし | eagle | まむし | a viper | |
| なかま | companions | むし | insects | |
| にんげん | human beings | もうふ | blanket | |
| はし | chopsticks | ゆうき | courage | |
| ひかり | light | ようふく | Western clothing | |
| ふね | ship | わた | cotton | |
| やみ | darkness | いきる | to live | |
| やきいも | roasted potatoes | あまい | sweet | |
| めがね | eye glasses | くも | spider, cloud | |
| れきし | history | にげる | to run away | |
| すうがく | mathematics | がきあみ | starved child (Buddhist term) | |
| いわし | sardines | じびき | dictionary | |
| りんご | apples | いきじびき | a walking dictionary | |
| れんが | bricks | ふかい | deep | |
| にく | meat | さんにん | three people | |
| なみだ | tears | だいじなひと | precious person | |
| ぬの | cloth | ちがい | difference | |
| はがき | postcards | べんきょうする | to study | |

Chapter 3 (A): Crossword Puzzle # 1 (Food)

Hiragana (all of them)

Find the following words in the box and circle/color them. The words can go
horizontally, vertically, diagonally, or backward.

1. ぎょうざ dumpling
2. ちらしずし chirashi-zushi
3. ほたて scallop
4. おべんとう boxed lunch
5. ていしょく assorted meal
6. みそしる miso soup

7. てんぷら tenpura
8. さらだ salad
9. はむ ham
10. たまご eggs
11. さんどいっち sandwich
12. そば buckwheat noodle

13. きゅうり cucumber

| ろ | さ | ゆ | き | ま | す | は | た |
|---|---|---|---|---|---|---|---|
| て | ん | ぷ | ら | み | む | む | ま |
| き | ど | み | そ | し | る | お | ご |
| ゅ | い | れ | ほ | た | て | べ | る |
| う | っ | だ | お | ま | い | ん | り |
| り | ち | ら | し | ず | し | と | め |
| ち | い | さ | い | ぎ | よ | う | ざ |
| な | そ | ば | し | い | く | せ | む |

Chapter 3 (A):  Crossword Puzzle # 2 (Expressions for ordering food & drink)

Hiragana (all of them)

Find the following words in the box and circle/color them.  The words can go horizontally, vertically, diagonally, or backward.

1.  きっさてん coffee shop
2.  ちゅうもんする to order
3.  いらっしゃいませ May I help you?
4.  なさいます polite form of "do する"
5.  しょうしょう a little
6.  おねがいします Please do me a favor.
7.  ください  Please give me.
8.  すみません Excuse me.
9.  なんですか What is it?
10.  どれですか Which one?
11.  これ this one (near the speaker)
12.  それ that one (near the listener)
13.  かしこまりました I understood.
14.  おまたせしました Thank you for waiting.
15.  おまちください Please wait.

| な | み | だ | そ | い | ら | る | れ | た | や | ゆ | よ |
|---|---|---|---|---|---|---|---|---|---|---|---|
| ね | ち | こ | れ | さ | お | ぬ | な | ひ | す | し | る |
| の | ゅ | ず | い | だ | ね | づ | に | ふ | み | た | り |
| で | う | づ | ら | く | が | ぢ | み | か | ま | せ | か |
| か | も | ど | っ | ち | い | ふ | し | へ | せ | そ | ち |
| す | ん | な | し | ま | し | こ | う | ほ | ん | は | ま |
| で | す | か | ゃ | お | ま | た | せ | し | ま | し | た |
| ん | る | も | い | り | す | け | あ | え | い | お | さ |
| な | さ | い | ま | す | し | よ | う | し | よ | う | か |
| ぷ | ぴ | し | せ | や | か | す | で | れ | ど | ま | な |
| ぺ | た | ぱ | い | さ | ん | て | さ | っ | き | ご | た |

ひらがなのきそく (Hiragana Rules)

1. Use "u う" for the second "o," unless it appears at the beginning of a word.

そう、そうじ、きのう、どうぞ、なんようび、ありがとう、

Exceptions (when "oo" appears at the beginning)
おおきい、おおさか、おおかみ

2. Use small hiragana "tsu っ" for double consonants (cc, kk, ss, pp, etc.), unless it is nasal "nn" (ex. o-n-na = おんな )

いっぱい、がっこう、さっき、きっと、いっち、はっぱ、かっぱ

3. Use small "ya や, yu ゆ, yo よ" for contracted sounds such as "kya, kyu, kyo; sha, shu, sho; cha, chu, cho; gya, gyu, gyo; pya, pyu,pyo, etc.)

きょう、やきゅう、しゃちょう、きゅう、じゅう、こんしゅう、としょかん、べんきょう、しゅくだい

4. Use "じ" for "ji," and "ず" for "zu." Only exception to this rule is when they are having to do with "chi ち(blood)" or "tsu つ" in such words as "tsuki (the moon), tsuku (arrival), tsuchi (hammer),  tsukai (use), tsume (nail)." In these cases, you use "ぢ" or "づ." But, these exceptions come one thing at a time as your vocabulary increase.

Normally, you write:
じびき、かず、はずかしい、じてんしゃ、ずうずうしい

Exceptions are:
みかづき、ちかづく、かなづち、こまづかい、ふかづめ

5. Use the same hiragana for repetition.
すず、すずしい、すずき、しじみ、つづき、つづく、ちぢみ

6. Particles are written differently.
   (1) particle "wa" is written in hiragana "ha は."
      あなたは、せんせいですか。いいえ、わたしは、がくせいです。

   (2) particle "e" is written in hiragana "he へ."
      どこへ、いきますか。がっこうへ、いきます。

   (3) particle "wo" is written in hiragana "を."
      なにを　たべますか。　おすしを　たべます。

ひらがなのれんしゅうもんだい (Hiragana Exercises) じず and ぢづ

1. どちらが　ただしいですか。ただしいほうに○をつけなさい。
   Which is correct?  Circle the correct ones.

(1) suzushii　　　　　すずしい、すづしい

(2) hazukashii　　　　はづかしい、はずかしい

(3) ijiwaru　　　　　　いぢわる、いじわる

(4) kaji　　　　　　　かじ、　かぢ

(5) jitensha　　　　　ぢてんしゃ、じてんしゃ

(6) shijimi　　　　　　しじみ、しぢみ

(7) jimi　　　　　　　ぢみ、じみ

(8) jibiki　　　　　　じびき、ぢびき

2. ただしいほうに○をつけなさい。 Circle the correct ones.

(1) tsuzuki　　　　　つづき、つずき

(2) suzu　　　　　　すづ、　すず

(3) chijimi　　　　　ちじみ、ちぢみ

(4) kazukazu　　　　かずかず、かづかづ

(5) guzuguzu　　　　ぐづぐず、ぐずぐず

2. ただしいほうに○をつけなさい。 Circle the correct ones.

(1) hanaji (nose blood; hana + chi ち)　　　はなぢ、はなじ

(2) kanzume (canned stuff; kan + tsume[ru]つめ[る])　　かんずめ、かんづめ

(3) kozukai (allowance; small こ + use つかい)　　こづかい、こずかい

(4) mikazuki (crescent moon; three days みっか + moon つき) みかずき、みかづき

Hiragana Practice:  Writing sentences in hiragana.  Copy the sentences below.
Do not forget to write a period (。　), too.

1.　おはよう。

　　------------------------------------------------

2.　いってきます。　　　　　　　　いっていらっしゃい。

　　----------------------------　　----------------------------

3.　おはようございます。

　　------------------------------------------------

4.　こんにちは。

　　------------------------------

5.　いただきます。　　　　　　　　どうぞ。

　　----------------------------　　--------------------------

6.　ごちそうさまでした。

　　----------------------------------------

7.　さようなら。

　　------------------------------

8.　こんばんは。

　　------------------------------

9.　ただいま。　　　　　　　　　　おかえりなさい。

　　----------------------------　　--------------------------

10.おやすみなさい。

　　------------------------------------

１１．はい、どうぞ。　　　　　どうも　ありがとう。

------------------------     ------------------------------

１２．ごめんなさい。　　　　　　すみません。

------------------------     ------------------

１３．おげんきですか。　　　　はい、げんきです。

------------------------     ------------------------

１４．みてください。

------------------------------------------

１５．もういちど、いってください。

------------------------------------------------

１６．かいてください。

------------------------------------------------

１７．よんでください。

------------------------------------------

１８．これは、にほんごで　なんといいますか。

------------------------------------------------

１９．それは、なんですか。

------------------------------------------------

## Particle "wo": を

１．それを　ください。

------------------------------------------------

2．わたしを　みてください。

\-------------------------------------------------

3．ほんを　よんでください。

\-------------------------------------------------

4．おすしを　たべます。

\-------------------------------------------------

Particle "e": へ

1.　　どこへ　いきますか。

\-------------------------------------------------

2.　　がっこうへ　いきます。

\-------------------------------------------------

3.　　うちへ　かえります。

\-------------------------------------------------

4.　　あしたも　ここへ　きますか。

\-------------------------------------------------

れんしゅう First read the passage and, once you understand the content, copy it.

１．きのう、がっこうへ　いきました。がっこうで、たなかさんに　あいました。たなかさんと　いっしょに、きっさてんへ　いきました。そこで、こうひいを　のみました。

２．あした、としょかんへ　いきます。そこで　ほんを　よみます。
にほんのほんです。わたしは、ほんを　よむのが　すきです。

```



```

３．きょう、えいがかんへ　いきました。そのえいがかんで、ともだちに　あいました。ともだちは、にほんのえいがを　みました。わたしは、あめりかのえいがを　みました。ふたりで、れすとらんへ　いきました。わたしは、そこで、ぱすたを　たべました。ともだちは、さんどいっちを　たべました。

```



```

４．
やまだ：あした、えいがを　みませんか。
たなか：いいですね。なんのえいがを　みましょうか。
やまだ：もちろん、にほんのえいがです。
たなか：わたしは、さむらいのえいがが　すきですけど、、
やまだ：「たそがれ　せいべい」が　いいですよ。
たなか：そうですか。じゃ、すぐ　いきましょう。

```



```

## こぶとりじいさん
## An Old Man with a Lump on the Cheek

1.

　むかしむかし、あるところに、ひとのよい　おじいさんが　いました。おじ

いさんの　ほっぺたには、おおきな　こぶが　ありました。

　おじいさんの　むらに、もうひとり、おじいさんが　すんでいました。この

おじいさんにも　こぶが　ありました。でも　このおじいさんは、とても　い

じわるでした。

　Once upon a time, somewhere there lived a kind-hearted old man.  He had a big lump
on his cheek.  In the same village, there lived another old man who also had a lump on
his cheek.  But this (latter) old man was very mean.

2.

　あるとき、ひとのよい　おじいさんが、もりのなかで　きを　きっていると、

あめが　ふってきました。そこで　おじいさんは、きのうろのなかで、あまや

どりを　しているうちに、すっかり　ぐうぐう　ねこんで　しまいました。そ

こへ、おにたちが　やってきて、おどりはじめました。あかおに、あおおに、

おおきいおに、みんな　たのしそうに、おどります。おどりがだいすきなおじ

いさんも、なかまに　はいって、おどりはじめました。

　One day, when the good old man was cutting wood in the forest, it began to rain.  So,
he went into a tree hollow to wait for the rain to stop.  Shortly, he fell asleep.  And ogres
came to dance.  There were red ogres, blue ogres, and big ogres.  All of them danced
happily.  The old man who loved dancing joined them and they all danced together.

3.

　びっくりしたおにたちは、おじいさんのおどりが　あんまりたのしかったの
で、おおよろこび。かえるときに、おじいさんのこぶを　あずかろう　と　い
って、こぶを　ほっぺたから、とってしまいました。

　「こんや　またこい。そうしたら、かえしてやるから。」

　と、おにが　いいました。

The ogres were surprised (having discovered the intruder), but since the old man's dancing was so funny, they were all entertained.  They decided to take the old man's lump as a token, saying,
"Come back tonight.  We will then return this to you."

4.

　おじいさんが、ほっぺたに　てを　やると、あれ、ふしぎ、いままで　あっ
た　おおきなこぶが　ありません。すっかりよろこんだおじいさんは、このこ
とを　となりの　いじわるな　おじいさんに　はなしました。

When the old man put his hand on his cheek, he found his big lump gone.  The old man was so happy, and told his neighbor, the mean old man, about what happened.

5.

　うらやましいのは、いじわるじいさん。

　「よっしゃ、わしもいって、おにに　このこぶをとってもらおう。」

　そういって、おにのくるのを　まちました。

The mean old man was envious.
"All right.  I shall go now and have them take my lump off, too."
Then, he went and waited for ogres to come.

6.

　ところが、いじわるじいさんは、おどりがへた。おこったおにたちは、

　「このやろう。せっかくのたのしみを　だいなしにしたな。おまえには、こ

のこぶをやろう。」

　といって、おじいさんの　もうひとつのほっぺたに、こぶをくっつけました。

いじわるじいさんは、それから、ほっぺたに　ふたつも　こぶを　もつことに

なりました。

　Unfortunately, the mean old man proved to be a terrible dancer.  The ogres got so
annoyed with the mean old man's clumsy dancing, and yelled,
"Darn!  You ruined our fun.  We're giving you this wen!"
They placed the good old man's lump on the mean old man's cheek.  And so the mean
old man ended up with two.

[Passive Vocabulary from reading section: "An Old Man with a Lump on the Cheek)"]
(Listed in the order of the story)

| | | |
|---|---|---|
| hoppeta | ほっぺた | cheeks |
| kobu | こぶ | lump |
| mura | むら | village |
| sunde imashita | すんでいました | was living |
| ijiwaru | いじわる | mean |
| mori | もり | forest |
| ki | き | tree |
| kitte iru | きっている | is cutting |
| ame ga futte kimashita | あめがふってきました。 | It started raining |
| ki no uro | きのうろ | tree hollow |
| amayadori | あまやどり | waiting rain for stop |
| sukkari | すっかり | completely |
| nekomu | ねこむ | to fall a sleep deeply |
| oni-tachi | おにたち | ogres |
| yatte kite | やってきて | coming and then |
| odori-hajimemashita | おどりはじめました。 | started dancing |
| tanoshisooni | たのしそうに | looking happily |
| daisuki | だいすき | loving so much |
| nakama | なかま | companion |
| haitte | はいって | join and |
| bikkuri shita | びっくりした | surprised |
| tanoshikatta | たのしかった | was joyful |
| oo-yorokobi | おおよろこび | pleased much |
| kaeru toki | かえるとき | at the time of returning |
| azukaroo | あずかろう (あずかる) | Let me keep it. |
| itte | いって | say and |
| totte | とって | take and |
| konya | こんや | tonight |
| mata | また | again |
| koi | こい。 | Come! |
| soo shitara | そうしたら | If you do so, |
| kaeshite yaru | かえしてやる。 | I'll return it to you. |
| iimashita | いいました。 | said |
| te wo yaru | てをやる | to touch with hand |
| fushigi | ふしぎ | wonder |
| imamade | いままで | until now |
| atta | あった | existed |
| ookina | おおきな | large |

| | | |
|---|---|---|
| yorokonda | よろこんだ | pleased |
| urayamashii | うらやましい | envious |
| washi | わし | I |
| kuru no wo matsu | くるのをまつ | to wait for coming |
| tokoroga | ところが | however |
| heta | へた | unskilled |
| okotta | おこった | angry |
| konoyaroo | このやろう！ | Darn! |
| sekkaku no tanoshimi | せっかくのたのしみ | fan that was anticipated |
| dainashi ni suru | だいなしにする | to ruin |
| omae | おまえ | you |
| yaru/yaroo | やる・やろう | to give/You shall have one. |
| moo hitotsu | もうひとつ | additional |
| kuttsukeru | くっつける | to attach |
| motsu | もつ | to have |
| koto ni naru | ことになる | to end up with ~ing |

\* \* \* \* \* \* \* \* \* \* Hayakuchi-kotoba はやくちことば(tongue-twisters)\* \* \* \* \* \* \* \*

Say the Japanese tongue-twisters as fast as you can!

1. nama-mugi nama-gome nama-tamago
   
   なまむぎなまごめなまたまご
   生麦生米生卵

2. tonari no kyaku wa yoku kaki kuu kyaku da
   
   となり きゃく かきく きゃく
   隣 の 客 は よく 柿食う 客 だ

3. tokkyo kyoka suru Tokyo tokkyo kyokakyoku
   
   とっきょきょか とうきょうとっきょきょかきょく
   特許許可する 東京特許許可局

4. boozu ga byoobu ni jyoozu ni boozu no e wo kaita
   
   ぼうず びょうぶ じょうず ぼうず え
   坊主が屏風に上手に坊主の絵を
   か
   書いた

5. kaeru pyokopyoko mi-pyokopyoko awasete pyokopyoko mu-pyokopyoko
   
   かえる み
   蛙 ぴょこぴょこ三ぴょこぴょこ
   あ む
   合わせてぴょこぴょこ六ぴょこぴょこ

Chapter 3(B)　　　　Ordering at McDonald's　ちゅうもんする
　　　　　　　　　　　　　　　　　　　　　　Chu-u-mo-n su-ru

てんいん：いらっしゃいませ。ごちゅうもんは？　　　　　　　　1
te-n-i-n　：i-ra-s-sha-i-ma-se.　go-chu-u-mo-n wa?

モニカ：　チーズバーガー　を　一つ　ください。　　　　　　2
Mo-ni-ka：chi-i-zu-ba-a-ga-a　wo hi-to-tsu　ku-da-sa-i

てんいん：はい、チーズバーガー　おーつ　ですね。　　　　　3
te-n-i-n　：ha-i,　chi-i-zu-ba-a-ga-a　o-hi-to-tsu　de-su ne

　　　　　おのみものは？　　　　　　　　　　　　　　　　　4
　　　　　o-no-mi-mo-no wa?

モニカ：　コーラを　おねがいします。　　　　　　　　　　　5
Mo-ni-ka：　ko-o-ra wo o-ne-ga-i shi-ma-su

てんいん：はい、コーラは、「大」、「中」、「小」ございますが、、、　6
te-n-i-n　：ha-i,　ko-o-ra wa, "dai,"　"chu-u,"　"sho-o" go-za-i-ma-su ga,,,

モニカ：　あ、「中」で　いいです。　　　　　　　　　　　　7
Mo-ni-ka：　a, "chu-u" de i-i de-su.

てんいん：わかりました。ありがとうございます。　　　　　　8
te-n-i-n　：wa-ka-ri-ma-shi-ta. A-ri-ga-to-o go-za-i-ma-su

　　　　　チーズバーガー　おーつ　と　　　　　　　　　　　9
　　　　　chi-i-zu-ba-a-ga-a　o-hi-to-tsu to

　　　　　コーラ　おーつ　で、三百六十円に　なります。　　10
　　　　　Ko-o-ra　o-hi-to-tsu de, sa-n-bya-ku ro-ku-jyu-u e-n ni na-ri-ma-su

（Monica handed 五百 yen to the salesperson）
　　　　　go-hya-ku
てんいん：百四十　円の　おかえしです。　　　　　　　　　　11
te-n-i-n　：hya-ku-yo-n-jyu-u e-n no o-ka-e-shi de-su

　　　　　ありがとうございました。　　　　　　　　　　　　12
　　　　　a-ri-ga-to-o go-za-i-ma-shi-ta

[English translation:]  Ordering at McDonald's

Salesperson:  Welcome.  May I take your order?  (Lit:  What would you like to order?)
Monica:        May I have a cheeseburger, please?  (Lit:  Please give me one
                    cheeseburger.)
Salesperson:  Yes, one cheeseburger, right?  How about something to drink?
Monica:         A coke, please.
Salesperson:  We have "large," "medium," and "small" options…
Monica:          Ah, "medium" is fine.
Salesperson:  Sure, thank you very much.  One cheeseburger and one coke come to 360
                    yen.
            (Monica hands 500 yen to the salesperson.)
Salesperson:  140 en is your change.  Thank you very much.

Chapter 3(B)                    Grammar and Cultural Notes

## 1. お ”o”, a prefix that expresses politeness

The polite prefix "o-" is used with verbs, adjectives and nouns to express politeness, modesty or respect. There are certain rules in its usage as follows:

(1) "O" cannot be attached to the following words:
   (A) Adjectives and nouns which begin with the [o] sound:

| | | | | | |
|---|---|---|---|---|---|
| おおきい | large | おもしろい | interesting | おいしい | tasty |
| おじさん | uncle | おび | sash | おおかみ | wolf |
| おにぎり | rice ball | おかみさん | wife; madam | | |

   (B) Long words:
   ほうれんそう spinach　じゃがいも potato（cf. おじゃが is acceptable.）

   (C) Foreign (loan) words:
   クリスマス Christmas　プレゼント present　エスカレーター escalator

Some exceptions:
   There are words with foreign origin that are exempt from the rule.
   おタバコ、おビール、おソース、おズボン
   tobacco　　　beer　　　　sauce　　　　trousers (Portuguese origin)
   They are used with "o" because they have become part of the Japanese vocabulary after so many years after adaptation to the Japanese life.

   "お O" can be an honorific polite expression (being addressed to a specific person), as in the following: おいそがしい "busy." おじょうず "skilled." おのみもの "a drink," おかばん "a bag," おはし "chopsticks," or as a simple polite expression in おにく　や　おさかな "meat" and "fish."

(2) Aside from "お o," there is another prefix that also adds politeness: "go （ご、御）." "ご Go" is used for words of Chinese origin, while "お o" is used for those of Japanese origin. In chapter dialogue 3 (B), the word "order" in its polite form is "go-chuumon," ごちゅうもん （ご注文）, and the word "drink" in its Japanese origin is "o-nomimono."

## 2. Particle "で de" to end the choices

Particle "で de" has various functions. This "de" works to end the choices. For example, If you say "kore de owari desu," that means "This is it (as the end of everything)." If you say, "kore de ii desu," it means "This is good (since it' the end of choices)." In the dialogue Chapter 3 (B), Monica says "A, 'chuu' de iidesu (Oh, "medium" is good) to a salesperson who says, "We have 'large,' 'medium' and 'small' options." Monica had three choices to choose from and she chose "medium" sized coke. The particle "de" indicates that "medium" is the end of choices.

Chapter 3 (B) Exercises

A. Each word in the groups below shares something in common with one another. With a partner: Add the one item that would naturally belong to its group.

1. はまち、うなぎ、さけ、たい、（　　　　　　）
   hamachi, unagi,  sake,  tai

2. ケーキ、パイ、アイスクリーム、（　　　　　）
   keeki,  pai,  aisukuriimu

3. ハンバーガー、チーズバーガー、フライドポテト、（　　　　　　）
   hanbaagaa,    chiizu-baagaa,    furaido-poteto

4. りんご、みかん、ぶどう、（　　　　　　）
   ringo,   mikan,   bodoo

5. きゅうり、きゃべつ、にんじん、（　　　　　　）
   kyuuri,    kyabetsu,  ninjin

6. コーラ、ペプシ、ジュース、（　　　　　　）
   koora,   pepushi,   jyuusu

7. バナナ、きゅうり、にんじん、（　　　　　）
   banana,   kyuuri,    ninjin

B. Fill in the blanks with your partner.

(A): いらっしゃいませ。（ gochuumon　　　）は？
   Irasshaimase　　　　　　　　　　　　wa

(B): チーズバーガーを　ひとつ　（ kudasai　　　）。
   Chiizu-baagaa  wo  hitotsu

(A): おのみものは？
   o-nomimono wa

(B): コーラを（ onegai  shimasu. ）
   Koora wo

(A): コーラは、（ dai ）（ chuu ）（ shoo ） ございますが、、、
   Koora wa,　　　　　　　　　　　　　gozaimasu ga

(B): あ、「小」（ で ） いいです。
   A,    shoo        ii desu.

(A): ありがとうございます。チーズバーガーを
   Arigatoo gozaimasu.    Chiizu-baagaa wo
   （ o ） ひとつ （ to ） コーラを （ a ） ですね。
       hitotsu      koora wo        desu ne.
   みんな（ de ）、三百六十円（ ni ） なります。
   Min'na         san-byaku-roku-jyuu-en    narimasu.

⚛ Chapter 3(B)'s Dict-A-Conversation (1):  At a Bakery
Listen to Chapter 3 (B)-1 the student CD and fill in the blanks with the information you hear.
At this point, you may write in Roma-ji; but later, practice hiragana.

A : _____

B : １２０えんです。
　　Hyaku ni-jyuu en desu.

A : _____

B : １００えんです。
　　Hyaku en desu.

A : _____

B : ありがとうございます。ふたつで　にひゃくえん　になります。
　　Arigatoo gozaimasu.　　Futatsu de  ni-hyaku en　　ni narimasu.

A : _____

B : ありがとうございました。
　　Arigatoo　　gozaimashita.

Chapter 3(B)'s Dict-A-Conversation (2) Conversation in a Restaurant Setting
Listen to each conversation and fill in the blanks with the appropriate words.

（A）
１．ここは、（　　　　　　　　　　　　） です。
２．おとこのひとは、（　　　　　　　　　　　） を　ちゅうもんします。
３．おんなのひとは、（　　　　　　　　　　　） を　ちゅうもんします。

（B）
１．ここは、（　　　　　　　　） の　レストランです。
２．おんなのひとは、（　　　　　） と （　　　　　　） を　ちゅうもんします。

（C）
１．ここは、（　　　　　　　　） の　レストランです。
２．おとこのひとは、（　　　　　　　　） を　たべます。
３．おんなのひとは、（　　　　　　　　） を　たべます。

## Chapter 3 (B): Crossword Puzzle # 1 (A General Counter for Small Items)

Hiragana: All of them

Find the following words in the box and circle/color them. The words can go horizontally, vertically, diagonally, or backward.

| | | | |
|---|---|---|---|
| 1. ひとつ | one | 6. むっつ | six |
| 2. ふたつ | two | 7. ななつ | seven |
| 3. みっつ | three | 8. やっつ | eight |
| 4. よっつ | four | 9. ここのつ | nine |
| 5. いつつ | five | 10. とお | ten |

| さ | と | お | き | ま | す | わ |
|---|---|---|---|---|---|---|
| む | ほ | ひ | き | い | む | か |
| ふ | っ | と | つ | の | こ | こ |
| み | っ | つ | た | ふ | て | り |
| さ | っ | っ | な | ま | す | ま |
| や | あ | よ | ち | な | つ | す |

Chapter 3 (B):  Crossword Puzzle in <u>Hiragana</u> # 2 (Vocabulary for Vegetables and Fruits)
 [Remember this is Hiragana crossword puzzle.  It's different from English crossword puzzle.]

<u>Across</u>

1. carrot
3. grape
4. cabbage
6. watermelon
7. banana
9. tomato

<u>Down</u>

2. tangerine
4. cucumber
5. apple
8. onion

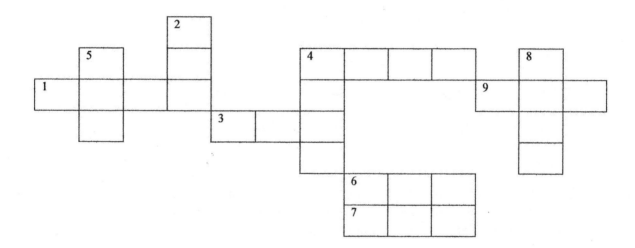

## つきに　すむ　うさぎ Rabbit in the Moon

A folktale that originated from the Konjyaku Monogatari –
a Collection from 12<sup>th</sup> century Buddhist stories

むかし　むかし、つきに　かみさまが　すんでいました。そのかみさまが、ちきゅうを　みおろすと、したに、さんびきの　どうぶつが　あそんでいるのが、みえました。それは、うさぎ　と　さる　と　きつね　でした。どうぶつたちは、とても　なかが　よかったのです。　かみさまは、

「どの　どうぶつが　いちばん　しんせつ　かな。」と、おもいました。

Once upon a time, there lived a god in the moon named "Kami-sama." When Kami-sama looked down to the earth, he spotted three animals happily playing: a rabbit, a monkey and a fox. They were good friends. Kami-sama wondered which animal was the kindest.

そこで、ちきゅうにおりて　ためしてみることにしました。かみさまは、まずしい　こじきの　ろうじんに　ばけて　つきから　おりてきました。こじきはいいました。「ああ、おなかが　すいた。だれか、たべものを　ください。」

He decided to test them. Descending to the earth in disguise, he became a poor old beggar and said to them, "Oh, how hungry I am. Please, someone give me something to eat."

それを　きいた　さると　きつねと　うさぎは、かわいそうに　おもって、こじきの　おじいさんのために、たべものを　さがしに　いきました。さるは、たくさんの　くだものを　もってきました。バナナ、かき、みかん、もも、すもも、などです。

きつねも、かわで、おおきいさかなを　つって　もってきました。

Hearing this, the monkey, fox and rabbit pitied him and went to fetch for food.
The monkey came back with a lot of fruits including bananas, persimmons, tangerines, peaches and plums.  The fox fished in the river and brought a big fish to him.

でも、うさぎは、なにも　さがすことが　できませんでした。うさぎは、いっしょうけんめい　かんがえました。どうしたら、このまずしいろうじんをたすけることが　できるでしょうか。そのとき、あるかんがえが、うさぎのあたまに　うかびました。そこで、うさぎは、いいました。

「さるさん、たきぎを　たくさん　あつめて　ください。」

「きつねさん、そのきを　つかって、おおきいたきびを　つくってください。」

But the rabbit could not find any food.  He thought hard; how could I help this poor old man?  Then, an idea dawned upon him.  The rabbit said to his friends,

>“Dear monkey, please collect firewood for me.”
>“Dear fox, please make a big bonfire with that firewood for me.”

たきびが　あかるく　もえあがったとき、うさぎは、こじきに　いいました。

「おじいさん、わたしは、あなたのために、なにもみつけられませんでした。でも、わたしを　さしあげることが　できます。このひのなかに　わたしをいれて、やきあがったら、わたしを　たべてください。」

When the big bonfire was made, the rabbit said to the old man:
>“Dear old man, I couldn't find anything for you to eat. But, I can offer me.  Please throw me into this fire, and eat when the cooking is done.”

うさぎは、そういうと、ひのなかに　とびこもうとしました。そのとき、か

みさまのすがたにもどった　ろうじんは、うさぎをとめて　いいました。

「うさぎさん、あなたのしんせつなことは、よくわかりました。わたしとい

っしょに、つきへ　いきましょう。」

そこで、かみさまは、うさぎを　うでに　かかえて、つきへ、のぼっていき

ました。

Once he said it, the rabbit jumped into the fire. In a flash, the old man transformed back into the form of Kami-sama, stopped the rabbit and said:

"Dear rabbit, I understood your sincerity. Let's go up to the moon together."

Then, Kami-sama held the rabbit in his arms and ascended to the moon.


------------Passive vocabulary from the reading section "Rabbit in the Moon"----------------

| | | |
|---|---|---|
| kamisama | かみさま | God |
| chikyuu | ちきゅう | the Earth |
| mi-orosu | みおろす | to look down |
| asonde-iru | あそんでいる | be playing （あそぶ） |
| miemashita | みえました | was seen （みえる） |
| totemo | とても | very |
| naka ga yokatta | なかがよかった | got along well |
| omoimashita | おもいました | thought （おもう） |
| orite | おりて | get down and （おりる） |
| tameshite miru | ためして　みる | try and see （ためす） |
| mazushii | まずしい | poor |
| kojiki | こじき | beggar |
| roojin | ろうじん | the old man |
| bakete | ばけて | disguised and （ばける） |
| orite kimashita | おりてきました | came down （おりる） |
| iimashita | いいました | said （いう） |
| onaka ga suita | おなかが　すいた | I'm hungry. （すく） |
| dareka | だれか | someone |
| tabemono | たべもの | food |
| kiita | きいた | heard （きく） |

kawaisooni omotte かわいそうにおもって    feeling pity and    （おもう）

tameni    ために    for the sake of

sagashi ni ikimashita さがしに　いきました    went to search    （さがす）

kudamono    くだもの    fruits

kaki    かき    persimmon

momo    もも    peach

sumomo    すもも    Japanese plum

tsutte    つって    fish（つる）and

motte kimashita もってきました    brought in    （もってくる）

isshoo kenmei いっしょうけんめい    with all one's might

kangaemashita かんがえました    contemplated    （かんがえる）

dooshitara    どうしたら    how

tasukeru koto ga dekiru たすけることができる    can help

kangae    かんがえ    idea

ukabimashita    うかびました    came to mind    （うかぶ）

takigi    たきぎ    firewood

atsumete    あつめて    gather（あつめる）and

tsukatte    つかって    use（つかう）and

tsukutte kudasai    つくってください    Please（つくる）make.

akaruku    あかるい    bright

moe-agatta    もえあがった    burst into flame    （もえあがる）

nani mo mitsuke-rare-masendeshita なにもみつけられませんでした。    couldn't find anything.

sashi-ageru    さしあげる    give humbly

dekimasu    できます    can    （できる）

hi    ひ    fire

irete    いれて    insert（いれる）and

yaki-agattara    やきあがったら    once it's roasted    （やきあがる）

tobi-komoo to shimashita とびこもうとしました。    tried to jump in（とびこむ）

sugata    すがた    figure

modotta    もどった    returned    （もどる）

tomete    とめて    stop and    （とめる）

ude    うで    arms

kakaete    かかえて    hold in one's arm and（かかえる）

nobotte    のぼって    climb and    （のぼる）

# **<u>Introduction to Katakana</u>**

Basic 46 Katakana Syllables

How we use Katakana

Guess who they are

Advanced Katakana Syllables

List of Katakana words from lessons in the textbook

## _Katakana_

Basic 46 Katakana Syllables

| a | i | u | e | o |
|---|---|---|---|---|
| ア | イ | ウ | エ | オ |
| ka | ki | ku | ke | ko |
| カ | キ | ク | ケ | コ |
| sa | *shi | su | se | so |
| サ | シ | ス | セ | ソ |
| ta | *chi | *tsu | te | to |
| タ | チ | ツ | テ | ト |
| na | ni | nu | ne | no |
| ナ | ニ | ヌ | ネ | ノ |
| ha | hi | *fu | he | ho |
| ハ | ヒ | フ | ヘ | ホ |
| ma | mi | mu | me | mo |
| マ | ミ | ム | メ | モ |
| ya | | yu | | yo |
| ヤ | | ユ | | ヨ |
| ra | ri | ru | re | ro |
| ラ | リ | ル | レ | ロ |
| wa | | | | **wo |
| ワ | | | | ヲ |
| n | | | | |
| ン | | | | |

*The syllables シ、チ、ツ and フ are Romanized as "shi, chi, tsu, and fu" to closely resemble English pronunciation.  **The use of ヲ "wo" is limited in modern Japan.

Almost all the hiragana rules can apply to katakana, except the way the 'long vowel' is transcribed:  Use a dash ー.  Write it horizontally if you are writing horizontally, and write it vertically if you are writing vertically.

Examples of horizontal writing:

スキー、 ボール、 カー、 キー、 スーツ
 (ski)      (ball)    (car)  ( key)    (suit)

Examples of vertical writing:

スキー　　　ボール　　カー　キー　スーツ

## 2. Katakana with "two dots" (voiced sounds) and "small circle" (p-sounds)

| ga ガ | gi ギ | gu グ | ge ゲ | go ゴ |
|---|---|---|---|---|
| za ザ | ji ジ | zu ズ | ze ゼ | zo ソ |
| da ダ | *ji ヂ | *zu ツ | de デ | do ド |
| ba バ | bi ビ | bu ブ | be ベ | bo ボ |

| pa パ | pi ピ | pu プ | pe ペ | po ポ |
|---|---|---|---|---|

*ヂ ji and ツ zu are pronounced the same as ジ ji and ズ zu, respectively, but they have limited use.

## 3. Katakana for contracted sounds.

| kya キャ | kyu キュ | kyo キョ |
|---|---|---|
| sha シャ | shu シュ | sho ショ |
| cha チャ | chu チュ | cho チョ |
| nya ニャ | nyu ニュ | nyo ニョ |
| hya ヒャ | hyu ヒュ | hyo ヒョ |
| mya ミャ | myu ミュ | myo ミョ |
| rya リャ | ryu リュ | ryo リョ |

| gya ギャ | gyu ギュ | gyo ギョ |
|---|---|---|
| jya ジャ | jyu ジュ | jyo ジョ |

| bya ビャ | byu ビュ | byo ビョ |
|---|---|---|
| pya ピャ | pyu ピュ | pyo ピョ |

## How we use Katakana

Aside from hiragana, there is another alphabets, <u>katakana</u>.  The syllable sounds are exactly the same as those in hiragana, but katakana symbols are typically used to write foreign borrowed, onomatopoeic and slang words.  Katakana usage is quite broad; and you will also see academic terms for animal species and plants written in katakana, despite their Japanese origin.  Thus the Japanese word for "wolf" can be written in hiragana (おおかみ), kanji (狼), and katakana (オオカミ).  Katakana is also used to add emphasis, similar to using Italicism in English.  In modern Japanese, there are many foreign-derived words, such as those for pen, taxi, bus, coffee, beer, radio, television, hamburger, among others.  Since these common words are written in katakana, it is extremely important for you to master katakana.

The same rules of writing hiragana apply for katakana.  For example, double consonants are indicated by a small "tsu," the contracted/combined sounds are written with small "ya," "yu," and "yo," and the "p" sounds are written with a diacritical mark on the top right of "ha, hi, fu, he, ho".  One difference from hiragana: katakana requires identical double vowels to be marked by a dash, as in チーズ "cheese" (read: chiizu), テーブル "table" (read: teeburu), and ボール "ball" (read: booru).

## Some hints in rendering English words into Japanese pronunciation.

1) English –er and –or are perceived as "aa" in Japanese.  Thus:

   エスカレーター    escalator (read: esukareetaa)
   リーダー         leader (read: riidaa)
   レコーダー       recorder (read: rekoodaa)

2) English [v] is heard in Japanese as "b'; therefore, "va, vi, vu, ve, vo" sound will be "ba, bi, bu, be, bo" in Japanese.  Thus:

   バイオリン       violin (read: baiorin)
   ビオラ          viola (read: biora)
   ビクター        Victor (read: Bikutaa)
   シルバー        silver (read: shirubaa)

3) English [l] and [r] sounds are both heard as an "r" sound in Japanese.  Thus:

   ライト          light (read: raito)
   ライト          right (read: raito)

4) English [th] as in "health" or "thank" is heard as "s" and its voiced counterpart is heard as "z." Thus:

   バス           bath (read: basu)

バス　　　　bus (read: basu)

サンキューThank you. (read: sankyuu)

5) If a word ends in a [k] or [g] sound, the vowel "u" follows in Japanese. The same is true for [m, f, v, l, s, z, th, p, b] sounds. This rule is also applied when the sounds are immediately followed by a consonant. Thus:

キング　　　king (read: kingu)
バンク　　　bank (read: banku)
リング　　　ring (read: ringu)
ミス　　　　short form of "mistake" (read: misu)
サーフ　　　surf (read: saafu)
キャロル　　Carol (read: kyaroru)
パブ　　　　pub (read: pabu)

6) If a word ends in a [t] or [d] sound, the vowel "o" would follow in Japanese. Thus:

ラスト　　　last (read: rasuto)
ファースト first (read: huaasuto) (* the English sound "f" is substituted by the Japanese　sound "h")
マスト　　　mast (read: masuto)
スタンド　　stand (read: sutando)
スピード　　speed (read: supiido)

## Compound symbols

To approximate foreign sounds, some symbols are combined. These compound symbols are not used in hiragana.

ウィ for a syllable as in "whisky" ウィスキー
ウェ　　　　　　　　　"waiter" ウェーター
ウォ　　　　　　　　　"water" ウォーター

ヴァ　　　　　　　　　"violin" ヴァイオリン （Also: バイオリン）
ヴィ　　　　　　　　　"viola" ヴィオラ （Also: ビオラ）

ファ　　　　　　　　　"fan" ファン
フィ　　　　　　　　　"Finland" フィンランド, "film" フィルム
フェ　　　　　　　　　"fencing" フェンシング
フォ　　　　　　　　　"Ford" フォード, "fork" フォーク

ティ　　　　　　　　　"party" パーティー, "tea" ティー
ディ　　　　　　　　　"Disneyland" ディズニーランド
デュ　　　　　　　　　"producer" プロデューサー

Guess who they are. だれですか。

Japanese have different sound system such as ending all the sounds with vowels (a, i, u, e, o) except "n." So, the key to figure out original English sounds is to drop the vowels from the Japanese sounds. Try the following.  Answers are found from the box below.

Boys' names

    1. ボブ　2．トム　3．マイク　4．ケン　5．ジョン　6．ベン
    7. クリス　8．ジョー　9．ジョージ　10．ケント　11．ケブン
    12. アイク　13．デボン　14．ブライアン　15．アラン 16．アレックス
    17. リック　18．ボール　19．ギルバート 20．ランス

> Gilbert, Ben, Mike, Lance, Ike, Devon, George, John, Bob, Alex, Kevin, Kent, Rick, Ken, Chris, Joe, Tom, Paul, Allen, Brian

Girls' names

    1. アン　2．ケイト　3．キャシー　4．キャロル　5．サラ 6．ルーシー
    7. ヘレン　8, マイラ　9．バネッサ　10．スーザン　11．エリカ
    12. アンジェリナ　13．ジェシカ　14．カレン 15．ローラ 16．レズリー
    17. ミシェル　18．バーバラ 19．ジェニファー　20．ジュディー

> Judy, Carol, Sarah, Kate, Jennifer, Lucy, Susan, Mira, Michele, Angelina, Leslie, Jessica, Karen, Vanessa, Laura, Helen, Cathy, Erica, Anne, Kate

Guess what they are. なんですか。

A. Food

    1. ピザ　　　2．ハンバーガー　　　3．サンドイッチ　　　4．スパゲッティ
    5. ビフテキ　6．ポテト　7．トマト　8．バナナ　9．パン　10．ポーク

B. Drinks

    1. ワイン　2．コーラ　3．コーヒー　4．ジュース　　　5．レモネード
    6. ミルク　7．ビール　8．ソーダ　9．ミルクシェイク　10．ココア

C. Countries　　　Which countries are these? どこですか。

    1. カナダ　2．アメリカ　3．メキシコ　4．スイス　　5．フランス
    6. イギリス 7．スペイン　8．ドイツ　　9．ギリシャ　10．イタリア

### Advanced Katakana:  More Syllables

| | | | | | | | | |
|---|---|---|---|---|---|---|---|---|
| **Voiceless syllables** | a | fa ファ | tsa ツァ | cha | sha | kwa クァ | kya | |
| | i | fi フィ | ti ティ | | | | | wi ウィ |
| | u | fu | | chu | shu | | kyu | |
| | e | fe フェ | tse ツェ | che チェ | she シェ | | | we ウェ  ye イェ |
| | o | fo フォ | tso ツォ | cho | sho | kwo クォ | kyo | wo ウォ |
| **Voiced syllables** | a | va ヴァ | | ja | | gwa グァ | gya | |
| | i | vi ヴィ | di ディ | | | | | |
| | u | vu ヴ | dyu デュ | ju | | | | |
| | e | ve ヴェ | | je ジェ | | | | |
| | o | vo ヴォ | | jo | | | | |

Examples:
1) folk (fo-o-ku)           フォーク
2) formal (fo-o-ma-ru)      フォーマル
3) fan (fua-n)              ファン
4) film (fi-ru-mu)          フィルム
5) Fatima (fa-ti-ma)        ファティマ
6) fencing (fe-n-shi-n-gu)  フェンシング
7) fifty (fi-fu-ti-i)       フィフティ
8) Vienna (u-i-i-n)         ウィーン
9) chain (che-e-n)          チェイン（チェーン）
10) Jane(je-i-n)            ジェイン（ジェーン）

11) tea (ti-i)                    ティー
12) party (pa-a-ti)               パーティー
13) water (u-o-o-ta-a)            ウォーター
14) violin (va-i-o-ri-n)          ヴァイオリン
15) viola (vi-o-ra)               ヴィオラ
16) Victor (vi-ku-ta-a)           ヴィクター
17) Vogue (vo-o-gu)               ヴォーグ
18) Vincent (vi-n-se-n-to)        ヴィンセント
19) guava (gua-va)                グァヴァ（グァバ）
20) Jeff (je-fu)                  ジェフ
21) Jet (je-t-to)                 ジェット
22) Duke (d[ey]u-u-ku)            デューク
23) producer (pu-ro-d[ey]u-u-sa-a)   プロデューサー
24) Disneyland (di-zu-ni-i-ra-n-do)ディズニーランド
25) agent (e-i-je-n-to)           エージェント

List of Katakana words from lessons in the textbook (excluding "Katakana Chapter")
Chapters 1~14

## Food

ケーキ、スパゲッティ、サンドイッチ、ミックスサンド、ハムサンド、バナナ、
cake, spaghetti, sandwich, mixed sandwich, ham sandwich, banana

アイスクリーム、ラーメン、カレーライス、チャーハン、ハンバーガー、
ice cream, ramen noodle, curried rice, fried rice, hamburger,

チーズバーガー、ビフテキ、オムライス、オムレツ、フライドポテト、サラダ、
cheese burger, beef stake, omelet w/rice, omelet, French fries, salad

パイ、パン、ステーキ、ミートソース、ナポリタン、　　　シリアル、トマト、
pie, bread, stake, meat sauce, spaghetti with tomato sauce, cereal, tomato

キャベツ、アーモンド、チョコレート、オレンジ、グレープ、ガム、チキン、
cabbage, almond, chocolate, orange, grapes, gum, chicken,

ポーク、ビーフ、クリーム、ポップコーン、レタス、ブロッコリ（ー）、
pork, beef, cream, pop corn, lettuce, broccoli,

レモン、メロン、プリン、スウィート・ポテト、スープ、サワークリーム、
lemon, melon, pudding, candied Japanese yam, soup, sour cream,

クリームチーズ、ジャム
cream cheese, jam

## Drinks

ミルク、ミルクシェーク、ホット、アイス、ワイン、ココア、
milk, milk shake, hot coffee, iced coffee, wine, cocoa

レモンスカッシュ、オレンジジュース、カプチーノ、ペプシ、コカコーラ、
lemonade, orange juice, Cappuccino, Pepsi cola, Coca cola,

コーラ、コーク、ビール、カクテル
cola, coke, beer, cocktail

## People
1) Proper Nouns
ブラウン、スミス、ホワイト、リー、ペリネール、モネ、チョウ、アラ、
Brown, Smith, White, Lee, Perrinelle, Monet, Cho(u), Ara

ゴンザレス、ガルシア、ロドリゲス、キム、シャン、ジョンソン、ジョーンズ、
Gonzalez, Garcia, Rodriguez, Kim, Shan, Johnson, Jones,

スミス、ウィリアムズ、モニカ、アポロ、プリンセス・ダイアナ、アン、ナン、
Smith, Williams, Monica, Apollo, Princess Diana, Ann(ne), Nan

アンジェラ、カレン、ミシェル、ボブ、ケン、トム、アラン、ジョン、
Angela, Karen, Michelle, Bob, Ken, Tom, Allan (Allen), John

アネット、ジョゼフ、ジョージ、デイナ、キャシー、メアリー、
Annett, Joseph, George, Dana, Cathy, Mary

シェイクスピア、ベートーベン、モーツァルト、レオナルド・ダヴィンチ、
Shakespeare, Beethoven, Mozart, Leonard・da Vinch

モナリザ
Mona Liza

2) General/Group Nouns.
ウェイトレス、ウェイター、スター、エンジニア、ボーイフレンド、
waitress, waiter, star, engineer, boy friend,

ガールフレンド、クラスメート、プロ（フェッショナル）、ゲスト、
girl friend, classmate, professionals guests

サラリーマン、インテリ、ヒスパニック
salaried man, intelligent, Hispanic

3) Words to describe people
キュート、セクシー、ハンサム
cute, sexy, handsome

## Places
1) General locations
カフェテリア、デパート、レストラン、ビアガーデン、コンビニ、スーパー、
cafeteria, department store, restaurant, beer hall, convenience store, super market,

マーケット、アパート、プール、クラス、アーケード、キャンパス、パブ、ロビー
market, apartment, swimming pool, class, almond, campus, pub, lobby

ディスコ、オフィス、トイレ、キッチン、ジム、モール、ビーチ、ホテル、
disco, office, toilet, kitchen, gym, shopping mall, beach, hotel,

2) Proper nouns
パサデナ、ロス、ロサンジェルス、ニューヨーク、アンカレッジ、ロンドン、
Pasadena, LA, Los Angeles, New York, Anchorage, London,

ローマ、 シカゴ、 パリ、 シシリー、 アムステルダム、 アメリカ、 イギリス、
Rome,　　Chicago, Paris, Sicily,　　　　Amsterdam,　America,　　England,

ロシア、 アラスカ、 フランス、 スペイン、 ドイツ、 イタリア、 インド、
Russia,　Alaska,　　France,　　Spain,　　Germany, Italy,　　　India,

ベトナム、 ナイル、 マッキンリー、 ミシシッピ（ー）、 エベレスト、 ハワイ、
Vietnam,　River Nile, Mt. McKinley,　Mississippi (River),　(Mt.) Everest,　Hawaii,

アフガニスタン、 タイ、 コペンハーゲン、 サンクト・ペテルブルグ、
Afghanistan,　　Thailand, Copenhagen,　　St. Petersburg,

リオデジャネイロ、 バグダット、 モスクワ、 ラスベガス、 カイロ、 オアフ、
Rio de Janeiro,　　Baghdad,　　Moscow,　Las Vegas,　Cairo,　Oahu,

サンディエゴ、 アジア、 ヨーロッパ、 ローズボール、 スターバックス
San Diego,　　Asia,　　Europe　　Rose Bowl,　　Starbucks

マクドナルド（マック）、 バーガーキング、 ハンティントン・ガーデン、
McDonald,　　　　　　　Burger King,　　Huntington Garden,

## Animals
ライオン、 ペンギン、 パンダ、 コアラ、 カンガルー、 ワンワン、　　　ペット、
lion,　　penguin,　panda,　koala bear, kangaroo,　kid's way to address dogs, pets

サル、 キリン
monkeys,　giraffe

## Transportations
バス、 エレベーター、 タクシー、 トラック、 フライト、 フリーウェイ、 ボート、
bus,　elevator,　　　taxi,　　truck,　　flight,　　free way,　　　boat,

オートバイ、 ヘリコプター
motorcycle,　helicopter,

## Clothing
ボタン、 シャツ、 ネクタイ、 スーツ、 セーター、 ハンカチ、 ハンドバッグ、
button, shirt,　neck tie　suit,　sweater, handkerchief, woman's purse,
アクセサリー、 ネックレス、 イヤリング、 ピアス、 ベルト、 ズボン、 コート、
accessories, necklace,　ear rings,　pierce,　belt,　trousers,　coat,

ブラウス、 スカート、 スカーフ、 ドレス、 ハイヒール、 ジーンズ、 ウエスト、
blouse,　skirt,　scarf,　dress,　high heels,　jeans,　waist,

コンタクト・レンズ、スニーカー、テニスシューズ、サンダル、マント、
contact lenses,              sneakers,       tennis shoes,       sandals,        mantle; cloak

ポリエステル、レーヨン、
polyester,               rayon,

## Miscellaneous

サイズ、センチ、ベッド、テーブル、テレビ、ラジオ、コンピューター、
size,    centimeters, bed,    table,        television, radio,    computer,

ノート、スタンド、カーテン、キー、キーホルダー、ギター、テレホンカード、
notebook, light stand,  curtain,        key,    key folder,      guitar,    telephone card,

ペン、ボールペン、スプーン、パーセント、ナイフ、フォーク、コップ、
pen,    ballpoint pen, spoon,       percent,       knife,     a folk,         a glass,

ポスター、ドル、セント、ブラシ、ヘローキティ、アイロン、アイデア、
poster,    dollar,   cent,    brush,     Hello Kitty,        iron,         idea,

スコア、プラント（プランツ）、クリスマス・ツリー、クリスマス・カード、
score,    plant(s)                        Christmas tree,              Christmas card

チューリップ、コンピューター・サイエンス、アニメ、テープ、セール、
tulip,               computer science,                animation, tape,  a sale,

ゴールデン・ウィーク、クーラー、ガン(cancer)、タバコ、カレールー、レシピ、
the Golden Week,            air conditioner, cancer,        cigarettes, curry roux,    recipe,

イラスト、グラム、メートル、ハリケーン、スイッチ、カード、ドッグフード、
illustration, gram,    meter,      hurricane,      switch,       card,       dog food,

キャットフード、ゲスト、スパイス、ハンドミキサー、オーブン、カメラ、
cat food,            guest,     spices,      hand mixer,        oven,         camera,

ビデオ、マイク、ニュース、プライベート・パーティー、サイン、イメージ、
video, microphone, news,        private party,                signature,   image,

アスピリン、ダイヤモンド、バックミラー、パーフェクト、プライド、
Aspirin,         diamond,        rear-view mirror,  perfect,              pride,

チャンバラ、エッセー、バランス、スクリーン
sword fight,    essay,        balance,     screen,

## Music

コンサート、チケット、ロック、ジャズ、バンド、ロック・グループ、ピアノ、
concert,      ticket,    rock & roll,  jazz,    a band,    a rock group,        piano,

バイオリン、オルゴール
violin        a music box (from old Portuguese)

## Sports & Activities
1) Verbs you say [～を]する
スポーツ、サッカー、バスケット・ボール、スキー、ゴルフ、ピンポン、
sports,      soccer,      basket ball,         ski,     golf,     ping pong,

フットボール、フラダンス、ジョギング、アルバイト、パーティー、ノック、
football,      hula dance,   jogging,     part-time job,  party,        knock,

テスト、コンピューター・ゲーム、スイミング、バケーション、プレゼント、
test,       computer game,          swimming,    vacation,       present,

ドライブ、メール、ミーティング、ランチ、リクエスト、ピクニック、
driving,    mail,    meeting,       lunch,   request,    picnic,

サーフィン、スノーケル、スノーボード、タイプ、シュート、パス、プレー、
surfing,      snorkeling,  snow-board,    type,    shoot,    pass,  play,

ドキッ（と）、ションボリ、セット、リラックス、ライトアップ、オーケー、
heart beat,      feeling down,  setting,  relax,        light-up,       OK,

スピーチ、チェック、デッサン、ジャンプ、デート
speech,    check,    sketching,  jump,     date

2) Others
ホームラン（をうつ）、シャワー（をあびる）、クラブ
hit a homerun,            take a shower,            club

## Mimetic adverbs and Onomatopoeia
ガシャン、サンサン、ニコニコ、シクシク、ニヤニヤ、キャッキャッ、
(loud noise) (sunny)    (smile)   (sob)    (evil smile)  (baby laughter)
シトシト、ゴクゴク、ピューピュー、ソヨソヨ、ハラハラ、チラチラ、
(quiet rain) (gulp-gulp) (swift wind)   (soft breeze) (nervous watching) (glance)
ドンドン、ドロドロ、トロトロ、　ブカブカ、　ポイ、　ボーッ（と）、
(spontaneous) (muddy) (sticky)    (size too big) (quick litter) (daydreaming)
ハッ（と）、　　ピクピク
(sudden awakening)   (scared)

Katakana Search: Crosswords Puzzle （１）
Find the following words:
テニス、ベースボール、ストライク、バッター、ホームラン、ファン、ボール、
tennis　　baseball　　strike　　　　batter　　homerun　　fan　　ball
チケット、ピッチャー、バスケット
ticket　　　pitcher　　　basket

| テ | タ | カ | ミ | キ | シ | チ | ア | ワ | ホ |
|---|---|---|---|---|---|---|---|---|---|
| ニ | ス | ト | ラ | イ | ク | ニ | タ | ー | フ |
| ス | フ | ト | ハ | ヒ | ロ | ム | ム | マ | ァ |
| ピ | ッ | チ | ャ | ー | ヌ | ラ | チ | ヤ | ン |
| ベ | エ | ホ | ナ | ブ | ン | ネ | テ | ラ | リ |
| ツ | ー | ム | ミ | マ | ヘ | バ | ッ | タ | ー |
| メ | モ | ス | ア | イ | ウ | ノ | ハ | ル | レ |
| エ | オ | ル | ボ | バ | ス | ケ | ッ | ト | カ |
| キ | ー | ク | サ | ー | シ | タ | セ | ツ | テ |
| ボ | ケ | コ | ス | ソ | ル | チ | ケ | ッ | ト |

Katakana Search: Crosswords Puzzle （２）
Find the following words:
バレンタインデー、キス、バニラ、アイスクリーム、チョコレート
Valentine day,　　　　kiss,　vanilla,　ice cream,　　　chocolate
ミルクチョコレート、プレゼント、デート
milk chocolate,　　　　　present,　　　date

| バ | ア | ス | ム | ー | リ | ク | ス | イ | ア |
|---|---|---|---|---|---|---|---|---|---|
| ナ | レ | ロ | キ | サ | タ | ナ | ハ | マ | ヤ |
| ラ | ワ | ン | ス | イ | シ | チ | ニ | プ | ウ |
| ク | ス | バ | タ | ツ | ヌ | ヒ | レ | ミ | イ |
| リ | ウ | ニ | エ | イ | ケ | ゼ | セ | テ | ネ |
| オ | コ | ラ | ソ | ト | ン | ノ | パ | チ | ン |
| ピ | プ | バ | ビ | ト | ベ | デ | ー | ト | キ |
| ミ | ル | ク | チ | ョ | コ | レ | ー | ト | ノ |
| ア | イ | シ | テ | ル | ヒ | ミ | ツ | ノ | コ |
| チ | ョ | コ | レ | ー | ト | イ | ビ | ト | サ |

Katakana Search:  Crosswords Puzzle    （３）
Find the following words:

キッチン、　トイレ、　　　　エアコン、　　マンション、リビングルーム、
kitchen,　　　toilet, bathroom,　air conditioner,  condominium,  living room,

ダイニング、アパート、エレベーター、ベランダ
dining room　apartment,  elevator,　　　　verandah

| キ | ア | カ | イ | ダ | ハ | ナ | ガ | サ | ア |
|---|---|---|---|---|---|---|---|---|---|
| ッ | リ | イ | タ | イ | ノ | ウ | レ | パ | シ |
| チ | ナ | ビ | マ | ニ | ミ | ム | ー | メ | モ |
| ン | ナ | ヌ | ン | ン | ネ | ト | ヒ | フ | ヘ |
| ホ | カ | キ | コ | グ | マ | ン | ショ | ョ | ン |
| ク | ケ | コ | ア | サ | ル | シ | ス | セ | ソ |
| ダ | チ | ツ | エ | レ | ベ | ー | タ | ー | テ |
| ト | ン | ワ | ン | イ | チ | ニ | ム | ネ | ラ |
| リ | ル | ラ | レ | ト | ロ | サ | ケ | タ | チ |
| ベ | ダ | グ | ベ | パ | ダ | ヘ | マ | ア | エ |

Katakana Search:  Crosswords Puzzle    （４）
Find the following words:

ヘルス、　ジョギング、　エアロビクス、　ダイエット、　マラソン、
health,　jogging　　　aerobics,　　　　diet,　　　　marathon,
ロッククライミング、ダイビング
rock-climbing,　　　　　diving

| イ | キ | シ | エ | ア | ロ | ビ | ク | ス | チ |
|---|---|---|---|---|---|---|---|---|---|
| ニ | ウ | ク | ス | ト | ッ | エ | イ | ダ | ツ |
| ヌ | ナ | ア | マ | ハ | ク | ヤ | ラ | ア | ワ |
| ラ | ル | レ | ロ | リ | ク | マ | ミ | ム | ダ |
| カ | ジ | ゾ | ジ | バ | ラ | ス | ズ | ゲ | ジ |
| パ | シ | ョ | エ | ア | イ | ロ | ビ | ク | ス |
| ダ | ギ | サ | ギ | タ | ミ | チ | ヘ | ツ | テ |
| ト | マ | ラ | ソ | ン | ン | ハ | キ | ル | シ |
| ヒ | フ | ヘ | ユ | コ | グ | ツ | テ | グ | ス |
| ホ | ヤ | ア | ン | ダ | イ | ビ | ン | グ | ヌ |

Chapter 3(C)   Shopping at a Department Store   デパートでかいものをする
de-pa-a-to de ka-i-mo-no wo su-ru

てんいん：　いらっしゃいませ。　　　　　　　　　　　　　　　　　　　1
te-n-i-n:　　　i-ra-s-sha-i-ma-se.

モニカ：　　あのう、くつうりばは、どこですか。　　　　　　　　　2
Mo-ni-ka:　　a-no-o,　ku-tsu-u-ri-ba wa, do-ko de-su ka.

*shoe section*

てんいん：　くつうりばは、三がいで　ございます。あちらにエレベーターが
te-n-i-n:　　ku-tsu-u-ri-ba wa, sa-n-ga-i de go-za-i-ma-su. a-chi-ra ni e-re-be-e-ta-a ga

ございます。　　　　　　　　　　　　　　　　　　　　　　　　　4
go-za-i-ma-su.

モニカ：　　わかりました。ありがとう。　　　　　　　　　　　　5
Mo-ni-ka:　　wa-ka-ri-ma-shi-ta. a-ri-ga-to-o.

てんいん：　いいえ。　　　　　　　　　　　　　　　　　　　　　6
te-n-i-n:　　i-i-e.

（At the shoe department）

モニカ：　　女ものの　くつが　ありますか。　　　　　　　　　　7
Mo-ni-ka:　　o-n-na-mo-no no　ku-tsu ga　a-ri-ma-su ka.

てんいん：　こちらです。どんなくつが　よろしいですか。　　　　8
te-n-i-n:　　ko-chi-ra de-su. do-n-na ku-tsu ga　yo-ro-shi-i de-su ka.

モニカ：　　色は、くろが　いいです。サイズは、アメリカのサイズで「7」
Mo-ni-ka:　　i-ro wa, ku-ro ga　i-i de-su.　　sa-i-zu wa, a-me-ri-ka no sa-i-zu de "7"

です。　　　　　　　　　　　　　　　　　　　　　　　　　　　10
de-su.

てんいん：　それでは、こちらのくろいくつは、いかがですか。サイズは、
te-n-i-n:　　so-re-de wa, ko-chi-ra no ku-ro-i ku-tsu wa, i-ka-ga de-su ka. sa-i-zu wa,
２３．５センチです。　　　　　　　　　　　　　　　　　　　　12
ni-jyu-u sa-n te-n go se-n-chi de-su.

モニカ：　　ちょっと　小さいです。もうすこし大きいのは、ありませんか。13
Mo-ni-ka:　　cho-t-to chi-i-sa-i de-su.　　mo-o su-ko-shi o-o-ki-i no wa, a-ri-ma-se-n ka.

てんいん：　こちらに　２４<ruby>セ<rt>せん</rt></ruby>ンチのくろいくつが　ございます。　　　　14
te-n-i-n:　　ko-chi-ra ni ni-jyu-u-yo-n se-n-chi no ku-ro-i ku-tsu ga go-za-i ma-su.

モニカ：　　あ、これで　ちょうどいいです。これにします。　　　　15
Mo-ni-ka:　　a, ko-re de　cho-o-do i-i de-su.　　ko-re ni shi-ma-su.

てんいん：　はこに　お<ruby>入<rt>い</rt></ruby>れしますね。　<ruby>一万五千円<rt>いちまんごせんえん</rt></ruby>　　いただきます。16
te-n-i-n:　　ha-ko ni o-i-re shi-ma-su ne. i-chi-ma-n go-se-n e-n  i-ta-da-ki-ma-su.

どうも、ありがとうございました。　　　　　　　　　　　　　17
do-o-mo, a-ri-ga-to-o  go-za-i ma-shi-ta.

モニカ：　　ありがとう。　　　　　　　　　　　　　　　　　　　18
Mo-ni-ka:　　a-ri-ga-to-o

[English translation]:

Store clerk: May I help you?
Monica:　　Yes… where is the shoe section?
Store clerk: The shoe section is on the third floor.  There is an elevator over there.
Monica:　　Understood. Thank you.
Store clerk: You're welcome.
(At the shoe department)
Monica:　　Do you have shoes for women?
Store clerk: Yes, right here.  What kind of shoes suits (you) best?
Monica:　　Black color works well.  (My) size is "7" in American size.
Store clerk: Then, how about the black shoes over here?  The size is 23.5 centimeters.
Monica:　　It's a bit too small.  Do you have ones a bit larger?
Store clerk: We have the black shoes of 24 centimeters here.
Monica:　　Oh, these are perfect.  I'll take these.
Store clerk: I'll put them in a box.  It'll be 15,000 yen.  Thank you very much.
Monica:　　Thank you.

**Chapter 3C.  Monica goes shopping for shoes to a department store.**

Chapter 3(C)                    Vocabulary List

## 1. Expressions

| | | |
|---|---|---|
| Kore de choodo ii desu. | | This is just fine. |
| | これでちょうどいいです。 | |
| ookii no | おおきいの | a big one |
| "Moo sukoshi ookii no wa arimasen ka." | | "Wouldn't you have ones a bit larger?" |
| | もうすこし　おおきいのは　ありませんか。 | |
| ~ de gozaimasu | でございます。 | formal expression of "~ desu." |
| ~ ni gozaimasu | にございます。 | formal expression of "~ ni arimasu." |

## 2. Nouns

| | | |
|---|---|---|
| depaato | デパート | department store |
| kaimono | かいもの | shopping |
| kaimono wo suru | かいものをする | to do shopping |
| kutsu | くつ | shoes |
| kutsu-uriba | くつうりば | shoe department |
| san-gai | さんがい | third floor ("kai" is a counter for the floor and "gai" is a phonetic change from a voiceless to a voiced sound) |
| kochira | こちら | this way, this side (close to the speaker) |
| sochira | そちら | that way, that side (close to the listener) |
| achira | あちら | over that way, over that side (far for both) |
| erebeetaa | エレベーター | elevator |
| on'na-mono | おんなもの | things for women |
| kuro | くろ | black (noun form) |
| saizu | サイズ | size |
| senchi | センチ | centimeter |
| sukoshi | すこし | a little (more formal than ちょっと chotto) |
| hako | はこ | box |

(Additional vocabulary for the floors)

| | | |
|---|---|---|
| i-k-kai | いっかい | first floor |
| ni-kai | にかい | second floor |
| san-gai, san-kai | さんがい、さんかい | third floor |
| yon-kai | よんかい | fourth floor |
| go-kai | ごかい | fifth floor |
| ro-k-kai | ろっかい | sixth floor |

| | | |
|---|---|---|
| nana-kai | なな かい | seventh floor |
| hachi-kai | はち かい | eighth floor |
| kyuu-kai | きゅうかい | ninth floor |
| jyu-k-kai | じゅっかい | tenth floor |

[Essential location words]

| | | |
|---|---|---|
| ue | うえ | above; top; on |
| shita | した | under; below |
| naka | なか | in; inside, center |
| soto | そと | outside |
| chikaku | ちかく | near; vicinity |
| tonari | となり | next (to the same group) |
| yoko | よこ | next (to the different group) |
| aida | あいだ | between |
| mae | まえ | front |
| ushiro | うしろ | behind |

| | | |
|---|---|---|
| kyooshitsu | きょうしつ | classroom |
| shawaa | シャワー | shower |
| kabe | かべ | wall |
| yuka | ゆか | floor |
| mado | まど | window |

| | | |
|---|---|---|
| [furniture] kagu | かぐ | furniture |
| beddo | ベッド | bed |
| isu | いす | chair |
| tsukue | つくえ | desk |
| hikidashi | ひきだし | drawer |
| terebi | テレビ | television |
| teeburu | テーブル | table |
| konpyuutaa | コンピューター | computer |
| todana | とだな | cabinet |
| oshiire | おしいれ | closet |
| tansu | たんす | chest |
| sutando | スタンド | electric stand |
| hontate | ほんたて | book shelf |
| hondana | ほんだな | book shelf |
| tana | たな | shelf |
| kaaten | カーテン | curtain |

| | | |
|---|---|---|
| tokei | とけい | clock |
| posutaa | ポスター | poster |
| gomi-bako | ごみばこ | trash bin |

## 3. Interrogative pronouns

| | | |
|---|---|---|
| don'na | どんな | What kind of ? |
| ~wa ikaga desuka. | ～はいかがですか。 | How about ~ ? |

## 4. Adjectives

| | | |
|---|---|---|
| kuroi | くろい | black (adjectival form) |
| chiisai | ちいさい | small |
| ookii | おおきい | big, large |
| ii | いい | good |
| yoroshii | よろしい | good (polite/formal form) |
| (~ ga) hoshii | ほしい | is desired; is wanted |

## 5. Verbs

| | | |
|---|---|---|
| arimasu | あります | to exist (inanimate things) |
| imasu | います | to exist (animate things) |
| suru | する | to do (dictionary form) |
| shimasu | します | to do (masu/polite form) |
| ~ ni shimasu | ～にします | decide on ~ |
| ireru | いれる | to insert, put in |
| iremasu | いれます | to insert, put in (masu/polite form) |
| o-ire-shimasu | おいれします | I shall put it in (humble form) |
| itadaku | いただく | to receive (humble form) |
| itadakimasu | いただきます | to receive (masu/polite form) |

## 6. Adverbs

| | | |
|---|---|---|
| choodo | ちょうど | exactly |
| moo sukoshi | もうすこし | a little more ("moo" in this context means "additional") |

## 7. Conjunctions

| | | |
|---|---|---|
| soredewa | それでは | in that case, then |
| | | formal expression of それじゃ "sorejya (a)" |

. . . . . . . . . . . . . . . . . . . . . . . . . . . . . . . . . . . . . . . . . . . . . . . . . . . . . .

## Additional Vocabulary from Grammar Notes, Exercises, and Dict-A-Conversation

. . . . . . . . . . . . . . . . . . . . . . . . . . . . . . . . . . . . . . . . . . . . . . . . . . . . . .

1. Nouns
[items in the room]

| | | |
|---|---|---|
| denwa | でんわ | telephone |
| hana | はな | flower |
| kabin | かびん | flower vase |
| shinbun | しんぶん | newspaper |
| zasshi | ざっし | magazine |

[items you put on yourself or carry with you]

| | | |
|---|---|---|
| megane | めがね | eye glasses |
| kutsushita | くつした | socks |
| shatsu | シャツ | shirt |
| T-shatsu | Tシャツ | T-shirt |
| zubon | ズボン | pants; trousers |
| kaban | かばん | bag; brief case |
| kasa | かさ | umbrella |
| saifu | さいふ | wallet |
| hankachi | ハンカチ | handkerchief |
| nekutai | ネクタイ | necktie |
| beruto | ベルト | belt |
| botan | ボタン | button |
| o-mamori | おまもり | (good luck) charm |
| kii-horudaa | キーホルダー | key holder |
| terehon-kaado | テレホンカード | telephone card |
| okane | おかね | money |

[other household items]

| | | |
|---|---|---|
| kitte | きって | stamps |
| hagaki | はがき | post card |
| sekken | せっけん | soap |

| | | |
|---|---|---|
| [clothing] fuku | ふく | western clothing |
| fujin-fuku | ふじんふく | women's clothing |
| burausu | ブラウス | blouse |

| | | |
|---|---|---|
| sukaato | スカート | skirt |
| shinshi-fuku | しんしふく | men's wear |
| | | |
| [materials] mono | もの | materials; things that are made of |
| poriesuteru | ポリエステル | polyester |
| (mo)men | （も）めん | cotton |
| kinu | きぬ | silk |
| reeyon | レーヨン | rayon |
| | | |
| [stationary] bunboogu | ぶんぼうぐ | stationary |
| man'nen hitsu | まんねんひつ | fountain pen |
| booru-pen | ボールペン | ballpoint pen |
| | | |
| [Department sections]  uriba | うりば | (selling) section |
| omocha | おもちゃ | toy |
| kutsu | くつ | shoes |
| kimono | きもの | Japanese kimono |

[people and animals]

| | | |
|---|---|---|
| tomodachi | ともだち | friend |
| kodomo | こども | child |
| inu | いぬ | dog |
| neko | ねこ | cat |
| boku | ぼく | I (used by male in casual situation) |
| koibito | こいびと | lover |
| o-ko-san | おこさん | child (polite form used for others' child) |
| otona | おとな | adult |
| otona-yoo | おとなよう | for adult |

[others]

| | | |
|---|---|---|
| jikan | じかん | time |
| seiseki | せいせき | grades |
| fukuro | ふくろ | sack; bag |

(For the vocabulary in the Department Directory, see Exercise C in this chapter)

Chapter 3(C)                    Grammar and Cultural Notes

## 1. Location に Something が "あります" or Someone が "います"

These verbs, "arimasu" and "imasu," are intransitive verbs that mean "exist." In English, arimasu and imasu may be translated to "have" or to "own." Essentially, "arimasu" is used for "inanimate" objects such as trees, rocks, houses, etc. and "imasu" for "animate" beings such as people and animals. For the location of existence, you use a particle "ni."

Examples:
A: つくえのうえに、なにが　ありますか。What's on the desk?
　　tsukue no ue ni,　nani ga　arimasuka.
B: ほんが　あります。　　　　　　　　There is a book.
　　hon ga　arimasu.

A:きょうしつに、だれが　いますか。　Who's in the classroom?
　　kyooshitsu ni,　dare ga　imasu ka.
B:がくせいと せんせいが　います。　　There are students and teacher.
　　gakusei to sensei ga　imasu.

## 2. Someone には S が "あります" or "います"

Though "arimasu" is the verb to be used for "inanimate" objects, people who may be considered by the speaker as his **belongings**, such as "family, pen-pals, and best friends," may be followed by "arimasu." Also, the sentence pattern of "~ **ni** wa, Subject ga arimasu/imasu" may often be used for expressing the speaker's belongings.

The sentence pattern to show belongings:

| Topic ni wa | Subject ga | Numbers | arimasu/imasu |
|---|---|---|---|
| (As for me) | (kids) | (how many) | (exist/have) |
| わたしには | こどもが | ふたり | います or あります。 |
| watashi ni wa | kodomo ga | futari | imasu/arimasu |

*Numerals and counters (such as "futari" or "ippiki") are inserted between the subjective case-marker "ga" and the verb (arimasu/imasu).

Examples:
(1)  I have two (older) brothers.  → わたしには　　　あにが ふたり　います/あります。
　　　　　　　　　　　　　　　　watashi ni wa　　ani ga futari imasu/arimasu.
(2)  I have two kids.　　　　　　  → わたしには　　こどもが ふたり　います/あります。
　　　　　　　　　　　　　　　　watashi ni wa　kodomo ga futari imasu.
(3)  This house has a red gate.  → このうちには あかいもんが　あります。
　　　　　　　　　　　　　　　　kono uchi ni wa akai mon ga arimasu.
(4)  There is a swimming pool in my house. → わたしのうちには プールが　あります。
　　　　　　　　　　　　　　　　watashi no uchi ni wa puuru ga arimasu.

### 3. こちら、そちら、あちら **to show the directions**.

Another example following the "ko-so-a-do" pattern, aside from the ones previously introduced, is "achira," which means "over there." Following the "ko-so-a-do" pattern will lead you a new set of expressions: "here, there, over there, where," or "kochira, sochira, achira, dochira." Look at the list of both formal and casual sets:

|  | Formal | Casual |
|---|---|---|
| Here (this direction) (near the speaker) | kochira こちら | kocchi こっち |
| There (that direction) (near the listener) | sochira そちら | socchi そっち |
| Over there (that direction) (far for both) | achira あちら | acchi あっち |
| Where (which direction) | dochira どちら | docchi どっち |

*Comparing to "koko, soko, asoko," "kochira, sochira, achira" convey a stronger sense of direction.

**They may also be used to address people politely. "こちらは、田中さんです。 Kochira wa Tanaka-san desu" means "This is Mr. Tanaka," and "あちらのかたは、どなたですか。 Achira no kata wa, donata desu ka" means "Who is that person over there?"

### 4. Particle "ni" to show the destination of movement

(1) はこに　いれます。　(おいれします in the dialogue is the exalted form.)
　　　　　　　　　　　o i r e s h i m a s u
　　hako **ni**　ire masu.　(I'll put [them] into a box.)

(2) ぽけっとに　てを　いれました。
　　poketto **ni**　te wo　ire mashita. (I put my hand into a pocket.)

(3) さいふに　おかねを　いれました。
　　saifu **ni**　o kane wo　ire mashita. (I put money into a wallet.)

### 5. ～がほしい (です)。 **I want that.**

When you express your desire to have something, you can make a sentence pattern of "X wa Y ga hoshii (adding "desu" to "hoshii" makes it formal)." It is equivalent to "X wants Y" in English. The conjugation of "hoshii" is the same as that of adjectives, which will be introduced shortly.
Ex.
わたしは、ともだちが　ほしいです。　I want friends.
　　　　　こいびとが　ほしいです。　I want a lover.
　　　　　じかんが　　ほしいです。　I want time.

| いぬが | ほしいです。 | I want dogs. |
| I-pad が | ほしいです。 | I want an I-pad. |

## 6. Japanese numerals beyond one thousand

1,000-digit

|  | Japanese numerals | hiragana | kanji |
|---|---|---|---|
| 1000 | (is)sen | （いっ）せん | （一）千 |
| 2000 | nisen | にせん | 二千 |
| 3000 | sanzen | さんぜん | 三千 |
| 4000 | yonsen | よんせん | 四千 |
| 5000 | gosen | ごせん | 五千 |
| 6000 | rokusen | ろくせん | 六千 |
| 7000 | nanasen | ななせん | 七千 |
| 8000 | hassen, hachisen | はっせん | 八千 |
| 9000 | kyuusen | きゅうせん | 九千 |

10,000-digit

|  | Japanese numerals | hiragana | kanji |
|---|---|---|---|
| 10,000 | ichiman | いちまん | 一万 |
| 20,000 | niman | にまん | 二万 |
| 30,000 | sanman | さんまん | 三万 |
| 40,000 | yonman | よんまん | 四万 |
| 50,000 | goman | ごまん | 五万 |
| 60,000 | rokuman | ろくまん | 六万 |
| 70,000 | nanaman | ななまん | 七万 |
| 80,000 | hachiman | はちまん | 八万 |
| 90,000 | kyuuman | きゅうまん | 九万 |

How to count numerals beyond "-man":

100,000 → 10, 0000
Move the dividing comma to the one after the fourth zero from the right. Read the numbers left of the comma. You read "10," which is "jyuu" in Japanese. Add "jyuu" to "man," making "jyuu man."じゅうまん（十万）

1,000,000 → 100, 0000
The numbers to the left of the comma (after you move the comma between the fourth and fifth zero from the right) is "100," which is "hyaku" in Japanese. Add "hyaku" to "man," making "hyaku man."ひゃくまん（百万）

Along the same token, 10,000,000 is 1000, 0000, which is "issen man," （いっ）せんまん（［一］千万）

The following digits are いちおく（一億）(100,000,000)、じゅうおく（十億）、ひゃくおく（百億）、（いっ）せんおく（一千億）、and いっちょう（一兆）.

If you are shown a box, and asked "what's in the box?" you certainly don't know what's in there. This pattern is used when you know the location, but you don't know what's inside. The pattern of the sentence is as follows:

はこのなかに　なにが
ありますか。

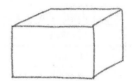

| **Location** に　**Subject (item)**　が |
|---|
| あります。 |

The location in this case may be "ここ koko" or "はこのなか in the box."

Variations of locations:

| | | うえ ue (above; on) |
|---|---|---|
| | | なか naka (in; inside) |
| | | した shita (below; under) |
| はこ | の | よこ yoko (side) |
| hako | no | まえ mae (front) |
| ↓ | | うしろ　(rear; behind) |
| box | | ちかく　(near) |
| | | あいだ　(between; among) |

Now, how would you ask what's on top of the desk?

Yes, you say つくえのうえに、なにが
ありますか。

The answer is スタンドがあります。
（すたんど）

What if you are looking for your key? You will ask かぎは、どこにありますか。 And if you are looking for your sister, you will say いもうとは、どこにいますか。

This pattern is used when you know what you are looking for, but don't know where it is. The pattern of the sentence is as follows:

| |
|---|
| **Item/ Topic** は　　**Location** に　　あります。<br>　　　　　　　　　　　　　　　　います。 |

If your money is in your wallet, the answer is:

サイフ　の　なかに　あります。

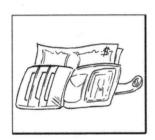

If your sister is behind a tree, the answer is:

　き　の　うしろに　います。

Now, a question for you.  How would you describe where the boy is?

He is next to a tree.  Would you say he is き の となり？ き の よこ？

Both となり and よこ means "next to it," but the better definitions are:

| |
|---|
| となり (next to items in the same group/category)<br>よこ (next to items in a different group/category) |

A human boy and a tree don't seem to belong to the same category, therefore, the better choice of word is: き の よこ

Japanese counters

| Non-classified items: chairs, desks, boxes, erasers, apples, bags, also ages | | Vehicles, machines, etc | | Flat items: paper, plates, leaf, etc. also shirts | |
|---|---|---|---|---|---|
| How many? = いくつ | | How many? = なんだい | | How many? = なんまい | |
| 1 | ひとつ | 1 | いちだい | 1 | いちまい |
| 2 | ふたつ | 2 | にだい | 2 | にまい |
| 3 | みっつ | 3 | さんだい | 3 | さんまい |
| 4 | よっつ | 4 | よんだい | 4 | よんまい |
| 5 | いつつ | 5 | ごだい | 5 | ごまい |
| 6 | むっつ | 6 | ろくだい | 6 | ろくまい |
| 7 | ななつ | 7 | ななだい | 7 | ななまい |
| 8 | やっつ | 8 | はちだい | 8 | はちまい |
| 9 | ここのつ | 9 | きゅうだい | 9 | きゅうまい |
| 10 | とお | 10 | じゅうだい | 10 | じゅうまい |
| 11 | じゅういち | 11 | じゅういちだい | 11 | じゅういちまい |
| 12 | じゅうに | 12 | じゅうにだい | 12 | じゅうにまい |
| Bound items: Books, magazines, etc. | | Cup-full, etc. | | Long items: pens, pencils, bottles, trees, also belts, neckties | |
| How many? = なんさつ | | How many? = なんばい | | How many? = なんぼん | |
| 1 | いっさつ | 1 | いっぱい | 1 | いっぽん |
| 2 | にさつ | 2 | にはい | 2 | にほん |
| 3 | さんさつ | 3 | さんばい | 3 | さんぼん |
| 4 | よんさつ | 4 | よんはい | 4 | よんほん |
| 5 | ごさつ | 5 | ごはい | 5 | ごほん |
| 6 | ろくさつ | 6 | ろっぱい | 6 | ろっぽん |
| 7 | ななさつ | 7 | ななはい | 7 | ななほん |
| 8 | はっさつ、はちさつ | 8 | はっぱい、はちはい | 8 | はっぽん、はちほん |
| 9 | きゅうほん | 9 | きゅうはい | 9 | きゅうほん |
| 10 | じゅっさつ | 10 | じゅっぽん | 10 | じゅっぽん |
| 11 | じゅういっさつ | 11 | じゅういっぱい | 11 | じゅういっぽん |
| 12 | じゅうにさつ | 12 | じゅうにはい | 12 | じゅうにほん |

Japanese counters

| People | Animals | Non-classified items that use Chinese numbers |
|---|---|---|
| | | |
| How many? = なんにん | How many? = なんびき | How many? = なんこ |
| 1　ひとり | 1　いっぴき | 1　いっこ |
| 2　ふたり | 2　にひき | 2　にこ |
| 3　さんにん | 3　さんびき | 3　さんこ |
| 4　よにん | 4　よんひき | 4　よんこ |
| 5　ごにん | 5　ごひき | 5　ごこ |
| 6　ろくにん | 6　ろっぴき | 6　ろっこ |
| 7　ななにん、しちにん | 7　ななひき | 7　ななこ |
| 8　はちにん | 8　はっぴき | 8　はっこ、はちこ |
| 9　きゅうにん、くにん | 9　きゅうひき | 9　きゅうこ |
| 10　じゅうにん | 10　じゅっぴき | 10　じゅっこ |
| 11　じゅういちにん | 11　じゅういっぴき | 11　じゅういっこ |
| 12　じゅうににん | 12　じゅうにひき | 12　じゅうにこ |

Tell how many there are. Use the appropriate numeral classifiers and the proper verb demonstrating existence.

| For inanimate things | [Item] ga [number]   arimasu |
|---|---|
| For animate things | [Item] ga [number]   imasu |

1. こども kodomo

2. りんご ringo

3. けしごむ keshigomu

4. ビール biiru

5. 本 hon

6. ハンカチ hankachi

7. 女の人 on'na no hito

8. スプーン supuun

9. えんぴつ enpitsu

10. ノート nooto

11. 男の人 otoko no hito

12. ネクタイ nekutai

13. ボタン botan

14. たまご tamago

15. きって kitte

16. ハンバーガー hanbaagaa

17. せっけん sekken

18. たまねぎ tamanegi

19. パン pan

20. ベルト beruto

Chapter 3(C) Exercises

A. Pair-work: Learn the following vocabulary and expressions.

もの materials、どこの of which（country/place）、〜せい made-in〜、〜がほしい

（です）I want 〜. Tシャツ T-shirt、シャツ shirt、ズボン pants、ネクタイ tie,

ポリエステル polyester,（も）めん cotton, きぬ silk, レーヨン rayon

## Conversation 1.

A: Looking at B's clothing, say

いい ┌──────────────────┐ ですね。ものは、なんですか。
       │ シャツ、Tシャツ、ズボン、 │
       │ ネクタイ、（　　　） │
       └──────────────────┘

B: ┌──────────────┐ です。
     │ ポリエステル、 │
     │ （も）めん、きぬ、 │
     │ レーヨン │
     └──────────────┘

A: ぼく／ わたし も （それが）ほしいです。
   (boku= "I," used by boys)

B: (You can find it at...)
┌──────────────────┐ に ありますよ。
│ Sears, Macy's, Target, │
│ etc. │
└──────────────────┘

## Conversation 2.

A: いい とけい ですね。どこのですか。(Besides とけい, use ペン、かばん、
                               ハンカチ etc.)

B: にほんせいです。

A: ぼく／わたしも ほしいです。

B: 〜にありますよ。

## Question/Answer:

いま、なにが いちばん ほしいですか。

   1. おかね (money)

   2. こいびと (lover)

   3. じかん (time)

   4. いい せいせき (good grade)

   5. 犬 (dogs) か 猫 (cats)

   6. その他 (others)

B. Shopping Task. Pair-work: Practice various shopping scenarios with your partner.
Switch partners between tasks. Fill in the blanks with your partner, switch roles, and
practice.
(C: customer, S: salesperson)

Task 1

C：＿＿＿＿＿＿＿ が ありますか。

S：＿＿＿＿＿は、ありません。＿＿＿＿＿は、どうですか。

C：そうですね。じゃ、＿＿＿＿＿を ください。
　　おいくらですか。

S：＿＿＿＿＿えん です。
　　(Customer pays ___yen) ありがとうございました。

C：どうも、ありがとう。

Hints: あかいかさ、あおいかさ
　　　　まんねんひつ、ボールペン
　　　　(fountain pen)　　(ballpoint pen)

Task 2

S：いらっしゃいませ。

C：あのう、＿＿＿＿＿が ほしいんですが。

S：＿＿＿＿＿ですか。こちらです。

C：これは、みんな <u>おとなよう</u>（大人用）　ですね。(for adults)

　　こども の ＿＿＿＿＿は、ありませんか。

S：<u>おこさん</u> の ＿＿＿＿＿は、二かい（二階）です。
　　(polite form for children)

C：ああ、そうですか。どうも。

Hints: かさ，ふく (clothing)

Task 3

  C：<u>こどもよう</u>（子供用）の ＿＿＿＿＿＿＿がありますか。(for kids)

  S：はい、いろいろ ございます。

  C：あおい （青い）＿＿＿＿＿＿が いいんですが。

  S：この あおい の は、いかが ですか。

  C：きれいな いろ ですね。おいくら ですか。

  S：＿＿＿＿＿＿えんです。

  C：じゃ、この あおい ＿＿＿＿＿＿ を、＿＿＿＿＿＿＿ ください。
               Number with a counter

  S：ありがとうございます。

  Hints: かさ，くつ(shoes), シャツ(shirt)、ズボン(pants)


Task 4 (At a coffee shop)

  S：いらっしゃいませ。
  C：*^_^*
  S：なんに なさいますか。

  C：＿＿＿＿＿＿を ください。
  S：かしこまりました。

  C：＿＿＿＿＿＿も ひとつ おねがいします。

  S：＿＿＿＿＿＿を おひとつと ＿＿＿＿＿＿＿を おひとつ ですね。

   ＿＿＿＿＿＿は、＿＿＿＿＿＿ と ＿＿＿＿＿＿があ りますが、、、

  C：＿＿＿＿＿＿を ください。
  S：はい。

  Hints: コーヒー、サンドイッチ、ハムサンド、ミックスサンド
     こうちゃ、スパゲティ、ナポリタン、ミートソース

C. Pair-work: First, study the floor directory of a typical Japanese department store. Then practice occurring dialogues between customers and clerks as cued in the next page.

| おくじょう<br>okujyoo<br>(R) | ゆうえんち (amusement park)　ビアガーデン (beer garden)<br>yuuenchi　　　　　　　　　　bia-gaaden |
|---|---|
| 八階はちかい<br>hachikai<br>(8 F) | レストラン<br>resutoran |
| 七階ななかい<br>nanakai<br>(7 F) | ぶんぼうぐ (stationery)、本、CD，おもちゃ (toys)<br>bunboogu　　　　　　　hon　shiidii　omocha |
| 六階ろっかい<br>rokkai<br>(6 F) | かぐ (furniture)、しょっき (tableware)、<br>kagu　　　　　　shokki<br>だいどころようひん (kitchenware)<br>daidokoro-yoohin |
| 五階ごかい<br>gokai<br>(5 F) | でんかせいひん (electrical appliances)<br>denka-seihin |
| 四階よんかい<br>yonkai<br>(4 F) | きもの、こうげいひん (arts and crafts)<br>kimono　koogeihin |
| 三階さんがい<br>sangai<br>(3 F) | ふじんふく (women's clothing)<br>fujin-fuku |
| 二階にかい<br>nikai<br>(2 F) | しんしふく (men's clothing)<br>shinshi-fuku |
| 一階いっかい<br>ikkai<br>(1 F) | ほうせき (jewelry)、けしょうひん (cosmetics)、ハンドバッグ<br>hooseki　　　　　　keshoohin　　　　　　　handobaggu<br>(lady's purses)、かばん (bags)、ネクタイ (ties)、ハンカチ<br>kaban　　　　nekutai　　　hankachi<br>(handkerchiefs)、こもの・アクセサリー (accessories)、くつ (shoes)<br>komono　akusesarii　　　　　　kutsu |
| 地下一階<br>ちかいっかい<br>chika-ikkai<br>(B1) | しょくひん (food)<br>shokuhin |
| 地下二階<br>ちかにかい<br>chika-nikai<br>(B2) | ちゅうしゃじょう (parking)<br>chuusha-jyoo |

うりば: "Departments" (sections) in a department store

**(1) Practice the following dialogue first.**

| | |
|---|---|
| Customer: | すみません、ふじんふくうりばは、どこ（or なんがい）ですか。<br>Sumimasen    fujinfuku-uriba    wa,   doko (nan-gai)      desuka. |
| Clerk : | はい、ふじんふくうりばですね。ふじんふくは、さんがいで<br>Hai,    fujinfuku-uriba      desune.   Fujinfuku-uriba wa, sangai de<br>ございます。<br>gozaimasu. |
| Customer: | どうも、ありがとう。<br>Doomo, arigatoo. |
| Clerk : | いいえ。<br>Iie. |

**(2) Replace "fujinfuku-uriba" with the following sections:**

しんしふくうりば、かばんうりば、CD うりば、ぶんぼうぐうりば、しょくひん
shinshifuku-uriba      kaban-uriba      CD-uriba      bunboogu-uriba       shokuhin-
うりば、ほうせきうりば、くつうりば、こものうりば、おもちゃうりば、
uriba    hooseki-uriba      kutsu-uriba    komono-uriba    omocha-uriba
きものうりば、かぐうりば
kimono-uriba      kagu-uriba

**(3) Guess where the various departments are found in a local, large department store.**
   **Then list a few items that are sold in each department.**

| | | うりば<br>uriba | Items |
|---|---|---|---|
| ななかい<br>nanakai | 7 F | | |
| ろっかい<br>rokkai | 6 F | | |
| ごかい<br>gokai | 5 F | | |
| よんかい<br>yonkai | 4 F | | |
| さんがい<br>sangai | 3 F | | |
| にかい<br>nikai | 2 F | | |
| いっかい<br>ikkai | 1 F | | |
| ちかいっかい<br>chika-ikkai | B 1 | | |

D. Role-play: Work with your partner and create dialogues under the following situations.

1. You are at a department store and want to know which floor you should go to find "たび tabi" (socks for kimono 足袋). Ask the person at the information desk.

2. You are at the kimono department. You want to ask if they have "たび tabi" for women.
   First, get the attention of a store clerk and ask him/her if they have women's tabi in 24 centimeters (American size 6).

3. A store clerk has shown you a sweater. Ask the clerk how much it is. If it is too expensive, ask for a more affordable one. Ask for ones in different colors. Ask for a bigger (or smaller) size.

   [Vocabulary help]:
   expensive: takai
   a little cheaper: もうすこし やすい moo sukoshi yasui
   a little smaller: もうすこし ちいさい moo sukoshi chiisai
   a little bigger : もうすこし おおきい moo sukoshi ookii

   color: いろ iro
   what color: なにいろ nani iro
   other colors: ほかのいろ hoka no iro

   Do you (or Don't you) have ~? : 〜が　ありますか。〜は　ありませんか。
   ~ ga (or wa) arimasu ka (or arimasen ka)

4. You are at the umbrella department and want to buy a present for your mother. Your budget is 5000 yen. Garner the attention of a store clerk and explain with what you need help. Respond to questions about size, color preferences, etc.

   [Vocabulary help]:
   umbrella: かさ kasa
   budget: よさん yosan
   mother (humble form; my mother): はは haha
   a present for my mother: ははへの　プレゼント haha e no purezento
   It's a present for my mother (as I explain to you why): ははへの　プレゼント なんです。 haha e no purezento nan desu.

E. Based on the information given below, figure out who lives in which apartment.

(1)
1. Aさんのへやは、Bさんのへやの　うえに　あります。
2. Eさんのへやは、さくらのき (cherry tree) の　ちかくに　あります。
3. Bさんのへやは、DさんとFさんの　あいだに　あります。
4. Fさんは、Cさんのへやの　したに　すんでいます。
5. Cさんのへやは、かいだん (stairs) の　ちかくです。
6. Dさんのへやは、Eさんのしたです。

(2)
1. Bさんは、Fさんのへやのとなりです。
2. Eさんは、Bさんのしたに　すんでいます。
3. Eさんのへやは、Dさんの　となりです。
4. Eさんのへやは、かいだんの　ちかくです。
5. Dさんのへやは、EさんとAさんの　あいだにあります。
6. Cさんは、Aさんのへやの　うえに　すんでいます。
7. CさんとFさんは、となりです。
8. Cさんのへやは、さくらのきのちかくです。

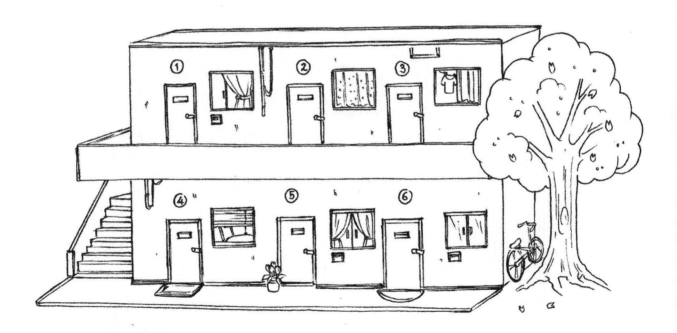

F. Pair-work.

(1) First, use Pictures A and B. Each student asks where missing items are. The items you are missing are in the box. Use "~ wa doko ni arimsuka?"

(2) Next, draw the furniture on the Picture C as the way you like. Ask each other where those items are.

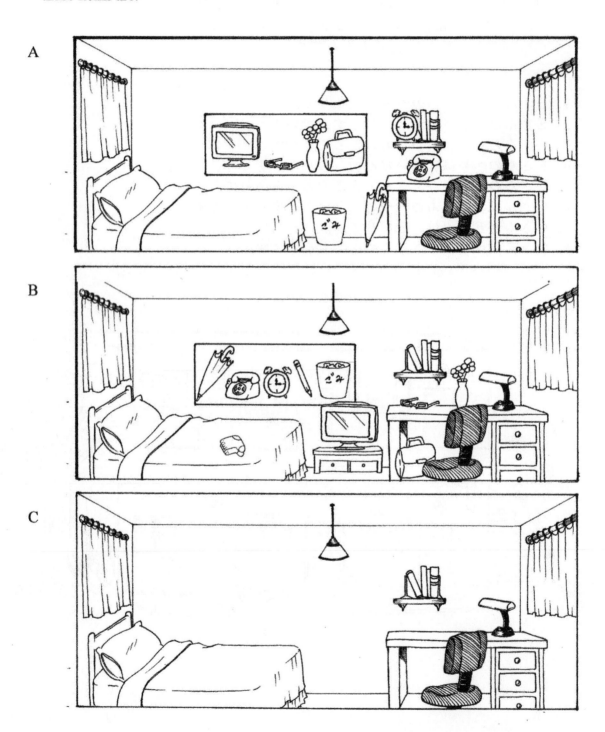

G. りんごは、ひとつ　いくらですか。How much is an apple?

1. ぶどうは、ひとつ　いくらですか。　　　こたえ＿＿＿＿＿＿＿＿＿＿
2. りんごは、ひとつ　いくらですか。　　　こたえ＿＿＿＿＿＿＿＿＿＿
3. すいかは、ひとつ　いくらですか。　　　こたえ＿＿＿＿＿＿＿＿＿＿
4. みかんは、ひとつ　いくらですか。　　　こたえ＿＿＿＿＿＿＿＿＿＿
5. にんじんは　いっぽん　いくらですか。　こたえ＿＿＿＿＿＿＿＿＿＿
6. きゃべつは、ひとつ　いくらですか。　　こたえ＿＿＿＿＿＿＿＿＿＿
7. バナナは、いっぽん　いくらですか。　　こたえ＿＿＿＿＿＿＿＿＿＿
8. たまねぎは、ひとつ　いくらですか。　　こたえ＿＿＿＿＿＿＿＿＿＿
9. トマトは、ひとつ　いくらですか。　　　こたえ＿＿＿＿＿＿＿＿＿＿
10. きゅうりは、いっぽん　いくらですか。　こたえ＿＿＿＿＿＿＿＿＿＿

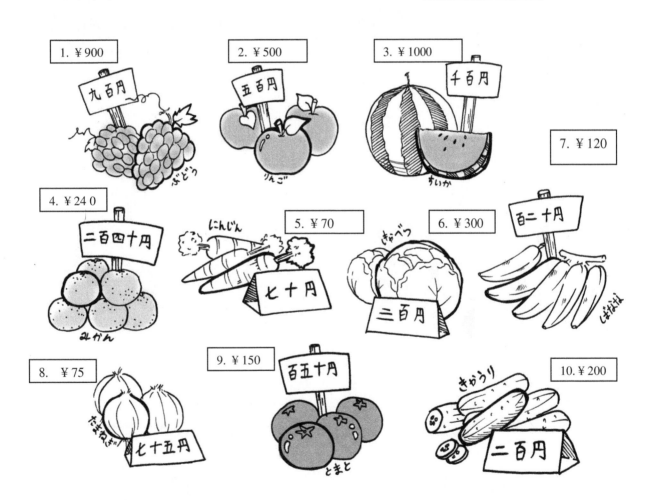

H: Draw pictures depicting various items at designated locations as your instructor or partner tells you. For example, as you hear "tukue no ue ni hon ga arimasu," you draw a book on the desk. Use the following items: pen, book, light stand, clock, bag, tree, cat, dog, telephone, etc. Vary the locations, i. e., under/top or front/rear of the desk, chair, door, outside of the window, or on the floor (yuka), etc.

A                                        B

C                                        D

E                                        F

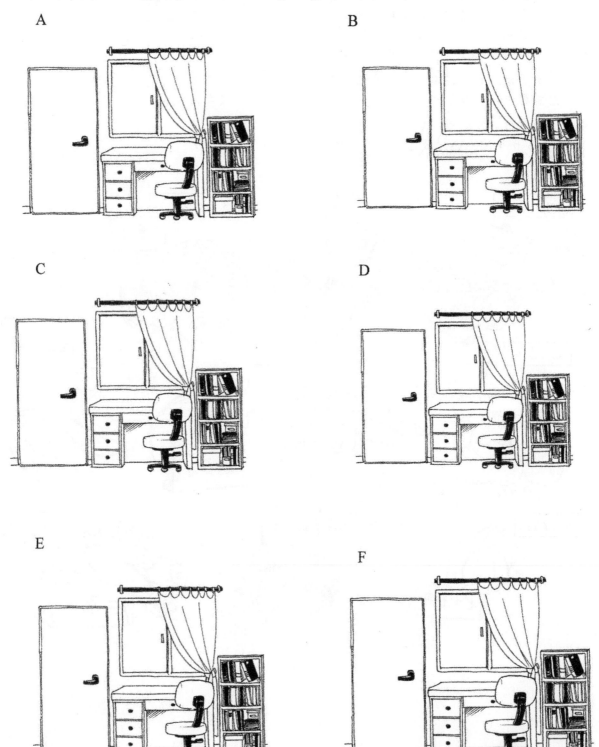

I. Entire-class activity. Your instructor will provide you with a picture. Find the person who has identical picture as yours, without showing each other the picture you have. Communicate only verbally to confirm whether the two of you hold the same pictures.

> You may use either of the following sentence patterns:
> (1) "Inu wa doko ni imasu ka." Or, "Inu wa tsukue no ue ni imasu ka."
> (2) "Tsukue no ue ni nani ga imasu ka." Or, "Tsukue no ue ni inu ga imasu ka."

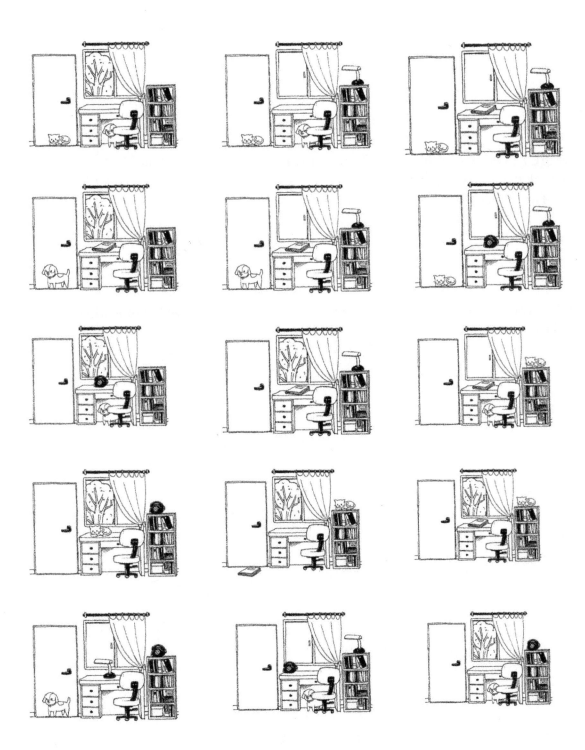

Chapter 3(C)'s Dict-A-Conversation (1)
Look at the 20 different illustration items in page 182 and answer the questions. You may first write answers in Roma-ji, then rewrite in hiragana.

1 .......................................     2 .......................................

3 .......................................     4 .......................................

5 .......................................     6 .......................................

7 .......................................     8 .......................................

9 .......................................     10 .......................................

Chapter 3(C)'s Dict-A-Conversation (2): Floor Directory of a Department Store
1. Look at the floor directory in page 186 and answer the questions. You may first write answers in Roma-ji, then rewrite in hiragana.

1) .......................................     2) .......................................

3) .......................................     4) .......................................

2. When you hear the chime, ask the appropriate question to receive the following answers.

5A : ＿＿＿＿＿＿＿＿＿＿＿＿＿＿＿＿＿＿＿＿＿＿＿＿

5B : レ
す
と
ら
ん
ストランは、はっかいに　ございます。

6A : ＿＿＿＿＿＿＿＿＿＿＿＿＿＿＿＿＿＿＿＿＿＿＿＿

6B : かばんうりばは、いっかいで　ございます。

7A : ＿＿＿＿＿＿＿＿＿＿＿＿＿＿＿＿＿＿＿＿＿＿＿＿

7B : おとこのひとのス
す
う
つ
ーツですか、しんしふくは、にかいに　ございます。

8A : ＿＿＿＿＿＿＿＿＿＿＿＿＿＿＿＿＿＿＿＿＿＿＿＿

8B : きものは、さんがいで　ございます。

9A : ＿＿＿＿＿＿＿＿＿＿＿＿＿＿＿＿＿＿＿＿＿＿＿＿

9B : ビ
ぴ
あ
が
あ
でん
アガーデンは、おくじょうで　ございます。

## Chapter 3(D)    Ordering at a Restaurant    レストランで　ちゅうもんする
re-su-to-ran de   chu-u-mo-n su-ru

ウェイトレス：いらっしゃいませ。何に　なさいますか。　　　　　　　　　1
u-e-i-to-re-su  : i-ra-s-sha-i ma-se.   na-n ni na-sa-i ma-su ka

モニカ：　　　わたしは、カレーライス。　　　　　　　　　　　　　　　2
Mo-ni-ka:        wa-ta-shi wa, ka-re-e-ra-i-su

ケン：　　　　ぼくは、チキンカレー。　　　　　　　　　　　　　　　　3
ken  :           bo-ku wa, chi-ki-n-ka-re-e

ウェイトレス：カレーおーつ　と　チキンカレーおーつ　ですね。　　　　4
u-e-i-to-re-su  : ka-re-e o-hi-to-tsu to chi-ki-n-ka-re-e o-hi-to-tsu  de-su ne

　　　　　　　おのみものは？　　　　　　　　　　　　　　　　　　　5
　　　　　　　o-no-mi-mo-no wa

モニカ：　　　わたしは、こうちゃを　おねがいします。　　　　　　　　6
Mo-ni-ka:        wa-ta-shi wa, ko-o-cha wo o-ne-ga-i  shi-ma-su

ウェイトレス：おさとう　と　クリームは、どうなさいますか。　　　　　7
u-e-i-to-re-su  : o-sa-to-o  to    ku-ri-i-mu  wa, do-o na-sa-i ma-su ka

モニカ：　　　おさとうは、けっこうです。クリームだけ　おねがいします。8
Mo-ni-ka:        o-sa-to-o wa, ke-k-ko-o de-su. ku-ri-i-mu da-ke  o-ne-ga-i shi-ma-su

ウェイトレス：かしこまりました。こちらさまは？　　　　　　　　　　9
u-e-i-to-re-su  : ka-shi-ko-ma-ri-ma-shi-ta.  ko-chi-ra sa-ma wa

ケン：　　　　ぼくは、水で　いいです。　　　　　　　　　　　　　10
ken  :           bo-ku wa, mi-zu de i-i de-su

ウェイトレス：それでは、こうちゃ　と　お水ですね。ありがとうございます。11
u-e-i-to-re-su  : so-re-de-wa, ko-o-cha to o-mi-zu de-su ne. a-ri-ga-to-o go-za-i-ma-su

Chapter 3 (D)
[English translation:]

Waitress: May I help you?  What would you like? (Lit: what will you decide on?)
Monica  :  I will have curry rice.
Ken      :  I will have chicken curry.
Waitress: One curry rice, and one chicken curry.  How about a drink?
Monica  :  May I have tea please?
Waitress: Would you like cream and sugar?
Monica  :  I don't take any sugar.  May I have just cream?
Waitress: Certainly.  How about you, sir?
Ken      :  I'm just fine with water.
Waitress: Then, one tea and one water.  Thank you very much.

Chapter 3 (D)                    Vocabulary List

1. Expressions

| | |
|---|---|
| Nan ni nasai masu ka.<br>なんに　なさいますか。 | a polite form of "nan ni shimasu ka" (What will you decide on?) |
| Doo nasai masu ka.<br>どう　なさいますか。 | a polite form of "doo shimasu ka" (What will you do?) |
| ~wa kekkoo desu.<br>〜は、けっこうです。 | I can do without ~.  No thank you ~. |

2. Nouns

| | |
|---|---|
| （レストラン）(resutoran) | restaurant |
| （カレーライス) (karee-raisu) | curry rice (curry on rice) |
| （ぼく)(boku) | I (used by a male speaker) |
| チキンライス chikin-raisu | chicken rice (fried rice with chicken) |
| さとう satoo | sugar |
| おさとう osatoo | polite form of "satoo" |
| クリーム　kuriimu | cream (possibly meant for "milk") |
| （こちらさま kochira-sama) | this person (polite form to address someone close to the speaker) |
| （みず mizu) | water |
| おみず o-mizu | polite form of "mizu" |

3. Particles

| | |
|---|---|
| だけ dake | |
| で de (in the context of "mizu de ii") | particle to "limit" choice/selection<br>"Mizu de ii desu" means "I am just fine with water." |

--------------------------------------------------------------------------------
Additional Vocabulary from Grammar and Exercises sections
--------------------------------------------------------------------------------

[Nouns]

| | |
|---|---|
| うどんやさん udon-ya-san | noodle shop |
| みせ mise | store |
| おつり otsuri | (the) change |
| おしながき oshinagaki | menu |
| ビール biiru | beer |
| おさけ osake | liquor; Japanese rice wine |
| ちゅうハイ chuuhai | "shochu" liquor mixed with soda water |
| ドル doru | dollar |

せ ん と
セント sento                                     cent

(うどんや noodle shop)
てんぷらそば tenpura soba                buckwheat noodles topped with tempura
ざるそば zaru soba                          buckwheat noodles served with a soup
つきみうどん tsukimi udon                udon noodles served with an egg
とりなんばん         tori-nanban            buckwheat noodles served with chicken


(わしょくのみせ) washoku わしょく         Japanese cuisine
やきとりていしょく yakitori teishoku    assorted meal with roasted chicken
てんぷらていしょく tenpura teishoku    assorted meal with tempura
とんかつていしょく tonkatsu teishoku    assorted meal with pork cutlet
すきやきていしょく sukiyaki teishoku    assorted meal with sukiyaki (thin-sliced beef,
                                                              kon'nyaku noodles, tofu, green onions, etc.
                                                              cooked in a soup)


ともだちと tomodachi to                      with (one's) friend
ひとつずつ hitotsu zutsu                      one by one
ぜんぶで zenbu de                              in all
いちど ichido                                       once

[な Adjectives]

けっこう kekkoo                                  fine; good
   けっこうな おてまえでした。
   kekkoo na o-temae deshita.                It was a fine cup of tea that you served.
   けっこうな おたくですね。
   kekkoo na otaku desune.                   You have a nice house.

[Expressions]

けっこうです。kekkoo desu.                No thank you.

おそれいります。Osore irimasu.              Excuse me/Thank you.

Chapter 3(D)                    Grammar and Cultural Notes

## 1. Particle "だけ dake;" only

The particle "dake" is equivalent in meaning to "only, alone, merely, just, or that's all" in English. It is used with nouns, adjectives or verbs.  Another particle "shika しか", which also means "only," will be introduced in later chapter, Chapter 4(D).

Example sentences:
(1) おみずだけ　おねがいします。
　　o-mizu dake　　onegaishimasu.　(Please give me only "water.")

(2) 五ドルだけ　ください。
　　go-doru dake　kudasai.　　(Please give me just five dollars.)

(3) いちどだけ、いきました。
　　ichido dake　　ikimashita. (I went [there] only once.)

## 2. Ambiguous word "けっこう kekkoo"

"Kekkoo" is a 'na-adjective', which means "fine" and can be used in two diversely different ways: One as a compliment meaning "It's beautiful," and the other as a gentle statement of refusal, "No thank you."  It is not too difficult to tell which meaning is being expressed in a real scenario.  In a situation where someone offers you something, your "Kekkoo desu" would mean "No thank you," while in a situation where you want to praise something, your "kekkoo" would mean "It's nice."
Examine the following examples. Do they make sense to you?

(1)
A:　ビールを（or は）　いかがですか。
　　biiru　wo (or wa)　ikaga desu ka. (Would you like to have some beer?)

B:　ありがとう、けっこうです。
　　arigatoo,　　kekkoo desu. (Thank you, but no.)

(2)
A:　けっこうな　おたくですね。
　　kekkoo na　　o-taku　desune. (It's a nice house [you have].)

B:　おそれいります。
　　osore　irimasu.　("Thank you" in a humble way.)

In-Class Activity:  Eating at a Restaurant

A.  Practice how to place orders:

Pattern:  Item　を　_____　ください。
　　　　　　Item  wo　　Number　　kudasai

Example:  はまち　を　ひとつ　ください。 Replace はまち with まぐろ, あなご, いか.
　　　　　　　"hamachi"  wo  hitotsu　　kudasai.　　　　　　　　　　　　　　tuna   sea eel   squid
　　　　　　　(yellow tale)

Pattern to be used when ordering more than one item:

(Item#)1 を _____ と (Item#2) を_____ と (Item#)3 を_____ ください 。
　#1  wo Number  to　　　#2  wo Number  to　　　#3　　wo Number  kudasai.

Practice ordering at a sushi-bar:
1)  May I have one yellow tale and two tunas まぐろ?
2)  What's good today?  May I have two?
3)  May I have one tuna, one sea eel あなご, and one squid いか?

B.  Count how many o-sushi you ate:

Pattern:  Item を _____ たべました。
　　　　　Item wo  Number　　tabemashita.

Example:  わたしは、はまちを　ひとつ　たべました。
　　　　　　watashi wa,  hamachi wo  hitotsu　　tabemashita.

Pattern to be used when ordering more than one item:

(Item#)1 を _____ と (Item#2) を_____ と (Item#)3 を_____ たべました。
　#1  wo Number  to　　　#2  wo Number  to　　#3　　wo Number  tabemashita.

Example:  わたしは、はまちをひとつ　と、まぐろをふたつ　と、あなごを　みっつ
　　　　　　たべました。　　　　　　　　　　(tuna)　　　　　　　(sea eel)

(*Note: No particle is used after the last counter: みっつ　たべました)
　　　　　　　　　　　　　　　　　　　　　　　　　　　　mittsu　　tabemashita.

C.  Pair/group work:  Figure out the totals.

1.マクドナルドで　ハンバー
ガーを二つと、コカコーラを
一つと、ミルクシェークを一
つ　ちゅうもんしました。
千円で、おつりは　いくらで
すか。

| はんばがー ハンバーガー | 240 円 |
|---|---|
| ちずばがー チーズバーガー | 300 円 |
| こかこーら コカコーラ | 120 円 |
| みるくしぇいく ミルクシェイク | 250 円 |
| ぼてと ポテト | 250 円 |

Answer_____

2.
うどんやさんで、あなたは、
てんぷらそばを一つと、つき
みうどんを　一つ　ちゅうも
んしました。五千円で　お
つりは　いくらですか。
Answer_____

3.わしょくのみせで、ともだちと　やきとりていしょくと
てんぷらていしょくを　ちゅうもんしました。ビールと
おさけも　ひとつずつ　ちゅうもんしました。ぜんぶで
いくらですか。Answer_____

<おしながき>
ていしょく千円
やきとりていしょく千円
てんぷらていしょく千円
とんかつていしょく千円
すきやきていしょく千円
おのみもの
| びーる ビール | 300 円 |
|---|---|
| おさけ | 400 円 |
| ちゅうはい | 300 円 |

にほんご 1    Particles Summary: Memorization  (Essential particles up to Chapter 3)

(Set 1) (wa は, ga が, no の, ka か)

A.  Kore **wa** hon desu.                          A. これは、ほんです。
B.  Dore **ga** hon desu **ka**.                   B. どれが　ほんですか。
A.  Kore **ga** hon desu.                          A. これが　ほんです。
B.  Sore **wa** nan **no** hon desu **ka**.        B. それは、なんのほんですか。
A.  Kore **wa** Nihongo **no** hon desu.           A. これは、にほんごのほんです。

(Set 2) (de で[by means of], to と [to connect two nouns])

A.  Steak **wa** nan **de** tabemasu ka.           A. Steak は、なんで　たべますか。
B.  Knife **to** folk **de** tabemasu.  Sashimi **wa** nan **de** tabemasu ka.
                        B. Knife と folk で　たべます。さしみは、なんで　たべますか。
A.  O-hashi **de** tabemasu.                        A. おはしで　たべます。

(Set 3) (wo を [for direct objects])

A.  Kore **wo** kudasai.                            A. これを　ください。
B.  Dore desu ka.                                   B. どれですか。
A.  Sono aoi hon desu.                              A. その　あおいほんです。
B.  Ah, kore desu ka. Hai, doozo.                   B. ああ、これですか。はい、どうぞ。

 (Set 4) (de で [to end the choices], mo も [also])

A.  Kore to kore to kore wo kudasai. Min'na **de** ikura desu ka.    A. これとこれとこれを
                                    ください。みんなで　いくらですか。
B.  Min'na **de** 500 en desu.                      B. みんなで 500 えんです。
A.  Ah, kore **mo** kudasai.                        A. あ、これも　ください。
B.  Hai, arigatoo gozaimasu.                        B. はい、ありがとうございます。

(Set 5) idiom (~ ni shimasu ～にします。[I've decided on ~.])

A.  Dore **ni shimasu** ka. (Which one will you decide on?) A. どれにしますか。
B.  Kore **ni shimasu**.  (I'll decide on this one.)         B. これにします。

A.  Nan **ni shimasu** ka. (What will you have?)             A. なんにしますか。
B.  Supagetti **ni shimasu**.  Anata wa? (I'll have spagetti.  How about you?)
                                    B. Supagetti にします。あなたは？
A.  Watashi wa sandoicchi **ni shimasu**. (I'll have a sandwich.)
                                    A. わたしは sandoicchi にします。

# <u>Introduction to Kanji</u>

Introduction to Kanji

Basic rules of Kanji writing

About Kanji radicals

Kanji practice for Chapter 1

Kanji practice for Chapter 2A

Kanji Bingo for Chapter 1 & Chapter 2A

Kanji practice for Chapter 2B

Kanji practice for Chapter 3B

Kanji practice for Chapter 3C

Vocabulary list from Introduction to Kanji Chapter

# Introduction to Kanji

(1) Three types of Japanese writing systems and two or more ways of reading characters in the Kanji system

The Japanese writing system consists of three types: two are alphabet-based, Hiragana and Katakana, and one is character-based, Kanji. Aside from Hiragana and Katakana, the Japanese writing system makes extensive use of Kanji, which borrows characters from the Chinese language. When the Japanese adopted the characters, they also borrowed the Chinese way of reading them; and simultaneously, they also gave the characters Japanese readings based on existing vocabulary. As a result, a Kanji character has two (or sometimes more than two) readings. The Chinese pronunciation of Kanji is the "on" reading, and the Japanese, the "kun" reading. See the example below.

The kanji 大 means "big," and the Japanese word for "big" is "ookii." However, unlike the Chinese language, Japanese carries an inflection in its adjectives. Therefore, only the root of adjectives is written in Kanji, and its inflectional ending retains itself in hiragana. Thus, "ookii" is written as follows.

おお
大きい

As you see in the above example, the inflectional parts are written in Hiragana to maintain the Japanese pronunciation.

The Chinese sound of "dai" for this Kanji returns when it is part of a Chinese compound noun, such as "dai-gaku" (university). The Japanese word for university (daigaku) is thus written as follows.

だいがく
大学

As a principle, the Kanji in Chinese compound words are based on the "on" reading. But note there are exceptions. Japanese last names adopt the "kun" reading despite how they feature a string of two or more Kanji characters.

(2) Which part of a sentence do you write in Kanji?

In Japanese, Kanji is used mostly in nouns, as well as the stems of verbs, adjectives, and adverbs. Grammatical markers, such as particles and inflectional endings, are not written in Kanji. For example, the noun "watashi" and "sakana" are written in Kanji, 私 and 魚, and the verb stem "ta" of "tabemasu" is also written in Kanji 食. The particles は and を, as well as the verb endings べます are written in Hiragana.

私は 魚を 食べます。 （わたしは　さかなを　たべます。I eat fish.)

(3) Kanji use is based on "meaning," not on "sound."

A Kanji can only be used to delineate a specific meaning. Therefore, the Kanji for rice field "ta" cannot be substituted for the Kanji that appears in the word "tabemasu" (to eat). The former features the Kanji 田 , and the latter the Kanji 食 .

(4) A Kanji's stroke order is fixed.
Kanji is always written accordingly to a fixed stroke order. The general rule is to write from top to bottom and left to right, and horizontal lines are usually drawn before vertical lines. Chinese stroke orders are not necessarily the same as those of Japanese.

(5) History of Kanji:

Kanji originated as pictographs, and some of them still retain their pictorial qualities. For example, 月(moon) developed from a picture of the moon with clouds in the middle, and 川(river) from the picture of streaming water , and 山(mountain) from its geographic appearance. Other Kanji are ideographs that express concepts, rather than visual shape, such as the numbers 一 (one), 二 (two), 三 (three), 上 (above), 下 (below) and so forth. The exact number of existing Kanji has never been clear, but it is estimated to be more than 40,000. Approximately 3,000 Kanji are commonly used in Japan, and 1,945 Kanji have been decided as essential by the Ministry of Education for use in publications including newspapers and magazines.

(6) One of the most effective ways to learn Kanji: Via "radicals"

Learning Kanji may require labor, but once a certain number of Kanji has been learned, it becomes easier through association of character components. Kanji are classified accordingly to 214 basic components. They are also called "radicals" or "elements" and have core meanings. Therefore, learning Kanji with their components in mind helps you learn Kanji quickly and systematically. For example, once you learn the Kanji 言("i" u), which means "to say," learning Kanji such as 語 (language), 話 (speech), 読 (reading ), 訳 (translation), will begin to make sense through association. The complete list of 214 components can be found in any Kanji dictionary.

## Basic Rules of Kanji Writings

1. Make every kanji in the same size.
   Examples:
   ( O ) Good

   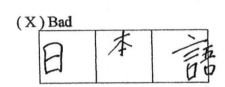

   ( X ) Bad

2. Follow the basic stroke order.
   (1) Write from left to right.

   (2) Write downward.

   (3) Write horizontal lines before vertical lines

   (4) Draw strokes from the top to the bottom.

   (5) Draw strokes from the left to the right.

   (6) Draw a square in the following way.

   (7) Where there is a figure in the square, the line which closes the square is
       drawn last.

   (8) When a stroke line passes through a square, draw that stroke last.

3. There are three basic ways to end a stroke.
   ① Stop ("tome")

   ② Hook ("hane")

   ③ Sweep ("harai")

## About Kanji Radicals ("bushu" 部首)

There are seven patterns in "bushu," based on their positions in the kanji characters. "Bushu" is not an absolute rule.  They only help us to learn kanji by classifications.

1) へん (left)

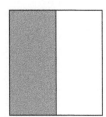

語池洋海神侍油作私
行後駅持低読飲秘校
知明帰初話押社動好
時住記切姉札晩妹助
曜和晴暗化信炊何強

2) つくり (right)

形　新
朝

3) かんむり (top; crown)

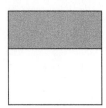

前家茶苦薬

花雪安赤
会合英若

4) たれ (top & left)

広　屋
度

5) にょう (left & bottom)

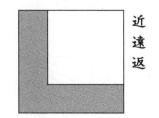

近　道
遠　通
返　週

6) あし (bottom)

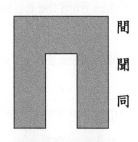

魚　怒
黒　思
煮

7) かまえ (enclosure)

間
聞
同

困
囚

医

Chapter 1

| 一<br>(one) | ひと（つ）<br>イチ | 一つ（ひとつ）one (thing)<br>一人（ひとり）one person<br>一月（いちがつ）January<br>一日（ついたち）1st day of the month |
| --- | --- | --- |
| | | (1) 一 |
| 二<br>(two) | ふた（つ）<br>ニ | 二つ（ふたつ）two (things)<br>二日（ふつか）2nd day of the month<br>二人（ふたり）two people<br>二月（にがつ）February |
| | | (2) 一 二 |
| 三<br>(three) | みっ（つ）<br>サン | 三つ（みっつ）three (things)<br>三日（みっか）3rd day of the month<br>三月（さんがつ）March<br>三人（さんにん）three people |
| | | (3) 一 二 三 |
| 四<br>(four) | よっ（つ）<br>よん／よ<br>シ | 四つ（よっつ）four (things)<br>四日（よっか）4th day of the month<br>四人（よにん）four people<br>四月（しがつ）April |
| | | (5) 丨 冂 冂 四 四 |
| 五<br>(five) | いつ（つ）<br>ゴ | 五つ（いつつ）five (things)<br>五日（いつか）5th day of the month<br>五月（ごがつ）May<br>五人（ごにん）five people |
| | | (4) 一 丁 五 五 |
| 六<br>(six) | むっつ<br>ロク<br>ロッ | 六つ（むっつ）six (things)<br>六日（むいか）6th day of the month<br>六月（ろくがつ）June<br>六人（ろくにん）six people |
| | | (4) 丶 亠 六 六 |

| 七<br>(seven) | なな（つ）<br>シチ<sub>しち</sub> | 七つ（ななつ）seven (things)<br>七日（なのか）7th day of the month<br>七月（しちがつ）July<br>七人（ななにん／しちにん）seven people |
| | | (2)<br>一 七 |
| 八<br>(eight) | やっ（つ）<br>ハチ<br>ハッ | 八つ（やっつ）eight (things)<br>八日（ようか）8th day of the month<br>八月（はちがつ）August<br>八人（はちにん）eight people |
| | | (2)<br>ノ 八 |
| 九<br>(nine) | ここの（つ）<br>ク<br>キュウ | 九つ（ここのつ）nine (things)<br>九日（ここのか）9th day of the month<br>九月（くがつ）September<br>九人（きゅうにん）nine people |
| | | (2)<br>ノ 九 |
| 十<br>(ten) | とお<br>ジュウ<br>ジュッ | 十（とお）ten (things)<br>十日（とおか）10th day of the month<br>十月（じゅうがつ）October<br>十人（じゅうにん）ten people |
| | | (2)<br>一 十 |
| 月<br>(moon, month) | つき<br>ガツ<br>ゲツ | 月（つき）the moon<br>三日月（みかづき）crescent moon<br>一月（いちがつ）July<br>一ヶ月（いっかげつ）one month<br>[月曜日（げつようび）Monday] |
| | | (4)<br>丿 刀 月 月 |
| 日<br>(day) | ひ／び／か<br>ニチ／ジツ<br>ニ | 日（ひ）the sun, a day<br>日本（にほん、にっぽん）Japan<br>一日（いちにち one day、ついたち 1st day of the month）<br>[日曜日（にちようび）Sunday] |
| | | (4)<br>丨 冂 日 日 |

Note: The reading superscript furigana beside シチ reads しち ち; beside ハチ reads はち; beside ハッ reads はっ; beside ク reads く; beside キュウ reads きゅう; beside ジュウ reads じゅう; beside ジュッ reads じゅっ; beside ガツ reads がっ; beside ゲツ reads げっ; beside ニチ／ジツ reads にち／じっ; beside ニ reads に.

**Kanji Practice for Chapter 1**   かんじの　れんしゅう (Months and Dates)

1.つぎの　かんじを　よみなさい。Read the following words aloud.

（１）　　一月、　二月、　三月、　四月、

（２）　　五月、　六月　、七月、　八月、

（３）　　九月、　十月、　十一月、　十二月

2.ただしいかきじゅんに　Oをつけましょう。Choose the one featuring the correct stroke order by placing a circle (O) in the space given.

1．四　　あ（　　）　　　　　4．七　　あ（　　）
　　　　い（　　）　　　　　　　　　い（　　）

2．五　　あ（　　）　　　　　5．九　　あ（　　）
　　　　い（　　）　　　　　　　　　い（　　）

3．六　　あ（　　）　　　　　6．十　　あ（　　）
　　　　い（　　）　　　　　　　　　い（　　）

3．よみかたを　ひらがなで　かきなさい。Write "yomigana" above each kanji.

①　一月一日　　　　　②　二月二日　　　　　③　三月三日

④　四月四日　　　　　⑤　五月五日　　　　　⑥　六月六日

⑦　七月七日　　　　　⑧　八月八日　　　　　⑨　九月九日

⑩　十月十日　　　　　⑪　十一月十一日　　　⑫　十二月十二日

⑬　一月二十日　　　　⑭　二月十四日　　　　⑮　四月二十四日

4. よみなさい。Read the following dates.

    a. 一日、二日、三日、四日、五日

    b. 六日、七日、八日、九日、十日

    c. 十一日、十二日、十三日、十四日

    d. 十五日、十六日、十七日、十八日、十九日

    e. 二十日、二十一日、二十二日、二十三日

    f. 二十四日、二十五日、二十六日、二十七日

    g. 二十八日、二十九日、三十日、三十一日

5. はじめに　よみなさい。それから、かんじに「よみがな（ふりがな）」を
かきなさい。Read the phrase, then write "yomigana" above each kanji.

    一. あつい日　　二. さむい日　　三. あたたかい日　　四. すずしい日

    五. きれいな月　　　六. アポロ<sup>あぼろ</sup>は、月に　いきました。
                       （Apollo went to the Moon.）

    七. お正月の一日、二日、三日は、三が日といいます。

    八. 一月は、「いく」の「い」です。
            （leave; go away）

    九. 二月は、「にげる」の「に」です。
            （run away; escape）

    十. 三月は、「さる」の「さ」です。It means that January, February,
          （leave）               and March go very quickly.

Kanji Practice for Chapter 1　かんじの　れんしゅう (Japanese numerals)

れんしゅう **1**. Write the following numbers in Arabic numerals.

① 十　　② 十六　　　③ 四十　　　④ 七十三　　⑤ 八十　　　⑥ 九十九

1.＿＿＿　2.＿＿＿　　3.＿＿＿　　4.＿＿＿　　5.＿＿＿　　6.＿＿＿

れんしゅう **2**. Write in kanji.

① ごじゅう　　② さんじゅうろく　　❸ よんじゅう　　　④ ななじゅうに
　　　　　　　　　　　　　　　　　　　　（よん＝し）　　　　（なな＝しち）

1.＿＿＿＿＿　2.＿＿＿＿＿　　　3.＿＿＿＿＿＿＿　　4.＿＿＿＿＿

⑤ ななじゅうきゅう　　⑥ きゅうじゅうきゅう　　⑦ ごじゅうはち
　（しちじゅうく）　　　　（くじゅうく）

5.＿＿＿＿＿　　　　6.＿＿＿＿＿　　　　　7.＿＿＿＿＿

Chapter 1 kanji (2)

| 本 | もと<br>ほ ん<br>ホ ン<br>ぼ ん<br>ポ ン<br>ぼ ん<br>ボ ン<br><br><br>(origin) | 山本（やまもと）a surname<br><br>日本（にほん、にっぽん）Japan<br>一本（いっぽん）one (long item)<br>三本（さんぼん）three (long items)<br>[本当（ほんとう）truth]<br>本人（ほんにん）the person him/herself |
| | | (5) 一 十 オ 木 本 |
| 円 | まる（い）<br>え ん<br>エ ン<br><br><br>(circle) | 円（えん）circle<br>十円（じゅうえん）ten yen (Japanese currency) |
| | | (4)<br>　丨 冂 冂 円 |

れんしゅう **3.**  Write the Japanese currency in kanji.

1. ごじゅうえん          2. よんじゅうえん          3. きゅうじゅうえん

-------------------          -------------------          -------------------

4. ろくじゅうえん          5. ななじゅうごえん          6. はちじゅうさんえん

-------------------          -------------------          -------------------


れんしゅう **4.** Write in kanji and hiragana.

1. にほん          2. いっぽん          3. さんぼん

-----------          -----------          -----------

4. こくばんに  えんを  かいてください。 (Please draw a circle on the blackboard.)

-----------------------------------------------------------------

5. ほんとうに  いいんですか。 (Are you sure [it's all right with you]?)

-----------------------------------------------------------------

6.  あれは、ほんやさんです。 (That's a bookstore.)

-----------------------------------------------------------------


れんしゅう **5.** Write yomigana to kanji.

-----------          -----------          -----------

1. 日本          2. 山本さん          3. 本<sup>や</sup>屋さん (bookstore)

-----------          -----------          -----------

4. 本当<sup>とう</sup>          5. 五十円          6. 円はまるいです。
   (truth)                                ("En" means round.)

Chapter 2 (A)

| 大 (large) | おお（きい）<br>ダイ<br>タイ | 大きい（おおきい）big<br>大学（だいがく）a college/university<br>*[大切（たいせつ）な important]<br>*大人（おとな）an adult |
|---|---|---|
| | | (3)<br>一 ナ 大 |
| 学 (to learn) | まな（ぶ）<br>ガク | 学ぶ（まなぶ）to learn<br>大学（だいがく）a college/university<br>学生（がくせい）a student |
| | | (8)<br>丶 ゛ ゛゛ ゛゛ 〩 学 学 学 |
| 生 (life, to live) | なま<br>い（きる）<br>き<br>セイ/ショウ | 生きる（いきる）to live<br>[生ビール（なまびいる）draft beer]<br>[生糸（きいと）raw silk]<br>大学生（だいがくせい）a college student |
| | | (5)<br>ノ ⺊ 牛 生 生 |
| 何 (what) | なに<br>なん<br>ナン | 何（なに、なん）what<br>何人（なんにん how many people、<br>　　　なにじん what nationality） |
| | | (7)<br>ノ イ 仁 仁 仔 何 何 |
| 白 (white) | しろ（い）<br>ハク/ビャク<br>パク | 白い（しろい）white<br>白人（はくじん）Caucasian |
| | | (5)<br>ノ イ 白 白 白 |
| 私 (I, private) | わたし<br>シ | 私（わたし）I<br>私学（しがく）a private school |
| | | (7)<br>一 ニ 千 矛 禾 私 私 |
| 犬 (a dog) | いぬ<br>ケン | 犬（いぬ）a dog<br>[秋田犬（あきたけん）Dogs from Akita<br>　　　　　prefecture] |
| | | (4)<br>一 ナ 大 犬 |

Kanji Practice for Chapter 2(A)
かんじの　れんしゅう

1. Read the following words to your classmates and ask them for the meaning of each word/phrase.

（1）　大きい

（2）　学ぶ、大学

（3）　生きる、学生、大学生

（4）　白い

（5）　私、私の大学

（6）　白い犬、私の犬

（7）　何月、何日

2. よんで、えいごでいいなさい。 Read first, then translate into English.

（1）　きょうは、四月一日です。きょうから、私は、大学生です。

（2）　「生きる」は、くろさわあきらの　えいがです。

（3）　十月十日は、私のたんじょう日です。

（4）　大学で　学ぶ。

（5）　私の大学は、大きい大学です。

3.  Fill in the blanks to complete a word or a phrase.

(1)  white dog

| | い | |
|---|---|---|

(2)  to live

| | き | |
|---|---|---|

(3)  college student

| 大 | | |
|---|---|---|

(4)  my dog

| | の | |
|---|---|---|

(5)  big dog

| | き | い | |
|---|---|---|---|

(6)  to learn

| | ぶ |
|---|---|

(7)  what month

| 何 | |
|---|---|

(8)  what day of the month

| | 日 |
|---|---|

これは、何<sub>なん</sub>ですか。犬<sub>いぬ</sub>ですか。

この木<sub>き</sub>は 私<sub>わたし</sub>の木<sub>き</sub>です。

これは、何<sub>なん</sub>の木<sub>き</sub>ですか。

この木<sub>き</sub>は、大<sub>おお</sub>きい木<sub>き</sub>ですね。

## Kanji Bingo Sheet (1) Chapter 1 & Chapter 2A
### Fill in the blanks with the kanji and play Bingo.

Kanji 一、二、三、四、五、六、七、八、九

| 四 | 三 | 二 |
|---|---|---|
| 一 | 六 | 八 |
| 九 | 五 | 七 |

| 五 | 一 | 四 |
|---|---|---|
| 二 | 八 | 六 |
| 七 | 三 | 九 |

| | | |
|---|---|---|
| | | |
| | | |

Kanji 大、学、生、本、何、円、月、日、十

| 大 | 本 | 何 |
|---|---|---|
| 学 | 月 | 十 |
| 生 | 日 | 円 |

| 学 | 何 | 本 |
|---|---|---|
| 生 | 月 | 日 |
| 大 | 十 | 円 |

| | | |
|---|---|---|
| | | |
| | | |

Kanji 大、学、生、私、何、白、月、日、犬

| | | |
|---|---|---|
| | | |
| | | |

| | | |
|---|---|---|
| | | |
| | | |

| | | |
|---|---|---|
| | | |
| | | |

Chapter 2 (B)

| 年<br><br>(a year, age) | とし<br>ねン<br>ネン | 年 （とし） a year, age<br><br>一年 （いちねん） one year<br>一年生 （いちねんせい） fresh man |
| | | (6)<br>丿 𠂉 仁 仁 年 年 |
| 語<br><br>(language,<br>to narrate) | かた（る）<br>ゴ | 語る （かたる） to narrate<br>［物語 （ものがたり） a story］<br><br>日本語 （にほんご） Japanese |
| | | (14)<br>丶 二 三 言 言 言 訂 訂 評 語 語<br>語 語 |
| 田<br><br>(rice field) | た<br>でン<br>デン | 田んぼ （たんぼ） rice field<br>田中 （たなか） a surname<br>山田 （やまだ） a surname<br>水田 （すいでん） a rice paddy |
| | | (5)<br>丨 冂 冊 田 田 |
| 山<br><br>(a mountain) | やま<br>さン<br>サン | 山 （やま） mountains<br>山々 （やまやま） mountains; having a strong<br>　　　　　　　　　desire to do~<br>［富士山 （ふじさん） Mt. Fuji］ |
| | | (3)<br>丨 山 山 |
| 来<br><br>(to come) | く（る）<br>き（ます）<br>こ（ない）<br>らイ<br>ライ | 来る （くる） to come<br>来ます （きます） come<br>来ない （こない） don't come<br>来日 （らいにち） coming to Japan |
| | | (7)<br>一 厂 厂 歪 平 来 来 |

Kanji Practice for Chapter 2 (B)
かんじの　れんしゅう

1．つぎの　かんじを　よみなさい。Read the following words.

    (1) 一年生と二年生 (freshman and sophomore)

    (2) 学年 (year at school)

    (3) 日本語

    (4) 語学 (languages)

    (5) 田んぼ (rice fields)、大田さん、山田さん

    (6) 来ます(to come)

2．はじめによんで、つぎにかんじにふりがな（よみがな）を　かきなさい。
Read first, then write hiragana above each kanji.

    （1）　あなたは、大学生ですか。

    （2）　学年は、二年生です。

    （3）　大田さんと山田さんが、来ます。

    （4）　日本語は、たのしいですか。(enjoyable)

    （5）　これは、私の大学です。

    （6）　何語を　はなしますか。（What language do you speak?）

Chapter 3 (B)

| 百 (a hundred) | ひゃ く<br>ヒャク<br>びゃ く<br>ビャク<br>ぴゃ く<br>ピャク | 百円 （ひゃくえん） one hundred yen<br>百年 （ひゃくねん） one hundred years<br>三百 （さんびゃく） three hundreds<br>六百 （ろっぴゃく） six hundreds |
| | | (6)<br>一 ｢ ｢ 百 百 百 |
| 小 (small) | ちい （さい）<br>こ<br>しょ う<br>ショウ | 小さい （ちいさい） small<br>[小鳥 （ことり） small birds]<br><br>小学生 （しょうがくせい） an elementary-<br>school student |
| | | (3)<br>亅 小 小 |
| 中 (in, inside, middle) | なか<br>ちゅ う<br>チュウ | 中 （なか） in, inside, middle<br>中学生 （ちゅうがくせい） a middle-school<br>student<br>中年 （ちゅうねん） middle age |
| | | (4)<br>丨 冂 口 中 |

ちゅうがくせい
中 学 生

## Kanji Practice for Chapter 3 (B)
かんじの　れんしゅう

1. よんでから、クラスメート<ruby>く<rt></rt>ら<rt></rt>す<rt></rt>め<rt></rt>え<rt></rt>と<rt></rt></ruby>にいみをききなさい。Read the following words to your classmates and ask them for the meaning of each word/phrase.

（１）　百年

（２）　三百円

（３）　小さい犬

（４）　小学生

（５）　中学生

（６）　うちの中

（７）　中田さんと山中さん

2. はじめによんで、それから、かんじにふりがな（よみがな）を　かきなさい。Read first, then write hiragana above each kanji.

（１）あなたは、中学生ですか。(junior high school student)

（２）小学生です。(an elementary school student)

（３）中田さんと山中さんが、来ます。

（４）これは、三百円です。

（５）小さい犬は、私の犬です。

（６）日本語を　二年　ならいました。(learned)

Chapter 3 (C)

| 千<br>(thousand) | ち<br>せん<br>セン | 千円（せんえん）a thousand yen<br>千年（せんねん）one thousand years |
| | | (3)　一　二　千 |
| 万<br>(ten thousands) | よろず<br>まん<br>マン | 一万円（いちまんえん）ten thousand yen<br>[八百万の神（やおよろずのかみ）millions of<br>deities] |
| | | (3)　一　フ　万 |
| 水<br>(water) | みず<br>すい<br>スイ | 水（みず）water<br>[水曜日（すいようび）Wednesday] |
| | | (4)　亅　オ　オ　水 |
| 女<br>(woman) | おんな<br>じょ<br>ジョ | 女の人（おんなのひと）a woman<br>女子（じょし）a girl<br>[女性（じょせい）women] |
| | | (3)　く　女　女 |
| 色<br>(colors) | いろ<br>しき<br>シキ<br>しょく<br>ショク | 水色（みずいろ）water color, light blue<br>色（いろ）えんぴつ color pencils<br>十二色（じゅうにしょく）a dozen color<br>[色彩（しきさい）coloring; a tint] |
| | | (6)　ノ　ク　ク　名　名　色 |
| 入<br>(to enter, insert) | はい（る）<br>い（れる）<br>にゅう<br>ニュウ | 入る（はいる）to enter<br>入れる（いれる）to insert<br>出入り（でいり）going in and out, entrance<br>and exit; regular visit<br>入学（にゅうがく）entrance to a school |
| | | (2)　ノ　入 |

## Kanji Practice for Chapter 3(C)
かんじの　れんしゅう

1．つぎの　ことばを　よみなさい。Read the following words to your partner
and ask for the English equivalents.

    （1）　　千年

    （2）　　千円

    （3）　　一万円

    （4）　　女の学生

    （5）　　お水

    （6）　　水色

    （7）　　うちの中に入る

2．かんじで　かきなさい。Write in kanji.

    （1）　　せんねん

    （2）　　せんえん

    （3）　　いちまんえん

    （4）　　おんなのがくせい

    （5）　　おみず

    （6）　　みずいろ

    （7）　　うちのなかにはいる

３．こえをだして、よみなさい。Read aloud.それから、かんじにふりがな
（よみがな）を　かきなさい。Then, write hiragana above kanji.

（１）この本は、水色です。

（２）お水を　ください。

（３）女のひとが、来ます。

（４）この本は、一万円です。

（５）「千と千尋の神隠し」の　えいがを　みましたか。
Did you see the movie, "The Spirited Away"?

（６）学生が、たくさん大学に　入りました。
Many students entered the college.

４．ひらがなとかんじで　かきなさい。
Write in hiragana and kanji, paying attention to particles and "okuri-gana."
The underlined words should be written in kanji.

    1.　Tanakasanwa kireina on'na no hito desu.

    2.　watashiwa daigakuni hairimashita.

    3.　sonohonwa mizuiro desu.

    4.　korewa, issenman'en no uchi desu.

Kanji Practice on Japanese Numerals (数かず).

**1.** Choose the correct numbers.

A. さんじゅうろく
   ① 306        ② 36        ③ 136        ④ 1036
   _____

B. ひゃくご
   ① 1005       ② 505       ③ 105        ④ 10005
   _____

C. さんびゃくにじゅうなな
   ① 327        ② 1327      ③ 3027       ④ 3207
   _____

D. せんごひゃくきゅうじゅういち
   ① 10591      ② 591       ③ 1591       ④ 15910
   _____

**2.** Read the following and translate into Arabic numerals.

1. ごじゅう          2. さんじゅうろく          3. よんじゅうはち

4. ななじゅうに    5. はちじゅうきゅう          6. きゅうじゅうきゅう

7. ひゃく    8. にひゃくろくじゅうご    9. さんびゃく  10. よんひゃく

11. ごひゃくにじゅう    12. ろっぴゃくさん          13. はっぴゃく

14. さんぜんごひゃく    15. ななひゃくきゅうじゅうよん

16. きゅうひゃくにじゅうなな          17. にせんよんひゃくろく

18. いっせん    19. ごせんさんびゃく    20. はっせんひゃくご

**3.** Write the following numbers in Arabic numerals.

① 五十    ② 三十六    ③ 四十八    ④ 七十二    ⑤ 八十九    ⑥ 九十九

1.___    2. _____    3. _____    4. _____    5. _____    6. _____

⑦ 百     ⑧ 三百     ⑨ 六百     ⑩ 千二百     ⑪ 三千五百     ⑫ 四千六百五

7._____     8. _____     9. _____ 10. _____     11. _____     12. _____

**4.**   Write in kanji.

① ごじゅう     ② さんじゅうろく     ③ よんじゅうはち     ④ ななじゅうに
                                    （よん＝し）             （なな＝しち）

1. _____     2. _____          3. _____          4. _____

⑤ はちじゅうきゅう     ⑥ きゅうじゅうきゅう   ⑦ ごひゃくにじゅう
   （はちじゅうく）        （くじゅうく）

5. _____     6. _____     7. _____

⑧ せんさんびゃく     ⑨ ななせんろっぴゃく   ⑩ さんぜんよんひゃく

8. _____     9. _____     10. _____

**5.** Read aloud in Japanese the following mathematical equations.  The plus sign (+) is pronounced "たす tasu", and the minus sign (-) is pronounced "ひく hiku." The topic marker は "wa" is used to pronounce the equal sign (=).

Examples:

$100 + 200 = 300$
         → ひゃく　たす　にひゃくは、さんびゃく　です。

$500 - 400 = 100$
         → ごひゃく　ひく　よんひゃくは、ひゃく　です。

Now try the followings in Japanese:

1. $200 + 500 =$               2. $300 - 100 =$

3. $650 + 70 =$                4. $1250 - 400 =$

5. $3910 + 90 =$               6. $47,000 - 2,000 =$

7. $304 + 88 =$                8. $9900 - 8800 =$

9. $500 + 600 =$               10. $128 - 28 =$

## Vocabulary List from Introduction to Kanji

1. Nouns

| | | |
|---|---|---|
| nama | なま | raw |
| eiga | えいが | movie |
| toshi | とし | age; year |
| monogatari | ものがたり | story; narrative |
| tanbo | たんぼ | rice field |
| Yamada | やまだ | last name |
| suiden | すいでん | rice paddy |
| rainichi | らいにち | coming to Japan |
| gakunen | がくねん | school year |
| gogaku | ごがく | languages |
| kotori | ことり | small bird |
| shoo-gakusei | しょうがくせい | elementary school students |
| chuu-gukusei | ちゅうがくせい | junior high school students |
| dai-gakusei | だいがくせい | college students |
| ichi-nichi-jyuu | いちにちじゅう | all-day long |
| jyoshi | じょし | girls |
| de-iri | でいり | coming in and out |
| iro | いろ | color |
| nani-iro | なにいろ | what color |
| mizu-iro | みずいろ | water color; light blue |
| nyuu-gaku | にゅうがく | entrance to school |

2. Adjectives

| | | |
|---|---|---|
| tanoshii | たのしい | enjoyable |

3. Verbs

| | | |
|---|---|---|
| nigeru | にげる | to run away; escape |
| saru | さる | to leave |
| manabu | まなぶ | to learn |
| ikiru | いきる | to live |
| kataru | かたる | to narrate |
| kuru | くる | to come |
| konai | こない | not come |
| naraimasu | ならいます | learn |
| hairu | はいる | to enter |

# **At a Campus Cafeteria**

Chapter 4A: Won't you eat with us?
*Expressions*
"Wont' you eat with us here?" "What is it that is called so and so?"
"What day is good for you?"
*Singing a Japanese song: "Under the Big Chestnut Tree"*
*Kanji practice from Chapter 4A*

Chapter 4B: How do you do? My major is Japanese.
*Expressions*
"My major is the same as you." "It's a school called Caltech."
"It's difficult; it's not difficult; it was difficult; it wasn't difficult."
"I know it." "I don't know it." "How do you say it in Chinese?"
*Kanji practice from Chapter 4B*
*Kanji Bingo from Chapter 4AB*
*Kanji Bingo from Chapters 3BC & 4AB*

Chapter 4C: Have you eaten spaghetti (here before)?
*Expressions*
"I haven't eaten it yet." "Which would you like better, coffee or tea?" "I like tea better."
"Which one is biggest among them?" "It's not as big as that."
*Kanji practice from Chapter 4C*

Chapter 4D: My family and hometown
*Expressions*
"How many siblings do you have?" "I'm a single child" "I'm the second child." "I have only five dollars." "I'll eat more because it's delicious."
*Kanji practice from Chapter 4D*

Chapter 4E: I get up at 6:30 A.M.
*Expressions*
"What time is it?" "It takes about 45 minutes by bus"
*Kanji practice from Chapter 4E*

*Kanji Review (Chapter 1 ~ 4E)*
*Review Exercise on Word Order and Particles*
*Kanji Bingo (Chapters 4CDE)*
*Kanji List for Japanese 1*

*Singing a Japanese song: The Ocean*

Ookina    kuri no ki no shita de   (Under the Big Chestnut Tree)
おおきなくりの きの　したで

> おおきな　くりの　きのしたで
> Under the big chestnut tree,
> あなたとわたし、なかよくあそびましょ
> Let's play together, you and I,
> おおきな　くりの　きのしたで。
> Under the big chestnut tree.

Chapter 4 (A)　　　At a Campus Cafeteria　　だいがく
大学のカフェテリアで

Won't you eat with us?　いっしょに　たべませんか。

せんせい：あら、モニカさん。　　　　　　　　　　　　　　　　　1

モニカ：　あ、せんせい。せんじつは、ありがとうございました。　2

せんせい：いいえ。きょうは、ひとりですか。　　　　　　　　　3

モニカ：　はい。　　　　　　　　　　　　　　　　　　　　　　4

せんせい：じゃ、あちらで　みんなと　たべませんか。　　　　　5

モニカ：　いいんですか。　　　　　　　　　　　　　　　　　　6

せんせい：もちろんですよ。　　　　　　　　　　　　　　　　　7

[English translation]:

Professor:　Oh, Monica.
Monica:　　Ah, professor.　Thank you so much (for the favor) the other day.
Professor:　Not at all.　Are you alone, today?
Monica:　　Yes.
Professor:　Then, won't you eat with us (= everybody) over there?
Monica:　　Is it all right?
Professor:　Of course.

Chapter 4 (A)  Vocabulary List

### 1. Expressions

| | |
|---|---|
| ～ませんか masen ka? | "Won't you ~?" (invitation) |
| たべませんか  tabemasen ka | "Won't you eat?" |
| ～んですか n desu ka? | (Adds a strong sense of inquiry in question form) |
| いいんですか Ii n desu ka | "Are you sure it is really all right?" |

| | |
|---|---|
| ～よ yo. (affirmation) | (= I tell you.) |
| もちろんですよ  mochiron desu yo | "Certainly it is all right." |
| いつ？ (interrogative pronoun) | When? |

(Interjections)

| | |
|---|---|
| あら ara | feminine "oh," to show surprise (Men should use "おや oya" instead.) |

### 2. Nouns

| | |
|---|---|
| せんじつ senjitsu | the other day |
| みんな min'na | everyone |
| ひとり hitori | one person, alone |

Important additional nouns to remember (days of the week)

| | |
|---|---|
| なんようび nan-yoobi | What day of the week? |
| にちようび nichi-yoobi | Sunday |
| げつようび getsu-yoobi | Monday |
| かようび ka-yoobi | Tuesday |
| すいようび sui-yoobi | Wednesday |
| もくようび moku-yoobi | Thursday |
| きんようび kin-yoobi | Friday |
| どようび do-yoobi | Saturday |

### 3. Adverbs

| | |
|---|---|
| もちろん mochiron | certainly, of course |

### 4. Particles

| | |
|---|---|
| で de | indicates the location in which an action takes place |
| あちらで　たべませんか Achira de tabemasen ka | "Won't you eat with us (at) over there?" |

| | |
|---|---|
| と to | with (someone) |
| みんなと min'na to | with everyone |

### 5. Essential verbs to remember

| | | | |
|---|---|---|---|
| みます mimasu (see) | | かいます kaimasu (buy) |

あげます agemasu (give)

あけます akemasu (open)

しめます shimemasu (close)

かります karimasu (borrow)

のります norimasu (ride)

あいます aimasu (meet; see)

します shimasu (do)

      しごと**(を)**します      shigoto (wo) shimasu (work)

      ちゅうもん（を）します     chuumon (wo) shimasu (order)

      かいもの（を）します     kaimono (wo) shimasu (shop)

かえします kaeshimasu (return s.t.)

すいます suimasu (smoke; inhale)

おどります odorimasu (dance)

およぎます oyogimasu (swim)

おります orimasu (get off)

(いきます) ikimasu (go)

(きます) kimasu (come)

(かえります) kaerimasu (return)

----------------------------------------------------------------------------------------------------

## Additional Vocabulary from Grammar Notes, Exercises, and Dict-A-Conversation

----------------------------------------------------------------------------------------------------

[Nouns]

(locations)

| | | |
|---|---|---|
| としょかん | toshokan | library |
| ゆうびんきょく | yuubin-kyoku | post office |
| えいがかん | eiga-kan | movie theater |
| さかや | saka-ya | liquor shop |
| さかなや | sakana-ya | fish market |
| どうぶつえん | doobutsu-en | zoo |
| ぎんこう | ginkoo | bank |
| こうえん | kooen | park |
| けいむしょ | keimusho | prison |
| びょういん | byooin | hospital |

コンビニ      konbini      convenience store

スーパー      uupaa      super market

プール      puuru      swimming pool

(food)

ごはん      gohan      cooked rice

おかず      okazu      dishes to go with the rice

ポップコーン      poppukoon      popcorn

(daily goods)

はみがき      ha-migaki      tooth paste

はブラシ      ha-burashi      tooth brush

かんでんち      kandenchi      batteries

てがみ      tegami      letters

チケット/けん      chiketto/ ken      ticket

セール      seeru      sale

(others)

あした      ashita      tomorrow

コンサート      konsaato      concert

[な Adjectives/Copula Nouns]

ひま      hima      free (time); not occupied

[Adjectives]

おもしろい      omoshiroi      interesting; fun

(いたい)      itai      painful

[Adverbs]

いっしょに      isshoni      together

また      mata      again

ぜひ      zehi      by all means

[Expressions]

よかった！      Yokatta!      Good!

どようびは、ちょっと      Doyoobi wa chotto...      I cannot make Saturday.

ざんねんですね。      Zan'nen desu ne.      That's too bad.

さそってください。      Sasotte kudasai.      Please invite me.

ほんと（う）ですか。      Honto(o) desu ka.      Is it true?

どうして？      Dooshite?      Why?

Chapter 4 (A)                    Grammar and Cultural Notes

## 1. ～ませんか。 "~ masen ka": Invitation/suggestion (Shall we~? Won't we~?)

You can suggest an action by using the expression "～ませんか masen ka." This form is obtained simply by changing the "ます masu" form of the verb to "ませんか masen ka." The expression is similar to "～ましょうか mashoo ka," though the latter is also used when the listener is not involved in the action. For example, you may offer help carrying a heavy luggage for an elderly person. It would be only you who carries the luggage when you use "～ましょうか mashoo ka" (おてつだいしましょうか。 otetsudai shimashoo ka, or わたしがもちましょうか。 watshi ga mochimashoo ka); so the focus is more on the speaker's action than that of the listener. Conversely, the expression "～ませんか masen ka" implies actions done together between the speaker and the listener; and thus focus is placed more on the listener's action than that of the speaker.

## 2. Particle "で de" to indicate place of action

| で |
|---|

In line 5 of Chapter 4 (A)'s dialogue, the professor indicated dining location in the following Japanese sentence: "あちら　で　たべませんか。 achira de tabemasen ka (Won't you eat [with us] over there?)" As such, particle "de" shows the location of action, whereas particle "ni" shows the location of existence. Thus, in the previous chapter [Chapter 3(C)], particle "ni" in such a sentence as "あちらにエレベーターがございます。 achira ni erebeetaa ga gozaimasu (polite form of 'arimasu')" shows the location where the elevator is; and in this chapter, particle "で de" in such a sentence as "あちらでたべませんか。 achira de tabemasen ka" indicates the location of the "eating" action.

Examples:
(1) ここで　たべませんか。          Won't we eat here?
    koko de    tabemasen ka.
(2) がっこうで　します。          I'll do it at school.
    gakkoo de        shimasu.
(3) うちで　おちゃを　のみます。      I'll drink tea at home.
    uchi de    ocha wo      nomimasu.
(4) カフェテリアで　サンドイッチを　たべませんか。 Won't we eat the
    kafeteria de        sandoicchi wo       tabemasen ka.      sandwich in the cafeteria?
(5) えいがかんで　えいがを　みませんか。 Shall we watch a movie at a movie
    eiga-kan de    eiga wo       mimasen ka.      theater?
(6) としょかんで　しゅくだいを　しませんか。 Shall we do the homework in the
    toshokan de    shukudai wo       shimasen ka.      library?

### 3. <u>Particle "の no" or "ん n" to enhance reasoning/explanation</u>

As the Professor suggested Monica to join her (and the others), Monica asked "いいんで
すか ii n desu ka" (Is it all right?)  A sense of inquiry is enhanced by the particle "の no";
or actually, its short form "ん n." Her statement sounds as if she is saying "Are you sure
it is truly all right?" while "いいですか ii desu ka," without "ん n," sounds more
affirmative, and at times aggressive.  But when an instructor asks his/her students
whether they have understood the materials, s/he would very appropriately ask, "いいで
すか ii desu ka," and not "いいんですか ii n desu ka." And lastly, if a speaker wants to
see whether his/her listener is ready, the former should ask "いいですか ii desu ka?"
Examine the following situations:

(1)
A: これを　あげましょう。 kore wo agemashoo. (I shall give this to you.)

B: いいんですか。 ii n desu ka?  (Are you sure it is really all right? [a strong sense of
<u>inquiry</u>])

A: いいんですよ。 ii n desu yo.  (Yes, it is [I have a good reason to do so] [speaker's
attempt to <u>explain</u>])

B: すみません sumimasen.  (Thank you very much. [Literally: Sorry to burden you.])

(2)
Professor: このもんだいを　してください。 kono mondai wo shite kudasai. (Please
do this problem.)

いいですか。　　　 ii desu ka?　(All right? [You heard me, right?] or [Are
you ready?])

Students: はい、わかりました。 hai. wakarimashita.  (Yes, we understood.)

(3)
A: まどを　しめなさい。いいですね。 mado wo shimenasai.  ii desu ne.
(Close your window.  All right?)

B: はい。 Hai.　　　　　　　　 (Yes.)

(4)
A: まどを　しめても　いいですか。 mado wo shimete mo ii desu ka.
(May I close the window?)

B: いいですよ。　　　　　　　 ii desu yo.　　(It's all right.)

(5)
A: まどを　しめても　いい<u>ん</u>ですか。 mado wo shimete mo ii <u>**n**</u> desu ka.

(Are you sure that I can close the window? [Are you sure? Because you normally don't like the window closed] or [Are you sure? You just told me to open it.]

B: いいですよ。ii desu yo. Or, いいんですよ。ii n desu yo.

(Its' all right [because I am going to sleep now.] or [It's all right [since it is cold tonight.]

The expression "んです n desu" (or "のです no desu,"formal style) implies a **"sense of inquiry"** when it is used in a question; and on the other hand, it implies a speaker's **"attempt to explain"** when it is used in an answer. A sentence with "ん n" also gives a more "personal" feeling to a statement, while a sentence without "ん n" or "の no" may sound more objective. Imagine which expression, with or without "ん n", will a doctor choose to inquire what is wrong with his/her patient. Doctors, who need to stand objectively to examine a patient's illness, will probably choose a sentence without "ん n." How about from friends or family? They may choose the expression using "ん n," upon trying to find out what's wrong with you. Using "ん n" sounds more personal and subjective.

(1)
Doctor: どうしましたか。doo shimashita ka. (What's wrong?)

Patient: ちょっと　おなかが　いたい<u>ん</u>です。chotto onaka ga itai n desu.
(It's because my stomach hurts.)

(2)
Your friend: どうした<u>ん</u>ですか。doo shita n desu ka. (What's wrong?)
　　　　　どうした<u>の</u>？　　　　doo shita no?

You: ちょっと　おなかが　いたい<u>ん</u>です。chotto onaka ga itai n desu. Or,
　　 ちょっと　おなかが　いたい<u>の</u>。　　chotto onaka ga itai no.
(It's because my stomach hurts.)

## 4. <u>Question word "When?"</u> いつ？

When you want to ask about the time frame, you can use "itsu" to make it non-specific, instead of asking exactly "what time," "what month," or "what year." See examples:

A: テストは　いつですか。　　　　　　A: テストは、何曜日ですか。
B: あしたです。　　　　　　　　　　　B: 金曜日です。

A: 誕生日は　いつですか。　　　　　　A: 誕生日は、何月何日ですか。
B: 五月十日です。　　　　　　　　　　B: 五月十日です。

Chapter 4(A) Exercises

A. Association exercises: Connect right (actions) and left (locations).

1.　えき　　　　　　　　　　　　A．ねます

2.　としょかん　　　　　　　　　B．コーヒーを　のみます

3.　えいがかん　　　　　　　　　C．さんぽをします

4.　スーパー　　　　　　　　　　D．べんきょうします

5.　さかや　　　　　　　　　　　E．サンドイッチをかいます

6.　デパート　　　　　　　　　　F．でんしゃに　のります

7.　きっさてん　　　　　　　　　G．スカートを　かいます

8.　コンビニ　　　　　　　　　　H．おさけを　かいます

9.　こうえん　　　　　　　　　　I．えいがを　みます

10.　ベッド　　　　　　　　　　　J．やさいを　かいます

B. Fill in the blanks with appropriate words and particles.

わたしは、きょう ほんやさんで、（　　　　　　）を　かいました。そして、それ
をとしょかんで（　　　　　　　　）。とてもおもしろい、いいほんでした。そ
れから、でんしゃに（　　　　）ました。でんしゃを　ぎんざ（　　）おりま
した。ぎんざのきっさてんで、コーヒーを（　　）ました。おいしかったです。
そのきっさてんで、ともだちに（　　　　　　）。ともだちは、きょねん
(last year) フランスから　（　　　　　　　　）。えいごとフランスごで、
（　　　　）ました。たのしかったです。

C. In-class Activity (group or a pair): そこで　なにを　しますか。
Place a deck of card face-down. Take turn in picking up one card at a time without
showing it to the rest of the group. Take turn in asking a question, using "masu-form"
verb. The card-holder answers only "yes," or "no." When you guessed the name of the
place, tell that to the card-holder. If you guessed right, you get that card.
[Places]:

ぎんこう bank、デパートdepartment store、スーパーsupermarket、きょうし
つ classroom、としょかん library、こうえん park、ほんや bookstore、えいが
かん movie theater、レストランrestaurant、プールswimming pool、ひこうき
airplane（のなか inside）、びょういん hospital、ゆうびんきょく post
office、けいむしょ prison、どうぶつえん zoo、でんしゃ train（のなか
inside）、きっさてん coffee shop、ビアガーデンbeer garden (often on the
roof-top of a department store where you can drink beer)、コンビニ
convenience store、さかや liquor store、さかなや fish market

[verbs]:

たべます eat、みます watch/see、のみます drink、ねます sleep、かいます buy、
はなします talk/speak、あるきます walk、しごとをします work、たばこをすいま
す smoke cigarettes、あそびます play、おどります dance、かります borrow、いれ
ます insert/put in、かえします return、およぎます swim、かきます write、よみま
す read、ちゅうもんします order、べんきょうします study、ききます listen

Example (1):

Student 2:  そこで　ごはんを　たべますか。
Student 1:  いいえ。
Student 3:  そこで　本を　よみますか。
Student 1:  いいえ。
Student 2:  そこで　ビールを　のみますか。
Student 1:  いいえ。
Student 4:  そこで　おさけを　かいますか。
Student 1:  はい、そうです。
Student 4:  コンビニですね？
Student 1:  いいえ。
Student 2:  そこで　おさけだけ　かいますか。
Student 1:  はい、そうです。
Student 2:  じゃ、さかやです。

Example (2):

Student 2:  そこで　あそびますか。
Student 1:  いいえ。
Student 3:  そこで　本を　よみますか。
Student 1:  はい。
Student 2:  きょうしつですか。
Student 1:  いいえ。
Student 4:  としょかんですか。
Student 1:  はい、そうです。

D. Guess what place is being described in the following statements. どこですか。

List of places:

レストラン、デパート，コンビニ，きっさてん、ほんや (bookstore)、
としょかん (library)、えいがかん (movie theatre)、きょうしつ(classroom)、
ゆうびんきょく (post office)、さかや(liquor store)、どうぶつえん(zoo)、
ビアガーデン(beer garden)、

1. ぞう(elephants) や さる(monkeys) や ライオン(lions)などが おり
(cage)のなかにいます。                                    etc.

    ------------------------------

2. こくばんや つくえや いすなどが、あります。ここに、せんせいと
   がくせいが います。ここで べんきょうします。

    ------------------------------

3. デパートのおくじょうにあります。ここで おとながビールをのみます。

    ------------------------------

4. おおきいたてものの なかで、みんなでえいがをみます。よく、ポップコ
   ーンをたべます。                                    often

    ------------------------------

5. ここで、コーヒーやこうちゃをのみます。サンドイッチやカレーもありま
   す。はじめに、ちゅうもんします。ウエイターやウエイトレスさんがいま
   す。at first

    ------------------------------

6. ここに、ほんが たくさんあります。ここで、ほんをよみます。べんきょ
   うも します。

    ------------------------------

7. ここに おさけが たくさんあります。ここで おさけを かいます。
   でも、ここで おさけを のみません。

    ------------------------------

8. ここに ほんやざっしが たくさんあります。ここで、ほんや ざっしを
   かいます。

    ------------------------------

9. ここは、ちいさいです。しんぶん、ざっし、パン、おかし(snacks, sweets)、
おにぎり(rice ball)、おかず(dishes to go with rice)、のみもの (drinks)、
はみがき(toothpaste)、はブラシ (toothbrush)、かんでんち (batteries)、など
が あります。ここで かいものを します。

-----------------------------

10. ここで、きって (stamps)を かいます。てがみを だします(send a letter)。

-----------------------------

11. おおきいたてものです。ここで かいものをします。ちかに たべもの
(food)が あります。いっかいに、ハンカチや、けしょうひん(cosmetics)
や、ネクタイがあります。

-----------------------------

12. ここで おいしいものをたべます。ワインものみます。はじめに、
メニューをみます。そして、ウエイターやウエイトレスさんに、ちゅう
もんします。

-----------------------------

E. Pair-work: Invitation ～ませんか (Shall we ～?) and respond ～ましょう (Let's ～).
First, practice the dialogues below; then alternate the underlined words with a different
ending and practice new dialogues with your partner.

[Basic Pattern]
Q: コンサートにいき<u>ませんか</u>。 Shall we go to a concert?
A: ええ、いき<u>ましょう</u>。　　　 Yes, let's go.

(1) Practice the dialogue A:

A: いっしょに、<u>えいが</u>に いきませんか。
B: いつ [when]ですか。
A: あしたなんですが、、
B: いいですよ。いきましょう。
A: よかった *^_^*

[Replace "movie" with your own words, such as "restaurant, shopping, driving, "etc.]

(2) Practice the dialogue B:

A:  コンサートの<ruby>けん<rt>こ ん さ と</rt></ruby>がありますから、いっしょにいきませんか。

B:   いつ [when]ですか。

A:   ２４<ruby>日<rt>にじゅうよっか</rt></ruby>のどようびです。

B:   すみません、どようびは、ちょっと、、

A:   そうですか。ざんねんですね。


(Vocabulary help: けん ticket, also <ruby>チケット<rt>ち け っ と</rt></ruby>)


[Replace "concert" with "movie, Kabuki, Sumo (Japanese wrestling), baseball," etc.]


(3) Practice the dialogue C:

A:  <u>きんようび</u>は、ひまですか。

B:  <u>きんようび</u>ですか。どうして？

A:  <ruby>パーティー<rt>ぱ あ て ぃ い</rt></ruby>に　いきませんか。

B:   すみません。その<ruby>日<rt>ひ</rt></ruby>は、ちょっと、、

A:   そうですか。

B:   また、さそってください。 (Please invite me again)

A:   そうします。

(Vocabulary help: ひま free, open, どうして why?)


[Replace "Friday" with any other day of the week, and "party" with different events: "rock concert, festival, shopping, movie," etc.]

(4) Fill in the blanks with your partner, following the below pattern.

```
A: _____は、ひまですか。
B: はい、ひまですが、、、
A: _____に　いきませんか。
   _____が _____んです。
B: ほんとですか。ぜひ！
```

Example 1:
   Ａ：（ど）ようび、ひまですか。
   Ｂ：はい、ひまですが、、、
   Ａ：（えいが）に　いきませんか。
      （あたらしい<ruby>アニメ<rt>あ に め</rt></ruby>）が　（おもしろい）んです。
   Ｂ：ほんとですか。ぜひ！

Example 2:

 A： （きん）ようび、ひまですか。

 B：はい、ひまですが、、、

 A： （デパート）に　いきませんか。

  （セーター）が　（セール）なんです。

 B：ほんとですか。ぜひ！

F. Group work:  Group up in teams of five and have each member create a deck of cards
 following the five themes: (1) Topic (Who), (2) Time (When), (3) With Whom
 (4) Location (Where), and (5) Verb or Object + Verb (what s/he will do or did).  Once
 everyone completes writing the five to ten words on their cards, line up each deck in
 the above order.  Then pick up a card at a time from each deck to frame a complete
 sentence.  You must use particles including "wa," "de," "to," and "wo."

Example, （１）けんじさんは、（２）きのう　（３）けいこさんと
    （４）レストランで　（５）ごはんを　たべました。

| (1) Who だれ （が→は） | (2) When いつ | (3) with whom だれと | (4) Where どこで | (5) What なにをします （しました）か |
|---|---|---|---|---|
| ～は | | ～と | ～で | |
| けんじさんは | きのう | けいこさんと | レストランで | ごはんをたべました。 |
| キムさんは | あした | ともだちと | デパートで | かいものをします。 |
| トムさんは | きょう | ひとりで | としょかんで | べんきょうしました。 |
| | | | | |
| | | | | |
| | | | | |

Chapter 4 (A): Dict-A-Conversation (1)   Counter for people.
Respond to the statements verbally, and then write down your replies.  Please answer in
<u>complete sentences,</u> writing in hiragana.

1 . _____    2. _____

3. _____    4. _____

5. _____    6. _____

7. _____    8. _____

9. _____    10. _____

Chapter 4 (A): Dict-A-Conversation (2)   Invitation/suggestion ~ masen ka?
Respond to the statements verbally, and write your answers in hiragana.

1. _____

2. _____

3. _____

4. _____

5. _____

6. _____

7. _____

8. _____

9. _____

10. _____

Chapter 4 (A)

| 先<br><br>(ahead) | さき、ま（ず）<br>せん<br>セン<br><br> | この先（さき）ahead of this point<br>先ず（まず）first of all<br>先生（せんせい）a teacher<br>先人（せんじん）a predecessor |
| --- | --- | --- |
| | | (6)<br>ノ 　 ┌ 　 ┴ 　 生 　 歩 　 先 |
| 人<br><br>(a person) | ひと<br>じん<br>ジン<br>にん<br>ニン<br> | いい人（ひと）a nice person<br>日本人（にほんじん）a Japanese<br>三人（さんにん）three people |
| | | (2)<br>ノ 　 人 |
| 今<br><br>(now, present) | いま<br>こん<br>コン<br> | ただ今（ただいま）right now; I'm home.<br>　　　　　　　　　　　　　　(greeting)<br>今日（きょう）today<br>今月（こんげつ）this month |
| | | (4)<br>ノ 　 ∧ 　 ∧ 　 今 |
| 上<br><br>(above, high) | うえ<br>のぼ（り、る）<br>じょう<br>ジョウ<br> | 目上（めうえ）social superiors, the older<br>上る（のぼる）to climb<br>上り（のぼり）trains that go to Tokyo |
| | | (3)<br>｜ 　 ┠ 　 上 |
| 下<br><br>(below, under) | した<br>くだ（り、る）<br>げ<br>ゲ<br>か<br>カ<br> | 目下（めした）social inferiors, the younger<br>下る（くだる）to descend<br>下り（くだり）trains that move away from<br>　　　　　　　　　　　　　　Tokyo<br>上下（じょうげ）rankings (the top and bottom<br>in social status) |
| | | (3)<br>一 　 丁 　 下 |

## Kanji Practice for Chapter 4(A)
かんじの　れんしゅう

1. つぎの　ことばを　よみなさい。Read the following words to your
   classmates and ask them for the meaning of each word/phrase.

| | | | | |
|---|---|---|---|---|
| （1） | えんぴつの先 | | （7） | 今日 |
| （2） | 先生 | | （8） | つくえの上 |
| （3） | 先月 | | （9） | いすの下 |
| （4） | 先日 | | （10） | 日本人の女の人 |
| （5） | 今 | | （11） | 来年 |
| （6） | 今月 | | （12） | 来月 |

2. かんじで　かきなさい。Write in kanji and hiragana.

（1）　えんぴつのさき

（2）　いすのうえ

（3）　ほんのした

（4）　おんなのがくせい

（5）　きょうのてんき

（6）　こんげつ

（7）　せんせい

3. よんでから、かんじによみがなを　かきなさい。それからえいごで
いいなさい。 **Read the sentence first, then write yomigana to kanji, and translate the sentence into English.**


(1) つくえの上の本は、水色です。


(2) つくえの下に大きい犬がいます。


(3) 今、女の人が、来ます。


(4) 先生は、きょうしつの中です。


(5) 今日は、学生が　先に、きょうしつに入りました。


(6) 今年は、たくさんの学生が　大学に　入りました。


(7) 日本語の本を　ください。


(8) 中山さんは、先月、日本から来ました。


(9) 来年は、何年ですか。


(10) 来月、日本へ　いきます。

**Chapter 4 (B)**　はじめまして。私のせんこうは、日本語です。
　　　　　　　　**How do you do?  My major is Japanese.**

せんせい：みなさん、こちらは、モニカさんです。　　　　　　　　　　　1

みんな：　はじめまして。　　　　　　　　　　　　　　　　　　　　　2

モニカ：　はじめまして。どうぞよろしく。　　　　　　　　　　　　　3

みんな：　こちらこそ。　　　　　　　　　　　　　　　　　　　　　　4

せんせい：モニカさんは、二年生です。あいこさんとおなじですね。　　5

あいこ：　モニカさん、せんこうは、何ですか。　　　　　　　　　　　6

モニカ：　日本語です。　　　　　　　　　　　　　　　　　　　　　　7

あいこ：　そう。私は、まだ　わかりません。　　　　　　　　　　　　8

てつや：　ぼくは、「てつや」と　言います。こう学ぶの　三回生です。　9

モニカ：　「三回生」って？　　　　　　　　　　　　　　　　　　　　10

せんせい：　きょうとでは、「三回生」と言いますが、ふつうは、　　　11

　　　　　　「三年生」と言いますよ。　　　　　　　　　　　　　　　12

モニカ：　ああ、そうなんですか。　　　　　　　　　　　　　　　　　13

みわ：　　わたしは、四回生の「みわ」です。せんこうは、ぶつり学です。　14

モニカ：　ぶつり？　むずかしいですか。　　　　　　　　　　　　　　15

みわ：　　すごく、むずかしいです。　　　　　　　　　　　　　　　　16

モニカ：　へえ、たいへんですね。　　　　　　　　　　　　　　　　　17

[English translation]:

Professor:  Everyone, this is Monica.
Everyone:  How do you do?
Monica:    How do you do?  Nice to meet you.
Everyone:  The pleasure is ours.
Professor:  Monica is a sophomore.  She is in the same grade as Aiko.
Aiko:       Monica, what is your major?
Monica:    Japanese.
Aiko:       Is that right?  I don't know (much about it) yet.
Tetsuya:   I am Tetsuya.  I'm a junior [majoring] in Engineering.
Monica:    (What is) "San-kai-sei"?
Professor:  In Kyoto, we say "san-kai-sei," but usually it is referred to as "san-nen-sei."
Monica:    Oh, is that right?
Miwa:      I am Miwa.  I'm a senior.  My major is in Physics.
Monica:    Physics?  Is it hard?
Miwa:      Very hard.
Monica:    Wow, (it) must be a lot of work.

Chapter 4 (B)                     Vocabulary List

## 1. Expressions

| | | |
|---|---|---|
| そうなんですか | Soo na n desu ka | "Is that so?"  That's the reason.  That's why. |
| へえ | Hee | "Hmm", "Wow" |
| って（なんですか） | ~tte (nan desu ka) | short form of "to (iu no wa)" quotation particle:  What is it that is called ~? |

## 2. Nouns

| | | |
|---|---|---|
| にねんせい | ni-nen-sei | sophomore; second-year student |
| おなじ | onaji | same |
| ~とおなじです | ~ to onaji desu | It's the same as ~ . |
| せんこう | senkoo | major |
| そう | soo | so |
| こうがくぶ | koogaku-bu | Engineering Department |
| さんかいせい | san-kai-sei | junior; the same as "san-nen-sei," third year student |
| よんかいせい | yon-kai-sei | senior; the same as "yo-nen-sei," fourth year student |
| ぶつり（がく） | butsuri-gaku | Physics |

## 3. な Adjectives/Copula nouns

| | | |
|---|---|---|
| たいへん | taihen | hard work, a lot of work |

## 4. Adjectives

| | | |
|---|---|---|
| むずかしい | muzukashii | hard, difficult |
| やさしい | yasashii | easy |

## 5. Verbs

| | | |
|---|---|---|
| いいます | ii masu | polite form of "iu" (to say) |
| ~といいます | ~ to iimasu | It is said that~  ("と to" is a quotation) |
| わかりません | wakarimasen | don't know; negative form of "wakarimasu" |

## 6. Adverbs

| | | |
|---|---|---|
| ふつう | futsuu | usually, ordinarily |
| すごく | sugoku | casual form "very," awesome |

..................................................................................................

Additional Vocabulary from Grammar Notes, Exercises, and Dict-A-Conversation

..................................................................................................

[Nouns]

| | | |
|---|---|---|
| かれ | kare | he, boyfriend |
| かれら | karera | they |

| | | |
|---|---|---|
| かのじょ | kanojyo | she, girlfriend |
| かのじょたち | kanojyo-tach | they |
| あのひとたち | ano-hito-tachi | they |
| たなかさんたち | Tanaka san tachi | Tanaka-san and his/her group |
| ど | ~do | degree |
| ひゃくど | hyaku-do | one hundred degrees |
| れいぞうこ | reizouko | refrigerator |
| プリンセス・ダイアナ | purinsesu daiana | Princess Diana |
| あめ | ame | rain |
| アイデア | aidea | idea |
| たんご | tango | vocabulary |
| しゅくだい | shukudai | homework |
| そら | sora | sky |
| まち | machi | town |
| おたく | otaku | fanatic |
| ぶしどう | Bushido | the way of warriors |
| いりぐち | iriguchi | entrance |
| でぐち | deguchi | exit |

(food)

| | | |
|---|---|---|
| あんパン | an-pan | bread with sweet red beans |
| なし | nashi | Japanese pear |
| とうもろこし | toomorokoshi | corn |
| （お）べんとう | o-bentoo | boxed lunch |
| かぼちゃ | kabocha | Japanese squash |

(insects/birds)

| | | |
|---|---|---|
| みみずく | mimizuku | horned owl |
| せみ | semi | cicada |
| とかげ | tokage | lizard |

(academic subjects)

| | | |
|---|---|---|
| すうがく | suugaku | Mathematics |
| こうがく | koogaku | Engineering |
| かがく | kagaku | Chemistry |
| おんがく | ongaku | Music |
| ぶんがく | bungaku | Literature |
| せいぶつ（がく） | seibutsu(-gaku) | Biology |
| ぶつり（がく） | butsuri(-baku) | Physics |
| けいざい（がく） | keizai(-gaku) | Economics |
| きょういくがく | kyooiku-gaku | Education |

げんごがく    gengo-gaku                    Linguistics
コンピューターサイエンス konpyuutaa saiensu    Computer Science

(frequency)
〜かい〜 kai                                 times
なんかい              nan kai                how many times
　　いっかい          i-k-kai                once
　　にかい            ni-kai                 twice
　　さんかい          san-kai                three times
　　よんかい          yon-kai                four times
　　ごかい            go-kai                 five times
　　ろっかい          ro-k-kai               six times
　　ななかい          nana-kai               seven times
　　はちかい          hachi-kai, ha-k-kai    eight times
　　きゅうかい        kyuu-kai               nine times
　　じゅっかい        jyu-k-kai              ten times

サッカー       sakkaa                        soccer
バスケットボール basuketto booru              basketball

[な Adjectives/Copula Nouns]
ゆううつ        yuu-utsu                     depressed; melancholic
ゆかい          yukai                        pleasing; fun
ハンサム        hansamu                      handsome

[Adjectives]
にがい          nigai                        bitter
ひもじい        himojii                      starving
すばらしい      subarashii                   wonderful
くらい          kurai                        dark

Antonyms
　　やさしい yasashii(easy;gentle)    ↔ むずかしい muzukashii(difficult)
　　まずい mazui(not tasty)           ↔ おいしい oishii(tasty)
　　わるい warui(bad)                 ↔ いい ii(good)
　　たかい takai(expensive; tall)     ↔ やすい yasui(cheap, reasonable)
　　あつい atsui (hot) samui (cold)   ↔ さむい samui
　　あたたかい atatakai (nice & worm) ↔すずしい suzushii (nice & cool)

[Verbs]

| | | |
|---|---|---|
| おもいます | omoimasu | (I) think. (masu form of "omou") |
| ちがいます | chigaimasu | is different (masu form of "chigau") |
| ふる | furu | to fall (dictionary form of "furimasu") |
| あめがふる | ame ga furu | It rains. |
| できました | dekimashita | finished; done (masu form of "dekiru") |
| なきました | nakimashita | barked; cried (masu form of "naku") |
| ノックしました | nokku shimashita | knocked |
| ドアをノックする | doa wo nokku suru | to knock the door |

[Adverbs]

| | | |
|---|---|---|
| まだ | mada | yet; still |
| ワンワン | wan-wan | onomatopoeia of a dog's bark |
| まいにち | mainichi | everyday |
| くるくる | kuru-kuru | onomatopoeia to express something is circulating; going around repeatedly |

[Expressions]

しっています。Shitte imasu          I know.

↕

しりません。Shirimasen          I don't know.

なんと　いいますか。Nan to iimasuka.          What/How do you say (it)?

～というのは、なんですか。
"～" to iu no wa nan desu ka.          What is it that is called "..." ? more formal way of saying "～" tte nan desu ka. ～って なんですか。

ブラウンさんという人          a person called Mr. Brown
Buraun-san to iu hito

Chapter 4 (B)                    Grammar and Cultural Notes

## 1. Adjectival Inflection

Unlike the negative form of nouns, which is "Noun jya arimasen," negative form of adjectives is "-ku arimasen," and its past tense affirmative is "- katta (desu), and past tense negative is "-ku nakatta (desu)" or "-ku arimasen deshita." Observe:

[Adjectival Inflection]

|  | **affirmative** | **negative** |
|---|---|---|
| **Non-past tense** | ---い（です）<br>   **---i (desu)** | ---くないです<br> **-ku nai desu) or**<br>--- くありません<br> **-ku arimasen** |
| **Past tense** | ---かった（です）<br> **---katta (desu)** | --- くなかったです<br> **-ku nakatta desu) or**<br>---くありませんでした<br> **ku arimasen deshita** |

Ex.

It is cold.  →  さむいです。 samui desu.

It is not cold. → さむくないです。　(samu-ku nai desu.)
　　　　　　Or さむくありません。 samu-ku arimasen.


It was cold.　 → さむかったです。 samu-katta desu.

It wasn't cold. → さむくなかったです。(samu-ku nakatta desu.)
　　　　　　　Or, さむくありませんでした。 samu-ku arimsen deshita.

How to make the **negative** form of adjectives?　　　　| ～　くない |

1. Change the last vowel (い"i") of the adjective to "く ku" and then,
2. Add "ない nai." ("ない nai" means "no")
   For example,
   おおきい→　おおきく→　おおきくない
   ookii　→ ookiku → ookiku nai

   Plain non-past affirmative →　Plain non-past negative
   　　　　ちいさい　→　ちいさくない
   　　　　あかい　　→　あかくない
   　　　　おもしろい→　おもしろくない

If you add "です desu" to casual form of adjective, you can make it "formal."
For example, おおきくない → おおきくないです。

How to make the **past tense**
(affirmative) form of adjectives?

| ～ かった |
| --- |

1. Change the last vowel (い"i") of the adjective to "かった katta"
For example,

  おおきい→ おおきかった
  ookii → ookikatta

| non-past → | past tense |
| --- | --- |
| ちいさい → | ちいさかった |
| あかい → | あかかった |
| おもしろい→ | おもしろかった |

How to make the **past tense negative**
form of adjectives?

| ～くなかった |
| --- |

1. Change the last vowel (い"i") of the adjective to "く ku"
  and then,

2. Add "ない nai." ("ない nai" means "no")

3. Change the last vowel (い"i") of the "ない nai" to "かった katta"
For example,

  おおきい→ おおきくない →おおきくなかった
  ookii → ookiku nai → ookiku na-katta

| non-past → | past negative |
| --- | --- |
| ちいさい → | ちいさくなかった |
| あかい → | あかくなかった |
| おもしろい→ | おもしろくなかった |

Practice the following:
Affirmative to Negative form of adjectives (Non-past tense casual without "desu")

1. あつい→　　あつくない
　　　　　　　あつかった / あつくなかった
2. さむい→　　さむくない
　　　　　　　さむかった / さむくなかった
3. むずかしい→ むずかしくない
　　　　　　　むずかしかった / むずかしくなかった
4. やさしい→　やさしくない
　　　　　　　やさしかった / やさしくなかった

5. おいしい→ おいしくない
     おいしかった ／ おいしくなかった

6. まずい→ まずくない
     まずかった ／ まずくなかった

7. いい→ よくない
    よかった ／ よくなかった

*Note the inflection of いい. You must use the original/formal style of "ii," which is "よい yoi" for inflection, whether for negative, past, or past negative forms.

8. わるい→ わるくない
    わるかった ／ わるくなかった

9. たかい→ たかくない
    たかかった ／ たかくなかった

10. やすい→ やすくない
    やすかった ／ やすくなかった

Now, learn "ten" adjectives in both their affirmative and negative forms. There are five sets of antonymic adjectives.

| Groups | | |
|---|---|---|
| weather | あつい(hot) | さむい(cold) |
| difficulty | むずかしい(difficult) | やさしい(easy) |
| taste | おいしい(tasty) | まずい(not tasty) |
| judgment | いい(good) | わるい(bad) |
| prices | たかい(expensive) | やすい(inexpensive) |

## 2. Personal Pronouns and their Omission

| | Singular | Plural |
|---|---|---|
| 1st person | わたし watashi (I) | わたしたち watashi-tachi (we) |
| 2nd person | あなた anata (you) | あなたたち anata-tachi (you) |
| 3rd person | かのじょ kanojyo (she) | かのじょたち kanojyo-tachi /ra (they) |
| | かれ kare(he) | かれら kare-ra(they) |
| | あのひと ano-hito (that person) | あのひとたち ano-hito-tachi (they) |
| | あのかた ano-kata (politer than ano- "hito") | あのかたたち ano-kata-tachi (politer than ano-hito-tachi) |
| | たなかさん Tanaka san | たなかさんたち Tanaka-san-tachi (Tanaka and his/her group) |

One of the characteristics of the Japanese language is omission, especially of personal pronouns. They are omitted if understood in context. In fact, the repetition of personal pronouns is considered unnatural. Look at Miwa's statement in line 14 in the Chapter 4(B) conversation. In the English translation, she says "I am Miwa. I'm a senior.

<u>My</u> major is in Physics." However, in Japanese, she said "I" only in the initial sentence, and the rest of the pronouns were omitted. Once obvious in context, personal pronouns are not repeated unless necessary. In line 8, Aiko says "わたしはまだわかりません。<u>watashi wa,</u> mada wakarimasen (I don't know [my major] yet)," hearing Monica's major being Japanese. She uses "は wa" to signal "わたし watashi" as the topic of the sentence, comparing with Monica who knows her major already. "わたし Watashi" was necessary to convey a strong sense of "comparison and contrast"; and the particle "は wa" enhances that sense of "comparison."

As for second and third person personal pronouns, they are seldom or never used in formal conversation – and especially in addressing a superior, because it carries a tone of arrogance. It is actually considered rude. The second person (for example, the listener) and third person are usually referred to by their names or social rankings/status instead of pronouns. Younger speakers never address adults "あなた anata," and social inferiors never address social superiors "あなた anata." It would be insulting to do so. However, toward strangers, "あなた anata" can be used as a polite expression. See the illustration.

## 3. <u>Particle "to" signaling quotation marks</u>

| と |
|---|

In Chapter 4(B) line 11, the professor says, "Kyoto dewa 'san-kai-sei' to iimasu" (In Kyoto we call it "san-kai-sei"). This particle "to" before the verb "iimasu" signals the preceding part in the sentence is quoted. The preceding word or sentence may be a quotation, one's thought, onomatopoeic expression, etc. Its casual form is "-tte" as in Monica's statement in the tenth line: " 「sankaisei」 tte (nan desu ka)?"
Examples:

　　　　　　　　　　　　　　　あめがふる　と　　　　いいました。
I said it will rain/I said "It will rain." → "<u>Ame ga furu</u>　　　to　　iimashita"
　　　　　　　　　　　　　　(It will rain = quotation,　as such, [I] said)
　　　　　　　　　　　　　　いぬが「わんわん」と　なきました。
A dog barked, "Ruff, ruff."　　　→　"Inu ga　wan wan　　to nakimashita"
　　　　　　　　　　　　　　(A dog,　　"ruff, ruff,"　as such, barked)
　　　　　　　　　　　　それはすばらしいアイデアだ　と　　おもいます。
I think it is a brilliant idea.　　→　"Sore wa subarashii aidea da　to　　omoimasu"
　　　　　　　　　　　　　　(It is a brilliant idea,　　　　as such, [I] think)

Note that "-tte" is a short form of "to iu no wa." Therefore, Monica's question in line 10
　　　　　　〜って　　　　　　　　というのは
will be " 「sankaisei」 <u>to iu no wa</u> nan desu ka" in formal speech.
　　　　「さんかいせい」というのは、なんですか。
Examples:
(1) A: 「おたく」って　なに？
　　　　"Otaku" tte nani?　(What's "otaku"?) (What is it that is called "otaku"?)

B:  「おたく」っていうのは、

"Otaku" tte iu no wa, .........(Otaku means someone who is absorbed in only one interest.  It is different from its original meanings, "somebody's house" or the honorific personal pronoun "you")

(2) A:  「こくばん」って　なんですか。

"Kokuban" tte nan desu ka.  (What is "kokuban"? What is it that is called "kokuban"?)

B:  「こくばん」は、"blackboard"です。

"Kokuban" wa "blackboard" desu.  ("Kokuban means "blackboard.")

(3) A:  「ブラウンさん」って　しってる？(Do you know a person called Mr. Brown?)

"Buraun-san" tte shitteru?

Or, more formally,

「ブラウンさん」というひとを　しっていますか。

"Buraun san" to iu hito wo shitte imasu ka.

B:  ええ、しっています。　　　　(Or, more casually: うん、しってる。)

Ee, shitte imasu. (Yes, I do [know].)                     un, shitteru.

## 4. Particle と "to" indicating similarity and difference

> ～と　おなじ

　　　"To" has many usages as a particle.  The particle "to" in the fifth sentence in Chapter 4(B) is different from the particle "to" that signals quotation marks. The particle "to" in "~ to onaji" or "~ to chigau" indicates that the preceding noun is "same as ~" or "different from ~."  Here the professor says to everyone that "Monica is in the same [grade] as Aiko," "(Monica san wa) Aiko san <u>to</u> onaji desu ne."

(モニカさんは)　あいこさんとおなじですね。

Examples:

A is the same as B.　→　A wa B <u>to</u> onaji desu.

Ａは、Ｂと　おなじです。

My major is the same as yours.　→　わたしのせんこうは、あなたとおなじです。

Watashi no senkoo wa anata <u>to</u> onaji desu.

This is different from that. →　　これは、それと　ちがいます。

Kore wa　sore <u>to</u>　chigaimasu.

　　　　　　　→　　これは、それと　おなじじゃありません。

Kore wa　sore <u>to</u>　onaji jya arimasen.

## Chapter 4(B)  A list of verbs in the dictionary form and ます form

(This list includes verbs from the dialogues and exercises from the past chapters)

| Dictionary form | English meaning | Affirmative non-past | Negative non-past |
|---|---|---|---|
| すむ（済む） | end, come to an end, to be done | すみます | すみません |
| たすかる | survive, escape, be saved | たすかります | たすかりません |
| くる | come | きます | きません |
| いく | go | いきます | いきません |
| たべる | eat | たべます | たべません |
| のむ | drink | のみます | のみません |
| ちゅうもんする べんきょうする おねがいする | place an order study ask a favor | ちゅうもんします べんきょうします おねがいします | ちゅうもんしません べんきょうしません おねがいしません |
| いたす | do: humble form | いたします | いたしません |
| まつ | wait | まちます | まちません |
| またせる | make someone wait | またせます | またせません |
| くださる | receive (someone gives me): humble form | くださいます | くださいません |
| なる | become | なります | なりません |
| ある | exist (inanimate) | あります | ありません |
| いう | say | いいます | いいません |
| わかる | understand | わかります | わかりません |
| みる | see, watch, look | みます | みません |
| ねる | sleep, go to bed | ねます | ねません |
| かう | buy | かいます | かいません |
| はなす | talk, speak | はなします | はなしません |
| あそぶ | play | あそびます | あそびません |
| おどる | dance | おどります | おどりません |
| かりる | borrow | かります | かりません |
| いれる | insert | いれます | いれません |
| かえす | return something | かえします | かえしません |
| およぐ | swim | およぎます | およぎません |
| かく | write, draw | かきます | かきません |
| よむ | read | よみます | よみません |
| きく | hear, listen | ききます | ききません |

Chapter 4 (B)
Exercises
A. Negate the following nouns and copula nouns, using じゃ　ありません。

１．そうです。　　　　　　　　２．たいへんです。
３．にねんせいです。　　　　　４．おなじです。
５．ぶつりです。　　　　　　　６．こうがくぶです。
７．せんこうです。　　　　　　８．わたしです。
９．よんかいせいです。　　　１０．ごまんえんです。

B. Negate the following adjectives, using ～くありません or ～くないです。

１．あついです。　　　　　　　２．さむいです。
３．すずしいです。　　　　　　４．あたたかいです。
５．むずかしいです。　　　　　６．やさしいです。
７．おいしいです。　　　　　　８．まずいです。
９．たかいです。　　　　　１０．やすいです。
１１．いいです。　　　　　　１２．わるいです。

C. Fill in the blanks with appropriate words.

１．A：きょうは、おてんきが（　　　　　　　）ですね。
　　　　　　　　　　　　　　　　good; nice
　　B：ええ、百ど　ありますねぇ。

２．A：にほんごのクラスは、（　　　　　　　）ですか。
　　　　　　　　　　　　　　　　a lot of work
　　B：ええ、ひらがなとかたかなと　かんじが　あります。しゅくだいも
　　　　ありますよ。

３．A：「れいぞうこ」（　　　　　　　）なんですか。
　　B：え？「れいぞうこ」ですか。refrigerator のことですよ。

４．A：blackboard は、にほんごで、なん（　　　　　　　）いいますか。
　　B：blackboard は、ね、「こくばん」って　いうんです。

５．A：え？五万円のくつですか。（　　　　　　　）ですねぇ。
　　B：でも、プリンセスダイアナのくつなんです。
　　A：ああ、それなら、（　　　　　　　）ですね。
　　　　　(If that is the case)

## D. Connect antonyms.

| | | | |
|---|---|---|---|
| 1. | むずかしい | A. | やすい |
| 2. | あつい | B. | まずい |
| 3. | いい | C. | やさしい |
| 4. | すずしい | D. | わるい |
| 5. | たかい | E. | あたたかい |
| 6. | おいしい | F. | さむい |

## E. Fill in the right adjectives in the blanks below.

1. きょうは、（　　　　　）ですね。３８ど　あります。

                        (38 Celsius temp. = 100 Fahrenheit temp.)

2. きょうは、（　　　　　）ですね。４ど　ですよ。

                        (4° C = 40 ° F)

3. きょうのテスト<ruby>テスト<rt>てすと</rt></ruby>は、（　　　　　）ですね。<u>たんご</u>が　たくさんあります。

                                       vocabulary

4. きょうのテストは、（　　　　）です。きのう　よく　べんきょうしました。

5. あなたのおかあさんのケーキ<ruby>ケーキ<rt>けえき</rt></ruby>は、すごく（　　　　　　）です。

                                   delicious

6. このパン<ruby>パン<rt>ぱん</rt></ruby>は、<u>まだ</u>（　　　　　）です。いま、<u>できました</u>。

          still                        done; finished

7. きょうは、おてんきが　（　　　　）ですね。<u>そら</u>が<u>きれい</u>です。

                      good         sky   clean, pretty

8. きょうは、おてんきが　（　　　　）ですね。<u>そら</u>が<u>くらい</u>です。

                      bad         sky   dark

9. このくつは、（　　　　）ですよ。<ruby>五万円<rt>ごまんえん</rt></ruby>です！

10. このくつは、（　　　　）ですよ。<ruby>三千円<rt>さんぜんえん</rt></ruby>です。

F.  What comes to mind when you hear the following adjectives and な na-adjectives?
Examples:

(1) やさしい (gentle, kind) ------ おかあさん

  (easy)  ------ テスト

(2) ゆうめい (famous) ---------- ケネディ、リンカーン

1.  むずかしい -----

2.  おいしい -----

3.  まずい -----

4.  さむい -----

5.  あつい -----

6.  あたたかい -----

7.  すずしい -----

8.  いい -----

9.  わるい -----

10. あたらしい -----
    (new)

11. ふるい -----
    (old)

12. ひとがおおい -----
    (having many people)

13. げんき -----

14. すき -----

15. きれい -----

16. しずか -----

17. じょうぶ-----
    (healthy; sturdy)

## G. Pair-work

1）Ask your partner whether the following things are difficult for her/him, using ～は、むずかしいですか。Write (O) for むずかしいです or (X) for むずかしくないです。

Example 1:
   Q: にほんごは、むずかしいですか。
   A: いいえ、むずかしくないです。

Example 2:
   Q: ぶつりは、むずかしいですか。
   A: はい、むずかしいです。

| しつもん | 1.<br>にほんご | 2.<br>ぶつり<br>physics | 3.<br>かがく<br>chemistry | 4.<br>こうがく<br>engineering | 5.<br>すうがく<br>math | 6.<br>せんたく<br>laundry | 7.<br>そうじ<br>cleaning | 8.<br>りょうり<br>cooking | 9.<br>うんてん<br>driving |
|---|---|---|---|---|---|---|---|---|---|
| むずかしいです。 | | | | | | | | | |
| むずかしくないです。 | | | | | | | | | |

(2) Ask if they are easy, using ～ は、やさしいですか。

Example:
Q: にほんごは、やさしいですか。
A: はい、やさしいです。むずかしくないです。

Example:
Q: りょうりは、やさしいですか。
A: いいえ、やさしくないです。むずかしいです。

H.  Adjectival inflection practice.  Fill in the blanks to complete the chart.

### 1)  Size

| | Non-past tense | | | Past tense | |
| | Affirmative | Negative | | Affirmative | Negative |
|---|---|---|---|---|---|
| large | おおきい | | | おおきかった | |
| small | | ちいさくない | | | ちいさくなかった |
| spacious | ひろい | | | ひろかった | |
| narrow | | せまくない | | | せまくなかった |

### 2)  Color

| | Non-past tense | | | Past tense | |
| | Affirmative | Negative | | Affirmative | Negative |
|---|---|---|---|---|---|
| red | あかい | | | | あかくなかった |
| blue | | あおくない | | | |
| white | しろい | | | しろかった | |
| black | くろい | | | | くろくなかった |
| yellow | | きいろくない | | | |
| brown | ちゃいろい | | | ちゃいろかった | |

### 3)  Length

| | Non-past tense | | | Past tense | |
| | Affirmative | Negative | | Affirmative | Negative |
|---|---|---|---|---|---|
| long | | | | | ながくない |
| short | みじかい | | | | |

### 4)  Weather

| | Non-past tense | | | Past tense | |
| | Affirmative | Negative | | Affirmative | Negative |
|---|---|---|---|---|---|
| hot | あつい | | | | |
| nice and warm | | あたたかくない | | | あたたかくなかった |
| nice and cool | | すずしくない | | | |
| cold | さむい | | | | |

### 5)  Interest

| | Non-past tense | | | Past tense | |
| | Affirmative | Negative | | Affirmative | Negative |
|---|---|---|---|---|---|
| interesting | | おもしろくない | | おもしろかった | |
| boring | つまらない | | | | |

6) Price

|  | Non-past tense | |
|---|---|---|
|  | Affirmative | Negative |
| expensive | たかい | |
| inexpensive | | やすくない |

| Past tense | |
|---|---|
| Affirmative | Negative |
| | |
| | |

7) Difficulty

|  | Non-past tense | |
|---|---|---|
|  | Affirmative | Negative |
| easy | | やさしくない |
| hard | | |

| Past tense | |
|---|---|
| Affirmative | Negative |
| | |
| むずかしかった | |

8) Taste

|  | Non-past tense | |
|---|---|---|
|  | Affirmative | Negative |
| tasty | おいしい | |
| not tasty | | |

| Past tense | |
|---|---|
| Affirmative | Negative |
| | |
| | まずくなかった |

9) Distance

|  | Non-past tense | |
|---|---|---|
|  | Affirmative | Negative |
| near | | |
| far | | とおくない |

| Past tense | |
|---|---|
| Affirmative | Negative |
| ちかかった | |
| | |

10) Emotions

|  | Non-past tense | |
|---|---|---|
|  | Affirmative | Negative |
| happy | うれしい | |
| sad | | かなしくない |

| Past tense | |
|---|---|
| Affirmative | Negative |
| | |
| | |

11) New/Old

|  | Non-past tense | |
|---|---|---|
|  | Affirmative | Negative |
| new | | あたらしくない |
| old | | |

| Past tense | |
|---|---|
| Affirmative | Negative |
| | |
| | ふるくなかった |

I. Ask a partner about the following places, using i-adjectives and na-adjectives.
Example:
A: パサデナは、しずかな　まち(town)ですか。
B: はい、しずかな　まちです。
   1. Los Angeles
   2. Tokyo

3. New York
4. Chicago
5. Kyoto
6. Las Vegas
7. Paris
8. London
9. Hong Kong
10. Beijin

Vocabulary Help:にぎやかな lively, きけんな（あぶない）dangerous, あんぜんな safe, きれいな（うつくしい）beautiful、あたらしい new、ふるい old、れきしてきな historic, ひとがおおい having many people, ゆたかな rich

J. Pair-work:  Ask your partner the meaning of the following words, with "～ってなんですか" phrased in a question, and "……は、～のことです" the reply.
Your partner would have the definitions of the words in question in his/her dictionary.

Example:
A：「とかげ」って、なんですか。
B：「とかげ」は、" lizard" のことです。

(1)

| The words A wants to ask: | Dictionary: (The words B wants to know) |
|---|---|
| 1．みみずく | 1. a cicada |
| 2．とうもろこし | 2. a squash |
| 3．ひもじい | 3. melancholy, the blues, gloom |
| 4．でぐち | 4. entrance |
| 5．おべんとう | 5. round bread with sweetened beans filling |
| The words B wants to ask: | Dictionary: (The words A wants to know) |
| 1．せみ | 1. a horned owl |
| 2．かぼちゃ | 2. corn |
| 3．ゆううつ | 3. hungry |
| 4．いりぐち | 4. exit |
| 5．あんぱん | 5. boxed lunch |

(2) Change your partner and do the same activity.

| The words A wants to ask: | Dictionary: (The words B wants to know) |
|---|---|
| 1．りんご | 1. rabbit |
| 2．すいか | 2. turtle |
| 3．いちご | 3. horse |
| 4．ぶどう | 4. monkey |
| 5．なし | 5. sheep |

| The words B wants to ask: | Dictionary: (The words A wants to know) |
|---|---|
| １．うさぎ<br>２．かめ<br>３．うま<br>４．さる<br>５．ひつじ | 1. apple<br>2. watermelon<br>3. strawberry<br>4. grapes<br>5. pear |

K. Go around the class to find answers to the following questions.

1. こんにちは」は、スペインごで、なんと　いいますか。

2. 「さようなら」は、ちゅうごくごで、なんと　いいますか。

3. 「えんぴつ」は、かんこくごで　なんと　いいますか。

4. 「おはよう」は、ドイツごで　なんと　いいますか。

5. 「おげんきですか」は、フランスごで　なんといいますか。

L. Ask your classmates what to say the words of your choice in other language. You may use the vocabulary in Exercise J.

Example: "Adios" は、えいごで　なんと　いいますか。
"Monkey" は、にほんごで　なんと　いいますか。

M. Ask your classmates the names of his/her parents.

Hint: おかあさん（orおとうさん）の　おなまえは、なんと　いいますか。

N. Task: Find the person who shares the same identity as you. Each student takes on an identity from the list of (a) to (r), which is now your hometown, year, and major. Once you remember your identity, find another person who shares the same hometown, year and major through questions and answers. Use sentence patterns of X は wa Y です desu, X も mo Y です desu, X は wa Y とおなじです to onaji desu, or X は wa Y じゃ ありません jya arimasen. Also ask if the major is difficult, using X は wa、むずかし いですか muzukshii desu ka.

List of majors せんこう

| Mathematics | すうがく | Education | きょういくがく |
|---|---|---|---|
| Physics | ぶつり | Literature | ぶんがく |
| Biology | せいぶつ | Linguistics | げんごがく |
| Engineering | こうがく | Economics | けいざいがく |

| History | れきし | Computer science | コンピューター・サイエンス |
| Music | おんがく | Japanese | にほんご |
| Chemistry | かがく | Psychology | しんりがく |
| Arts | びじゅつ | Undecided | まだわかりません (みてい) |

Sample dialogue:

A: はじめまして。Bob です。

B: はじめまして。Tom です。どちらから、ですか。

A: New York からです。どちらから？

B: Chicago です。なんねんせいですか。

A: にねんせいです。なんねんせいですか。

B: いちねんせいです。せんこうは、なんですか。

A: すうがくです。せんこうは？

B: Bob さんとおなじです。（Or, わたしも すうがくです。）

A: すうがくは、むずかしいですか。

B: はい、すごく。どうですか。

A: まあまあです。

B: そうですか。じゃ、また。

A: じゃ、また。

Activity sheet

(a)

| hometown | Pasadena |
| year | にねんせい |
| major | こうがく |

(b)

| hometown | Seattle |
| year | いちねんせい |
| major | ぶんがく |

(c)

| hometown | Tucson |
| year | さんねんせい |
| major | けいざいがく |

(d)

| hometown | Chicago |
| year | にねんせい |
| major | れきし |

(e)

| hometown | Los Angeles |
| year | いちねんせい |
| major | まだわかりません |

(f)

| hometown | San Diego |
| year | にねんせい |
| major | すうがく |

(g)

| hometown | Denver |
| year | さんねんせい |
| major | ぶつり |

(h)

| hometown | Pomona |
| year | よねんせい |
| major | せいぶつ |

(i)

| hometown | New York |
| year | さんねんせい |
| major | コンピューター・サイエンス |

| (j) | hometown | San Francisco |
|---|---|---|
| | year | いちねん せい |
| | major | きょういく がく |

| (k) | home town | Miami |
|---|---|---|
| | year | にねんせい |
| | major | おんがく |

| (l) | home town | Atlanta |
|---|---|---|
| | year | にねんせい |
| | major | げんごがく |

| (m) | hometown | Houston |
|---|---|---|
| | year | さんねん せい |
| | major | にほんご |

| (n) | home town | Honolulu |
|---|---|---|
| | year | よねんせい |
| | major | かがく |

| (o) | home town | Boston |
|---|---|---|
| | year | さんねんせい |
| | major | しんりがく |

| (p) | hometown | Salt Lake |
|---|---|---|
| | year | いちねん せい |
| | major | れきし |

| (q) | home town | St. Paul |
|---|---|---|
| | year | にねんせい |
| | major | けいざいが く |

| (r) | home town | Minneapolis |
|---|---|---|
| | year | にねんせい |
| | major | びじゅつ |

O. The use of "の no" to replace a noun.

(1). Look at the chart below and write appropriate statements, using the information given about each item. Use "i-adjective + の no" or "na adj + な na +の no."

| ヘローキティ | としょかん | にほんのおかし | ふじさん | まっちゃ |
|---|---|---|---|---|
| かわいい ゆうめい | しずか おおきい | きれい ちいさい たかい おいしい | (せが) たかい ゆうめい | おいしい にがい |

れい Examples :
1) おいしいのは、にほんのおかし と まっちゃです。
2) ゆうめいなのは、へろうきてぃ と ふじさんです。

1. かわいい ....................................................................................

2. しずか ....................................................................................

3. おおきい ....................................................................................

4. ちいさい ....................................................................................

5. きれい　　.......................................................................................

6. たかい　　.......................................................................................

7. せがたかい　.....................................................................................

8. にがい　　.......................................................................................

(2). Complete the sentences with your own thoughts.

1. むずかしいのは、.................................................................................

2. やさしいのは、　　.............................................................................

3. きれいなのは、　　.............................................................................

4. ハンサムなのは、..............................................................................

5. ゆかいなのは、　.............................................................................
   (amusing; fun)

6. しあわせなのは、..............................................................................
   (happy)

7. あぶないのは、..............................................................................
   (dangerous)

8. きたないのは、..............................................................................
   (dirty)

9. おもしろいのは、..............................................................................

10. たのしみなのは、..............................................................................
    (something to look for)

Chapter 4 (B): Dict-A-Conversation (1)  Predicate Types (masu & masen)
Respond to the statements verbally, and write in your answers.  Please answer "yes" or "no" first; then reply in <u>complete sentences</u> in hiragana.  Write your answers on a separate sheet.

1. _____
2. _____
3. _____
4. _____
5. _____
6. _____
7. _____
8. _____
9. _____
1 0. _____

Chapter 4(B): Dict-A-Conversation (2): Predicate Types – Affirmative & Negative forms of Adjectives.  Respond to the questions verbally, and write in your answers.  Please answer "yes" or "no" first; then reply in <u>complete sentences</u> in hiragana.  Write your answers on a separate sheet.

1. _____
2. _____
3. _____
4. _____
5. _____
6. _____
7. _____
8. _____
9. _____
10. _____

Dict-A-Conversation (3): Listen to Dict-A-Conversation (3) in Chapter 4 (B) on the student CD,  and answer the questions in <u>complete sentences</u>.  Write answers on a separate sheet.

1. _____    2. _____
3. _____    4. _____
5. _____    6. _____
7. _____    8. _____
9. _____    10. _____

Chapter 4 (B)

| 回 (to go round, ~times) | まわ（る）<br>まわ（す）<br>か い<br>カイ | 目（め）が回（まわ）る eyes go round<br>一回（いっかい）once<br>今回（こんかい）this time<br><br>(6)<br>  l 冂 冋 冋 回 回 |
|---|---|---|
| 言 (to say) | い（う）<br>こと<br>げ ん<br>ゲン<br>ご ん<br>ゴン | 言う（いう）to say<br>*［言葉（ことば）words, a language］<br>言語（げんご）a language<br>二言（にごん）correction of the first statement<br>ぶ し　 に ごん<br>「武士に二言はない」Samurai don't lie.<br><br>(7)<br>  、　二　亠　言　言　言　言 |
| 分 (minutes, to divide) | わ（かる）<br>わ（ける）<br>ふ ん ぶ ん ぶん<br>フン/プン/ブン | 分かる（わかる）to understand<br>分ける（わける）to divide<br>一分（いっぷん）one minute<br>二分（にふん）three minutes<br>私の分（わたしのぶん）my share<br><br>(4)<br>  ノ　八　今　分 |
| 口 (mouth, entrance) | くち<br>ぐち<br>こ う<br>コウ | 口（くち）the mouth<br>入口（いりぐち）an entrance<br>川口（かわぐち）a surname<br>口先（くちさき）the mouth; lips; talk; the snout (of animals)<br><br>(3)<br>  l　口　口 |
| 同 (same; identical) | おな（じ）<br>ど う<br>ドウ | 同じ（おなじ）the same<br>一同（いちどう）all of us<br>同一（どういつ）the same<br>同一人物（どういつじんぶつ）the same person<br><br>(6)<br>  l　冂　冂　同　同　同 |

Kanji Practice for Chapter 4 (B)
かんじの　れんしゅう

1．つぎの　ことばを　よみなさい。それから、クラス<ruby>メ<rt>く</rt></ruby><ruby>ー<rt>ら</rt></ruby><ruby>ト<rt>す</rt></ruby><ruby><rt>め</rt></ruby><ruby><rt>え</rt></ruby><ruby><rt>と</rt></ruby>にいみをきき
なさい。Read the following words to your classmates and ask them the
meaning of each word/sentence.

（1）　一回、二回、三回、何回？

（2）　先生のおなまえは、田中先生と　言います。

（3）　一分、二分、三分

（4）　日本語が　分かります。

（5）　口で　たべます。

（6）　入口は、あそこです。

（7）　今日のそらの色は、きのうと　同じ色です。

（8）　一回生と一年生は、同じです。

（9）　私は、四回生です。

（10）　くるくる回る、目が回る。(くるくる onomatopoeia)

2．よんでから、よみがなをかいて、えいごでいいなさい。Read first, write
yomigana above kanji, and translate into English.

（1）　私のなまえは、田中と言います。

（2）　今、十じ三分すぎです。

（3）　私は、山田さんと同じ年です。

（4）　何回ぐらい、<ruby>ド<rt>ど</rt></ruby><ruby>ア<rt>あ</rt></ruby>を<ruby>ノ<rt>の</rt></ruby><ruby>ッ<rt>っ</rt></ruby><ruby>ク<rt>く</rt></ruby>(knock)しましたか。

（5）　今、何と、言いましたか。

## Bingo Sheet for Chapter 4AB
## [Adjectives & な Adjectives (Copula Nouns)]

| | | | |
|---|---|---|---|
| おいしい | ふるい | いい | ゆかい |
| あつい | げんき | わるい | しずか |
| ゆうめい | むずかしい | すき | あたらしい |
| まずい | すずしい | たかい | あたたかい |

| | | | |
|---|---|---|---|
| むずかしい | やさしい | やすい | たいへん |
| にがい | きれい | あたらしい | わるい |
| すき | おいしい | すずしい | あたたかい |
| げんき | しずか | まずい | かわいい |

| | | | |
|---|---|---|---|
| | | | |
| | | | |
| | | | |
| | | | |

| | | | |
|---|---|---|---|
| | | | |
| | | | |
| | | | |
| | | | |

## Bingo Sheet for Chapter 4AB
### Verbs in the "masu" form. When you play, change them to the "Dictionary" form & vice versa

| | | | |
|---|---|---|---|
| あります | はなします | よみます | きます |
| のみます | かきます | します | ききます |
| ちゅうもんします | いきます | みます | べんきょうします |
| いいます | います | たべます | あるきます |

| | | | |
|---|---|---|---|
| のみます | はなします | きます | よみます |
| ちゅうもんします | ききます | かきます | します |
| べんきょうします | います | みます | いきます |
| いいます | たべます | あります | あるきます |

| | | | |
|---|---|---|---|
| | | | |
| | | | |
| | | | |
| | | | |

| | | | |
|---|---|---|---|
| | | | |
| | | | |
| | | | |
| | | | |

## Bingo Sheet for Chapter 4AB
### Verbs in the "Dictionary form."  When you play, change them to the "masu" form & vice versa

| | | | |
|---|---|---|---|
| ある | はなす | よむ | くる |
| のむ | かく | する | きく |
| ちゅうもんする | いく | みる | べんきょうする |
| いう | いる | たべる | あるく |

| | | | |
|---|---|---|---|
| のむ | はなす | くる | よむ |
| ちゅうもんする | きく | かく | する |
| べんきょうする | いる | みる | いく |
| いう | たべる | ある | あるく |

| | | | |
|---|---|---|---|
| | | | |
| | | | |
| | | | |
| | | | |

| | | | |
|---|---|---|---|
| | | | |
| | | | |
| | | | |
| | | | |

## Kanji Bingo Sheet (2)  Chapter 3BC & Chapter 4AB
### Fill in the blanks with the kanji and play Bingo.

Kanji 百、小、中、千、万、水、女、色、入

| 百 | 小 | 中 |
|---|---|---|
| 千 | 万 | 水 |
| 女 | 色 | 入 |

| 入 | 色 | 女 |
|---|---|---|
| 水 | 千 | 万 |
| 中 | 小 | 百 |

|  |  |  |
|---|---|---|
|  |  |  |
|  |  |  |

Kanji 先、人、今、上、下　（女、色、水、入）

| 先 | 人 | 今 |
|---|---|---|
| 女 | 下 | 上 |
| 色 | 水 | 入 |

| 入 | 水 | 色 |
|---|---|---|
| 上 | 下 | 女 |
| 今 | 人 | 先 |

|  |  |  |
|---|---|---|
|  |  |  |
|  |  |  |

Kanji 回、分、言、口、同（今、先、上、下）

| 回 | 分 | 言 |
|---|---|---|
| 今 | 同 | 口 |
| 先 | 上 | 下 |

| 下 | 今 | 先 |
|---|---|---|
| 同 | 口 | 上 |
| 回 | 言 | 分 |

|  |  |  |
|---|---|---|
|  |  |  |
|  |  |  |

## Chapter 4 (C) Have you eaten spaghetti (here before)?

スパゲティを　たべましたか。

あいこ：　　モニカさん、ここのスパゲティを　食べましたか。　　　　1

モニカ：　　いえ、まだです。　　　　2

あいこ：　　なっとうスパゲティが　おいしいですよ。　　　　3

てつや：　　カプチーノも　まあまあです。　　　　4

みわ：　　　おにぎりべんとうも、人気が　あります。　　　　5

モニカ：　　うれしい。私、日本の食べものが　大好きなんです。　　　　6

みわ：　　　日本の食べもの　の　方が　好きなんですか。　　　　7

モニカ：　　ええ、アメリカりょうりより…　　　　8

てつや：　　ぼくは、ハンバーガーの　方が　好きだな…　　　　9

[English translation]:
Aiko:　　　Monica, have you eaten spaghetti here?
Monica:　　No, not yet.
Aiko:　　　Nattoo spaghetti is good (= tasty).
Tetsuya:　Cappuccino isn't bad, either.
Miwa:　　　Onigiri-bentoo is also popular.
Monica:　　I'm delighted!  Because I like Japanese food so much!
Miwa:　　　You like Japanese food better (than other cuisines)?
Monica:　　Yes, more than American food…
Tetsuya:　I like hamburger better…

---

どんなあじが　しますか: あまい sweet、すっぱい sour、しおからい salty、
にがい bitter.

チョコレート、あめ-------　あまい
レモン、うめぼし　--------　すっぱい
うめぼし　　　　　--------　しおからい
コーヒー、まっちゃ--------　にがい

## Chapter 4 (C)                    Vocabulary List

### 1. Expressions
| | | |
|---|---|---|
| まだです | mada desu | Not yet. |
| まあまあ | maa maa | so so |
| なんです | ~ na n desu | It is because ~ . |
| だいすきなんです | daisuki na n desu | It is because I like it so much. |

### 2. Nouns
| | | |
|---|---|---|
| なっとう | nattoo | fermented soybeans |
| カプチーノ | kapuchiino | cappuccino |
| おにぎりべんとう | onigiri bentoo | boxed lunch with rice balls |
| にんき | ninki | popularity |
| たべもの | tabemono | food |
| アメリカりょうり | Amerika ryoori | American food |

### 3. な Adjectives /Copula nouns
| | | |
|---|---|---|
| だいすき | daisuki | like very much ("likable" or "pleasing") |

### 4. Adjectives
| | | |
|---|---|---|
| うれしい | ureshii | (I am) happy, glad |

### 5. Verbs
| | | |
|---|---|---|
| にんきがあります | ninki ga arimasu | It is popular. |

### 6. Particles
| | | |
|---|---|---|
| より | ~ yori | ~ than |
| ほう | ~ (no) hoo | side |
| な | "na" sentence final | shows a personal feeling/sentiment |

---

Additional Vocabulary from Grammar Notes, Exercises, and Dict-A-Conversation

---

[Nouns]

| | | |
|---|---|---|
| にく | niku | meat |
| やさい | yasai | vegetables |
| チーズ | chiizu | cheese |
| チョコレート | chokoreeto | chocolate |
| あめ | ame | candy |
| うめぼし | ume-boshi | soured pickled plum |
| テスト | tesuto | test |
| チーズケーキ | chiizu-keeki | cheesecake |
| くだもの | kudamono | fruits |
| ぎゅうにゅう | gyuunyuu | milk |
| あじ | aji | taste |
| みどり | midori | green |
| むらさき | murasaki | purple |
| せ | se | height (せがたかい se ga takaii: tall) |
| コンピューターゲーム | konpyuutaa-geemu | computer game |
| しつもん | shitsumon | question |
| おせじ | o-seji | flattery |
| はやくちことば | hayakuchi-kotoba | tongue twister |
| すいえい | suiei | swimming |
| うんてん | unten | driving |
| アイロンがけ | airon-gake | ironing |
| そうじ | sooji | cleaning |
| りょうり | ryoori | cooking |
| スポーツ | supootsu | sports |
| スター | sutaa | stars; celebrity |
| かしゅ | kashu | singer |
| バンド | bando | (music) band |
| ばしょ/ ところ | basho/tokoro | place (specific/ broad sense) |
| かぞく | kazoku | family |
| ロック | rokku | rock |
| ジャズ | jyazu | jazz |
| ジョギング | jogingu | jogging |
| パーティー | paatii | party |

| | | |
|---|---|---|
| せかい | sekai | world |
| しんかんせん | shin-kan-sen | bullet train |
| がっか | gakka | academic subjects |
| おくさん | okusan | wife (polite form) |
| ごしゅじん | go-shujin | husband (polite form) |
| スキー | sukii | ski |
| フラダンス | fura-dansu | hula dance |

[な Adjectives/Copula Nouns]

| | | |
|---|---|---|
| きらい | kirai | dislikable; unpleasant |

[Adjectives]

| | | |
|---|---|---|
| たのしい | tanoshii | enjoyable; fun |
| つまらない | tsumaranai | boring; uninteresting |
| あまい | amai | sweet |
| しおからい | shio-karai | salty |
| すっぱい | suppai | sour |
| にがい | nigai | bitter |
| かわいい | kawaii | cute |

[Adverbs]

| | | |
|---|---|---|
| はじめに | hajime ni | at first |
| つぎに | tsugi ni | next |

[Verbs]

| | | |
|---|---|---|
| きにいりました。 | ki ni irimashita | I liked it./ It's my liking. |
| きにいる | ki ni iru | to like; suit to one's taste |
| ～ドル します | ～ shimasu | It costs ~dollars. (~suru: to cost) |
| あじが します | | It tastes (sweet, bitter, sour, salty) |

----------------------- Vocabulary from Dict-A-Conversation-----------------------------------

[Nouns]

| | | |
|---|---|---|
| あさ | asa | morning |
| ばん | ban | evening |
| ゆうがた | yuugata | dusk |
| にんじん | ninjin | carrots |
| ブロッコリ | burokkori | broccoli |
| レタス | retasu | lettuce |
| くに | kuni | country |
| ナイルがわ | Nairu-gawa | River Nile |
| マッキンリー | Makkinrii | Mt. McKinley |

Chapter 4 (C)                    Grammar and Cultural Notes

## 1. <u>Comparative:  I like A better than B.</u>

Q:  Which do you like better, A or B?

> ＡとＢと　どちら（のほう）が　すきですか。

A:  I like A better than B.     (A ＞B)  ＝  (B ＜A)

> Ｂ　より　Ａ（のほう）が　すきです。
> Ａ（のほう）が　Ｂ　より　すきです。

The idea of comparison is expressed via the following format within a complete sentence.

> わたしは、コーヒーより　おちゃのほうが　すきです。
> Watashi wa koohii <u>yori</u>      ocha <u>no hoo ga</u>     suki desu.
> (コーヒー＜ おちゃ[すき]) ＝ I like tea better than coffee.)

However, "のほう no hoo" may be dropped to simply read "コーヒーよりおちゃがすきです。 koohii yori ocha ga suki desu." If the object being compared is obvious, then omit "コーヒーより koohii yori," and say "おちゃのほうがすきです。 ocha no hoo ga suki desu." You may also switch the order between things being compared: "おちゃのほうがコーヒーよりすきです。 Ocha no hooga koohii yori suki desu." Also, any predicate may be used, rather than "すきです suki desu."

Examples:
1. にく　＜　やさい　（すき favorable）
   わたしは、にくより　やさいのほうが　すきです。
   Watashi wa niku yori     yasai no hoo ga   suki desu. (I prefer vegetables to meat.)
2. バス　＜　タクシー　　（はやい fast）
   バスよりタクシーのほうが　はやいです。
   Basu yori takushii no hoo ga hayai desu.  (Taxi is faster than bus.)
3. チーズ　＜　にく　（たかい expensive）
   にくのほうが　チーズより　たかいです。
   Niku no hoo ga chiize yori takai desu. (Beef is more expensive than cheese.)
4. ミシシッピ川　＜　ナイルがわ　（ながい long）
   ナイル川のほうが　ミシシッピがわより　ながいです。
   Nairu-gawa no hoo ga Mishishippi-gawa yori nagai desu. (The Nile River is longer than the Mississippi River.)

## 2. <u>Superlative: I like A best</u>.

Q: Which one do you like best?

> AとBとC（のなか）で、どれが　いちばん　すきですか。

A: I like A best.

> Aが　　いちばん　すきです。

In Japanese, there is no superlative form equivalent to "~ est" or "most" in English.  The adverbial phrase "いちばん ichiban ~" is equivalent to "~ est" or "~ most."
"いちばん Ichiban" can modify a noun, an adjective, a copula noun, an adverb and a verb.
Examples:
いちばん　いい (the best) ,　　　　　いちばん　すき (the most favorite)
　ichiban　ii　　　　　　　　　　　　ichiban　　suki

いちばん　はやく (the fastest, or the earliest) , いちばんあたまがいい (the smartest)
ichiban　　hayaku　　　　　　　　　　ichiban　　atama ga ii

いちばん　いきたい (the most desired place to go)
Ichiban　　ikitai

> Particle で　in superlative

When you have a list of choices, such as "among the fruits" or "among apples, bananas, and oranges," use "~ のなかで no naka de." This particle "で de" has the function of "ending the choices."   See the following examples:

1) りんごとバナナとオレンジ（のなか）で、どれが　いちばんすきですか。
   ringo to banana to orenji　(no naka)　de,　dore ga　ichiban　suki desu ka.
   Among apples, bananas, and oranges, which one do you like best?

2) うさぎとライオンとうまでは、どれが　いちばん　はやいですか。
   usagi to raion to uma de wa,　　dore ga　ichiban　　hayai desu ka.
   Among rabbits, lions, and horses, which one is fastest?
   Of course, you answer:
   うまが　いちばん　はやいです。Horses are the fastest.
   uma ga　ichiban　　hayai desu.
   Or, you may say, うまです。
   　　　　　　　　　uma desu.

A hint of how to respond to questions in general:

> For questions that have an "interrogative pronoun" ('question words' such as "when," "who," what," "which," "where," or "how"), you may answer with a copula verb (です). For example: For above sentence (1) asking you "which" fruit you liked best, you may answer with either pattern (A) or (B) shown below:
>
> (A)　りんご　が　いちばん　すきです。
>
> 　　　ringo　ga　ichiban　suki desu.
>
> (B)　りんご　です。
>
> 　　　ringo　desu.

3）にほんで　いちばん　たかいやまは、どれですか。

　　nihon de　ichiban　takai yama　wa, dore desu ka.

　　Which mountain in Japan is the highest?

　　ふじさん　です。It's Mt. Fuji

　　Fuji-san　desu.

4）ホンダと　トヨタと　マツダで、どのくるまが　いちばんすきですか。

　　Honda to Toyota to Matsuda de, dono kuruma ga ichiban suki desu ka.

　　Which car do you like best, among Honda, Toyota, and Matsuda?

　　わたしは、トヨタです。I like Toyota (best).

　　watashi wa  Toyota desu.

　　ぼくは、ホンダです。　I like Honda (best).

　　boku wa Matsuda desu.

5）あか、しろ、きいろ、くろ、みどり、あお、むらさきのなかで、

　　aka,　shiro,　kiiro,　kuro, midori,　ao,　murasaki no naka de,

　　どのいろが　いちばん　きれいですか。

　　dono iro ga ichiban　kirei　desu ka.

　　Which color is most beautiful among red, white, yellow, black, green, blue and purple?

　　みどりが　いちばん　きれいです。Green is most beautiful.

　　midori ga ichiban　kirei　desu.

　　みどりです。　　　　　　　　Green is.

　　midori desu.

## 3. Comparative: as ~ as

| ～と　おなじ　ぐらい |

(ぐらい is also pronounced くらい.)

In Chapter 4 (B), we learned the word "～とおなじ (the same as~)." For example,

Monica's academic year is the same as Aiko's. モニカは、あいことおなじ（がくねん）です。 In this chapter, we'll use it as a comparative, " ～とおなじぐらい," A is as ~ as B. For example. If Monica is as tall as Aiko,

モニカは、あいこと　おなじぐらい　せがたかい([height is] tall)です。
Monica wa Aiko to onaji gurai se ga takai desu.

Examples:

1. ほっかいどうは、カナダと　おなじぐらい　さむいです
   Hokkaidoo wa Kanada to onaji gurai samui desu. (Hokkaido is as cold as Canada.)

2. ここは、もりのなかと　おなじぐらい　しずかです。
   koko wa mori no naka to onaji gurai shizuka desu.(Here is as quiet as in the forest.)

3. きょうしつは、アーケードとおなじぐらい　にぎやか(lively)です。
   kyooshitsu wa aakeedo to onaji gurai nigiyaka desu.
   (The classroom is as lively as an arcade.)

4. にほんごのべんきょうは、コンピューターゲームとおなじぐらい
   ゆかい(amusing) です。
   nihongo no benkyoo wa konpyuutaa-geemu to onaji gurai yukai desu.
   (Studying Japanese is as fun as playing a computer game.

5. あたらしい (new)アニメは、ふるい (old)アニメとおなじぐらい　おもしろ
   い(fun)です。
   atarashii anime wa furui anime to onaji gurai omoshiroi desu.
   (The new animation is as interesting as the old one.)

## 4. Comparative: not as ~ as

| A　は　Bほど、～　ない |
|---|
| ありません |

When A is bigger than B, you may also say "B is not as big as A." This is the expression we learn here. Its Japanese equivalent is "A wa B hodo ~ nai (negative predicate)." See the examples:

（1）Aは　Bより　おおきいです。→Bは、Aほど　おおきくありません。
   A is bigger than B.　　　　　　　　B is not as big as A.

（2）AはBよりおもしろいです。→Bは、Aほど　おもしろくありません。
   A is more fun than B.　　　　　　　B is not as fun as A.

（3）Aは、Bより　すきです。　→Bは、Aほど、すきじゃありません。
   I like A better than B.　　　　　　I don't like B as much as I like A.

（4）Aは、Bより　しずかです。→Bは、Aほど、しずかじゃありません。
   A is quieter than B.　　　　　　　B is not as quiet as A.

## 5. だいすきなんです: **"na n desu" to give an explanation**

As explained in Chapter 4(A), "んです n desu" expresses the speaker's attempt to "explain." You have also seen そうなんですか soo nan desu ka (that's why; that's the reason), in Chapter 4(B)'s. な **is added to** んです after nouns. Observe Monica's statement in line six of this chapter:

うれしい！わたし（は）、にほんのたべものが　だいすきなんです。
"Ureshii!　watashi [wa],　nihon no tabemono ga　daisuki <u>na'n</u> desu."
　(I'm so delighted!  [Because] I like Japanese food very much.)

Examine the following:
a. これなんです。
b. わたしなんです。
c. だめなんです。(だめ no good; can't be)
d. きらいなんです。きらい(unfavorable; disliked)

## 6. もうたべました **Completion of action**

Japanese past tense verbs also indicate the "completion" of action (which is "have done" in English).  It is expressed by the final verb"た ta" or "-ました mashita." Therefore, if you want to ask "Have you eaten lunch?," you may say:

"（もう）ランチをたべ<u>ました</u>か。(Moo) ranchi wo tabe-<u>mashita</u> ka."
And, if the answer is Yes, it is "はい、（もう）たべ<u>ました</u>。Hai, (moo) tabe-<u>mashita."</u>
　　　　　　　　　　　　　　[もう moo means "already"]
If the answer is No, it is, "いいえ、まだです。Iie, mada desu (No, not yet)." The complete sentence of this negative form is "いいえ、まだ たべていません。Iie, mada tabeteimasen," which will be officially introduced later.

Observe the following:
1. A: もう　よみましたか。
　　"Moo yomi-mashita ka" (Have you read [it] already?)

　B: はい、よみました。　　　　　Or、いいえ、まだです。
　　"Hai, yomimashita. (Yes, I have.)　　　"Iie, mada desu"　(No, not yet.)

2. A: もう　いきましたか。
　　"Moo ikimashita ka"　(Have you been there already?)

　B: はい、いきました。　　　　　Or, いいえ、まだです。
　　"Hai, ikimashita"　(Yes, I have.)　　　"Iie, mada desu"　(No, I haven't.)

## Chapter 4 (C) Exercises

A. Pair-work:

（1）Ask your partner whether s/he likes the following, using ～がすきですか。
Write the answers in the chart: (O) for すきです and (X) for すきじゃありません.

| しつもん | 1. くだもの | 2. チーズケーキ Cheesecake | 3. アイスクリーム ice cream | 4. やさい | 5. にく | 6. （お）すし | 7. べんきょう | 8. しゅくだい | 9. テスト test |
|---|---|---|---|---|---|---|---|---|---|
| すきです | | | | | | | | | |
| すきじゃ ありません | | | | | | | | | |

（2）Ask your partner whether s/he is good at the following things, using ～がじょうずですか。Write the answers in the chart: (O) for じょうずです and (X) for じょうず じゃありません.

| しつもん | 1. りょうり cooking | 2. そうじ cleaning | 3. せんたく laundry | 4. アイロンかけ ironing | 5. じ handwriting | 6. うんてん driving | 7. すいえい swimming | 8. はやくちことば talking fast/ tongue twister | 9. おせじ flattery |
|---|---|---|---|---|---|---|---|---|---|
| じょうず です | | | | | | | | | |
| じょうずじゃ ありません | | | | | | | | | |

B. In-class activity:  Ask four classmates and find what they like to eat and drink; who their favorite persons are; what sports they like; and also ask what they don't enjoy in general.  Fill in the chart with the information you obtain.

Pattern of questions/answers to be used in this activity:
Q:  いちばん　すきなたべものは、なんですか。（〜ひとは、だれですか。）
A:  （　　　　）です。

| | いちばん すきな たべもの | いちばん すきな のみもの | いちばん すきな ひと | いちばん すきな スポーツ | いちばん きらいな もの(thing) |
|---|---|---|---|---|---|
| A さん | りんご | おちゃ | おかあさん | サッカー | しゅくだい |
| さん | | | | | |
| さん | | | | | |
| さん | | | | | |
| さん | | | | | |

Report to class what you have found from your four classmates, using the following pattern:

（１）〜さんが、いちばん　すきな　たべものは、＿＿＿＿＿＿です。

（２）〜さんが、いちばん　すきな　のみものは、＿＿＿＿＿＿です。

（３）〜さんが、いちばん　すきな　ひとは、　＿＿＿＿＿＿です。

（４）〜さんが、いちばん　すきな　スポーツは、＿＿＿＿＿＿です。

（５）〜さんが、いちばん　きらいな　ものは、＿＿＿＿＿＿です。

C. Form sentences comparing two items, using the adjectives in the parentheses.

　1.　にく　　　　さかな　　（おいしい）

→　　にくより　　　さかなのほうが　おいしいです。

＿＿＿＿＿＿＿＿＿＿＿＿＿＿＿＿＿＿＿＿＿＿＿

2. とうきょう　　おおさか　　（おもしろい fun）

_____

3. おとうさん　　おかあさん　　（せがたかい tall）

_____

4. ＭＩＴ　　カ<ruby>カルテック<rt>かるてっく</rt></ruby>　　（<ruby>大<rt>おお</rt></ruby>きい）

_____

5. しんかんせん　　でんしゃ　　（はやい fast）

_____

6. ひらがな　　かたかな　　（むずかしい）

_____

_____

D. In-class Activity: Interview your classmate and report what you learn to the class.
The information you need to obtain is as follows:
1. Which s/he prefers: vegetables or fruits, meat or fish, coke or milk, rock or jazz,
jogging or swimming, partying or studying

You can use the comparative pattern:
Q: Ａ と Ｂ と（で，or では），どちらのほうが、すきですか。
A:（　　）のほうが　すきです。

Reporting format: ～さんは、Ａより Ｂ（のほう）が　すきです。

2. His/her most favorite star/singer/band, class, and place:

[Vocabulary help]
<ruby>スター<rt>すた</rt></ruby>（はいゆう）star、かしゅ singer、<ruby>バンド<rt>ばんど</rt></ruby>band、ばしょ place
だれ who、どれ which one／どの ＋noun、どこ where

You can use the superlative pattern:
Q:（かしゅ）で、（　だれ　）が　いちばん　すきですか。Or
　　いちばん　すきな　（かしゅ）は、（だれ）ですか。
A:（　　　　　）が　いちばん　すきです。

Reporting format: ～さんが　いちばんすきな（かしゅ）は、～です。
Caution: Question words can vary なに、だれ、どこ

[Vocabulary help]:

> food たべもの, drink のみもの, family かぞく, friend ともだち, place ばしょ,
> vegetables やさい, fruits くだもの, meet にく, fish さかな, milk ミルク or
> ぎゅうにゅう, rock ロック, jazz ジャズ, jogging ジョギング,
> swimming スイミング or すいえい, partying パーティー, studying べんきょう

E. Write in your answers for each of the questions using 〜の中で、いちばん.

1. スポーツの中で、どのスポーツがいちばん　すきですか。

　　_____

2. べんきょうの中で、どのがっかが　いちばん　おもしろいですか。
　　　　　　　　　　　　　(subject)　　　　　　　　(interesting)

　　_____

3. やさいの中で、どのやさいが　いちばん　おいしいですか。

　　_____

4. くだものの中で、どれが　いちばん　すきですか。

　　_____

5. かぞくの中で、だれが　いちばん　すきですか。

　　_____

6. きっさてんで、なにを　いちばん　よく　ちゅうもんしますか。

　　_____

F. Fill in the appropriate question for each of the following answers. Use いちばん and a fitting adjective.

[Vocabulary list]: せかい world, ながい long, はやい fast, ひとがおおい populated

1. ふじさん
　　日本で　いちばん　たかい山は、どの山ですか。

　　_____

2. マッキンリー山

　　_____

3.　エベレスト山
　　えべれすとさん

　_____

4.　ちゅうごく

　_____

5.　しんかんせん

　_____

6.　ミシシッピ川
　　みししっぴがわ

　_____

G. Reading comprehension: Read the following passage and answer the questions.

　田中さんのおくさんは、なつがにがて(weak point)です。あついのがいや(unpleasant)なんです。ふゆのほうが、すきです。田中さんのおくさんは、本がだいすきです。そして、しずかなところ (place)が　すきです。きょねんのなつは、ほっかいどうへ　いきました。ほっかいどうは、とうきょうよりすずしいんです。すずしいところで、たくさん本をよみました。

　田中さんのごしゅじんも、なつよりふゆのほうが　すきです。スキーがだいすきです。きょねんのクリスマスに　ながのへ、スキーにいきました。ながのは、　　　　　　　　　　　　　Nagano prefecture in central Japan
とうきょうから　それほどとおくありません。

1.　なつがにがてなひとは、だれですか。

2.　本がだいすきなひとは、だれですか。

3.　田中さんのおくさんは、きょねんのなつ　どこへ　いきましたか。

4.　そこで、何をしましたか。

5.　田中さんのごしゅじんは、きょねんのクリスマスに、どこへ　いきましたか。

　６．ながのは、とうきょうからとおいですか。


　７．田中さんのごしゅじんは、そこで、何をしましたか。


H.  Answer the questions with either Yes（はい、もう〜ました。）or No（いいえ、まだです。）.
Example:　　あさごはんを　たべましたか。
　　　　　　　→ はい、<u>もう</u>たべ<u>ました</u>。Or, → いいえ、まだです。

　（１）しゅくだいを　しましたか。

　（２）ぶつりのせんせいに　あいましたか。

　（３）コーヒーを　のみましたか。

　（４）日本語の本を　かいましたか。

　（５）としょかんの本を　かえしましたか。
　　　　　　library　　　　　　　　return

　（６）おひるごはんを　たべましたか。

　（７）クラスメートと　はなしましたか。

　（８）ミステリーを　よみましたか。
　　　　　mystery

　（９）きっさてんに　はいりましたか。
　　　　　　　　　　　　enter

　（１０）ともだちに　てがみを　かきましたか。
　　　　　　　　　　　　a letter

I. Change the comparative form from "A wa B yori ~" to the "B wa A hodo ~ nai" pattern.
　Example:

　　　ごはん<u>は</u>、パン<u>より</u>　おいしいです。
　→　　パン<u>は</u>、ごはん<u>ほど</u>　おいしく<u>ない</u>です。

　　（１）たなかさんは、かとうさんより、せがたかいです。
　　　　　→

（２）これは、あれより、おいしいです。
→

（３）ロックは、クラシックより、にんきがあります (is popular)。
→

（４）スーパー(supermarket)は、やおや(green-grocer)より、おおきいです。
→

（５）まきこさんのじ(handwriting)は、わたしのじより、きれいです。
→

（６）としょかんは、カフェテリアより、しずかです。
→

（７）わたしのいぬは、となり(neighbor)のいぬより、かわいいです。
→

（８）ぶつり(Physics)は、すうがく(Mathematics)より、おもしろいです。
→

（９）母は、父より　やさしいです。
→

（１０）すうがくは、せいぶつ(Biology)より　むずかしいです。
→

J. Reading comprehension practice: Read the following passage with your partner and figure out the answers to the questions below. Put an (O) next to the correct statement(s), and (X) next to the incorrect statement(s).

きのうは、ともだちのたんじょうびパーティーに　いきました。パーティーのまえに、デパートへ　いきました。そして、プレゼントをかいました。はじめは、セーターを　みました。きれいなセーターは、いちまい　五千円しました。つぎに、スカーフをみました。たかいスカーフは、一万円しました。そこで、ハンカチうりばにいきました。ハンカチは、いちまい　三千円しました。わたしは、きれいなハンカチを　にまい　ともだちに　かいました。

1. （　）ハンカチにまいは、セーターいちまいより、やすいです。
2. （　）セーターいちまいは、ハンカチにまいほど、たかくありません。
3. （　）スカーフいちまいは、ハンカチにまいより、たかいです。
4. （　）このひとは、セーターより、ハンカチのほうが、きにいりました。
   liked, favored
5. （　）このひとは、プレゼントに　ハンカチを　かいました。

Chapter 4(C): Dict-A-Conversation (1): Comparative
Answer the questions verbally and write your answers in hiragana
on a separate sheet.

1. _____
2. _____
3. _____
4. _____
5. _____
6. _____
7. _____
8. _____
9. _____
10. _____

Chapter 4(C): Dict-A-Conversation (2): Superlative
Answer the questions verbally and write your answers in hiragana
on a separate sheet.

1. _____
2. _____
3. _____
4. _____
5. _____
6. _____
7. _____
8. _____
9. _____
10. _____

Chapter 4 (C)'s Dict-A-Conversation (3): Superlatives
Listen to Chapter 4 C(3) on the student CD and fill in the blanks.

1. おとうさんは、「わたしは、だれよりも（　　　　　　　　）」といいました。
                                    (more than anyone)

2. こどもは、きょう　おとうさん（　　　　　　）おおきいものをみました。

3. でも、おとうさんは、「わたしが（　　　　　　　　）で　いちばん
おおきい。」といいました。

4. おとうさんは、こどもに、「それは、どの（　　　　　　　　）おおきいのか
ね？」と　いいました。

5. こどもは、「おとうさん（　　　　　　）、（　　　　　　　）おおきいんだ。」
といいました。

6. おとうさんは、がんばって、（　　　　　　　　）を　いっぱいにしました。
                        (worked very hard)                  (made it full)

7. そして、もっと、もっとおおきい（　　　　　　　　）になりましたが、

8. とうとう、（　　　　　　　）と　おおきいおとがして、はちきれて
(finally)              (made a loud noise)        (has exploded)
しまいました。

Chapter 4 (C)

| 食 | た（べる）<br>ショク<br><br>(food, to eat) | 食べる（たべる）to eat<br>日本食（にほんしょく）Japanese food<br>[朝食（ちょうしょく）breakfast]<br>[昼食（ちゅうしょく）lunch]<br>[夕食（ゆうしょく）　dinner]<br><br>(9)<br>ノ　入　𠆢　今　今　仒　食　食　食 |
|---|---|---|
| 気 | キ<br>ケ<br><br>(mind, air) | 気分（きぶん）feelings, mood<br>気もち（きもち）feelings<br>大気（たいき）atmosphere<br><br>(6)<br>ノ　ᅳ　气　气　気　気 |
| 好 | この（む）<br>す（く）<br>す（き）<br>コウ<br><br>(to favor, likable) | 好ましい（このましい）likable<br>好き（すき）　　　　likable<br><br>(5)<br>く　夕　女　女　好　好 |
| 方 | かた<br>ホウ<br>ボウ<br><br>(direction, a person) | あの方（かた）that person<br>あちらの方（ほう）that direction<br>一方（いっぽう）one side; while ~ing<br><br>(4)<br>丶　ᅳ　方　方 |
| 校 | コウ<br><br><br><br><br><br><br>(school) | 学校（がっこう）a school<br>　小学校（しょうがっこう）elementary<br>　　　　　　　　　　　　　　school<br>　中学校（ちゅうがっこう）junior high-<br>　　　　　　　　　　　　　　school<br>　[高校（こうこう）high school]<br>母校（ぼこう）one's old school<br>校内（こうない）school grounds<br><br>(10)<br>ᅳ　十　オ　木　杧　杧　栌　栌　校　校 |

## Kanji Practice for Chapter 4 (C)
かんじの　れんしゅう

1. つぎの　ことばを　よみなさい。それから、<ruby>クラスメート<rt>くらすめえと</rt></ruby>にいみをきき　なさい。 Read the following words to your classmates and ask them the meaning of each word/sentence.

 （１）　口で　食べます。

 （２）　食べるのが　好きです。

 （３）　好きな人は、あの人です。

 （４）　大好きです。

 （５）　日本の食べものの方が、好きです。

 （６）　おすしやおそばは、日本食です。

 （７）　今日は、気分がいいです。

 （８）　学校からうちへかえるのは、「下校」と言います。

 （９）　"Atmosphere" は、日本語で、「大気」と言います。

 （１０）　今回は、<ruby>和<rt>わ</rt></ruby>食にします。

2. よんでから、よみがなをかいて、えいごでいいなさい。 Read first, write yomigana above kanji, and translate into English.

 （１）　日本食が　好きです。

 （２）　今、とてもいい気分です。

 （３）　今回の日本語の<ruby>テスト<rt>てすと</rt></ruby>の<ruby>スコア<rt>すこあ</rt></ruby>は、山田さんと同じです。

 （４）　学校の中を　校内と　言います。

 （５）　下校の　じかんです。

## Chapter 4 (D) My family and hometown　私のかぞく　と　まち

せんせい：モニカさんの　お父さん　と　お母さんは、アメリカですか。　1

モニカ：　ええ、りょうしんは、ロサンジェルスの　ちかくにいます。　2

みわ：　　そのまちは、なんといいますか。　3

モニカ：　パサデナです。　4

あいこ：　パサデナは、どんなところですか。　5

モニカ：　きれいなところです。しずかですよ。びじゅつかん　や　こうえんが

　　　　　あります。フットボールで　ゆうめいなローズボールもあります。 7

せんせい：ごきょうだいは？　8

モニカ：　三人います。兄が一人　と　妹　が　二人です。　9

あいこ：　じゃ、「四人きょうだい」ですね。いいな、、、　10

モニカ：　どうして？　11

あいこ：　わたしは、一人っ子ですから、うらやましいです。　12

モニカ：　「一人っ子」って？　13

せんせい：「一人だけの子ども」のいみですよ。　14

モニカ：　ああ、わかりました。　15

みわ：　　あ、クラスのじかん。今から、ぶつりのクラスがありますから、　16

　　　　　先生、これで　しつれいします。　17

せんせい：はい、じゃまたあとで。　18

Chapter 4 (D)                    Vocabulary List

### 1. Expressions
いいなあ　　　Ii na...                    "I am envious."
なんといいますか。Nan to iimasu ka        "What is it called?"

### 2. Nouns
(おとうさん otoosan)                      father (respect form)
(おかあさん okaasan)                      mother (respect form)
りょうしん　ryooshin                          parents
　ごりょうしん go-ryooshin               polite form of "ryooshin"
ロサンジェルスRosanjerusu                Los Angeles
ちかく　　　　chikaku                    near
(まち machi)                             town
(ところ tokoro)                          place
びじゅつかん bijyutsukan                 museum
(こうえん kooen)                         park
フットボールfuttobooru                   football
ローズボールroozu booru                  Rose Bowl
きょうだい　kyoodai                      siblings
　ごきょうだい go-kyoodai                siblings; polite form of "kyoodai"
　よにんきょうだい yonin-kyoodai         four-siblings (including yourself)

あに　　　　ani                          older brother (polite form is "oniisan")
いもうと　　imooto                       younger sister (polite form is "imooto-san")
ひとりっこ　hitori-k-ko                  single child
(こども kodomo)                          child, children
クラス　　　kurasu                       class, lecture, classroom
　ぶつりのクラス　butsuri no kurasu      Physics class

### 3. Copula nouns
(きれい[な])kirei [na]                    pretty; beautiful
(しずか[な]shizuka [na])                  quiet
(ゆうめい[な]yuumei [na])                famous

### 4. Interrogative pronoun
(どうして dooshite)                       Why?

### 5. Adjective
うらやましい urayamashii                 envious

6. Verbs

しつれいします shitsurei shimasu       Please excuse me.

7. Particles

| から | kara | conjunctive particle "because" |
|---|---|---|
| だけ | dake | only |
| ひとりだけいます。hitori dake imasu | | There's only one person. |
| しか〜ない | shika ~ nai | only |
| ひとりしかいません。hitori shika imasen | | There's only one person. |
| で | de | particle to show limit |
| これで | kore de | with this |
| "Kore de shitsurei shimasu." | | "It's time for me to leave." (polite form) |
| これでしつれいします。 | | |

-------------------------------------------------------------------------------

Additional Vocabulary from Grammar Notes, Exercises, and Dict-A-Conversation

-------------------------------------------------------------------------------

[Nouns]

| ばん | - ban | ordinal numbers |
|---|---|---|
| ばんめ | - ban-me | one's order within a group such as the first, the second, etc. |
| いちばんうえいちばんうえ ichiban-ue | | the highest; the oldest |
| まんなか | ichiban-shita | the lowest; the youngest |
| まんなか | man-naka | the middle |
| うえからにばんめ ue kara ni-ban-me | | second highest; second oldest |
| したからにばんめ shita kara ni-ban-me | | second lowest; second youngest |
| なんにんかぞく nan-nin kazoku | | how many family members (total numbers) |
| さい | - sai | - years old (counter for age) |
| ニキロ | ni kiro | two kilometers |
| はちうえ | hachi-ue | potted plants |
| かいしゃ | kaisha | company |
| ハリウッド | Hariuddo | Hollywood |
| ないしょ | naisho | secret |
| クリスマスツリー kurisumasu-tsurii | | Christmas tree |
| かじ | kaji | fire |

(family tree vocabulary) (humble--polite)

| そふ--おじいさん sofu-ojiisan | grandfather |
|---|---|
| そぼ--おばあさん sobo-obaasan | grandmother |
| ちち--おとうさん chichi-otoosan | father |
| はは--おかあさん haha-okaasan | mother |

あに--おにいさん ani-oniisan      older brother
あね--おねえさん ane-oneesan      older sister
おとうと--おとうとさん otooto-otooto san      younger brother
いもうと--いもうとさん imooto-imooto san      younger sister
おじ--おじさん oji-ojisan      uncle
おば--おばさん oba-obasan      aunt

## Vocabulary from Dict-A-Conversation

### [Nouns & Noun phrases]
なんさいうえ nan-sai ue      how much older
なんさいした nan-sai shita      how much younger
まちのなまえ machi no namae      name of the town
きれいなところ kirei na tokoro      pretty places
しずかなところ shizuka na tokoro      quiet places
(びじゅつかん bijyutsukan)      museum

### [Copula Nouns]
りっぱ      rippa      splendid; great; well-built
むり      muri      impossible

### [Question word]
どなた      donata      who (casual form of "dare" だれ)

### [Adjectives]
さみしい      samishii      lonely
かなしい      kanashii      sad

### [Adverbs]
いそいで      isoide      in a hurry

### [Particle]
しか〜ありません shika (+ ~ nai)      only; have nothing but ~

### [Verbs]
と いいます。 ~ to iimasu      It's said ~
いそぎましょう。 isogimashoo      Let's hurry up. (いそぐ isogu to hurry)
のこりました。 nokorimashita      It remained. (のこる nokoru to remain)

### [Conjunction]
だから      dakara      therefore; connects two sentences when the preceding sentence shows a reason for the second. See Exercise A in this chapter.

Chapter 4(D)                    Grammar and Cultural Notes

## 1.  Particle "から kara" to show reasons

The particle "kara" signals the preceding sentence is a reason for, or explains, the main clause.  In a formal sentence structure, the subordinate clause followed by the "kara" particle comes before the main clause.  Observe:

| Reason (Subordinate clause) | | Consequence(Main clause) |
|---|---|---|
| Kurasu ga arimasu (I have a class [to go to]) | | Shitsurei shimasu (Please excuse me.) |
| Hitorikko desu (I am a single child) | kara (because), | Urayamashii desu (I am envious.) |
| Ki ga arimasen (There are no trees) | | Atsui desu (It's hot.) |

However, in real conversation, the order of subordinate and main clauses may switch, just as often as the phenomenon happens in the English language, where the main clause (consequence) is stated first.  It is also possible where the main clause may be omitted.  Let us look at a variation of dialogue now.  Take a look at line 10 through line 12 in Chapter 4(D).  Observe:

Aiko:      Then, there are "four-siblings" (all together).  Oh, I am envious…
Monica:  Why?
Aiko:      Because I am a single child.

Aiko:      じゃ、よにんきょうだいですね。いいな、      Jya, "yonin-kyoodai" desu ne.  Ii na…
Monica:  どうして？                                        Dooshite?
Aiko:      わたしは、ひとりっこですから。              Watashi wa hitorikko desu kara.

Miwa's statement (in lines 16-17) is in an ordinary order:

| Subordinate clause (reason)  kara  +  Main clause (consequence) |
|---|

Miwa:  Because I have engineering class now, please excuse me.
　　　　いまから　こうがくのクラスがありますから、しつれいします。
　　　　Ima kara, koogaku no kurasu ga arimasu kara, (korede) shitsurei shimasu.

Observe another variation in the following pattern:

わたしは、ひとりっこです。だから、うらやましいです。
Watashi wa,     hitori-k-ko desu.   Dakara (because of that),   urayamashii desu.

This sentence conveys the exact message in a connected sentence form as follows.
→   わたしは、ひとりっこですから、うらやましいです。
　　　Watashi wa, hitori-k-ko desu kara,   urayamashii desu.

## 2. <u>Particle "だけ dake"</u>

The particle "dake" indicates that the preceding noun or sentence shows restriction or limitation. It is equivalent to "just" or "only" in English. In line fourteen of Chapter 4(D), the professor explains the meaning of "ひとりっこ hitori-k-ko," saying it means a "single-child," "ひとりだけのこども hitori dake no kodomo" in Japanese. Literally, "hitori dake" means "only one-person."

Examples:

1．やさしいかんじ<u>だけ</u>、べんきょうしました。I studied only easy kanji.
2．ロシアには、一回<u>だけ</u>、いきました。 I went to Russia only once.
3．きょうは、テレビをみた<u>だけ</u>です。   I only watched TV today.
   (みた：past tense casual of "miru," to watch)
4．げんきな<u>だけ</u>が、とりえです。      My strong point is that I'm healthy.

## 3. <u>Particle "しか shika" + negative predicate</u>

The particle "shika + negative predicate" is equivalent to "only" or "nothing but" in English. While it means the same as "dake," the difference is observed in the following: "Shika + negative predicate" strongly focuses upon negativity. For example, if you have five dollars in your pocket and you focus on what you don't have, or on what you are lacking in order to buy an item of fifty dollars, you use "shika+ arimasen," which conveys a feeling of incompletion, disappointment or dissatisfaction.

Examples:

1．きょう、いえには、私<u>しか</u> いません。I'm the only one at home today.
2．とおいですが、五分<u>しか</u> かかりませんでした。It's far, but it took me
                                                    only five minutes.
3．パンがひとつ<u>しか</u>ありませんが、いっしょにそれを食べましょう。
                  A piece of bread is the only thing I have, but let me share it
                  with you.
4．えい語<u>しか</u> 分かりません。English is the only language I understand.
5．ポケットには、一ドル<u>しか</u>ありません。I have nothing but a dollar in my
                                               pocket.
6．田中さんは、サラダ<u>しか</u> 食べません。Ms. Tanaka eats nothing but salad.

## 4. <u>Ordinal numbers:</u> 何番（なんばん）、何番目（なんばんめ）

You may know how to say "No. 1" in Japanese. Yes, "ichiban いちばん"! The counter for order is "-ban 番," therefore, number 1 is "ichi-ban 一番," number 2 is "ni-ban 二番," number 3 is "san-ban 三番," number 4 is "yon-ban 四番," and so forth. Thus, this counter "ban 番"converts cardinal numbers to ordinal numbers, and "-ban me 番目" illustrates one's order within a group. This "me 目" is used for other numeral classifiers as well, including "ひとりめ（一人目）" (the first person), "ひとつめ（一つ目）" (the first one), "いっけんめ（一軒目）" (the first house), and so forth.

### Counters for people and age, and ordinal numbers

|  | ～にん (~people) | ～さい (~years old) | ～ばん（め）(ordinal, ~th) |
|---|---|---|---|
| 何 | なんにん　　　何人 | なんさい　　　何才<br>（お）いくつ？ | なんばん（め）　　何番（目） |
| 一 | ひとり　　　一人 | いっさい　　　一才 | いちばん（め）　　一番（目） |
| 二 | ふたり　　　二人 | にさい　　　二才 | にばん（め）　　二番（目） |
| 三 | さんにん　　　三人 | さんさい　　　三才 | さんばん（め）　　三番（目） |
| 四 | よにん　　　四人 | よんさい　　　四才 | よんばん（め）　　四番（目） |
| 五 | ごにん　　　五人 | ごさい　　　五才 | ごばん（め）　　五番（目） |
| 六 | ろくにん　　　六人 | ろくさい　　　六才 | ろくばん（め）　　六番（目） |
| 七 | しちにん　　　七人 | ななさい　　　七才 | ななばん（め）　　七番（目） |
| 八 | はちにん　　　八人 | はっさい　　　八才 | はちばん（め）　　八番（目） |
| 九 | きゅうにん　　九人 | きゅうさい　　九才 | きゅうばん（め）　　九番（目） |
| 十 | じゅうにん　　十人 | じゅっさい　　十才 | じゅうばん（め）　　十番（目） |
| 百 | ひゃくにん　　百人 | ひゃくさい　　百才 | ひゃくばん（め）　　百番（目） |

Examples:
    (1) 一番上（いちばんうえ）the eldest (literally: the first from the top)
    (2) 一番下（いちばんした）the youngest (literally: the first from the bottom)
    (3) 上（うえ）から二番目（にばんめ）the second oldest
    (4) まん中（なか）　　　　　　the right in the middle
    (5) 下（した）から二番目（にばんめ）the second youngest

Look at the illustration of Monica's family and read the following dialogue.

あいこ：モニカさんは、なんにんかぞくですか。
モニカ：わたしは、ろくにんかぞくです。
あいこ：モニカさんは、いちばんうえですか。
モニカ：いいえ、わたしは、うえから　にばんめです。うえに　あにがいます。
あいこ：そうですか。したは、いもうとさんですか、おとうとさんですか。
モニカ：いもうとが、ふたり　います。
あいこ：そうですか。よにんきょうだいですね。
モニカ：はい、きょうだいは、みんなで　よにんです。

Chapter 4 (D) Exercises

A. Combine two sentences into one, using から.

1. あしたは、テスト<ruby>テスト<rt>てすと</rt></ruby>です。だから、きょうは、べんきょうします。
                (Therefore)

_____

2. お金<rt>かね</rt>がありません。だから、ぎんこうへ いきます。

_____

3. おいしいです。だから、たくさん食<rt>た</rt>べます。

_____

4. ひとりだけのいもうとです。だから、<u>かわいい</u>です。
                           adorable

_____

5. 一人<rt>ひとり</rt>っ子<rt>こ</rt>です。だから、<u>さみしい</u>です。
                      lonely

_____

B. Fill in the blanks with appropriate words.

1. 田中<rt>たなか</rt>さんが、きますから、あなたも（            ）か。

2. もう（       ）ですから、おひるごはんを食<rt>た</rt>べませんか。

3. 今日<rt>きょう</rt>は、一月四日<rt>いちがつよっか</rt>ですから、あしたは、（       ）です。

4. いえから、がっこうまで、二十キロ<rt>にじゅっきろ</rt>（メートル<rt>めえとる</rt>）ありますから、
   （       ）です。

5. （       ）から、 かいません。

6. （       ）から、食<rt>た</rt>べません。

7. お金が（       ）から、ぎんこうへ いきます。

C. Combine two sentences, using な adjectives (= copula nouns.

1. これは、きれいです。いえです。

   →  これは、きれいな いえです。

２．いもうとは、げんきです。こどもです。
<br>　　　　　　　　　　　　　　(child)
<br>　　→

３．あには、しずかです。ひとです。

　　→

４．これは、ゆうめいです。だいがくです。

　　→

５．これは、たいへんです。しごとです。
<br>　　　　　　　　　　　　　(job, work)
<br>　　→

６．あの人<sup>ひと</sup>は、りっぱです。人<sup>ひと</sup>です。

　　→

７．これは、じょうぶです。つくえです。
<br>　　　　　(sturdy; strong)
<br>　　→

D.  Pair-work: Work together in choosing the correct verbs （あります or います）for each listed item.

　　１．　犬<sup>いぬ</sup>
　　２．　ねこ
　　３．　はちうえ（プラント<sup>ぷらんと</sup> potted plants）
　　４．　かぞく
　　５．　ひと
　　６．　あに
　　７．　がっこう
　　８．　しごと
　　９．　だいがく
　１０．　きょうだい
　１１．　ライオン<sup>らいおん</sup>
　１２．　いもうと under a tree

E. Pair-work: Ask your partner the following questions.

1. あなたには、おにいさんが ありますか。

2. あなたには、いもうとさんが ありますか。

3. あなたのうちには、<ruby>プール<rt>ぷうる</rt></ruby>が ありますか。
swimming pool

4. あなたには、おねえさんが、ありますか。

5. あなたには、おとうとさんが、ありますか。

6. いま、おかあさんは、うちに いますか。

7. いま、おとうさんは、<u>かいしゃ</u>に いますか。
company

F. Fill in the blanks with appropriate particles.

1. いま、<u>じかん</u>がありません（    ）、<u>いそいで</u><ruby>コーヒー<rt>こうひい</rt></ruby>
（    ）のみます。

2. わたし（    ）（    ）、こどもが ふたり あります。

3. これは、おいしくない（    ）、<ruby>食<rt>た</rt></ruby>べません。

4. おかあさん（    ）、いま どこ（    ）いますか。

5. きょう（    ）おてんき（    ）いいですね。

6. ぎんざ（    ）しんじゅく（    ）あるきました。

7. うち（    ）でんしゃ（    ）えき（    ）、じてんしゃ
（    ）いきました。

8. きっさてん（    ）、<ruby>サンドイッチ<rt>さんどいっち</rt></ruby>（    ）<ruby>食<rt>た</rt></ruby>べました。

9. <ruby>ハリウッド<rt>はりうっど</rt></ruby>[Hollywood]（    ）、えいが（    ）みました。

10. みたかえき（    ）でんしゃ（    ）のりました。

<ruby>たんご<rt></rt></ruby><ruby>ヘルプ<rt>へるぷ</rt></ruby>(Vocabulary Help)

| |
|---|
| じかん time, いそいで in a hurry, のみます drink, こども children, おいしい tasty, たべます eat, おてんき weather, ぎんざ&しんじゅく places in Tokyo, あるきます walk, でんしゃ train, えき station, じてんしゃ bicycle, いきます go, きっさてん coffee shop, えいが movie, みます watch, のります get on, ride |

G. You are Kinoshita Shinobu.  Look at the family tree and answer each question as
   Shinobu.  Since you will be addressing your own family members, you must use
   "in-group" family vocabulary (humble form).

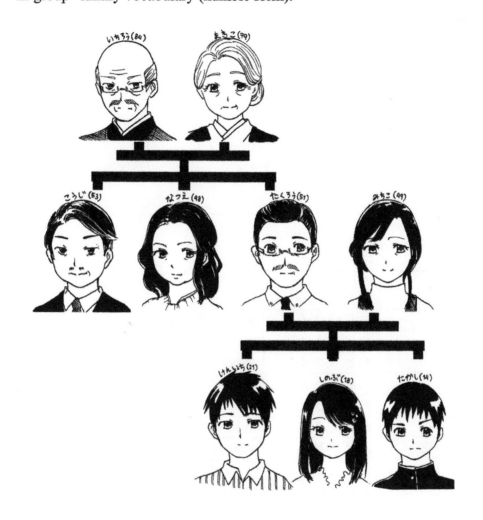

しつもん：

1.   木下けんいちさんは、どなたですか。
     <u>けんいちは、私の　あにです。</u>

2.   たくろうさんは、どなたですか。

     _____

3.   みちこさんは、どなたですか。

     _____

4.   まきこさんは、どなたですか。

     _____

5.　　たかしさんは、どなたですか。

　　　　_____

6.　　こうじさんは、どなたですか。

　　　　_____

7.　　なつえさんは、どなたですか。

　　　　_____

8.　　いちろうさんは、どなたですか。

　　　　_____

[Family tree vocabulary]

| In-group vocabulary | Polite way to address family | English equivalents |
|---|---|---|
| そふ | おじいさん | grandfather |
| そぼ | おばあさん | grandmother |
| ちち | おとうさん | father |
| はは | おかあさん | mother |
| あに | おにいさん | older brother |
| あね | おねえさん | older sister |
| おとうと | おとうとさん | younger brother |
| いもうと | いもうとさん | younger sister |
| おじ | おじさん | uncle |
| おば | おばさん | aunt |

H. Group work

(1). Work in groups of three or four. Take turns asking your classmates how many people are in their family. Comment on with いいですねえ、うらやましいです、さみしくありませんか、etc.

Example:

A：～さんの　ごかぞくは、なんにんかぞくですか。

B：ちちと　ははと　わたしだけです。

C：へぇ、さんにんかぞくですか。

D：きょうだいは、いないんですね。

B：ええ、ひとりっこです。

A：さみしくありませんか。

B：ええ、さみしいです。でも犬（いぬ）がたくさんいますから。

Practice:

A:（      ）さんの　ごかぞくは、なんにんかぞくですか。

B:　五人かぞくです。（　）と（　）と私と、あにが　ふたりいます。

C:　へぇ、<u>にぎやか</u>ですね。
　　　　　（lively）

B:　いえ、<u>けんか</u>しますから、<u>やかましい</u>です。
　　　　　（fight; quarrel）　　　　（noisy）

A:　私は、ひとりっこですから、うらやましいです。

C:　私も　です。

Create your own:

A:

B:

C:

etc.


(2). Work in groups of four or five.  Take turns asking your classmates how many siblings they have, and also inquire their sibling birth order.

Example:

A：～さんは、ごきょうだいが　ありますか。

B：はい、ふたり　あります。

C：～さんは、なんばんめですか。

B：わたしは、まんなかです。

D：うえは、おにいさんですか、おねえさんですか。

B：あねです。

A：したは、いもうとさんですか、おとうとさんですか。

B：おとうとです。

C：じゃ、～さんは、さんにんきょうだいのまんなかですね。

B：はい、そうです。

Create your own:

A:

B:

C:

etc.


(3). Work with a partner.  Take turns to describe the members of your family by name and age.  Fill in the chart with information about your partner's family.
Example:

わたしには、あねがひとりと　おとうとが　ひとりいます。あねのなまえは、
アンです。２５さいです。おとうとは、ジョンで、１８さい。ちちのなまえは、
アランです。いま、５４さい。ははは、アネットといいます。５０さいです。

| ごかぞく | おなまえ | ねんれい age（～さい） |
|---|---|---|
|  |  |  |
|  |  |  |
|  |  |  |
|  |  |  |
|  |  |  |
|  |  |  |

I. Choose either だけ or しか

（１）えいご（　　　　　）わかります。

（２）えいご（　　　　　）わかりません。

（３）わたし（　　　　　）が、きょうだいの中で、女の子です。

（４）あなたに（　　　　　）はなしますよ。みんなには、ないしょですから。
　　　　　　　　　　　　　　　　　　　　　　　　　　a secret

（５）いえには、パン（　　　　　）ありませんから、マーケットにいきました。

（６）かとうさんは、サラダ（　　　　　）たべました。そしてステーキは、
　　　おとうとに　やりました。　　　　　　　　　　　　steak
　　　　　　やる to give

（７）じかんが　ありませんから、しゅくだい（　　　　　）しましょう。

（８）クリスマスツリーには、この木（　　　　　）ありません。とても、
　　　りっぱな木ですから。
　　　magnificent

（９）あと五分（　　　　　）ありませんから、いそぎましょう。
　　　　　　　　　　　　　　　　　　　　　いそぐ to rush; hurry up

（１０）火事のあと、このたてもの（　　　　　）が　のこりました。
　　　　fire　　　　　　　　　　　　　　　　　　　remained

Choose the right one.

（１）五ドル（だけあります、しかありません）から、えいがは、むりですね。
　　　　　　　　　　　　　　　　　　　　　　　　　　　impossible

（２）五ドル（だけあります、しかありません）から、うれしいです。
　　　　　　　　　　　　　　　　　　　　　　glad

（３）五ドル（だけあります、しかありません）から、かなしいです。
　　　　　　　　　　　　　　　　　　　　　　sad

J. Guess what surnames are most popular in the U.S.? どの<ruby>姓<rt>せい</rt></ruby>が<ruby>一番<rt>いちばん</rt></ruby>おおいですか。

Please place them in descending order as 1<sup>st</sup>, 2<sup>nd</sup>, 3<sup>rd</sup>, 4<sup>th</sup>, and 5<sup>th</sup> in Japanese いちばん、
にばん、さんばん、よんばん、ごばん．

<ruby>ジョンソン<rt>じょんそん</rt></ruby>、<ruby>スミス<rt>すみす</rt></ruby>、<ruby>ジョーンズ<rt>じょおんず</rt></ruby>、<ruby>ブラウン<rt>ぶらうん</rt></ruby>、<ruby>ウィリアムズ<rt>うぃりあむず</rt></ruby>
Johnson,     Smith,     Jones,        Brown,      Williams

| | |
|---|---|
| ジョンソン | |
| スミス | |
| ジョーンズ | |
| ブラウン | |
| ウィリアムズ | |

(For answers, see the end of Chapter 14.)

いちばんは、（　　　　　　　）です。

にばんは、（　　　　　　　）です。

さんばんは、（　　　　　　　）です。

よんばんは、（　　　　　　　）です。

ごばんは、（　　　　　　　）です。

K. Guess what surnames are most popular in Japan.? どの<ruby>姓<rt>せい</rt></ruby>が<ruby>一番<rt>いちばん</rt></ruby>おおいですか。
なまえのしたに、ばんごうをかいてください。

| たなか | すずき | さとう | たかはし | わたなべ |
|---|---|---|---|---|
| | | | | |

こたえ：<ruby>一番<rt>いちばん</rt></ruby><ruby>多<rt>おお</rt></ruby>いのは、「<ruby>佐藤<rt>さとう</rt></ruby>」です。<ruby>二番目<rt>にばんめ</rt></ruby>に<ruby>多<rt>おお</rt></ruby>いのは、「<ruby>鈴木<rt>すずき</rt></ruby>」、<ruby>三番目<rt>さんばんめ</rt></ruby>が「<ruby>高橋<rt>たかはし</rt></ruby>」、<ruby>四番目<rt>よんばんめ</rt></ruby>が、「<ruby>田中<rt>たなか</rt></ruby>」、<ruby>五番目<rt>ごばんめ</rt></ruby>が、「<ruby>渡辺<rt>わたなべ</rt></ruby>」です。このあと、「<ruby>伊藤<rt>いとう</rt></ruby>」、「<ruby>山本<rt>やまもと</rt></ruby>」、「<ruby>中村<rt>なかむら</rt></ruby>」、「<ruby>小林<rt>こばやし</rt></ruby>」、「<ruby>斉藤<rt>さいとう</rt></ruby>」と　つづきます。

Chapter 4(D)'s Dict-A-Conversation (1)
Look at the family tree in Chapter 4(D), Exercise G. Answer the following questions as
Shinobu Kinoshita. You can answer in short phrases, rather than complete sentences.

1 _____

2 _____

3 _____

4 _____

5 _____

6 _____

7 _____

8 _____

9 _____

10 _____

11 _____

12 _____

Chapter 4(D)'s Dict-A-Conversation (2)
Answer the following questions in complete sentences.

1

_____

2

_____

3

_____

4

_____

5

_____

6

_____

7

_____

8

_____

9

_____

Chapter 4 (D)

| 父<br>(father) | ち ち<br>ふ フ | 父（ちち）father (humble form)<br>お父さん（おとうさん）father (respect form)<br>父子（ふし）father and children |
| | | (4)<br>ノ ハ グ 父 |
| 母<br>(mother) | は は<br>ぼ ボ<br>も モ | 母（はは）mother (humble form)<br>お母さん（おかあさん）mother (respect form)<br>父母（ふぼ）parents |
| | | (5)<br>乚 口 母 母 母 |
| 近<br>(near) | ち か（い）<br>きん キン | 近い（ちかい）near<br>近く（ちかく）near, neighborhood<br>[近所（きんじょ）neighborhood] |
| | | (7)<br>ノ イ 斤 斤 斤 近 近 |
| 子<br>(a child) | こ<br>し シ | 女の子（おんなのこ）a girl<br>[子供（こども）a child]<br>子女（しじょ）women and children<br>女子（じょし）a girl |
| | | (3)<br>フ 了 子 |
| 兄<br>(an older brother) | あ に<br>け い ケイ<br>きょう キョウ | 兄（あに）an older brother<br>兄弟（きょうだい）brothers |
| | | (5)<br>ノ 口 口 尸 兄 |
| 妹<br>(a younger sister) | い も う と<br>し シ | 妹（いもうと）a younger sister<br>姉妹（しまい）sisters |
| | | (8)<br>く 夕 女 女 女 好 妹 妹 |
| 目<br>(eyes) | め<br>がん ガン | 目（め）eyes<br>目上（めうえ）social superiors<br>目下（めした）social inferiors |
| | | (5)<br>丨 冂 日 目 目 |

## Kanji Practice for Chapter 4 (D)
かんじの　れんしゅう

1. つぎの　ことばを　よみなさい。それから、クラスメート<sup>くらすめえと</sup>にいみをきき
   なさい。 Read the following words to your classmates and ask them the
   meaning of each word/sentence.

   （１）　父と母

   （２）　お母さん

   （３）　お父さん

   （４）　学校から近い

   （５）　母と子

   （６）　兄と妹

   （７）　お兄さん

   （８）　目上の人

   （９）　目下の人

   （１０）　日本語で、「父母」と「りょうしん」は、　同じです。

   （１１）　この近くに、すんでいます。

   （１２）　私は、一人っ子です。

   （１３）　兄が一人と、妹が二人います。

2. よんでから、よみがなをかいて、えいごでいいなさい。 Read first, write
   yomigana above kanji, and translate into English.

   （１）　私の父のなまえは、「たろう」と言います。

   （２）　母には、きょうだいが、三人あります。

（３）　四人の子どもが、生まれました。
　　　　　　　　　　（was born）

（４）　女子学生が　十五人います。

（５）　妹さんのおなまえは、何と、言いますか。

（６）　うちから、学校まで、近いですか。

3.　ひらがなとかんじで　かきなさい。Write in kanji and hiragana.

（１）　ちちとははは、パサデナに　すんでいます。

（２）　このちかくに、にほんしょくのレストランがあります。

（３）　あにのなまえは、あなたとおなじなまえです。

（４）　めうえのひとには、ていねいなにほんごで、はなします。
　　　　　　　　　　　　　（polite）

（５）　わたしは、めがいいです。

（６）　このクラスのがくせいは、みんなで、にじゅうろくにんです。

（７）　おんなのこは、いま　アイスクリームを　たべています。
　　　　　　　　　　　　　　　　　　　　（is eating）

（８）　ひとりめのこは、おんなのこ　でした。
　　　　（The first child was a girl.）

4. かぞくのことを　かきましょう。Write about your family. Follow the instructions by filling in the blanks with your own information, then summarize them in the box.

(1) I live in (name of the city).
　私は、（パサデナ）に　すんでいます。

(2) I am in a family of (three, four, five, etc.).
　（五人）かぞく です。

(3) My father's name is (　　　). He is (number) years old.
　父のなまえは、（ジョゼフ）です。（四十五）さいです。

(4) My mother's name is (　　). She is (number) years old.
　母のなまえは、（デイナ）です。（四十一）さいです。

(5) I am the (ordinal number, e.g., 2nd or 3rd) among my siblings.
　私は、（三人きょうだい）の　（まん中）です。
　Or（いちばん上、二ばん目、いちばん下）

(6) I have (number of) (brothers, sisters) or I am an only child.
　（私には）（あね）が（一人）と、（おとうと）が　（一人）います。
　Or（私は、一人っ子です）

(7) We have a dog/cat/fish etc.
　（うちには、）（かわいい犬）も、います。
　Or（うちには、大きいねこが　います。）（ペットは、いません。）

[Summary]
私は、五人かぞくです。父のなまえは、ジョゼフ<u>で</u>、四十五さいです。母のなまえは、デイナ<u>で</u>、四十一さいです。私は、三人きょうだいの　まん中です。あねが一人と、おとうとが　ひとりいます。うちには、かわいい犬も　います。
　（で connects two sentences when the first sentence ends with a noun.）
Now try your composition.

Chapter 4 (E)　　　　　I get up at 6:30 A.M.　六時半に　おきます。

せんせい：モニカさんは、毎日　何時ごろに　おきますか。　　　　　　　　1

モニカ：　六時半ごろ　です。りょうのあさごはんは、七時ですから。　　　2

せんせい：だいがくのりょうは、とおいですね。　　　　　　　　　　　　　3

モニカ：　はい、キャンパスまで　バスで、四十五分　かかります。　　　　4

せんせい：四十五分は、ながいですね。　　　　　　　　　　　　　　　　　5

モニカ：　先生、大学のちかくに　アパートか、げしゅくがありますか。　　6

せんせい：きっと　ありますよ。　　　　　　　　　　　　　　　　　　　　7

モニカ：　でも、学生課では、もうありませんでした。　　　　　　　　　　8


せんせい：ああ、それで　先日　学生課に？　　　　　　　　　　　　　　　9

モニカ：　はい、きのうも　行きました。でも、むずかしいです。　　　　　10

せんせい：そうですか。モニカさんは、くるまを　うんてんしますか。　　　11

モニカ：　いいえ、しません。　　　　　　　　　　　　　　　　　　　　　12

せんせい：じゃ、ふどうさんやに　たのみましょう。　　　　　　　　　　　13

モニカ：　「ふどうさんや」は、「Realtor」のことですか。　　　　　　　14

せんせい：モニカさんは、ことばを　たくさん　しっていますね。　　　　　15
　　　　　しりあいの　ふどうさんやさんに、きいてみましょう。　　　　　16

モニカ：　ありがとうございます！　　　　　　　　　　　　　　　　　　　17

[English translation]:

Professor: Monica, what time do you get up everyday?
Monica: About six thirty. My dormitory breakfast is at seven o'clock.
Professor: The college dormitory is (located) far, isn't it?
Monica: Yes, it takes forty five minutes by bus to get to campus.
Professor: Forty five minutes is (a) long (time).
Monica: Professor, are there any apartments or boarding houses near campus?
Professor: I'm sure there are.
Monica: But there were none (left) at the Student Office.
Professor: Oh, was it why you were there the other day?
Monica: Yes, I went there yesterday (too). But, it's been difficult.
Professor: I see. Do you drive, Monica?
Monica: No, I don't.
Professor: Then, let's ask a realtor.
Monica: Does "fu-do-o san ya" mean a "realtor"?
Professor: That's right. You have a good vocabulary. I know someone who is a realtor
Monica: Thank you so much!

バスで ４５分
かかります。

[Vocabulary]:

1. Expressions

| | | |
|---|---|---|
| しっています | Shitte imasu | I know. |
| ～のことですか | ~ no koto desuka. | Are you talking about~? |
| きいてみましょう | Kiite mimashoo | Let's (try and) ask. |

2. Nouns

| | | |
|---|---|---|
| りょう | ryoo | dormitory |
| あさごはん | asa-gohan | breakfast |
| だいがくのキャンパス | daigaku no kyanpasu | college campus |
| ちかく | chikaku | near by, vicinity |

| | | |
|---|---|---|
| アパート<br>あぱあと | apaato | apartment building |
| げしゅく | geshuku | boarding house |
| (くるま kuruma) | | car |
| こと | koto | thing(s) [abstract things] |
| ~のこと | ~ no koto | about ~ |
| しりあい | shiriai | acquaintance |
| ふどうさんや | fudoosan ya | realtor |

[time words]

| | | |
|---|---|---|
| まいにち | mainichi | everyday |
| きのう | kinoo | yesterday |
| なんじごろ | nan-ji goro | around what time |
| ろくじはんごろ | roku-ji han goro | around six thirty |
| しちじ | shichi-ji | seven o'clock |
| よんじゅうごふん | yon-jyuu-go fun | forty five minutes |

## 3. Adjectives

| | |
|---|---|
| (とおい tooi) | far (↔ちかい chikai) |
| (ながい nagai) | long (↔みじかい mijikai) |

## 4. Adverbs

| | | |
|---|---|---|
| きっと | kitto | surely, certainly, probably |
| それで | sore de | because of that, due to that |

## 5. Verbs

| | | |
|---|---|---|
| おきます | okimasu | get up (おきる okiru: to get up) |
| かかります | kakarimasu | take (かかる kakaru: to take) |
| うんてんします | unten shimasu | drive (うんてんする unten suru: to drive) |
| しません | shimasen | don't do |
| たのみましょう | tanomimashoo | Let's ask for a favor. (たのむ tanomu: to ask for a favor) |

## 6. Particles

| | |
|---|---|
| (まで made) | up to, until, as far as |

-----------------------------------------------------------------------

Additional Vocabulary from Grammar Notes, Exercises, and Dict-A-Conversation

-----------------------------------------------------------------------

[Nouns]

| | | |
|---|---|---|
| じ | ~ji | o'clock |

| | | |
|---|---|---|
| ふん/ぶん | ~ fun/pun | minutes |
| はん | ~ han | half-hour; thirty minutes |
| ごぜん | gozen | a.m. |
| ごご | gogo | p.m. |
| ごろ/ぐらい | goro/gurai | about; approximately (goro is used only for time) |
| これぐらい | kore-gurai | this much; about this size |
| しょうご | shoogo | noon |
| ひる | hiru | daytime |
| よなか | yonaka | midnight |
| おおきさ | ookisa | size |
| フライト | furaito | flight |
| て | te | hand |
| じゅぎょう | jyugyoo | lecture |
| ひるごはん | hiru-gohan | lunch |
| ばんごはん | ban-gohan | dinner |
| アルバイト | arubaito | part-time job; side job |
| よる | yoru | night |
| がくちょう | gakuchoo | university president |
| はやおき | hayaoki | early bird; early riser |
| ねぼう | neboo | late riser |
| おなまえ | o-namae | name (polite form) |

[Verbs]

| | | |
|---|---|---|
| シャワーをあびる | shawaa wo abiru | to take a shower |
| じゅぎょうをうける/ | jyugyoo wo ukeru | to attend a class |
| じゅぎょうにでる | jyugyoo ni deru | to attend a class |
| のる | noru | to ride; get on~ (~ni noru) |
| おりる | oriru | to get off (~ wo oriru) |
| かえる | kaeru | to return; go home |
| あらう | arau | to wash |
| はいる | hairu | to enter ~ (~ ni hairu) |
| (ねる neru) | | to go to bed; sleep |
| (~を)でる | (~ wo ) deru | to leave a place |
| はじまる | hajimaru | to begin (intransitive verb) |
| おわる | owaru | to end (intransitive verb) |

Chapter 4(E)　　　　　　　　　Grammar and Cultural Notes

## 1. <u>Time expressions</u>

### (1) 〜じ o'clock , 〜ふん minute

When you tell time, the suffix for "o'clock" is じ（時）and the suffix for "minute" is
ふん（分）. Phonetic change occurs (from ふん to ぷん) for the following minutes:
1, 3, 4, 6, 8, and 10, and also for "how many minutes?" which is なんぷん。

| | 〜じ | 〜ふん |
|---|---|---|
| 1 | いちじ | いっぷん |
| 2 | にじ | にふん |
| 3 | さんじ | さんぷん |
| 4 | ＊よじ | よんぷん |
| 5 | ごじ | ごふん |
| 6 | ろくじ | ろっぷん |
| 7 | しちじ | ななふん |
| 8 | はちじ | はっぷん（はちふん） |
| 9 | ＊くじ | きゅうふん |
| 10 | じゅうじ | じゅっぷん（じっぷん） |
| 11 | じゅういちじ | じゅういっぷん |
| 12 | じゅうにじ | じゅうにふん |
| ? | なんじ | なんぷん |

### (2) Particle "ni に" indicating specific time

The particle "ni" marks a point in time. It corresponds to "at," "in" or "on" in English. It
follows the time expressions which need "at," "in" or "on" in English, such as "at one
o'clock," or "on Sunday," and "in August."

Since it indicates a "specific time," it cannot follow a "vague" time expression such as
"today," "tomorrow," "last week" and "next year." In other words, "ni" does not follow
time words which do not need preposition in English.

Examples:

①私は、まいあさ　六時<u>に</u>　おきます。 I get up at 6 o'clock every morning.

②七時ごろ（<u>に</u>）あさごはんを　たべます。 I eat breakfast around 7 o'clock.

　　　　　* Particle "ni" is optional when it is used with "goro" or "gurai."

③ 七月<u>に</u>　日本へ　行きます。　　　　I am going to Japan in July.

④ 母は、昭和３６年（１９６１年）<u>に</u>　生まれました。　My mother was born in 1961.

Important to remember!  Do not add particle に to these words.

---

Since the particle "ni" indicates time specificity, words that express "ambiguous time frames" do not usually pair with the particle "ni."
Those words are:
あさ(morning)、 ひる(daytime), よる/ ばん (evening)、
きのう(yesterday)、 きょう(today)、 あす（あした）(tomorrow)、
きょねん(last year)、 ことし(this year)、 らいねん(next year)、
せんげつ(last month)、 こんげつ(this month)、 らいげつ(next month)、
せんしゅう(last week)、 こんしゅう(this week)、 らいしゅう(next week)、
いつか(some time)、 ときどき(sometimes)、 こんど(this time, last time)、
いつも(always)、 たいてい(usually)
まいねん、 (every year)、まいあさ (every morning) ,  まいにち(everyday)
And several others

---

① 父は、毎朝(**X**)　ジョギングをします。 My father jogs every morning.

② 私は、去年(**X**)、大学を　そつぎょうしました。 I graduated from college last year.

③ 祖母は、夜(**X**)　三十分ぐらい　およぎます。 My grandmother swims about half an hour at night.

## (3) ごろ、ぐらい **approximately, around**

Both words indicate the approximation of time.  The difference is, while ごろ is used only for "time," ぐらい is applied to all other concepts, including amount, distance, time, etc.
Examples:

①五時ごろ、行きませんか。 Why don't we go around five o'clock?

②五時ぐらいに、行きませんか。 Why don't we go around five o'clock?

③「その犬は、どのぐらいの大きさでしたか。」 How big was that dog?

　　「この犬ですか。これぐらいでした。」 "You mean this dog?  It's about
　　　　　　　(also このぐらい)　　　　　　　　　　　　　　this big."

④わたしのうちまで、百メートルぐらいです。

　　　　　　　　　　　　　It's about 100 meters to my house.

(4)  **a.m.** =ごぜん（午前）,  **p.m.**=ごご（午後）
Note the word order:  The bigger unit is placed first.

Examples:

| | |
|---|---|
| 1:05 a.m. | ごぜん　いちじ　ごふん |
| 4:09 p.m. | ごご　　よじ　　きゅうふん |
| 12:00 noon | しょうご（正午）、ひるのじゅうにじ |
| 12:00 midnight | ごぜん　れいじ（零時）, よなかのじゅうにじ |

Note that "half an hour" is either さんじゅっぷん or はん（"half", 半）

## 2. <u>ちかい & ちかく</u>: **Location words**

Both ちかい and ちかく mean "near," while ちかい is an adjective and ちかく is a noun.  The same is true also with とおい and とおく, "far."
Examples:
My house is near the college.
1. わたしのうちは、だいがくの<u>ちかく</u>　にあります。
2. わたしのうちは、だいがくに　<u>ちかい</u>です。

There's Yoshinoya near the college.
1. がっこうの<u>ちかく</u>に、「よしのや」が　あります。
2. がっこうから<u>ちかいところ</u>に、「よしのや」があります。

## 3. <u>しっています</u> **I know**.

The "te" form verb will be officially introduced in Chapter 6D.  Every verb has its "te" form.  By adding something to the "te" form, you can expand the meaning.  The "te" form of verb "shiru" is "shitte" and by adding "imasu," you can express your current state such as "I'm hungry," "I know him," and "I am married."

| | |
|---|---|
| 田中さんを知っていますか。 | Do you know Mr. Tanaka? |
| A：ええ、よく知っています。 | A:  Yes, I know him well. |
| B：私は、知りません。 | B:  I don't know (him). |

## 4. <u>きいてみましょう</u> **Let's ask and see**.

The construction of this sentence also uses the "te" form verb.  "Kiite" is the "te" form of "kiku," to "ask" or "inquire" (it also means to "listen").  The verb "miru" is to "see."  Therefore the combination creates the meaning of "Let's ask to see what it is like."  This pattern of "te + miru" is widely used and will be explored in detail in Chapter 10A.  For now, just learn that きいてみましょう is "Let's ask to find out."

## 5. ごはん（ご飯）& こめ（米）

あさごはん means "breakfast," ひるごはん, "lunch," and ばんごはん（ゆうごはん、ゆうはん）, dinner. ごはん means "cooked rice," while こめ refers to "raw/uncooked rice." So, before you start cooking rice, you address rice as こめ, but once it's cooked, call it ごはん. Rice is still a main diet for the Japanese, and おにぎり（おむすび）serves as a quick and convenient lunch and snack.

## 6. げしゅく（下宿）Boarding house

College students who live away from home have several residence options: dormitory, apartment or boarding house. The arrangement for げしゅく is typically made between someone you know and the landlord, although in recent years it can be managed by a realtor. Some げしゅく offers meals and some don't; some offers only a room, and others a separate guest house, depending upon arrangement. As the Western influence of individualism has increasingly saturated modern Japan, apartment living has popularized for college students.

がくせいのせいかつ   **Student's Life**

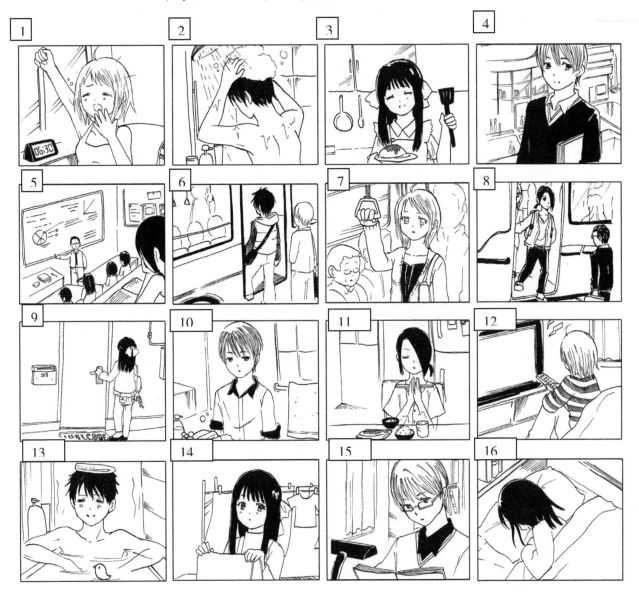

1. おきます    2. シャワーをあびます    3. あさごはんをつくります
4. がっこうへ いきます。
5. クラス（じゅぎょう）に でます（じゅぎょうをうけます）
6.&7. バスにのります      8. バスをおります
9. うちに かえります    10. てを あらいます     11. ごはんをたべます
12. テレビをみます     13. おふろに はいります 14. せんたくを します
15. べんきょうします    16. ねます

## Chapter 4(E) Exercises

A.　Pair Work:　なんじ　なんぷん　ですか。

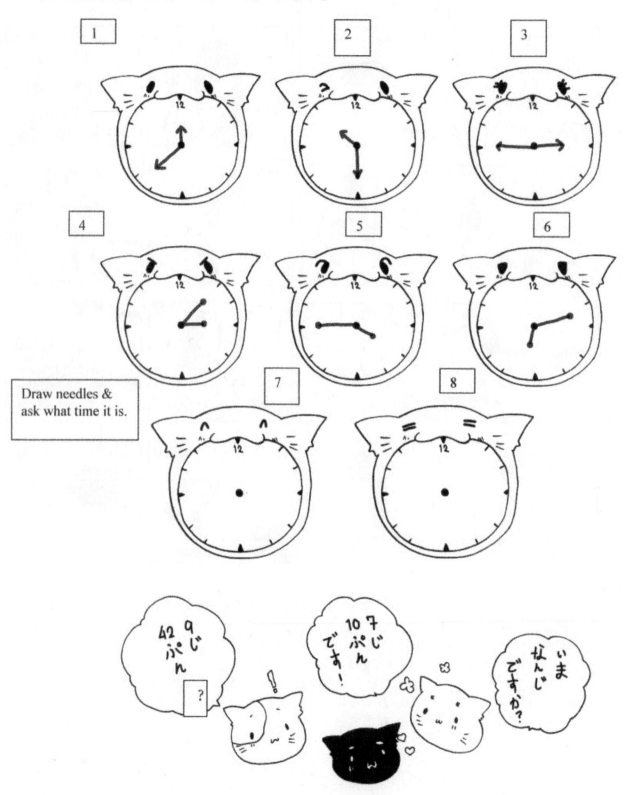

B-1.  Match up the vocabulary with its definition.

1.  おきる                                                a. to go to bed
2.  シャワーを　あびる f                                 b. to go home
3.  あさごはんを　たべる I                               c. to wash one's hands
4.  がっこうへ　いく h                                   d. to get up
5.  じゅぎょうに　でる                                   e. to end
6.  バスに　のる k                                      f. to take a shower
7.  うち（りょう/アパート）に　かえる b                   g. to take a bath
8.  てを　あらう C                                      h. to go to school
9.  はじまる                                            i. to attend class
10. べんきょう（を）する j                               j. to study
11. おわる                                              k. to take a bus
12. おふろに　はいる                                     l. to eat breakfast
13. ねる                                                m. to begin

B-2.  Come up with the "masu" form verbs

1.  おきる→          2.  あびる→          3.  たべる→          4.  かかる→
5.  いく →           6.  でる→            7.  のる→            8.  かえる→
9.  あらう →         10. する→            11. はいる→          12. ねる→

C. Fill in the first column under わたし and find a classmate who got at least five same answers to the following questions.  S/he is your partner for the next exercise.
Examples:

Q:  うちから　学校まで　近いですか。

A:  いいえ、近くありません。とおいです。


Q:  アパートに　すんでいますか。

A:  はい、アパートに　すんでいます。


Q:  ねぼう (late riser) ですか。

A:  いいえ、はやおき (early bird) です。

| | わたし | なまえ(          ) |
|---|---|---|
| 1. うちから学校まで　近い | | |
| 2. うちから学校まで　とおい | | |
| 3. アパートに　すんでいます | | |

| | | |
|---|---|---|
| 4. りょうに　すんでいます<br>　　dormitory | | |
| 5. うちに　すんでいます | | |
| 6. くるまを　うんてんします | | |
| 7. はやおき　です<br>　　early bird | | |
| 8. ねぼう　です<br>　　late riser | | |
| 9. よく　おふろに　入ります | | |

D. Write down your daily schedule under the column of わたし. Then, ask your partner for the following information and write down his/her schedules on the table.
Examples:

（１）　　Ｑ：なんじに　おきますか。
　　　　　Ａ：しちじに　おきます。

（２）　　Ｑ：なんじに　うちを　でますか。
　　　　　Ａ：はちじ　です。

| Activities | わたし | （　　　　　　）さん |
|---|---|---|
| 1. おきます | ………じ………ふん | ………じ………ふん |
| 2. シャワーを　あびます | ………じ………ふん | ………じ………ふん |
| 3. あさごはんを　たべます | ………じ………ふん | ………じ………ふん |
| 4. うちを　でます<br>　　(leave home) | ………じ………ふん | ………じ………ふん |
| 5. がっこうに　きます | ………じ………ふん | ………じ………ふん |
| 6. じゅぎょうに　でます | （　　　）じから<br>（　　　）じまで | （　　　）じから<br>（　　　）じまで |
| 7. ひるごはんを　たべます | ………じ………ふん | ………じ………ふん |
| 8. アルバイトを　します<br>　　(side/part-time job) | （　　　）じから<br>（　　　）じまで | （　　　）じから<br>（　　　）じまで |
| 9. うちに　かえります | ………じ………ふん | ………じ………ふん |

| 10. ばんごはんを　たべます | ………じ………ふん | ………じ………ふん |
|---|---|---|
| 11. テレビを　みます | （　　　）じから<br>（　　　）じまで | （　　　）じから<br>（　　　）じまで |
| 12. しゅくだいをします | （　　　）じから<br>（　　　）じまで | （　　　）じから<br>（　　　）じまで |
| 13. ねます | ………じ………ふん | ………じ………ふん |

E. Pair-work: Ask your classmate the following questions.

（１）きょう　あさごはんを　たべましたか。

（２）きょうのあさ、なにを　のみましたか。

（３）きのうの<u>よる</u>は、<u>よく</u>　ねましたか。
　　　　　　night　　well

（４）きのう、アルバイトを　しましたか。

（５）きのう、なんのしゅくだいを　しましたか。

Now, change partners and continue.

（６）きのう、テレビを　みましたか。

（７）きのう、ばんごはんは、なにを　たべましたか。

（８）きのう、せんたくを　しましたか。

（９）きのう、バスに　のりましたか。

（１０）きのうのてんきは、<u>あめ</u>でしたか。
　　　　　　　　　　rain

（１１）きのうは、げつようびでしたか。

（１２）<u>学長</u>のなまえを　しっていますか。
college/university president

Chapter 4 (E): Dict-A-Conversation (1)   Daily Life

    (A) Respond to the statements verbally, and then write down your replies.  Please answer in <u>short sentences,</u> writing in hiragana.

1

_____

2

_____

3

_____

4

_____

5

_____

6

_____

7

_____

(B) When you hear the chime, ask the appropriate questions verbally before you hear the answers.  Please write in <u>complete sentences</u> in hiragana.

8    Please ask me if I ate breakfast today.

_____

9    Please ask me if my house is far from school.

_____

10  Please ask me what I ate dinner.

_____

11  Please ask me what time I usually go to bed.

_____

12  Please ask me if today was cold.

_____

13  Please ask me if I had coffee this afternoon.

_____

14  Please ask me if there's Yoshinoya near the college.

_____

Chapter 4 (E)

| 毎<br>(every) | ごと<br>まい<br>マイ | 日毎に（ひごとに）day by day<br>毎日（まいにち）every day<br>毎月（まいつき）every month<br>毎回（まいかい）every time<br>毎朝（まいあさ）every morning |
| | | (6)<br>ノ ﾉ ﾄ 亡 勾 毎 毎 |
| 時<br>(time, o'clock) | とき<br>じ<br>ジ | いい時（いいとき）a good time<br>あつい時（あついとき）when it's hot<br>何時（なんじ）what time?<br>一時（いちじ）one o'clock<br>一時間（いちじかん）one hour |
| | | (10)<br>l 冂 日 日 旷 旷 昨 昨 時 時 |
| 半<br>(half, middle) | なか（ば）<br>は ん<br>ハン | 二月の半ば（にがつのなかば）mid February<br>半日（はんにち）half a day<br>半月（はんつき）half a month<br>一時半（いちじはん）one thirty |
| | | (5)<br>丶 丷 ﾞ 半 半 |
| 行<br>(to go, a line) | い（く）<br>こ う<br>コウ<br>ぎ ょ う<br>ギョウ | 行く（いく）to go<br>学校（がっこう）a school<br>一行（いちぎょう）one line<br>一行目（いちぎょうめ）the first line<br>銀行（ぎんこう）a bank |
| | | (6)<br>ノ ﾞ 彳 彳 行 行 |
| 知<br>(to know,<br>knowledge) | し（る）<br>ち<br>チ | 知る（しる）to discover, to find out<br>知人（ちじん）an acquaintance |
| | | (8)<br>ノ 느 ﾝ 午 矢 知 知 知 |

Kanji Practice for Chapter 4 (E)
かんじの　れんしゅう

1．つぎの　ことばを　よみなさい。それから、クラス<ruby>メート<rt>くらすめえと</rt></ruby>にいみをきき
なさい。Read the following words to your classmates and ask them the
meaning of each word/sentence.

(1)　　毎日

(2)　　毎年

(3)　　毎月

(4)　　四時半

(5)　　半分、　半日、　半月、　半年

(6)　　行きます。

(7)　　知っています。

(8)　　一行目

(9)　　二行目半

(10)　山中さんは、母の知人です。

2．よんでから、よみがなをかいて、えいごでいいなさい。Read first, write
yomigana above kanji, and translate into English.

(1)　　毎日、あさごはんを　食べます。

(2)　　毎あさ、学校へ　行きます。

(3)　　一時半にともだちが　来ます。

(4)　　りんごを　ともだちと半分ずつ、分けました。

(5)　　あの方を　知っています。

(6)　　一行目から　五行目まで　よんでください。

3. かんじをかいてから、しつもんに　こたえなさい。Write the underlined words
   in kanji and answer the questions.

    （１）　　<u>まいにち</u>　<u>がっこう</u>へ　<u>き</u>ますか。

    （２）　　この<u>ちかく</u>のレストラン<sup>れすとらん</sup>を　<u>し</u>っていますか。

    （３）　　<u>なんじ</u>に　としょかんへ　<u>い</u>きますか。

    （４）　　<u>ろくじはん</u>ごろ、ここへ　<u>き</u>ますか。

    （５）　　お<u>とう</u>さんとおかあさんは、<u>まいつき</u>、お<u>てら</u>へ　<u>い</u>きますか。

    （６）　　このクラス<sup>くらす</sup>は、<u>まいにち</u>　<u>くじ</u>から　<u>じゅうじはん</u>まで　ありますか。

    （７）　　<u>まいかい</u>、このクラス<sup>くらす</sup>で　だれに　<u>あ</u>いますか。
        (every time)　　　　　　　　　　　　　　　(meet)

    （８）　　<u>きょう</u>は、<u>なんじ</u>に　<u>がっこう</u>に　<u>き</u>ましたか。

    （９）　　この<u>だいがく</u>の　がくちょうの　おなまえを　<u>し</u>っていますか。
        (college president)

日本語1　かんじのまとめ Kanji Review (Chapters 1 ~ 4E)
The answers for A and B correspond to each other so that you can check yourselves.
A.　Read the following and write yomigana:

1．日本、百円、千円、一万円

2．大学生、何年、山田さんの白い犬が来ます。

3．大中小、小学生、中学生

4．女の人、水色、入ります

5．えんぴつの先、私の先生、今、今日、上と下

6．一回、今回、分かる、言います、同じ

7．口で食べます、気分がいい時、お母さんが好き。妹の方がやさしい。

8．学校へ行きます。お父さん、この近くの子、お兄さんは目がいい。

9．毎日、何時、四時半、半分、知っています

B.　Write the following in kanji

1．にほん、ひゃくえん、せんえん、いちまんえん

2．だいがくせい、なんねん、やまださんの　しろい　いぬが　きます。

3．だいちゅうしょう、しょうがくせい、ちゅうがくせい

4．おんなのひと、みずいろ、はいります

5．えんぴつのさき、わたしのせんせい、いま、きょう、うえとした

6．いっかい、こんかい、わかる、いいます、おなじ

7．くちでたべます。きぶんがいいとき、おかあさんがすき。いもうとのほう
　　が　やさしい。

8．がっこうへいきます。おとうさん、このちかくのこ、おにいさんはめがいい。

9．まいにち、なんじ、よじはん、はんぶん、しっています

にほんご１のまとめ　　　　Review Exercise on Word Order and Particles

Place the words in the right order so that the sentences become coherent.  You also need
to choose the particles from below so that each sentence is complete.

1．ともだち、しました、へや、コンピューター・ゲーム
　　　（を、で、と）

2．かえりました、あるいて、りょう、がっこう
　　　（まで、から）

3．てがみ、おとうさん、おかあさん、かきました
　　　（と、に、を）

4．いま、しました、へや、きのう、そうじ、きれいです
　　　（の、から、は、を）

5．パーティー、あります、しけん、いきません
　　　（から、に、が）

6．でんわ、じかん、きょう、ありました、ともだち、はなしました
　　　（から、で、が、と、は）

7．たのしくありませんでした、きっさてん、コーヒー、ひとり、のみました
　　　（から、を、で、で）

8．たべました、たべませんでした、きのう、あさごはん、きょう
　　　（は、は、を、が）

9．ひとり、ぶつり、むずかしい、きょう、テスト、よる、べんきょうします
　　　（の、の、は、は、で、から）

10．シャツ、しました、きれいじゃありませんでした、せんたく
　　　（を、から、が）

Kanji Bingo Sheet (3) Chapter 4CDE
Fill in the blanks with the kanji and play Bingo.

Kanji 食、気、好、方、校　（山、日、田、生）

| 食 | 気 | 好 |
|---|---|---|
| 方 | 校 | 山 |
| 生 | 田 | 日 |

| 山 | 生 | 日 |
|---|---|---|
| 方 | 校 | 田 |
| 好 | 気 | 食 |

|  |  |  |
|---|---|---|
|  |  |  |
|  |  |  |

Kanji 父、母、近、子、兄、妹、目　（色、気）

| 父 | 母 | 近 |
|---|---|---|
| 妹 | 兄 | 子 |
| 目 | 色 | 気 |

| 気 | 目 | 色 |
|---|---|---|
| 子 | 兄 | 妹 |
| 近 | 母 | 父 |

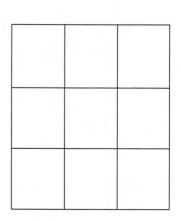

Kanji 毎、時、半、行、知　（近、子、兄、妹）

| 毎 | 時 | 半 |
|---|---|---|
| 近 | 知 | 行 |
| 子 | 兄 | 妹 |

| 妹 | 兄 | 子 |
|---|---|---|
| 半 | 行 | 近 |
| 知 | 時 | 毎 |

|  |  |  |
|---|---|---|
|  |  |  |
|  |  |  |

Kanji list for Japanese 1: (Ch.1, 2A, 2B, 3B, 3C, 4A, 4B, 4C, 4D, 4E)

1) Size
　　　　大、中、小
2) Numbers
　　　　一、二、三、四、五、六、七、八、九、十、百、千、万
3) Locations, Distance & Directions
　　　　上、（中）、下、方、先、近い、学校
4) People and animals
　　　　私、人、女、父、母、兄、妹、子、犬、学生、先生
　　　　目、口
5) Nature
　　　　日、月、山、田、水
6) Time
　　　　今、時、分、年
7) Actions
　　　　来ます、入ります、言います、回ります、食べます、行きます、

　　　　知ります、（語ります）
8) Feelings
　　　　気、好き
9) Concepts & Others
　　　　何、毎、半、色、白
10) Products of Human Activities
　　　　本


よみがなヘルプ：
１）だいちゅうしょう（おおきい、なか、ちいさい）
３）うえ、（なか）、した、ほう、さき、ちかい、がっこう
４）わたし、ひと、おんな、ちち、はは、あに、いもうと、こ、いぬ、がくせい、
　　せんせい、め、くち
５）ひ、つき、やま、た、みず
６）いま、じ（とき）、ふん（ぶん、ぶん）、ねん（とし）
７）きます、はいります、いいます、まわります、たべます、いきます、しります、
　　（かたります）
８）き、すき
９）なに（なん）、まい、はん、いろ、しろ
１０）ほん

## うみ (The Ocean)

うみ

うみは、ひろいな おおきいな
つきが のぼるし ひがしずむ

うみは、おおなみ あおいなみ
ゆれて どこまで つづくやら

うみに おふねを うかばせて
いって みたいな よそのくに

海は 広いな 大きいな
月が 昇るし 日が沈む

海は 大波 青い波
揺れて どこまで 続くやら

海に お船を 浮かばせて
行ってみたいな よその国

Umi wa hiroi na ookii na
Tsuki ga noboru shi hi ga shizumu

Umi wa oonami aoi nami
Yurete dokomade tsuzuku yara

Umi ni ofune wo ukabasete
Itte mitai na yoso no kuni

Oh, how big you are, the ocean.
The moon rises and the sun sets from you.

The waves are big and deep blue,
They sway back and forth eternally.

Oh I wish I could sail out to a foreign country,
in a ship I float on those waves.

# **Invitation to Kabuki**

*Expressions*
"It begins at one o'clock and ends at five thirty"
"Always, often, sometimes, occasionally, seldom, never"
"Once a day, once a week, once a month, once a year"
"Won't we go see a movie?"

*About Japanese Verbs*

*Kanji practice from Chapter 5*

*Golden Week*

*Reading a Japanese story: The Story of Urashima*

*Reading a Japanese story: The Grateful Crane*

歌舞伎に　行きませんか。

Chapter 5　　　Invitation to Kabuki　かぶき　に　行きませんか。

てつや：モニカさん、こんしゅうの土曜日は、ひまですか。　　　　　　　1

モニカ：え？いつですか。土曜日ですか。午前中は、としょかんへ　　　2

　　　　行きますが、午後は、何もありません。　　　　　　　　　　　3

てつや：じゃ、かぶき　に　行きませんか。　　　　　　　　　　　　　4

モニカ：「かぶき」って、何ですか。　　　　　　　　　　　　　　　　5

てつや：「かぶき」の　せつめい　は、、、むずかしいなあ、、　　　　6

　　　　あのう、おしばいなんです。日本の　古い　おしばいですが、、。

モニカ：ああ、かぶき？　おもいだしました。　　　　　　　　　　　　8

　　　　アメリカの大学で、ならいました。えどじだいに、さかんでしたね？

　　　　「おくに」さん　の　なまえを　知っています。　　　　　　10

てつや：そうです、そうです。今は、男の人だけですが、、、　　　　11

　　　　その「かぶき」です。　　　　　　　　　　　　　　　　　　12

モニカ：でも、私には、日本語が　むずかしくありませんか。　　　　13

てつや：むずかしくないですよ。だいじょうぶです。　　　　　　　　14

モニカ：かとうさんは、いつも　どこで　かぶきを　みるんですか。　15

てつや：「みなみざ」です。三じょうかわらまちの。　　　　　　　　16

モニカ：あ、川のそば　ですね。何時に　はじまりますか。　　　　　17

てつや：一時です。　五時半ごろに　おわります。　　　　　　　　　18

モニカ：じゃ、行きましょう。十五分ぐらい前に　行きましょうか。　19

てつや：それがいい。十二時四十五分<ruby>じゅうにじよんじゅうごふん</ruby>に、みなみざの前<ruby>まえ</ruby>で、会<ruby>あ</ruby>いましょう。    1

[English Translation]:

Tetsuya:  Monica, are you free this Saturday?
Monica:  Eh?  When?  (You mean) this Saturday?  I will be going to the library in the
         morning, but I won't have anything (to do) in the afternoon.
Tetsuya:  Then, won't you go to Kabuki (with me)?
Monica:  What's "Kabuki"?
Tetsuya:  It's hard to explain "Kabuki" ….Well, it's a play.  It's an old play in Japan…...
Monica:  Oh, Kabuki?  I remember (now).  I learned (about it) in college in the US.
         It was poplular during the Edo Period, right?  I know the name of "Okuni."
Tetsuya:  That's right.  There are only male performers nowadays though…  That's the
         one I am talking about…
Monica:  But, isn't the Japanese (language) too difficult for me?
Tetsuya:  It's not difficult.  (You'll be) all right.
Monica:  Where do you usually see Kabuki, Mr. Kato?
Tetsuya:  (I see Kabuki) at Minami-za.  It's at Sanjyo-Kawaramachi.
Monica:  Ah, it is the one near the river, isn't it?  What time will it start?
Tetsuya:  At one o'clock.  It ends around five thirty.
Monica:  Then let's go.  Shall we go there about fifteen minutes early?
Tetsuya:  That sounds good.  Let's meet at twelve forty-five in front of the Minami-za.

Chapter 5                    Vocabulary List

1. Expressions

| | |
|---|---|
| 〜んですか。 | A question form that adds personal (feelings of) involvement in the inquiry (or surprise). |
| （どこで）みるんですか。 | Where do you see (it)? |
| え？ | An expression showing surprise or question |
| あのう | An expression showing hesitance at the beginning of a speech |
| 〜が..... | Originally "but." However, it is often used at the end of speech to add softness; i.e., to avoid strong and determined undertones, or to encourage a listener to speak. |
| そう（です）,そう（です）。 | That's right. |

2. Nouns

| | |
|---|---|
| かぶき | Kabuki theater, a performance onstage that flourished during the Edo period. |
| せつめい | explanation |
| しばい | a play (=おしばい) |
| えどじだい | the Edo Period (A.D. 1603~ 1865) |
| おくに（さん） | A girl from Shikoku who danced in an exotic costume; an originator of Kabuki |
| みなみざ | a Kabuki theater in Kyoto |
| さんじょうかわらまち | a location in Kyoto where Sanjo St. and Kawaramachi St. meet |
| （としょかん） | a library |
| （かわ） | a river |
| （そば） | nearby |
| （まえ） | front |

Time words

| | |
|---|---|
| こんしゅう | this week |
| せんしゅう | last week |
| らいしゅう | next week |
| いま | now |
| ごぜんちゅう | during the morning (hours) (ごぜん A.M.) |
| （ごご） | P.M.  afternoon |
| （〜じ） | o'clock |
| （〜ふん、ふん） | minutes |
| （ごろ・ぐらい） | about, around |

3. な Adjectives/Copula Nouns

| | |
|---|---|
| さかん | prosperous, flourish |
| (だいじょうぶ) | all right |
| (ひま) | free (time) |

4. Adjectives

| | |
|---|---|
| むずかしくない | (It's) not difficult (むずかしい difficult) |
| (ふるい) | old |
| (いい) | good |

5. Verbs

| | |
|---|---|
| おもいだします（おもいだす） | remember; recall |
| ならいます（ならう） | learn |
| はじまります（はじまる） | begin |
| おわります（おわる） | end |
| あいます（あう） | meet |
| します | |
| メール、でんわ、そうじ、せんたく、べんきょう、しんぱい＋します | email, telephone, clean, laundry, study, worry |
| かぜをひきます | catch a cold（かぜをひく） |
| ごはんを　つくる | to cook |
| うんどうする | to exercise |
| いしゃにいく | go to see a doctor |
| (しっています/しっている) | I know (S/he knows). |
| (みます/みる) | see, look, watch |

6. Adverbs
(adverbs of frequency)

| | |
|---|---|
| いつも | always |
| よく | often |
| たいてい | usually |
| ときどき | sometimes |
| たまに | occasionally |
| あまり〜ない | not very (much) |
| ぜんぜん〜ない | not at all |

(time words)

| | |
|---|---|
| しゅうまつ | weekend |
| いっしゅうかん | for one week |
| いっかげつ | for one month |

7.  Particles
    に                                          A particle showing a specific time; "at~"
        ごじ　に　はじまります    It begins at five o'clock.

    に                                          A particle demonstrating "purpose" of going
        かぶき　に　いきます      I'll go "for" Kabuki.

        [Vocabulary often used with particle "ni" to show a purpose]
        かいもの                          shopping
        しょくじ                          meal
        デート                            date
        べんきょう                        study
        えいが                            movie
        しごと                            work
        ドライブ                          drive
        あそび                            pleasure; leisure

    で                                          A particle showing the location of action;  "at" or
                                                "in" in English where actions take place
        うちで　べんきょうします I (will) study at home.
        としょかんで　ほんを　よみます。 I (will) read books in the library.

8.  が                                          Conjunctive Particle which means " but" or
                                                "although."  It's used when content between
                                                two sentences contradict.
9.  いつ                                        A question word meaning "when." While "なんじ、
                                                なんがつ、なんにち" express very specific times,
                                                "いつ" is used in a  much broader and vague sense.

--------------------------------------------------------------------------------
Additional Vocabulary from Grammar Notes, Exercises, and Dict-A-Conversation
--------------------------------------------------------------------------------

[Nouns]
せいかつ                                  life; life style
パブ                                      pub
つき                                      the moon
やすみ                                    holiday; absent; rest　（おやすみ）
くもり                                    cloudy
ふろ                                      (hot) bath　（おふろ）
テープ                                    tape
いしゃ                                    medical doctor (おいしゃさん)
しんぱい                                  worry

[な Adjectives/Copula Nouns]
(いや)                                          dislikable; unpleasant

[Adjectives]
ひろい                                          spacious
せまい                                          small/narrow-spaced

[Adverbs]
きのう                                          yesterday
あす                                            tomorrow

きょねん                                        last year
ことし                                          this year
らいねん                                        next year

せんげつ                                        last month
こんげつ                                        this month
らいげつ                                        next month

いつか                                          some time
こんど                                          this time; last time

まいねん                                        every year
まいあさ                                        every morning
まいばん                                        every night

[Verbs]
うまれる                                        to be born
まつ                                            to wait

[Particles]
に                                              per (short form of "に 付き")
　　いちにちに　なんかい                        how many times a day
　　いっしゅうかん　に　なんかい                how many times a week
　　いっかげつ　に　なんかい                    how many times a month

も                                              for emphasis; even
Question words + mo + nai    = total negation
　　なにも　ない。    There's nothing.
　　だれも　いない。    There's nobody.
　　どこにも　いない。 He's nowhere.

-----------------------Vocabulary from Dict-A-Conversation----------------------------

[Nouns]

| | |
|---|---|
| りょこう | trip |
| ほか | other |
|     ほかのともだち | other friends |
|     なんにんのひと | how many people |

[Verbs]

| | |
|---|---|
| よぶ/ よびます | to invite; call |

-----------------------Vocabulary from the Golden Week ----------------------------

[Nouns]

| | |
|---|---|
| ミーティング/ かいぎ | meeting |
| りょこうちゅう | during the trip |
| きこく | returning to the country |
| つぎのひ/よくじつ | the next day |
| れんきゅう | consecutive holidays |
| きん | gold |
| さいしょのしゅう | the first week |
| おわり | end |
| まいとし | every year |
| とびいし | stepping-stone |

[Adjectives]

| | |
|---|---|
| すばらしい | wonderful |

[Verbs]

| | |
|---|---|
| つづく | to continue |
| ジャンプする | to jump |

Chapter 5                    Grammar and Cultural Notes

## 1. <u>Expressing a strong sense of inquiry or surprise:</u> "…んですか **n desu ka**"

You have already seen the usage of "~n desuka" in Monica's reply to the Professor in Chapter 4 (A). When Monica was invited to join her, she asked "Ii n desu ka?" (Are you sure it is really all right?). In this case, the preceding word is the adjective "ii." In Chapter 5, we will use a verb instead. As "ii" is a plain form of adjective, you will need the casual form of a verb (which is also a dictionary form) before adding "n desu ka."

How to form the "…n desu" style:

> Casual form verb (dictionary form) + n desu ka

Examples:

Dictionary form verb "taberu" + n desu (ka) 食べるんですか。
"iku"   + n desu (ka) 行くんですか。
"yomu"   + n desu (ka) 読むんですか。

You can render your speech emotionally expressive and alive by appropriately using "…n desu." This is most impactful in question form, "…n desu ka," which conveys a strong sense of inquiry or surprise. On the other hand, the "…masu ka" ending at times conveys feelings of distance and excessive formality. For example, "どこへ行きますか。 Doko e ikimasu ka" does not convey the vivacity and liveliness of "どこへ行くんですか。 Doko e iku-n-desu ka" (Where are you going? [I really want to know] or [I am totally shocked]). Certainly, one must be careful not to overuse the "n desu" form. A better sense of when to use "んです n desu" will come naturally through exposure and experience. The first step to take is to **master the dictionary form verb**.

## 2. <u>Expressing speaker's attempt to explain:</u> "…んです **n desu.**"

When you try to explain, to someone who is concerned with your health since you look ill, you use "んです n desu." It is equivalent to "It's because...." in English. So, if you are having a headache, you say "あたまが　いたいんです。 atama ga itai n desu" to explain why you don't look well. When your reply with a verb, you use a dictionary form with "んです n desu," e.g., テストが<u>ある</u>んです。 Observe:

A: どうしたんですか。          Why are you looking so gloomy?
B: テストが　あるんです。      (It's because) I have a test.

A: どうしたの。               Why are you looking so happy?
B: デートが　あるんです。      (It's because) I have a date.

**Note:　After a noun (& な Adjectives/Copula Nouns)**, you need to supply な before ん です。 Remember the following formula:

(Non-Past Tense)

| Adjectives | （いた）　い | | んです。 |
|---|---|---|---|
| Verbs (Dictionary form) | ある | | んです。 |
| Nouns | ひま | な | んです。 |

A:　どうしたんですか。　　　　　Why are you looking unhappy?

B:　ひま<u>な</u>んです。　　　　　　(It's because) I'm bored.

## 3.　<u>Total negation (nothing, nowhere, nobody): Interrogative Pronouns and Particle "も mo"</u>

| | |
|---|---|
| なにも　　ない | There's nothing. |
| だれも　いない | There's nobody. |
| どこにも　　ない | It's nowhere. |

There are several ways to express "total negation," e.g., "It's not funny at all," or "I don't have even one cent," such as "ぜんぜん～ない or　一セントもありません." In this chapter you learn the expression that uses Interrogative Pronouns (question words such as "when," "what," "where," "who," and "how") and particle "も mo" with a negative predicate (ない；ません).

For example,

(1)

なに　　　も　たべません。

"nani" + mo + tabemasen　　　　　→ (He) doesn't eat anything.

("what") mo　Negative of "tabemasu"

(2)

どこ　に　　も　いません。

"doko" ni　+ mo + imasen

("where") (at)　mo　Negative of "imasu"　　→ (He) is not anywhere.

(3)

だれ　も　いません。

"dare" + mo + imasen

("who")　mo　Negative of "imasu"　　　→ No one is here.

In the Chapter 5 dialogue, Monica said to Tetsuya who asked her out for a Kabuki viewing:

午前中は、としょかんへ　行きますが、午後は、<u>何も　ありません</u>。

I will go to a library in the morning, but <u>I have nothing</u> in the afternoon.

## 4. <u>Particle "ni" to demonstrate purpose</u>

しょくじ <u>に</u> 行<sup>い</sup>きます
来<sup>き</sup>ます
帰<sup>かえ</sup>ります

"に Ni" is used to show a "purpose" in motion verbs (such as "go," "come," and "return")
Thus, the above sentence means "I will go/come/return for a meal."

Examples

(1) えいが に 行<sup>い</sup>きませんか。　　Won't we go see a movie?

(2) かいもの に 行<sup>い</sup>きました。　　I went for shopping.

(3) ドライブ に 行<sup>い</sup>きましょう。　　Let's go for a drive.

(4) しごと に 行<sup>い</sup>ってきます。　　I'm leaving for work.

Aside from "movie," "shopping," "driving" and "work" as mentioned above, you can add "purpose" to any motion verb by following the formula: V-stem + ni + motion verbs: 食べに行く (go to eat)、飲<sup>の</sup>みに行く (got to drink)、泳<sup>およ</sup>ぎに行く (go to swim)、休<sup>やす</sup>みに帰<sup>かえ</sup>る (return to rest)、遊<sup>あそ</sup>びに来<sup>く</sup>る (come to visit), and so forth, and this expression will be introduced in Chapter 11B.

## 5. <u>Adverbs of frequency</u> いつも、よく、ときどき、たまに、あまり、ぜんぜん いちにちになんかい

How often do you eat hamburgers? Everyday? Sometimes, or never? In this chapter, you practice the adverbs that express the frequency. You use the following adverbs with an affirmative verb such as 食べます：いつも (always)、たいてい(usually)、よく (often)、ときどき(sometimes)、たまに(occasionally)、while, the adverbs あまり (not so much)、そんなに(not so much), and ぜんぜん (not at all) are used with a negative verb such as 食べません。

| 0 % | 5~10 % | 10~15 % | 20%~30 % | | 90~% | 95% | 100 % |
|---|---|---|---|---|---|---|---|
| ぜんぜん | あまり | たまに | ときどき | | よく | たいてい | いつも |

(いつも、たいてい、よく、ときどき、たまに) ハンバーガーを食べ<u>ます</u>。
(あまり、そんなに、ぜんぜん) ハンバーガーを食べ<u>ません</u>。

## About Japanese Verbs

### Casual versus Formal

Would it be awkward to speak with your close friends and family in the "ます masu" form? Yes. People in modern Japan speak more casually among family members and friends. The "ます masu" form is used in formal situations and toward your social superiors, guests and customers, and also strangers to whom you share no hierarchy. In this chapter, we focus on verbs in casual form.

### Remember: Casual non-past form verb is **Dictionary form**.

The dictionary form verb of "いきます ikimasu" is "いく iku," and the dictionary form of "みます mimasu" is "みる miru." It is under this form that dictionaries list the verbs "to go" and "to see." So to close friends and family, you ask "いく iku?" for "Will you go?" instead of "いきますか ikimasu ka?" and "みる miru?" instead of "みますか mimasu ka?" for "Will you see it?"

### How to find the Dictionary form?

It depends whether the verbs are Vowel verbs, Consonant verbs, or Irregular verbs.

### [Vowel verbs]

Vowel verbs are also called the "る ru" or "non-conjugating" verbs. As the name indicates, they have no conjugation and their stems remain the same. The stem of the vowel verb precedes the "ます masu" form. It is easy to figure out the dictionary form of a vowel verb: simply change "ます masu" to "る ru." For instance, the dictionary form of "たべます tabe-masu" would be "たべる tabe-ru," and that of "みます mi-masu" would be "みる miru."

The unchanged part ("tabe" or "mi" in these cases) is called the "Stem."

### [Consonant verbs]

Consonant verbs are also called "う u" or "conjugating" verbs. They do conjugate. In Japanese, verb conjugation is quite different from inflection in the Indo-European languages (e.g., Spanish, French, German, etc). Rather than affected by gender, Japanese verb conjugations show **formality** or allow **linkage to Auxiliaries** (such as "can," "want to," "intend to" that gives additional meanings to the verb).

Are verb conjugations hard to figure out? Not at all! In fact, you know them already! They can be found on the Hiragana chart. That Hiragana chart "あいうえお a-i-u-e-o," "かきくけこ ka-ki-ku-ke-ko," "さしすせそ sa-shi-su-se-so," "たちつてと ta-chi-tsu-te-to," etc. actually show verb conjugations for consonant verbs. Recall all consonants are followed by five vowels, "あ a," "い i," "う u," "え e," and "お o." For example, if you look at the second vertical line in the Hiragana chart, you will see "か ka," "き ki," "く ku," "け ke," and "こ ko." "か ka" is Base 1, "き ki" is Base 2, "く ku" is Base 3, "け ke" is Base 4, and "こ ko" is Base 5. The dictionary form is Base 3, "く ku." So, given the verb "かきます ka-ki-masu," change "き ki" to "く ku" to derive the dictionary form, which is "かく ka-ku." It's easier to understand if you look at the hiragana chart below.

### Basic 46 Hiragana Chart

|           |         | k        | s         | t         | n        | h        | m        | y        | r        | w        | n       |
|-----------|---------|----------|-----------|-----------|----------|----------|----------|----------|----------|----------|---------|
| Base 1    | あ a    | か ka    | さ sa     | た ta     | な na    | は ha    | ま ma    | や ya    | ら ra    | わ wa    | ん **n** |
| Base 2    | い i    | き ki    | し shi    | ち chi    | に ni    | ひ hi    | み mi    |          | り ri    |          |         |
| Base 3    | う u    | く ku    | す su     | つ tsu    | ぬ nu    | ふ fu    | む mu    | ゆ yu    | る ru    |          |         |
| Base 4    | え e    | け ke    | せ se     | て te     | ね ne    | へ he    | め me    |          | れ re    |          |         |
| Base 5    | お o    | こ ko    | そ so     | と to     | の no    | ほ ho    | も mo    | よ yo    | ろ ro    | を wo    |         |

The Dictionary form (casual form) is the 3$^{rd}$ Base.
The "masu" form (formal form) is the 2nd Base.

Besides showing formality, Japanese verb conjugations allow **linkage to Auxiliaries** (such as "can," "want to," "intend to" that gives additional meanings to the verb).

Here is how the verb conjugation is used to expand expressions by adding "can, want to, intend to," and such.

か ka  ＋ ない nai (casual negative form)

き ki  ＋ ます masu (polite form), tai (want to)

い i   く ku ＋ つもりです tsumori desu (intend to), ことができます (can)

け ke  ＋ ば ba (if), or strong command as "いけ ike"

こ ko  ＋ "う o" (casual form of "Let's")

These steps for each expression will be introduced gradually and one by one in the chapters to come.

In summary, follow these steps to discover the Dictionary form:

(1) Distinguish verb types:  Is it a Consonant or Vowel verb?
(2) If it's a Vowel verb, use the Stem of the verb and add "る ru."
(3) If it's a Consonant verb, refer to the verb conjugation chart (Hiragana chart).
    The Dictionary form is the 3rd Base.

---

| How to Distinguish Consonant verbs from Vowel verbs |
|---|

The following rule normally works well.

1. If the verb ends with "e る ru" or "i る ru," then it is a Vowel verb.

   They are "たべる taberu (eat), ねる neru (sleep), おきる okiru (get up), みる miru (see), みえる mieru (be visible), [シャワーを]あびる [shawaa wo] abiru (to take a shower), おしえる oshieru (teach), なげる nageru (throw), いる iru (stay; exist), あける akeru (open), しめる shimeru (close), あげる ageru (give; raise), さげる sageru (lower), くれる kureru (receive), いれる ireru (insert), おさえる osaeru (press), にげる nigeru (escape), なめる nameru (lick)," etc.

2. Remember the exceptions. (Consonant verbs whose endings are "eru" or "iru," like vowel verbs):  They are:

   ちる chiru (scatter), きる kiru (cut), はいる hairu (enter), いる iru (need), しる shiru (get to know), はしる hashiru (run), かえる kaeru (return, go home), にぎる nigiru (grasp), まいる mairu (humble form of "come" and "go").  And a few more to come such as "しゃべる shaberu (chat).

Here is a hint to remember the verbs of this type.  Practice the following passage.

チリチリ（散り散り）の髪を切りに、とこ屋へ　入りましたが、お金が要ると
知って、家へ走って帰り、お金を握って　また参ります。

"Chiri-chiri" no kami wo "kiri" ni, tokoya e "hairimashita" ga, okane ga "iru" to "shitte," uchi e "hashitte" "kaeri," okane wo "nigitte," mata "mairimasu."

(English:  I entered a barber shop to get my curly hair cut.  But I found it costs (needs) money.  So, I will run home, and with money in my hand, will return humbly.)

**[Irregular verbs]**

There are two irregular verbs in Japanese: "します shimasu (do)" and "きます kimasu (come)." Their dictionary forms are "する suru" (do) and "くる kuru" (come), respectively.  These two verbs do not follow any system.

Chapter 5 Exercises

A. Pair-work: なんようび？ Ask your partner the following questions and checkmark the days of the week in the chart.

    1. なんようびが　いちばん　すきですか。
    2. なんようびが　いちばん　いそがしいですか。
    3. なんようびが　いちばん　ひまですか。
    4. なんようびに　がっこうへ　きますか。
    5. なんようびに　パーティーに　いきますか。
    6. なんようびに　デートを　しますか。
    7. なんようびに　アルバイトを　しますか。
    8. (Create your own question) ?

| | にちようび<br>日曜日 | げつようび<br>月曜日 | かようび<br>火曜日 | すいようび<br>水曜日 | もくようび<br>木曜日 | きんようび<br>金曜日 | どようび<br>土曜日 |
|---|---|---|---|---|---|---|---|
| 1.<br>　すき | | | | | | | |
| 2. いそ<br>がしい | | | | | | | |
| 3.<br>　ひま | | | | | | | |
| 4.がっこ<br>うへ<br>きます | | | | | | | |
| 5.パーティ<br>ーに<br>いきます | | | | | | | |
| 6.デート<br>をします | | | | | | | |
| 7.アルバイ<br>トを<br>します | | | | | | | |
| 8. | | | | | | | |

B. Which adverbs are correct?  Choose the right ones.
Remember the adverbs that are used with affirmative verbs, and the adverbs that are sued with negative verbs?
(いつも、たいてい、よく、ときどき、たまに) ハンバーガーを食べ<u>ます</u>。
(あまり、そんなに、ぜんぜん) ハンバーガーを食べ<u>ません</u>。

1a.  私は、（いつも、そんなに）朝早く　おきます。
1b.  私は、（いつも、そんなに）朝早く　おきません。

２a. 田中さんは、（たいてい、あまり）バスで　学校へ　来ます。

２b. 田中さんは、（たいてい、あまり）バスで　学校へ　来ません。

３a. リサさんは、（よく、ぜんぜん）としょかんへ　行きます。

３b. リサさんは、（よく、ぜんぜん）としょかんへ　行きません。

４a. キャシーさんは、（ときどき、あまり）あさごはんを　食べます。

４b. キャシーさんは、（ときどき、あまり）あさごはんを　食べません。

５a. ボブさんは、（たまに、そんなに）すきやきを　作ります。

５b. ボブさんは、（たまに、そんなに）すきやきを　作りません。

C. Change to the 〜んですか style

　Example: あなたも　<u>いきますか</u>。→ いくんですか。

　　1．ここに　ありますか。　　　　2．いつ　いきますか。

　　3．なんじごろ　かえりますか。　　4．あしたも、まちますか。

　　5．いつしゅくだいを　しますか。　6．どこで、あいますか。

　　7．いつも　おすしをちゅうもんしますか。

　Answer with 〜んです。

　　1：きぶんが　わるいんですか。
　　　ええ、（　　　　　　　　　　　　　）I have a headache.

　　2：すうがくが　きらいなんですか。
　　　いいえ、でも（　　　　　　　　　　　）It's difficult.

　　3：なにか　いいことが　あるんですか。
　　　はい、（　　　　　　　　　　　　　）I have a date today!

　　4：あたまが　いたいんですか。
　　　いいえ、でも（　　　　　　　　　　　）I'm bored!

　　5：たくさん　食べるんですねぇ〜！
　　　はい、チョコレートが（　　　　　　　　）I love chocolate!

D. In-class activity: First, fill in the column under "わたし," then ask three classmates what they do on weekends (holidays, or day-offs), やすみに　なにをしますか。Add up your points and compare.  The higher the points, the more active you are.
ワークシートに　こたえをかきましょう。それからクラスメートにしつもんしてください。なんてん (how many points)でしたか。

| いつも | (always) | 5 points | ときどき | | (sometimes) | 3 points |
| たいてい | (usually) | 5 points | あまり/たまに | | (seldom) | 2 points |
| よく | (often) | 4 points | ぜんぜん | | (never) | 1 point |

| 0 % | 5～10 % | 20 % | | 90～% | 95% | 100 % |
| ぜんぜん | あまり | ときどき | | よく | たいてい | いつも |
| | たまに | | | | | |

Examples:
A: やすみに　そうじをしますか。　　　A: やすみに　かいものをしますか。
B: いいえ、ぜんぜん　しません。　　　B: はい、ときどき　します。

| | わたし | （　　）さん | （　　）さん | （　　）さん |
|---|---|---|---|---|
| ①そうじをします | | | | |
| ②せんたくをします | | | | |
| ③デートをします | | | | |
| ④アルバイトを　します | | | | |
| ⑤ほんをよみます | | | | |
| ⑥ともだちにあいます | | | | |
| ⑦おさけをのみます | | | | |
| ⑧かいものにいきます | | | | |
| ⑨えいがをみます | | | | |
| ⑩うちでテレビをみます | | | | |
| ⑪にほんごをべんきょうします | | | | |

E. Pair-work:  The chart below shows Monica's weekly schedule.  Based on the information, create dialogue with your partner(s) (with questions and answers).

Examples: Q: モニカは、よくおさけを　のみますか。
　　　　　A: いいえ、あまりのみません。きんようびだけ　のみます。

　　　　　Q: モニカは、なんようびに　はやくうちに　かえりますか。
　　　　　A: げつようび　です。

[Vocabulary help]: たんごヘルプ

まいにち everyday、あさ morning（あさごはん breakfast, まいあさ every morning）、ひる daytime（ひるごはん lunch)、ばん evening（ばんごはん dinner, まいばん every night）、しゅうまつ weekend

[ モニカのスケジュール]

|  | 日曜日 | 月曜日 | 火曜日 | 水曜日 | 木曜日 | 金曜日 | 土曜日 |
|---|---|---|---|---|---|---|---|
| 1. get up early |  | O | O | O | O |  |  |
| 2. go to bed early | O | O | O | O | O |  |  |
| 3. take a shower |  | O | O | O | O | O | O |
| 4. eat breakfast |  | O | O | O | O | O |  |
| 5. take a bath | O |  |  |  |  |  | O |
| 6. have Japanese classes |  | O |  | O |  | O |  |
| 7. listen to tapes |  | O | O |  | O |  |  |
| 8. go to the library |  | O |  |  | O |  |  |
| 9. come home early |  | O |  |  |  |  |  |
| 10. study |  | O | O | O | O | O |  |
| 11. read books | O |  |  |  |  |  | O |
| 12. watch TV | O |  |  |  |  | O | O |
| 13. drink liquor |  |  |  |  |  | O |  |
| 14. date |  |  |  |  |  | O | O |
| 15. laundry | O |  |  |  |  |  |  |

Japanese translation for Ex. E's 1 to 15

1. はやくおきます 2. はやくねます 3. シャワーをあびます 4. あさごはんをたべます 5. おふろに　はいります 6. にほんごのクラスが　あります 7. テープをききます 8. としょかんへ　いきます 9. はやく　うちに　かえります 10. べんきょう（を）します 11. ほんをよみます 12. テレビを　みます 13. おさけをのみます 14. デートを　します 15. せんたくを　します

F.  Ask your partner what day(s) of the week (or how often), (s) he does the following activities and put checkmarks on those days.  Use the same chart for Ex. E.

Examples:  Q: あなたは、よくおさけを　のみますか。
         A: いいえ、あまりのみません。どようびだけ　のみます。

         Q: あなたは、まいにち　にほんごのクラスに　きますか。
         A: いいえ、かようびともくようびは、きません。
Continue:

G.  Answer with the total negation form "Interrogative Pronouns + も + negative predicate"
    Example:
      なにが　ありますか。 → なにも　ありません。

1. どこに　いきますか。             2. だれが　いますか。

3. どれが、すきですか。             4. どこが、いいですか。

5. なにが、ほしいですか。           6. なにか、いますか。

7. だれが、いきましたか。           8. なにを　みましたか。

9. なにを　しましたか。            10. だれが、きましたか。

H. 日本語で　言ってください。 Translate into Japanese.

1. I sometimes go to a park.            2. Tom always studies in the library.

3. I occasionally <u>use</u> taxi.           4. Lisa never eats meats.
   （つかいます）

5. We don't have that many tests.        6. Kathy doesn't drink coffee so much.

I. つぎの文を読んで、英語で 言ってください。Translate into English

私はときどき、近くのこうえんへ、行きますが、そこの池におおきなこいがいます。あまり えさをやりませんが、たまに パンを やります。いちばん大きいこいは、金色のこいで、よく私の近くまで 来ます。ほかのこいは、たいてい池のまんなかに いますが、私がパンを持って行くので、そのときだけは、私の近くに 来て、パンを食べます。ちょっとおもしろいです。

[Vocabulary Help]
えさ bate; food for fish and animals やります（やる）give something to lower beings
ほか other　まんなか right in the middle

[English Translation]


J. Interview your classmates about their life style (せいかつ)

Give (O) for "yes", and (X) for "no. (O) is "maru," and (X) is "batsu" in Japanese.

[Vocabulary preparation]:

1. うんどうする　　　　　　to exercise
2. りょうしん　　　　　　　parents
   でんわ（を）する　　　　to make a phone call,
3. まいにち　　　　　　　　everyday,
   ごはんをつくる　　　　　to cook
4. こうこう　　　　　　　　high school,
   こうこうのとき　　　　　when you're in high school,
   きっさてん　　　　　　　coffee shop
5. せんしゅう　　　　　　　last week,
   おいしゃさん　　　　　　medical doctor
6. しんぱいだ　　　　　　　I am worried.
7. かぜをひく　　　　　　　to catch a cold

| しつもん | さん | さん | さん | さん |
|---|---|---|---|---|
| 1. よく うんどうを　　しますか。 | | | | |
| 2. ときどき りょうしんに　　でんわを かけますか。 | | | | |
| 3. まいにち ごはんを　　つくりますか。 | | | | |

| | | | | |
|---|---|---|---|---|
| ４．こうこうのとき　よく<br>きっさてんへいきましたか。 | | | | |
| ５．せんしゅう、おいしゃ<br>さんに　いきましたか。 | | | | |
| ６．テスト（のこと）が<br>しんぱいですか。 | | | | |
| ７．よく　かぜをひきます<br>か。 | | | | |

## K. Interview on life style (continued)

[Vocabulary preparation]:

1. いちにちに　なんかい　　　how many times a day
2. メールをする　　　　　　　 to email
3. いちにちに　どれぐらい　　how much/often a day
4. いっしゅうかんに　なんかい how many times a week
5. にしゅうかんに　なんかい how many times per two weeks / every other week,
   せんたく（を）する　　　　 to do laundry
6. いっかげつに　なんかい how many times a month,
   へやのそうじ（を）する clean (your) room

| しつもん | さん | さん | さん | さん |
|---|---|---|---|---|
| １．いちにちに　なんかい<br>　　たべますか。 | | | | |
| ２．きのうは、だれに<br>　　メールをしましたか。 | | | | |
| ３．いちにちに　どれぐらい<br>　　べんきょうしますか。 | | | | |
| ４．いっしゅうかんに　なん<br>　　かい　きっさてんへ<br>　　いきますか。 | | | | |
| ５．にしゅうかんになんかい<br>　　せんたくをしますか。 | | | | |
| ６．いっかげつに　なんかい<br>　　へやのそうじをしますか。 | | | | |

L. Match left and right columns to pair up the Casual verbs and Formal verbs.

## "Casual" and "Formal" Verbs

| | Dictionary form (Casual form) | | Masu form (Formal form) |
|---|---|---|---|
| 1. go | いく | A | します |
| 2. come | くる | B | なります |
| 3. do | する | C | はいります |
| 4. is saved | たすかる | D | かえります |
| 5. get up | おきる | E | きます |
| 6. pour over oneself | あびる | F | のります |
| 7. understand | わかる | G | いれます |
| 8. become | なる | H | いいます |
| 9. enter | はいる | I | あびます |
| 10. exist | ある | J | あります |
| 11. ride | のる | K | おもいだします |
| 12. get off | おりる | L | いきます |
| 13. insert | いれる | M | あらいます |
| 14. eat | たべる | N | たべます |
| 15. say | いう | O | たすかります |
| 16. wait | まつ | P | ねます |
| 17. exist | いる | Q | おわります |
| 18. return | かえる | R | みます |
| 19. recall | おもいだす | S | まちます |
| 20. wash | あらう | T | あいます |
| 21. sleep | ねる | U | おきます |
| 22. begin | はじまる | V | ならいます |
| 23. end | おわる | W | はじまります |
| 24. see | みる | X | わかります |
| 25. meet | あう | Y | います |
| 26. learn | ならう | Z | おります |
| 27. hear | きく | a | よみます |
| 28. read | よむ | b | のみます |
| 29. leave | でる | c | ききます |
| 30. drink | のむ | d | かけます |
| 31. drink | かう | e | つくります |
| 32. drink | つくる | f | かいます |
| 33. drink | かける | g | でます |

だい五か　　かいわ　の　れんしゅう　　Chapter 5 Conversation Practice

Make a group of three.
Ask your classmate(s) on the following topics and practice the conversation.  Take turn.

1.
A：にほんごのクラスは、<u>たいへん</u>ですか。　（たいへん hard work）
B：そんなに　たいへんじゃ　ありません。
C：私には、たいへんです。


2.
B：ぶつりのクラスは　たいへんですか。
A：すごく　たいへんです。
C：私にも、たいへんです。しゅくだいが　たくさんあるんです。


3.
A：しゅうに　なんかい、にほんごのクラスが　ありますか。
　　（しゅう　に＝いっしゅうかん　に）
B：しゅうに　（　　　　　）かいです。すうがくのクラスは？
A：しゅうに　（　　　　　）かいです。せいぶつのクラスはどうですか。
C：しゅうに（　　　　　）かいです。（せいぶつ Biology）


4.
C：いちにちに　なんかい　たべますか。
A：私は、にかいです。
B：私は、さんかい　たべます。
C：私は、いっかい　だけ　です。
AB：え～！


5.
C：いっかげつに　なんかいぐらい　スターバックスへ　いきますか。
B：私は　まいにち　いきます。
A：私は、ぜんぜん　いきません。
C：そうですか。私は、たまに　いきます。


6.
B：テストが　しんぱいですか。
A：ええ、しんぱいです。あした<u>な</u>んです。
C：私は　しんぱいじゃありません。テストは、<ruby>来年<rt>らいねん</rt></ruby>ですから。
A：いいですねぇ～
　　（Say this enviously）

Chapter 5: Dict-A-Conversation (1)   Listening comprehension practice
Listen to the CD and answer the following questions based on what you hear.  You will
be listening to a conversation among Matt, Josh and Sensei.

Vocabulary Preparation:

りょこう trip、アルバイト/バイト part-time job、ひま free time、
いそがしい busy、ゴールデンウィーク Golden Week、ほかの other, others,
ほかのともだち other friends、よぶ/よびます to invite

1. だれが　ながのへ　りょこうしましたか。

   _____

2. アルバイトで　いそがしいのは、だれですか。

   _____

3. ジョシュさんは、いつ　ひまが　ありますか。

   _____

4. だれが、すきやきパーティーを　しましょうと　いいましたか。

   _____

5. ほかの　ともだちも　よびますか。

   _____

Chapter 5: Dict-A-Conversation (2)
Answer the following questions in short answers. Base answers on your daily life and
write in hiragana.

Vocabulary preparation:

うんどう exercise、いちにち one day、いっかげつ one month、こんげつ this month、
こんしゅう this week、なんかい how many times、せんたく laundry、
ごはんをつくる to cook、なんにんのひと how many people、メールをする to
email、おいしゃさん medical doctor、いそがしい busy、ひま free time

1. _____    2. _____
3. _____    4. _____
5. _____    6. _____
7. _____    8. _____
9. _____    10. _____

Chapter 5 – (1)

| | | |
|---|---|---|
| 曜<br><br>(days of the week) | ヨウ | 日曜日（にちようび）Sunday |
| | | **(18)**<br>丨 冂 日 日 日ヿ 日ヿ 日ヨ 日ヨヿ 日ヨヿ 日ヨヿ<br>日ヨ 日ヨ 日ヨ 日ヨ 日ヨ 日ヨ 曜 曜 |
| 火<br><br>(fire) | ひ<br>カ | 大きい火（おおきいひ）a big flame<br>火曜日（かようび）Tuesday<br>大火（たいか）a big fire<br>火災（かさい）a fire<br>火事（かじ）a fire |
| | | **(6)**<br>丶 丷 少 火 |
| 木<br><br>(a tree) | き<br>モク<br>ボク | 小さい木（ちいさいき）a small tree<br>木曜日（もくようび）Thursday<br>大木（たいぼく）a big tree |
| | | **(4)**<br>一 十 才 木 |
| 金<br><br>(money, gold) | かね<br>キン<br>ゴン | お金（おかね）money<br>金曜日（きんようび）Friday<br>大金（たいきん）large amount of money<br>黄金（おうごん）gold |
| | | **(8)**<br>ノ 人 亼 仐 仐 全 全 金 |
| 土<br><br>(soil, ground) | つち<br>ド | 赤土（あかつち）red soil<br>土曜日（どようび）Saturday<br>土木工学（どぼくこうがく）civil engineering |
| | | **(3)**<br>一 十 土 |
| 川<br><br>(river) | かわ<br>セン | 大きい川（おおきいかわ）a big river<br>川上（かわかみ）the upper reaches of a river<br>河川（かせん）rivers<br>川柳（せんりゅう）a free-style haiku poem |
| | | **(3)**<br>ノ 川 川 |

Chapter 5- (2)

| 古 (old) | ふる（い）<br>コ | 古い学校（ふるいがっこう）old school<br>古里（ふるさと;故郷）birth place; a place<br>dear to one's heart<br>中古（ちゅうこ）used |
| | | (5)<br>一 十 十 古 古 |
| 男 (a male) | おとこ<br>ダン<br>ナン | 男の子（おとこのこ）boys<br>男子（だんし）boys, 男性（だんせい）men<br>美男（びなん）handsome |
| | | (7)<br>丿 口 冂 田 田 甼 男 |
| 会 (to meet, a party) | あ（う）<br>カイ | 会う（あう）to meet<br>クラス会（くらすかい）reunion |
| | | (6)<br>ノ 入 人 会 会 会 |
| 午 (noon) | ひる<br>ゴ | 正午（しょうご） |
| | | (4)<br>丿 一 二 午 |
| 前 (before, ago) | まえ<br>ゼン | お前（おまえ）you (informal)<br>手前（てまえ）beforehand<br>午前（ごぜん）a.m.; morning<br>前回（ぜんかい）a previous time<br>前方（ぜんぼう）front; forward |
| | | (9)<br>丶 丷 艹 广 芇 前 前 前 前 |
| 後 (after, later) | あと<br>うし（ろ）<br>のち<br>ゴ | 後で（あとで）later (time)<br>後ろ（うしろ）behind (location)<br>曇り後雨（くもりのちあめ）cloudy –later-rain<br>午後（ごご）p.m.; afternoon<br>後日（ごじつ）a few days later<br>後方（こうほう）back; behind |
| | | (9)<br>丿 彳 彳 彳 彳 徍 衻 後 後 |

## Kanji Practice for Chapter 5
かんじの　れんしゅう

1．つぎの　ことばを　よみなさい。それから、クラスメートにいみをききなさい。 Read the following words to your classmates and ask them for the meaning of each word/sentence.

|   |   |   |   |
|---|---|---|---|
| （1） | 日曜日 | （8） | 古い川、　中古 |
| （2） | 月曜日 | （9） | 午前と午後 |
| （3） | 火、　火曜日 | （10） | 午前中に　会いましょう。 |
| （4） | 水、　水曜日 | | |
| （5） | 木、　木曜日 | （11） | あの木の下の　男の人を　知っています。 |
| （6） | お金、　金曜日 | （12） | くるまの前と後ろ |
| （7） | 土、　土曜日 | （13） | テストの前と後 |

2．よんでから、よみがなをかいて、えいごでいいなさい。 Read the kanji, write in the yomigana above it, and translate its meaning into English.

（1）　毎月、金曜日に、おすしを　食べに行きます。

（2）　きのう、その男の人に　会いました。

（3）　午前十一時半に、来ました。

（4）　午後は、何も　食べませんでした。

（5）　プラントには、日と水と土が　要ります(~ is needed)。

（6）　古い車を　中古車と　言います。

（7）　毎日、ランチに　十ドルぐらい、お金がかかります。

（8）　川のそばに、古いうちが　あります。

（9）　学校の後ろに、古い大木が　あります。

（１０）　　また、後でね〜！

（１１）　　クラスの前に、ラボへ　行きました。


3. かんじとひらがなで　こたえなさい。 Answer the questions in complete sentences using kanji and hiragana.  In your answers, use kanji for the underlined words.

（１）　　<u>まいにち</u>　クラスの<u>まえ</u>に　ラボへ　<u>いきます</u>か。

（２）　　あなたの<u>うしろ</u>に　だれが　いますか。<u>しって</u>いますか。

（３）　　にほんごのクラスの<u>あと</u>で、どこへ　<u>いきます</u>か。

（４）　　<u>まいにち</u>ランチに　なんドルぐらい、かかりますか。

（５）　　あなたのお<u>とう</u>さんのくるまは、<u>ふるい</u>ですか。

（６）　　きのうの<u>ごご</u>は、どこに　いましたか。

（７）　　きのうの<u>ごぜんちゅう</u>に　なにを<u>たべ</u>ましたか。

（８）　　にほんごのクラスに　<u>おとこ</u>の<u>がくせい</u>は、なん<u>にん</u>ぐらい
　　　　　いますか。

（９）　　<u>きょう</u>は、なん<u>ようび</u>ですか。

（１０）　あなたのうちの<u>うしろ</u>に、<u>ふるいき</u>が　ありますか。

（１１）　あなたのうちから　<u>がっこう</u>まで　なん<u>ぷん</u>ぐらい　かかりますか。

## Kanji Review (Chapters 1 ~5)　漢字
かんじ

A. Find the matching compound words from the box below and write them in each box.

1. a college student

2. A.M.

3. Japanese language

4. What language?

5. teachers

6. What school year?

7. 4:04

8. Friday

9. acquaintance

10. this time; last time

11. school

12. puppy

先生（せんせい）、子犬（こいぬ）、何年生（なんねんせい）、大学生（だいがく
せい）、何語（なにご）、学校（がっこう）、四時四分（よじよんぷん）、今回
（こんかい）、知人（ちじん），金曜日（きんようび）、日本語（にほんご）

B.  Match-up English and Japanese and write the appropriate alphabets in the blanks.

| | Japanese | Answers (matching English words) | | | English |
|---|---|---|---|---|---|
| 1 | 日 | | | a | mountains |
| 2 | 山 | | | b | books; origin |
| 3 | 川 | | | c | person |
| 4 | 色 | | | d | old |
| 5 | 好 | | | e | soil; ground |
| 6 | 大 | | | f | fire |
| 7 | 小 | | | g | favorite; likable |
| 8 | 中 | | | h | the moon |
| 9 | 月 | | | i | female |
| 10 | 火 | | | j | the sun |
| 11 | 水 | | | k | behind; later |
| 12 | 木 | | | l | male |
| 13 | 金 | | | m | front; before; ago |
| 14 | 土 | | | n | small |
| 15 | 前 | | | o | color |
| 16 | 口 | | | p | middle; center |
| 17 | 人 | | | q | mouth |
| 18 | 本 | | | r | gold |
| 19 | 古 | | | s | tree |
| 20 | 男 | | | t | time; o'clock |
| 21 | 女 | | | u | rivers |
| 22 | 時 | | | v | water |
| 23 | 後 | | | w | large |
| 24 | 妹 | | | x | rice fields |
| 25 | 田 | | | y | younger sister |
| 26 | 年 | | | z | minutes; to divide |
| 27 | 先生 | | | A | everyday |
| 28 | 毎日 | | | B | parents |
| 29 | 父母 | | | C | teachers |
| 30 | 分 | | | D | years |

Kanji list from Chapter 1 to Chapter 5

一、二、三、四、五、六、七、八、九、十、百、千、万、日、月、火、水、
木、金、土、曜、人、入、本、口、言、語、兄、妹、子、何、父、母、山、
川、中、食、気、大、犬、小、時、寺、分、男、女、田、先、生、好、方、
先、今、上、下、年、学、円、白、来、色、回、同、校、近、目、毎、半、
行、知、午、前、後、古、会

C. Which of the following kanji or compound refer to nature? Which refer to people or animals? Product of human activities? Numbers? Sizes? Time? Or, days of the week? Write each kanji or compound under its correct category. You may use the same kanji more than once.

A. Nature ....................................................................................

B. People, animals...........................................................................

C. Activities....................................................................................

D. Numbers....................................................................................

E. Sizes, shapes, colors....................................................................

F. Time .........................................................................................

G. Days of the week.........................................................................

D. Make compounds from the kanji above. You may use the kanji from the list or you can use other kanji to make compounds.
Examples:
月 ＋ 曜 ＋ 日 ＝月曜日 、 何 ＋ 語 ＝ 何語

E. Match the kanji compounds with their pronunciations by writing the letters of the correct pronunciations in the blanks.

| | | | | | |
|---|---|---|---|---|---|
| 1. _____ 父母 | 2. _____ 水色 | 3. _____ 先生 |
| 4. _____ 十日 | 5. _____ 大火 | 6. _____ 日本語 |
| 7. _____ 一日 | 8. _____ 日本人 | 9. _____ 午後 |
| 10. _____ 男女 | 11. _____ 学校 | 12. _____ 子犬 |
| 13. _____ 三分 | 14. _____ 日曜日 | 15. _____ 毎日 |
| 16. _____ 大金 | 17. _____ 先生 | |

| | | |
|---|---|---|
| a. せんせい | b. みずいろ | c. まいにち |
| d. にほんご | e. さんぶん | f. にちようび |
| g. にほんじん | h. たいきん | i. こいぬ |
| j. ごご | k. せんせい | l. ついたち |
| m. だんじょ | n. とおか | o. がっこう |
| p. たいか | q. ふぼ | |

F. Fill in the blanks with appropriate words in kanji.  Do not forget "okuri-gana."

1. (          ) の (        ) は、(          ) です。
   わたし          いぬ          ちいさい

2. お (        ) の (          ) に、(        ) んぼが、あります。
   てら          ちかく          た

3. いま、(            ) なん (          ) ですか。
   なんじ          ぶん

4. (              ) は、(        ) の (            ) です。
   やまなかせんせい          おとこ          せんせい

5. (          ) のが (          ) です。
   たべる          すき

6. (            ) くんが、あちらから (          )。
   やまだ          きます

7. (          )、お (        ) をください。
   おかあさん          みず

8. あの (      ) の (          )で、やすみましょう。
   き          した

9. (          ) が いますか。いいえ、(            ) だけです。
   おにいさん          いもうと

# Golden Week　ゴールデンウィーク

What is "Golden Week"?
May in Japan is blessed with beautiful weather and greenery; but above all, several national holidays in a row.  Green Day (April 29,　みどりの日), Constitution Day (May 3, けんぽうきねんび), Children's Day（May 5, 子どもの日）, and two weekends compose Golden Week, a time which provides people with a chance to travel and enjoy outdoor leisure activities.

Phrases to remember for the "Golden Week" season:
"Satsuki-bare," meaning "Sunny May."  Satsuki is an old name for May and means Japanese azalea.  "Bare" is the result of a phonetic change to the second word, when it's attached to the first word.  The initial sound of the second word becomes voiced.  Why? It becomes easier to pronounce!  In this case, the root word attached to Satsuki is "hare," that came from the verb "hareru (become clear). "  The voiceless sound "ha" is altered to its voiced counterpart "ba," changing "hare" to "bare."

<u>My schedule during Golden Week</u>　ゴールデンウィークのよてい

| 月 | 火 | 水 | 木 | 金 | 土 | 日 |
|---|---|---|---|---|---|---|
| 4/22 | 4/23 | 4/24 | 4/25 ミーティング 8:00 A.M.12:00 P.M. | 4/26 ハワイ りょこう 旅行 → なりた 成田 7:00 P.M. | 4/27 → りょこうちゅう 旅行中 | 4/28 → りょこうちゅう 旅行中 |
| 4/29 みどりの日 → りょこうちゅう 旅行中 | 4/30 → りょこうちゅう 旅行中 | 5/1 → りょこうちゅう 旅行中 | 5/2 → りょこうちゅう 旅行中 | 5/3 けんぽう きねんび → りょこうちゅう 旅行中 | 5/4 → りょこうちゅう 旅行中 | 5/5 こどもの日 きこく ← 帰国 なりた 成田 10:00 A.M. |
| 5/6 ミーティング 9:00 A.M. 〜 | 5/7 | 5/8 | 5/9 | 5/10 | 5/11 | 5/12 |

単語ヘルプ

ミーティング meeting、ハワイ Hawaii、りょこう（旅行）trip、旅行中during the trip、帰国returning to the country、成田 Narita International (Airport)

Based on the calendar and "my" schedule in the previous page, answer the following questions.

1. ことしの「みどりの日」は、なんようびですか。

2. ことしの「けんぽうきねん日」は、なんようびですか。

3. ことしの「子どもの日」は、なんようびですか。

4. ことしのゴールデンウィークに、わたしは、どこへいきますか。

5. ことしのゴールデンウィークに、わたしは、なんにちから　なんにちまで
   おやすみですか。("o-yasumi" means holiday, absence or rest)

6. わたしは、なんにちに、ハワイへ　いきますか。

7. わたしは、なんにちに、ハワイから、かえりますか。

8. わたしが、ハワイからかえるのは、ごぜんですか、ごごですか。

9. 「子どもの日」の　つぎの日（よくじつ）は、なんようびですか。

10. 「子どもの日」の　つぎの日（よくじつ）は、なんじから　ミーティン
    グ（かいぎ）が、ありますか。

Practice the following dialogue with your partner.

A：もうすぐ　ゴールデンウィークですね。

B：え？ゴールデンウィークって、なんですか。

A：ゴールデンウィークは、五月の　「れんきゅう」のことですよ。

B：「れんきゅう」って、やすみの日が　つづくことですね。

A：ええ。

B：でも、なぜ　ゴールデンなんですか。

A：う～ん、それは、ね、「金」って、すばらしいでしょう？「金」とおなじ
　　ように、すばらしいウィーク（しゅう）って、いみです。

B：ああ、わかりました。それで、ゴールデンウィークは、まいとし、おなじ
　　日なんですか。

A：ええ、だいたい　おなじです。五月のさいしょのしゅうですよ。四月のお
　　わりから、はじまりますが、、、
　　　まえは、「とびいしれんきゅう」って、言ったんですけど、、

B：え？「とびいし」？

A：「とびいし」は、のことです。ほら、四月二十九日、五月三日、五月五日
　　　とやすみが、とびいしのように、ジャンプするでしょう？だから、です。

B：ああ、それで、よくわかりました。

単語ヘルプ：
れんきゅう　（連休）consecutive holidays, やすみ　（休み）holidays; day off
さいしょのしゅう　（最初の週）the first week, おわり　（終わり）the end
はじまります　（始まります）It begins. まいとし　（毎年）every year
おなじひ　（同じ日）the same day
とびいしれんきゅう　（飛び石連休）consecutive holidays with intervals

## うらしまたろう　の　おはなし
## The Story of Urashima

1.

　　むかし　むかし　あるところに　うらしまたろう　という　わかものが

すんでいました。たろうは、りょうし　でした。

まいにち　うみへ　でて、さかなを　とってくらしを　たてて　いました。

たろうは、としおいた　おかあさんと　いっしょに　うみべの　むらで

くらして　いました。

　　Once upon a time, there lived a young man named Urashima Taro.  He was a fisherman.  He went to the sea everyday and made a living by fishing.  He lived with his elderly mother in a village near the sea.

2.

　　あるとき、たろうが　りょうを　おえて　うみべに　かえってくると、

こどもたちが　なにかを　かこんで　さわいでいます。たろうが　ちかよる

と、それは　いっぴきの　おおきな　かめでした。こどもたちは、かめの

こうらを　いしで　たたいたり、ぼうで　あしを　つついたり　していまし

た。

　　One day on his way home from fishing, he found children making a commotion around something at the beach.  When Taro approached, he discovered it was over a big turtle.  The children were striking the turtle with stones on his back and poking his legs with sticks.

3.

　　「これこれ、なにを　しているのだね。かわいそうな　かめを　ゆるして

やりなさい。」

と、うらしまは、こどもたちに　いいました。でも、こどもたちは、きこう

と　しません。

　　「おれたちが　みつけた　かめだ。だから、どうしたって　いいんだ。」

そういって、いじめるのを　やめませんでした。

"What are you doing? Why don't you pardon the poor turtle?" Urashima said to the children, but they wouldn't listen to him.
"We found it, so it's our business whatever we do to it," said the children, and they did not stop attacking the turtle.

4.
「それでは、わたしが　おまえたちに　さかなを　やるから、それで

かわいそうな　かめを　はなして　おやり。」

と　うらしまが　いうと、こどもたちは、

「わあっ」

と　よろこんで、さかなを　もらうと、さっさと　いってしまいました。

"I will give you fish, if you free the poor turtle," said Urashima. The children shouted happily and left it alone as soon as they received the fish from Urashima.

5.
のこされた　かめを、うらしまは、いとおしそうに　みながら、

いいました。

「かめさんよ。かわいそうに。いたかっただろう。」

そういいながら、うらしまは、かめの　せなかを　なでました。

「さあ、はやく　うみへ　おかえり。わるい　こどもたちが、ふたたび

もどってこない　うちに。」

うらしまが　そう　いうと、かめは、うれしそうに　おきへ　むかって

およいで　いきました。

Looking at the turtle with sorrow and compassion, Urashima said to it,
"Poor turtle. How painful it must be." He caressed its back gently.
"Why don't you go back to the sea before the bad children return?" Taro asked; and then the turtle left the shore and happily swam away.

6.

　それから　すうじつごの　あるひの　ことです。うらしまが　うみで

つりを　していると、うしろで、だれか　よぶ　もの　が、　あります。

「うらしまさん、うらしまさん。」

「はて、こんな　ところで、だれだろう。わたしの　なまえを　よぶもの

　は。」

たろうが　ふりかえると、そこに　いたのは、せんじつの　あの　おおきな

かめでした。

　　A few days later, when Taro was fishing in the sea, someone called his name
behind him; "Mr. Urashima, Mr. Urashima."
　　"Hmmm, I wonder who's calling my name at such a place as this."
　　When Taro turned his back, he saw the big turtle he saved the other day.

7.

　「うらしまさん。せんじつの　おれいに　りゅうぐうじょうへ　ごあんない

いたします。」と、かめが　もうします。

　「りゅうぐうじょう。はて、、はなしには　きいたことが　あるが。わたし

は、まだ　いったことが　ない。」

　「どうぞ、わたしの　せなかに　おのりください。あっというまに　つき

ますよ。」

そこで、たろうは、かめの　せなかに　のりました。

　　"Mr. Urashima.  I will take you to the Dragon Palace as
a token of my gratitude," the turtle said.
　　"The Dragon Palace?  I wonder.  I have heard of it in a story,
but I have never been there."
　　"Please ride on my back.  I will get you there in a second."
　　Then Taro got on its back.

8.

たろうを　せなかにのせた　かめは、どんどん、ふかい　うみのそこを

めざして、およいで　いきました。あたりは、すっかり　くらくなりました。

うらしまは、すこし　しんぱいになって、かめに　たずねました。

「かめさん、りゅうぐうじょうは、まだ　とおいのかい。」

「いえいえ、もう　すぐ　です。ほら、あそこに　みえて　きました。」

かめの　いう　ほうを　みると、りゅうぐうじょうの　うつくしい

もんが　みえてきました。

The turtle and Taro proceeded deeper and deeper to the bottom of the sea.  It was completely dark around them.  Urashima, who started to get a bit worried, asked the turtle,
"Mr. Turtle.  Is the Dragon Palace still far?"
"No, it is very close.  Look, it's starting to show over there."
When Taro looked in the direction the turtle pointed, he saw the gate of the beautiful Dragon Palace.

9.

りゅうぐうじょうに　つくと　うつくしい　おとひめさまが、うらしまを

でむかえました。

「うらしまさん。せんじつは、かめを　たすけてくださって、ほんとうに

ありがとうございました。おれいに　おまねきいたしました。」と、おと

ひめさまが　いいました。そして、おとひめさまは、うらしまのてをとると、

しずかに　りゅうぐうじょうの　なかへ　うらしまを　あんないしてくれました。

When Taro arrived at the Dragon Palace, Princess Otohime welcomed him.
"We are grateful that you have saved the turtle the other day. We have invited you
here as a token of our appreciation, "said the princess. She took his hand gently and
guided him inside the Palace.

10.

どこからか、うつくしい　おんがくが　きこえてきます。はしらは、さん

ごでできています。いたるところが　かがやくような　うつくしさです。そ

こへ　おいしい　ごちそうが、つぎつぎに　はこばれてきました。うつくしい

おんなのひとや、たいや　ひらめ　が、おどりを　みせてくれます。たろうは、

あまりの　たのしさ　と　うつくしさに　ときを　わすれて　しまいました。

Beautiful music can be heard emanating from somewhere. The pillars of the
Palace were made of coral. Everywhere was beautiful, illustriously. Delicious feasts
were carried in one after another. Lovely women, red snapper, and flounder entertained
him with dancing. It was so enjoyable and so enchanting that Taro forgot about the time.

11.

あるとき、きゅうに　うみべの　むらに　のこしてきた　はは　のことが、

しんぱいに　なりました。もう　すでに、みっか　みばんも　たってい

ます。たろうは、おとひめさまに　いいました。

「おとひめさま。わたしは、うちが　こいしくなりました。そろそろ

おいとま　いたします。」

One day, Taro suddenly became worried about his mother left in the village near the shore.  Three days and three nights have gone by already.  Taro said to the princess, "Princess Otohime, I am homesick.  It's time for me to leave."

12.
　　これを　きいて、おとひめさまは、おくから　ちいさな　はこを　もって

きました。

「うらしまさま。これを　おみやげに　さしあげます。でも、どんなことが

あっても、このはこを　あけては　いけません。」

たろうは、おれいを　いって、みなに　わかれを　つげました。

そして、また、おおきな　かめの　せなかに　のって、うみの　うえを　め

ざして、およいで　いきました。

　　　　Hearing it, the princess went to fetch a little box from the back of the Palace. "Mr. Urashima, this is a souvenir for you.  But you shall not open it no matter what happens."
Taro thanked and bid farewell; and riding on the turtle's back, they headed back to shore.

13.
　　あたりは、しだいに　あかるくなってきました。うみべは　もうすぐです。

「これで　おわかれです。」

すなはまに　たろうを　おろすと、かめは　また　ふかい　うみのそこを

めざして　かえって　いきました。

　　　　The surrounding began to brighten around them. It's a sign the shore must be near. "Farewell, Mr. Urashima." The turtle swam back to the sea as soon as he dropped off Taro at the shore.

14.
　　たろうは、あたりを　みわたしました。でも、なぜか　なつかしい　ふる

さとの　においが　しません。たろうは、しんぱいに　なりました。

「かめさんは、わたしを　まちがえて、ちがうむらに　つれてきたのだろうか。」

たろうは、あるきはじめました。いえの　あるほうを　めざして。でも、いくら　いっても、たろうの　いえは、みつかりません。そこへ、おばあさんが、とおりかかりました。たろうは、たずねました。

Taro looked around, but for some reason it didn't seem like his hometown. Taro's anxiety grew. He wondered if the turtle has mistakenly taken him to the wrong shore. Taro started walking, with hopes of returning to his hometown. But no matter how far he went, he could not find his house. Then he came across an old lady.

15.
「すみません。おばあさん。ちょっと　おたずねしますが。」

やさしそうな　おばあさんは、あしをとめ、たろうをみながら、いいました。

「はい、なんでしょうか。」

「このへんに、うらしまたろうのうちのものが　すんでいるはずですが、どこでしょうか。」

「うらしまたろう。きいたことが　ある。はあはあ、おもいだしました。たしか、こどものころきいた　おはなしでは、むかし　そんなひとがいたそうですが、りょうに　うみへ　でたまま、かえってこなかったそうですよ。」

これをきいた　たろうは、びっくりして　こえも　でませんでした。ふしんにおもった　おばあさんは、また　こう　いいました。

「でもね、それは　もう　さんびゃくねんも　まえの　むかし　の　はなしですよ。」

"Excuse me, old lady. May I ask you a question?" Taro asked. The kind-looking old lady stopped walking, looked at him, and said,

"Yes, what is it that you want to ask me?"
"The Urashima Taro residence must be around here. Where is it?" Taro inquired.
"Urashima Taro? I have heard of the name. Ah, I remember now. According to the story I heard when I was a little child, there was a man with that name long ago. I heard he never returned after he left to the sea for fishing."
Hearing this, Taro was astounded and speechless. The old lady felt it strange and said, "But you know, the story took place three hundred years ago."

16.

　　こえもなく　たろうは、ふらふらと　あるきはじめました。そして、

たしかに　じぶんの　いえが　あったと　おもわれる　ばしょに　きました。

しかし、そこに　あるのは、ぼうぼうと　はえた　くさだけでした。

　　Taro staggered to the place where he thought his house used to be. But all he found was grass.

17.

　　たろうは、どうしていいのか　わからずに、とぼとぼと　うみべに　もど

りました。そこで、きのしたに　こしを　おろすと、おとひめさまから　い

ただいたはこの　ことを　おもいだしました。たろうは、はこを　あけまし

た。すると、なかから、とつぜん　むらさきいろの　けむりが　たちこめ、

そのけむりは、たろうを　あっというまに、はくはつの　おじいさんに　か

えてしまいました。たろうは、とおくで　おとひめさまの　こえを　きいた

ような　きが　しました。きがつくと、おとひめさまに　てをとられた　た

ろうは、つるに　かわって、ふたりは、そらたかく、まいあがって　いきま

した。

　　Taro, not knowing what to do, trudged his weary way and returned to the shore. When he sat down under a tree, he remembered the box he received from the princess. The desperate Taro opened the box. Purple smoke came out of the box and instantly changed Taro into a white-haired old man. He felt as if he heard the voice of the princess. Then Taro felt his hand taken by the princess, and he was transformed into a crane. Together with the princess, he flew away higher and higher into the sky.

## つるのおんがえし
## The Grateful Crane

1.

　むかしむかし、びんぼうな　わかものが、ひとりで　すんでいました。ふゆになり、ゆきが　たくさん　ふっていました。あるひ、ふかい　ゆきの　なかを、しごとから　いえに　かえる　とちゅう、へんな　おとが　きこえました。その　うめきごえの　ような　おとが、どこから　くるのかを　さがしに、むこうの　はたけに　いって　みました。すると　そこには　きずついた　いちわの　つるが　いました。　そのつるは、はねに　やを　うけて、ないて　いたのです。わかものは、つるを　かわいそうに　おもい、やを　ぬいて　やりました。じゆうに　なった　つるは、そらへ　とびたち、そらの　むこうへきえて　いきました。

　　Once upon a time, there lived a young man who was very poor. It was winter time and a lot of snow was falling. One day, the young man was walking home in the deep snow when he heard a strange groaning noise. Wondering where this sound was coming from, he walked towards it into surrounding fields. What he found was a crane moaning and groaning. Its wing had been pierced by an arrow. The young man felt sorry for the crane and pulled the arrow out. The crane now freed, flew away and vanished in the sky.

2.

　わかものは、いえへ　かえりました。かれは、まずしくて　ひとりぼっちで、じんせいは、さみしい　もの　でした。だれも　たずねて　くれる　ひとは　ありません。しかし、そのよ、いえの　とを、とんとんと　たたく　おとが　しました。こんな　ゆきの　よる、しかも　こんなに　おそい　じかんに、だれが　きたのだろう。わかものは、ふしぎに　おもいました。おどろいた　ことに、わかものが　とを　あけると、そこには　うつくしい　むすめが　たっていた　のです。むすめは、みちに　まよったので、こんや　とめて　ほしい　と　たのみました。むすめは、つぎの　よるも　とまりました。そして、その　つぎの　よるも。

　　The young man returned home.  He was poor and lonely and his life was miserable.
No one even visited him.  But on that night, someone came and knocked at the door.  He
was wondering who would call on him so late on a snowy evening.  When he opened the
door, to his surprise, there stood a beautiful young woman.  She was lost and begged him
to let her stay that night.  She stayed the next night, and the night after.

3.

　わかものは、とうとう　むすめに　にょうぼうに　なって　ほしいと　いいました。そして、むすめは、はいと　こたえて、ふたりは、ふうふに　なりました。ふたりは、びんぼうでしたが、しあわせ　でした。きんじょの　ひとたちも、ふたりの　しあわせを　よろこんで　いました。しかし、ふゆは、ながく　つめたく、とうとう　いきて　いく　ための　たべものも　おかねも　なくなりました。そこで、あるひ　にょうぼうは、はたを　おる　ことに　しました。そして　おくの　へやに　はたおりきを　そなえて　くれる　ように　おっとに　たのみました。

　　Finally, the young man asked the lady to marry him.  She agreed and they became a man and wife.  Although they were poor, they were happy.  The neighbors were also delighted with their happiness.  Nevertheless, winter was long and cold and one day it came that there was neither food nor money left to go on living.  So, the young woman made up her mind to weave a piece of cloth and asked her husband to prepare a loom for her in a room at the back of the house.

4.

　はたを　おる　まえに、にょうぼうは、わかものに　ある　やくそくを　さ
せました。

　「わたしが　はたを　おっている　あいだは、ぜったいに　のぞいては、
いけません。」

　にょうぼうは、おくの　へやの　とを　しめて、はたを　おりはじめました。
おっとは、みっかみばん　の　あいだ、まちましたが、にょうぼうは、やすみ
なく　おりつづけました。みっかめ　の　よる、つかれはてた　にょうぼうは、
おりものを　もって　でてきました。それは、だれも　これまで　みた　こと
の　ない　ほど、うつくしい　おりもの　でした。わかものは、おりものを
うりに　いちばん　ちかい　まちへ、でかけましたが、それは、とても　めず
らしい　きちょうな　ぬの　でした　ので、とても　たかく　うれました。

Before she started weaving, she said to her husband, "You shall not come and peep in while I am weaving." The husband promised that he would not. The young woman then shut herself in the room, and started weaving. The young man waited for three days and three nights, but his wife kept weaving without rest. At the end of the third day the bride, wan and exhausted, brought in her work. It was such a gorgeous and beautiful piece of cloth that no one had ever seen. The young man traveled to the nearest town to sell it, and as it was a very precious and rare piece of cloth, he was able to sell it for a great amount of money.

5.

　その　おかね　の　おかげで、ふたりは　しばらく　の　あいだ、へいわに
くらす　ことが　できました。しかし、ふゆは　ながく、また　おかねも　た
べものも　なくなって　しまいました。そこで　にょうぼうは、もう　いちど、
はたを　おる　ことに　しました。ふたたび、おっとに　のぞかない　ことを
やくそく　させて、しごとに　かかりました。ふつかふたばんが、すぎました。
でも、まだ、おわりません。よっかめ　の　ばん、つかれはてて　でてきた
にょうぼうは、まえ　より　もっと　うつくしい　おりものを　てにしていま

した。わかものが　まちへ　うりに　でかけると、まえより　もっと　いいね
で、うれました。

Thanks to this money, they were able to live peacefully for a while. But, winter was yet very long and again there was no more food or money left. So the bride decided to weave one more piece of cloth. She warned her husband again not to peep in and started weaving. Two days and two nights went by, and it was not over yet. The night of the fourth day the bride appeared, more tired and wan, produced a piece of cloth much more beautiful than the first one. The young man left for the nearest town and sold this magnificent piece of cloth for an amount of money he would have never dreamt of.

6.

こうして　つまの　おかげで　しあわせに　なった　のに、おっとは、もっ
と　もっと　おかねが　ほしく　なりました。そのうえ、きんじょの　ひとも
いとも　かわずに　どうやって　そんなに　すばらしい　おりものが　できる
のか、おっとを　しつもんぜめに　しました。おっとも　それを　ふしぎな
ことだと　おもって　いました。もっと　たくさんの　おかねが　ほしい　と
おもった　おっとは、にょうぼうに　もう　いちまい　ぬのを　おってくれ
と　たのみました。やつれた　にょうぼうは、なぜ　おっとが　そんなに　お
かねを　ほしがるのか　りかい　できませんでしたが、しぶしぶ　しょうち
しました。

Thanks to his wife, the young man's life was no longer miserable. But, he came to wish he had more money. Moreover, the neighbors were harassing him with questions about his wife and her weaving. They thought it was very queer that she could weave such gorgeous pieces of cloth without even buying a singe thread. The young man too was wondering how she managed. Wanting more money, he asked his wife for another piece of cloth. The emaciated wife did not understand why her husband wanted more money, but she reluctantly agreed.

7.

「けっして　のぞいては　いけません。」
にょうぼうは、ふたたび　おっとに　やくそく　させて、おくの　へやに
はいりました。しかし、にょうぼうが　どのようにして　はたを　おるのか
しりたくて　たまらなくなった　おっとは、やくそくを　わすれ、にょうぼう

が　はたを　おっている　こべやの　ちいさな　あな　から、なかを　のぞき
ました。そこに　いたのは、かれの　にょうぼう　ではなく、つるでした。つ
るが　その　からだから、いっぽん　いっぽん、はねを　ぬき、それを　おり
こんで　うつくしい　ぬのに　していたのです。おっとは、とうとう　にょう
ぼうが　どうやって　あんなに　うつくしい　ぬのを　おることが　できたの
か、りかいしたのです。あまりの　おどろきに、おっとは、こえを　あげて
しまいました。そのとき、つるは、おっとに　きづき、にんげんの　すがたに
もどりました。

"You shall not come and peep in," she reminded him of his promise and entered the
back-room to work.　But the young man grew impatient and inquisitive:　he wanted so
much to find out how she weaved.　He forgot about his promise, crept into the back of the
little room where his wife was weaving and peeped inside through a little hole.　Instead
of his wife, a crane was there, tearing out one after the other its feathers and weaving a
beautiful piece of cloth out of them.　The young man finally understood how his wife
could weave such pieces of cloth.　The scene he saw made him gasp and then the bird
noticed his peeping and changed back to its human form.

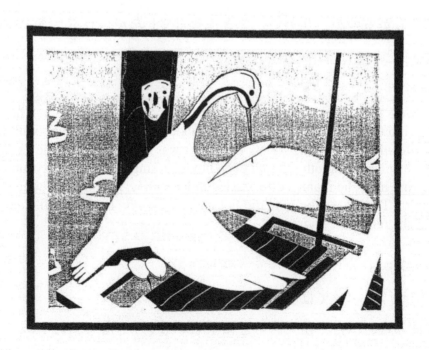

8.

おどろいている　わかものに、にょうぼうは、せつめい　しました。じぶんは、わかものに　いのちを　たすけられた　つる　であること。そして、そのおんに　こたえる　ために、わかい　おんなの　すがたに　なって、かれのもとへ　きたこと。そして、じぶんの　はねを　つかって　ぬのを　おり、まずしい　かれを　たすけよう　と　したことを。しかし、わかものが、やくそくを　やぶって　かのじょの　ほんとうの　すがたを　みた　いじょう、もういっしょに　いる　ことは、ゆるされません。わかものは、おかね　ほしさのために、やくそくを　やぶった　ことを　こうかい　しましたが、もう　おそいのです。いまとなっては、ふたりは　わかれる　しか　ありません。にょうぼうは、ふたたび　つるの　すがたに　もどって、そらへ　とんで　いきました。

The bride told her story to the astonished young man. She was the crane he had once saved from death. Taking a form of a young woman, she returned in order to pay him back for his kindness. She weaved those pieces of cloth, using her own feathers, to save him from poverty. But since the young man failed to keep his promise and now he knew the truth about her, they were not allowed to live together any more. The young man was deeply sorry that he had failed to keep his promise because of his greed, but there was no way to change things and they had to part. The young woman became one more time a crane, and flew away.

# **Finding an Apartment**

Chapter 6A:  At a Realtor's office
*Expressions*
"I prefer smaller (one) though…."
"I prefer quieter"
*Kanji practice from Chapter 6A*

Chapter 6B:  Looking for an apartment
*Expressions*
"If it's a bicycle, it takes fifteen minutes"
"I have one of each"  "I slept as long as ten hours"
"The window is on the south side"
"You'll be a millionaire"
"It's yours, right?"
"I can see it"
*Kanji practice from Chapter 6B*

Chapter 6C:  Meeting the landlord
*Expressions*
"Japanese is fun and easy"
"It is nice and quiet, and moreover, it is close to the station"
*Kanji practice from Chapter 6C*

Chapter 6D:  There is a carp!
*Expressions*
"Please eat it"  "It's not that far"
"There's a carp at such a place like this"
"Please show me your passport"
*Kanji practice from Chapter 6D*

Chapter 6          Finding an Apartment        アパートさがし

(A). At a realtor's office    ふどうさんや　の　オフィスで

ふどうさんや：(pointing on a map) ここに　きれいな　アパートが　一つ　　　1

　　　　　　　あります。このアパートは、ほんとうに　新しいですよ。　　2

モニカ：　　　大きい　たてもの　の　中　ですか。　　　　　　　　　　　3

ふどうさんや：ええ、アパートが　ぜんぶで　二十ぐらい　ありますよ。　　4

モニカ：　　　わたしは、小さいほうが、いいんですけど、、、　　　　　　5

ふどうさんや：そうですか。どれぐらいの　大きさですか。　　　　　　　　6

モニカ：　　　そうですね。みんなで　八つか、それぐらいのアパートの方が、

　　　　　　　いいです。　　　　　　　　　　　　　　　　　　　　　　8

ふどうさんや：じゃ、ちょっと　えきから　遠いですが、このアパートは、　9

　　　　　　　どうですか。　　　　　　　　　　　　　　　　　　　　　10

　　　　　　　一けんのたてものの中に、アパートが　みんなで、八つあります。

　　　　　　　大家さんも、しんせつな人ですよ。　　　　　　　　　　　12

モニカ：　　　へやに、トイレがありますか。　　　　　　　　　　　　　13

ふどうさんや：あります。小さいですが、キッチンも　あります。　　　　14

モニカ：　　　じゃ、ぜひ　おねがいします。　　　　　　　　　　　　　15

ふどうさんや：今から、行きましょう。　　　　　　　　　　　　　　　　16

Chapter 6(A)
[English translation]:

Realtor: (pointing on a map) Here is a pretty apartment. This apartment is really new.
Monica: Is it inside a large building?
Realtor: Yes, there are twenty (apartments) total.
Monica: I prefer a smaller one…
Realtor: Is that right? How small?
Monica: Well, I prefer the one with eight or so apartments in all.
Realtor: Then, how about this one? It's a bit far from the station though. There are eight of them in one building. The landlord is a very kind man, too.
Monica: Is there a toilet in the room (apartment)?
Realtor: Yes, there is. There is a kitchen, too, though it's small.
Monica: Then, by all means.
Realtor: Let's go now.

[Vocabulary List]

1. Expressions
   ちいさいほうが　いいんですが、、　　　I prefer smaller.
   どれぐらいの　おおきさですか。　　　How big is it?
   おねがいします。　　　Please do me a favor.

2. Nouns
   アパート　　　　　　　　　　apartment
   アパートさがし　　　　　　　search for an apartment
   　　さがします　　　　　　　2nd Base of verb "さがす" (search)
   オフィス　　　　　　　　　　office
   ふどうさんや　　　　　　　　realtor
   (たてもの)　　　　　　　　　building
   おおや（大家）　　　　　　　landlord
   ぜんぶ/みんな　　　　　　　everything
   へや　　　　　　　　　　　　room
   トイレ　　　　　　　　　　　toilet, bathroom
   キッチン　　　　　　　　　　kitchen
   --- けん　　　　　　　　　　counter for houses/buildings

3. Copula Nouns
   (きれい)　　　　　　　　　　pretty, clean
   しんせつ　　　　　　　　　　kindhearted

4. Interrogative Pronoun
   どう　　　　　　　　　　　　how
   　　どうですか。　　　　　　How is it? How about that?

5.  Adjectives
（ 新 <ruby>しい<rt>あたら</rt></ruby>）                   new

（ 遠い<rt>とお</rt>）            far

6.  Adverbs
ほんとうに           truly
ちょっと            a little
（ぜひ）            by all means
ぜんぶで(＝みんなで)    in all

7.  Particles
Ａ か Ｂ           A or B
〜　けど、      Conjunctive Particle: though, but…

--------------------------------------------------------------------------------

Additional Vocabulary from Exercises, Dict-A-Conversation, and Kanji sections

--------------------------------------------------------------------------------

[Nouns]

| | |
|---|---|
| ながし | kitchen sink |
| とおく （遠く） | place that is far |
| ちかく （近く） | place that is near |
| じぶん （自分） | oneself |
| しんしゃ （新車） | new car |
| ちゅうこしゃ （中古車） | used car |
| じてんしゃ （自てん車） | bicycle |
| じどうしゃ （自どう車） | car; automobile |
| だいしょう （大小） | size (big & small) |
| じょうげ （上下） | top and bottom (high and low) |

[Copula Nouns]

| | |
|---|---|
| ふしんせつ | unkind |
| にぎやか | lively |

[Adjectives]

| | |
|---|---|
| きたない | dirty |

--------------------------------------------------------------------------------

Chapter 6 (A)         **Grammar and Cultural Notes**

## 1. Comparative form of Adjectives

 The sentence pattern is very similar to that used with Comparative forms of Nouns, 〜のほうが　いいです。 Be careful not to use particle の before ほう. See the example sentences:

      I prefer (it to be) smaller. <u>ちいさい</u>ほうが　いいです。

I like (it) cheaper.　やすいほうが　いいです。

I like (it) hotter.　あついほうが　すきです。

## 2. ～けど....(though)

It is used the same way as が at the end of sentences.  Just like が in Chapter 5, けど is also used at the end of sentences in avoiding assertiveness.　It is a short form of けれども; and its other variations are けれど、だけど.

Compare the following statements. Which sounds more definite and which more hesitant?

    A.　わたしは、ケーキが　いいです。

    B.　わたしは、ケーキが　いい（ん）ですけど、、

B implies feelings of hesitance and may mean: "I like cake better, but if you don't like my choice, I don't mind choosing something else," or "I like cake; what do you think?"

Read the below conversation among the three students and their teacher, and follow how they come to decide the date of the party.

先生　　：みなさん、パーティーは　何曜日がいいですか。

学生Ａ：わたしは、土曜日が　いいんですけど、、

学生Ｂ：わたしは、ほんとうは、金曜日がいいんですけど、
　　　　土曜日でも　いいです。

学生Ｃ：わたしは、日曜日がいいんですけど、、、じつは、
　　　　金、土　は、しごとなんです。

学生Ａ：わたしは、ほんとうは、土曜日がいいんですけど、
　　　　日曜日でも　いいです。

先生　　：Ｂさん、日曜日でも　いいですか。

学生Ｂ：はい！

Guess what is implied after けど.

    1．私は、いきますけど、、

    2．ここに　パンがあるんですけど、、、

    3．あしたは、ひまなんですけど、、

    4．きょうなら、いいんですけど、、

    5．このくつが　ほしいんですけど、、

Chapter 6 (A) Exercises

A. Choose the adjective of your preference, saying ～ほうが　いいんですけど...

（1）ケーキは、（おおきい、ちいさい）ほうが　いいんですけど、、

（2）テストは、（むずかしい、やさしい）ほうが　いいんですけど、、

（3）へやは、（あたらしい、ふるい）ほうが　いいんですけど、、
　　　　room

（4）学校は、（ちかい、とおい）ほうが　いいんですけど、、
　　　がっこう

（5）アイスクリームは、（あまい、あまくない）ほうが　いいんですけど、、
　　　　　　　　　　　　　sweet

Choose a copula noun or adjective of your preference, saying ～ほうが　いいんですけど...

（1）人は、（しんせつな、ふしんせつな）ほうが　いいんですけど、、
　　　ひと　　　　　　　　　unkind

（2）たてものは、（きれいな、きたない）ほうが　いいんですけど、、
　　　　　　　　　　　　clean　　　　dirty

（3）こうえんは、（しずかな、にぎやかな）ほうが　いいんですけど、、
　　　park　　　　　quiet　　　lively

（4）学校は、（ゆうめいな、ゆうめいじゃない）ほうが　いいんですけど、、
　　　がっこう　　famous

（5）こどもは、（げんきな、しずかな）ほうが　いいんですけど、、

（6）日曜日は、（ひまな、いそがしい）ほうが　いいんですけど、、
　　　にちようび　　　　　busy

B. Ask your classmates the following questions in Japanese.

1.  How many buildings are in this school?
2.  How many rooms does s/he have in her/his apartment/house?
3.  Is her/his apartment/house far from the station?
4.  Is his/her room pretty?
5.  Which does s/he prefer, a smaller or a bigger room?
6.  Does s/he have a bathroom in her/his room?
7.  Does s/he have a kitchen in her room?
8.  Is there a landlord in her/his apartment/house?  If there is, is s/he kind?

Hints:
1 & 2: Use the sentence pattern "Location に item が　いくつ　ありますか。"
5: Use "Ａ と Ｂ と、どちらのほうが、.....ですか。"

C. Pair-work (or in groups): Role play. Take turns with your partner in role playing the student and realtor. Using the Chapter 6(A) dialogue as example, create a conversation between the two of you. But first, have each one of you mentally decide your preferred size, location, age of building, apartment quantity in the building, and as well as the existence or absence of bathroom, kitchen, and so forth. Then exchange the information with each other by asking and answering questions. See if the two of you can find preference similarities.

Essential vocabulary:

ふどうさんや realtor　アパート apartment　へや room たてもの　building
ぜんぶで　いくつ how many in all
どれぐらいの　おおきさ how big?
とおい/ちかい(far/near),　ふるい/あたらしい(old/new),
おおきい/ちいさい(big/small)　ひろい / せまい (spacious/narrow)
しずか(quiet)/ にぎやか(lively)
トイレ or おてあらい (bathroom)
キッチン or だいどころ (kitchen)　ながし (sink)　れいぞうこ(refrigerator)
ながめ (view)
～は　どうですか。(How about ~? How would you like it?)
おねがいします。(Please do me a favor. )

♬
Chapter 6 (A) Dict-A-Conversation
Listen to the dialogue between a student and a realtor in the Chapter 6 (A) on the student CD, and circle the right answers.

Q1: (1) おおきい　(2) ちいさい

Q2: (1) よっつ　(2) やっつ　(3) むっつ

Q3: (1) ちょっと とおい　(2) とても とおい (3) とおくない

Q4: (1) きれい　(2) きれいじゃない

Q5: (1) あります　(2) ありません

Q6: (1) あります　(2) ありません

Q7: (1) toilet　(2) bath tub (3) kitchen sink

Q8: (1) しました　(2) しませんでした

Chapter 6 (A)

| 家 <br><br> (a house; home) | いえ<br>うち<br>や<br>カ<br>ケ | 家 （いえ、うち） a house; home<br>大家 （おおや） landlord<br>[家族 （かぞく） a family]<br>田中家 （たなかけ） The Tanaka<br>家内 （かない） my wife<br>一家全員 （いっかぜんいん） everyone in the family |
|---|---|---|
| | | (10)<br>丶 丶 宀 宀 宀 宁 宇 穻 家 家 |
| 遠 <br><br> (far) | とお （い）<br>エン | 遠い （とおい） far<br>遠足 （えんそく） excursion; picnic<br>遠近 （えんきん） near and far; distance; perspective |
| | | (13)<br>一 十 土 キ 吉 吉 声 声 章 章 袁 遠 遠 |
| 新 <br><br> (new) | あたら （しい）<br>シン | 新しい （あたらしい） new<br>[新聞 （しんぶん） newspaper]<br>新人 （しんじん） new face<br>新学期 （しんがっき） new semester/term<br>新入生 （しんにゅうせい） freshmen |
| | | (13)<br>丶 亠 卉 立 立 辛 辛 亲 亲 新 新 新 |
| 車 <br><br> (a car; a wheel) | くるま<br>シャ | 車 （くるま） a car; wheel<br>日本車 （にほんしゃ） Japanese cars<br>外車 （がいしゃ） foreign cars<br>車内 （しゃない） inside a car<br>車外 （しゃがい） outside a car<br>新車 （しんしゃ） new car |
| | | (7)<br>一 厂 厅 戸 百 亘 車 |
| 自 <br><br> (oneself) | みずか （ら）<br>ジ | 自ら （みずから） of one's own accord<br>自分 （じぶん） oneself<br>自信 （じしん） confidence<br>自身 （じしん） oneself |
| | | (6)<br>丿 亻 白 白 自 自 |

## Kanji Practice for Chapter 6(A)

かんじの　れんしゅう

1. つぎの　ことばを　よみなさい。それから、クラスメートにいみをきき
なさい。Read the following words to your classmates and ask them for the
meaning of each word/sentence.

（1）　家

（2）　私の家

（3）　家<sub>ぞく</sub>族

（4）　遠く　と　近く

（5）　新しい

（6）　車

（7）　新車　と　中古車

（8）　自分

（9）　自<sup>てん</sup>転車　と　自<sup>どう</sup>動車

2. Write antonymous kanji in the box.

(1) large ↔ small

| 大 | 小 |
|---|---|

(2) top (above) ↔ bottom (below)

| | 下 |
|---|---|

(3) water ↔ fire

| 水 | と | |
|---|---|---|

(4) oneself ↔ others

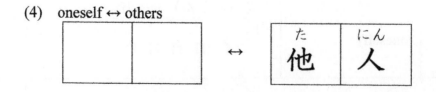

| | | ↔ | 他<sup>た</sup> | 人<sup>にん</sup> |

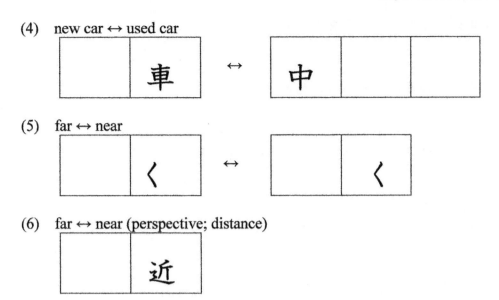

(4)　new car ↔ used car

(5)　far ↔ near

(6)　far ↔ near (perspective; distance)

3．よんでから、よみがなをかいて、えいごでいいなさい。Read first, then write yomigana above each kanji, and translate into English.

（1）　私の家から学校まで、遠くありません。近いです。

（2）　今日、新しい車を　かいました。

（3）　家族は、みんなで　五人です。

（4）　午後は、自分一人で、べんきょうしました。

（5）　兄が　遠くから　来ました。

（6）　私は、中古車を　かいましたが、とてもいい車です。

（7）　毎日、電車で　学校に　行きます。

(8) 川のそばの、古い家を　よく知っています。

(9) その家の色は、私の家の色と　同じ色です。

(10) 遠くからでも、分かります。あれは妹です。

4. かんじとひらがなで　かきなさい。
Write in kanji and hiragana.  Write the underlined words in kanji, while paying attention to the "okurigana."

（１）　　いえから　がっこうまで、なんで　きますか。

（２）　　「くるま」と「じどうしゃ」は、おなじです。しっていましたか。

（３）　　そのきっさてんは、とおいですね。ちかくのきっさてんにしましょう。

（４）　　じぶんのおかねで、アラスカに　いきました。

（５）　　あなたのおとうさんのくるまは、あたらしいですか。

（６）　　あたらしいくるまを　「しんしゃ」といいます。

（７）　　しんにゅうせいは、かわいいですね。
　　　　　　　freshmen (students who newly entered)

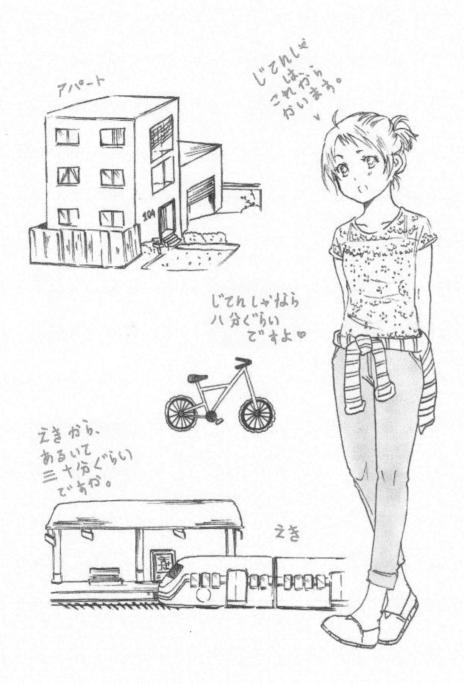

アパート

じてんしゃ
はぐらい
これがいます、

じてんしゃなら
八分ぐらい
ですよ♡

えきから、
あるいて
三十分ぐらい
ですが。

えき

Chapter 6 (B)　　　　Looking for an Apartment　アパートを見る

| | | |
|---|---|---|
| ふどうさんや： | つきました。ここです。 | 1 |
| モニカ： | えきから、歩いて 三十分ぐらいですか。 | 2 |
| ふどうさんや： | あなたなら、二十分ぐらいでしょう。 | 3 |
| | じてんしゃは、どうですか。 | 4 |
| モニカ： | じてんしゃは、ありませんが、これから買います。 | 5 |
| ふどうさんや： | じてんしゃなら、八分ぐらいですよ。 | 6 |

〔中に入る〕

| | | |
|---|---|---|
| モニカ： | うわあ、かなり 広いですね。 | 8 |
| ふどうさんや： | それに、明るいでしょう？　南 がわですから。 | 9 |
| モニカ： | まどが 二つも ありますね。 | 10 |
| ふどうさんや： | ええ、東と南に 一つずつ ありますから、朝は、日光がよく | |
| | 入りますよ。 | 12 |
| モニカ： | おふろも ありますか。 | 13 |
| ふどうさんや： | おふろは、ありません。でも、近くに 銭湯がありますから。 | 14 |
| モニカ： | そうですか。まどから公園が見えます。木がたくさんありますね。 | |
| ふどうさんや： | しずかでしょう？ | 16 |
| モニカ： | ええ、気に入りました。 | 17 |
| ふどうさんや： | じゃ、これから 大家さんに 会いましょうか。 | 18 |
| モニカ： | はい、おねがいします。 | 19 |

Chapter 6 (B)
[English translation:]

Realtor:  Here we are.  It's right here.
Monica:  Is it about thirty minutes by foot from the station?
Realtor:  It'll take about twenty minutes for you.  How about by bicycle?
Monica:  I don't have a bicycle, but I will buy one.
Realtor:  It'll take about eight minutes by bicycle.

[They both enter inside]
Monica:  Wow, it's pretty big.
Realtor:  Aside from that, it's bright, isn't it?  Because it's (facing) the south (side).
Monica:  There are even two windows.
Realtor:  Yes, there is one of each at the East and South ends, so you get a lot of sunshine
              in the morning.
Monica:  Is there a bath?
Realtor:  No, there isn't a bath, but there is a "sentoo (public bath)" nearby.
Monica:  Is that right?  I can see a park through the window.  There are lots of trees,
              aren't there?
Realtor:  Isn't it quiet?
Monica:  Yes, I like it.
Realtor:  Then, shall we meet the landlord?
Monica:  Yes, please.

Chapter 6 (B)                    Vocabulary List

1. Expressions

   <ruby>二十分<rt>にじゅっぷん</rt></ruby>ぐらいでしょう。          It will probably take about 20 min.

   しずかでしょう？                      It is quiet, isn't it?

   じてんしゃなら、八分ぐらいです。        If by bicycle, it would take 8 minutes.

   <ruby>歩<rt>ある</rt></ruby>いて、三十分です。            It takes 30 minutes by foot.

   うわあ                            Wow!

2. Nouns

   まど                              window

   <ruby>南<rt>みなみ</rt></ruby>                               South

   <ruby>南<rt>みなみ</rt></ruby>がわ                            south side

   <ruby>東<rt>ひがし</rt></ruby>                               East

   Additional vocabulary:  <ruby>北<rt>きた</rt></ruby>        North

                           <ruby>西<rt>にし</rt></ruby>        West

   <ruby>日光<rt>にっこう</rt></ruby>                             sunshine, sunlight

   せんとう（銭湯）                     public bath

   <ruby>大家<rt>おおや</rt></ruby>                              landlord

   （<ruby>木<rt>き</rt></ruby>）                            tree

   （こうえん　公園）                   park

   （おふろ）                         bath

   （<ruby>近<rt>ちか</rt></ruby>く）                          vicinity, nearby

   （<ruby>朝<rt>あさ</rt></ruby>）                           morning

   （じてんしゃ）                      bicycle

   （<ruby>歩<rt>ある</rt></ruby>いて）                         walking, by foot

   （えき）                          station

3. Adjectives

   （<ruby>広<rt>ひろ</rt></ruby>い）                          wide, broad, spacious

   （<ruby>明<rt>あか</rt></ruby>るい）                         bright

4. Verbs

   つく（着く）                        to arrive

   <ruby>見<rt>み</rt></ruby>える                             to be visible

   （<ruby>歩<rt>ある</rt></ruby>く）                          to walk

| | |
|---|---|
| (買う) | to buy |
| (気に入る) | to like |
| (入る) | to enter |

5. Adverbs

| | |
|---|---|
| かなり | quite |
| たくさん | many, a lot |
| これから | now, from now on |

6. Particles

| | |
|---|---|
| も | for emphasis, as many as ~ |
| 　二つも　あります | There are as many as two. |
| ずつ | each; a particle that indicates equal distribution of quantity |
| 　一つずつ　あります | It has one of each. |
| Ｎなら、 | if it is ~, |
| 　あしたなら、だいじょうぶ | If tomorrow, it will be all right. |

7. Conjunction

| | |
|---|---|
| でも | But; However (used between two Sentences) |

-------------------------------------------------------------------------------------
Additional Vocabulary from Grammar Notes, Exercises, and Dict-A-Conversation
-------------------------------------------------------------------------------------

[Nouns]

| | |
|---|---|
| ラボ | lab |
| てん　（くろいてん） | dot; point; spot (black dots) |
| ひゃくてん | one hundred points |
| だれか | someone |
| おこさん | child (polite form) |
| にわ | yard; garden |
| くうき | air |
| さんがいだて | three-story building |
| すみ | in-corner |
| にしび | afternoon sun from the West |
| どちらがわ | which side |

[Adverbs]

| | |
|---|---|
| たぶん、おそらく、おおかた | perhaps, probably |

[Verb]

| | |
|---|---|
| とる | to get; receive |

Chapter 6 B                    Grammar and Cultural Notes

## 1. <u>Sentence + でしょう (stated with a parallel or falling tone) : Probably</u>

| Sentence (Informal) | |
|---|---|
| (1) あれは、田中さん | でしょう。 |
| (2) あしたは、あつい | でしょう。 |
| (3) たぶん、来る | でしょう。 |

でしょう（だろう in casual form）is an auxiliary that expresses a speaker's conjecture. It is usually not based on evidence or particular information, though often accompanied by adverbs that show "probability." The adverbs include たぶん、おそらく、たいてい、おおかた、きっと。 The speakers' conjecture sounds certain when paired with たぶん、おそらく、 and even more confident with きっと.

In the Chapter 6 B dialogue, a realtor guessed how long Monica's commute might take by foot (line 3). He said,

あなたなら、二十分ぐらいでしょう。("It will probably take about twenty minutes for you.") in response to the question, えきから歩いて三十分ぐらいですか。("Will it take about half an hour by foot from the station?"). Certainly, the realtor did not measure how long it would take Monica, but simply estimate how long it would take her, given she's a young adult.

The example sentences in the box are all non-past tense. Regardless of tense, "でしょう" always follows sentences in their "informal" forms.

## 2. <u>Sentence + でしょう (with rising tone)? : Isn't it?</u>

"でしょう" with a rising intonation asks for a listener's consent.
Examples:
  （１）これは、あなたの本でしょう？        This is your book, isn't it?
  （２）この本は、たかいでしょう？          This book is expensive, isn't it?
  （３）あなたも、いくでしょう？            You are going, too, aren't you?

## 3. <u>Noun なら: If it is ~, ...</u>

なら is a conjunction which means; "If it is the case…"
Examples:
  （１）あなたなら、どうしますか？          What will you do if it were you?
  （２）あしたなら、だいじょうぶですよ。     If it's tomorrow, it will be all right.
  （３）でんしゃなら、（バスより）はやいですよ If it's a train, it would be faster
                                              (than a bus).

## 4. 〜も for emphasis: even; as many as; not even one; not any

The particle も can be used for added emphasis.

### (1) も with multiple numbers

Examples:

1．え？あなたは、ごはんを毎日　五杯も食べるんですか！？
     What?  You eat as many as five bowls  of rice?

2．チャンさんは、中国人ですから、漢字を五千も知っています。
     Mr. Chan knows as many as five thousands Chinese characters, since he is Chinese.

### (2) も with interrogative pronouns (what, where, who, etc) means "total negation;" nothing, nowhere, nobody, etc.

1. きのうのよるは、何も　食べませんでした。
     I didn't eat anything last night.

2. きのうの日曜日は、どこにも　行きませんでした。
     I didn't go anywhere this Sunday.

3. きょうしつには、だれも　いません。
     No one is in the classroom.

### (3) も with number "one" with counters (such as ひとりも、ひとつも、いちまいも、いちだいも、etc.) means also total negation; not even one.

1. きょうしつには、学生が　一人もいません。
     There's not even one student in the classroom.

2. 今日は、ごはんを　一杯も　食べませんでした。
     I didn't eat even one bowl of rice today.

3. ここには、くるまが、一台も　ありません。

     There's  not even one car here.

In order to come up with this expression properly, you must refresh your memory of counters that you learned in Japanese 1.  Here is the list of the essential counters you must know.

1．一人（ひとり）(counter for people)

２．一枚（いちまい）(counter for sheets and thin items such as paper)
３．一ドル、一円（いちえん）、一セント（いっせんと）(money)
４．一杯（いっぱい）(counter for glassful/cupful)
５．一本（いっぽん）(counter for long items such as pens)
６．一冊（いっさつ）(counter for books)
７．一台（いちだい）(counter for cars/machines)
８．一つ（ひとつ） or 一個（いっこ） (general counters)

Now, how would you say the following in Japanese?
1. There isn't even one person (here).
2. I don't have even one cent (with me).
3. I don't have even one pencil.
4. I don't have even one car.
5. I don't have even one candy.
6. I didn't drink alcohol at all, not even one glass.
7. I didn't read even one book of Shakespeare.
8. I didn't buy even one T-shirt.

Answers:
１．人は、ひとりも いません。
２．私（に）は、（おかねが）一セントも ありません。
３．私（に）は、えんぴつが いっぽんも ありません。
４．私（に）は、くるまが いちだいも ありません。
５．私（に）は、おかしが ひとつも ありません。
６．私は、おさけを いっぱいも のみませんでした。
７．私は、シェイクスピアを いっさつも よみませんでした。
８．私は、Ｔシャツを いちまいも かいませんでした。

## 5. でも Conjunction that connects two sentences where content disagrees

| Sentence<br>おふろはありません。 | でも、 | Sentence<br>ちかくにせんとうが あります。 |
|---|---|---|
| There is no bath. | But, | there is a public bath nearby. |

| Sentence<br>そうじは できます。 | でも、 | Sentence<br>りょうりは できません。 |
|---|---|---|
| I can clean up. | But, | I cannot cook. |

| Sentence<br>きょうは いそがしい です。 | でも、 | Sentence<br>あしたは、ひまです。 |
|---|---|---|
| Today I am busy. | But, | tomorrow I am free. |

## 6. Particle は to show contrast

Particle "は" is used for contrast and comparison.  Original particles including "が" and "を" may be switched out with "は" for contrast effect.  For example, in the Chapter 6B dialogue where Monica was asked if she had a bicycle, she answered:

じてんしゃ<u>は</u>、ありませんが、これから　買<sup>か</sup>います。(Line 5)
　　"I have no bicycle, but I will buy one soon."

Another example can be found in the realtor's reply to her question, おふろも　ありますか。 "Is there a bath, too?" and he answered, おふろ<u>は</u>、ありません。 "No, there is no bath.  But there is a public bath in the neighborhood."
See the following examples:

　　（１）　　お金<sup>かね</sup><u>は</u>、ありませんが、ひま<u>は</u>、あります。
　　　　　　　I have no money, but I have (plenty of free) time.

　　（２）　　コーヒー<u>は</u>、すきじゃありません。でも。おちゃ<u>は</u>、すきです。
　　　　　　　I don't like coffee, but I like tea.

　　（３）　　午後<sup>ごご</sup>は、クラス<u>は</u>ありませんが、ラボがあります。
　　　　　　　I don't have classes in the afternoon, but I have (to go to) lab.

In sentence (1), money and time are being compared.  In sentence (2), coffee and tea are.  And, in sentence (3), the speaker is comparing what s/he has to do and what s/he doesn't in the afternoon.  Therefore, if you were asked whether you drink coffee,

コーヒー<u>を</u>　飲<sup>の</sup>みますか。(Do you drink coffee?)

it is more natural to answer with は, if you don't drink coffee (but drink something else):

コーヒー<u>は</u>、飲<sup>の</sup>みません。(I don't drink coffee.)

## 7.　～が　見<sup>み</sup>えます: ～ is visible (Intransitive Verb) (Dictionary form: 見<sup>み</sup>える)

Do not confuse the verb "mieru" with "miru."  The latter is a transitive verb, meaning to "look at something," and the former is an intransitive verb, meaning that "something is visible."  Since "mieru" is an intransitive verb, it is preceded by a Subject and the subjective marker "ga."  Let's compare:

(1) ～　を　見<sup>み</sup>る/見<sup>み</sup>ます
　　私<sup>わたし</sup>の目<sup>め</sup>を　見<sup>み</sup>てください。
　　Please look at me in the eyes.

(2) ～　が　見<sup>み</sup>える/見<sup>み</sup>えます
　　黒<sup>くろ</sup>い点<sup>てん</sup>が　見<sup>み</sup>えますか。
　　Can you see the black dots?

Sentence (1) uses the verb "miru" because it involves a person's "intent" to look at another in the eyes; while in sentence (2), the verb "mieru" is used because the visibility of black dots is being questioned.  "Mieru" has nothing to do with "will," but rather the "fact" or the ability of seeing the black dots.

Chapter 6 (B) Exercises

A. You are a fortuneteller. Use 〜でしょう (with a falling pitch ⟍) to predict your classmates' future. Practice the following "predictions" first:

(1) あなたは、あす <u>だれか</u>しんせつな<u>人</u>に <u>会う</u>でしょう。
　　　　　　　　　 someone　　　　　　　　 to meet

(2) あなたは、テストで <u>百</u>てんを <u>とる</u>でしょう。
　　　　　　　　　　　　　　　　　　　　 to get

(3) あなたの<u>未来</u>の <u>ご主人</u>は、<u>ハンサム</u>でしょう。
　　　　　　 future　　 husband　 handsome

(4) あなたの<u>未来</u>の <u>おくさん</u>は、きれいでしょう。
　　　　　　 future　　　 wife

(5) あなたの<u>未来</u>の <u>お子さん</u>は、<u>かわいい</u>でしょう。
　　　　　　　　　　　　 child　　　　　 cute

(6) あしたは、テストが <u>ない</u>でしょう。
　　　　　　　　　　　　 negative form of "aru"

B.

1. Add でしょう？ (with a rising tone ⟋) to the end of each sentence to make them "tag questions."

Example: あの<u>人</u>は、<u>田中</u>さん ＋ でしょう？ (He's Mr. Tanaka, isn't he?)

（１）きょうは、げつようび

（２）あしたは、はれ

（３）ここは、<u>日光</u>が、よく<u>入る</u>

（４）うちに、おふろは、ない

（５）きょう、<u>大家</u>さんに <u>会う</u>

（６）あなたの<u>にわ</u>には、<u>木</u>がたくさんある
　　　　　　 yard

（７）としょかんは、しずか

（８）あなたのへやは、きれい

（９）<u>おてあらい</u>は、<ruby>明<rt>あか</rt></ruby>るい
   bathroom

（１０）ここは、<u>くうき</u>が　いい
         air

2. Pair-work: Ask your partner the phrases in Section 1 using でしょう ? and attain yes/no answers based on reality.  Be careful how you answer number (4).  In Japanese, when you are asked a question in the negative form, your answer isn't derived from reality, but on whether you agree with the inquiry or not: In other words, if you agree with what's been (negatively) asked, you would answer "yes, (I agree with what you said. In fact, I don't have a bath-tub in my house). But if you disagree with what's been (negatively) asked, you would answer, "no (I don't agree with you.  I have a bath-tub in my house)."

Examples:

(1)

A: きょうは、げつようびでしょう？

B: はい、そうです。Or,
   いいえ、げつようびじゃありません。かようびです。

(2)

A: テストは、ないでしょう？

B: はい、テストは、ないですよ。Or,
   いいえ、テストは、ありますよ！

C. Pair-work: Create a dialogue in Japanese with your partner, commenting on the apartment below. Use both the か question and tag question ね ? forms to discuss about the apartment: its location, how many windows it has, from which window it gets sun, what you can see from the window, etc.

D. Choose either でも (But, …) or そして (And,…) to connect the given sentences.

（１）あさごはんを食べます。（　　　　　）、おちゃをのみます。

（２）おちゃが好きです。（　　　　　）、コーヒーは、きらいです。

（３）デパートへ行きました。（　　　　　）、なにも買いませんでした。

（４）あさ、おきます。（　　　　　）、シャワーを　あびます。

（５）えきで、バスにのりました。（　　　　　）、ここまで、来ました。

（６）日本語ができます。（　　　　　）、ちゅうご語は、できません。

E. Brag what you can do to impress your classmates, using も to the amount, degree, etc. that you are able to do something (e.g., eat, drink, walk, lift, run, etc).
   Examples:

（１）私は、ごはんを三杯も　食べます。

（２）きのうは、十二時間も　ねました。

（３）私は、かんじを　五百も　知っています。

Fill in the blanks:

(1) ぼくは、がいこく語を（　　　　　）も　知っています。
　　　　　　　foreign languages　as many as four

(2) 私は、がいこくへ　（　　　　　）も　行きました。
　　　　　　　foreign countries　as often as five times

(3) 私は、ビールを（　　　　　）も　のみました。
　　　　　　　　as many as ten glasses

Now make your own:

(1)

(2)

(3)

(4)

(5)

F. Make a sentence of "total negation," using the ひとつ (and other counters with "one") + も…ない pattern.
   Example:

（１）ぼくは、かんじをひとつも　知らないんです。
　　　　I don't even know one kanji.

（２）私は、ゆうめいな人を　ひとりも　知りません。
　　　　I don't even know one famous person.

（３）私は、アフリカの国のなまえを、<u>ひとつも</u>、<u>知りません</u>。
                      （くに country）

    I don't know any countries' names in Africa.

（４）私は、デザイナーのふくが、<u>いちまいも</u>  <u>ありません</u>。

    I don't have any designer clothes.

Fill in the blanks:

(1) ぼくは、がいこく語を（           ）も  知りません。
          foreign languages  <u>not even one</u>

(2) 私は、がいこくへ  （         ）も  行っていません。
          foreign countries  <u>not even once</u>

(3) 私は、ビールを（       ）も  のみません。
             <u>not even one glass</u>

Now make your own:

(1)

(2)

(3)

(4)

(5)

G. Recommend restaurants, classes, places, etc., using the ～なら，…がいいですよ pattern.

   Examples:

   (1) うどんなら、「さぬきうどん」が  いいですよ。

   (2) カレーなら、「カレーハウス」が  いいですよ。

   (3) えいがなら、日本のえいがが  いいですよ。

   Now make your own:

(1)

(2)

(3)

(4)

(5)

Chapter 6 (B) Dict-A-Conversation: Listen to the CD and answer the following questions in Japanese based on the content you hear.

[Vocabulary help]: You must learn to let go of unfamiliar words and capture the general idea without being held up by what you do not know. Here are four vocabulary words from the CD perhaps new to you. 三階建て three-story building, 隅 in-corner, 西日 the afternoon sun from the West, 南 の日 (or 陽) the sunshine from the South

Questions:

1．はじめの　アパートは、どのへんに　ありますか。えきから遠いですか。

　　　．．．．．．．．．．．．．．．．．．．．．．．．．．．．．．．．．．．．．．．．．．．．．．

2．そのアパートは、新しいですか。

　　　．．．．．．．．．．．．．．．．．．．．．．．．．．．．．．．．．．．．．．．．．．．．．．

3．そのたてものには、アパートが　なんけんぐらい　ありますか。

　　　．．．．．．．．．．．．．．．．．．．．．．．．．．．．．．．．．．．．．．．．．．．．．．

4．そのアパートは、たてものの北にありますか、それとも、南にありますか。

　　　．．．．．．．．．．．．．．．．．．．．．．．．．．．．．．．．．．．．．．．．．．．．．．

5．そのアパートのまどは、どちらのほうに　ありますか。

　　　．．．．．．．．．．．．．．．．．．．．．．．．．．．．．．．．．．．．．．．．．．．．．．

6．モニカは、そのアパートが、気に入りませんでした。どうしてですか。

　　　．．．．．．．．．．．．．．．．．．．．．．．．．．．．．．．．．．．．．．．．．．．．．．

7．二つ目のアパートは、古いですか、新しいですか。

　　　．．．．．．．．．．．．．．．．．．．．．．．．．．．．．．．．．．．．．．．．．．．．．．

8．二つ目のアパートは、まどが、どちらがわに　ありますか。
　　　　　　　　　　　　　　　　which side

　　　．．．．．．．．．．．．．．．．．．．．．．．．．．．．．．．．．．．．．．．．．．．．．．

9．二つ目のアパートの、東がわには、なにが　ありますか。

　　　．．．．．．．．．．．．．．．．．．．．．．．．．．．．．．．．．．．．．．．．．．．．．．

10．二つ目のアパートの　東がわから、なにが　見えますか。

　　　．．．．．．．．．．．．．．．．．．．．．．．．．．．．．．．．．．．．．．．．．．．．．．

11．モニカは、二つ目のアパートが　気に入りました。どうしてですか。

　　　．．．．．．．．．．．．．．．．．．．．．．．．．．．．．．．．．．．．．．．．．．．．．．

Chapter 6 (B) – (1)

| 見 | み（る）<br>ケン<br><br>(to see, to look) | 見る（みる）to see; to watch; to look<br>見学（けんがく）a field trip; a study tour<br>一見する（いっけんする）take a glance |
| | | (7)<br>丨 冂 冃 月 目 貝 見 |
| 歩 | ある（く）<br>ホ<br>ポ<br><br>(to walk, steps) | 歩く（あるく）to walk<br>一歩（いっぽ）one step<br>歩行（ほこう）walking<br>[徒歩（とほ）walking] |
| | | (8)<br>丨 卜 止 止 牛 爿 歨 歩 |
| 買 | か（う）<br>バイ<br><br>(to buy) | 買う（かう）to shop; to buy<br>[買い物（かいもの）a shopping]<br>[売買（ばいばい）selling and buying] |
| | | (12)<br>丶 冂 皿 皿 皿 罒 罒 胃 冒 冒 買 買 |
| 広 | ひろ（い）<br>コウ<br><br>(wide, spacious) | 広い（ひろい）wide; spacious<br>広々（ひろびろ）として いる being spacious<br>広大（こうだい）な spacious |
| | | (5)<br>丶 亠 广 広 広 |
| 明 | あか（るい）<br>ミョウ<br>メイ<br><br>(bright) | 明るい（あかるい）bright<br>明日（みょうにち、あす、あした）<br>tomorrow<br>[明快（めいかい）な clear] |
| | | (8)<br>丨 冂 日 日 囙 明 明 明 |
| 南 | みなみ<br>ナン<br><br>(south) | 南の方（みなみのほう）to the south<br>[南天（なんてん）the south sky]<br>南東（なんとう）south-east |
| | | (9)<br>一 十 冇 冇 肉 肉 肉 南 南 |

Chapter 6 (B) – (2)

| 東<br><br>(east) | ひがし<br>トウ | 東の方（ひがしのほう）the direction of east<br>東京（とうきょう）Tokyo, capital of Japan |
| :--: | :-- | :-- |
| | | (8)<br>一 厂 冂 両 亘 車 東 東 |
| 朝<br><br>(morning) | あさ<br>チョウ | 今日の朝（きょうのあさ）this morning<br>朝日（あさひ）morning sun<br>朝食（ちょうしょく）breakfast<br>[朝刊（ちょうかん）morning newspaper]<br>＊今朝（けさ） |
| | | (12)<br>一 十 古 古 古 直 卓 朝 朝 朝 |
| 光<br><br>(a light, beam) | ひかり<br>ひか（る）<br>コウ | 朝の光（あさのひかり）morning sun<br>光る（ひかる）to shine<br>光明（こうみょう）light, hope<br>日光（にっこう）the sunlight |
| | | (6)<br>丨 丬 业 业 光 |
| 西<br><br>(west) | にし<br>サイ<br>ザイ<br>セイ | 西の方（にしのほう）the direction of west<br>東西（とうざい）the east-west<br>[西方浄土（さいほうじょうど）paradise in<br>Pure-land Buddhism]<br>関西（かんさい）Kansai; Kyoto, Osaka, Kobe<br>area<br>[西高東低（せいこうとうてい）high in the<br>west and low in the east in climate] |
| | | (6)<br>一 厂 冂 丙 西 西 |
| 北<br><br>(north) | きた<br>ホク | 北の海（きたのうみ）the sea in the north<br>北海（ほっかい）the North Sea<br>北海道（ほっかいどう）Hokkaido district<br>東北（とうほく）the north-east, Tohoku<br>district |
| | | (5)<br>一 十 北 北 |

## Kanji Practice for Chapter 6 (B)
かんじの れんしゅう

1. つぎの ことばを よみなさい。それから、クラスメートにいみをきき
   <sup>くらすめえと</sup>
   なさい。Read the following words to your classmates and ask them for the
   meaning of each word/sentence.

   （１）　見る、歩く、買う

   （２）　朝の光

   （３）　日光

   （４）　明るいへや

   （５）　明日

   （６）　広いへや

   （７）　南のまど

   （８）　まどから南の日が入る

   （９）　東のそら
   　　　　 (sky)

   （１０）南東の方

   （１１）西日が入る

   （１２）気に入る

   （１３）北の方

   （１４）北西のかぜ
   　　　　 (wind)

2. よんでから、よみがなをかいて、えいごでいいなさい。Read the kanji,
   write in the yomigana above it, and translate its meaning into English.

   （１）　私のアパートは、南と東に　まどがあります。

（２）　まどから　朝の光が　入ります。

（３）　明るいへやが　好きです。

（４）　おさいふの中を見て、買いました。

（５）　広いへやは、気もちが　いいです。

（６）　朝です。東のそらが、明るいです。

（７）　北がわのへやは、さむいですね。

（８）　毎朝、近くのこうえんまで　歩きます。

（９）　朝、買いものに　行きました。

（１０）　遠くから、歩いて来ました。

3. かんじとひらがなで　こたえなさい。Answer the questions in complete sentences using kanji and hiragana.

（１）　あなたのへやのまどから　なにが<u>みえます</u>か。

（２）　<u>まいあさ</u>、なん<u>じ</u>ごろに　おきますか。

（３）　あなたのへやの<u>にし</u>がわに　まどが　ありますか。

（４）　あなたのへやは、<u>ひろい</u>ですか。

（５）　がっこうまで　あるいてきますか。

（６）　さいきん(recently)　「しんしゃ」をかいましたか。

（７）　あさのひかりが　すきですか。

（８）　かいものが　すきですか。

（９）　あなたのへやの　みなみがわに　なにが　みえますか。

（１０）　あなたのいえは、がっこうから、ひがしにありますか、にしに
ありますか、それとも、きたですか、みなみですか。
（or）

4. どちらのおくりがなが　正しいですか。Choose the one featuring the correct "okurigana" by placing a circle (O) in the space given.

(1) （　）a. 明るい　　　(2) （　）a. 歩るく　　　(3) （　）a. 広い
　　（　）b. 明かるい　　　（　）b. 歩く　　　　　（　）b. 広ろい

5. Match up: Choose the correct English translation for each kanji compound and write your answer in the space given.

(1) （　）東北（とうほく）　　a. Northeast

　　（　）北東　（ほくとう）　　b. One of the administrative districts in Japan located in the northeast of the main island, south of Hokkaido.

(2) （　）東南（とうなん）アジア　　　　a. the Middle East

　　（　）中近東　（ちゅうきんとう）　　b. the Middle and Near East

　　（　）中東　（ちゅうとう）　　　　　c. Southeast Asia

Chapter 6 (C)　　　Meeting the Landlord　　大家さんに　会う

| | | |
|---|---|---|
| 不動産屋： | ごめんください。 | 1 |
| 大家： | は〜い。あ、三井さん、おひさしぶりですね。 | 2 |
| 不動産屋： | ごぶさたしています。こちらは、留学生のモニカさんです。 | 3 |
| モニカ： | はじめまして。モニカです。 | 4 |
| 大家： | 大家の高木です。どうぞ　よろしく。 | 5 |
| モニカ： | こちらこそ。どうぞ　よろしく　おねがいします。 | 6 |
| 不動産屋： | モニカさんに、あの南東のへやは、どうでしょうか。 | 7 |
| 大家： | あのへやは、いいへやですよ。まどが　二つありますしね。 | 8 |
| | 明るくて、ながめがいいし、、、 | 9 |
| モニカ： | それに、南のまどから、公園も　見えます。 | 10 |
| 大家： | あの公園は、木が多くて、しずかで、私も　よく | 11 |
| | さんぽを　しますよ。 | 12 |
| モニカ： | そうですか。 | 13 |
| 大家： | あの公園のうらに、古いお寺があります。 | 14 |
| | 有名なお寺じゃありませんが、、 | 15 |
| | 境内が　広くて、気持ちがいいですよ。 | 16 |
| モニカ： | ありがとうございます。私は　お寺が　大好きです。 | 17 |

Chapter 6 (C)
[English translation:]

Realtor:   Hello.

Landlord: Yes. Oh, Mr. Mitsui. It's been a while (since I last saw you).

Realtor:   It's been a while (for me as well). This is Monica-san. She is a student from abroad.

Monica:   How do you do? I'm Monica.

Landlord: I am Takagi, the landlord. Pleased to meet you.

Monica:   The pleasure is mine.

Realtor:   I wonder if the apartment in the Southeast is good for her.

Landlord: That is a nice room. It has two windows, and (what's more) it's bright, and also has a nice view…

Monica:   Moreover, I can see a park from the window in the south end.

Landlord: There are many trees in the park, and it's very quiet. I often go there for a stroll.

Monica:   Is that so?

Landlord: There is an old temple behind the park. It's not famous, but it has a spacious courtyard, which is very pleasant.

Monica: Thank you very much. I like temples very much.

Chapter 6 (C)                    Vocabulary List

1. Expressions

ごめんください。                        Excuse me.  (Often used as a greeting to
                                       visit someone's house)

おひさしぶりです（ね）。               It's been a while since I last saw you.
ごぶさたしています。                    Excuse me for the long absence.
おあがりください。                      Please come in. (あがる step up)
おじゃまします。                        Expression used as you enter someone's
                                       house. (Literally: Sorry to intrude.)

2. Nouns

南東 (なんとう)                         Southeast

    Additional Vocabulary for directions

    南西 (なんせい)                 Southwest

    北東 (ほくとう)                 Northeast

    北西 (ほくせい)                 Northwest

ながめ（ながめがいい）               view, scenery (The view is nice.)
さんぽ（をする）                        stroll, walking (to stroll)
うら                                    back, backyard
（お）寺 (てら)                         Buddhist temple
境内（けいだい）                        temple yard

3. Adverbs

それに                                 in addition to, on top of it

4. Particles

し                                     and what's more, in addition to;
                                       Conjunctive Particle connecting
                                       sentences

----------------------------------------------------------------------

Additional Vocabulary from Grammar Notes, Exercises, and Dict-A-Conversation

----------------------------------------------------------------------

[Nouns]
りょう（量）                            amount
かいしゃいん / サラリーマン           company employee
だいがくいんせい                        graduate student
なきむし                                crybaby
あかちゃん                              baby
なか（仲）                              relationship (仲 (なか) がいい = get along well)
おかねもち                              rich
さばく                                  desert

| | |
|---|---|
| しゅと | capital |
| デザイン | design |
| せいのう | performance |
| ディスコ | disco |
| からだ | body |
| ちょきん | savings |
| やおや | greengrocer |
| ごぼう | burdock root |
| まっすぐ | straight |
| だいこん | daikon radish |
| さんま | mackerel |
| は | leaf |
| キャベツ | cabbage |
| ペット | pet |

[な Adjectives/Copula Nouns]

| | |
|---|---|
| いたずら | mischievous |
| しあわせ | happy |
| キュート | cute |
| セクシー | sexy |
| べんり ↔ ふべん | convenient ↔ inconvenient |
| あんぜん ↔ きけん | safe ↔ dangerous |
| ようき | happy-go-lucky |
| しなやか | supple |

[Adjectives]

| | |
|---|---|
| つめたい | cold (by touch) |
| あぶない | dangerous |
| きもちが いい | pleasant; feeling good |
| まずしい | poor |
| うつくしい | beautiful |
| ふとい | thick |
| かたい | firm |

[Verbs]

| | | |
|---|---|---|
| わらう | （わらいます） | to smile |

[Expression]

| | |
|---|---|
| だれにも | to everyone |

キャシーさんは、だれにもしんせつです。 Cathy is kind to everybody.

Chapter 6 (C)                    Grammar and Cultural Notes

## 1. <u>Connecting words and sentences: when they are complementing each other.</u>

How would you describe your dog, which is black and big?  You cannot use a particle "to と" since this particle connects two nous such as "pencils and erasers," or "you and I." For the adjective that is connected to the next word, we can use "kute くて" form. Therefore, your "black and big" dog in Japanese will be "くろくて　おおきい"

It is easy to derive the "くて kute" form.  Simply change "い i" in the end of an adjective to "くて kute." For example:

たかい　　→　たかくて
やすい　　→　やすくて
おいしい　→　おいしくて
おおい　　→　おおくて
やさしい　→　やさしくて
おもしろい→　おもしろくて
＊ いい　　→　＊ よくて

See the examples:
（１）りんごは、やす<u>くて</u>、おいしいです。
（２）山田さんは、やさし<u>くて</u>、おもしろい人ですね。
（３）ボブさんは、あたまがよ<u>くて</u>、しんせつです。

**\* Remember "ii" is a casual form of "yoi."  You must use "yoi" for its inflection.**

- **Also important to remember is that the words connected with "kute" must be supporting each other in their meanings.  In other words, if you are speaking "positively" both words must be positive, and if you are speaking "negatively," both words must be negative.**

More example sentences:

**(4)** やすくて　おいしい　カレーのみせを　知っていますか。
Do you know a curry restaurant that serves good and reasonably priced curry?

**(5)** このへやは、あかるくて、しずかないいへやですね。
This room is bright and quiet; it's so nice.

**(6)** あのみせは、たかくて、<u>まずくて</u>、よくありませんよ。
（まずい not tasty）
That restaurant is expensive and not tasty; it's no good.

(7) あそこのラーメンは、りょうがおおくて、おいしいですよ。
        (量 amount)
    That restaurant serves ramen in large quantities and (its food) is also delicious.

(8) さとうさんは、あたまがよくて、しんせつです。
        Mr. Sato is smart and kind.

## 2. <u>Connecting Noun-ending sentences with で: when they are complementing each other.</u>

How would you express, in Japanese, your "healthy and cute" dog? The word "healthy" is "genki げんき" and "cute" is "kawaii かわいい." You cannot use "kute" connective since "genki" is not an adjective. "Genki" is a copula noun. In that case, the connective is "de で," instead. Therefore, your "healthy and cute dog" in Japanese is "genki de kawaii げんきで　かわいい" inu いぬ. Remember the words need to be complementing each other when you use the "de" connective.

It is easy to derive the "de で" form. Simply add "de で" to the end of a noun or a copula noun." For example:

きれい　　→　きれいで
げんき　　→　げんきで
じょうず　→　じょうずで
へた　　　→　へたで
にぎやか　→　にぎやかで
しずか　　→　しずかで

Examples:
きれいで　やさしい　　　　pretty and kind
    メリーさんは、きれいで　やさしい人です。
    Mary is a pretty and kind lady.
字がじょうずで、はやい　　fast and skilled handwriting
    ケンさんは、字が上手で、はやいです。
    Ken has a good penmanship and he also writes fast.

にぎやかで　たのしい　　lively and fun
    キャシーさんは、にぎやかで　たのしい人ですね。
    Cathy is a lively and fun person.

しずかで　きれい　　quiet and clean
    私はしずかで　きれいな　アパートがいいです。
    I like a quiet and clean apartment.

See the examples below for connecting two sentences.

(1) これは、私の本で、あれは、あなたのです。
This is my book and that is yours.

(2) 私は、アメリカ人で、大学一年生です。
I am an American, and a college student.

(3) きのうは、雨で、きょうは、晴れでした。
Yesterday was a rainy day, and today was a nice day.

(4) ぼくは、コーヒーで、ともだちは、こうちゃです。
I ordered coffee and my friend ordered tea.

(5) キャシーは、いつもしずかで、よく本をよみます。
Cathy is always quiet, and she often reads books.

## 3. <u>Connecting sentences with particle し: and, moreover, in addition</u>

(1) You can connect two sentences if they are consistent in meaning. In other words, if a sentence comments on the good quality of a book, the second sentence must also speak of a "good" quality. The content of the two sentences must not contradict. Particle "shi" is similar to "and," though it further enhances meaning. "し" structure also implies the "reason," as you see in the example sentences below.

(2) The "shi" conjunctive particle can be preceded by both the formal and informal styles of speech; but in daily conversation, it is more common to use the informal style with し – unless the situation demands otherwise.

<u>Casual Predicate Patterns in non-past tense</u>:

```
Noun +　です。→ だ
Adjective い　です。→ い
Verb　(Dictionary form such as 行く, 見る, 食べる)
```

Examples:

1．この本は、やすいですし、おもしろいですし、とてもいい本です。
　　　　やすいし、　　おもしろいし、

2．かとうさんは、きれいですし、あたまも　いいです。
　　　　きれいだし、

3．田中さんも<u>行きます</u>し、山田さんも行きますから、私も行きます。
　　行くし、

4. Q: どうして　日本語が　すきなんですか。
　　　 Why do you like Japanese language?
　　A: 日本語は、<u>やさしいし</u>、おもしろいから、（すきです）。
　　　 (I like it) because it's easy and fun.

5. Q: どうして　毎日やさいを　食べるんですか。
　　　 Why do you eat vegetables everyday?
　　A: やさいは、<u>おいしいし</u>、からだに　いいんです。
　　　 Because they are delicious and good for our health (=body).

6. A: いつも　同じカバンですね。
　　　 You always carry the same bag.

　　B: このカバンは、<u>じょうぶだし</u>、色が<u>きれいだし</u>、とても
　　　 かるくて、いいカバンなんですよ。
　　　 (It's because) this bag is sturdy, and the color is pretty; and it is also
　　　 very light-weight.  It's such a good bag.

Now, tell whether or not you need "da だ" in the blanks.  You need "da" after copula nouns, and do not need "da" after adjectives.  Write an X when you don't need "da だ," and write down "da だ" in the blanks when it's appropriate.

(1) 私のいもうとは、げんき（　）し、おもしろいです。
　　 My younger sister is energetic and fun.

(2) このクラスは、おもしろい（　）し、やさしい（　）し、だいすきです。
　　 This class is fun and easy, so I love it.

(3) トムさんは、目がきれい（　）し、あたまがいい（　）し、やさしいから、
　　 女の子に　人気があります。
　　 Tom has pretty eyes, and he is smart and kind.  So, he is popular among girls.

(4) エドさんは、ハンサム（　）し、しんせつ（　）し、クラスで　いちば
　　 んすきな人です。
　　 Ed is handsome and kind, so he is my most favorite person in class.

(5) ぶつりは、むずかしい（　）し、テストの点がわるいから、にがてです。
　　 Physics is difficult and my test scores are bad, so that's my weakness.

[Answers]:
(1) だ, (2) X, X, (3) だ, X (4) だ, だ, (5) X

Note:  Is the sentence with "…shi" different from the sentence with "…te"?  Observe the following to find out the differences.

A.

私は、とても健康です。(I am very healthy)

朝は、早く起きるし、ジョギングをするし、朝ごはんを食べます。

[The reason I am staying healthy is because] I get up early in the morning, do joggings, and eat breakfast.)

B.

私は、

朝早く　起きて、ジョギングをして、朝ごはんを食べます。

(I wake up early in the morning, do joggings, and eat breakfast.)

As you have observed in the example A, "shi" structure exemplifies the reason. In this statement, three reasons are mentioned as a proof or a convincing evidence for the speaker being healthy.

On the other hand, the example B simply makes a list of "sequential" activities to tell what the speaker "does" in the morning in that "order."

Now, translate the following into Japanese.
1.  I like apples.  (Because) they are sweet, juicy, delicious, and healthy!

   [Sample answers]
   　私はりんごが好きです。りんごは、あまいし、みずみずしいし、おいし
   いし、体にいいし、、、。
   　　　(good for [our] health)
   Or,
   私はりんごが好きです。りんごは、あまくて、みずみずしくて、おいし
   くて、体にいいから。

2.  I am so melancholic because I have to write a composition for homework.  I don't like it (=composition) (because) I am not good at grammar, don't have many vocabulary, and I don't know what to write about!

   [Sample answers]
   　私はとても　ゆううつです。なぜなら、作文の宿題があるから。　作文が
   きらいです。文法ができないし、言葉をたくさん知らないし、書くこと
   がないし、、、。
   　　　(or ないから。)

Chapter 6 (C)  Exercises れんしゅうもんだい

## A. Practice "で"
Look at Monica's family information below and fill in the blanks.

モニカは、十八<sup>じゅうはっさい</sup>才<u>です。そして、</u>大学生<sup>だいがくせい</sup>です。

→モニカは、十八才<sup>じゅうはっさい</sup><u>で</u>、大学生<sup>だいがくせい</sup>です。

モニカのかぞく

| | | |
|---|---|---|
| お父<sup>とう</sup>さん | ４９才<sup>さい</sup> | かいしゃいん(company employee) |
| お母<sup>かあ</sup>さん | ４２才<sup>さい</sup> | しゅふ (homemaker)、いそがしい(busy) |
| お兄<sup>にい</sup>さん | ２３才<sup>さい</sup> | 大学<sup>だいがく</sup>いん生<sup>せい</sup> (graduate student)、　あたまがいい(smart) |
| モニカ | １８才<sup>さい</sup> | 大学生<sup>だいがくせい</sup>、　やさしい(gentle)、しんせつ (kind to others) |
| 上<sup>うえ</sup>の妹<sup>いもうと</sup> | ７才 | 小学生<sup>しょうがくせい</sup> (elementary school student)、いたずら(mischievous)、なきむし(crybaby) |
| 下<sup>した</sup>の妹<sup>いもうと</sup> | １才<sup>さい</sup> | あかちゃん (baby)、元気<sup>げんき</sup>、かわいい(cute) |

（１）お父<sup>とう</sup>さんは、４９才<sup>さい</sup>で、＿＿＿＿＿＿＿＿です。

（２）お母<sup>かあ</sup>さんは、４２才＿＿＿＿＿、しゅふです。

（３）お兄<sup>にい</sup>さんは、＿＿＿＿＿才<sup>さい</sup>＿＿＿＿、大学<sup>だいがく</sup>いん生<sup>せい</sup>＿＿＿＿＿。

（４）モニカは、１８才<sup>さい</sup>＿＿＿＿、大学生<sup>だいがくせい</sup>です。

（５）上<sup>うえ</sup>の妹<sup>いもうと</sup>は、７才<sup>さい</sup>＿＿＿＿＿、小学生<sup>しょうがくせい</sup>です。

（６）下<sup>した</sup>の妹<sup>いもうと</sup>は、一才<sup>さい</sup>＿＿＿＿＿、＿＿＿＿＿＿です。

（７）モニカは、四人<sup>よにん</sup>きょうだい＿＿＿＿、上<sup>うえ</sup>から二人目<sup>ふたりめ</sup>です。

（８）下の妹は、あかちゃん_____、とてもかわいいです。

（９）お母さんは、しゅふ_____、毎日いそがしいです。

（１０）お父さんは、かいしゃいん_____、毎日かいしゃに行きます。

（１１）上の妹は、とても元気_____、いたずらです。でも、

　　　 なきむし_____、よくなきます。

　　　　　　　　　　crybaby　　　　　　　　　　　　　　　　to cry

（１２）モニカは、だれにもしんせつ_____、やさしい子です。

　　　　　　　　to everyone

赤ちゃん

泣き虫

やさしい

B. Practice "くて": Base the following on Monica's family information as well.

（１）モニカは、_____くて、しんせつな子です。

（２）お母さんは、いつも_____くて、あまり家にいません。

（３）お兄さんは、あたまが、_____くて、よくべんきょうします。

（４）あかちゃんは、_____くて、よくわらいます。

　　　　　　　　　　　　　　　　　　smile

（５）モニカのかぞくは、仲が_____くて、しあわせなかぞくです。

　　　　　　　　　　　　to get along well　　　　happy

C. Practice "し"

Select topics from group A, and connect them with the most appropriate choices from groups B and C to form complete sentences. Use the "shi" conjunctive particle as featured in the example. You may create additional sentences with other vocabulary.

Example:

Group A　　　アイスクリーム

Group B　　　つめたい

Group C　　　おいしい

　　　　　　Completed sentence: アイスクリームは、つめたいし、おいしい。

Example:

| | |
|---|---|
| Group A | ボーイフレンド |
| Group B | ハンサム |
| Group C | おもしろい |

Completed sentence: ボーイフレンドはハンサムだ<u>し</u>、おもしろい。

Group A: Topic ～は、

私の家，私のアパート、私のへや、私の学校、としょかん、きっさてん、スターバックス、こうえん、この本、日本語のクラス、ガールフレンド、ボーイフレンド、りんご、バナナ、アイスクリーム、コーヒー

Group B

とおい(far)、ちかい(near)、ふるい (old)、あたらしい(new)、大きい、小さい、やすい(cheap)、たかい(tall, expensive)、つめたい(cold)、あつい(hot), ひろい(spacious)、せまい (narrow)、にぎやか (lively; bustling)、しずか (quiet)、きれい(pretty, clean)、ゆうめい、やさしい(kind, easy)、おいしい(tasty)，ハンサム、キュート(cute)、セクシー(sexy)

Group C

りっぱ(magnificent)、たのしい(enjoyable)、おもしろい(interesting, fun)、あたまがいい(smart)、かわいい(cute)、ふべん(inconvenient)、べんり(convenient)、きたない(dirty)、つまらない(boring)、きもちがいい(it feels good)，からだにいい(good for health)，おいしい(tasty)，きれい(pretty, clean)，あぶない (dangerous)

D. Practice connecting sentences with "くて" and "で."

Do the same as 1, using the "kute" or "de" connectives in combining Groups B and C.
Example with "kute":

| | |
|---|---|
| Group A | アイスクリーム |
| Group B | つめたい |
| Group C | おいしい |

Completed sentence using "kute": アイスクリームは、つめた<u>くて</u>、おいしい。

Completed sentence using "de": 私のアパートは、しずか<u>で</u>、きれいです。

E. Choose a place from the list below and describe it to your partner. Use "kute" or "de" connectives when describing the place as "All favorable" or "All unfavorable," and "ga" when mixing favorable and unfavorable descriptive words.
For example:

| | |
|---|---|
| All favorable: | ふる<u>くて</u>、れきしがあります。 |
| All unfavorable: | ふる<u>くて</u>、きたないです。 |
| Mixing favorable and unfavorable: | ふるくて、れきしがあります<u>が</u>、あぶないです。 |

Example:

Topic: きょうと

Copula Nouns: しずか

Adjective:　　うつくしい

　　　　　Completed sentence: きょうとは、しずか<u>で</u>　うつくしい。

---

1. パサデナ　2. ロサンジェルス　3. とうきょう　4. きょうと　5. おおさか
6. ラスベガス　7. ニューヨーク　8. ホノルル　9. モスクワ
10. サンクト・ペテルブルグ　11. リオデジャネイロ　12. バグダッド
13. 中国（ちゅうごく）　14. アフガニスタン　15. タイ　16. アムステルダム
17. コペンハーゲン　18. パリ　19. カイロ　20. シンガポール

---

Vocabulary help:

| Adjectives | | Copula Nouns | |
|---|---|---|---|
| 1．人が多い（ひと おお） | (lots of people) | 1．あんぜん （な） | (safe) |
| 　（木が多い）（き おお） | (lots of trees) | 2．きけん （な） | (dangerous) |
| 2．人が少ない（ひと すく） | (few people) | 3．ゆたか （な） | (abundant) |
| 3．ひろい | (spacious) | 4．にぎやか （な） | (lively) |
| 4．せまい | (not spacious) | 5．しずか （な） | (quiet) |
| 5．まずしい | (poor) | 6．ようき(陽気) （な） | (happy-go-lucky) |
| 6．うつくしい | (beautiful) | 7．ゆうめい （な） | (famous) |
| 7．あぶない | (dangerous) | 8．うみがきれい （な） | (ocean is pretty) |
| 8．きたない | (dirty) | | |
| 9．おもしろい | (interesting, fun) | | |
| 10．つまらない | (boring) | | |
| 11．あたらしい | (new) | | |
| 12．ふるい | (old) | | |
| 13．たべものがおいしい | (food is tasty) | | |

| Nouns | |
|---|---|
| 1．おかねもち(の) | (rich) |
| 2．さばく(の) | (desert) |
| 3．しゅと(の) | (capital) |

F. Learn the pattern: "S₁ し, S₂ から, 〜 " (because not only S₁, but also S₂)

Examples:

(1)　　にほんごは、やさしいです。（そのうえ、）おもしろいです。

　　　　　　　　　　　　　　　　　moreover

　　だから、だいすきです。

　→　にほんごは、<u>やさしいし、おもしろいから</u>、すきです。

(2)　田中さんが、来ます。（そのうえ）かとうさんも来ます。
　　　だから、私も　来ます。

　　→　田中さんが、来るし、かとうさんも来るから、私も　来ます。

（1）きょうは、どようびです。（そのうえ）じかんがあります。
　　　だから、デートに行きます。
　　　→　＿＿＿＿＿＿＿＿＿し、＿＿＿＿＿＿＿から、

　　　　＿＿＿＿＿＿＿＿＿＿＿＿＿＿＿＿＿＿。

（2）きょうは、しゅくだいが　あります。（そのうえ）あしたは、テストが
　　　あります。だから、家で　べんきょうします。

　　　→　＿＿＿＿＿＿＿＿＿し、＿＿＿＿＿＿＿から、

　　　　＿＿＿＿＿＿＿＿＿＿＿＿＿＿＿＿＿。

（3）たなかさんは、きれいです。（そのうえ）やさしいです。
　　　だから、人気があります。
　　　　　　　　to be popular

　　　→　＿＿＿＿＿＿＿＿＿し、＿＿＿＿＿＿＿から、

　　　　＿＿＿＿＿＿＿＿＿＿＿＿＿＿＿＿＿。

（4）日本車は、デザインがいいです。（そのうえ）せいのうが　いいです。
　　　だから、買います。　　　　　　　　　performance

　　　→　＿＿＿＿＿＿＿＿＿し、＿＿＿＿＿＿＿から、

　　　　＿＿＿＿＿＿＿＿＿＿＿＿＿＿＿＿＿。

（5）うたがすきです。（そのうえ）おどりが　すきです。
　　　だから、ディスコに　行きます。

　　　→　＿＿＿＿＿＿＿＿＿し、＿＿＿＿＿＿＿から、

　　　　＿＿＿＿＿＿＿＿＿＿＿＿＿＿＿＿＿。

G.  Fill in the blanks with the correct Japanese connectives.

（1）このじしょは、たか（　　　　　）、よくない。

（2）パサデナは、ふる（　　　　　）、おもしろい。

（3）お母さんは、きれい（　　　　　）、やさしい。

（4）りんごは、おいし（　　　　　）、からだに　いい。

（5）月曜日のこうえんは、しずか（　　　　　）、人が少ない。

（6）ちょきんがすくな（　　　　　）、つまらない。
　　　(savings)

（7）パサデナは、ローズパレードがゆうめい（　　　　　）、一月一日は、
　　　まちに　人が多い。

H.  Complete the dialogue.

（1）A：＿＿＿＿＿＿＿＿＿＿＿＿＿＿＿＿。(You are at the door, greeting and
　　　　　calling out to someone in the house.)
　　　B：はい、どなたですか。あ、田中さん。

（2）A：おひさしぶりです。
　　　B：＿＿＿＿＿＿＿＿＿＿＿＿＿＿。

（3）A：私、りゅうがくせいのモニカと言います。はじめまして。
　　　B：＿＿＿＿＿＿＿＿＿＿＿＿＿＿＿。

（4）A：どうぞ　よろしくおねがいします。
　　　B：＿＿＿＿＿＿＿＿＿＿＿＿。

（5）A：どんな　へやが　いいんですか。
　　　B：＿＿＿＿＿＿＿＿＿＿＿＿＿＿。

（6）A：このアパートのうらに、きれいなこうえんが　あるんですよ。
　　　B：＿＿＿＿＿＿＿＿＿＿＿＿＿。

（7）A：いらっしゃい。どうぞ　おあがりください。
　　　B：＿＿＿＿＿＿＿＿＿＿＿＿＿。

I.  Your host-family asked you to get the following things from the やおや, the green-grocer.  Pick the descriptive words consistent with those made by your host-family.

> ................さん、どうもありがとう。やおやさんでつぎのものを、かってきて
> ください。
>
> 　1）　　ふとくなくて、ながくて、くろい　ごぼう
> 　2）　　ふとくて、まっすぐで、しなやかな　だいこん
> 　3）　　あたらしくて、めがきれいな　さんま
> 　4）　　おおきくて、かたくて、はがみどりの　キャベツ

Japanese-English dictionary:
　　　ふとい thick, ふとくない not thick, ながい long, ごぼう burdock root
　　　まっすぐ straight,　しなやか supple,　だいこん daikon radish
　　　めがしろい　eyes are white, さんま mackerel
　　　かたい firm,　は leaf,　みどり green,　キャベツ cabbage

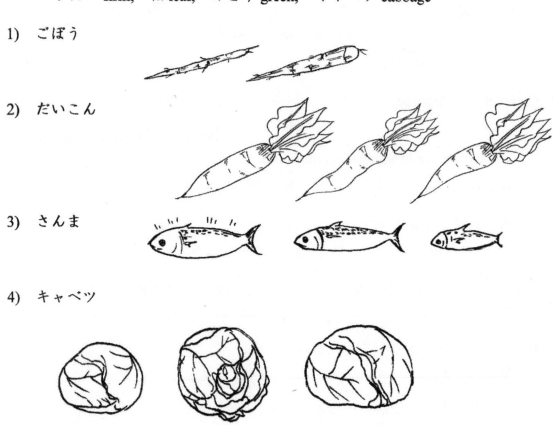

1)　ごぼう

2)　だいこん

3)　さんま

4)　キャベツ

J.  Draw and describe your room/apartment/house.  Include the following information: its location in the neighborhood, its interiors, including its window placement, kitchen and bathroom, whether or not sun rays permeate, and if so, from which window or direction you get the sun.

Chapter 6C In-class activity: pair-work interview.  Ask your partner the questions 1 to 6 and circle the answers your partner chose about your facial feature.  Then work on the number 7; combine the answers from 2 to 4, then combine 5 and 6.  See the example.

なまえ（　　　　　　　　　　　　　　　　）

1．わたしのかおを　みてください。

2．わたしのかおは、<u>まるい</u>ですか、<u>しかくい</u>ですか、<u>たまごがた</u>ですか。
                round        square        egg-shaped
    A．　まるい
    B．　しかくい
    C．　たまごがた

3．わたしの目（め）は、おおきいですか、ちいさいですか、ふつうですか。
    A．　おおきい
    B．　ちいさい
    C．　ふつう

4．わたしのはなは、おおきいですか、ちいさいですか、たかいですか、ひくいですか。
    A．　おおきい
    B．　ちいさい
    C．　たかい
    D．　ひくい

5．わたしの口（くち）は、<u>おおきいほう</u>ですか、<u>ちいさいほう</u>ですか。
                rather big        rather small
    A．　おおきいほう
    B．　ちいさいほう

6．わたしの耳（みみ）は、おおきいほうですか、ちいさいほうですか。

    A．　おおきいほう
    B．　ちいさいほう

7．Connect answers from 2 to 4 to make a combined sentence, first.  Then combine 5 and 6.

    Example: わたしのかおは、まる<u>くて</u>、目は、ふつう<u>で</u>、はなは、ちいさいです。くちは、ちいさいほう<u>で</u>、みみは、おおきいほうです。

Chapter 6 (C) Dict-A-Conversation
Listen to the CD and create a dialogue based on what you hear. You must not only answer the questions Mr. A presents, but also ask him questions by role playing person "B." Mr. A will initiate the conversation.
Fill in the dotted lines for "B" below. There is no need to transcribe Mr. A's half of the dialogue.

1A:

1B: ...............................................................................................................

.................................................?
How about your mother?
2A:

2B: ...............................................................................................................

3A:

3B: ...............................................................................................................

.................................................?
How about you?
4A:

4B: ...............................................................................................................

Chapter 6 (C) – (1)

| 井<br><br>(a well) | い<br>セン<br>セイ | 井戸（いど）a well<br>土井（どい）a surname<br>井上（いのうえ）a surname<br>*天井（てんじょう）a ceiling<br>[市井の人（しせいのひと）an ordinary citizen] |
| | | (4)<br>一 二 井 井 |
| 多<br><br>(more) | おお（い）<br>タ | 多い（おおい）more<br>多大（ただい）a great deal; considerable |
| | | (6)<br>ノ ク タ タ 多 多 |
| 寺<br><br>(temple) | てら<br>ジ | お寺（おてら）a temple<br>寺院（じいん）a temple<br>[金閣寺（きんかくじ）The Golden Pavilion] |
| | | (6)<br>一 十 土 寺 寺 寺 |
| 有<br><br>(to exist; to have) | あ（る）<br>ユウ | 有る（ある）to exist; to have<br>有する（ゆうする）to own<br>所有（しょゆう）する to own |
| | | (6)<br>ノ ナ ナ オ 有 有 有 |
| 名<br><br>(name) | な<br>メイ | 名前（なまえ）a name<br>有名（ゆうめい）な famous<br>名刺（めいし）business card<br>名人（めいじん）an expert<br>氏名（しめい）a full name |
| | | (6)<br>ノ ク タ タ 名 名 |

Chapter 6 (C) – (2)

| 持 | も（つ）<br>ジ<br><br><br>(to have; to hold) | 持つ（もつ）to have; to hold<br>気持ち（きもち）feelings<br>[所持（しょじ）する to have; to own]<br><br>(9)<br> ー 十 扌 扌 扩 扩 持 持 持 |
|---|---|---|
| 内 | うち<br>ナイ<br><br><br>(inside; within) | 内々（うちうち）private<br>家内（かない）(my) wife<br>内科（ないか）internal medicine<br><br>(4)<br> 丨 冂 内 内 |
| 外 | そと<br>ガイ<br>ゲ<br><br>(outside) | 家の外（いえのそと）outside of a house<br>内と外（うちとそと）in and out<br>外出（がいしゅつ）する to go out<br>外科（げか）surgery<br><br>(5)<br> ノ ク タ 夘 外 |
| 少 | すくな（い）<br>ショウ<br><br><br>(fewer, less) | 少ない（すくない）fewer; less<br>少し（すこし）a little<br>多少（たしょう）a little<br>少年（しょうねん）a young boy<br><br>(4)<br> 亅 小 小 少 |

Kanji Practice for Chapter 6 (C)
かんじの　れんしゅう

1．つぎの　ことばを　よみなさい。それから、クラスメートにいみをきき
なさい。 Read the following words to your classmates and ask them for the
meaning of each word.

（１）　内と外

（２）　名前

（３）　有名

（４）　多い

（５）　少ない

（６）　お寺

（７）　井戸

（８）　＊天井

（９）　気持ち

（１０）　持っている

2．よんでから、よみがなをかいて、えいごでいいなさい。Read first, then
write yomigana above each kanji, and translate into English.

（１）　土井さんの家には、南と東に　まどがあります。

（２）　この近くに　小さなお寺が　あります。

（３）　有名なスターが、家の外にいます。

（４）　今日は、買いものが　多かったです。

（５）　車が少ないと、気もちが　いいです。

（６）　古い井戸は、あぶないです。

（７）　妹は、内気です。あまり外に行きません。

3．かんじとひらがなで　こたえなさい。Answer the questions in complete sentences
using kanji and hiragana.

（１）　あなたのかぞくに、だれかゆうめいなひとが　いますか。

（２）　てんじょうに　なにがありますか。

（３）　にほんごのクラスで、おおいのは、おとこのがくせいですか、
　　　　おんなのがくせいですか。

（４）　あなたは、きょうおかねを　たくさんもっていますか。

（５）　きょうのあさ、いえのそとで、だれかにあいましたか。

（６）　あなたのいえに、ふるいいどのしゃしんが、ありますか。
　　　　　　　　　　　　　　　　　戸

4. Choose the one featuring the correct "okurigana" by placing a circle (O) in the space given.

(1)　(　　) a. 多い　　　　　　　　　　　(2)　(　　) a. 少ない
　　　(　　) b. 多おい　　　　　　　　　　　　　(　　) b. 少い

5. Write antonymous kanji in the box.
　　(1)　more ↔ fewer　　　　　　　　　(4)　go

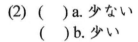

　　(2)　in (inside/within) ↔ out (outside)

come

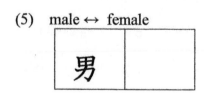

　　(3)　social superior

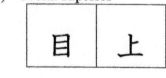

social inferior

(5)　male ↔ female

(6)　front ↔ rear

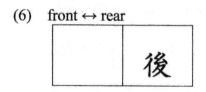

Chapter 6 (D)　　　　　　　There is a Carp! 鯉が　いる！

不動産屋：じゃ、高木さん、おじゃましました。　　　　　　　　　　1

大家：　　いえいえ、ありがとうございました。　　　　　　　　　2

モニカ：　よろしく　おねがいします。　　　　　　　　　　　　　3

大家：　　こちらこそ。　　　　　　　　　　　　　　　　　　　4

(On the way out, passing by the front garden)

モニカ：　えきから、そんなに遠くありませんし、明るいし、このアパートに　5
　　　　　します。　　　　　　　　　　　　　　　　　　　　　　　6

不動産屋：わかりました。じゃ、わたしのじむしょで、けいやくしょに、　　7
　　　　　サインしてください。　　　　　　　　　　　　　　　　　8

モニカ：　わかりました。あ、あんなところに、池が　あります。　　　9

　　　　　魚が　いるんですか。　　　　　　　　　　　　　　　　10

不動産屋：ええ、鯉が　いますよ。　　　　　　　　　　　　　　　11

モニカ：　え？　こい？　「こい」は、英語で　何と言うんですか。　　12

不動産屋：英語で　ですか。わたしは、英語が苦手なんですがね、、、　　13
　　　　　え～と、たしか、「こい」は　"CARP"ですね。もっと近くに　14
　　　　　行きましょう。　　　　　　　　　　　　　　　　　　　15

モニカ：　あ、います！赤いのや、白いのが！　あれ、金色のも　いますよ。　16

不動産屋：ずいぶん大きくてりっぱな鯉だなあ。あの黒いのは、珍しいです　17
　　　　　よ。　　　　　　　　　　　　　　　　　　　　　　　　18

モニカ：　何才ぐらいですか。　　　　　　　　　　　　　　　　　19

不動産屋：え？鯉の年ですか。う～ん、大きいのは、若くありませんよ。　　　　1

二十年ぐらい、ここにいますから。　　　　2

モニカ：　えっ！この鯉が　わたしと同じ年なんですか？　　　　3

[English translation:]

Realtor　 : Well then, thank you, Mr. Takagi.  We will be leaving. (Sorry to have bothered you.)
Landlord: Not at all.  Thank you very much.
Monica　 : Thank you.  (Please be favorable with me.)
Landlord: The pleasure is mine.

(On the way out, passing by the front garden)

Monica:　(The apartment) is not so far from the station and is brightly lit.  I've decided on this apartment.
Realtor:　I see.  In that case, please sign the contract in my office.
Monica:　Will do. (I understand.)  Oh, there is a pond in a place like this?
Realtor:　Yes, there are "koi."
Monica:　Eh?  "Koi"?  What is "koi" in English?
Realtor:　In English?  Well, English isn't my strongest language (subject), but…hmm…"koi" is probably "carp," if I'm not mistaken.  Let's take a closer look.
Monica:　Yes, there they are!  There are red and white ones.  Oh, there's a gold one, too!
Realtor:　How big and splendid (is the gold one)!  The black one over there is rare, you know.
Monica:　 How old is it?
Realtor:　Eh?  You mean the age of the carp?  Hmm…the big one isn't that young since it's been here for about twenty years.
Monica:　 Oh, my!  Is that carp as old as me?

Chapter 6 (D)                    Vocabulary List

1.  Expressions
    おじゃましました。                    Greeting: Sorry to have bothered you.
    いえいえ。                          No,  not at all.
    え～と、                            Well,…, hmm..
    えっ！                              What? (Surprised)

2.  Nouns
    じむしょ                            office
    けいやくしょ                        contract
    サイン                              signature
    こい (鯉)                           carp (koi/fish)
    きんいろ （金色）                    gold (golden color)
    とし （年）                          age
    (おなじ      同じ)                  same
        ～と  おなじ                     the same as ～
    ところ                              place

    (Counters)
    ～  さい （才）                      ～ year old
    ～  ねん （年）                      ～ years

3.  Copula Nouns
    にがて （苦手）                      not good at
    (りっぱ)                            magnificent

4.  Demonstrative Pronoun
    あんな                              such ～ as that
        あんなところ                    such a place like that
        Additional vocabulary こんな    such ～ as this
                         そんな         such ～ as that
                         どんな         what kind of?

5.  Dependent Pronoun
    の
        Adjective + の     くろいの the black one
                         あかいの the red one
                         大きいの the big one

6.  Adjectives
    めずらしい                          rare
    わかい （若い）                      young

7.  Adverbs

| | |
|---|---|
| そんなに + negative predicate | not very/so ~ |
| そんなに遠<ruby>遠<rt>とお</rt></ruby>くありません | (It's) not so far. |
| | |
| ずいぶん | extremely (with an objective overtone) |
| たしか | probably; if I am not mistaken |

8.  Verb

| | |
|---|---|
| サインする | to sign |

--------------------------------------------------------------------

Additional Vocabulary from Grammar Notes, Exercises, and Dict-A-Conversation

--------------------------------------------------------------------

[Nouns]

| | |
|---|---|
| ふかざけ | excessive drinking |
| スピードうんてん | speeding |
| ひるね | nap |
| おてつだい | help; assistance |
| あくま | devil |
| きんぎょ | gold fish |

[な Adjectives/Copula Nouns]

| | |
|---|---|
| だめ | no good |

[Adverbs]

| | |
|---|---|
| さいきん | recently |
| しずかに | quietly |
| ゆっくり | slowly |
| とても | very |

[Verbs]

| | |
|---|---|
| さいている | is blooming ("te" form of "saku") |
| あった | occurred; happened (past tense of "aru") |
| おしえる | to teach |
| かりる | to borrow |
| おどる | to dance |
| あう | to meet |
| なる | to become |
| おねがいする | to ask a favor |
| リクエストする | to request |
| (いる) | to exist |
| (おりる) | to get off |
| (あそぶ) | to play; to have a good time |
| (くる) | to come |

Chapter 6 D                    Grammar and Cultural Notes

## 1. 〜てください。 **Polite request form**

The expression of "V-てください te kudasai" is equivalent to "please do such and such" in English.  Remember in early chapters the "….をください wo kudasai" expression in shopping and ordering?  In those chapters, you were requesting for "materialistic items," such as food, drink, shoes, etc.; but in this chapter you will be asking for "actions" to be done for you.

---
| The te-form verb |
---

It is extremely important for you to learn how to derive the "te" form verb.  There are three steps toward mastering them:

(1) Distinguish **Irregular, Vowel, and Consonant verbs**
(2) Use the **stem + te-form** for **Vowel verbs** (Stem is found by dropping "ru" in the end.)
(3) Use the **"te-form" (Silver Bell song) rules for Consonant verbs**

   (1)  3 Irregular verbs: "do," "come," and "go"

"Do" (する/します) and "come" (くる/きます) are irregular verbs.
Their te-form verbs are "して" and "きて" respectively.  The te-form of the verb "go" (いく/いきます) is also irregular when it comes to the te-form.  Its te-form is いって.

   (2) Vowel verbs: If the verb's dictionary form ends with "eru" or "iru," it is most likely a vowel verb.  (There are exceptions, which are listed in this section.)

     たべる　　(tabe-ru) →　たべて
     みる　　　(m-iru)　→　みて
     おしえる (oshi-eru) →　おしえて
     ねる　　　(n-eru) →　ねて
     いる　　　(iru) →　いて

   (3) If the verb endings are not "eru" or "iru," and they are not exceptions, they would be consonant verbs.  Apply the rules of "how to make the te-form verb" shown below.

---
| How to make the "Te-Form" of Consonant Verbs |
---

   1. Dictionary form (Base 3) ending in MU, BU, NU: change to "-NDE."
   2. Ending in U, TSU, RU: change to "-TTE."
   3. Ending in KU: change to "-ITE."
   4. Ending in GU: change to "-IDE."
   5. Ending in SU: change to "-SHITE."

## The "te-form" rules for Consonant Verbs

1. **MU, BU, NU ending verbs → NDE**
   む
   | | | | | |
   |---|---|---|---|---|
   | よむ | → | よんで | よむ | (read) |
   | かむ | → | かんで | かむ | (bite) |
   | はさむ | → | はさんで | はさむ | (pinch) |
   | やむ | → | やんで | やむ | (cease) |

   ぶ
   | | | | | |
   |---|---|---|---|---|
   | とぶ | → | とんで | とぶ | (jump; fly) |
   | ころぶ | → | ころんで | ころぶ | (fall; trip over) |
   | しのぶ | → | しのんで | しのぶ | (endure) |
   | さけぶ | → | さけんで | さけぶ | (scream) |

   ぬ
   | | | | | |
   |---|---|---|---|---|
   | しぬ | → | しんで | しぬ | (die) |

2. **U, TSU, RU ending verbs → TTE**
   う
   | | | | | |
   |---|---|---|---|---|
   | すう | → | すって | すう | (smoke) |
   | うたう | → | うたって | うたう | (sing) |
   | あう | → | あって | あう | (meet) |
   | あらう | → | あらって | あらう | (wash) |

   つ
   | | | | | |
   |---|---|---|---|---|
   | たつ | → | たって | たつ | (stand up) |
   | まつ | → | まって | まつ | (wait) |
   | かつ | → | かって | かつ | (win) |

   る
   | | | | | |
   |---|---|---|---|---|
   | うる | → | うって | うる | (sell) |
   | しゃべる | → | しゃべって | しゃべる | (chat) |
   | ける | → | けって | ける | (kick) |
   | まわる | → | まわって | まわる | (circle) |

3. **KU ending verbs → ITE**
   く
   | | | | | |
   |---|---|---|---|---|
   | かく | → | かいて | かく | (write) |
   | きく | → | きいて | きく | (hear) |
   | おく | → | おいて | おく | (put down) |
   | さく | → | さいて | さく | (boom) |
   | はく | → | はいて | はく | (wear shoes) |

4. GU ending verbs → IDE
   ぐ

| | | | | |
|---|---|---|---|---|
| ぬぐ | → | ぬいで | ぬぐ | (write) |
| いそぐ | → | いそいで | いそぐ | (write) |
| およぐ | → | およいで | およぐ | (write) |

5. SU ending verbs → SHITE
   す

| | | | | |
|---|---|---|---|---|
| はなす | → | はなして | はなす | (speak) |
| かす | → | かして | かす | (loan) |
| だす | → | だして | だす | (submit) |
| とおす | → | とおして | とおす | (let ~through) |

Let's learn the te-form rules through a parody of the Christmas song, "Silver Bells."

---

"Te-form" Song
(A parody of "Silver Bells")

---

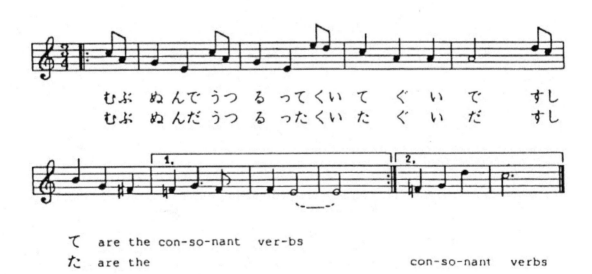

む ぶ ぬ ん で う つ る って く い て　ぐ い で　　す し
む ぶ ぬ ん だ う つ る った く い た　ぐ い だ　　す し

て　are the con-so-nant ver-bs
た　are the　　　　　　　　　　con-so-nant　verbs

Deceptive-looking Consonant Verbs:

Remember there are some consonant verbs that have "eru" or "iru" endings. These are:

"ちる chiru (scatter)," "きる kiru (cut)," "はいる hairu (enter)," "いる iru (need)," "しる shiru (get to know), "はしる hashiru (run)," "かえる kaeru (return, go home)," "にぎる nigiru (grasp)," "まいる mairu (humble form of "come" and "go")," "しゃべる shaberu (chat)," and several more.

Here is a hint to remember some of the verbs of this type. Practice the following passage.

---

チリチリ（散り散り）の髪を切りに、とこ屋へ　入りましたが、お金が要ると
知って、家へ走って帰り、お金を握って　また参ります。

"Chiri-chiri" no kami wo "kiri" ni, tokoya e "hairimashita" ga, okane ga "iru" to "shitte," uchi e "hashitte" "kaeri," okane wo "nigitte," mata "mairimasu."

(English:  I <u>entered</u> a barber shop to get my curly hair <u>cut</u>.  But, I found it costs (<u>needs</u>) money.  So, I will <u>run home,</u> and <u>with money in my hand,</u> will <u>return humbly</u>.)

---

## 2.  そんなに〜negative ない: Partial negation; not very/so much

When the adverb "son'nani" is used with a negative predicate, it means "not so much," "not often," or "not enough" in English.  It is interchangeable with "あんまり anmari + ない negative predicate."

Examples:

（1）ここから、えきまで、そんなに　遠くありません。
　　　It's not so far from here to the station.

（2）そんなにたくさんはありませんが、みんなで分けましょう。
　　　I don't have that much, but let's share it among us.

（3）ジムへは、そんなに　行きません。ときどき行きますが、、
　　　I don't go to the gym that often.  I only go sometimes…

（4）お金は、そんなに要りません。
　　　I don't need a lot of money/ Or, It doesn't cost that much.

（5）そんなに　人は、　いませんでした。
　　　There weren't a lot of people.

## 3.  こんな、そんな、あんな、どんな (+ Noun)

Another "ko-so-a-do" line in this chapter is: Demonstrative Pronouns, こんな such ~ as this、そんな such ~ as that、あんな such ~ as that、どんな what kind of?

Note that "そ so" and "あ a" have secondary meaning.  They are not only to suggest the physical distance and position, but also are used in the following manner:

(1)
A: 田中さんをしっていますか。
B: いいえ、そのひとは、Aさんのおともだちですか。
A: はい、そうなんです。

(2)
A: 田中さんをしっていますか。
B: はい、あのひとは、ほんとうに　いいひとですね。
A: そうですね。

In example (1), B who didn't know Mr. Tanaka used "その sono" to refer to the statement A made, which is 田中さん. This is a new usage of "そ so," which is used to refer to what has been previously mentioned. You can use それ、その、そこ, referring to what's been stated previously.

On the contrary, in example (2), B who knew Mr. Tanaka used "あの ano" to refer to him. In this case, Mr. Tanaka is "commonly shared information" between A and B. You can use あれ、あの、あそこ to refer to the information shared between listener and speaker.

Observe more:
(1)
A: 「きっさアキ」のコーヒーは　おいしいですね。
B: そのきっさてんは、どこにありますか。
A: 大学のまえですよ。

(2)
A: 「きっさアキ」のコーヒーは　おいしいですね。
B: はい、あそこのーヒーは、ほんとうに　おいしいですね。
A: こんどいっしょに行きましょう。

Again, "そ so" is referred to the previously mentioned information, since B in example (1) doesn't know that coffee shop, and "あ a" is used by B in example (2) since B knows that coffee shop (=commonly shared information).

Let's see how そんな and あんな are used:
(1)
A: ハンサムで　あたまがよくて、しんせつで、スーパーマンのようなひとを
　　しっていますか。　　　　　　　　　　　　　　　　　　like
B: そんなひとは、しりません。
A: そうでしょうね。

(2)
A: きのう　またダウンタウンのカラオケボックスへ　行きました。
B: え？また？あんなやかましいところが　すきなんですか。

A: はい！こんどいっしょに行きましょう。

B: ...........

(3) こんなところに　本がありますよ。だれのでしょうか？
(on a refrigerator)　There's a book at such a place like this.  Whose is it?

## 4. こ（そ、あ、ど）んなに＋**affirmative predicates: showing the extent**

When こんなに、そんなに、あんなに、どんなに are followed by the affirmative predicates, they show the degree, how much (or how deep, shallow, red, painful, etc.) it is. See the examples below:

(1) A:　見てください。手がこんなに　赤い！ Please look.  My hands are this red!

　　B:　そんなに赤いのは、さむいからでしょうね、かわいそうに。
　　　　It must be due to the cold weather that your hands are that red.  Poor thing!

　　(Later)

　　A:　あんなに　手が赤くなったのは、はじめてです。
　　　　It's the first time that my hand got that red.

　　B:　ほんとうに、そうでしたね。 It's so true~!

　　C:　どんなふうに、赤かったんですか。 How red were they?

　　A:　こんなふうに～ (pointing at her red bag)　As red as this red bag!

(2) A:　あんなにべんきょうしたけれど、テストはだめでした。
　　　　I studied so hard, but my test was bad.

　　B:　どんなにべんきょうしたの？ How hard did you study?

　　A:　三十分ぐらい、、　　　　　　About thirty minutes…..

　　B:　う～ん、それじゃあ、ちょっと、、、、 Well…. that won't do!

(3) A:　見て、見て。チョコレートが　こんなに　ある！
　　　　Look! There're this many chocolates!

　　B:　すごい！　すぐ　食べましょう！ Splendid!  Let's eat them right now!

## 5. Adjectives＋の，Copula Nouns (な Adjectives) ＋ なの

We have observed this type of "の" used with nouns in Chapter 2 (A), あなたの (yours)、わたしの (mine)、せんせいの (teacher's).  While it was "Noun + の" in Chapter 2(A), we will use "の" with Adjectives in this chapter, such as 大きいの、くろいの、あかいの. We also learn that "な Adjectives/Copula Nouns" with の.  In that case, you should say なの after "な Adjectives/Copula Nouns": りっぱなの、げんきなの、きれいなの and such.

Examples:

　　A:　あそこに、おおきい鯉がいますよ。
　　　　There's a big carp over there!

　　B:　あ、あそこにも、おおきいのが　いますよ。
　　　　Oh, there's another big one there!

C:　あの、しろいのは、りっぱですねぇ。
That white one over there is splendid.

D:　あのりっぱなのを、ちかくで 見たいですね。
I want to see that splendid one closer.

E:　あっ！あのきんいろのを　見てください。
Oh! Please look at that gold one.

## 6. **The particle に for the Indirect Objects**
Examples:

A: 私に　そのりんごを　ください。　　Please give me an apple.
B: だれに　でんわを　しましたか。　　To whom did you call?
C: 私に、日本語を　おしえてください。Please teach me Japanese.

This is equivalent to the English sentence pattern: Subject + Verb + Indirect Object + Direct Object, SVOO pattern.  Since Japanese verbs come at the end of a sentence, it is SOOV in Japanese.  Note, however, that you don't normally say "Subject" in Japanese in a request/order.  You say O + O + V.  For example, 私に　そのりんごを　ください。 O (私に)　+O (そのりんごを) +V (ください).　 The verbs used in SVOO (or SOOV in Japanese) are limited: Remember the following; "giving + receiving verbs あげる、くれる、もらう," "teach おしえる," "show みせる," and "do する."

**(1)** ブラウンさんは、妹に英語を　おしえました。
Mr. Brown taught my sister English.（It is more natural to say おしえてくれました when you are thankful about it）

**(2)** 私はブラウンさんに、日本語を　おしえました。
I taught Mr. Brown Japanese.（おしえてあげました may be used if Mr. Brown is not your social superior.）

**(3)** 山田さんは、私にパスポートを　見せました。
Mr. Yamada showed me his passport.　（見せてくれました may be used if you are thankful about it.)

**(4)** 父は、私たちに、むかしのはなしを　しました。
Our father told us the stories of his past.（してくれました may be used if you are thankful about it.)

Chapter 6 (D) Exercises

A. Replace あまり with そんなに, and translate into English.

（１）この本は　あまり　むずかしくありませんよ。

（２）きょうは、あまり　お金がないんです。

（３）お肉は、あまり　食べません。

（４）このじしょは、あまり　よくありませんね。

（５）<u>さいきん</u>、あまり　ゴルフを　しません。
　　　　lately

B. Group-work:  Ask three classmates how often they do the following, using よくします すか, and place a checkmark in each column for each person, depending on their responses.  Answer with よくします、そんなにしません or ぜんぜんしません。

| | よくします(often) | そんなにしません (rarely) | ぜんぜんしません (never) |
|---|---|---|---|
| そうじ(clean, vacuum) | | | |
| せんたく(laundry) | | | |
| アルバイト(part-time job) | | | |
| ふかざけ（深酒） excessive drinking | | | |
| かいもの (shopping) | | | |
| べんきょう (studying) | | | |
| スピードうんてん speeding | | | |
| うんどう exercises | | | |
| ひるね　nap | | | |
| お母さんのおてつだい helping mother | | | |

C. Translate into English.

（１）こんなところに、花が　咲いている。
　　　　　　　　　　　　flowers　blooming

（２）あんなところに、犬が　いますよ！

（３）悪魔？そんなのは、いませんよ。
　　　devil

（４）え？そんなたいへんなことが、あったんですか。

（５）見て、見て。私のはな。こんなに　あかい！


D. Fill in the blanks with a noun that works in all.

(At a wine shop)

A：　おいしい　ワインを　ください。

B：　このしろい（　　）が　いいですよ。

A：　たかい（　　）は、だめなんです。

B：　あ、そう。じゃ、このあかい（　　）は、どうですか。

A：　あかい（　　）は、きらいなんです。

B：　おや、むずかしいですね。じゃ、このせのたかい（　　）は、どう？
　　　せは、たかいが、ねだんは、たかくないよ。

A：　アハハ、せのたかい（　　）は、しろい（　　）より　やすいですか。

B：　そう、しろい（　　）より、やすいです。

A：　じゃ、それを　ください。

B：　どうも、まいど　ありがとう。
　　　　　　Thank you for your patronage.


E.  Make a polite request sentence, using "~ てください." Make your sentences more realistic by adding direct objects to transitive verbs, and adverbs or adverbial phrases to intransitive verbs.

For example:　　Please look at me. → わたしを　みてください。

　　"miru" (vowel verb) → "te" form of "miru" = "mite" → "mite kudasai" →
　　+"watashi wo" → "watashi wo mite kudasai"

　　みる→　みて→　みてください→わたしを　みてください。


[Pre-study]: You must identify the verb type before adding information to it.  There are intransitive and transitive verbs, and only the transitive verb takes a direct object.  Such verbs as "miru" and "taberu" are transitive, and they are preceded by direct objects such as "television" for "miru" and "bread" for "taberu." The particle "wo を" precedes the transitive verb. On the other hand, intransitive verbs do not take direct objects.  Examples of intransitive verbs include "aruku," "iku," "kaeru," "aru," "iru," "au," "wakaru" and so forth.  They are preceded by particles "ga" or "wa," and are followed by adverbs or adverbial phrases. The sign "t.v." stands for a transitive verb and "i.v." stands for an intransitive verb.

(t.v.)

みる→　みて→　みてください→　　わたしを　　　　みてください。
　　　　　　　　　　　　　　　　　　　direct object　　　transitive verb

(i.v.)

ねる→　ねて→　ねてください→　　ここで、　　　　　ねてください。
　　　　　　　　　　　　　　　　　　adverbial phrase　　intransitive verb

---

**1. Vowel verbs**

(1) たべる（食べる）(eat)　　　　　(2) おしえる（教える）(teach)

(3) いる（居る）(stay, exist)　　　　(4) おりる（降りる）(get off)

　　(Attention: the particle "wo" in ～をおりる does not indicate a direct object, but a
　　departing point for a motion verb. "Oriru" is an intransitive verb.)

(5) いれる（入れる）(insert)　　　　(6) かりる（借りる）(borrow)

　(place s.t. into a location に～を　いれる)　　(s.o から s.t. を　かりる)

(7) ねる（寝る）(sleep)　　　　　　(8) みる（見る）(look, see, watch)

(9) おきる（起きる）(get up)　　　　(10) シャワーをあびる（浴びる）(take a shower)

(11) あける（開ける）(open)　　　　(12) しめる（閉める）(close)

(13) あげる (give; raise)

---

Translate into Japanese, using the vocabulary in the box 1 above.

1. Please eat more vegetable.
2. Please teach me Japanese.
3. Please stay here.
4. Please get off the train at next station.
5. Please put your books into a bag.
6. Please borrow a pen from your classmate.
7. Please lie down here.
8. Please look at the blackboard/whiteboard.
9. Please get up at 6 AM.
10. Please take shower before me.
11. Please open the door.
12. Please close the window.
13. Please raise your hand.

---

**2. Consonant verbs**: Remember the "te" form song (Silver Bells)?

「むぶぬ→んで、うつる→って、く→いて、ぐ→いで、す→して are the consonant
　verbs～～～!」

(1) のむ（飲む）(drink)　　　　　＊ Exception (2) いく（行く）(go) → 行って
　　　　　　　　　　　　　　　　　　　　　　　　　　（～に or へ　いく）

(3) もつ（持つ）(bring, hold, have)　(4) あるく（歩く）(walk)
　　　　　　　　　　　　　　　（しずかに quietly、はやく quickly、ゆっくり slowly）

Chapter 6D: There is a Carp!  461

---

(5) はなす（話す）(talk, speak, tell)  (6) おどる（踊る）(dance)

(7) あそぶ（遊ぶ）(play)          (8) のる（乗る）(ride, get on)

(9) あう（会う）(meet)（〜にあう）(10) かえる（帰る）(i.v., return)

（〜に or へ　かえる）

(11) まつ（待つ）(wait)          (12) なる（成る）(become)（〜になる）

(13) いう（言う）(say)（〜と いう）(14) かう（買う）(buy)

(15) わかる（分かる）(be understandable) (16) かく（書く）(write)

(17) およぐ（泳ぐ）(swim) (18) よむ（読む）(read) (19) きく（聞く）(listen, hear, ask)

---

Translate into Japanese, using the vocabulary in the box 2 above.
1. Please drink your coffee outside of classroom.
2. Please go to the library this afternoon.
3. Please hold this bag (for me).
4. Please walk slowly.
5. Please speak in Japanese.
6. Please dance on the stage.
7. Please play with me.
8. Please get on the bus here.
9. Please meet Mr. かとう at the station.
10. Please return at 3 p.m.
11. Please wait one second.
12. Please become a policeman.
13. Please say "Ah~."
14. Please buy me a T-shirt.
15. Please understand me.
16. Please write your name on this paper.
17. Please swim in the ocean.
18. Please read it <u>aloud</u>（おおきい　こえで）
19. Please listen <u>carefully</u>.（ちゅういして）

---

**3. Irregular verbs**
(1) する (do)

べんきょう（勉強）する (study)        でんわ（電話）する (to call)
ちゅうもん（注文）する (order)
うんてん（運転）する (drive)
せんたく（洗濯）する (laundry)

(2) くる（来る）(come)

Translate into Japanese, using the vocabulary in the box 3 above.
1. Please study Japanese everyday.
2. Please order coffee (for me).
3. Please drive to the station.
4. Please do the laundry this shirt.
5. Please come to my office tomorrow morning.
6. Please call 911.

F. Pair-work: Request your partner to perform various activities, using てください form. Make as many requests as possible.
 Examples:
あなたのなまえを　かいてください。
 それを　よんでください。
 となりの人<ruby>人<rt>ひと</rt></ruby>を　じっと見<ruby>見<rt>み</rt></ruby>てください。(じっと見<ruby>見<rt>み</rt></ruby>る to gaze intently)
 こくばん（のところ）まで、あるいてください。

(When you are out of ideas → More possible requests below)
  1. Please lie down. (Use "ねる")
  2. Please get up.
  3. Please look at the person next to you.
  4. Please say something in Japanese to the person to your right.
  5. Please look behind you.
  6. Please show me your keys.
  7. Please tell me your best friend's name.
  8. Please stand up.
  9. Please sit down.
  10. Please raise your right hand. (Use "みぎてをあげる")
  11. Please ask for a sheet of paper from your classmate. (Use "もらう")

G. Look at the following chart and write appropriate statements with the information provided. Use either the "adjective + no" or "copula noun + na + no" pattern.

| まど | にわ | きんぎょ<br>gold fish | だいどころ<br>kitchen | おふろ |
|---|---|---|---|---|
| おおきい<br>あかるい<br>あたらしい | ひろい<br>ふるい<br>しずか | おおきい<br>りっぱ | ちいさい<br>せまい<br>くらい | あたらしい<br>きれい<br>あかるい |

Examples:
(1)　おおきい<u>の</u>は、まどと、きんぎょです。
(2)　きれい<u>なの</u>は、おふろです。

 1. ちいさい・・・・・・・・・・・・・・・・・・・・・・・・・・・・・・・・・・・・・・・・・・・・
 2. りっぱ・・・・・・・・・・・・・・・・・・・・・・・・・・・・・・・・・・・・・・・・・・・・

3. ひろい・・・・・・・・・・・・・・・・・・・・・・・・・・・・・・・・・・・・・・・・・・・・・・・・・・・・・・・・・・・・・・・・・・・・

4. しずか・・・・・・・・・・・・・・・・・・・・・・・・・・・・・・・・・・・・・・・・・・・・・・・・・・・・・・・・・・・・・・・・・・・・

5. あかるい・・・・・・・・・・・・・・・・・・・・・・・・・・・・・・・・・・・・・・・・・・・・・・・・・・・・・・・・・・・・・・・・・・

6. あたらしい・・・・・・・・・・・・・・・・・・・・・・・・・・・・・・・・・・・・・・・・・・・・・・・・・・・・・・・・・・・・・・・

H.　Use the same chart above and connect two modifiers for each of the below.
　Examples:
　　（1）　おおき<u>くて</u>、あかるいのは、まどです。
　　（2）　しずか<u>で</u>、ひろいのは、にわです。

1. ・・・・・・・・・・・・・・・・・・・・・・・・・・・・・・・・・・・・・は、まどです。

2. ・・・・・・・・・・・・・・・・・・・・・・・・・・・・・・・・・・・・・は、にわです。

3. ・・・・・・・・・・・・・・・・・・・・・・・・・・・・・・・・・・・・・は、きんぎょです。

4. ・・・・・・・・・・・・・・・・・・・・・・・・・・・・・・・・・・・・・は、だいどころです。

5. ・・・・・・・・・・・・・・・・・・・・・・・・・・・・・・・・・・・・・は、おふろです。

I.　Pair-work: Look at the chart below describing the conditions of different buildings.
Discuss the questions and answers with your partner, paying attention to はい、いいえ、
とても、そんなに、and あまり.
Examples:
A:　このたてものは、あたらしいですか。
B:　いいえ、あたらしくありません。
A:　としょかんは、きれいですか。
B:　はい、とてもきれいです。

| | きっさてん | このたてもの | たなかさんの アパート | としょかん |
|---|---|---|---|---|
| あたらしい | はい | いいえ | そんなに | はい |
| いい | とても | あまり | はい | はい |
| りっぱ | いいえ | あまり | いいえ | はい |
| きれい | はい | そんなに | はい | とても |
| しずか | とても | いいえ | はい | はい |
| ゆうめい | はい | いいえ | いいえ | はい |

J. Fill in the blanks with appropriate particles or predicates.

[Pre-exercise]

For the transitive verbs such as "teach おしえる," "show みせる," "give あげる," "tell a story はなしをする," use the sentence pattern SVOO in English, and SOOV in Japanese.

Examples:

Tom showed me his photo.  →  トムは、　私に　しゃしんを　見せました。
S    V    I.O  D.O            S (=Topic)    I.O      D.O        V

Please show me your photo. → 私に　しゃしんを　見せてください。
V   I.O  D.O            I.O      D.O          V

Now try to fill in the blanks:

1. 私 (　　　) そのじしょ (　　　) みせてください。
    Please show me that dictionary.

2. 私の子ども (　　　) 英語を　おしえてください。
    Please teach English to my child.

3. 私 (　　　) でんわばんごうを、(　　　) ください。
    Please tell me (= teach me) your telephone number.

4. 私のちち (　　　) その話 (はなし) を (　　　) ください。
    Please tell that story to my father.

5. あなた (　　　) この本 (　　　) あげましょう。
    I shall give you this book.

6. お母さん、私 (　　　) このおかしを　(　　　) ください。
    Mom, please buy me this candy.

7. 私 (　　　) あなたの車を五百ドルで　(　　　) ください。
    Please sell me your car with five hundred dollars. (to sell = うる)

8. お母さんのこどものときのはなし (　　　) してください。
    Please tell us about you when you were a little girl.

Chapter 6D Presentation: Create a dialogue under the given situations and act out.

1. You are at a shoe shop. Greeting takes place between a customer and a salesperson. A customer asks a salesperson to <u>show</u> him/her red shoes (in distance). Salesperson comments on them saying that they are very nice and <u>asks the customer to</u> <u>put them on</u> (haku). The customer says they are good, but asks him/her to <u>show</u> black shoes, too. Salesperson brings them and says please <u>try them on</u>. The customer says s/he has decided on them (kore ni shimasu), and asks the salesperson to <u>put them in the box</u>. Salesperson says certainly (kashikomarimashtia) and hands them to the customer. They thank each other.

2. The same situation as Number 1 except you are at an umbrella shop. Instead of putting the umbrella in the box, you request to put it in the bag (fukuro).

3. Create a dialogue between you and your neighbor in the following situation.

A: You visit your neighbor (during the day; greet appropriately)
B: You politely ask your neighbor to <u>cut his/her tree in his/her backyard</u> since it is blocking your view of the beautiful mountains from his house.
A: Your neighbor agrees or disagrees.
C: Farewell greetings.

4. Create a dialogue between you and your neighbor in the following situation.

A: You visit your neighbor (at night; greet appropriately)
B: You politely ask your neighbor to <u>cut the noise of his/her TV down</u> since you have a baby in your household. (cut the noise → make the noise smaller → oto wo chiisaku suru)
A: Your neighbor agrees or disagrees.
C: Farewell greetings.

5. You are at a train station and an old person asks you to <u>read</u> the sign for him/her since s/he cannot read the sign (due to his/her eye conditions: use "me ga warui" for the reason). You read it for him/her and s/he thanks to you. Then s/he asks you to <u>tell</u> you what time it is (use ~ <u>wo oshiete kudasai</u>"). You tell him/her what time it is. Then s/he asks you to <u>hold</u> his/her luggage (nimotsu or just say "kore") for a moment. You hold it for a moment and s/he thanks you as you return his/her luggage. Farewell greetings.

6. You are outside of Japanese classroom. It's raining heavy, but you have no umbrella. You see a kind-looking classmate who starts walking toward the parking lot, so you ask him/her to <u>walk/go</u> (together) with him/her to the parking lot (chuushajyoo). Your classmates agrees. During your walk to the parking lot, you carry on a conversation about Japanese class being fun and easy, kanji is not so difficult, etc. Once you got to your car, you thank your classmate and do farewell greetings.

7. You're struggling with kanji, so you ask a kind-looking classmate to <u>help</u> you. S/he agrees and asks you to <u>write</u> kanji that means "suffering" three times. After you wrote them, s/he asks you to <u>read</u> them. You read them, then s/he asks you to <u>put that paper into your pocket.</u> You do as s/he said. S/he tells you to <u>look at</u> that sheet once more at home. You promise you will do that. Farewell greeting. (help = transitive verb ~ wo tasukeru)

8. You are searching for a ticket (kippu; "I don't have a ticket" is "There is no ticket."). So, your friend suggests you to <u>look into</u> your bag. You follow his advice but finds no ticket. S/he suggests you to <u>look into</u> your wallet (saifu), but it's not there. So, you asks him/her to <u>look into</u> his/her pocket. Here it is! S/he finds the ticket in his/pocket (Use "arimashita!" when you found it.)

9. You are looking for a station. You ask a passerby where it is. S/he tells you to do the followings: Please go strait (massugu), make a right turn (migi ni magaru) at the traffic signal (shingoo), then <u>look at</u> the mountains. The station is right there.

10. You are in the Japanese classroom. your classmates asks you how to get to the Students Office. So you give him/her the instruction: please <u>leave</u> this building, and <u>walk</u> toward the mountains (that is North), then <u>look at</u> the building in front of him/her, the Students Office is in that building. S/he asks you if s/he recognizes it right away. You assure him/her. S/he thanks you and you say "good luck."

Chapter 6 (D): Dict-A-Conversation (1)   About Yourself

(A) Respond to the statements verbally, and then write down your replies.  Please answer in <u>short sentences,</u> writing in hiragana.

1.

_____

2.

_____

3.

_____

4.

_____

5.

_____

6.

_____

7.

_____

Chapter 6 (D) – (1)

| 池<br><br>(a pond) | いけ<br>チ | 池（いけ）a pond<br>池田（いけだ）a surname<br>治水（ちすい）flood control |
| | | (4)<br>`ヽ ゝ ⺡ 汀 沖 池` |
| 魚<br><br>(fish) | さかな<br>うお<br>ギョ | 魚（さかな）fish<br>金魚（きんぎょ）gold fish<br>人魚（にんぎょ）a mermaid |
| | | (10)<br>`ノ ク 勹 匃 甪 角 甶 魚 魚 魚` |
| 英<br><br>(brave) | ひで<br>エイ | 英語（えいご）English<br>[英国（えいこく）England]<br>[英雄（えいゆう）a hero] |
| | | (8)<br>`一 十 艹 艹 苎 苹 英 英` |
| 苦<br><br>(bitter; to suffer) | にが（い）<br>くる（しい、<br>　　しむ）<br>ク | 苦い（にがい）bitter<br>苦しい（くるしい）suffering<br>苦しむ（くるしむ）to suffer<br>苦心（くしん）する to make strenuous efforts<br>[苦労（くろう）する to endure; suffer] |
| | | (8)<br>`一 十 艹 艹 芢 芢 苦 苦` |
| 手<br><br>(a hand) | て<br>で<br>シュ | 苦手（にがて）one's weak point<br>手先（てさき）the fingers; a cat's-paw<br>男手が足りない（おとこでがたりない）<br>　　　　　need (the help of) more men<br>手話（しゅわ）sign language<br>[握手（あくしゅ）a handshake] |
| | | (4)<br>`ノ 二 三 手` |

Chapter 6 (D) – (2)

| 赤<br><br>(red) | あか（い）<br>セキ | 赤い（あかい）red<br>赤字（あかじ）deficit<br>赤十字（せきじゅうじ）the Red Cross<br>[赤面（せきめん）する to blush; to turn red; to<br>feel ashamed] |
| | | (7)<br>一 十 土 亍 亣 赤 赤 |
| 黒<br><br>(black) | くろ（い）<br>コク | 黒い（くろい）black<br>黒板（こくばん）blackboard<br>大黒[天]（だいこく[てん]）the God of Wealth;<br>one of the Seven Deities of Good Fortune |
| | | (11)<br>丶 口 円 日 甲 甲 里 里 黒 黒 黒 |
| 才<br><br>(talent, year-old) | サイ | 一才（いっさい）one year old<br>*二十才（はたち）twenty years old<br>[才能（さいのう）talent]<br>[天才（てんさい）genius] |
| | | (3)<br>一 十 才 |
| 若<br><br>(young) | わか（い）<br>ジャク<br>ニャク | 若い（わかい）young<br>若者（わかもの）young people<br>[若輩（じゃくはい）] a youngster;<br>a greenhorn<br>[老若男女（ろうにゃくだんじょ）] everyone |
| | | (8)<br>一 十 艹 艹 艻 若 若 若 |
| 足<br><br>(foot, counter for socks and shoes) | あし<br>ソク<br>ゾク | 足（あし）foot, leg<br>一本足（いっぽんあし）one-leg (scarecrow)<br>一足（いっそく）one pair (of socks, shoes,<br>etc.)<br>[足袋（たび）] socks cloven at the big toe |
| | | (7)<br>丶 口 口 ア 平 足 足 |

Kanji Practice for Chapter 6 (D)
かんじの　れんしゅう

1．つぎの　ことばを　よみなさい。それから、<sup>くらすめえと</sup>クラスメートにいみをきき
なさい。Read the following words to your classmates and ask them for the
meaning of each word.

（１）　手と足

（６）　上手

（２）　赤と黒

（７）　下手

（３）　池の魚

（８）　英語

（４）　苦い

（９）　十九才

（５）　苦手

（１０）　若い人

2.　Write kanji in the box to complete the word.

(1)　English

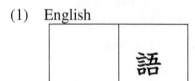

(4)　one's weak point

(2)　skilled/skillful

(5)　hands and feet

(3)　unskilled/unskillful

(6)　mermaid

3. よんでから、よみがなをかいて、えいごでいいなさい。Read first, then write
yomigana above each kanji, and translate into English.

(1) 池に　魚が　います。

(2) 私は、魚が　好きです。

(3) 今日のコーヒーは、苦かったです。

(4) スタンダール(Stendhal)は、「赤と黒」(Le Rouge et le Noir) をかきました。

(5) 辛いものが　苦手です。

(6) 「中古車」は、英語で　何と言いますか。

(7) 犬には　足が　四本　あります。

(8) 日本語で　「二十才」を「はたち」と言います。

(9) 私の犬の年は、十二才です。そんなに若くありません。

(10) 年は、何才ですか。


4. かんじとひらがなで　かきなさい。Write in kanji and hiragana.

（１）　　やまださんは、えいごが　じょうずです。


（２）　　わたしは、かんじが　にがてでしたが、いまでは、すきになりました。


（３）　　このいけのさかなは、「はたち」ですから、わたしとおなじとしです。


（４）　　あかいかさと　くろいかさと、どちらのほうが、すきですか。


（５）　　あなたのいぬのとしは、なんさいですか。


（６）　　モールでくろいズボンを　にほん　かいました。


（７）　　にほんごで、「しょうねん」は、なんさいぐらいですか。

Ch. 6 D　　　Kanji Review: 四角に　てきとうな　漢字を　書きなさい。

1.
□ い □
black　　fish

2.
□ い □　と　□ の □
red fish　　and　golden　fish

3.
□ の □　は、　□ □ □　で　す。
pond　fish　　　　twenty-years-old

4.
□ □　な　お　□　の　□
famous　　　　temple's　　pond

5.
□ □ □　は、　□ □　で　す。
Japanese language　is　my weakness.

6.
□ い □　は、　元 □　で　す。
Young people　are　energetic.

7.
□ い　か　ら　□ い　て　□　き　ま　す。
Because it's close,　　by walking,　　I will go.

8.
□　し　い　□　を　□　い　ま　す。
(I)　new　　　house　　　will buy. (I'll buy a new house.)

# **My Dormitory Life**

*Expressions*
"I go to bed some time between twelve and one o'clock"
"I slept from ten to five"
"I live in a dormitory"
"Is it truly you?"
"Yes, that's why"
"I missed breakfast because I was late"
"I'll become an English teacher in the future"
"Japanese has become harder"

*Kanji practice from Chapter 7*

Chapter 7　　　　　　　　My Dormitory Life

<ruby>私<rt>わたし</rt></ruby>のりょう<ruby>生活<rt>せいかつ</rt></ruby>

<ruby>先生<rt>せんせい</rt></ruby>　：モニカさんは、いつ　きょうとに　<ruby>来<rt>き</rt></ruby>ましたか。　　　　　　1

モニカ：<ruby>今年<rt>ことし</rt></ruby>の<ruby>一月<rt>いちがつ</rt></ruby>です。

みわ　：どこに　<ruby>住<rt>す</rt></ruby>んでいますか。　　　　　　　　　　　　　　　3

モニカ：<ruby>大学<rt>だいがく</rt></ruby>の　りょう　に　<ruby>住<rt>す</rt></ruby>んでいます。　　　　　　　4

<ruby>先生<rt>せんせい</rt></ruby>　：りょうの　<ruby>食事<rt>しょくじ</rt></ruby>は、どうですか。　　　　　　　　　　5

モニカ：おいしいです。

<ruby>先生<rt>せんせい</rt></ruby>　：<ruby>今日<rt>きょう</rt></ruby>の　<ruby>朝<rt>あさ</rt></ruby>は、<ruby>何<rt>なに</rt></ruby>を　<ruby>食<rt>た</rt></ruby>べましたか。　　　　7

モニカ：え〜っと、ごはん　と　おみそしる、のり　と　<ruby>魚<rt>さかな</rt></ruby>です。

みわ　：え〜！？　<ruby>和食<rt>わしょく</rt></ruby>なんですか。　　　　　　　　　　　9

モニカ：ええ、<ruby>洋食<rt>ようしょく</rt></ruby>も　あるんですが、、、　　　　　　　　10

<ruby>先生<rt>せんせい</rt></ruby>　：おいしくないんですか。　　　　　　　　　　　　　　11

モニカ：いえ、すごく　おいしいんです。でも、<ruby>私<rt>わたし</rt></ruby>が「あさねぼう」なので、

もう　ないんです。　　　　　　　　　　　　　12-13

<ruby>先生<rt>せんせい</rt></ruby>　：じゃ、とっても　<ruby>人気<rt>にんき</rt></ruby>が　あるんですね。　　　　　14

モニカ：ええ、パンが　やわらかくて、ジャムが　ほんのり<ruby>甘<rt>あま</rt></ruby>くて、コーヒー
　　　　　も　おいしいです。

みわ　：　モニカは、<ruby>何時<rt>なんじ</rt></ruby>ごろ　おきるの？　　　　　　　　17

モニカ：七時ごろ、、、

みわ　：りょうの朝ごはんは、七時から八時まで、、、でしょう？

モニカ：そう。だから、七時半には、もう洋食は、ないんです。人気が

　　　　あるから、、、　　　　　　　　　　　　　　　　　　　　　20-21

みわ：　ねえ、モニカ、何時に　ねるの？　　　　　　　　　　　　　22

モニカ：たいてい　十二時から一時ぐらいの間に、、、

みわ：　う〜ん、それじゃ、ちょっと、、、

モニカ：私は、まだ日本語が　下手なので、しゅくだいに　時間がかかるん
　　　　です。　　　　　　　　　　　　　　　　　　　　　　　　25-26

先生　：分かります。でも、すぐに上手になりますよ。

Chapter 7 [English translation]:

Professor:  Monica, when did you come to Kyoto?
Monica  :  January.
Miwa    :  Where do you live?
Monica  :  I live in a college dormitory.
Professor:  How's the dormitory food?
Monica  :  (It's) delicious.
Miwa    :  What did you eat this morning?
Monica  :  Hmm…(cooked) rice, miso-soup, seaweed, and fish.
Miwa    :  Wow, is it Japanese food?
Monica  :  Yeah, they have Western food, too, but…
Professor:  Is it not tasty?
Monica  :  No, (it's not that) it is very tasty.  But, it (the food) is gone by the time I get
              up, since I am not an early-riser.
professor:  Then, it is very popular, isn't it?
Monica  :  Yes, the bread is very soft, jam is subtly sweet, and coffee is delicious.
Miwa    :  What time do you get up, Monica?
Monica  :  Around 7 o'clock…
Miwa    :  Dormitory breakfast is from seven to eight o'clock…
Monica  :  Yes, that's why.  Western food is all gone by seven thirty, since it is so
              popular.
Miwa    :  Monica, what time do you go to bed?
Monica  :  Sometime between twelve and one o'clock.
Miwa    :  Hmm… then it's a bit difficult.
Monica  :  My Japanese still isn't good.  So, it takes time to do my homework.2
Professor:  I understand, but you'll improve soon.

Chapter 7 [Vocabulary List]

1. Expressions
   え～っと                        Well, let me see.(=え～と)
   え～！                         What?!(=えっ！)
   そう。                          Is that right?
   ねえ                           Listen!
   う～ん                          Well, let me think…
   それじゃ、ちょっと、、           That won't do.

2. Nouns
   きょうと                        Kyoto, ancient capital of Japan
   (りょう寮)                      dormitory
   せいかつ（生活）                 life, lifestyle
   ことし（今年）                   this year
   しょくじ（食事）                 meal
   (ごはん)                        meal, cooked rice

| | |
|---|---|
| みそしる | miso soup |
| のり | seaweed |
| (さかな 魚) | fish |
| (わしょく和食) | Japanese food |
| (ようしょく洋食) | Western food |
| (あさねぼう) | late riser |
| にんき(人気) | popularity |
| (パン) | bread |
| ジャム | jam |
| あさごはん(朝ごはん) | breakfast |
| (しゅくだい) | homework |
| (じかん 時間) | time |

3. Copula Nouns

| | |
|---|---|
| じょうず(上手) | good, skilled |
| へた (下手) | poor, unskilled |

4. Interrogative Pronouns

| | |
|---|---|
| (いつ) | when |
| (どう) | how |

5. Adjectives

| | |
|---|---|
| (おいしい) | tasty |
| やわらかい | soft |
| (あまい) | sweet |
| ない | nonexistent |

6. Adverbs

| | |
|---|---|
| もう〜ない | no longer exist |
| とっても | very (casual form of "totemo") |
| ほんのり | slightly |
| (たいてい) | usually |

7. Verbs

| | |
|---|---|
| (にんきが) ある | is popular |
| (ねる) | go to bed, sleep |
| (じかんが) かかる | (It) takes (time). |
| (わかる 分かる) | to understand |
| (〜に なる) | to become ~ |

8. Particles
   Conjunctive Particle

| | |
|---|---|
| ので | because |

| | |
|---|---|
| あいだ | during; throughout that time |
| あいだに | while: some time during the time period |

9. Conjunctions

| | |
|---|---|
| じゃ | in that case, then |
| （でも） | but, however |
| （だから） | therefore, for that reason |

---
Additional Vocabulary from Grammar Notes, Exercises, and Dict-A-Conversation
---

[Nouns]

| | |
|---|---|
| じこ | accident |
| チューリップ | tulip |
| けいたいでんわ | cell phone |
| どろぼう | thief |
| おたまじゃくし | tadpole |
| （おとな） | adult |
| せいじんしき | ceremony for coming of age |
| しんごう | traffic lights |
| （ねぼう） | late riser |
| しけん | examination |
| じかん | hours; duration of time (八時間 eight hours) |
| （そと） | outside |

[Adjective]

| | |
|---|---|
| はずかしい | shy; embarrassed |

[Adverbs]

| | |
|---|---|
| しょうらい | in the future |
| もうすぐ | pretty soon |
| ずっと | throughout the time |

[Verbs]

| | |
|---|---|
| ちこくする | to become late |
| れんしゅうする | to practice |
| そつぎょうする | to graduate |
| たす　（足す） | to add |
| ひく（引く） | to subtract |
| すんでいる　　（すむ） | to live; living |
| たべている　　（たべる） | is eating |
| まっている　　（まつ） | is waiting |
| ないている　　（なく） | is crying |

Chapter 7                    Grammar and Cultural Notes

## 1. ので **Conjunctive Particle showing reason or cause**

| （1）いい　てんき　な | ので | こうえんは、人が　おおい。 |
|---|---|---|
| （2）てんきが　いい | | うみに　行きました。 |
| （3）日本へ　行く | | 日本語のべんきょうを　はじめました。 |

English translation:
(1) Since it's a nice day, there are a lot of people in the park.
(2) Since the weather was nice, I went to the beach.
(3) I began to study Japanese, because I will go to Japan.

"Node" is a subordinate conjunction which expresses a "cause" or a "reason."  We have learned before a similar subordinate conjunction, "kara."  Both of them are subordinate conjunctions that express a "cause" or a "reason.  But they differ in the following:
(1) "ので node" sounds politer in case you need to make an excuse.
(2) After nouns "な na" is used before "ので node."

   e.g. こども<u>だ</u>から、できません。    (I cannot do it since I'm merely a kid.)
   　　こども<u>な</u>ので、できません。    (I cannot do it since I'm merely a kid.)

Observe the example sentences below.
   A) Noun/Copula Noun + ので
   　The plain non-past copula "da" is replaced by "na" when the statement in the "node" clause is in the present tense.

   （1）日本のうたが、好きなので、よくＣＤをききます。
   　　　I like Japanese songs, so I often listen to (Japanese) CDs.

   （2）日本語がへたなので、はずかしい。
   　　　I'm embarrassed because my Japanese is not good.

   （3）そのチューリップが、きれい<u>だった</u>ので、買いました。
   　　　　　　　　　　　(datta: past tense of copula "da")
   　　　Because those tulips were pretty, I bought them.

   （4）私は、じがきれい<u>じゃない</u>ので、れんしゅうしました。
   　　　　　　　　　(jyanai: negative form of copula "da")
   　　　Since my penmanship is poor, I practiced (writing).

   B) Adjective +　ので
   　（1）そのシャツは、高いので、買いません。
   　　　　That shirt is expensive, so I won't buy it.

（２）へやが　せまいので、ちいさいつくえを　買いました。

Since my room is small, I bought a small desk.

（３）新しいギターがほしいので、アルバイトをしています。

I want a new guitar, so I took on a side-job (part-time job).

（４）お金がないので、こんしゅうは、えいがに　行きません。

Since I have no money, I won't go see a movie this week.

C) Verb +　ので

（１）明日しけんがあるので、今日は、べんきょうします。

Since I have an examination tomorrow, I will study today.

（２）毎日べんきょうするので、テストは、いつも百てんです。

Since I study everyday, my tests are always a perfect hundred.

（３）午後、友だちが　来るので、へやを　そうじします。

Since my friends are coming this afternoon, I will clean up my room.

## 2. んです to enhance/inquire/explain ：じかんが　かかるんです。

As we saw in Chapter 4 (A) Grammar 4, "〜んです"is more emotionally expressive than the simple "〜です." It enhances the speaker's feelings of inquiry in question form, and also his attempt to explain in answer form. In the previous chapters, we saw "~ n desu" preceded by a noun (~na n desu) and an adjective (~ i n desu). In this chapter "~ n desu" will be preceded by a verb.

Examples:

(Noun)

（１）ひまなんです。(As an answer to "Why are you looking bored?")

（２）日曜日なんです。(As an answer to "Why are you not at school?")

(Adjective)

（１）高いんです。(As an answer to "Why don't you buy what you want?")

（２）ないんです。(As an answer to "Why do you look so disappointed?")

(Verb)

（１）じかんがかかるんです。(As an answer to "Why can't you do it quickly?")

（２）母が来るんです。(As an answer to "Why are you looking so happy?")

### 3.  あいだ & あいだに **Conjunctive Particle meaning "between, while"**

While "aida" expands for an entire duration of time, "aida ni" focuses at the end-period.
Therefore, the sentence "クラスの 間<sup>あいだ</sup> は、けいたいでんわを けしておきましょう
(During class, I will shut my cell phone off)," refers to the entire duration of class; "先生<sup>せんせい</sup>
がこくばんに 書<sup>か</sup>いている 間<sup>あいだ</sup> に、しゅくだいをしてしまいましょう(Let's finish
homework while the teacher is busy writing on the board)" indicates the student wishes to
complete his homework anytime **before** the teacher finishes writing on the board.

Examples of あいだ
    (1) ビルとビルのあいだは、くらいです。It's dark between buildings.
                     (This "aida" is a spatial term.)
    (2) 四時<sup>よじ</sup>から六時<sup>ろくじ</sup>までのあいだ、しごとをしました。I worked between four
        and six o'clock.

    (3) 私<sup>わたし</sup> が本<sup>ほん</sup>をよむあいだ、あなたは、まっていてください。Please wait while
        I read the book.

Examples of あいだに
    (1) 毎日<sup>まいにち</sup>、十二時<sup>じゅうにじ</sup>から一時<sup>いちじ</sup>のあいだに、ねます。I go to bed sometime
        between twelve and one o'clock everyday.

    (2) 私<sup>わたし</sup> が、学校<sup>がっこう</sup>にいるあいだに、（うちに）どろぼうが 入<sup>はい</sup>りました。
        While I was at school, a burglar got into my house.

    (3) 四時から六時のあいだに、来<sup>き</sup>てください。Please come some time
        between four and six o'clock.

### 4. の **Sentence Final, concluding a question with a rising tone** なんじにねるの？
"No" is a soft and casual ending to an inquiry.  Simply add "no" with a rising tone to a
plain form ending, regardless of tense.

|  | Affirmative | Negative |  |
|---|---|---|---|
| Non-past tense | あなた　な | あなたじゃない | |
| | いい | よくない | |
| | ねる | ねない | の？ |
| Past tense | あなた　だった | あなたじゃなかった | |
| | よかった | よくなかった | |
| | ねた | ねなかった | |

Compare formal and casual (soft sounding) speech.

(1) Noun

       Formal:        あなたですか。

       Casual soft:   あなたなの？

(2) Adjective

       Formal:        いいですか。

       Casual soft:   いいの？

(3) Verb

       Formal:        いつ　行きますか。

       Casual soft:   いつ　行くの？

       Formal:        なんじに　ねますか。

       Casual soft:   なんじに　ねるの？

## 5. 〜になる **to become ~**

The verb "naru" is preceded by particle "ni" after a noun and a copula noun.  Therefore, to express the idea that you will become an engineer, say: エンジニアになります。
Examples:

（１）今年、十九さいになります。I will become nineteen years old this year.
(Or, I have become nineteen years old this year.)

（２）しょうらい、英語の先生になります。I'll be an English teacher in the
(in the future)                        future.

（３）もうすぐ、十二時になります。It'll be twelve o'clock soon.

（４）おたまじゃくしは、かえるになりました。A tadpole became a frog.

（５）まいどありがとうございます。みんなで五千円になります。
Thank you for your patronage.  The total would be five thousand yen.

（６）１０＋９０は、百になります。Ten plus ninety makes one hundred.
      足す(to add)

（７）日本語が　じょうずになりましたね。Your Japanese has improved.

（８）かなこちゃんは、おとなになって、とてもきれいになりました。
Kanako has grown up and become very pretty.

（９）二月になりました。だから、さむいんですね。
               (therefore, for that reason)
It's become February.  That's why it's cold.

## 6. ～くなる: **to become so and so**

When "naru なる" is preceded by an adjective, its form is " –ku naru く なる." Just as "-ni naru になる" shows a change from one stage to another, it also describes a change in state or condition. For example, with the increase of temperature, change is expressed in the form of "stem of adjective (without 'i') + "ku" + "naru," （おんどが）たかくなりました。 If expressing a yearly phenomenal change in the spring, you may say 春は、あたたかくなります。

| Stem of Adjectives (no final 'i') たか≠、あたたか≠、さむ≠、etc. From (たかい、あたたかい、さむい) | + く なる |
|---|---|

- （１）さむくなりましたね。もう冬ですね。
  It's become cold. It's already winter.
- （２）もうすぐ四月ですから、あたたかくなりますよ。
  It will be nice and warm because it's almost April.
- （３）きょうは、おんどが　たかくなるかな。
  I wonder if the temperature today will become higher.
- （４）さとうを入れてみました。おいしくなりました。
  I tried adding sugar. It became more delicious.

## 7. ～に住んでいます **I live in ~.**

Particle "ni に" is used with static verbs such as "live," since living is considered a static action, as with the idea that plants do not change location of existence, unlike how animals can move around. "Sunde すんで" is the "te" form of the verb "sumu すむ (to live) and when the "te" form is followed by "imasu います," it expresses either an "on-going action," or a "present state of being." "Sunde imase すんでいます" would be the case of the latter. In chapter 4(E), we observed another example, "shitte imasu しっています," which means "I know (it)."

Read the following dialogue and answer the questions:

A: らいねん、パサデナに　住むんですよ。

B: いいですね。私の妹がパサデナに　住んでいますが、とてもいいところ
　　ですよ。

A: たのしみです。

Question 1: Does A-san now live in Pasadena?
Question 2: Who lives in Pasadena now?

The answer for Q 1 is "No," since A said "すむ" (will live) in Pasadena "next year," and the answer for Q 2 is B's younger sister.

Chapter 7 Exercises れんしゅうもんだい

A-1. <u>Practice on "node"</u>

"Node" shows a reason and it is followed by a main clause that shows a consequence. Choose the right answer in the following exercises.  Remember the following rules: (In a non-past tense sentence)

> 1.  Adjective (い) +  node
> 2.  Noun & Copula Noun + (な) node
> 3.  Dictionary form Verb (non-past) + node

1. おいしい（ので、なので）、もっとたべます。

2. たかい（ので、なので）、かいません。

3. げんき（ので、なので）、うれしいです。
glad

4. ひま（ので、なので）、ひるねをします。
   (free of time)                 nap

5. 日本へ行く（ので、なので）、おみやげを　かいます。
souvenir

6. さむい（ので、なので）、まどを　しめます。
close

7. きれい（ので、なので）、かいます。

8. たんじょうび（ので、なので）、プレゼントが　ほしいです。

9. ともだちがくる（ので、なので）、そうじします。
clean up

10. じかんが　ない（ので、なので）、いそいでください。
    time                                Please hurry.

A-2. Combine sentences with "node." The first sentence is the reason for the second.

1. わたしは、ねぼうです。おいしいパンは、もうありません。

2. そのセーターは、たかいです。かいません。

3. キャシーさんは、きれいです。うらやましい(envious)です。

4. どようびです。クラスは、ありません。

5. カレーライスをつくります。マーケットへいきます。

6. あしたは、ひまです。いっしょにえいがを　みましょう。

B. かっこの中にことばを入れなさい。 Fill in the blanks with suitable words.

1. きせつは（　　　　　　　）になりました。だから、あたたかいです。

2. （　　　　　　　）になりました。だから、あついです。

3. （　　　　　　　）になりました。だから、すずしいです。

4. （　　　　　　　）になりました。だから、さむいです。

5. へやをそうじしました。だから，（　　　　　　　）になりました。
   (heya: room) (sooji: clean, vacuum)

6. 日本語を毎日れんしゅうしました。だから，（　　　　　　　）になりました。

7. クリスマスの日、お父さんは、（　　　　　　　）になりました。

8. 姉は、こどもが　好きなので、（　　　　　　　）になりました。

9. 兄は、りょうりが　好きなので、（　　　　　　　）になりました。

10. 成人式の日に（　　　　　　　）になりました。
   (Seijin-shiki: Ceremony for Coming of Age)

11. 3＋5は、（　　　　　　　）になります。
   （3 足す 5）

12. 9－7は、2 に （　　　　　　　）。
   （9 引く 2）

13. 「まいどありがとうございます。みんなで二千円（　　　　　　　）。」

C. Change the following sentences into ones using "naru."

れい：日本語は、むずかしいです。 →　日本語は、むずかし<u>くなりました</u>。

1. しゅくだいを見て、あたまがいたいです。 →

２．くるまは、古いです。→
　　car　　　　old

３．さいきん、さむいです。→
　　recently

４．このごろ、あついです。→
　　recently

５．となりのむすこさんは、大きいです。→
　　our next-door neighbor's son

６．へやが、広いです。→
　　　　　　spacious

７．スカートが　みじかいです。→
　　　　　　　　　short

８．かみが　ながいです。→
　　　　　　long

９．スパイスを入れて、カレーがおいしいです。→
　　spices

１０．しおを入れて、からいです。→
　　　　salt

D. Change the question from its formal form to a soft casual form.
(Change "desu ka/masu ka" to the "plain form + no")

Example:

例：今、行きますか。→　今、行くの？
　１．　　ここに　いますか。→
　２．　　どこに　ありますか。→
　３．　　今、食べますか。→
　４．　　明日は、どうしますか。→
　５．　　ビールを飲みますか。→
　６．　　これから、来ますか。→
　７．　　でんしゃに　のりますか。→
　８．　　日本語を話しますか。→
　９．　　あの信号で、曲がりますか。→
　１０．このズボンを買いますか。→

E. Change to "~ n desu ka," or "~ n desu," so that the new sentences include strong sense of "inquiry or surprise" (~ n desu ka) or speaker's attempt to "explain" (~ n desu).

1. 明日、行きますか。

2. 今、食べますか。

3. 一時間かかりますか。

4. テストが　むずかしいです。

5. おいしくないです。

6. ひまです。

7. びょうき (ill)です。

F.  Answer with " ~ n desu," to show your attempt to explain why.

1. どうしてクラスを　休むんですか。→

Hints:　あたまがいたい (my head hutts)

ねつがある (have a fever)

裁判所 (court) へいく

2. どうして　まどを　あけるんですか。→

Hints:

あつい

きれいな空気 (air) がほしい

3. 食べないんですか。→

Hints:

食欲 (appetite) がない

今食べたところ (I've just eaten.)

4.よく食べますねぇ～！→

Hints:

おいしい

すきだ

5. 元気がないですねぇ～　→

Hints:

びょうきだ

クラスがむずかしい

お金が　ない

G.  Combine sentences using "node."

1. (1) 私は、ねぼうです。

(2) ときどき、クラスに遅れます (become late)。

2. (1) 花火 (firework) がきれいです。
   (2) 見に行きました。

3. (1) そのとけいは 高いです。
   (2) 買いませんでした。

4. (1) その駅まで、遠いです。
   (2) 車で 行きました。

5. (1) ピクニックがあります。
   (2) おべんとう (boxed lunch) をつくりました。

6. (1) 暗い へや (dark room) の中にいます。
   (2) よく 見えません。

H. Choose "aida" or "aida ni" for each sentence as appropriate.

1. 私が食べている (          )、ここでまっていてください。
   (am eating)                              (please wait)

2. クラスの (          )、ずっと ねていました。
                        (throughout the time)

3. 六時から九時の (          )、ここに 来てください。

4. 私は、たいてい、十時半から十一時の (          )、ねます。

5. しけんの (          )、ずっと ないていました。
   (examination)              (was crying)

I. Fill in the blanks with appropriate words.

1. あなたは、(          ) 住んでいますか。

2. あなたは、(          ) ロサンジェルスに来ましたか。

3. りょうの食事は、(          ) ですか。

4. 今日の朝ごはんは、(          ) を食べましたか。

5．和食〔わしょく〕（　　　　）洋食〔ようしょく〕（　　　　）あります。

6．みんなが買〔か〕うんですか。とても（　　　　　　　）があるんですね。

7．りょうの朝〔あさ〕ごはんは、七時〔しちじ〕（　　　　　）八時〔はちじ〕（　　　　）でしょう？

8．今年〔ことし〕で、何才〔なんさい〕（　　　　　　）なりますか。

9．まだ日本語が（　　　　　　）なので、しゅくだいに時間〔じかん〕がかかるんです。

10．あなたなら、すぐ、（　　　　　　　）になりますよ。

11．私〔わたし〕は、まだこどもです。（　　　　　）、Ｒえいがは、だめなんです。
　　　　　　　　　　　　　　R-rated movie

J. Pair-work: Ask your classmates the following questions and report the answers to the class.

1. Ask if s/he is an early bird or a late-riser.
2. Ask how old s/he will become on the next birthday.
3. Ask where s/he lives.
4. Ask if s/he lives in a dormitory.
5. Ask which s/he prefers, Western or Japanese food
6. Ask what s/he will become in the future.

K. Fill in the bubbles in the illustration with Japanese statements.

Chapter 7: Dict-A-Conversation
Listen to Chapter 7's Dict-A-Conversation on the student CD, and write in the checkmark in either "Truth" or "False" columns, after judging the credibility of each statement.

| statements | Truth （ほんとう） | False （うそ） |
|---|---|---|
| 1 | | |
| 2 | | |
| 3 | | |
| 4 | | |
| 5 | | |
| 6 | | |
| 7 | | |
| 8 | | |
| 9 | | |
| 10 | | |

Chapter 7– (1)

| 住<br>(to live) | す（む）<br>ジュウ | 住む（すむ）to live<br>[住所（じゅうしょ）an address]<br>住人（じゅうにん）a resident |
| | | (7)<br>ノ イ イ 广 仠 仹 住 |
| 和<br>(harmony;<br>Japanese) | かず<br>ワ | 和子（かずこ）girl's name<br>和（わ）sum, harmony<br>[平和（へいわ）peace]<br>和食（わしょく）Japanese food<br>[和風（わふう）Japanese style]<br>[和室（わしつ）a Japanese style room] |
| | | (8)<br>一 ニ 千 千 禾 禾 和 和 |
| 洋<br>(ocean) | ヨウ | [太平洋（たいへいよう）the Pacific Ocean]<br>洋食（ようしょく）western food<br>[洋風（ようふう）western style]<br>[洋室（ようしつ）a western style room] |
| | | (9)<br>丶 氵 氵 泸 泮 泮 洋 洋 |
| 甘<br>(sweet) | あま（い）<br>カン | 甘い（あまい）sweet<br>甘味（あまみ）sweetness |
| | | (5)<br>一 十 廿 甘 甘 |
| 間<br>(between, room) | あいだ<br>ま<br>カン<br>ケン | この間（あいだ）the other day<br>日本間（にほんま）a Japanese style room<br>洋間（ようま）a western style room<br>間に合う（まにあう）to make in time<br>時間（じかん）time<br>間食（かんしょく）snacks |
| | | (12)<br>｜ 冂 冂 冂 冃 門 門 門 門 間 間 間 |

Chapter 7 – (2)

| 事 (matters, events) | こと ジ | いい事（いいこと）a good thing<br>人事（じんじ）human matters<br>[用事（ようじ）an errand]<br>知事（ちじ）a governor<br>食事（しょくじ）meal<br>火事（かじ）a fire<br>大事（だいじ）important |
|---|---|---|
| | | (8)<br>一 亇 亇 亖 亖 写 写 事 |
| 戸 (door, household) | と コ | 戸（と）a door<br>戸口（とぐち）an entrance<br>戸田（とだ）a surname<br>井戸（いど）a well<br>一戸（いっこ）one household |
| | | (4)<br>一 ラ ヨ 戸 |
| 所 (a place) | ところ ショ ジョ | 所（ところ）a place; an address<br>住所（じゅうしょ）an address<br>[所在（しょざい）one's whereabouts] |
| | | (8)<br>一 ラ ヨ 戸 戸 所 所 所 |

## Kanji Practice for Chapter 7
かんじの　れんしゅう

1. つぎの　ことばを　よみなさい。それから、クラスメートにいみをきき
   なさい。 Read the following words/sentences to your classmates and ask them
   for the meaning of each word/sentence.

   （1）アパートに住んでいる。

   （2）甘いおかし

   （3）ロサンジェルスとパサデナの間

   （4）時間がない。

   （5）よく間食をします。（= おやつを食べます）

   （6）何かいい事が、ある。

(7)　　　火事、大事、用事

(8)　　　<u>おすしのような</u>和食が好きです。
　　　　　sushi-like

(9)　　　カレーライスは、洋食です。

(10)　　　ケーキは、洋<ruby>菓<rt>がし</rt></ruby>子です。

(11)　　　その戸をあけて、<u>まっすぐ</u>行きなさい。
　　　　　　　　　　　　　　　　straight

(12)　　　古い井戸

(13)　　　パサデナは、いい所です。

(14)　　　住所は、パサデナです。

2. Write kanji in the box to complete the compound word.

(1)　important/precious

(2) fire

(3)　address

(4) Japanese food

(5)　Western food

(6) snacks between meals

(7)　a well

3. かんじとひらがなで　こたえなさい。 Rewrite the sentences with kanji and hiragana and answer the questions in complete sentences.

(1) あなたは、だいがくのりょうにすんでいますか。

(2) わしょくが　すきですか。

(3) あまいものを　よくたべますか。

(4) きょうのごご、じかんが　ありますか。

(5) きょうしつの　と　は、どこに　ありますか。

(6) どんなところで　たべるのが　すきですか。

(7) こくばん　と　がくせいのあいだに　なにが　ありますか。
(Use kanji "kuro" for the first portion of the word, "blackboard.")

(8) きょう　なにか　いいことが　ありましたか。

(9) あなたのじゅうしょは、パサデナですか。

(10) まいにち　なんじかんぐらい　ねますか。

(11)　「<u>かんしょく</u>」って、<u>なん</u>ですか。

(12)　<u>かじ</u>は、どこで　ありましたか。

(13)　「オムライス」は、<u>ようしょく</u>ですか。

4.かんじとひらがなで　かきなさい。Write in kanji and hiragana.

(14)　それは、<u>わたし</u>の　<u>だいじ</u>な<u>ほん</u>です。

(15)　<u>てまえ</u>の　<u>と</u>を　あけてください。

(16)　<u>なまえ</u>と　<u>ところ</u>を　かいてください。

(17)　<u>ふるい</u><u>いど</u>は、あぶないですよ。

(18)　あそこに、<u>いのうえ</u>さんが　<u>みえます</u>。

(19)　"Ceiling"は、「天井」（てんじょう）と　<u>いいます</u>。

(20)　ガスの<u>ひ</u>を　<u>ちいさく</u>してください。

# <u>Ouch!</u>

*Expressions*
"What's wrong?"
"Does it hurt?"
"Do you have eye drops?"
 "I wonder if something got in my eye"

*Casual forms*

*Kanji practice from Chapter 8*

Chapter 8          Ouch!     いたい！

モニカ：あっ、いたい！                                              1

あいこ：どうしたの？                                                2

モニカ：目<sub>め</sub>が、、、                                        3

あいこ：目<sub>め</sub>がどうしたの？   いたいの？   何<sub>なに</sub>か　入<sub>はい</sub>ったの？   4

モニカ：目薬<sub>めぐすり</sub>が　ありますか。                            5

あいこ：ええ、持<sub>も</sub>っています。ここに、、、、                    6

モニカ：ありがとう。ちょっと　かしてください。                        7

　　　　あ〜、助<sub>たす</sub>かった！                                 8

あいこ：虫<sub>むし</sub>か、ほこりでも入<sub>はい</sub>ったのかな？   もう　いたくない？   9

モニカ：はい、だいじょうぶです。でも、いたかった！                   10

Chapter 8
[English translation:]
Monica: Ouch!
Aiko:    What's the matter?
Monica: My eye…
Aiko:    What happened to your eye?  Did something get in?
Monica: Do you have eye drops?
Aiko:    Yes, I do.  (It's) right here.
Monica: Thank you.  Please let me use it.  Wow, (you) saved me!
Aiko:     I wonder if it's caused by insect or dust.  Does it still hurt?
Monica: I am fine now.  But…Boy!  Was it painful!

[Vocabulary List]
1. Expressions

| | |
|---|---|
| あっ！ | expression of surprise |
| あ〜 | expression of relief |
| （かな？） | I wonder… |

2. Nouns

| | |
|---|---|
| （め　目） | eye(s) |
| めぐすり　（目薬） | eye drop |
| むし(虫) | bugs, insects |
| ほこり | dust |

3. Copula Nouns

| | |
|---|---|
| （だいじょうぶ　大丈夫） | all right, no problem |

4. Adjectives

| | |
|---|---|
| いたい | painful, |
| いたくない | is not painful |
| いたかった | was painful |
| いたくなかった | wasn't painful |

5. Verbs

| | |
|---|---|
| （はいる　入る） | to enter |
| はいった | entered |
| （もつ　持つ） | to hold, have |
| もっている（持っている） | (I) have, own |
| かす(貸す) | to loan |
| 　　かして | "te" form of "kasu" |
| （たすかる　助かる） | to be rescued, saved (Chapter 2[C]) |
| 　　たすかった | was saved; past tense of "tasukaru" |
| した | did; past tense of "suru" |

6. Particles

| | |
|---|---|
| でも | or something like that |
| ほこりでも | dust or something like that |

----------------------------------------------------------------------------

Additional Vocabulary from Grammar Notes, Exercises, and Dict-A-Conversation

----------------------------------------------------------------------------

[Nouns]

| | |
|---|---|
| みち | street |
| かぜ | a cold |
| くすり | medicine |
| かぜぐすり | cold medicine |
| クラブ | club activities at school |
| にほんえん （日本円） | Japanese currency |
| デジカメ | digital camera |
| ぼうし | hat |

[Adjectives]

| | |
|---|---|
| すくない | fewer |

[Verbs]

| | |
|---|---|
| とぶ | to fly; jump |
| しぬ | to die |
| ならう | to learn |
| たつ | to stand up |
| ぬぐ | to remove; take off |
| またせる | to make someone wait |
| ([～を] でる) | to leave a place |
| みえる | to be visible |
| でかける | to go out |
| いらっしゃる | to go, come, & stay in a polite form |
| かける | to hung |
| なさる | to do (polite form) |
| いただく | to receive |
| (かえす) | to return something (transitive verb) |

[Conjunctive Particle]

| | |
|---|---|
| とき | time; when |

Chapter 8                    Grammar and Cultural Notes

## 1. <u>Casual and Formal</u>

To learn casual form is important not only because we want to speak casually with our friends, but also it is grammatically necessary in certain expressions (such as before "n desu," before "node," before "kara," before "kana" and before "deshoo ka," and also in sentence modifiers [relative clauses] that we will learn later).

## [Formal]

### <u>Nouns</u>

How does the verb end after nouns in formal speech?  Look at the chart below.

|          | affirmative | negative |
|----------|-------------|----------|
| Non-past | です | じゃありません |
| Past | でした | じゃありませんでした |

### <u>Adjectives</u>

How does the verb end after adjectives in formal speech?

|          | affirmative | negative |
|----------|-------------|----------|
| Non-past | です | くありません |
| Past | かったです | くありませんでした |

### <u>Verbs</u>

How about the verbs in formal speech?

|          | affirmative | negative |
|----------|-------------|----------|
| Non-past | ます | ません |
| Past | ました | ませんでした |

## [Casual]
## <u>Nouns</u>

Casual Predicate Patterns that come after Nouns.

|          | affirmative | negative |
|----------|-------------|----------|
| Non-past | だ | じゃない |
| Past | だった | じゃなかった |

### <u>Adjectives</u>

Casual Predicate Patterns that come after Adjectives.

|          | affirmative | negative |
|----------|-------------|----------|
| Non-past | ----(い) | くない |
| Past | かった | くなかった |

## Verbs

Examine how Japanese verbs end in casual speech.  This is a formula:

|  | affirmative | negative |
|---|---|---|
| Non-past | **Dictionary form** | **-nai form** |
| Past | **"ta" form** | **na-katta** |

For example, if the verb is a Consonant Verb (Regular Conjugating Verb) such as "aru-ki-masu あるきます," its casual form is "aru-ku. あるく," and its negative form is "aru-ka-nai."  Since this verb "aru-ki-masu" belongs to a Consonant Verb, its conjugation is "ka-ki-ku-ke-ko," and the Base 1 is used for a negative form and the Base 3 is used for an affirmative form.  Take a look at the conjugation chart of this verb "aru-ki-masu."

```
        Base 1 (ka)  + nai
        Base 2 (ki)  + masu
aru-    Base 3 (ku)
        Base 4 (ke)
        Base 5 (ko)
```

What if the verb is in the past tense?  In that case, you need to use one more conjugation called the "te て" form.  The casual past tense verb in Japanese is called the "ta た" form, and its formation is simply change the "e" of the "te" form to "a" to make the "ta" form.  As you have learned how to make the "te て" form in Chapter 6D, you know the "te て" form of "aruku あるく" is "aruite あるいて," so simply change "te て" to "ta た" to make its past tense, "aruita あるいた."  See the chart below:

|  | affirmative | negative |
|---|---|---|
| Non-past | あるく | あるかない |
| Past | あるいた | あるかなかった |

See another example of a consonant verb, "hanashi-masu はなします":

|  | affirmative | negative |
|---|---|---|
| Non-past | はなす | はなさない |
| Past | はなした | はなさなかった |

If the verb belongs to Vowel Verbs (Non-Conjugating Verbs [that typically end with "-eru" or "-iru"]), then it's much simpler.  If you wish to find the casual form of "tabe-masu たべます," for example, change "masu ます" to "ru る" for its casual non-past tense and change "ru る" to "ta た" for its past tense, while keeping the stem part, "tabe たべ," unchanged.

|  | affirmative | negative |
|---|---|---|
| Non-past | たべる | たべない |
| Past | たべた | たべなかった |

The formation of negative form is also simple: Add "nai ない" to the stem. The outcome is "tabe-nai たべない," and its past tense is "tabe-na-katta たべなかった."

Look at another example of a Vowel Verb, "mi-masu みます"

|  | affirmative | negative |
|---|---|---|
| Non-past | みる | みない |
| Past | みた | みなかった |

For the detailed information about the Japanese Verbs, read "About Japanese Verbs" in the grammar section of Chapter 5.

## 2. <u>How to make the た form verb: Casual Past tense verb</u>

Remember you learned the "te" form verbs in Chapter 6D? You can easily derive the "ta" form from the same rules. Simply change "te" to "ta" to make the verb past tense casual. Remember the "te" form rule song in Chapter 6D?

```
むぶぬ  →  んで
うつる  →  って
く     →  いて
ぐ     →  いで
す     →  して  are the consonant verbs
```

The "te" to "ta": た form song (Casual past tense)

```
むぶぬ  →  んだ
うつる  →  った
く     →  いた
ぐ     →  いだ
す     →  した  are the consonant verbs
```

Examples:

| Ending syllables | Casual Non-past tense verbs | | Casual Past tense verbs |
|---|---|---|---|
| む | よむ | read | よんだ |
|  | のむ | drink | のんだ |
|  | すむ | live | すんだ |
| ぶ | とぶ | fly | とんだ |
| ぬ | しぬ | die | しんだ |
| う | かう | buy | かった |
|  | ならう | learn | ならった |
|  | あう | meet | あった |

| つ | たつ | stand up | たった |
|---|---|---|---|
| る | はしる | run | はしった |
| | ある | exist | あった |
| | わかる | understand | わかった |
| | はじまる | begin | はじまった |
| | おわる | end | おわった |
| | しる | discover | しった |
| く | かく | write | かいた |
| | あるく | walk | あるいた |
| ぐ | ぬぐ | take off | ぬいだ |
| す | はなす | speak | はなした |
| | おもいだす | recall | おもいだした |

- There is one exception among the listed consonant verbs that doesn't follow the same rules: "go" 行く. Its "te" form is 行って, and "ta" form is 行った.

The above rules apply only to consonant verbs (regular conjugating verbs). Vowel verbs don't follow complex rules. Simply use the <u>stem</u> of the vowel verb (after dropping "ru" or "masu") and add "ta." The vowel verbs typically end with "eru" or "iru." Examples:

たべる taberu　→　たべた　　　　　おきる okiru　→　おきた

みる　miru　→　みた　　　　　　　ねる　neru　→　ねた

みえる mieru　→　みえた　　　　　いる　iru　→　いた

- There are exceptions to the "eru" and "iru" rule, as some consonant verbs have "eru" or "iru" endings. Examples were shown in the Chapter 5 Grammar and Culture Notes. They include:
  はいる(enter)　　　→　　はいった
  はしる(run)　　　→　　はしった
  かえる(return)　　→　　かえった
  しる(get to know)　→　　しった

- There are two irregular verbs in Japanese: する "do" and くる "come." Their "te" and "ta" forms are して、きて、and also した、きた respectively.

## 3. <u>How to make かった Past tense affirmative form of Adjectives</u>

The tense of an adjective is expressed in either the "i" or "katta" portion of it, and not in the "desu." While "desu" after a noun performs as a copula verb, "desu" after an adjective would become an auxiliary verb expressing formality. Thus, "oishii" is casual and "oishii desu" is formal; and "oishikatta" is casual and "oishikatta desu" is formal.

Examples of Affirmative Adjectives:

| Adjectives | Non-past tense | Past tense |
|---|---|---|
| painful | いたい | いたかった |
| desirable | ほしい | ほしかった |
| want to go | いきたい | いきたかった |

## 4. How to make くなかった Past tense negative form of Adjectives

The "nai" form is adjectival since it ends with "i." Its past tense is "na-katta."
The plain negative past tense of an adjective is "~ ku nakatta."

＊Since the negative form of verb is also "-nai" form, you can apply this adjectival conjugation to the negative verbs. See the bottom three lines of the chart below.

Negative Adjectives and Verbs

| Adjectives | Non-past tense | Past tense |
|---|---|---|
| not painful | いたくない | いたくなかった |
| not desirable | ほしくない | ほしくなかった |
| don't want to go | いきたくない | いきたくなかった |
| won't go | いかない | いかなかった |
| won't see | みない | みなかった |

- Note the "tai form" (such as "iki-tai 行きたい") and the negative verb form (such as "ika-nai 行かない") are adjectival. Therefore, their past tense form is "katta," as in "iki-ta-katta 行きたかった" and "ika-na-katta 行かなかった," respectively. The Auxiliary Adjective "tai" form will be formally introduced in Chapter 10A.

- The word "hoshii ほしい" is also adjectival. It means "I want (it)," but it should be best translated into English as "something being desirable," as it is preceded by the particle "ga が," a subjective case marker.

  Example:
  パンがほしい（です）。I want bread. (Bread is desirable.)

  パンがほしかった（です）。I wanted bread. (Bread was desirable.)

## 5. How to make だった: casual form of copula verb でした

だった is a **past** tense of だ and it is used after nouns and copula nouns. Its English equivalent is "(it) was."
For example,

| | (Formal) | (Casual) |
|---|---|---|
| It was me. | 私でした。 | 私だった。 |

| | | |
|---|---|---|
| It was summer. | 夏<ruby>なつ</ruby>でした。 | 夏<ruby>なつ</ruby>だった。 |
| It was pretty. | きれいでした。 | きれいだった。 |
| This park was famous. | 有名<ruby>ゆうめい</ruby>でした。 | 有名<ruby>ゆうめい</ruby>だった。 |

[Caution] Distinguish the past tense of Adjectives and Copula Nouns.
Which is correct?

１．きのうは、さくらが　きれい（a. だった、b. かった）です。
２．きょうは、とても　いそがし（a. だった、b. かった）です。
３．ともだちは、きのう　げんき（a. だった、b. かった）です。
４．パサデナは、きょうも　あつ（a. だった、b. かった）です。

(Correct answers are: a, b, a, and b.)

**6. Expressing "ownership" or "possession": もっています**

The "te" form of "motsu" (to hold) + "imasu" means "possession" or "ownership,"
aside from its original meaning, "holding something."
Examples:
(1) ハンカチをもっています。I have a handkerchief (with me).
(2) 女<ruby>おんな</ruby>の子<ruby>こ</ruby>は、（手<ruby>て</ruby>に）ぬいぐるみを　もっています。
A girl has a stuffed animal in her hand.
(3) かぞくを　もっています。I have a family.
(4) くるまを　もっています。I have a car.
(5) お金<ruby>かね</ruby>を　もっています。I have some money.
(6) 家<ruby>いえ</ruby>を　もっています。I have a house.

**7. Sentence Final Particle "kana? かな" to express "wondering"**

If you add "kana かな" to the end of a sentence, you can express wondering. In
that case, the end of a preceding sentence is usually in a casual form. Remember not
to use "da だ" ending before "kana かな." See the examples:

[Adjectives]
(1)　この本は　たかいかな？　　　　　　I wonder if this book is expensive.
(2)　この本は　たかかったかな？　　　　I wonder if this book was expensive.
[Verbs]
(1)　田中さんは　あした、日本へ行くかな？ I wonder if Tanaka-san will go to
　　　　　　　　　　　　　　　　　　　　　　Japan tomorrow.
(2)　田中さんは　きのう、日本へ行ったかな？ I wonder if Tanaka-san went to
　　　　　　　　　　　　　　　　　　　　　　Japan yesterday.

[Nouns]
(1)　午後は、雨かな？（雨だかな is wrong.）I wonder if it will rain this afternoon.
(2)　午前中は、雨だったかな？　　　　　　I wonder if it rained in the morning.

Chapter 8 Exercises

A. Change the formality from formal to casual.
    Hint: notice that the end of each sentence is a noun. Thus, change "desu" to "da"
    for non-past tense, and "deshita" to "datta" for past tense.

１．きれいな月<sup>つき</sup>ですね。        ２．もう、十時<sup>じゅうじ</sup>です。

３．あしたは、木曜日<sup>もくようび</sup>ですね。    ４．きょうも、雨<sup>あめ</sup>ですね。

５．だいじょうぶですよ。        ６．これ、あなたのですよ。

７．きみの本<sup>ほん</sup>ですよ。        ８．きみのノートです。

９．いいお天気<sup>てんき</sup>ですね。      １０．もう　よるです。

１１．きょうは　いいお天気<sup>てんき</sup>でしたね。  １２．とても　いいえいがでしたよ。

１３．むずかしい本でした。      １４．ひどい雨<sup>あめ</sup>でした。

B. Change the formality from formal to casual. (Hint: omit "desu" for adjectives)

１．あついです。          ２．やさしいです。

３．たかいです。          ４．むずかしいです。

５．やすいですよ。        ６．おもしろいですね。

７．つまらなかったです。     ８．ほしいです。

９．ほしくないです。      １０．ほしかったです。

１１．めずらしくなかったです。   １２．さみしかったです。

C. Change the formality from formal to casual. (Hint: use the dictionary form.)

１．行きます。           ２．かきます。

３．つくります。         ４．はなします。

５．よみます。           ６．あそびます。

７．およぎます。         ８．はいります。

９．ねます。            １０．みます。

１１．おしえます。        １２．おきます。

１３．おります。         １４．あびます。

１５．たべます。         １６．でます。

D. Change the tense from non-past to past.
[Adjectives]  (Change い to かった).

１．いたい      ２．ほしい        ３．ほしくない

４．さむい      ５．はやい        ６．たのしくない

７．あたたかい    ８．すずしい      ９．むずかしくない

１０．わるい     *１１．いい        １２．おもしろくない

１３．おそい     １４．うらやましい    １５．はずかしい

１６．かわいい    １７．わかい        １８．あぶない

１９．あまい     ２０．からい        ２１．はずかしくない

E. Change the tense from non-past to past.
[Adjectives] (Change the dictionary form to the "た" form).

(1) Consonant verbs
1. いく       2. かく        3. はなす
4. つくる      5. よむ        6. あそぶ
7. およぐ      8. はいる       9. かえる
10. いう      11. ある       12. はじまる
13. おわる     14. しる       15. はしる
16. のむ      17. あるく      18. すむ
19. なる      20. しぬ       21. わかる

(1) Vowel verbs (Change "る" to "た").

1. ねる       2. みる        3. おしえる
4. おきる      5. あびる       6. たべる
7. でる       8. みえる       9. おりる
10. いる      11. でかける     12. はじまる
13. あける     14. しめる      15. とじる
16. うまれる    17. にげる      18. あげる
19. うける     20. くれる      21. いきる

(3) Irregular verbs
1. する                    2. くる

F. What would Caesar have said if he said "I came, I saw, and I won" in Japanese?
   Hint: use past tense casual of "くる、みる、かつ."

G-1. Add かな to the end of each sentence, so that you can include the idea of
"wondering." Remember to use "casual form" ending before you add かな?

1. I wonder if this test is difficult.
2. I wonder if homework is boring.
3. I wonder if this test is easy.
4. I wonder if this cake is sweet.
5. I wonder if my mother is well（げんき）.
6. I wonder if this school is famous.
7. I wonder if flowers（はな）in the park are pretty.
8. I wonder if Mr. Saitoo is good（じょうず）at English.
9. I wonder if the bus will leave（でる）soon（もうすぐ）.
10. I wonder if my dogs have already（もう）eaten.
11. I wonder if train has already left.

G-2. [Past-tense adjectives] Come up with a Japanese response for each given situation, ending with かな、、. Write in complete sentences.

12.  Looking at the students struggling with the test he gave, the teacher says:

13.  After splitting cake for Kate and Kevin, Mom wonders whether she's given more to Kate, saying: ☺

14.  After missing today's party, you say:

15.  After choosing between two streets, you wonder if you made a dangerous decision:

16.  After choosing a taxi, you get into a traffic jam.  You mumble to yourself, wondering if going by subway would be faster:

H. [Non-past verbs] Add かな and translate into English.

１．田中さんも行きます。
２．きょうは、テストがあります。
３．トムは、もうすぐ きます。
４．きょうは、クラスで、本をよみます。
５．カレンは、ドレスを買います。

[Past-tense verbs] Add かな and translate into English.

１．ともだちは、もうおひるごはんを食べました。

２．でんしゃは、もうえきを出ました。
　　　　　　　　　　　　　（でる to leave）

３．なにか、目に入りました。

４．母は、もう　かぜの 薬 を飲みました。
　　　　　　　to take a cold medication

５．父は、もうかいしゃへ　行きました。
　　　　　　　company

I. Pair-work: create dialogue with your partner with the given situations.

1.  Suddenly your eye hurt.  So you ask your partner for eye drops.  Luckily, s/he has them and they help you out.  You thank your partner, but s/he is still wondering if a bug or something else got into your eye.

2.  You wonder if you have a cold, and ask your partner if s/he has cold medicine.  Your partner, who doesn't have any medication with him/her, apologizes.  You wonder if your teacher has some instead.

3.  You wonder if you have a vocabulary test today in Japanese class.  You ask your classmate, and the response you receive is yes.  Needing to check on one vocabulary word, but not having a dictionary with you, you try borrowing one from your classmate.  S/he allows you to borrow it.  Now that you have a dictionary, you quickly look it up, and return it to him/her, thanking for his/her help.

J. Ask your classmates if they have the following items.  Mark (X) when someone doesn't have the item and (O) when someone does.

A：　〜さん、〜を　もっていますか。

B：　ええ、もっています。Or,
　　　いいえ、もっていません。

| | さん | さん | さん | さん |
|---|---|---|---|---|
| とけい | | | | |
| 日本円 | | | | |
| 日本語のじしょ | | | | |
| かぜぐすり | | | | |
| デジカメ | | | | |
| コンピューター | | | | |
| けいたいでんわ | | | | |
| 百ドル | | | | |
| iPod | | | | |
| iPhone | | | | |

K.  Pair-work: What did you do and how was it?
Today is Friday, November 30<sup>th</sup>.  The calendar below shows what you did and how
things were.  If the picture shows an X, you didn't do something.  Create a conversation
with your partner, describing your schedule.

Example:
A:十一月一日の木曜日は、何をしましたか。
B:その日は、テストをうけました。
A:どうでしたか。
B:ひどかったです。２５点でした。
A:５０点満点で？
B:いえ、１００点満点で、、、
A:それは　ざんねんでしたね。
B:ええ、こんどは、がんばります。

[１１月のカレンダー]

| Sunday | Monday | Tuesday | Wednesday | Thursday | Friday | Saturday |
|---|---|---|---|---|---|---|
| | | | | | 1 | 2 |
| 3 | 4 | 5 | 6 | 7 | 8 | 9 |
| 10 | 11 | 12 | 13 | 14 | 15 | 16 |
| 17 | 18 | 19 | 20 | 21 | 22 | 23 |
| 24 | 25 | 26 | 27 | 28 | 29 | 30 |

おととい　　きのう　　きょう

Practice on Non-Past Casual Verb Forms:  Fill in the blanks.

Group 1 (Vowel Verbs)

| Affirmative | Negative |
|---|---|
| たべる | たべない |
| ねる | |
| おきる | |
| いる | |
| あびる | |
| あける | |

| Affirmative | Negative |
|---|---|
| しめる | |
| あげる | |
| くれる | |
| にげる | |
| おりる | |
| まける | |

Group 2 (Consonant Verbs)

| Affirmative | Negative |
|---|---|
| のむ | のまない |
| はなす | |
| よむ | |
| かく | |
| つくる | |
| すわる | |

| Affirmative | Negative |
|---|---|
| たつ | |
| 行く （いく） | |
| 言う （いう） | |
| あるく | |
| のる | |
| 勝つ （かつ） | |

Group 3 (Deceptive-looking Consonant Verbs)

| Affirmative | Negative |
|---|---|
| 切る （きる） | 切らない |
| 入る （はいる） | |
| 走る （はしる） | |
| 知る （しる） | |
| 帰る （かえる） | |
| 要る （いる） | |

| Affirmative | Negative |
|---|---|
| 散る （ちる） | |
| しゃべる | |
| 参る （まいる） | |
| | |
| | |
| | |

Group 4 (Mixed group)

| Affirmative | Negative |
|---|---|
| あげる | |
| もつ | |
| はしる | |
| 返す （かえす） | |
| 帰る （かえる） | |
| あるく | |

| Affirmative | Negative |
|---|---|
| たべる | |
| ねる | |
| 知る （しる） | |
| しぬ | |
| いれる | |
| かく | |

Practice on Non-Past Adjectives: Fill in the blanks.
<u>Group 1</u> (Change from formal to Casual form)

| Formal | Casual |
|---|---|
| あついです | あつい |
| さむいです | |
| あたたかいです | |
| すずしいです | |
| むずかしいです | |
| やさしいです | |

| Formal | Casual |
|---|---|
| うれしいです | |
| さみしいです | |
| つまらないです | |
| たかいです | |
| やすいです | |
| おいしいです | |

<u>Group 2</u> (Change from Affirmative to Negative)

| Affirmative | Negative |
|---|---|
| あつい | あつくない |
| さむい | |
| あたたかい | |
| すずしい | |
| むずかしい | |
| やさしい | |

| Affirmative | Negative |
|---|---|
| うれしい | |
| さみしい | |
| つまらない | |
| たかい | |
| やすい | |
| おいしい | |

Past Tense Negative
<u>Group 3</u> (Change from non-past negative to past-tense negative)

| Non-Past | Past |
|---|---|
| あつくない | あつくなかった |
| さむくない | |
| あたたかくない | |
| すずしくない | |
| むずかしくない | |
| やさしくない | |

| Non-Past | Past |
|---|---|
| うれしくない | |
| さみしくない | |
| つまらなくない | |
| たかくない | |
| やすくない | |
| おいしくない | |

Past Tense Affirmative
<u>Group 4</u> (Change from non-past to past tense **affirmative**: Use stem + "katta")

| Non-past | Past |
|---|---|
| あつい | あつかった |
| さむい | |
| あたたかい | |
| すずしい | |
| むずかしい | |
| やさしい | |

| Non-past | Past |
|---|---|
| うれしい | うれしかった |
| さみしい | |
| つまらない | |
| たかい | |
| やすい | |
| おいしい | |

Chapter 8: Dict-A-Conversation

Listen to Chapter 8's Dict-A-Conversation on the student CD, and write in the checkmark in either "Truth" or "False" columns, after judging the credibility of each statement.

| statements | Truth （ほんとう） | False （うそ） |
|:---:|:---:|:---:|
| 1 | | |
| 2 | | |
| 3 | | |
| 4 | | |
| 5 | | |
| 6 | | |
| 7 | | |
| 8 | | |
| 9 | | |
| 10 | | |

Chapter 8

| 力 (power, strength) | ちから<br>リキ<br>リョク | 力 (ちから) power, strength<br>力持ち (ちからもち) a person with great physical strength<br>体力 (たいりょく) physical strength<br>強力 (きょうりょく) powerful<br>[怪力 (かいりき) superhuman strength] |
|---|---|---|
| | | (2)<br>フ 力 |
| 薬 (medicine) | くすり<br>ヤク | 薬 (くすり) medicine<br>薬屋 (くすりや) drug store<br>目薬 (めぐすり) eye drop<br>薬学 (やくがく) pharmaceutics<br>薬局 (やっきょく) drug stores |
| | | (16) 一 十 卝 艹 艹 ヴ 芦 苩 苩 茸 荢 萐 薴<br>萐 萐 薬 薬 |
| 虫 (bugs, insects) | むし<br>チュウ | 虫 (むし) insects<br>虫めがね a magnifying glass<br>[昆虫 (こんちゅう) insects] |
| | | (6)<br>丶 口 口 中 虫 虫 |
| 助 (to assist; rescue) | たす (ける)<br>たす (かる)<br>ジョ | 助ける (たすける) to help<br>助かる (たすかる) to be saved<br>助手 (じょしゅ) an assistant<br>[救助 (きゅうじょ) rescue] |
| | | (7)<br>１ Π Ή Ħ 且 助 助 |
| 強 (strong) | つよ (い)<br>こわ (い)<br>キョウ<br>ゴウ | 強い (つよい) strong<br>手強い (てごわい) tough; formidable<br>強大 (きょうだい) powerful<br>強力 (きょうりょく) powerful; mighty<br>勉強 (べんきょう) studying |
| | | (11)<br>フ コ 弓 号 号 弧 弭 弸 弹 強 強 |
| 楽 (enjoyable; to enjoy) | たの (しい)<br>らく<br>ガク | 楽しい (たのしい) enjoyable<br>楽 (らく) ないす a comfortable chair<br>[音楽 (おんがく) music]<br>[楽器 (がっき) musical instruments] |
| | | (13)<br>丶 ｆ 自 自 自 泊 泊 迫 渾 渾 楽 楽 |

Kanji Practice for Chapter 8
かんじの　れんしゅう

1．つぎの　ことばを　よみなさい。それから、クラスメートに　いみを
　ききなさい。Read the following words to your classmates and ask them for the
　meaning of each word/sentence.

（１）　力がある

（２）　語学に強い

（３）　強力

（４）　勉強

（５）　助ける

（６）　薬

（７）　目薬

（８）　虫

（９）　楽しい所

2．よんでから、よみがなをかいて、えいごでいいなさい。Read first, then
　write the yomigana above each kanji and translate into English.

（１）　土井さんは、　力があります。

（２）　私は、生物学に強い。

（３）　薬の力で　かぜを　なおしました。

（４）　妹のしゅくだいを　助けました。

（５）　デートは　楽しかったです。

（６）　兄は、力は強いですが、勉強は、苦手です。

（７）　英語の "assistant" を日本語で「助手」と言います。

3. The following are incomplete. Add the necessary strokes to complete the kanji.

(1) 助     (2) 弹     (3) 楽

(4) 薬     (5) 虫     (6) ⁷

4. 四角にことばを入れなさい。Write kanji in the box to complete the compound word.

(1)  powerful

| | 力 |
|---|---|

(4)  strong (adjective)

| | い |
|---|---|

(2)  study(ing)

| べん 勉 | |
|---|---|

(5)  enjoyable (adjective)

| | し | い |
|---|---|---|

(3)  assistance

| | 力 |
|---|---|

(6)  to help; assist

| | け | る |
|---|---|---|

5. かんじとひらがなで　こたえなさい。Answer the questions in complete sentences using kanji and hiragana.

（1）　あなたは、ときどき　くすりをのみますか。

（2）　よく　かぞくを　たすけますか。

（3）　あなたは、ちからが　つよいですか。

（4）　あなたは、むしが　すきですか。

（5）　なにをすることが　たのしいですか。

（6）　なんのべんきょうが　たのしいですか。

# **At the Station**

Chapter 9A:  It's raining
*Expressions*
"The boy gave me his umbrella"
"I got a watch from my mother"
"Tom gave me flowers"
"Wow, does he eat well!" ("na" or "naa" sentence final particle)
Feminine speech: sentence final particle "wa"

Chapter 9B:  It's all right
*Expressions*
"He's gone"
"To see is to believe"
"I've been to Japan"
"Isn't it so?"

Chapter 9C:  Monica's diary
*Expressions*
"He must have gotten soaked wet"
"I intend to return it to him"
"I wonder how I can do it"

*Additional Exercises: Diary in Casual Form*

*Kanji practice from Chapter 9ABC*

## Chapter 9A   At the Station   駅<sup>えき</sup>で

### It's raining!   雨<sup>あめ</sup>だ！

| | | |
|---|---|---|
| モニカ : | あら、雨<sup>あめ</sup>だわ、、、困<sup>こま</sup>ったな、かさがない。 | 1 |
| 若<sup>わか</sup>い 男<sup>おとこ</sup>の子<sup>こ</sup>： | あのう、これ、、 | 2 |
| モニカ ： | え？ | 3 |
| 若<sup>わか</sup>い 男<sup>おとこ</sup>の子<sup>こ</sup>： | これ、どうぞ。ぼくは、だいじょうぶだから。 | 4 |
| モニカ ： | でも、あなたが、困<sup>こま</sup>るでしょう？ | 5 |
| 若<sup>わか</sup>い 男<sup>おとこ</sup>の子<sup>こ</sup>： | ぼくは、いいから。それ、きみに あげるよ。 | 6 |
| モニカ ： | このかさ？ | 7 |
| 若<sup>わか</sup>い 男<sup>おとこ</sup>の子<sup>こ</sup>： | うん、じゃ。 | 8 |

[English translation]: It's raining!

Monica:  Oh, it's raining. I'm in trouble.
          I don't have an umbrella.
A young
    boy: Umm…this one….
Monica: Huh?
A boy : Please take this. I'll be all right.
Monica: But then you'll get wet.
          (Lit: You'll get in trouble).
A boy : I'll be all right. You can have it.
          (Lit: I'll give it to you.)
Monica: This umbrella?
A boy : Yes, see you.

Chapter 9 (A)　　　　　　　Vocabulary List

1. Expressions
   あら　　　　　　　　　　　Oh; a feminine expression of faint surprise
   え？　　　　　　　　　　　What? ("Did you say something?")
   これ、どうぞ。　　　　　　Please take this.
   ぼくは、いいから。　　　　I'm all right, so (you can go ahead).
   うん　　　　　　　　　　　casual expression of "Yes"
   じゃ　　　　　　　　　　　short form of それじゃ, and casual form of
   　　　　　　　　　　　　　それでは, then, in that case, bye.

2. Nouns
   あめ（雨）　　　　　　　　rain
   かさ　　　　　　　　　　　umbrella
   （ぼく）　　　　　　　　　male form of "I" (used by males in casual
   　　　　　　　　　　　　　situations)
   （きみ）　　　　　　　　　casual form of "you"

3. Copula nouns
   （だいじょうぶ）　　　　　no problem, all right

4. Adjectives
   ない　　　　　　　　　　　negative form of "aru," doesn't exist, not to have

5. Verbs
   だ　　　　　　　　　　　　casual form of the copula verb "desu," after nouns
   こまる（困る）　　　　　　to be troubled
   あげる　　　　　　　　　　to give
   someone に something をあげる　give something to someone

6. Particles
   わ　　　　　　　　　　　　sentence final, particle used by women
   な（あ）　　　　　　　　　sentence final, particle showing a speaker's
   　　　　　　　　　　　　　murmur

---------------------------------------------------------------------------------
Additional Vocabulary from Grammar Notes, Exercises, and Dict-A-Conversation
---------------------------------------------------------------------------------

[Nouns]
ゆきだるま　　　　　　　　　snowman
オルゴール　　　　　　　　　music box (Portuguese origin)
こづかい (おこづかい)　　　allowance
いとこ　　　　　　　　　　　cousin
[Verbs]
もらう　　　　　　　　　　　to receive
くれる　　　　　　　　　　　someone gives me/my in-group person
かしてあげる　　　　　　　　to loan something as a favor

Chapter 9 (A)                    Grammar and Cultural Notes

## 1. Giving & Receiving Verbs: あげる、くれる、もらう

### (1) あげる: **I'll give it to you.**
あげる means "to give." Its "masu" form is あげます, past tense あげました、and casual past tense あげた.

Examples:

(1)  I gave Mary a book.

| Topic (subject) | | Indirect Object | | Direct Object | | Verb |
|---|---|---|---|---|---|---|
| わたし<br>（トム） | は | メアリーさん | に | 本<br><sup>ほん</sup> | を | あげました。 |

(2)  Mr. Tanaka gave Cathy flowers.

| Topic (subject) | | Indirect Object | | Direct Object | | Verb |
|---|---|---|---|---|---|---|
| 田中さん<br><sup>たなか</sup> | は | キャシーさん | に | 花<br><sup>はな</sup> | を | あげました。 |

あげる is within a set of giving and receiving verbs.  The set involves seven verbs, with usage contingent on hierarchy and in-group / out-group. The verb あげる is not always interchangeable with the concept of "give" in English.  For example, あげる cannot be used when the indirect object is in the first person (I or we).  (For example, no such a sentence as 私にあげる？exists in Japanese.)  In such a case, you must use another verb くれる.  Therefore, when you say "someone gives/gave **me** something," use くれる.  Its "masu" form is くれます, past tense くれました, and casual past くれた.
If you look at past sentence examples using あげました, and rephrase them from Mary and Cathy's point of view, you can state the same ideas using くれる.  The "giver" would then become the subject of the sentence.

### (2) くれる

Examples:

(1)  (Mary's statement) Tom gave me a book.

| Topic (subject) | | Indirect Object | | Direct Object | | Verb |
|---|---|---|---|---|---|---|
| トム | は | わたし | に | 本<br><sup>ほん</sup> | を | くれました。 |

(2)  (Cathy's statement) Mr. Tanaka gave me flowers.

| Topic (subject) | | Indirect Object | | Direct Object | | Verb |
|---|---|---|---|---|---|---|
| 田中さん<br><sup>たなか</sup> | は | わたし | に | 花<br><sup>はな</sup> | を | くれました。 |

**(3) もらう**

There is another point of view: that of the "receiver." It can also be viewed from different perspectives: from that of the giver, observer (the third person), and receiver. Let's take a look from the point of view of the "receiver." In the above example sentences, Mary and Cathy are the receivers. To express the ideas from their point of view, the receivers would become subjects of the sentence, using the verb もらう (to receive). Observe:

Examples:
(1) I (Mary) received a book from Tom

| Topic (subject) | | Indirect Object | | Direct Object | | Verb |
|---|---|---|---|---|---|---|
| わたし<br>（メアリー） | は | トムさん | に／<br>から | 本 | を | もらいました。 |

(2) I (Cathy) received flowers from Mr. Tanaka.

| Topic (subject) | | Indirect Object | | Direct Object | | Verb |
|---|---|---|---|---|---|---|
| わたし<br>（キャシー） | は | 田中さん | に／<br>から | 花 | を | もらいました。 |

The "masu" form of もらう is もらいます, past tense もらいました, and casual past tense もらった.

In Chapter 9 (B), you'll see examples of もらう and くれる used in dialogue

**2. だ: casual form of です copula verb "to be"**

だ is a casual form of です and is used only after nouns and copula nouns. Be careful not to confuse it with its use with casual adjectives. Compare:

| | Formal | Casual |
|---|---|---|
| Nouns | わたしです | わたしだ |
| Copula Nouns | すきです | すきだ |
| Adjectives | おおきいです | おおきい |

The casual form of an adjective is obtained by dropping "desu" from its formal style.

いそがしいです　→　いそがしい

ちいさいです　　→　ちいさい

Watch copula nouns that end with い, which share the same endings as adjectives.

きれいです　→　きれいだ

ゆうめいです→　ゆうめいだ

\* How does one distinguish a copula noun from an adjective?
　Here is the secret. Look at the end of the word. Typically, the "ei" ending words are copula nouns. Many Chinese compound nouns are copula nouns. See the examples:

kir<u>ei</u> (綺麗), yuum<u>ei</u> (有名), soom<u>ei</u> (聡明 intelligent), tein<u>ei</u> (丁寧 polite), etc.

### 3. だった : casual form of copula verb でした

<u>だった</u> is a **past** tense of <u>だ</u> and it is used after nouns and copula nouns. Its English equivalent is "(it) was."

For example,

|  | (Formal) | (Casual) |
|---|---|---|
| It was me. | 私でした。 | 私だった。 |
| It was summer. | 夏<sup>なつ</sup>でした。 | 夏<sup>なつ</sup>だった。 |
| It was pretty. | きれいでした。 | きれいだった。 |
| This park was famous. | 有名<sup>ゆうめい</sup>でした。 | 有名<sup>ゆうめい</sup>だった。 |

[Caution] Distinguish the past tense of Adjectives and Copula Nouns. Which is correct?

1. きのうは、さくらが きれい （a. だった、 b. かった） です。
2. きょうは、とても いそがし （a. だった、 b. かった） です。
3. ともだちは、きのう げんき （a. だった、 b. かった） です。
4. パサデナは、きょうも あつ （a. だった、 b. かった） です。

(Correct answers are: a, b, a, and b.)

### 4. な（あ） : Sentence Final particle expressing sentiments such as surprise, happiness, uneasiness, envy, pity, etc.

Intended originally for casual male speech, the expression is now used in casual settings by both male and female speakers. Do not confuse it with (another) particle な, forbidding action. The exclamatory particle なあ is usually spoken with a prolonged elongation like "naa," unlike the aforementioned "na," which is normally pronounced in a brief and strong manner in command form at the end of a statement. The extended "na(a)" expresses the speaker's feelings as if s/he is murmuring to him/herself, or even sighing.

Examples:

| | |
|---|---|
| （1） なかむらさんは、よく食<sup>た</sup>べるなあ！ | Nakamura-san eats a lot! |
| （2） たかいなあ、このくるまは！ | Boy, how expensive is this car! |
| （3） よく飲<sup>の</sup>んだなあ！ | Wow, we drank a lot! |
| （4） 困<sup>こま</sup>ったなあ、あめだ。 | I'm troubled…it's raining. |
| （5） 家<sup>いえ</sup>がほしいなあ。 | Oh, I wish so much to own a house. |
| （6） きれいなきものだなあ、、、 | What a beautiful kimono that is! |
| （7） あつかったなあ、ことしのなつは、 | How hot it was this summer! |
| （8） いいなあ、犬<sup>いぬ</sup>は、しゅくだいがないから。 | Oh, I envy dogs. They have no homework (to do). |

## 5. わ **Sentence Final particle in feminine speech**

We have seen other Sentence Final particles such as よ and ね. Both よ and ね are neutral, as they are used by both genders; but わ is used by female speakers and gives a feminine sound. Among Japanese males of the older generation, わ may be used in casual and rather bold speech, but it differs in approach, and with its variation being わい.

| | Neutral よ、ね | Feminine わ | Masculine ぞ |
|---|---|---|---|
| だめです。 | だめですよ。<br>だめですね。<br>だめだよ。<br>だめだね。 | だめだわ。 | だめだ。だめだぞ。 |
| いいです。 | いいですよ。<br>いいですね。<br>いいよ。<br>いいね。 | いいわ。 | いいぞ。 |
| いきます。<br><br>いく。 | いきますよ。<br>いきますね。<br>いくよ。<br>いくね。 | いくわ。 | いくぞ。 |

## Feminine and masculine words:

There aren't many gender-oriented vocabulary in Japanese, but here are some examples.

| Feminine words | Neutral words | Masculine words |
|---|---|---|
| あら<br>おいしい<br>すてき | ----------<br>おいしい<br>すてき | おや<br>うまい<br>---------- |

## あげる、もらう、くれる

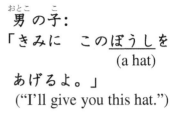

男の子:
「きみに　このぼうしを
　　　　　　　(a hat)
　あげるよ。」
("I'll give you this hat.")

男の子は、雪だるまにぼうしを
あげました。
(A boy gave a snowman a hat.)

雪だるまは、男の子にぼうしを
もらいました。
(A snowman received a hat from
　a boy.)

雪だるま:
「あのね、男の子がね、
　ぼくに　ぼうしを
　くれたよ。
　とても　あったかいよ。」

(Snowman:
　"A boy gave me a hat.
　　It's so nice and warm.")

## もらう、くれる

母： どうしたの、そのサンドイッチ？

子供：うん、おねえちゃんに、もらった。

母： おねえちゃんが、くれたの？

いいおねえちゃんね。

## あげる、もらう、くれる

**Exercise:**  Fill in the blanks with appropriate particles and giving-receiving verbs.

あきらくんは、けいこさん（　　　）
　花を（　　　　　　　　　）。

けいこさんは、あきらくん（　　　）
　花を（　　　　　　　　）。

かなさんは、のぼるくん（　　　　）
ハンカチを（　　　　　　　　）。

のぼるくんは、かなさん（　　　　）
ハンカチを（　　　　　　　　）。

お父さんは、お母さん（　　　　）
ネックレス（　　　　）
（　　　　　　　　　　　）

お母さんは、お父さん（　　　　　）
ネックレスを（　　　　　　　　）。

お母さんが、子供に言いました。

「お父さんが、ネックレス（　　　　　）
　ので、とっても、うれしい　わ。」

Chapter 9 (A) Exercises

A. Pair-work:

(1) First, practice the model dialogue in the middle column of the table with your pair.

(2) Practice feminine or masculine speech, based on your gender.

Model dialogue

| Feminine speech | Neutral (both genders) | Masculine speech |
|---|---|---|
| A：こまったわ。 | A：こまったな（あ） | |
| | B：どうしたの？ | B：どうしたんだ（い）？ |
| A：かさが　ないの。 | A：かさがない。 | A：かさが　ないんだ。 |
| | B：これ、どうぞ。 | |
| | A：あなたは？ | A：きみは？ |
| B：わたしはいいの。 | B：わたしは、いいよ。 | B：ぼくは、いいんだ。 |
| | A：ほんとにいいの？ | |
| | B：だいじょうぶ。 | |

B. Pretend that you are both male speakers and good friends. Speak the given sentences casually and boyishly.

> A：なんか　あった？ 　　　　(Did anything [bad] happen?)
> B：うん、きょう　テストなんだ。
> A：で？ 　　　　　　　　　　(So?)
> B：むずかしすぎる。 　　　　([It's] too difficult.)
> A：べんきょうした？
> B：いや、それが、、、 　　　(Well.....)
> A：じゃ、しょうがないな。 　(Then, no way.)

C. Pair-work: Pass around items around you, and frame a conversation accordingly.

Example 1:

A：あ、<u>ノート</u>がない。
B：これ、あげるよ。
A：いいの？
B：うん。
A：ありがとう。

- Replace ノート with other items such as eraser（けしごむ）, pencil（えんぴつ）, pen（ペン）, etc.
- The Japanese expression, "I'll loan it to you." is かしてあげる.

D. Describe who gave what to whom according to the illustration.  Start each sentence with わたしは、and use the particle 〜から or 〜に for someone who gave you the gift, and end the sentence with もらいました。

> わたしは、〜　から、、、を　もらいました。

まなぶ　　おかあさん　　おいしゃさん　　おばさん

１．わたしは、_____から、プレゼントを　_____。

２．わたしは、_____から、_____を　もらいました。

３．わたしは、_____から、くすり　　　を　_____。
medicine

４．わたしは、_____から、おべんとうを　_____。
boxed lunch

Replace particle から to に and practice these sentences again.

E. Describe who gave you what according to the illustration.  Start each sentence with **the name of a giver** and end the sentence with くれました。

~が、（わたしに）~を　くれました。

| まなぶ | おかあさん | おいしゃさん | おばさん |
|---|---|---|---|

1. ＿＿＿＿＿＿＿＿　が、わたしに、＿＿＿＿＿＿＿＿＿を　くれました。

2. ＿＿＿＿＿＿＿＿　が、わたしに、アイスクリーム　を　＿＿＿＿＿＿＿＿。

3. ＿＿＿＿＿＿＿＿　が、わたしに、＿＿＿＿＿＿＿　を　＿＿＿＿＿＿＿＿。
　　　　　　　　　　　　　　　　medicine

4. ＿＿＿＿＿＿＿＿　が、わたしに　＿＿＿＿＿＿＿＿　を　＿＿＿＿＿＿＿＿。
　　　　　　　　　　　　　　　boxed lunch

F. Describe who gave what to whom according to the illustration.  Look at the first
picture on top-left and read the sentences that describe.  Make two sentences, using あげ
ました and もらいました。

| 1．～は、～に　～を　あげました。 |
| 2．～は、～に　～を　もらいました。 |

田中さんは、スミスさんに　プレゼントを　あげました。
スミスさんは、田中さんに　プレゼントを　もらいました。

1．おかあさんは、＿＿＿＿＿＿に、アイスクリームを　＿＿＿＿＿＿＿。
2．こどもは、おかあさん＿＿＿＿、＿＿＿＿＿＿＿を　もらいました。

1．おいしゃさんは、キムさん＿＿＿、＿＿＿＿＿＿を　あげました。
2．キムさんは、＿＿＿＿＿＿に、　くすり　　を　＿＿＿＿＿＿＿。

1．みせのひとは、＿＿＿＿＿＿に、＿＿＿＿＿＿＿を　あげました。
2．山田さんは、＿＿＿＿＿＿に、おつり　　　を　もらいました。

1．おばさんは、トムさん　　に、＿＿＿＿＿＿＿を　あげました。
2．トムさんは、＿＿＿＿＿＿に、＿＿＿＿＿＿＿を　もらいました。

1．＿＿＿＿＿は、おとうさん＿＿＿、ネクタイ　＿＿＿＿　あげました。
2．おとうさんは、＿＿＿＿＿＿に、＿＿＿＿＿＿＿を　＿＿＿＿＿＿＿。

G. Pair Work: Practice original dialogue first, and then replace the underlined words.

1. もらう/もらった

A: いい<u>デジカメ</u>ですね。いつ買(か)ったんですか。

B: いいえ、もらったんです。

A: だれに　もらったんですか。

B: <u>姉(あね)</u>に　もらったんです。

    1.　ハンドバッグ、ともだち

    2.　ペン、父(ちち)

    3.　さいふ、母(はは)

    4.　とけい、祖父(そふ)

    5.　けいたい、兄(あに)

2. あげる/あげた、あげませんでした/あげなかった

A: <u>お母(かあ)さん</u>の誕生日(たんじょうび)に　何をあげたんですか。

B: なにも、、、あげませんでした。

A: え？何もあげなかったんですか。

B: 忘(わす)れていたんです。

    1.　お父(とう)さん

    2.　お兄(にい)さん

    3.　お姉(ねえ)さん

    4.　おじいさん

    5.　おばあさん

3. くれる/くれた

A: クリスマスに、<u>サンタ</u>は、何をくれると思う？

B: <u>サンタ</u>は、去年(きょねん)　<u>オルゴール</u>をくれたから、今年(ことし)は、何かな？

A: きっと、もっと　いいものだよ。

B: 車(くるま)とか、、、

    1.　両親(りょうしん)、おこづかい

    2.　いとこ、ハンカチ

    3.　妹(いもうと)、スカーフ

    4.　弟(おとうと)、CD

H. Exercises on Casual form

| Reminder of the rules: |
| --- |
| [Nouns & Copula Nouns] |
| N. です　　→ N. だ |
| N. でした　→ N. だった |
|  |
| [Adjectives] |
| Adj. おいしいです　　　　→ Adj. おいしい |
| Adj. おいしかったです　→ Adj. おいしかった |
|  |
| [Verbs] |
| V. (non-past) 行きます　→　行く |
| V. (past)　　　行きました→　行った |

H-1. Change the formality from formal to casual.

1. きれいな月ですね。

2. もう、十時です。

3. あしたは、木曜日ですね。

4. きょうも、雨ですね。

5. だいじょうぶですよ。

6. これ、あなたのですよ。

7. きみの本ですよ。

8. きみのノートです。

9. いいお天気ですね。

10. もう　よるです。

11. きょうは　いいお天気でしたね。

12. とても　いいえいがでしたよ。

13. むずかしい本でした。

14. ひどい雨でした。
(terrible)

H-2. Change the following diary into casual form.

今日は、四月十日、月曜日です。雨です。さくらが　きれいです。空は、くらいですが、空気がおいしいです。こうえんへ　行きました。人が多かったです。そこで友だちも見ました。お母さんといっしょでした。買い物の帰りでしょうか、大きなバッグを　持っていました。私も買い物に行きたいですが、時間がありません。姉から　ブラウスをもらいましたから、それを着ました。まあまあおしゃれに　見えました。

[Vocabulary help]
空がくらい the sky is dark, 空気 air, 買い物の帰り on the way home from shopping, でしょう probably (its casual form is だろう ), まあまあ so-so, おしゃれ fashionable
[Grammar note] Casual form of ありません is ない. The verb ある doesn't have the 1st base (あらない is ungrammatical.)

Chapter 9 (A)'s Dict-A-Conversation

1．Fill in the missing parts to make the dialogue coherent.

A：＿＿＿＿＿＿＿＿＿＿＿ (Inquire what's wrong with B-san.)
B：ペンが　ないんです。
A：＿＿＿＿＿＿＿＿＿＿＿ (Offer a pen to B.)
B：え？いいんですか。
A：＿＿＿＿＿＿＿＿＿＿＿ (Confirm it's all right to B.)
B：ありがとう。

2．Listen carefully and fill in the missing parts of the dialogue.

A：あめだよ。
B：＿＿＿＿＿＿＿＿＿＿＿＿＿＿＿＿＿＿．
A：どうして？
B：＿＿＿＿＿＿＿＿＿＿＿＿＿＿＿＿＿＿．
A：これ、かしてあげる。
B：＿＿＿＿＿＿＿＿＿＿＿＿＿＿＿＿＿＿．
A：だいじょうぶ。

3．Fill in the missing parts to make the dialogue coherent.

A：＿＿＿＿＿＿＿＿＿＿＿＿＿＿＿＿．
B：はい？なんでしょうか。
A：あのう、＿＿＿＿＿＿＿＿＿＿＿＿＿＿、いま、なんじですか。
B：いまですか。三時（さんじ）ちょっとすぎです。
A：＿＿＿＿＿＿＿＿＿＿＿＿＿＿＿＿＿．

4．Listen carefully and fill in the missing parts of the dialogue.

A：＿＿＿＿＿＿＿＿
B：なに？
A：＿＿＿＿＿＿＿＿＿＿＿＿＿＿＿＿
B：ぼくもないんだ。
A：あ、そう。

Chapter 9 (B) It's all right!　だいじょうぶよ！

みわ：　あら、モニカさん。今、おかえり？　　　　　　　　　　　1

モニカ：ええ、みわさん。　　　　　　　　　　　　　　　　　　　2

みわ：　どうしたの？　何か、困ったことがあったの？　　　　　　3

モニカ：いえ、そうじゃないんですけど。　　　　　　　　　　　　4
　　　　このかさをもらったの、知らない人から。　　　　　　　　5

みわ：　あら、しんせつね。　　　　　　　　　　　　　　　　　　6

モニカ：でも、その人は、私にかさをくれたので、雨にぬれてしまうでしょ
　　　　う？　　　　　　　　　　　　　　　　　　　　　　　　　8

みわ：　いいんじゃないの、このていどの雨なら。　　　　　　　　9

モニカ：そうでしょうか。　　　　　　　　　　　　　　　　　　　10

みわ：そうよ、そうよ。だいじょうぶよ。さあ、いっしょにかえりましょう！11

English translation:

Miwa:　　Oh, Monica.　Are you on your way home now?
Monica: Yes, Miwa.
Miwa:　　What's the matter?　Is something on you mind? (Lit: Is something of trouble to
　　　　you?)
Monica: No, that's not it.　Some stranger's just given me this umbrella (Lit:　I've
　　　　just received this umbrella from an unknown person).
Miwa:　　Ah, that's nice.
Monica: Since he's given me his umbrella, he'll get wet, right?
Miwa:　　Things will be all right (for him).
　　　　There's not much rain.
Monica: Do you think so? (Lit: Is that so?)
Miwa:　　It'll be all right!　Let's go home together.

Chapter 9 (B)                    Vocabulary List

1.  Expressions
    いま、おかえり？              Are you on your way home now?
    いいんじゃないの？            It's all right, isn't it?
    そうでしょうか。             I wonder if it is.
    そうよ、そうよ。             Sure thing!
    さあ                      Let's~.

2.  Nouns
    ていど                    degree
        そのていどのあめなら      If it's only that much rain.
    なにか                    something, anything
    こと                      (abstract) thing(s)
                             Nominalizer: changes a verb into a noun
        こまったこと            something that troubles you

3.  Copula nouns
    （しんせつ）               kindhearted

4.  Verbs
    じゃない                   casual form of では（じゃ）ありません; negative
                             copula verb that means "It's not ~"; negative form
                             of a noun + だ/です
                             It's not ~. (in a falling tone)
        ～じゃない？            Isn't it?   (in a rising tone)

    （もらう）                 to receive (when the Subject is the receiver)
    （くれる）                 to give (me/my in-group) (when the Subject is the
                             giver)
    て　しまう                 completion of action: the "te" form verb + shimau

--------------------------------------------------------------------------------

Additional Vocabulary from Grammar Notes, Exercises, and Dict-A-Conversation

--------------------------------------------------------------------------------

[Nouns]
せんそう                      war
きょうじゅう（今日中）          within today
うそ                         a lie
フリーウェイ                   freeway
（じこ）                      accident
おと（音）                    sound; noise （おおきいおと loud noise）

ガシャン                          crack!

[Copula Nouns]
ひつよう（必要）                 necessary
へん（変な）                     strange
とくい                           strong point; good at
へいき                           unconcerned; nonchalant
にがて                           weak point; not good at
（いや）                         disliking; unpleasant

[Adjectives]
こわい                           scared; scary
（かなしい）                     sad

[Verbs]
やる（やって）                   to do
わすれる（わすれて）             to forget
（かぜをひく［ひいて］）         to catch a cold
しんじる（信じる）               to believe
ゆるす（ゆるして）               to forgive
　　　ゆるしてあげない           I won't forgive you.
かんじる                         to feel

[Adverbs]
しょうじきに                     honestly

[Expressions]
よかったら                       If you would like.  If you don't mind.
おきのどくですね。               I am sympathetic.

-----------------------Vocabulary from Dict-A-Conversation----------------------------
うえのゆき                       Ueno-bound
かたち                           shape
しかくい                         square
じゅうしょ                       address
おしらせします                   I'll let you know.
じつは                           To tell you the truth.
だいじなもの                     something important
きっと                           for sure
あとで　もういちど               once more later
チェックする（チェックしてもいい）  to check (It's good to check.)
みつかる（みつかって）           to be found

Chapter 9 (B)                    Grammar and Cultural Notes

## 1. て + しまう : the Completion form

The completion "V-te shimau" is primarily used to express two ideas: the completion of action, and the speaker's feelings derived from the completion.  It can be feelings of happiness from a sense of accomplishment, or those of negativity, such as sorrow, regret, disappointment or embarrassment over a consequence, action or event.  It all depends on context.

How to make the "te shimau" form:
     "て te" form verb + しまう shimau (past tense: しまった shimatta)
          + しまいます shimaimasu (past tense: しまいました shimaimashita)


     contracted/short form "te" + shimau → chau ちゃう
               "te" + shimatta → chatta ちゃった


Examples:
(1) しゅくだいを　やってしまいました。            I'm done with my homework.
          (やる  do)
(2) 今日中にこの本を　読んでしまいます。        I'll finish reading this book
                                              before tomorrow.

(3) かとうさんの、電話番号を忘れてしまった。     I've forgotten Mr. Kato's
          (わすれる to forget)                    telephone number
                                              (unfortunately, regrettably).
(4) かぜを　ひいてしまった。                     (Too bad,) I've caught a cold.
          (かぜをひく to catch a cold)
(5) 友だちが　戦争に行ってしまった。             (I'm distressed because) my
          (せんそう war )                         friend has gone to war.

(6) 私の犬が、死んでしまった。                   (I'm sad because) my dog's
                                               dead.

(7) ちがう電車に乗ってしまった。                 (I ate it by mistake.)
     (a wrong train)
(8) まちがって、食べてしまった。                 (I ate it by mistake.)
     (by mistake)
(9) 恋人が他の人を好きになってしまった。         (My lover fell in love with
                                               someone else [sadly])
(10) 狼が　赤頭巾ちゃんに　言いました。「食べちゃうぞ」
               The wolf said to Little-Red-Riding-Hood, "I will devour you!"
(11) 試験に　受かってしまいました。        (I've passed the exam [to my surprise])
     (しけんにうかる  to pass the exam)

(12) 試験に　失敗してしまいました。　(I've unfortunately failed my exam.)

　　　　(しっぱいする to fail)

(13) 主人は、かさを忘れて行ってしまいました。

　　　　　　　　(My husband has left his umbrella at home [by accident; unfortunately])

(14) もっと勉強しないと、Fになってしまいますよ。

　　　　　　　　　　　　(You'll end up with an F if you don't study harder.)

(15) こども：「お母さん、　弟が私のケーキを食べちゃったよ。」

　　　母　　：「あらあら、いけない子ね。明日あなたに二つあげますよ。」

　　　　(Kid said, "Mom, my younger brother has eaten up my cake!")

　　　　(Mom said, "Oh, my! What a bad kid.  I will give you two [cakes] tomorrow.")

(16) トトロに　会っちゃった！　(I'm so excited that) I met Totoro!

(17) トトロ、かさ　もって（い）っちゃった！Totoro has taken (accidentally)

　　　　　　　　　　　　　　　　　　my umbrella with him.

(18) このかさ、買っちゃったけど、後悔してる。I regret I bought this umbrella (in
　　　　　　　　　　　　　　　　　　haste)

(19) このジュース、きみのだったの？もう飲んじゃったよ、、、Oh, was it your
　　　　　　　　　　　　　　　　　juice?  (Sorry,) I've drank it (already).

(20) あ、ちがう電車に乗っちゃった。　　　Oh, I got on a wrong train.


## 2.　こと the Nominalizer: changing a verb to a noun

Japanese verbs can be changed to nouns by attaching "koto" or "no" to the plain form.  It corresponds to the infinitive or gerund in English.  "Koto" and "no" are not always interchangeable. Use "koto" to indicate "fact."  Therefore, the fact that you ate is たべたこと, the fact that you drank is のんだこと, and the fact that you went is いったこと.

It can certainly be used with non-past tense verbs such as たべること(to eat, eating), のむこと(to drink, drinking), いくこと(to go, going).

"Koto" is often associated with factual, logical, general, and abstract things, while "no" is often used in context of human "perceptions" (hearing, seeing, smelling, tasting, sensing) and feelings. The nominalizer "no" will be learned in detail in Chapter 10 (A).

こと and もの: Both means "things" in English, but their usages are different.  Use "mono" for concrete and tangible things, and use "koto" for abstract things.

The, which will you use for the following things? もの or こと?

　　(1) money
　　(2) shoes
　　(3) books

    (4) theft
    (5) accident
    (6) fight; quarrel; argument
    (7) death

 You will use もの for (1) (2) (3) and こと for (4) (5) (6) (7), since the first three items are concrete things you can touch, and the last four are abstract things that you cannot touch.

Examples:

（１）見ることは、信じることだ。　　　　To see is to believe.

（２）りょうりをすることと、食べることと、どちらのほうが、いいですか。
　　　　　　　　　　　　　　　　　Which do you prefer, cooking or eating?

（３）子どものときに、てをつかうことは、あたまをよくします。
　　　　　　　　　　　　Using one's hands during childhood makes one smart.

（４）毎朝、同じ時間に起きることが、必要です。It's necessary to get up at the
　　　　　　　　　　　　　　　　　　　　　same time every morning.

（５）正直に話したことは、よかった。It's good that you spoke honestly.

Variation:

Since "koto" is a noun denoting an (abstract) thing, you can simply use this word to expand your vocabulary. You can create noun phrases by adding "koto" to nouns, adjectives and copula nouns.

Noun phrases

| Adjectives | いい | こと |
|---|---|---|
| Nouns | きのう　の | |
| Copula nouns | へん　な | |

Examples:

（１）なにか、いいことがありましたか。　Did something good happen?
（２）きのうのことを　おしえてください。　Please tell me about yesterday.
（３）へんなことが、あったんです。　Something odd happened.
（４）ちょっとたのしいことが　ありました。Something fun happened (to me).
（５）かぞくのことが、知りたいです。　　I want to know about my family.
（６）いろいろなことが、ありました。　Various things happened.
（７）そのことは、またこんど、はなしましょう。Let's talk about it next time.

**3.** V た こ と が　あ る **showing past experience: have done it before**
You can express your past experience, whether you have eaten certain food or have met someone, in the form of "TA form verb + koto ga aru."
See the examples below:

(1) I have been to Hawaii.

ハワイに行ったことがあります。

(2) I have camped in the mountains.

山でキャンプをしたことがあります。

(3) I have climbed Mt. Fuji.

富士山<ruby>富士山<rt>ふじさん</rt></ruby>にのぼったことがあります。

(4) I have eaten sushi.

おすしを　食べたことがあります。

Then, how would you say, "I have seen the photo of Einstein?"

Yes. 私はアインシュタインの写真<ruby>写真<rt>しゃしん</rt></ruby>を見たことがあります。

How would you say, then, that you have met Cleopatra in the dream.

Yes. 私は夢<ruby>夢<rt>ゆめ</rt></ruby>の中で、クレオパトラに会<ruby>会<rt>あ</rt></ruby>ったことがあります。

### 4. じゃない: Negative Copular verb

"Jya nai" is a non-past negative copula verb used after nouns or copula nouns. It is the casual equivalent of "jya arimasen じゃありません or dewa arimasen ではありません."

Examples:

（１）きょうは、月曜日じゃない。 　　Today isn't Monday.
（２）あすは、あめじゃない。 　　　　Tomorrow won't rain.
（３）これは、私の本じゃない。 　　　This isn't my book.
（４）それは、うそじゃない。 　　　　That isn't a lie.
（５）きょうしつは、きれいじゃない。 　The classroom isn't clean.
（６）わたしは、話すのがじょうずじゃない。 I'm not good at talking.
（７）そのえいがは、ゆうめいじゃない。 That movie isn't famous.
（８）ぼくは、ぶつりが、とくいじゃない。 I'm not good at Physics.

### 〜んじゃない？: Asking for affirmation

In the Chapter 9 (B) dialogue, Miwa said to Monica, いいんじゃないの, in line nine. She means, "It's all right, isn't it?" "いいんじゃない？" adding a rising tone at the end to express her perspective, as well as ask her listener to agree. The usage is similar to でしょう？with a rising tone at the end.
See the examples below.

（１）そうじゃない？ 　　　　　　Isn't it right? Am I right?
（２）そうなんじゃない？ 　　　　I think I'm right, am I not?
（３）きれいじゃない？ 　　　　　Isn't it pretty? I think it's pretty.
（４）きれいなんじゃない？ 　　　Isn't it pretty? (though I don't really care.)
（５）あたらしいんじゃない？ 　　Isn't it new? I think it's new.
（６）ふるいんじゃない？ 　　　　Isn't it old? I think it's old.
（７）行くんじゃない？ 　　　　　I think he'll go.
（８）行かないんじゃない？ 　　　I don't think he'll go.
（９）行ったんじゃない？ 　　　　I think he went.
（１０）　したんじゃない？ 　　　I think s/he did.

### 5. そうよ、そうよ: Repetition

You may have noticed some repetitive Japanese expressions; especially short phrases said twice, including どうぞ　どうぞ、いえ　いえ、どうも　どうも、おや　おや、まあ　まあ、そう　そう、よし　よし、そうだ　そうだ、and the like. The repetition is used to emphasize the speaker's feelings, while adding rhythm. As they are often used in conversation, many of them have become set expressions.

Examples:

(1) A : ごめんなさい。　　　　　　　　　I'm sorry.
　　 B : いいよ、いいよ。　　　　　　　　It's all right.

(2) A : ごめん、ごめん。　　　　　　　　Sorry, sorry.
　　 B : だめ、だめ。ゆるしてあげない。　No, no.  I won't forgive you.

(3) A : どうも、どうも。　　　　　　　　(Hello)
　　 B : いやぁ、おひさしぶりですね。　　Well, long time no see.

(4) A : むずかしくて、うまく　できないよ。It's too difficult to do.
　　 B : だいじょうぶ、だいじょうぶ。ゆっくり、ゆっくり。
　　　　　 It's all right.　　　　　　　　　Slowly......

(5) A : これで、いい？　　　　　　　　　Is this all right?
　　 B : ちがう、ちがう。　　　　　　　　No, no.
　　　　 Or,　そう　そう。　　　　　　　Yes, yes.

(6) A : あ、まちがえた！　　　　　　　　Oh, I made a mistake!
　　 B : へいき、へいき。　　　　　　　　Never mind!

Note:  When something or someone you have been waiting for finally came, or become reality, the past tense is often repeated to form this type of phrase. Examples:

(7) A : バス、おそいね。　　　　　　　　Isn't the bus late?
　　 B : あ、来た、来た。　　　　　　　　Oh, it (finally) came.

Repetition occurs often as an expression of excitement.

(8) A : きっぷ、ある？　　　　　　　　　Do you have a ticket
　　 B : あれ、どこかな？あ、あった、あった。Oh? Where is it?
　　　　　　　　　　　　　　　　　　　　 Ah, here it is!

(9) A : やった、やった。　　　　　　　　Yeah, we did it.
　　 B : すごいね。　　　　　　　　　　　Awesome!

(10) A : ちょっと、ちょっと。　　　　　　Wait a  minute.
　　 B : なんですか。　　　　　　　　　　What is it?

(11) A : まあ、まあ、こどものことですから。Kids are kids (why don't you
　　　　　　　　　　　　　　　　　　　　 forgive them?)
　　 B : それは　そうだが、、、。　　　　Yeah, it may be true...

Chapter 9 (B) Exercises

A. Change the following polite negative nouns into their casual forms.
Example:

それは、わたしのでは <u>ありません</u>。
↓
<u>じゃない</u>。

**(1)** きょうは、水曜日<sup>すいようび</sup>では、ありません。

(2) ここは、ドイツ語<sup>ご</sup>のクラスでは、ありません。

(3) わたしは、ひまでは、ありません。

(4) 話<sup>はな</sup>すのが、じょうずでは ありません。

(5) 聞<sup>き</sup>くのは、にがてでは ありません。

**(6)** このまち (town) は、ゆうめいでは、ありません。

(7) そのえいがは、すきじゃありません。

(8) その 話<sup>はなし</sup> (story) は、うそ (a lie) では ありません。

(9) すきなのは、ぶつりでは ありません。

(10) きらいなのは、トマトでは ありません。

B. Translate into casual Japanese, using <u>じゃない</u>。or <u>じゃない?</u>
Examples:

That is not true. それは、ほんとうじゃない。

Isn't today Wednesday? きょうは、水曜日じゃない？

(＝きょうは、水曜日でしょう？)

(1) This room is not clean.

(2) I'm not free (of time).

(3) I'm not good at speaking in public (to be good at とくい, in public 人前<sup>ひとまえ</sup>で)

(4) I'm not bad at listening to people. (to be bad at にがて, listen to people 人<sup>ひと</sup>の 話<sup>はなし</sup> を 聞<sup>き</sup>く)

(5) Bob doesn't like a scary movie. (scary movie こわいえいが)

(6) Isn't it German class?

(7) Isn't he Mr. Brown?

(8) Isn't today a test?

C. Follow the instruction to polish the vocabulary from this chapter:

1) Find the Japanese expressions from the dialogue that match the following.

 a). the way home

 b). something troubling

 c). someone I don't know

 d). to get wet in the rain

 e). rain of this degree

2)  Replace the words with the underlined words.
 (1). このていどの<u>雨</u>なら、だいじょうぶ。

　　　けが、　　かぜ、　　失敗（ミス）、　遅刻
　　　injury,  cold (or wind)  (mistake)　　(tardy)

 (2). なにか　<u>困ったこと</u>が　あったの？
　　　　わるいこと、いいこと、しんぱいなこと、うれしいこと
　　　　　　　　　　　　　　　　　(something to worry you)

 (3). なにか　<u>わるいもの</u>　を、みたの？
　　　　こわいもの、いやなもの、へんなもの、おもしろいもの

 (4). だれか　<u>わるいひと</u>　に　会ったの？
　　　　いいひと、やさしいひと、こわいひと、知らないひと

3)  Translate into Japanese.
  a). Are you on the way home?
  b). Did you have something that troubled you?
  c). I got this from someone I don't know.
  d). He will get wet in the rain, won't he?
  e). It's all right if the rain is this much (=degree).

D.  Change the completion form "te shimatta" to its contracted sound "chatta."

[Vowel Verbs]
1.  たべてしまった　　　2.  みてしまった　　　3.  ねてしまった

4.  あけてしまった　　　5.  しめてしまった　　6.  にげてしまった

7.  落ちてしまった　　　8.  おきてしまった　　9.  ぬれてしまった

10. おりてしまった　　 11. 負けてしまった　　12. 見てしまった

[Consonant Verbs]
13.  いってしまった　　 14.  のんでしまった　 15.  踏んでしまった（踏む）

16.  死んでしまった　　 17.  帰ってしまった　 18.  やってしまった

19.  乗ってしまった　　 20.  買ってしまった　 21.  読んでしまった

[Irregular Verbs]

1. べんきょうしてしまった　　　2. きてしまった

E.  Change the verb into "te form verb + shimatta," so that they can become more vividly expressive of speaker's emotions.  The vocabulary help is given below.

1. クラスに　おくれる
2. ねぼうする
3. テストで　０点を取る
4. 苦手な人に　会う
5. こわいものを　見る
6. 悪い言葉を　使う
7. 失礼なことを　言う
8. 遠いところに　来る
9. かぜを　ひく
10. 赤信号で　渡る

---

1. おくれる to be late  2. ねぼうする to wake up late  3. れいてんをとる to get zero points  4. にがてなひと a person that you feel uncomfortable with
6. わるいことば bad language  7. しつれいな rude  9. かぜをひく to catch a cold
10. あかしんごうでわたる to cross the red light.

---

F.  Translate into Japanese, using "te shimatta."

1. I have fallen into a ditch. (Hint: fall into a ditch 穴に落ちる)

2. I have made a mistake (Hint: make a mistake ミスをする, 失敗する)

3. Tom (unexpectedly) woke up early in the morning (and he regrets it).

4. I've lied to my father. (Hint: lie うそをつく)

5. Mary has already done her homework.

6. Bob (unfortunately) missed his bus.  (Hint: misses one's bus バスにのりおくれる)

7. I bit my tongue! (Hint: bite one's tongue舌をかむ)

8. Everyone's gone and no one is home. (go out でかける、no one 's home だれもいなくなる)

9. My car has broken down. (break down こわれる)

10. Cherry blossoms have fallen (to scatter). (cherry blossoms さくら（のはな）, fall and scatter ちる[consonant verb])

11. I burnt my hand (by accident). (burn やけどをする)

G. Fill in the blanks with appropriate words in the following sentences.

（１）なにか　いい（　　　　　　）が　ありましたか。

（２）たのしい（　　　　　　）を　しました。

（３）おいしい（　　　　　　）を　食べました。

（４）こどものときに、手をつかう（　　　　）は、
　　　あたまをよくします。

　　　　Using your hands when you are a child makes you smarter.

（５）しゅくだいを　わすれて（　　　　　　　　）。

　　　　　　　　（wasureru: to forget）

（６）ペットが　しんで（　　　　　　　）ので、かなしい。

　　　　　　　（shinu: to die）　　　　　　　　　　sad

（７）いやな（　　　　　）がありましたが、ともだちとあそんで、

　　　　unpleasant

　　　わすれました。

（８）ともだちから　クリスマスカードを（　　　　　　）ました。

（９）母が、クリスマスにプレゼントを（　　　　　　）ました。

（１０）かぜをひいて（　　　　　　　　）。

　　　　（kaze wo hiku: to catch a cold）

H. Pair-work: Practice example dialogues first and then create your own dialogue, asking each other what happened and how the experience was.

Example (1):

A: なにか　いいことがあったんですか。

B: ええ、ふふふ

A: どんな　いいことがあったんですか。

B: デートを　したんです。

A: え？デートですか。それはよかったですね。

B: はい、とてもたのしかったです。

Hints: Something good happened

1. I had 100 pts in the test.　（テストで百点をとる）

2. I bumped into a movie star.　（えいがスターに会う）

3. I ate something delicious.

4. I received a letter from my favorite person.

Example (2):

A: なにか　よくないことが　あったんですか。

B: ええ、、、

A: どんな　わるいことが　あったんですか。よかったら、話してください。

B: じつは、わたしの犬が、死んでしまったんです。

A: え？それは、、おきのどくですね。さみしいでしょうね。
                     (I feel bad for you./My deepest sympathies.) (You must miss it.)
B: はい、ほんとうに。わたしが ちいさいときに、もらったんです。

Hints: Something bad happened

1. I had bad scores in the test. （テストでわるい点<sup>てん</sup>をとる）
2. I bumped into someone I don't like.
3. I ate something bad.
4. I got a traffic ticket. （こうつういはんのチケットをもらう）

I. Write a short composition with the following topic:

    きょう、朝<sup>あさ</sup>　おきてから、どんなことがありましたか。

Brainstorm to answer the questions below.
    一．　　　どんなことを　しましたか。


    二．　　　どんなものを　見<sup>み</sup>ましたか。


    三．　　　どんな音<sup>おと</sup>が　聞<sup>き</sup>こえましたか。Or, どんなにおいがしましたか。
               (sounds)                          (smell)


    四．　　　どのように　感<sup>かん</sup>じましたか。
    (How did you feel?)


Summarize your answers above.まとめなさい。

    (Ex. きょう、学校<sup>がっこう</sup>へ来<sup>く</sup>るとき、フリーウェイで　じこを　見<sup>み</sup>ました。

    ガシャンという　大<sup>おお</sup>きい音<sup>おと</sup>が　しました。こわかったです。)

Your answer:

Practice on Casual Form Verbs (non-past & past tense, affirmative & negative):
Fill in the blanks.

## Group 1 (Vowel Verbs)

Non-Past

| Affirmative | Negative |
|---|---|
| たべる | たべない |
| ねる | |
| おきる | |
| いる | |
| あびる | |
| あける | |

Past Tense

| Affirmative | Negative |
|---|---|
| たべた | たべなかった |
| ねた | |
| おきた | |
| いた | |
| あびた | |
| あけた | |

| Affirmative | Negative |
|---|---|
| しめる | しめない |
| あげる | |
| くれる | |
| にげる | |
| おりる | |
| まける | |

| Affirmative | Negative |
|---|---|
| しめた | しめなかった |
| あげた | |
| くれた | |
| にげた | |
| おりた | |
| まけた | |

## Group 2 (Consonant Verbs)

Non-Past

| Affirmative | Negative |
|---|---|
| のむ | のまない |
| はなす | |
| よむ | |
| かく | |
| つくる | |
| すわる | |

Past Tense

| Affirmative | Negative |
|---|---|
| のんだ | のまなかった |
| はなした | |
| よんだ | |
| かいた | |
| つくった | |
| すわった | |

| Affirmative | Negative |
|---|---|
| たつ | |
| 行く （いく） | |
| 言う （いう） | |
| あるく | |
| のる | |
| 勝つ （かつ） | |

| Affirmative | Negative |
|---|---|
| たった | たたなかった |
| 行った | |
| 言った | |
| あるいた | |
| のった | |
| かった | |

## Group 3 (Deceptive-looking Consonant Verbs)

Non-Past

| Affirmative | Negative |
|---|---|
| 切る（きる） | 切らない |
| 入る（はいる） | |
| 走る（はしる） | |
| 知る（しる） | |
| 帰る（かえる） | |
| 要る（いる） | |

Past Tense

| Affirmative | Negative |
|---|---|
| 切（き）った | 切らなかった |
| 入（はい）った | |
| 走（はし）った | |
| | 知らなかった |
| | 帰らなかった |
| 要（い）った | |

| Affirmative | Negative |
|---|---|
| 散る（ちる） | |
| しゃべる | しゃべらない |
| 参る（まいる） | |
| | |
| | |
| | |

| Affirmative | Negative |
|---|---|
| 散（ち）った | 散（ち）らなかった |
| しゃべった | |
| 参（まい）った | |
| | |
| | |
| | |

## Group 4 (Mixed group)

Non-Past

| Affirmative | Negative |
|---|---|
| あげる | あげない |
| もつ | |
| はしる | |
| 返す（かえす） | |
| 帰る（かえる） | |
| あるく | |

Past Tense

| Affirmative | Negative |
|---|---|
| あげた | あげなかった |
| もった | |
| | はしらなかった |
| 返（かえ）した | |
| | |
| | あるかなかった |

| Affirmative | Negative |
|---|---|
| たべる | たべない |
| ねる | |
| 知る | |
| しぬ | |
| いれる | |
| かく | |

| Affirmative | Negative |
|---|---|
| たべた | たべなかった |
| ねた | |
| 知った | |
| | しななかった |
| いれた | |
| | かかなかった |

Chapter 9 (B) Dict-A-Conversation (1)
Listen to the CD and answer the following questions in Japanese.

1. 田中さんは、どこに　かばんをわすれてきましたか。(わすれる to forget)

2. 田中さんは、そのことを　だれに　たずねました（orききました）か。

3. 田中さんのでんしゃは、何時何分のでんしゃで、どこまで行く（or どこ
   行きの）でんしゃでしたか。

4. 田中さんのかばんは、どんなかばんですか。

5. えきいんさんは、田中さんに、何かをかいてくださいと言いました。田
   中さんは、そのかみに、なにを　かきましたか。


Chapter 9 (B) Dict-A-Conversation (2)
Listen to the CD and answer the following questions in Japanese.

1. きんじょの人が、田中さんにあいさつをしましたね。何と言って、あい
   さつをしましたか。

2. 田中さんのかばんの中には、何が、はいっていましたか。

3. きんじょの人が、田中さんに　なにかアドバイスをしました。どんなア
   ドバイスでしたか。


Chapter 9 (B) Dict-A-Conversation (3)
Listen to the CD and answer the following questions in Japanese.

1. 田中さんは、自分のかばんを　見つけることができましたか。
   (to find)

2. だれが、そのかばんを　とどけてくれたんですか。(とどける to deliver)

Chapter 9 (C)　　　　　Monica's Diary　モニカの日記

---

六月六日（木曜日）　　　　　　　　　　雨のち晴れ

今日、駅で　かさを　もらった。その人は、雨にぬれたはずだ。
いつか、このかさを　返すつもりだ。でも、どうやって返すことができるだろう。

---

[English Translation]:  Monica's Diary

June 6th, Thursday:  Initial downpour, followed by clear skies

Today, someone gave me an umbrella.  (But because of that) he must have gotten wet in the rain. I intend to return this umbrella some day. But I wonder how I can return this (to him)?

Vocabulary List

1. Nouns
   えき　　　　　　　　　　　　　　　(train station)

2. Verbs
   ぬれる　　　　　　　　　　　　　　to get wet

3. Auxiliaries
   〜つもり（だ）　　　　　　　　　　intend to 〜
   〜はず（だ）　　　　　　　　　　　is expected (supposed) to 〜
   〜ことが、できる　　　　　　　　　is able to 〜 , can do 〜
   〜だろうか。　　　　　　　　　　　I wonder if 〜

-------------------------------------------------------------------------
## Additional Vocabulary from Grammar Notes, Exercises, and Dict-A-Conversation
-------------------------------------------------------------------------

[Nouns]

| | |
|---|---|
| おみあい | match-making |
| ギタリスト | guitarist |
| ゆき | snow |
| ロックグループ | rock group |
| こんがっき | this semester |
| いちじく | figs |
| クーラー | air conditioner |
| ガン（がん） | cancer |
| アニメ | animation |
| とうきょうタワー | Tokyo Tower |
| あさって | the day after tomorrow |
| さくらのはな | cherry blossoms |
| ファッション | fashion |
| せいせき | grades |
| うに | sea urchin eggs |
| がっき | musical instruments |
| がいこくご | foreign languages |
| イラスト | illustration |
| サーフィン | surfing |
| スノーケル | snorkeling |
| じょうだん | joke |
| スノーボード | snowboard |

[な Adjectives; Copula Nouns]

| | |
|---|---|
| かんたん | easy; simple |

[Adverbs]

| | |
|---|---|
| たしか | if I'm not mistaken |

[Verbs]

| | |
|---|---|
| うかる（しけんにうかる） | to pass (the examination) |
| ひく　（がっきをひく） | to play (musical instruments) |
| けす | to erase |
| やめる | to quit |

Chapter 9 (C)                     Grammar and Cultural Notes

## 1. つもり（だ）: showing the speaker's intention

"Tsumori" is a noun expressing "intention," and when it is used with a plain form non-past verb, it works as an Auxiliary Noun. It is equivalent to "intend to do such and such" in English. Since "tsumori" is a noun, its negative form is つもりじゃありません, past affirmative form つもりでした, and past negative form つもりじゃありませんでした. Note it is more common to use つもりはありません when you negate intentions strongly. Unless you need to express strong negation, however, people usually use Verb + ないつもりです, and the pattern of "Verb + つもりじゃありません" is slightly less commonly used.

Formation of "tsumori つもり" with Verbs:

| | |
|---|---|
| Plain non-past affirmative verb | ＋つもりです |
| 行く | つもりでした |
| | つもりは　ありません（でした） |
| Negative plain non-past verb | ＋つもりです |
| 行かない | つもりでした |

[Affirmative]

行くつもりです            I intend/plan to go.

食べるつもりです          I intend/plan to eat.

見るつもりです            I intend/plan to see it.

[Negative]

行かないつもりです→ (stronger)   行くつもりは、ありません。

食べないつもりです→ (stronger)   食べるつもりは、ありません。

見ないつもりです  → (stronger)   見るつもりは、ありません。

Examples:

（１）今年こそ、漢字を毎日れんしゅうするつもりです。
I intend to practice kanji everyday for sure this year.

（２）そのコンサートに、行くつもりでしたが、つごうがわるくなってしまいました。
I meant to go to the concert, but something came up.

（３）きょうは、お酒は、飲まないつもりです。
I plan not to drink liquor today.

（４）絶対に、お見合いするつもりは、ありません。
I have absolutely no intention to meet someone through match-making.

（５）試験勉強がありますから、今日は寝ないつもりです。
I won't sleep tonight since I have to study for my examination.

## 2. はず（だ）: showing expectation

The noun "hazu" shows one's expectation of someone's action or of something to come, independent of the speaker him/herself. The expression "~ hazu da" is equivalent to "someone is expected to do something," or "something is expected to happen" in English.

Formation:

Verb + はずです。

|  | Affirmative | Negative |
|---|---|---|
| Non-Past | 行く　　はずです。 | 行かない　　はずです。 |
| Past | 行った　はずです。 | 行かなかった　はずです。 |

Noun + の　はずです。

|  | Affirmative | Negative |
|---|---|---|
| Non-Past | 明日の　　　はずです。 | 明日じゃない　　はずです。 |
| Past | 明日だった　はずです。 | 明日じゃなかった　はずです。 |

な Adj. + な　はずです。

|  | Affirmative | Negative |
|---|---|---|
| Non-Past | 上手な　　はずです。 | 上手じゃない　　はずです。 |
| Past | 上手だった　はずです。 | 上手じゃなかった　はずです。 |

Adj.い　+　はずです。

|  | Affirmative | Negative |
|---|---|---|
| Non-Past | 白い　はずです。 | 白くない　　はずです。 |
| Past | 白かった　はずです。 | 白くなかった　はずです。 |

Examples:

（1）あの子は、たしか今年、十九才のはずです。
　　　　She should be nineteen years old this year, I suppose.

（2）もうバスが来るはずです。The bus should come very soon.

（3）きのうさいとうさんが、ここへ来たはずなんですが、、
　　　　I suppose Mr. Saito must have come here yesterday…

（4）ここにいないはずです。今、遠くから電話がありました。
　　　　No wonder he's not here.  He just called from a distant place.

（5）さちこさんは、きれいなはずです。お父さんは、ハンサムで、お母さん
も　きれいでしたから。

No wonder Sachiko is pretty; her father was handsome and mother
beautiful.

（6）きょうは、テストは　ないはずです。きのうありましたから。

We shouldn't have a test today since we just had one yesterday.

（7）それは、わたしの犬じゃないはずです。わたしの犬は、ここにいますか
ら。

That dog cannot be mine, since my dog is right here with me.

## 3. ことができる: potential form

The expression "Verb (plain non-past) + koto ga dekiru" indicates potentiality and is
equivalent to "can + Verb" or "be able to do such and such" in English.  Its "masu" forms
are できます，できました，できません, formal style できませんでした, and casual
forms できない and できなかった.

Examples:

（1）雨で、帰ることが　できない。

I cannot go home because of the rain.

（2）そのセーターは、高いので、買うことができません。

Since that sweater is expensive, I cannot buy it.

（3）お金がなくて、りょこうに　行くことが、できませんでした。

I didn't have enough money to go on a trip.

（4）その漢字を読むことは、できますが、書くことはできません。

I can read that kanji (character), but cannot write it.

（5）ひまがなくて、えいがをみることができなかった。

I couldn't see the movie, because I had no spare time.

（6）まだ若いので、車をうんてんすることが　できない。

He is too young to drive.

（7）水がなくて、シャワーをあびることが　できません。

Since there's no water, I am not able to take a shower.

## 4. だろうか :showing conjecture, "I wonder"

"Daroo" is an auxiliary indicating a speaker's conjecture. There are other Japanese expressions accentuating conjecture, but "daroo" does not need to be based on information or evidence to come across as a personal articulation. "Daroo ka" simply means "I wonder," and is attached to the plain form sentence.

Examples:

（1） きょうは、雨だろうか。
I wonder if it's going to rain.

（2） きょうは、お天気がいいだろうか。
I wonder if it's going to be a nice day.

（3） あとで、雪がふるだろうか。
I wonder if it's going to snow later.

（4） 明日のテストは、むずかしいだろうか。
I wonder if tomorrow's test will be hard.

（5） しけんにうかることが、できるだろうか。
I wonder if I can pass the examination.

（6） としょかんは、しずかだろうか。
I wonder if the library is quiet.

（7） おとうとは、今ごろ　だいじょうぶだろうか。
I wonder if my brother is all right.

（8） もうひこうきは、出ただろうか。
I wonder if the airplane has left already.

（9） どうやって、お金をかえすことができるだろう（か）。
I wonder how I can repay the debt.

Chapter 9 (C) Exercises

A. Use either "tsumori" or "hazu" for the following sentences.

（１）そのロックグループが　大好きなので、ききに行く（　　　　　）です。
　　　　　　rock group　　　　　　　　　　　　to go listen

（２）わたしは、こんがっきは、アルバイトをする（　　　　　）です。
　　　　　　　　　this semester　　side job, part-time job

（３）日本のケーキなら、あまくない（　　　　　）です。
　　　　にほん

（４）今年の夏は、暑かったので、いちじくがおいしい（　　　　）です。
　　　こas とし なつ あつ　　　　　figs

（５）としょかんは、クーラーが入っているので、すずしい（　　　　）です。
　　　　　　　　　air conditioner　はい

（６）今から、としょかんで　べんきょうする（　　　　　）です。
　　　いま

（７）ガンになるのがこわいので、タバコはすわない（　　　　　）です。
　　　cancer　　　　　scared　　　cigarette

（８）この電話を使うのは、かんたんな（　　　　　）です。
　　　　でんわ つか　　　　easy, simple
　　　　to use

（９）ないとうさんは、父ととしが、同じなので、４８さいの（　　　）です。
　　　　　　　　　ちち　age　おな

（１０）来年は、お正月に　日本へ行く（　　　　　）です。
　　　らいねん　しょうがつ　にほん い

B. Think of something you planned to do, but couldn't. Express that idea in Japanese, using ～つもりでしたが、～ませんでした。

（V3 [dictionary form]つもりでしたが、V2nd Base ませんでした。）

Examples:

(1) きのう、としょかんへ　行くつもりでしたが、行きませんでした。
　　　　　　　　　　　　い
I planned to go to a library, but I didn't.

(2) お母さんのたんじょうびに、花をあげるつもりでしたが、あげませんでした。
　　　かあ　　　　　　　はな
I intended to give flowers to my mom for her birthday, but I didn't.

(3) きょうは、えいがをみるつもりでしたが、みませんでした。
I was going to see a movie today, but I didn't.

Continue:
1.
2.
3.

C. Change "ます" to "つもりです."

Example: 日曜日に、プールで　泳ぎます。→　　泳ぐつもりです。

1. 明日、かとうさんに、会います。→
2. 今日は、はやく　ねます。　　　　→
3. お昼に、ラーメンを　食べます。→
4. 母に、てがみを　書きます。　　→
5. 父に、電話をします。　　　　　　→

D. Change "ません" to "ないつもりです."

Example: この夏は　泳ぎません。→　　泳がないつもりです。

1. 今夜は、はやく　ねません。　→
2. 今日は、日記を　書きません。→
3. 明日は、テレビを　見ません。→
4. もう　まんがを　読みません。→
5. もう　クラスで　おしゃべりをしません。→

E. Change "ます" to "はずです."

Example: えいがは、三時に始まります。→　えいがは、三時に始まるはずです。

1. かぶきは、四時に　終わります。　　→
2. ボブさんは、日本語がわかります。　→
3. トムさんは、としょかんにいます。　→
4. ケンさんは、田中さんを知っています。→
5. 今日は　単語のテストがあります。　→

(たんご: vocabulary)

F. Change "ません" to "ないはずです."

Example:　今日は雨が　ふりません。　　　→　今日は雨が　ふらないはずです。

1. キャシーさんは、日本語がわかりません。→
2. 前田さんは、私の電話番号を知りません。→
3. リンダさんは、今日クラスに来ません。　→
4. 鈴木さんは、お酒は、飲みません。　　　→
5. 斉藤さんは、うそは、つきません。　　　→

(うそをつく: to lie)

G. Change "Copula Noun です" to "Copula Noun なはずです."
Examples:

にぎやかです。パーティーをしていますから。 →
にぎやかなはずです。パーティーをしていますから。

クリスさんは、日本語が上手だ。日本に住んでいたから。 →
クリスさんは、日本語が上手なはずだ。日本に住んでいたから。

1. このたてものは、りっぱです。知事さんの家ですから。 →
(Governor)

2. さとこさんは、きれいだ。お父さんはハンサムで、お母さんはきれいだ
から。 →

3. このジーンズは、じょうぶです。布が厚いから。    →
(布が厚い: the cloth [material] is thick)

4. リサさんは、ひまです。今週は、お休みですから。 →

5. この犬は元気だ。まだ若いから。              →

H. Change "Noun です" to "Noun のはずです."
Example: 今日は日曜日です。 →    今日は日曜日のはずです。

I. かとうさんは、会社の社長です。 →
(company president)

2. 友だちは、留守です。          →
(not home)

3. あの人は、１９才です。        →

4. ウィルさんは、今 東京です。   →

5. 来週は、試験です。          →
(examination)

I. Change "Adjective "〜いです to "Adj. いはずです."
Example: これは高いです。シルク（絹）ですから。    → これは高いはずです。
シルクですから。

1. あついです。９０度もありますから。        →

2. さむいです。外は、雪がふっています。        →
(Its' snowing outside.)

3. あの人は頭がいいです。ご両親も頭がいいから。 →

4. お金がないです。今月は、たくさん使いましたから。→
(使う to use)

5. やさしいです。小学生の数学ですから。              →

J. Change かな to だろうか.
Examples:

(1) きょうは雨かな　→　きょうは　雨だろうか。(I wonder if it'll rain.)

(2) 午後は、晴れるかな→　午後は、晴れるだろうか。
(I wonder if it'll clear up in the afternoon.)

(3) そのアニメはおもしろいかな→　そのアニメは　おもしろいだろうか。
(I wonder if that anime is interesting.)

(4) いもうとは、もう家を出たかな→　いもうとはもう家を出ただろうか。
(I wonder if my sister has left the house already.)

Continue:

（１）明日は、くもりかな。→
　　　　　cloudy

（２）ばんごはんは、カレーライスかな。

（３）ともだちは、きょう来るかな。

（４）ともだちは、もう来ないかな。

（５）とうきょうタワーからふじさんが　見えるかな。

（６）おとうとは、あさって　ひまかな。
　　　　　the day after tomorrow

（７）さくらの花は、まだ　きれいかな。
　　　cherry blossoms　still

（８）かぞくは、もう　ばんごはんを　食べたかな。

（９）この秋の　六本木の　ファッションは、なにかな。
　　　　Roppongi in Tokyo　　fashion

（１０）こんがっき　の　せいせきは、どうかな。
　　　　　　　　　grades

K. Find someone who can do it!  Go around the class to find someone who can do the
following and write down their names.  Add ことができますか to each question.
Example:
上手に　車をうんてんする　＋　ことができますか。...................

1. 朝、早く　おきる　　　　　　　.....................................
2. 上手に　かんじを　書く　　　　.....................................
3. うにを　食べる　　　　　　　　.....................................
　　sea urchin eggs
4. じてんしゃに　のる　　　　　　.....................................
　　bicycle
5. 海で　およぐ　　　　　　　　　.....................................

6. デパートで　一日中　買い物をする
   いちにちじゅう　か　もの
   all day long                                     .....................................

7. うたを　うたう
   to sing a song                                   .....................................

8. 一日中コンピューターゲームをする
   いちにちじゅう                                    .....................................

9. 自分のへやを　そうじする
   じぶん
   one's own room                                   .....................................

10. 一日中　ねている
    いちにちじゅう                                   .....................................

11. 和食をつくる
    わしょく
    Japanese food                                   .....................................

12. なにか　がっきを　ひく
    to play a musical instrument                    .....................................

13. 外国語を三つ話す
    がいこくご　　みっ　はな
    foreign languages                               ......................................

14. イラスト　を　かく
    illustration                                    .....................................

15. 上手に　しゃしんをとる
    じょうず
    to take a photo                                 .....................................

16. この数学の問題を解く (solve the math problem) ...........................
    すうがく　もんだい　と
    $x^2 - 3x + 2 = 0$

17. 早口で　しゃべる (speak fast)                    .....................................
    はやくち

18. 「生麦、生米、生卵」と早く言う                  .....................................
    なまむぎ　なまごめ　なまたまご　はや　い
    (Say the tong-twister

L.  Group Project and Role Play:  Form groups of three to four and decide which occupation from the list below your group will practice interviews for.  Come up with interview questions, based on the required skills for that job. Take turns between interviewers and interviewees.  Present your role play in class.

(1) Child Care (hints: can sing, dance, play the piano, play with kids, draw, etc.)
(2) Travel Agent (hints: can type, speak foreign languages, communicate with people, manage multi tasks, explain things clearly, etc.)
(3) Math teacher (hints: can explain simply, teach patiently, pay attention to every student, write neatly on the board, etc.)
(4) Publisher (hints: can speak/read/write Japanese and foreign languages, read fast, etc.)
(5) Broadcasting Company (hints: can get up early in the morning, stay up late at night, speak Japanese and English clearly, catch the world news swiftly, etc.)

M. Pair-work:  Converse with your partner to find out your travel plans.  Make sure you tell where you are going, with whom, how long, and what you plan to see and do there.  The plans can be fictional.

[Vocabulary]:
[How long will be your stay? (How many nights and days)]
一泊二日　（いっぱくふつか）　one night two days
二泊三日　（にはくみっか）　　two nights three days
三泊四日　（さんぱくよっか）　three nights four days
四泊五日　（よんはくいつか）　four nights five days
五泊六日　（ごはくむいか）　　five nights six days
六泊七日　（ろっぱくなのか）　six nights seven days
七泊八日　（ななはくようか）　seven nights eight days
一週間　　（いっしゅうかん）　for one week

泊まる to stay overnight, ホテルに　泊まるつもりです。

ともだちの家に　泊まるつもりです。

Example:
　　　Ａ：おやすみは、どこへ　行くつもりですか。
　　　Ｂ：ハワイです。
　　　Ａ：いいですねぇ。何日ぐらい行くつもりですか。
　　　Ｂ：五泊六日です。オアフ島に　行くんです。
　　　　　five nights and six days
　　　Ａ：かぞくといっしょですか。
　　　Ｂ：ええ、みんなで　行きます。
　　　Ａ：オアフ島で、どんなことをするつもりですか。
　　　Ｂ：毎日サーフィンをするつもりです。それから、スノーケルをして、
　　　　　　　surfing　　　　　　　　　　　　　　　　　snorkeling
　　　　　きれいな海や魚を見るつもりです。
　　　Ａ：うらやましいです。
　　　　　I'm envious.
　　　Ｂ：Ａさんは、おやすみは、何をするつもりですか。
　　　Ａ：わたしは、、、、(continue)
Your own dialogue:

N. Group-work:  Ask each other what kind of person you plan to marry, using〜つもりですか。

　[Vocabulary]:
けっこんする to marry, おかねもち　the rich, たいせつ　important
それは、ないでしょう？That can't be.　　じょうだん　　a joke

Example:

A：Ｃさん、どんな人とけっこんするつもりですか。

C：もちろん、おもしろい人とけっこんするつもりです。

B：どうして？

C：まいにちが　たのしいから。Ｂさんは？

B：わたしは、おかねもちの人とけっこんするつもりです。

A：それは、ないでしょう？おかねよりたいせつなものがあるはずです。

B：じゃ、Ａさんは、どんな人とけっこんするつもりですか。

A：わたしは、ゆうめいな人とけっこんするつもりです。

C：え？それじゃ、Ｂさんとおなじでしょ？

A：じょうだんです。わたしは、やさしい人とけっこんするつもりです。

B：わたしも、やさしい人とけっこんするつもりです。

Your own conversation:

O.  In-class activity:  A Magic Bag.

The class is to be divided into several groups for a competitive game. A representative from one group comes to the front of the classroom and picks an item from a magic bag that contains many things.  The students in the other groups ask him/her, "それで　なにをするつもりですか," with the student answering, これで，…（する）つもりです." S/he can go back to his/her group to solicit help.  Students are also allowed time to check the dictionary, but taking too long can incur a loss of points. The instructor determines the points to give, and calculates point totals determining the winning group.

Examples:

1.  (When a student picks a pencil form the bag, s/he will say これで（まんがを）かくつもりです。

2.  (When a student picks an eraser, s/he will say これで、（わるいことを、みんな）けすつもりです。

    (to erase)

Inside of A Magic Bag　そとからは　みえないふくろに、いれるもの
たとえば：
あめ、ガム、てぶくろ、とけい、ペン、えんぴつ、けしごむ
しゅうせいえき (white out)、じょうぎ(a ruler)、ものさし、はさみ、リボン
フラッシュカード、ちいさなはこ、おはし、ナイフとフォーク、はブラシ、
ハンカチ、CD、ちず、本、めがね、ドッグ・ビスケット、五ドルさつ

P.　Write in your schedule below, and then ask your partner for his/her schedule using the expression あしたのごご、なにをするつもりですか, and vice versa.

わたしの予定(スケジュール)表：

|  | きょう | あした | あさって |
|---|---|---|---|
| 午前中 |  |  |  |
| 午後 |  |  |  |
| 夕方 |  |  |  |
| 夜 |  |  |  |

パートナーのスケジュール表：Ask your partner for his/her schedule and write it in the table below.

|  | きょう | あした | あさって |
|---|---|---|---|
| 午前中 |  |  |  |
| 午後 |  |  |  |
| 夕方 |  |  |  |
| 夜 |  |  |  |

If the two of you happen to have the same plans at the same time, why don't you ask him/her to join you?

Chapter 9 Additional Exercises:  Diary in casual form.

Read the following diaries and answer the questions in Japanese.  Then, check the formal style sentences and compare with the casual form in the diaries.

1.

---

十二月二十四日　（月曜日）　（くもり）

今日は、クリスマスイブだ。雪<sub>ゆき</sub>がふるかな。そらがくらいから。今日は月曜日だが、学校は休みなので、買い物に行った。一人で行ったので、ちょっとさみしかった。明日はクリスマスだ。でも、パーティーには行きたくない。一人もさみしいし、パーティーには行きたくないし、困<sub>こま</sub>った自分だ。

---

**Vocabulary Help:**

雪<sub>ゆき</sub>がふる　　　to snow

そらがくらい　sky is dark

困<sub>こま</sub>った　　　　　troubled

しつもん Questions:

(1) 今日のお天気<sub>てんき</sub>は、どんなお天気<sub>てんき</sub>ですか。

(2) どうして、雪<sub>ゆき</sub>がふるかな、と思<sub>おも</sub>いました (thought) か。

(3) 今日は学校がありましたか。

(4) 何をしましたか。

(5) 一人で、買<sub>か</sub>い物<sub>もの</sub>をしたことを、どう思<sub>おも</sub>いましたか (what did s/he think of?) 。

(6) 一人でいることを、どう思<sub>おも</sub>っていますか (how is s/he thinking of it?) 。

(7) パーティーが好<sub>す</sub>きですか。

(8) この人は、自分のことを　どう言っていますか。

**Additional help: formal style ("masu" and "desu" verbs)**

今日はクリスマスイブです。

ゆきがふります。(It will snow.) →ゆきがふるでしょうか。(I wonder if it will snow.)そらがくらいですから。

今日は月曜日ですが、学校は休みなので、買<sub>か</sub>い物<sub>もの</sub>に行きました。一人で行きましたから、すこしさみしかったです。明日はクリスマスです。でも、パーティーには行きたくないです。一人もさみしいですし、

パーティーには行きたくありませんし、困<sub>こま</sub>った自分です。

**\*Remember to use casual form in your diary.**

2.

> 十二月三十一日（月曜日）　（はれ）
> 今日は、あまりさむくない。あたたかい日だ。
> 先週の月曜日も、一人で買い物に行った。今日こそは、
> だれかといっしょに行きたかった。一人は、つまらなか
> った。明日は、新年だ。新しい年が来る。新しい年に
> はたくさんいいことがあるかなぁ。

**Vocabulary Help:**

先週　　　　last week

新年　　　　new year

(1) 今日のお天気は、どんなお天気ですか。
(2) この人は、今日、一人で何をしましたか。
(3) そのことを　どう思っていますか。
(4) 新年はいつですか。
(5) 新年にどんな　期待を　もっていますか。
　　　　　　　　　(expectations)

**Additional help: formal style ("masu" and "desu" verbs)**

今日は、さむくないです。あたたかい日です。先週の月曜日も、一人で
買い物に行きました。今日こそは、だれかといっしょに行きたかったです。一
人は、つまらなかったです。明日は、新年です。新しい年が来ます。新しい
年には　たくさんいいことがあるでしょうか。(I wonder if something good may
happen.)

3.

> 一月一日（火曜日）　（はれ）
> あけましておめでとう！去年は、そんなにわるい年ではなか
> ったが、今年はもっといい年になりますように！
> かぞくといっしょに、じんじゃへ行った。みんながきものを
> 着て、とてもきれいだった。いつか着物を着てみたい。お
> 正月なので、「百人一首」をして、あそんだ。「かるた」
> と同じようなゲームだが、もっとむずかしい。来年はかぞく
> に勝ちたいから、昔の和歌を勉強しよう。

**Vocabulary Help:**

今年はもっといい年になりますように I wish this year will be a better year!

| | |
|---|---|
| じんじゃ | shrine |
| きもの | traditional Japanese clothing |
| お正月 | new year |
| 百人一首 | ancient card game from the Heian era based on waka poems |
| かるた | pre-modern card game; simplified card game |
| 勝ちたい | want to win |
| 昔の和歌 | old-time poem |

(1) 今日のお天気は、どんなお天気ですか。

(2) 今日は、なんの日ですか。

(3) 去年は、どんな年でしたか。

(4) 今年について、どんな期待をもっていますか。

(5) 新年にだれと、どこへ　行きましたか。

(6) お正月だから、<u>とくべつな</u>ことをしました。それは、なんですか。
(special)

(7) 「かるた」と「百人一首」と、どちらのほうが、むずかしいですか。

(8) この人は、どうして「昔の和歌」を<u>勉強したい</u> (want to study) のですか。

**Additional help: formal style ("masu" and "desu" verbs)**

あけましておめでとうございます。去年は、そんなにわるい年ではありませんでしたが、（そんなにわるい年ではなかったですが）今年はもっといい年になりますように！かぞくといっしょに、じんじゃへ　行きました。みんながきものを着て、とてもきれいでした。いつか着物を着てみたいです。お正月なので、百人一首をしてあそびました。「かるた」とおなじようなゲームですが、もっとむずかしいです。来年はかぞくに勝ちたいので、昔の和歌を勉強しましょう。

4.

---

一月三日（木曜日）（雨）

今日はさむくて、つめたい日だ。雨がふっている。せっかくお正月のさいごの日なのに、ざんねんだ。

昨日は、「<u>書初め</u>」をした。その年で初めて、筆で書くことをそう言うのだ。書初めには、一年の<u>誓い</u>を書く。

私の誓いは、今年こそ、もっと<u>積極的</u>になることだ。パーティーにもどんどん行くし、ともだちとも、もっと話す。自分から、<u>何でもやる</u>。

---

**Vocabulary Help:**

| | |
|---|---|
| せっかく | long-[eagerly-] awaited; precious; valuable |
| 書初め | first blush-ink writing of a year |
| 一年の誓い | new year resolution: a pledge of a year |
| 積極的に | assertively |
| どんどん | one after another; spontaneously |
| 何でもやる | will do anything |

(1) 今日のお天気は、どんなお天気ですか。

(2) 昨日は何をしましたか。

(3) それは、なにをすることですか。

(4) この人の新年の誓いは、どんなことですか。

**Additional help: formal style ("masu" and "desu" verbs)**

今日はさむくて、つめたい日です。雨がふっています。せっかくお正月のさいごの日なのに、ざんねんです。

昨日は、「かきぞめ」をしました。その年で初めて、筆で書くことをそう言うのです。書初めには、一年のちかいを　書きます。私のちかいは、今年こそ、せっきょくてきになることです。

パーティーにもどんどん行きますし、ともだちとももっと話します。

自分から　なんでも　やります。

Chapter 9 (C) Dict-A-Conversation
Listen to the CD and answer the following questions in Japanese.

1. みちこさんは、こんどのやすみに、なにをするつもりですか。

2. さのさんは、なにをするつもりですか。

3. さのさんは、はじめは、なにをするはずでしたか。

4. さのさんは、どうして　スノーボードりょこうを　<u>やめた</u>んですか。
   やめる to quit

5. さのさんは、いつか　たくさんあそぶつもりですか。それは、いつでしょう
   か。

Chapter 9 (A) (B) (C) – (1)

| 雨<br><br>(rain) | あめ<br>ウ | 雨（あめ）rain<br>大雨（おおあめ）heavy rain<br>小雨（こさめ）light rain<br>雨天（うてん）a rainy day<br>* [梅雨（つゆ）a rainy season] |
| :---: | :--- | :--- |
| | | (8)<br>一　厂　冂　币　雨　雨　雨　雨 |
| 困<br><br>(to become troubled) | こま（る）<br>コン | 困る（こまる）to become troubled<br>[困難（こんなん）a hardship]<br>[貧困（ひんこん）poverty] |
| | | (7)<br>丨　冂　冂　用　困　困　困 |
| 駅<br><br>(train station) | えき | 駅（えき）station<br>駅員（えきいん）a station master |
| | | (14)<br>丨　厂　𠂆　𠃌　𠃌　馬　馬　馬　馬　馬　馬<br>馿　馿　駅 |
| 帰<br><br>(to return; go home) | かえ（る）<br>キ | 帰る（かえる）to return; go home<br>帰宅（きたく）する to go home<br>帰国（きこく）する to return to one's country |
| | | (10)<br>丨　刂　刂　刂　刂　刂　归　帰　帰　帰 |
| 記<br><br>(to record) | しる（す）<br>キ | 記す（しるす）to record<br>日記（にっき）a diary<br>記事（きじ）an article |
| | | (10)<br>、　亠　亖　亖　言　言　言　記　記　記 |

Chapter 9 (A) (B) (C) – (2)

| 晴 (to become clear) | は（れる）<br>セイ | 晴れ　（はれ）a clear/sunny day<br>晴れる（はれる）to become clear<br>晴天（せいてん）a sunny (blue-sky) day |
| --- | --- | --- |
| | | (12)<br>丨 刀 日 日 日- 日+ 日上 晒 晴 晴 晴 |
| 返 (to return) | かえ（す）<br>ヘン | 返す（かえす）to return something<br>[仕返し（しかえし）revenge]<br>返事（へんじ）をする to reply<br>[返却（へんきゃく）する to return something<br>　　　　　　　　　　　　you borrowed] |
| | | (7)<br>一 厂 厅 反 反 返 返 |
| 海 (sea; ocean) | うみ<br>カイ | 海（うみ）ocean<br>日本海（にほんかい）the Japan Sea<br>海外（かいがい）abroad<br>海水（かいすい）sea water<br>[海岸（かいがん）the seashore] |
| | | (9)<br>丶 冫 氵 汀 汇 汒 海 海 海 |

Kanji Practice for Chapter 9 ABC
かんじの　れんしゅう

1. つぎの　ことばを　よみなさい。それから、クラスメートに　いみを
   ききなさい。Read the following words to your classmates and ask them for the
   meaning of each word.

   （1）雨

   （2）困る

   （3）駅

   （4）晴れる

   （5）帰る

   （6）返す

（７）日記

（８）しんぶんの記事をよみました。

（９）広い海

（１０）てがみに、返事をしました。

（１１）妹は、いつも「はい」と返事をします。

（１２）「井の中の 蛙 <sup>かえる</sup> 大海を知らず」
　　　　　(蛙 かえる, frog)(知らず＝知らない、知りません)
　　　　　"かはず" [kawazu] in archaic Japanese

2. Write kanji in the box to complete the compound word.

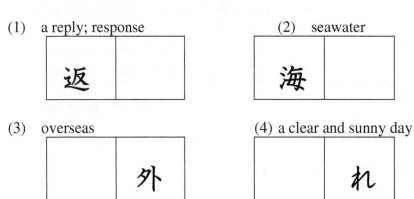

(1)  a reply; response　　返□

(2)  seawater　　海□

(3)  overseas　　□外

(4) a clear and sunny day　　□れ

(5)  diary　　日□

(6)  (newspaper) article　　記□

(7)  (clear-later-rain [weather forecast])

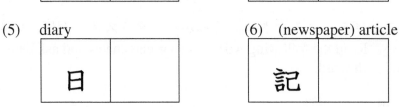

□後<sup>のち</sup>□

3. Choose the one featuring the correct "okurigana" by placing a circle (O) in the space given.

(1)  (　) a. 帰る
　　 (　) b. 帰える

(2)  (　) a. 返す
　　 (　) b. 返えす

(3)  (　) a. 晴れる
　　 (　) b. 晴る

4. よんでから、よみがなをかいて、えいごでいいなさい。 Read first, then write yomigana above each kanji, and translate into English.

（１）毎日、雨がふって、困ります。せんたくができませんから。

（２）前田さんは、今、家に　帰りました。

（３）はずかしくて、返事ができませんでした。

（４）若者
は、<u>かわいそうな</u>　<u>かめを</u>　海に　返してやりました。
（もの）                   (poor turtle)

（５）駅から家まで、歩いて十分ぐらいです。

（６）海上は、かぜが、強かったです。
　　　（風　wind)

（７）新しい駅が　できます。

（８）目に虫が、入って、困りました。

（９）その薬は　ねだんが高くて、人気がありません。
　　　　　　　　　　　　（たか）

（１０）　今日は、「雨　後　晴れ」　の　お天気でした。
　　　　　　　　　　（のち）　　　　　　　　（てん）

（１１）　遠足の日に、晴れて、助かりました。
　　　　（えんそく）
　　　　（遠足 school picnic)

# **Inviting a Friend**

Chapter 10A:  Why don't you come and see?
*Expressions*
"I saw her eating"  "Smoking is bad (for health)"  "I can drive"
"I want to eat it"  "Try and see"  "I'm glad I came"  "It may perhaps be cold"
"I like both cats and dogs"  "It's neither a human nor an animal"
Onomatopoeic and mimetic adverbs
*Kanji practice from Chapter 10A*

Chapter 10B:  Shopping at a market
*Expressions*
"I made the curry spicy"
"Curry looks like chocolate"
*Kanji practice from Chapter 10B*

Chapter 10C:  Recipe for curry rice
*Expressions*
"Do you know how to make it?"  "The depth of this river is about two meters"
"I took a shower, ate, and came to school"
*Kanji practice from Chapter 10C*

Chapter 10D:  Too spicy!
*Expressions*
"It looks delicious"  "It's too spicy"  "The hot bath is ready for you" "Pleas don't do it"
"I'm not married"
*Three Types of Adverbs*

Chapter 10E:  Writing composition:  "A Recent Event"
*Expressions*
"It means such and such"
"I prefer eating to sleeping"
"After finishing my homework, I watched a movie"
*Additional Exercises: Connecting Sentences with Adverbs*
*Kanji practice from Chapter 10E*

*Singing a Japanese song:  Tanabata*

たなばたさま
七夕

作詞：権藤花世、林柳波
作曲：下総 皖一

1.さ さ の は　　さ ら さ ら　　の き ば に　　ゆ れ る
2.ご し き の　　た ん ざ く　　わ た し が　　か い た

1.お ほ し さ ま　　き ら き ら　　き ん ぎ ん　　す な ご
2.お ほ し さ ま　　き ら き ら　　そ ら か ら　　み て る

The "Tanabata" Song

Leaves of bamboo rustle
Under the eaves, swaying in harmony
Stars of the night, twinkling, glittering
Gold, silver, and gold dust

Twinkling stars
Looking down at the poetry strips
Hung on the bamboo leaves
Shining from the Heavens

たなばた (tanabata)
July 7th

Originated from Chinese mythology, the two stars Vega in Lyre and Altair in Aquila (the eagle) were forced to be separated by the Milky Way under decree of the Heavenly God. Once a year, however, they were allowed to meet on this day. Children in Japan hang on the bamboo trees several rectangular papers with their wishes written on them.

Chapter 10          Inviting a Friend    友だちを　さそう

(A) Why don't you come and see?    来<sub>き</sub>てみて！

あいこ： 新<sub>あたら</sub>しいアパートは　どう？        1

モニカ： すごく、いいよ。へやは、新<sub>あたら</sub>しくないけど、まどが二<sub>ふた</sub>つも　あって。

だから、明<sub>あか</sub>るくて、お日<sub>ひ</sub>さまが、サンサンと　入<sub>はい</sub>るし、、、    3

それに、へやが　広<sub>ひろ</sub>いから、気持<sub>きも</sub>ちが　いい！    4

あいこ： よかったね！　見<sub>み</sub>たいな！    5

モニカ： うん、来<sub>き</sub>てみて！    6

あいこ： いつが　いい？    7

モニカ： あしたは、どう？    8

あいこ： あしたは金曜日<sub>きんようび</sub>だから、学校<sub>がっこう</sub>は　二時<sub>にじ</sub>までね。あしたの　午後<sub>ごご</sub>で　9
いい？

モニカ： いいよ。いっしょに　ばんごはんを　食<sub>た</sub>べる？    11

あいこ： りょうりが、　できるの？    12

モニカ： カレーライスなら、できるかも、、、    13

あいこ： 私<sub>わたし</sub>が　てつだうね！　アパートに、にんじんや　玉<sub>たま</sub>ねぎが　ある？

モニカ： ない、、、    15

あいこ： お肉<sub>にく</sub>も？    16

モニカ： やさいも　肉<sub>にく</sub>も　ない、、、。でも、お米<sub>こめ</sub>は、ある。    17

あいこ： じゃ、マーケットで　ざいりょうを、買<sub>か</sub>うのが、さいしょのしごと
ね。

Chapter 10 (A)
[English translation:]

Aiko:      How's your new apartment?

Monica:  It's fantastic!  My room isn't new, but it is bright with two windows.  It gets a lot of sunshine.  And (what's more), my room is very spacious, and that makes me feel good.

Aiko:      That's nice.  I want to see it!

Monica:  Yup. Please come and see it!

Aiko:      When is a good time?

Monica:  How about tomorrow?

Aiko:      Tomorrow is Friday, so school ends at two o'clock. Is tomorrow afternoon good?

Monica:  Sure.  Shall we eat dinner together?

Aiko:      Can you cook?

Monica:  If it's curry rice, maybe I can make it.

Aiko:      I will help you.  Do you have carrots and onion in your apartment?

Monica:  No.

Aiko:      No meat, either?

Monica:  No meat and no vegetables…but, I have rice.

Aiko:      In that case, our first job is to buy the ingredients at the market.

Chapter 10 (A)                    Vocabulary List

1. Expressions
    すごく　いいよ。          It's awesome.  It's great.
    きてみて！(来てみて)     Come and see!

2. Nouns
    おひさま（お日さま）     the sun, sunshine
    きもち（気持ち）        feelings
    ばんごはん             dinner
    りょうり              cooking
    カレーライス          curry rice
    にんじん              carrots
    たまねぎ（玉ねぎ）      onions
    にく（肉）           meat
    やさい               vegetables
    こめ（米）           rice
    ざいりょう            ingredient
    さいしょ             first
    しごと               job, work

3. Verbs
    できる               can do, able to do
    てつだう            to help

4. Adverbs
    Onomatopoeic adverb
    サンサン              the way the sun shines

Chapter 10 (A)　　　　　　　　Grammar and Cultural Notes

## 1. の **Nominalizer**

We have seen another nominalizer, "koto," in Chapter 9 (B).  While "koto" is associated with factual, general, and abstract concepts, "no" is often used in accordance with personal feelings and perceptions.

Examine the following sentence that uses both "koto" and "no."

（１）　何かを借りることは、はずかしいことじゃない。でも、だまって借りる
　　　　のは、よくない。
　　　　Nothing is bad about borrowing something (from others), but to do so silently is
　　　　not good.

Use "no" when verbs of perception (see, hear, feel) follow.  It is equivalent to English expressions of "I felt ~," I saw ~," "I heard ~."

（２）　私は、キャシーがそのパンを食べるのを　見ました。 I saw Cathy
　　　　　　　　　　　　　　　　　　　　　　　　　　　　　eat the bread.

（３）　キャシーがピアノを弾いているのが、聞こえました。 I heard Cathy
　　　　　　　　　　　　　　　　　　　　　　　　　　　　playing the piano.

（４）　田中さんの手が震えているのに、気がつきました。 I noticed Mr. Tanaka's
　　　　　　　　　　　　　　　　　　　　　　　　　　　hands were trembling.

（５）　むねがどきどきしているのを、感じました。 I felt my heart beating fast.

The pattern of "Plain verb + no wa ….da" corresponds to "It is ~ to do such and such" in English.

（６）　医者に行くのは、いやなんです。　　　　　　 I don't like going to see a doctor.

（７）　タバコをすうのは、よくないよ。　　　　　　 Smoking is bad (for the health).

（８）　日本語を話すのは、そんなに　むずかしくない。 Speaking Japanese is not
　　　　　　　　　　　　　　　　　　　　　　　　　so difficult.

The expression "X wa Plain verb no ga …da" often takes place with predicates such as すきだ(X likes ~), きらいだ(X dislikes ~), じょうずだ(X is good at~), へjust だ (にがてだ is not good at ~).

（９）　わたしは、朝はやく起きるのが、きらいです。 I don't like to get up early
　　　　　　　　　　　　　　　　　　　　　　　　　in the morning.

（１０）花子さんは、絵を描くのが、じょうずだ。 Hanako is good at drawing
pictures.

（１１）わたしは、人と話すのが、苦手だ。 I am not good at speaking with
people.

## 2. ～ができる  **can do ～**

> Noun + ga + dekiru
> 日本語　が　できる

できる originally means something is completed, finished, or done.  That's why students
say "できました" when they finished the test.  できる also means "possibility" and
"ability."

Certain nouns can be used with the potential verb できる.  They often involve skills in
academics, sports, work, etc.

| | |
|---|---|
| べんきょう | studying |
| しごと | work |
| スポーツ | sports |
| 語学 | language |
| タイプ | typing |
| コンピューター | computer |
| （車の）うんてん | driving |

You can also use  かいもの (shopping) with the verb できる, not inferring skills of
shopping per se, but in a sense of "possibility"; that is, "You can shop here" or "It's
possible to shop here."(ここで　かいものが　できますよ.)

Examples:

（１）かとうさんは、しごとが　できる。 Mr. Kato is a skilled worker.

（２）田中さんは、べんきょうは、できるが、スポーツは、できない。
Mr. Tanaka is good at academics, but not good at sports.

（３）タイプができますか。　　　　　 Can you type?

（４）トラックのうんてんができますか。　 Can you drive a truck?

（５）フランス語が、できますか。　　 Can you speak French?

（６）かれは、コンピューターが　できる。 He is good at the computer.

## 3. 〜たい : Auxiliary Adjective showing the speaker's desire

If you want a glass of water, you can express desire in the form of "〜 ga hoshii desu. (水が　ほしい [です])" What if you want to express your desire to <u>drink</u> (an action)? To express desire to perform, you can use the formula, "masu form verb + tai (desu)," （水が　のみたい [です]）. The "tai" form is adjectival; thus its inflection is the same as that of an adjective. Its negative form is "kunai," past tense "katta," and negative past tense "ku nakatta."

Adjectival inflections

|  | Non-Past | Past |
|---|---|---|
| Affirmative | 〜たい（です） | 〜たかった（です） |
| Negative | 〜たくない（です） | 〜たくなかった（です） |

As with the case of adjectives, the final "desu" shows only formality. The "masu" form verb is the 2nd base verb in the Consonant verb group, and the stem of the Vowel verb. Simply change "masu" to "tai (desu)" to show desire.

| 行きます　→　行きたい（です） |
|---|
| 見ます　　→　　見たい（です） |

\* Use particle "ga" for "personal matter."

Examine the change in particles below. Since "tai" expresses "personal" desire, the direct object case marker "wo" is often changed to "ga." However, it is not wrong to maintain "wo."

(1) 何かおいしいものを　食べます。→　　何かおいしいものが　食べたいです。
I (will) eat (meals).　　　　　　　I want to eat (meals).

(2) えいがを　みます。→　えいがが　みたいです。
I (will) watch a movie.　　　I want to watch a movie

(3) しゅくだいを　します。→しゅくだいが　したいです。
I (will) do my homework.　　　I want to do my homework

(4) さくぶんを　かきます。→　さくぶんが　かきたいです。
I (will) write a composition.　　I want to write a composition.

(5) シェイクスピアを読みます。→　シェイクスピアが　読みたいです。
I (will) read Shakespeare.　　　　　I want to read Shakespeare.

(6) そのシャツを買います。→　そのシャツが　買いたいです。
I (will) buy that shirt.　　　I want to buy that shirt.

If you have no direct object in the sentence, there is no need to change the particle.

(7) 日本へ　行きます。→　日本へ　行きたいです。
I (will) go to Japan.　　　　I want to go to Japan.

(8) 家に　帰ります。→　家に　帰りたいです。
I (will) go home.　　　　I want to go home.

(9) 学校に　来ます。→　学校に　来たいです。
I (will) come to school.　　I want to come to school.

(10)　　六時に　おきます。→　六時に　おきたいです。
I (will) get up at six o'clock.　I want to get up at six o'clock.

(11)　　十二時にねます。→　十二時に　ねたいです。
I (will) go to bed at twelve o'clock.　I want to go to bed at twelve o'clock

## 4. ～てみる : Try and see
The Japanese expression of "try and see" is the "te form verb + miru."

> 食べてみる　try and eat (to see what it tastes like)
> 行ってみる　try and go (to find out)
> 飲んでみる　try and drink (to see what it tastes like)
> やってみる　try and do (to see what it is like)
> 　　　　　It is slightly more colloquial than してみる
> 書いてみる　try and write (to see how it writes)

## 5. なにか、どこか、だれか、いつか
You can come up with the expressions such as "something, somewhere, someone, and someday," by adding "ka か" particle to the question words such as なに、どこ、だれ、いつ.
Examples:

(1) どこか　きれいなところへ　行ってみたい。I want to go somewhere beautiful.
(2) だれか　ハンサムな人を　知りませんか。　Do you know someone handsome?
(3) いつか　月へ　行ってみたい。　　　　　　I want to go the Moon someday.
(4) なにか　あまいものが　食べたいです。　　I want to eat something sweet.

## 6. ～て form showing reason
As an adverbial phrase, "te" form verbs, adjectives, and nouns can show reason.

| The te form of verbs | ～て |
| The te form of adjectives | ～くて |
| The te form of nouns/copula nouns | ～で |

See the examples below.

（1） 行<sub>い</sub>って<u>みて</u>、よかったです。
I'm glad I went. (Implication: I wasn't sure until I went.)

（2） 書<sub>か</sub>いて<u>みて</u>、とてもいいペンだと　わかりました。
When I wrote (with it), I found it's a very good pen.

（3） <u>来<sub>き</sub>て</u>、よかった。
I'm glad I came.

（4） まどが<u>広<sub>ひろ</sub>くて</u>、とてもいいです。
It's so nice because the window is so wide.

（5） <u>明<sub>あか</sub>るくて</u>、好<sub>す</sub>きです。
I like it since it's so bright.

（6） <u>新<sub>あたら</sub>しくて</u>、さいこうです。
It's new, so I'm elated.

（7） <u>元気<sub>げんき</sub>で</u>、よかったです。
I'm glad you are well.

（8） <u>きれいで</u>、きもちがいいですよ。
It's clean, so it makes me feel good.

（9） <u>事故<sub>じこ</sub>で</u>、大変<sub>たいへん</sub>でした。
There was an accident, and it was very tragic (difficult).

## 7. ～かもしれない: I suspect, it may ~ perhaps, probably

The expression "~ kamo shirenai" indicates "conjecture," and it corresponds to "may~" in English. Its polite form is ～かも　しれません.

It also indicates "probability" and can be used toward both future and past events and actions. The probability expressed by かもしれない is about 50 % or less.

Formation:

Simply add "kamoshirenai" to the plain form of verbs, adjectives, and nouns/copula nouns. The non-past copula verb "da" is not used with "kamoshirenai." That being the case, omit "da" (casual form of "desu" after noun) before adding "kamoshirenai." You can add "kamoshirenai" to sentences ending in the plain form, whether in the non-past or past tense.

> Verb:  Plain form (both non-past & past tense) ＋ かもしれない
> Adjective:  Plain form "i" ＋ かもしれない
> Noun:  Noun ＋ かもしれない ( without "da" before かもしれない )
> Copula Noun:  Plain form ＋ かもしれない
> ( without "na"/ "da" before かもしれない )

Take a look at the plain form endings below.

|  | い Adjective | な Adj. (copula noun) | Noun | Verb |
|---|---|---|---|---|
| Non-past Affirmative | さむい | しずか | 先生だ | 食べる |
| Non-past Negative | さむくない | しずかじゃない | 先生じゃない | 食べない |
| Past Affirmative | さむかった | しずかだった | 先生だった | 食べた |
| Past Negative | さむくなかった | しずかじゃなかった | 先生じゃなかった | 食べなかった |

Add "kamoshirenai" to express conjecture/probability
Pay attention: No だ before かもしれない

| ～かもしれない | | | | |
|---|---|---|---|---|
|  | い Adjective | な Adj. (copula noun) | Noun | Verb |
| Non-past Affirmative | さむい かもしれない | しずか かもしれない | 先生 かもしれない | 食べる かもしれない |
| Non-past Negative | さむくない かもしれない | しずかじゃない かもしれない | 先生じゃない かもしれない | 食べない かもしれない |
| Past Affirmative | さむかった かもしれない | しずかだった かもしれない | 先生だった かもしれない | 食べた かもしれない |
| Past Negative | さむくなかった かもしれない | しずかじゃなかった かもしれない | 先生じゃなかった かもしれない | 食べなかった かもしれない |

Examples:

1. 明日雨が<u>降る</u>かもしれない。　　　　　It may rain tomorrow.

2. 昨日雨が<u>降った</u>かもしれない。　　　　It might have rained yesterday.

3. あのレストランは、オムレツが　<u>おいしい</u>かもしれない。
   The omelet at that restaurant may be good.

4. あのレストランは、オムレツが　<u>おいしかった</u>かもしれない。
   (According to memory), that restaurant's omelet may have been good.

5. 田中さんは、字が<u>じょうず</u>かもしれない。
   Tanaka san's handwriting may be good (as guessed).

6. 花子さんは、昔 は、<u>きれいだった</u>かもしれない。
   Hanako san may have been pretty when she was young.

## 8. だから: **A conjunction showing reason**

When the initial sentence states a reason, and the next expresses consequence, the two sentences can be conjoined with "dakara." Unlike with "kara," the two sentences being connected with the "dakara" conjunction are not compound sentences. Instead, they are sentences independent of one another.

Examples:

(1) きょう、あさごはんを<u>食</u>べませんでした。<u>だから</u>、おなかがすいています。
   Today, I didn't eat breakfast. Therefore, I'm hungry.

(2) べんきょうしませんでした。<u>だから</u>、テストは、わるかったです。
   I didn't study. That's why my test (performance) was bad.

(3) このみちは、くるまが少ないです。<u>だから</u>、しずかです。
   This street does not have many cars (frequenting it), so it's quiet.

(4) はやく　ねました。<u>だから</u>、はやく　おきました。
   I went to bed early, so I got up early.

(5) そこは、とおいです。だから、くるまで　<u>行</u>きました。
   That place is far. So I went by car.

## 9. サンサン: **Onomatopoeia**

One of the great features of the Japanese language is Onomatopoeia, and they are abundant in the daily lives of the Japanese people. Learning them is one of the quickest ways to mastering the language.  They are often repetitions of the same sound, such as "shiku shiku," "gan gan," "doki doki," "niko niko," "kuyo kuyo," etc.  These Japanese onomatopoetic adverbs fall into two categories:  Onomatopoeia and Mimesis.  The former is based on sound, and latter on appearance; so in other words, some are auditory based and others visual.  The expression "san san" is always associated with the bright sun, meaning the sun shines abundantly.  "Gan gan" expresses loud noise. And typically, "voiced sounds" such as "gan gan" (with the hard "g") expresses a stronger sound/manner than "voiceless sounds" such as "kan kan."  Both express noise: the former louder, latter softer.  Sound-based onomatopoeia and visual-based mimesis are not always in align with one another, but there are occasions when they are.  "Gan gan" can express both loud noise and throbbing headache, and also that of a strong scorching sun.  In a similar vein, "kan kan" expresses (1) soft clanging when you hit a bell, (2) scorching sun or glowing red-hot charcoal, and (3) extreme anger or rage.

## 10.  <u>Ａ も Ｂ も</u>: **Both A and B, Neither A nor B**
The repetition of the particle "mo" in an affirmative sentence is equivalent to "both A and B"; and in a negative sentence "neither A nor B" in English.
Examples:

(1) わたしもあなたも、大学生ですね。Both you and I are college students, aren't we?

(2) わたしもあなたも、こうこうせいじゃありませんね。Neither you nor I are high school students, are we?

(3) 犬もねこも、すきです。                  I like both cats and dogs.

(4) へびも、とかげもすきじゃありません。I don't like either snakes or lizards.

(5) とうきょうへも、きょうとへも、行きました。I went to both Tokyo and Kyoto.

(6) おおさかにも、ほっかいどうにも、いました。I was both in Osaka and Hokkaido.

(7) にくもさかなも、たべなさい。       Eat both meat and fish.

(8) たかくも、やすくも　ありません。      It's neither expensive nor cheap.

(9) いたくも、かゆくも　ありません。      It's neither painful nor itchy.

(10) にんげんでも、どうぶつでも　ありません。It's neither a human nor an animal.

(11) 犬でも　サルでも　ありません。       It's neither a dog nor a monkey.

(12) 木でも、石でも　ありません。          I am neither a tree nor a rock. (I have feelings.)

## Onomatopoeia and Mimesis

どんどん

<u>たいこを</u>　<u>どんどん</u>　<u>たたく</u>。
(a drum)　ドンドン　(to hit, beat)

もぐもぐ（モグモグ）

もぐもぐ：
To chew without opening the mouth widely
むしゃむしゃ：
The sound or action of chewing on a large amount of
ばくばく：
A vigorous eating motion

ハンバーガーを　もぐもぐ　食べる

かんかん（に）（カンカンに）

母は、かんかんに　おこりました。
　My mother became furious.

そらがピカッとひかりました。
　I saw the flash of lightening.
あめが　ザーザーふりました。
　It poured.
かぜが　ピューピューふいています。
　It's very gusty.

More onomatopoeic and mimetic adverbs:

## Onomatopoeia: Smile わらう（わらいます）　& Crying　なく（なきます）

Which onomatopoeic adverbs best fit each illustrations?

[Smiling]

1. にこにこ
2. きゃっきゃっ
3. くすくす
4. あはは
5. にやにや

5

[Crying] 1. しくしく　2. （う）わ〜ん

Chapter 10 (A) Exercises

A.  Choose either "koto" or "no" to complete the following sentences.
Hint: "Koto" is often used for a general, universal, and abstract idea, while "no" is often used for more personal statement.  Also, when the verbs of perception (such as "hearing" and "seeing") are accompanied, only "no" should be used with the verb.

（1）タバコをすう（　　　　）は、からだによくないです。
　　　smoking a cigarette　　　　　　body

（2）まだ、八時ですから、ねる（　　　　　）は、いやです。
　　　　　　　　　　　　　　　　　　　　　　I don't like

（3）子どもが、バイオリンをひいている（　　　）が　聞こえてきます。
　　　violin　　　　　(is) playing

（4）たんごは、しょっちゅう使う（　　　　　）が、たいせつです。
　　　　　　　all the time　　to use　　　　　　　　　important

（5）三分でシャワーをあびる（　　　　）が　できますか。
　　　　　　　　　　　　　(Hint: you cannot change the existing "formula.")

（6）人前で、話す（　　　　　）が、にがてです。
　　　in public

（7）家に、プールがあるので、毎日およぐ（　　　　　）が　できます。

（8）日本語を読む（　　　）は、とくいですが、話す（　　　）は、苦手です。

（9）見る（　　　　）は、信じる（　　　　）です。(Hint: Proverb)
　　　　　　　　　　　　　to believe

B.  Change the following into sentences with potentiality or possibility.  And, ask your classmates if they can do those things.
Example: サッカーをします→　サッカーが　できます。

（１）べんきょうをします。
（２）しごとをします。
（３）ピンポンをします。(ping pong)
（４）タイプをします。　(typing)
（５）うんてんをします。(driving)
（６）りょうりをします。(cooking)
（７）やきゅうをします。(baseball)
（８）コンピューターをします。
（９）日本語で電話をします。
（１０）さかだちをします。(standing on the head)

C. Change the following underlined into "probable" expressions using "kamoshirenai."

Ex.　明日は晴れます。　→　晴れるかもしれません。
　　　It will be a nice day tomorrow.  It may be a nice day tomorrow.

1.　彼女は、もうすぐ結婚します。　＿＿＿＿＿＿＿＿＿＿＿＿＿＿
　　She'll get married soon.　　　　　　　　She may get married soon.

2.　このへんは、家が少ないから、静かです。　＿＿＿＿＿＿＿＿＿＿
　　This neighborhood is quiet since there aren't many houses.

3.　勉強しなかったから、試験は、よくできませんでした。
　　　　　　　　　　　　　examination

　　　　　　　　　　　　　＿＿＿＿＿＿＿＿＿＿＿＿＿＿＿＿

4.　今日の午後、友だちが来ます。　＿＿＿＿＿＿＿＿＿＿＿＿＿＿

5.　私が留守の間に、だれか来ました。　＿＿＿＿＿＿＿＿＿＿＿＿
　　When I wasn't home, someone came.

6.　今日のおみそしるは、おいしいです。＿＿＿＿＿＿＿＿＿＿＿＿
　　　　　　　　miso soup

7.　きのうの花火は、きれいでしたね。＿＿＿＿＿＿＿＿＿＿＿＿＿
　　　　　　　　fireworks

D.  Combine two sentences, using the "kara" conjunctive particle.
Example:
　　　きょうのあさ、はやくおきました。だから、ねむいです。
　　　→　きょうのあさ、はやくおきましたから、ねむいです。

（1）田中さんは、日本から来ました。だから、きれいな日本語を話します。
　　　→

（2）おそいです。だから、ちかみちにしましょう。
　　　　　　　　　　　　（近道 a shortcut）
　　　→

（3）その犬は、小さいです。だから、あまり食べないでしょう。
　　　→

（4）このみちは、まえに、とおりました。だから、よく知っています。
       (street)          (passed through)

     →

（5）だれもいません。だから、しずかです。

     →

E.  Come up with Japanese equivalents, using "te miru."
Examples:

  1.  I will eat it to see what it tastes like.  食べてみます。

  2.  I will try to cook curry rice.

  3.  I will drink it to see what it is like.

  4.  I will wear this (piece of) clothing to see how I look.  (use the verb to wear "kiru" [vowel verb] with "fuku" for western clothing)

  5.  I will wear these shoes to see how they fit.  (use the verb to wear "haku" [consonant verb] for items under the waist line and "kutsu" for shoes)

  6.  I will wear this hat to see how I look. (use the verb to wear on one's head "kaburu" [consonant verb] and "booshi" for hat)

  7.  Mr. Saito went to the park to see what's going on.

F.  Fill in the blanks.
Examples:

      （せいせきがよくて）、　　うらやましいです。
      Since your grades are good,   I'm envious.
      （びょうきじゃなくて）、よかったです。
      Since you're not sick,    I'm glad.

1.  (　　　　　　　　　　　　)、うらやましいです。
   Since you have good eyesight (use "me ga ii"), I'm envious.

2.  (　　　　　　　　　　　　)、きもちが　いいですね。
   Since the weather is nice, it feels good.

3.  (　　　　　　　　　　　　)、よかった。
   Since it wasn't an accident (use "jiko"), I'm relieved.

4.  (　　　　　　　　　　　　)、よかったですね。
   It's nice that you are number one.

5.  (　　　　　　　　　　　　)、いいですね。
   It's nice that your house is close.

G-1. Change "masu" to "tai" form. (Change from "I will" to "I want to")
To show a speaker's desire: "Vb2 (masu form) + tai desu"

| | | |
|---|---|---|
| 1. みます | 11. あいます | 21. でかけます |
| 2. たべます | 12. かきます | 22. たちます |
| 3. ねます | 13. よみます | 23. すわります |
| 4. おしえます | 14. はいります | 24. かいます |
| 5. います | 15. 切ります | 25. なります |
| 6. わすれます | 16. いきます | 26. ききます |
| 7. 着ます | 17. のみます | 27. いいます |
| 8. します | 18. あそびます | 28. まちます |
| 9. 来ます | 19. つくります | |
| 10. あらいます | 20. でます | |

G-2. Practice negative form of "tai"(desu): "taku-nai" (desu) (I don't want to do it.)
Non-past tense Affirmative: たいです→ Negative: たくないです (たくありません)

Task (1) Interview your classmates and fill in the blanks

| なまえ | 食べたいもの | 食べたくないもの |
|---|---|---|
| | | |
| | | |

A: 食べたいものは、何ですか。　　A: 食べたくないものは、何ですか。
B: おすしです。　　　　　　　　B: ハンバーガーです。

Task (2)

| なまえ | のみたいもの | のみたくないもの |
|---|---|---|
| | | |
| | | |

A: 飲みたいものは、何ですか。　　A: 飲みたくないものは、何ですか。
B: おみずです。　　　　　　　　B: ウイスキーです。

Task (3)

| なまえ | 会いたい人 | 会いたくない人 |
|---|---|---|
| | | |
| | | |

A：会いたい人は、だれですか。　　A: 会いたくない人は、だれですか。
B: 母です。　　　　　　　　　　　　B: いじわるな人です。

Task (4)

| なまえ | したいこと | したくないこと |
| --- | --- | --- |
|  |  |  |
|  |  |  |

A: したいことは、何ですか。　　A: したくないことは、何ですか。
B: ねることです。　　　　　　　　B: しゅくだいです。

G-3. Ask your classmates which s/he prefers.

1. やさいとくだものと　どちらのほうが　食べたいですか。
2. コーヒーとコーラと　どちらのほうが　のみたいですか。
3. ジョギングと水泳と　どちらのほうが　楽しいですか。

G-4. Practice Past tense Affirmative (V たかったです) and Past Negative (V たくなかったです or V たくありませんでした。) by asking your classmates the following.

1. 今日、したかったけど、しなかったことは、何ですか。
2. きのう、したくなかったけど、したことが、ありますか。どんなことですか。
3. ちいさいとき、したくなかったけど、したことは、何ですか。

G-5. Translate into Japanese, using "tai desu."
1. I want to see that movie.

2. I want to go to Japan next year.

3. I don't want to go <u>alone</u>.
　　　　　　　　（ひとりで）
4. I wanted to go to the party yesterday.

5. I want to buy that T-shirt.

G-6. Pair-work: Ask each other the following questions.
   1. What do you want to drink most now?
[Hint]: Use either pattern given below.
　　　　　今、何が一番、飲みたいですか。
　　　　　今、一番、飲みたいものは、何ですか。

   2. What do you want to eat most now?

3.  What do you want to do most now?

4.  Who do you want to see most now? (use ～に　会<ruby>会<rt>あ</rt></ruby>う)

5.  Which movie do you want to see most now?

6.  Where do you want to be most now?

7.  In what century have you <u>wanted</u> to live most? (use 何世紀<ruby>何世紀<rt>なんせいき</rt></ruby>に、生<ruby>生<rt>い</rt></ruby>きる)

H.  Fill in the blanks.
1．ここで（　　　　　　　　　）できますか。Can we shop here?

2．あなたは、（　　　　　　　　　　）できますか。Are you good at academics?

3．ないとうさんは、（　　　　　　　　　）できます。Mr. Naito is a good worker.

4．山田さんは、（　　　　　　　　）できます。Ms. Yamada is good at French.

5．わたしは、くるまの（　　　　　　　）できます。I can drive.

I.  Fill in the blanks with particles.
1．わたしも、あなた（　　　　）、二年生<ruby>二年生<rt>にねんせい</rt></ruby>ですね。
2．きょう（　　　）あしたも、おてんきがいいでしょう。
3．田中<ruby>田中<rt>たなか</rt></ruby>さんも、かとうさん（　　　　）、そこに　いません。
4．こうえんにも、家<ruby>家<rt>いえ</rt></ruby>に（　　　）、わたしの犬<ruby>犬<rt>いぬ</rt></ruby>は、いませんでした。
5．やさい（　　　　）、にくも、好<ruby>好<rt>す</rt></ruby>きです。
6．スキー（　　　）できますか。
7．さいりょう（　　　　）買<ruby>買<rt>か</rt></ruby>う（　　　　）が、さいしょのしごとです。
8．バス（　　　）行<ruby>行<rt>い</rt></ruby>く（　　　　）は、たいへんでした。
9．歩<ruby>歩<rt>ある</rt></ruby>いて行<ruby>行<rt>い</rt></ruby>く（　　　　）も、バスで行く（　　　　）も　たいへんです。
10．本当<ruby>本当<rt>ほんとう</rt></ruby>は、今日<ruby>今日<rt>きょう</rt></ruby>がいいんですが、あしたの午後<ruby>午後<rt>ごご</rt></ruby>（　　　）（　　）いいです。

J.  Fill in the blanks with appropriate onomatopoeia or mimesis from the box in the next page.
1．南<ruby>南<rt>みなみ</rt></ruby>のまどから、あたたかいお日<ruby>日<rt>ひ</rt></ruby>さまが、（　　　　　　）と、入<ruby>入<rt>はい</rt></ruby>る。

2．今日は、（　　　　　　）と、春<ruby>春<rt>はる</rt></ruby>のように、あたたかい。
                              like spring
3．おなかが すいて、（　　　　　　）です。

4. のどが　かわいたので、水を　（　　　　　　　）飲みました。

5. しけんのまえは、むねが　（　　　　　　　）します。
before the exam.　heart/chest

6. 強いお日さまが、（　　　　　　）と　照っています。
shine

7. 私がうそをついたので、母は、（　　　　　　）に　怒りました。
because I lied　　　　　　　　　　　　　　got angry

8. おなかがすいていたので、パンを（　　　　　　）食べました。

9. 祭りの日は、たいこを　（　　　　　　）たたきます。
festival

10. 悲しくて、（　　　　　　）泣きました。

11. 田中さんは、いつも　（　　　　　　）笑っています。

> かんかん、にこにこ、ぺこぺこ、ぽかぽか、しくしく、どんどん、ばくばく、
> ごくごく、ぽかぽか、さんさん

K. Translate into Japanese. Use ～がありますか in the ending of each sentence.
　1. Do you have something you want to eat?

　2. Is there any place you want to go?

　3. Do you have someone you want to meet now?

　4. Is there any movie you want to watch?

L.　Interview your classmate and report the information to class. The information you need to obtain is the following:

(1) his/her favorite food, drink, person, color, and place

(2) which s/he prefers: vegetables or fruits, meat or fish, coke or milk, reading books or watching television, swimming or jogging, writing papers or doing a research.

(3) what s/he is good at and not good at.
　苦手なのは、何ですか。得意なのは、なんですか。(i.e., academic subjects, sports, cooking, driving, etc.)

　苦手なことは、何ですか。得意なことは、なんですか。(i.e., public speech, eating fast, convincing others, finding someone in the crowds, etc.)

## Chapter 10 (A): Dict-A-Conversation

Respond orally to the following statements and write down your answers. Please answer in <u>complete sentences</u>, writing in hiragana and in kanji where applicable.

1. _____

2. _____

3. _____

4. _____

5. _____

6. _____

7. _____

8. _____

9. _____

10. _____

Chapter 10 (A)

| 玉 (sphere; gem) | たま<br>ギョク | 水玉（みずたま）a drop of water; a polka-dot pattern<br>玉ねぎ（たまねぎ）an onion<br>十円玉（じゅうえんだま）ten-yen coin<br>玉子（たまご）eggs<br>目玉（めだま）eyeball<br>　［目玉焼き（めだまやき）sunny-side egg］<br>［宝玉（ほうぎょく）jewel］ |
| | | (5)<br>　一　丁　干　王　玉 |
| 肉 (flesh; meat) | ニク | 肉（にく）meat; flesh<br>牛肉（ぎゅうにく）beef<br>［鶏肉（とりにく、けいにく）chicken］<br>［豚肉（ぶたにく）pork］<br>肉食（にくしょく）meat diet |
| | | (6)<br>　｜　冂　内　内　肉　肉 |
| 米 (rice) | こめ<br>マイ<br>ベイ<br>（メートル） | 米（こめ）rice<br>白米（はくまい）white rice<br>日米（にちべい）Japan-US<br>米国（べいこく）the United States<br>一米（いちメートル）　one meter |
| | | (6)<br>　ヽ　ソ　ユ　半　米　米 |
| 友 (a friend) | とも<br>ユウ | 友（とも）だち a friend<br>友人（ゆうじん）a friend<br>親友（しんゆう）best friend |
| | | (4)<br>　一　ナ　方　友 |

## Kanji Practice for Chapter 10 A

かんじの　れんしゅう

1. つぎの　ことばを　よみなさい。それから、クラスメートに　いみを
   ききなさい。Read the following words to your classmates and ask them for the
   meaning of each word.

（１）　牛<sup></sup>肉　　　　　　　　（６）　白米

（２）　日米　　　　　　　　　（７）　友だち

（３）　目玉　　　　　　　　　（８）　友人

（４）　肉　　　　　　　　　　（９）　玉ねぎ

（５）　白い米　　　　　　　　（１０）　玉子

　　　　　　　　　　　　　　　（１１）　米国

2. Write kanji in the box to complete the compound word.

(1) Japan and US

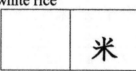

(2) white rice

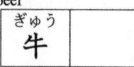

(3) beef

(4) best friend

しん
親

(5) U.S.

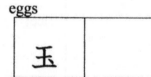

(6) eggs

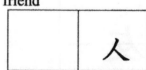

(7) friend

(8) eye balls (casual) [kun-
kun(Japanese-Japanese) reading]

3. よんでから、よみがなをかいて、えいごでいいなさい。 **Read first, then write yomigana above each kanji, and translate into English.**

    （１）    いちばんいい友だちを　親友と　言います。

    （２）    カレーライスに、肉や玉ねぎを　入れました。

    （３）    ジョンさんは、米国の友人です。

    （４）    白いお米を　「白米」と　言います。

    （５）    牛肉と　とり肉と　ぶた肉で、どれがいちばん好きですか。

4. クラスメートに日本語できwきなさい。 **Ask your classmate the following questions in Japanese.**

  (1) Brown rice is 「玄米」 in Japanese.  Then, what is "write rice" in Japanese?

  (2) Friends in Japanese is 「友人」.  Then, what is "the best friend" in Japanese?

  (3) What is "sunny-side egg" in Japanese?

  (4) "Japan-US" is 「日米」, then what would you say "Japan-China"?

  (5) I put beef in my curry.  What kind of meet do you put in your curry?

  (6) How many <u>coins</u> are there in <u>Japanese currency</u>?
        コイン        日本のお金（貨幣）

Chapter 10 (B)   Shopping at a Market   マーケットで 買い物を する

(At a market)

あいこ： ここで やさいと 肉を 買いましょう。   1

お肉は、何がいい？ 牛肉、ぶた肉、とり肉？   2

モニカ： 私は、チキンがいい。   3

あいこ： じゃ、お肉は、とり肉ね。   4

アパートに お米は あるから、、、あとは、やさい と チキン。

モニカ： カレーって、初めから、ドロドロなの？   6

あいこ： ドロドロ？ ああ、カレールー の こと？ ちがいます。   7

カレーの はこ を さがしてね。いろいろ あるでしょう？   8

モニカ： はこの中に、カレールーが あるの？   9

あいこ： そう、チョコレートみたいに見える。   10

モニカ： なるほど。あのね、わたしは 辛いのが苦手だから、甘くしてね。   11

あいこ： だいじょうぶ。甘口のカレールーを 買うから。   12

モニカ： ここに、レシピが あるから 見てみて！   13

[English translation:]

Aiko:     Let's buy meat and vegetables here.  What kind of meat do you like?  Beef, pork, or chicken?
Monica:  I like chicken.
Aiko:     Then the meat is chicken meat.  Since you have rice in your apartment, the remaining is chicken and vegetables.
Monica:  Is curry muddy from the beginning?
Aiko:     Muddy?  Oh, you mean curry roux?  No, it's not.  Please find a box of curry. There are many kinds, right?

Monica:   Is curry roux inside the box?
Aiko:      Yes, it looks like a chocolate bar.
Monica:   I see.  Well, since I am not good at spicy food, please make it mild.
Aiko:      It's all right.  I'll buy a mild curry roux.
Monica:   Here is a recipe!  Please look!

[Vocabulary List]

## 1. Expressions

| | |
|---|---|
| なるほど | I see. |
| あのね | May I say something? |
| みてみて！(見てみて) | Please take a look. |

## 2. Nouns

| | |
|---|---|
| ぎゅうにく(牛肉) | beef |
| ぶたにく　(豚肉) | pork |
| とりにく　(とり肉) | chicken |
| チキン | chicken |
| はじめ　(初め) | the beginning, first |
| 　　はじめから | from the beginning |
| カレールー | curry roux |
| 　　　カレールーのこと | about curry roux |
| はこ | box |
| チョコレート | chocolate |
| あまくち　(甘口) | sweet side, not spicy |
| レシピ | recipe |
| あと | the rest, remaining |

## 3. Copula Nouns

| | |
|---|---|
| いろいろ　(な) | various |

## 4. Verbs

| | |
|---|---|
| ちがいます | is different |
| 　　ちがう | dictionary form; differ |
| ～みたいに みえる　(見える) | looks like～, seems like ～ |
| さがす | to look for, seek |
| 　　さがして | the "te" form of "sagasu" |
| 　　さがします | "masu" form of "sagasu" |
| あまくする | to make it sweet |
| 　　あまくしてね。 | Please make it sweet. |

## 5. Adjectives

| | |
|---|---|
| からい　(辛い) | spicy |

あまい　（甘い）                           sweet

## 6. Adverbs
みたいに                                   adverbial form of "mitai" (seems like)

[Onomatopoeic Adverb]
ドロドロ                                   muddy, thick

## **Grammar and Cultural Notes**

### 1. ～くする **to make things a certain state**

The verb "suru" is used "to cause action," and in English it corresponds to "do," or "make." "Suru" denotes causative change within human control, whereas "naru" (to become) spontaneous change beyond human control. For example, we cannot make winter come after spring. It is nature's doing beyond our grasp. Therefore, we express that idea in Japanese, はるになる or はるがくる. On the contrary, we can influence the change of taste; you can make something spicier or sweeter. This is the expression we learn in this chapter. Making food spicier is からくする, and sweeter あまくする. If you are a math tutor, you can make questions harder or easier. むずかしくする for making a test harder, and やさしくする when making it easier.

Formation:

> Drop 'i' from Adjectives + 'ku' + 'suru'
> から／く　する

Examples:
（１）わたしは、カレーをからくしました。
      I made the curry (curry rice) spicy.

（２）チーズケーキに　さとうをたくさん入れて、あまくしましょう。
      Let's add more sugar to the cheesecake to make it sweeter.

（３）先生は、こんどのテストを　もっと　むずかしくしました。
      Our teacher made this test harder.

（４）イラストをかくとき、目を　大きくしました。
      When I drew the illustration (of people), I made their eyes bigger.

（５）イラストでアメリカ人をかくときは、はなを　高くしますが、日本人
      をかくときは、たいてい　はなを　低くします。
      When you illustrate Americans, you draw their noses taller, but when you draw the Japanese, you usually make them shorter.

## 2. ～みたいに <u>looks like, seems like</u>

チョコレートみたいに見える means that something looks like chocolate. There are other words that mean "looks like, seems like" in Japanese including "yoo, soo, rashi," but "mitai" is most casual and most versatile. It appears in three forms: みたいだ、みたいな、and みたいに. The first form is with a copula verb (だ，です), the second a copula noun (な), and the last an adverb (に).

Examples:

（1） 茶色いカレーは、チョコレートみたいだ。
The curry brown in color looks like chocolate.

（2） チョコレートみたいな　色ですね。
It's a chocolate-like color, isn't it?

（3） カレーって、チョコレートみたいに　見えますね。
Curry looks like chocolate.

（4） 今日は、あたたかくて、春みたいですね。
Today is nice and warm, and spring-like.

（5） ぽかぽかと、春みたいな、お天気ですね。
The weather is spring-like today.
("poka-poka" is a mimesis used to describe a typical spring day)

（6） わたしの犬は、ライオンみたいに、大きいです。
My dog is so big, it looks like a lion.

トマトみたいに、見えますが、
ほんとうは、りんごなんです。

Chapter 10 (B) Exercises

A. Match up the column entries.

| | | | |
|---|---|---|---|
| 1. | beef | A. | カレールー |
| 2. | pork | B. | みず |
| 3. | chicken | C. | チョコレート |
| 4. | vegetables | D. | ぎゅうにく |
| 5. | curry roux | E. | （お）ゆ |
| 6. | chocolate | F. | あまくち |
| 7. | water | G. | ぶたにく |
| 8. | hot water | H. | からくち |
| 9. | sweet-taste | I. | とりにく |
| 10. | spicy-side | J. | やさい |

B. Change the following adjectives to the <u>くする form</u>. (to make things a certain way)

1．あまい　→　あまくする (make it sweet)
2．からい　→
3．むずかしい→
4．やさしい→
5．たかい→
6．ひくい→
7．<ruby>大<rt>おお</rt></ruby>きい→
8．<ruby>小<rt>ちい</rt></ruby>さい→
9．<ruby>冷<rt>つめ</rt></ruby>たい→
１０．あたたかい→

C. Change the following words into expressions containing ～みたいです.
Example れい：かえります　→　かえるみたいです

（１）<ruby>日本人<rt>にほんじん</rt></ruby>です　→

（２）<ruby>好<rt>す</rt></ruby>きです　→

（３）あの<ruby>大学<rt>だいがく</rt></ruby>に<ruby>入<rt>はい</rt></ruby>ります　→

（４）<ruby>先生<rt>せんせい</rt></ruby>と<ruby>話<rt>はな</rt></ruby>します　→

（５）ひまです　→

（６）<ruby>高<rt>たか</rt></ruby>いです　→

（7）しんせつです　→

（8）行<sub>い</sub>きます　→

D. First, change のように to みたいに. Second, find words from the list below, matching with the given statements to form familiar expressions.

Example れい：石<sub>いし</sub>のように→ 石<sub>いし</sub>みたいに→

石<sub>いし</sub>みたいに＋ かたい(as hard as a rock)

1．こどものように→

2．花<sub>はな</sub>のように→

3．春<sub>はる</sub>のように→

4．アメリカ人<sub>じん</sub>のように→

5．こおり(ice)のように→

6．ひまわり(sunflower)（の花<sub>はな</sub>）のように→

7．蜜<sub>みつ</sub>(honey)のように→

8．借<sub>か</sub>りてきた猫<sub>ねこ</sub>(borrowed cat)のように→

| A．あまい | B．おとなしい | C．あかるい | D．英語<sub>えいご</sub>がうまい |
|---|---|---|---|
| | quiet/docile | bright/cheerful | skillful |
| E．つめたい | F．あそぶ | G．美<sub>うつく</sub>しい | H．あたたかい I．かたい |
| | | | hard, firm |

E. What is your family like? Do they remind animals, insects, or supernatural beings? Do you have siblings? What is your younger brother like, if you have any? What is your mother or father like? Use みたい to come up with similes.

Example れい：私<sub>わたし</sub>の母<sub>はは</sub>は、ふだんは、天使<sub>てんし</sub>みたいにやさしいですが、怒<sub>おこ</sub>るときは、鬼<sub>おに</sub>みたいです。父<sub>ちち</sub>は、たいてい、犬<sub>いぬ</sub>みたいによくねますが、サッカーをするときは、獅子<sub>しし</sub>のように、速<sub>はや</sub>く走<sub>はし</sub>ることができて、強<sub>つよ</sub>いです。祖父<sub>そふ</sub>は、石<sub>いし</sub>みたいに、無口<sub>むくち</sub>で、あまりしゃべりません。でもプロの歌手<sub>かしゅ</sub>みたいに、歌<sub>うた</sub>がうまいです。

(My mother is usually like an angel, except when she gets angry. Then she becomes like an ogre. My father usually sleeps like a dog (like a cat, in English); but when he plays soccer, he is as fast and as strong as a lion. My grandfather is as quiet (still) as a rock, but he sings like a professional vocalist.)

F. Fill in the blanks with appropriate simile.＿＿＿＿にことばを　いれなさい。

1．＿＿＿＿＿＿のように、白い。

2．＿＿＿＿＿＿のように、青<sub>あお</sub>い。

3．＿＿＿＿＿＿のように、赤<sub>あか</sub>い。

4．＿＿＿＿＿＿のように、黒<sub>くろ</sub>い。

5．＿＿＿＿＿＿のように、やさしい。

6．＿＿＿＿＿＿のように、こわい。

7．＿＿＿＿＿＿のように、かたい。

8．＿＿＿＿＿＿のように、強<sub>つよ</sub>い。

9．＿＿＿＿＿＿のように、せがたかい。

10．＿＿＿＿＿＿のように、英語がうまい。

11．＿＿＿＿＿＿のように、せまい。

12．＿＿＿＿＿＿のように、美<sub>うつく</sub>しい。

13．＿＿＿＿＿＿のように、明<sub>あか</sub>るい。

Make your own sentences with simile ～のように

14．＿＿＿＿＿＿

15．＿＿＿＿＿＿

16．＿＿＿＿＿＿

Chapter 10 (B): Dict-A-Conversation
Listen to Chapter 10 (B)'s Dict-A-Conversation on the student CD, and write in the checkmark in either "Truth" or "False" columns, after judging the credibility of each statement.

[Vocabulary Help]:

    せのたかい人 a tall person
    せがたかい　　(height is) tall
    キリン　　　　　giraffe
    シュートを　きめる to sink a shot
    はしる　　　　to run
    プレー　　　　a play; to play
    パスする　　　to pass the ball

| statements | Truth （ほんとう） | False （うそ） |
|:---:|:---:|:---:|
| 1 | | |
| 2 | | |
| 3 | | |
| 4 | | |
| 5 | | |
| 6 | | |
| 7 | | |
| 8 | | |
| 9 | | |
| 10 | | |

Chapter 10 (B)

| 物 (thing) | もの<br>ブツ<br>（モツ） | 物（もの）a thing<br>持ち物（もちもの）one's possessions<br>[品物（しなもの）a merchandise; an article]<br>[物事（ものごと）events/things in life]<br>見物（けんぶつ）sightseeing<br>名物（めいぶつ）noted products<br>大好物（だいこうぶつ）most favorite food<br>食物（しょくもつ）food<br>[怪物（かいぶつ）a monster] |
|---|---|---|
| | | (8)<br>ノ ー ナ 牛 牜 牜 物 物 |
| 牛 (a cow, beef) | うし<br>ギュウ | 牛（うし）a cow<br>水牛（すいぎゅう）a water buffalo<br>牛肉（ぎゅうにく）beef<br>牛丼（ぎゅうどん）beef bowl |
| | | (4)<br>ノ ー 二 牛 |
| 初 (first) | はじ（めて）<br>はつ<br>ショ | 初めて（はじめて）the first time<br>初物（はつもの）first food of the season<br>初日の出（はつひので）the first sun of a year<br>初回（しょかい）first time<br>初日（しょにち）first day; opening day<br>[最初（さいしょ）first; beginning] |
| | | (7)<br>丶 ﾗ ｵ ｵ ｵ 初 初 |
| 辛 (spicy; salty; harsh) | から（い）<br>つら（い）<br>シン | 辛い（からい）spicy; salty<br>辛い（つらい）difficult to bear<br>　辛い目に会う（つらいめにあう）have a<br>　　　　　　　　　　　　　　　hard time<br>辛口（からくち）spicy side<br>香辛料（こうしんりょう）spices<br>辛抱（しんぼう）する to be patient |
| | | (7)<br>丶 ー ｳ ｳ 立 产 辛 |

## Kanji Practice for Chapter 10 B

かんじの　れんしゅう

１．つぎの　ことばを　よみなさい。それから、クラスメートに　いみを
ききなさい。Read the following words to your classmates and ask them for the
meaning of each word.

（１）　大事な物

（２）　好きな物

（３）　大好物

（４）　物事

（５）　食物

（６）　牛

（７）　牛肉

（８）　牛乳

（９）　初めて

（１０）　初回

（１１）　辛い

２．Write kanji in the box to complete the compound word.

(1)   the first day

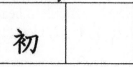

(2)   beef

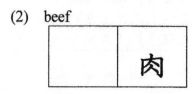

(3)   food

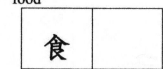

(4)   one's favorite food

3. よんでから、よみがなをかいて、えいごでいいなさい。 Read first, then write yomigana above each kanji, and translate into English.

    （１）    何か　おいしい物が　ありますか。

    （２）    私の　大好物は、スウィートポテトです。

    （３）    友人と「よしのや」で、「牛どん」を　食べました。

    （４）    初めて、アラスカへ　行きました。

    （５）    辛くないメキシコりょうりは、ありますか。

    （６）    「辛口」のカレーと「甘口」のカレーと、どちらの方が好き
             ですか。

    （７）    Buffalo は、「水牛」のことです。

    （８）    やきゅうで、初回から、ホームランを　うちました。
             (baseball)                              (to hit)

4. 日本語で書きなさい。 Translate into Japanese, writing the underlined words in kanji.

(1) Which do you <u>like</u> best among <u>beef</u>, pork, lamb, and chicken?

(2) What is "curry roux"?

(3) Which do you <u>prefer</u>: <u>spicy</u> curry or <u>mild</u> curry?

(4) What is your <u>utmost favorite food</u>?

Chapter 10 (C)   Recipe for Curry Rice   カレーライスのつくりかた

---

おいしいカレーのつくりかた

ざいりょう：〔四人分〕

やさい

      にんじん　　　（中）　　　二本
      玉ねぎ　　　　（大）　　　一こ

にく

      チキン(鶏肉)、ビーフ(牛肉)、または、ポーク(豚肉)　二百グラム

カレールー　一はこ

ごはん　　　四人分

つくりかた：

  1）　　　まず、にんじんと玉ねぎを　二センチの　大きさに　切ります。
  2）　　　大さじ　一ぱいの油で　炒めます。
  3）　　　肉を入れて、さらに　炒めます。
  4）　　　水　七百CCを　入れて、煮ます。
  5）　　　一度、火を止めて、カレールーを　入れます。
  6）　　　とろ火で、十分ぐらい　煮ます。
  7）　　　ごはんの上に　かけます。

      できあがり〜！

Chapter 10 (C)
[English translation:]

---

### How to make good curry rice

**Ingredients**: (four servings)

Vegetables

        Carrots (medium)  two
        Onions (large)     one

Meat

        Chicken (breast), beef, or pork    200 g

Curry roux     one box

Cooked rice     four servings

**How to prepare**:

  (1) Cut carrots and onions into two centimeter cubes.
  (2) Cook vegetables with one tablespoon of oil.
  (3) Add meat and cook further.
  (4) Pour 700 cc water and cook until ingredients become soft.
  (5) Turn off and remove from the heat and add curry roux.
  (6) Simmer for ten minutes.
  (7) Pour over cooked rice.
         It's done~!

---

[Vocabulary List]

1. Expressions

| | |
|---|---|
| つくりかた | how to make |
| できあがり～！ | It's done~! |

2. Nouns

| | |
|---|---|
| ビーフ | beef |
| ポーク | pork |
| グラム | gram |
| センチ(メートル) | centimeter |
| おおきさ　(大きさ) | size |
| おおさじ | one tablespoon |
| おおさじ　いっぱい(一杯) | one tablespoonful (15 cc) |
| あぶら　(油) | oil, cooking oil |
| ＣＣ | cubic centimeter, milliliter |

| | |
|---|---|
| いちど　（一度） | once, one time |
| ひ　（火） | fire |
| とろび　（とろ火） | low heat |

[Counter for serving]

| | |
|---|---|
| ～にんぶん　（～人分） | servings (a counter) |
| 　ひとりぶん | one serving (for one person) |
| 　ふたりぶん | two servings (for two persons) |
| 　さんにんぶん | three servings (for three people) |
| 　よにんぶん | four servings (for four people) |

[Other counters]　　　See Chapter 3 (C)

| | |
|---|---|
| いっぽん　（一本） | counter for long items |
| いっこ　　（一個） | counter for non-flat, small items |
| ひとはこ　（一箱） | counter for boxes |

3. Verbs

| | |
|---|---|
| つくります　（作ります） | make ("masu" form) |
| 　つくる　（作る） | to make (dictionary form) |
| きります　　（切ります） | cut |
| 　きる　　（切る） | to cut |
| いためます　（炒めます） | stir-fry |
| 　いためる　（炒める） | to stir-fry |
| にます（煮ます） | cook in a sauce or soup |
| 　にる　（煮る） | to cook in a sauce or soup |
| とめます　（止めます） | stop |
| 　とめる　（止める） | to stop |
| 　とめて　（止めて） | the "te" form of "tomeru" |
| かけます | pour over something |
| 　かける | to pour over something |

4. Adverbs

| | |
|---|---|
| まず | at first |
| さらに | moreover |

Chapter 10 (C)                    Grammar and Cultural Notes

## 1. 〜かた **how to; a way of; a manner of**

"- kata" is a noun-forming suffix that indicates a way or a manner in which one does something. For example, if you want to know how to write a kanji, you may ask in Japanese, このかんじの かきかたを おしえてください。 The formation is as follows:

> Masu form verb (2<sup>nd</sup> base Consonant verb or stem of Vowel verb) + kata
> かき＋かた (how to write)
> たべ＋かた (how to eat)

Examples:
（１）このケーキのつくりかたを おしえてください。
    Please teach me how to make this cake.

（２）先生、このかんじの書き方が、分かりません。
    Professor, I don't know how to write this Chinese character.

（３）日本語のべんきょうのしかたが、分かりません。
    I don't know how to study Japanese.

（４）このたんごの発音のしかたは、むずかしいです。
    It is difficult to pronounce this vocabulary word.

（５）えきまでの みちの行きかたが、分かりません。
    I don't know how to get to the station.

## 2. 〜さ : **–ness, -ty**

"-sa" is a suffix that creates a noun out of an adjective. It describes the intensity presented by an adjective. For example, an adjective むずかしい means "difficult," while むずかしさ means "how difficult it is."
Formation:

> Drop 'i' from adjectives + 'sa'
> むずかし (/) ＋ さ
> やさし (/) ＋ さ

When an adjective can be paired with another adjectival antonym as with "おおきい (big)" and "ちいさい(small)", the positive counterpart (おおきい in this case) tends to acquire a state/meaning of "absolute degree" when the suffix 'sa' is attached, as in おおきさ 'size'.

Examples:

Adjectives

| Positive meaning | Negative meaning |
|---|---|
| たかさ tallness, height | ひくさ shortness, lowness |
| あつさ(暑さ)hotness, heat | さむさ coldness |
| おおきさ largeness, size | ちいささ smallness |
| つよさ strength | よわさ weakness |
| ひろさ wideness of space | せまさ smallness of space |
| たのしさ　うれしさ happiness | かなしさ sadness |
| ふかさ deepness, depth | あささ shallowness |
| むずかしさ difficultness | やさしさ easiness |
| あつさ(厚さ)thickness | うすさ（薄さ）thinness |
| おもさ heaviness, weight | かるさ lightness |
| こさ(濃さ) thickness, density | うすさ（薄さ）thinness |

The left hand-side (positive) adjectives take on a meaning of absolute degree.
Examples:

（１）きみに、日本語のむずかしさが　分かるの？
Do you understand how difficult the Japanese language is?

（２）社長、コーヒーの濃さは、これぐらいでよろしいでしょうか。
President, is it all right to make your coffee this strong?

（３）このへやの広さは、さいこうです。きょうしつより広いです。
This room's spaciousness is wonderful.  It's wider than our classroom.

（４）日本語をべんきょうする楽しさを、知りました。
I learned the joy of studying Japanese.

（５）この川の深さは、ニメートルぐらい　ありますよ。
The depth of this river is about two meters.

（６）このにもつの重さは、１０キロ以上ありますよ。
This luggage weighs more than ten kilograms.

（７）台風の強さは、風速で　分かります。
We can measure the strength of a hurricane from the speed of wind.

（８）その本の厚さは、三センチぐらいです。
The width of that book is about three centimeters.

（９）そのはしの高<sub>たか</sub>さは、ナニメートルぐらいです。
      The height of the bridge is about twelve meters.

（１０）ことしの夏<sub>なつ</sub>の暑<sub>あつ</sub>さは、ひどかったです。
      This summer heat was terrible.

Note:

Copula nouns do not use the suffix 'sa' as often as adjectives. Do not assume 'sa' is immediately applicable to copula nouns. Only small batch of copula nouns are used with the suffix 'sa." Here are some frequently used "copula nouns + sa":

1）きれいさ (how pretty it is)
2）たいへんさ (how much work it is)
3）べんりさ (how convenient it is)
4）おだやかさ (how calm/peaceful it is)
5）りっぱさ (how dignified it is)
6）しずかさ (how quiet it is)
7）にぎやかさ (how lively it is)
8）あさはかさ (how stupid the person is)
9）みじめさ (how miserable the person is)
１０）せいかくさ/たしかさ (how accurate it is)
１１）ちゅうじつさ (how loyal it is)
１２）ぶきみさ (how eerie it is)

## 3. て form verb as a connective showing "sequential action"

The "te" form defines the sequence of actions in a sentence. Except for the main verb which comes at the end of a sentence, all verbs take the "te-form," and they connect the other verbs into a sequence of action. The "te" form verb has nothing to do with tense. Tense is always expressed in the main verb at the end of the sentence.

Examples:

１．六時<sub>ろくじ</sub>におきて、あさごはんを　食<sub>た</sub>べました。
    I got up at six o'clock and ate breakfast.

２．シャワーをあびて、ごはんを食<sub>た</sub>べて、学校<sub>がっこう</sub>に来<sub>き</sub>ました。
    I took a shower, ate, and came to school.

３．モールで　ともだちに会<sub>あ</sub>って、おしゃべりをしました。
    I met my friend at a shopping mall, and chatted with her.

４．としょかんへ行<sub>い</sub>って、しゅくだいをします。
    I will go to the library and do my homework.

5．ごはんをつくって、食べました。

I cooked and ate.

6．お米を洗って、水といっしょに、すいはんきに入れて、スイッチを入れました。

(raw rice) (洗う to wash)　　　　　(rice cooker)　　　　　to turn on a switch

I washed rice, placed it with water into the rice cooker, and turned on the power
switch.

アイスクリームをちゅうもんして、
食べました。

ガラスを割って、叱られました。

(I broke the window glass and was
scolded.)

Chapter 10 (C) Exercises

A.  Change the verb phrase below into noun phrases using "〜かた."

Example れい：日本語<u>を</u>話す→　日本語<u>の</u>話しかた

1）ことばを　おぼえる→
2）おはしを　つかう→
3）カレーを　つくる→
4）コーヒーをいれる→
5）じしょを　ひく　→
6）かんじを　よむ　→
7）きれいに　あるく→　きれいな
8）字を　きれいに　書く→
9）美しく　話す　→　美しい
10）ていねいに　聞く→　ていねいな
　　　　politely　　to ask　　polite

B.  Pair-work:  Practice the following dialogues with your pair and create your own
dialogues, using 〜かた (how to do it).

　　1.
　　(A)：Bさん、おいしいおちゃのいれかたを　おしえてください。
　　(B)：え？おいしいおちゃのいれかたですか。いいですよ。
　　(A)：ありがとう。

　　2.
　　(B)：Aさん、このかんじのかきかたが、わからないんですけど、、
　　(A)：あ、そのかんじですか。それはね、じつは、こうかくんです。
　　(B)：あ〜そうなんですか。ありがとう。

　　3.
　　(A)：Bさん、がくせいかの行きかたを　しっていますか。
　　(B)：あ、がくせいかですか。がくせいかはね、このビルのまえです。
　　　　このきょうしつをでて、すぐです。
　　(A)：ありがとう。

C. Find someone who can do it!  Go around the class to find someone who knows how to
do the followings.  Write down their names and tell the class in the format of 〜さん

　　は、、、、のしかたを　知っています。

　　Ask "〜の、、、かたを　知っていますか。"

　　(1) how to fold "origami" （おりがみ、　折る）　................................................

(2) how to fold "crane"　（つる、折る）　……………………………………

(3) how to cook curry　（カレー、つくる）　……………………………………

(4) how to saw a button　（ボタン、つける）　……………………………………

(5) how to use a kanji dictionary（かんじじしょ、　つかう）……………………

(6) how to make a cocktail　（カクテル、つくる）……………………………

(7) how to make a reservation at a hotel　（ホテルの予約をする）…………………

D-1. Change adjectives to "~sa" ending nouns.
Example れい：あつい→　あつさ

1）さむい　　　　2）たかい　　　　3）こわい　　　　4）大きい

5）小さい　　　　6）きびしい　　　7）おもしろい　　8）やさしい

9）むずかしい　10）あたたかい　　11）よい　　　　　12）ない

D-2.　（　）にてきとうな言葉を入れなさい。Fill in the blanks with appropriate words.

1．この　にもつの　（　　　　　　）　がわかりません。(hint: heavy おもい)
　　　　　luggage　　　　weight

2．この橋の　（　　　　　　）　は、何メートルありますか。(hint: long ながい)
　　　　　bridge　　　　length

3．この川の　（　　　　　　）　は、どれぐらいですか。(hint: deep ふかい)
　　　　　　　　　　depth

4．マザーテレサの　（　　　　　）　は、すべての人に、理解されました。
　　　　　　　kindness; gentleness　　(was understood by everyone)

5．かぶきの　（　　　　　）　は、最高ですよ！
　　　　　how interesting it is

E.　「あつさ、さむさも　ひがんまで（暑さ、寒さも　彼岸まで）」ということば
　　が　あります。どんないみか、しらべてみましょう。

F. Connect sentence using the "te" form verb.
Example れい：としょかんへ行きます。そして、本を借ります。
　　　　　　→　としょかんへ行って、本を借ります。

（1）朝はやくおきます。そして、ジョギングをします。

（2）しゅくだいをしました。そして、ねました。

（3）ごはんをつくりました。そして、食べました。

（4）学校に来ました。そして、ともだちに会いました。

（5）きっさてんに行きます。そして、コーヒーを飲みます。

（6）ジムで 泳ぎます。そして、うちに帰ります。

G.（　）にてきとうな言葉を入れなさい。Fill in the blanks with appropriate words.

1．あさ（　　　　　）、あさごはんを（　　　　）、しんぶん（　　　　　）
　　　　　get up　　　　　　　　　　　　　eat　　　　　　　　　　read
から、うちを 出ます。

2．しんじゅくで でんしゃに（　　　　）、ぎんざで（　　　　　）、
　　　　　　　　　　　　　　ride; get on　　　　　　　　get off
かいものをしました。

3．ＣＤを（　　　　）もんだいを（　　　　）、こたえを（　　　　）くだ
　　　　　listen　　　　　　　　　read　　　　　　　　　write
さい。

4．はらじゅくでともだちと（　　　　）、レストランで食事を
　　　　　　　　　　　　　　　meet
（　　　　）から、えいがを 見に行きました。
　　do

5．テレビを（　　　　）から、ごはんを（　　　　）、おみそしるを
　　　　　watch　　　　　　　　　　cook (rice)
（　　　　）、それからともだちを（　　　　）、いっしょに食べました。
　make　　　　　　　　　　　invite; call; summon

6．にんじんとたまねぎを（　　　　）、なべで（　　　　）から、お水を入
　　　　　　　　　　　　cut　　　　　　　stir-fry
れます。それをよく（　　　　）から、火を（　　　　）、カレールーを
　　　　　cook in a soup　　　　　　turn off; shut off
（　　　　）、できあがりです！
　put in; insert

H-1. Change the form as the example shows below. 例のように、変えなさい。

例　Sentence → Noun Phrase

あたまがいい　→　あたまのよさ

目がいい→　目の

耳がいい→

ひとがいい→

仲がいい→

きもちがいい→

感じがいい→

Vocabulary Hint: あたま head, 目 eyes, 耳 ears, ひと（がら）personality, 仲 relationship, きもち feelings, 感じ impressions given to others

Next, add to the noun phrases you created "〜に　感心しました。(I was impressed with ~.)" For example, あたまのよさに、感心しました。You may also add the subject of the sentence such as 彼 (he), 彼女 (she), 主人公 (protagonist) with a particle の, i.e. あなたの、キャシーさんの、彼女の, etc. 彼のあたまのよさに感心しました。(I was surprised how smart he was.)

H-2. Change the form as the example shows below. 例のように、変えなさい。

例　Sentence → Noun Phrase

やる気がない　→　やる気のなさ

元気がない→

欲がない→

人気がない→

おもいやりがない→

Vocabulary Hint: やる気 willingness (to do; to achieve), 欲 greed, 人気 popularity, おもいやり consideration for others

Next, add to the noun phrases you created "〜に　びっくりしました。(I was surprised at ~.)" For example, やる気のなさに　びっくりしました。You may add the subject of the sentence such as 彼、彼女、主人公 with a particle の, i.e. 彼のやる気のなさに びっくりしました。(I was surprised at his unenthusiastic attitude.)

I. グループ・プロジェクト (group project) & はっぴょう (presentation)

Make a group of two to four people in class. Discuss and decide on what item, people, animals, or anything you want to "describe" and let the class figure out what that is. So, be careful not to tell the class "what" you are describing, until someone in class guessed it right. Everyone in your group must participate in your activity and must say something at the time of presentation.

You may want to use the following information, but don't need to use all of them, and also feel free to add more. Choose the item from something which is known to people or someone who is famous enough that people recognize.

...................の　おおきさは、ーーーーです。

おもさは、ーーーーです。

ながさは、ーーーーです。

はやさは、ーーーーです。

たかさは、ーーーーです。

ふかさは、ーーーーです。

................. は、ーーーーーーが　好きです。

ーーーーが　上手 (得意) です。or　ーーー　が　できます。

ーーーーーーーに　住んでいます。or　ーに　います (あります)。

Chapter 10 (C): Dict-A-Conversation
Respond orally to the following statements and write down your answers. Please answer in <u>complete sentences</u>, writing in hiragana and in kanji where applicable.

1. _____

2. _____

3. _____

4. _____

5. _____

6. _____

7. _____

8. _____

9. _____

10. _____

Chapter 10 (C)

| 切<br>(to cut) | き（る）<br>き（れる）<br>セツ | 切る（きる）to cut; chop<br>切れる（きれる）to be sharp; break, snap<br>切手（きって）postage stamps<br>切れ目（きれめ）gap; break<br>大切（たいせつ）important |
| | | (4)<br>一 七 切 切 |
| 油<br>(oil) | あぶら<br>ユ | ごま油（あぶら）sesame oil<br>石油（せきゆ）petroleum<br>油田（ゆでん）an oil field (well) |
| | | (8)<br>丶 ニ 氵 氵 汩 油 油 油 |
| 煮<br>(to boil) | に（る）<br>シャ | 煮る（にる）to cook<br>[煮立つ（にたつ）start boiling]<br>[煮沸（しゃふつ）boiling] |
| | | (12)<br>一 十 土 耂 者 者 者 者 者 者 煮 煮 |
| 止<br>(to stop) | と（まる）<br>と（める）<br>シ<br>や（める） | 止まる（とまる）something stops<br>止める（とめる）you stop something<br>中止（ちゅうし）する to interrupt; to terminate a plan/activity<br>止める（やめる）to quit; to discontinue |
| | | (4)<br>｜ 卜 止 止 |
| 炊<br>(to cook) | た（く）<br>スイ | ごはんを炊く（たく）to cook rice<br>炊事（すいじ）をする to cook and clean up<br>自炊（じすい）cooking for oneself |
| | | (8)<br>丶 ゛ 少 火 火 炒 炒 炊 |
| 作<br>(to make) | つく（る）<br>サク | 作る（つくる）to make<br>作文（さくぶん）a composition<br>[作曲（さっきょく）(musical) composition] |
| | | (7)<br>丿 イ 仁 仁 竹 作 作 作 |

Kanji Practice for Chapter 10 C

かんじの　れんしゅう

　１．つぎの　ことばを　よみなさい。それから、クラスメートに　いみを
　　　ききなさい。Read the following words and sentences to your classmates and
　　　ask them for their meanings.

（１）　手を切る

（２）　大切な人

（３）　サラダ油

（４）　さとうとしょうゆで煮る

（５）　ごはんを　炊く

（６）　炊飯器
　　　　　はんき

（７）　炊事

（８）　友だちを作る

（９）　火を止める

（１０）花火大会が、中止になる
　　　　はなび

（１１）タバコを止める

　２．Write kanji in the box to complete the compound word.

(1)　suspension; cancellation

(2)　cooking; kitchen work

(3)　writers

(4)　important

(5) house chores (cleaning, cooking, etc.)

(6) rice cooker

3. よんでから、よみがなをかいて、えいごでいいなさい。 Read first, then write yomigana above each kanji, and translate into English.

（１）　　母は、私の大切な人です。

（２）　　肉や玉ねぎを、油で　炒めます。

（３）　　よく煮えましたから、火を止めてください。

（４）　　兄が　炊事当番のルールを作りました。
　　　　　(当番［とうばん］turn)

（５）　　父がタバコを止めたのは、とてもいい事です。

（６）　　スポーツ大会が　中止になったのは、ざんねんです。

（７）　　そうじ、せんたくなど、家の中の仕事を「家事」と言います。

（８）　　やさいをフライパンで油で炒めてから、おなべに入れて、さとう
　　　　　としょうゆとだしで、煮ます。
　　　　　(フライパン frying pan, おなべ pot, さとう sugar, しょうゆ soy sauce,
　　　　　だし soup stock)

## Chapter 10 (D)　　　Too Spicy!　辛すぎる！

| | | |
|---|---|---|
| モニカ： | あまり　辛くしないでね。 | 1 |
| あいこ： | だいじょうぶ。これ、甘口だから。 | 2 |
| モニカ： | わあ、トロトロになってる。おいしそう！ | 3 |
| あいこ： | ごはんも　できました。 | 4 |
| モニカ： | いただきま〜す！ | 5 |
| あいこ： | どうぞ。私も、いただきます。 | 6 |
| モニカ： | う！　から〜い！　からすぎる！ | 7 |
| あいこ： | え？　どうして？　甘口のはずだけど。 | 8 |
| | む？　からい！カレールーのはこを、見せて？ | 9 |
| | これ、「辛口」って　書いてある。 | 10 |
| モニカ： | ごめん。「甘口」と「辛口」を　まちがえました。 | 11 |
| あいこ： | 私は、いいけど。ずいぶん辛くなったね。モニカ、だいじょうぶ？ | |
| モニカ： | うん。辛口のカレーも、けっこうおいしい。 | 13 |
| | 私にも、辛口のカレーを食べることが　できました！ | 14 |

Chapter 10 (D)
[English translation:]

Monica: Please don't make it spicy.
Aiko:    It should be all right since this is mild.
Monica: Wow, it's becoming thick, looking delicious!
Aiko:    Rice is ready, too.
Monica: I will dig in!
Aiko:    Help yourself.  I am going to eat, too.
Monica: Oooo….spicy!  Too spicy!
Aiko:    What?  Why?  It has to be mild.  Hmmm…it is spicy!  Please show me the box
         of curry roux.  This (box) reads "spicy."
Monica: I'm sorry.  I got confused with the "mild" and "spicy" labels on the box.
Aiko:    I'm all right though…It's become really spicy.  Are you all right, Monica?
Monica: Yeah.  Spicy curry tastes pretty good, too. I succeeded in eating spicy curry!

[Vocabulary List]

1.  Expressions
    からくしないで                   Please don't make it spicy.
    いただきます                     I'm going to eat.
    からすぎる                       (It's) too spicy.
    おいしそう                       (It) looks delicious.
    かいてある                       (It's) been written (for you).
    からくなる                       to become spicier
    ごめん                           a casual form of "I'm sorry"

2.  Nouns
    からくち(辛口)                   spicy (taste)

3. Verbs
    まちがえる                       to make a mistake
        まちがえました               past tense of まちがえる
    (できる)                         to finish; accomplish
        できました                   It's finished. It's done.

4.  Adverbs
    ずいぶん                         very, extremely
    けっこう                         fairy well, the same as かなり

    Onomatopoeic adverb
    トロトロ                         thick and syrupy

## Additional Vocabulary from Grammar Notes, Exercises, and Dict-A-Conversation

------------------------------------------------------------------------------

[Nouns]

| | |
|---|---|
| ドッグフード | dog food |
| ゲスト | guest |
| おんど | temperature |
| ボート | boat |
| しあい | games; match |
| じゅぎょうちゅう | during the class |
| せんたくもの | laundry |
| むすこ | son |
| スパイス | spices |
| しお | salt |
| がけ | cliff |
| おたんじょうカード | birthday card |
| めざましどけい | alarm clock |
| わからないところ | things that one doesn't understand |
| じゅんび | preparation |
| （かびん） | vase |
| でんとう（電灯） | lamp; light |
| こたえ | answer |

[Copula Nouns]

| | |
|---|---|
| めんどう | troublesome |
| たいくつ | boring |

[Adjectives]

| | |
|---|---|
| くるしい | suffering |
| くやしい | regrettable; vexing |

[Adverbs]

| | |
|---|---|
| ブカブカ | It describes that things worn are too big. |
| さいきん/このごろ | recently |
| あまりにも | unbearably; extremely |

[Verbs]

| | |
|---|---|
| 行き過ぎる | to pass; go too far |
| もどる | to return |
| （ふろを）わかす | to boil the hot-bath water |
| （ふとんを）しく/ひく | to make a futon-bed; spread |
| ふとる /ふとっている | to gain weight/ is fat |

| | |
|---|---|
| やせる ／やせている | to lose weight/ is thin |
| こんやくする/こんやくしている | to get engaged/ is engaged |
| おなかがすく/すいている | to become hungry/ is hungry |
| こまる/こまっている | to become troubled/ is troubled |
| ドキッとする/ドキッとしている | to get startled/is startled |
| ションボリする/ションボリしている | to be downhearted/is downhearted |
| ぬれる/ ぬれている | to get wet/ is wet |
| かわく/ かわいている | to become dry/ is dry |
| 　（のどが　かわいている） | is thirsty) |
| こむ/ こんでいる | to become crowded/is crowded |
| （戸、ハンドバッグが）あく/あいている | to open / is open |
| しまる/しまっている | to close/ is closed |
| （でんとう　が）きえる/きえている | to extinguish/ is extinguished |
| （火、でんとう、テレビが）つく/ついている | to turn on/ is turned on |
| おちる/おちている | to fall/ is on the ground |
| はいる/はいっている | to enter/ is in |
| （かぎが）かかる/かかっている | to lock/ is locked |
| にげる | to escape |
| さわる | to touch |
| （えさを）やる | to feed (the animals) |
| （かみを）とく | to comb |
| つかれる/ つかれている | to get tired/is tired |
| （なく　泣く） | to cry |
| しっぱいする | to fail |
| （うかる） | to pass |
| かざる | to decorate |
| だす（しゅくだいを出す） | to turn in (homework etc.) |
| セットする | to set |
| ひやす（冷やす） | to cool something |
| しらべる | to check; investigate |
| よういする（＝じゅんびする） | to prepare |
| もる（お皿に盛る） | to dish up; heap; serve; fill |

[Expressions]

| | |
|---|---|
| ちょうどいい | just right; perfect |
| つぎのこたえのなかで | among the following answers |

Chapter 10 (D)                    Grammar and Cultural Notes

### 1. ～そう **It looks ~; It seems ~**
The stem of an adjective plus "soo" expresses in English "It looks ~" or "It seems ~ ". "Soo" indicates a speaker's subjective conjecture based on what s/he sees or how s/he feels.

Formation: Adjectives

| Stem of Adjectives (take final "i" from an adjective) | そうだ。 |
| --- | --- |
| | そうな + noun |
| | そうに + adv., adj., or verb |

Examples:
[そうだ]
（１）このカレー、おいしそうですね。　　　The curry looks delicious.
（２）このセーターは、たかそうですね。　　The sweater looks expensive.
（３）このパンは、かたそうだから、食べません。
　　　The bread looks hard, so I won't eat it.

[そうな]
（１）やわらかそうな　かみだなぁ。　　　How soft her hair looks!
（２）おいしそうなコーヒーですね。　　The coffee looks delicious, doesn't it?
（３）そこに　あたたかそうなコートが　あります。
　　　There is a coat over there that looks nice and warm.

[そうに]
（１）その人は、さむそうに、立っていました。
　　　He was standing there looking cold.
（２）田中さんは、あそこで　つまらなそうに　外を見ています。
　　　Appearing bored, Mr. Tanaka is looking outside over there.
（３）母は、いそがしそうに、おすしを　つくっていました。
　　　My mother was making o-sushi.  She looked busy.

**Attention**: ない and よい are adjectival.

ない＋そう→ なさそう (It appears not to have ~.)
よい＋そう→ よさそう (It appears to be good ~.)

Examples:
1. あの人は、あたまがよさそうですよ。　　　He looks smart.
2. 父は、あまりお金がなさそうです。 My father doesn't seem to have money.

This usage of "soo" is also used with copula nouns, but not nouns.

Formation: Copula Nouns (な Adjectives)

| Copula Nouns (な Adjectives) げんき、ひま、たいくつ、じょうぶ etc. | そうだ。 |
| --- | --- |
| | そうな + noun |
| | そうに + adv., adj., or verb |

げんき (healthy; energetic)、ひま (having too much free time)、たいくつ (bored)、じょうぶ (strong and sturdy; healthy)

Examples:
[そうだ]

(1) 小林さんは、今日も元気そうですね。 Mr. Kobayashi looks energetic today, too.

(2) ひまそうですね。 You seem nothing to do.

(3) このつくえは、たいへん じょうぶそうです。 This desk looks very sturdy.

[そうな]

(1) 元気そうなこどもたちですね。 Children look very healthy.

(2) あのひまそうな大学生に聞いてみましょう。
Let's ask the student who seems to be free.

(3) ずいぶん じょうぶそうなつくえですね。 What a sturdy looking desk!

[そうに]

(1) 元気そうにしていますが、じつは、病気なんです。
He is acting well, but the truth is he is ill.

(2) 社員は、仕事がなくて、ひまそうに しています。
Company employees look bored since they have no work to do.

(3) そのこどもは、たいくつそうに、外をみていました。
The child was looking out as if he was totally bored.

This usage of "soo" is also used with verbs in the "masu" form.
Formation: Verbs

| "ます"form Verbs あり、死に、降り、勝ち、転び、負け、落ち、太り | そうだ。 |
| --- | --- |
| | そうな + noun |
| | そうに + adv., adj., or verb |

ある (exist; have)、死ぬ (die)、降る (rain, snow)、勝つ (win)、転ぶ (fall; trip over)、太る (gain weight) 、負ける (to lose [the games, etc.])、落ちる (fall; decline)

Examples:

[そうだ]

(1) 試合に負けそうだ。　　　　　　　　We are about to lose the game.

(2) 今日は雨が降りそうです。　　　　　It seems going to rain today.

(3) ハイヒールが高くて、転びそうです。 Her high-heels are so high that she
looks she might tumble.

(4) こんなにカロリーの高いものを食べると、太りそうです。 I'll gain weight
if I eat such a high-calorie food.

[そうな]

(1) 負けそうな試合だったが、勝った。 It looked as if we're about to lose, but we
ended up with winning.

(2) 雨が降りそうな空だから、かさを持って行きなさい。
Take an umbrella with you since the sky looks as if it's going to rain.

(3) 試験に落ちそうな気がする。　　　 I feel like failing the exam.

(4) どろぼうは、お金がありそうな家を　ねらう。
A thief usually targets a house that looks having a lot of money.

[そうに]

(1) 負けそうに見えたが、がんばって　勝った。
They appeared to be losing, but won after fighting back.

(2) そのドレスがあまりすてきだったので、おもわず買いそうになった。
The dress was so wonderful that I was so tempted to buy it.

(3) 悲しくて泣きそうになったが、がまんした。
I felt like crying since I was so sad, but pushed tears back.

There is another "そうです" that is used with the dictionary form, featuring a totally different meaning. The "dictionary form + soo" is used to express "hearsay" or "I have heard that~."

## 2. ～すぎる; It's too (much) ～

The verb すぎる (過ぎる) is highly productive in forming compound verbs. It also functions as an auxiliary attached to the stem of an adjective or copula noun. "Sugiru" means "to exceed," enhancing the meaning of the preceding word. Thus when added to the stem of an adjective, verb or copula noun, something would become excessive.

1). Formation of "sugiru" with an adjective:

| Stem of Adjectives (no final "i")<br>たか≠、やす≠、むずかし≠, etc.<br>From (たかい)(やすい)(むずかしい) | ＋すぎる |
|---|---|

Examples:　（１）　このケーキは、甘<sub>あま</sub>すぎる。
This cake is too sweet.

（２）　このかばんは、高<sub>たか</sub>すぎますね。
This bag is too expensive.

（３）　このくつは、小<sub>ちい</sub>さすぎて、はくことができません。
These shoes are too small for me to fit in.

（４）　このテストは、むずかしすぎて、よくできませんでした。
This test was so hard I couldn't do well.

（５）　このズボンは、大<sub>おお</sub>きすぎて、ブカブカです。
This pair of pants is too big (and I am swimming in them).

2). Formation of "sugiru" with a verb:

| The "masu" form Verb (2<sup>nd</sup> base of consonant verbs/stem of vowel verbs) 買<sub>か</sub>い≠、し≠、食<sub>た</sub>べ≠、etc. From (買います)(します)(食べます) | + すぎる |
|---|---|

（１）　おさけを飲<sub>の</sub>みすぎました。
I drank too much.

（２）　ごはんを食<sub>た</sub>べ過<sub>す</sub>ぎて、おなかがくるしい。
I ate too much and I feel my stomach's being squeezed.

（３）　ちょっと行<sub>ゆ</sub>き過<sub>す</sub>ぎました。さっきの信号<sub>しんごう</sub>のところまで、もどりましょう。
We went too far.  Let's go back to where the traffic signal was.

（４）　今月<sub>こんげつ</sub>は、ドッグフードを買<sub>か</sub>いすぎましたね。来月<sub>らいげつ</sub>は、少<sub>すこ</sub>しにしましょう。
We bought too much dog food this month.  Let's buy less next month.

3). Formation of "sugiru" with a copula noun

| Copula Nouns without "na" ゆうめい、げんき、ひま、etc. | + すぎる |
|---|---|

（１）　こどもは、元気<sub>げんき</sub>すぎて、昼寝<sub>ひるね</sub>をしてくれない。
The kids have so much energy; they won't take a nap (for me).

（２）　きょうは、お客<sub>きゃく</sub>さんがなくて、ひますぎる。
I'm so bored today since I have no customers.

（３）　あの人<sub>ひと</sub>は、有名<sub>ゆうめい</sub>すぎて、ゲストに呼<sub>よ</sub>ぶことができません。
He is too famous to invite as our guest.

（４）　つかいかたが、<u>めんどう</u>すぎて、つかいませんでした。
　　　　　　　　　　　　(troublesome)
How to use it was too complicated, so I didn't use it.

### 3. ～てある **to express things done in advance for future use or benefit**

The "te" form verb with "aru" expresses the idea that things have been done in preparation for future use or benefit. For example, if you are expecting family members to come home late, hungry and tired, you would prepare their meal, bed, and, if in Japan, hot bath. The expression focuses on the phenomena, rather than the people, so the subject of the sentence involves inanimate items, like food, the bed, and bath. See the following example sentences.

(1) おふろが　わかしてありますよ。
The hot bath is ready for you.

(2) ばんごはんが、つくってあります。
Dinner is ready for you.

(3) おふとんが、しいてありますよ。(ふとんをしく to make a bed)
Your bed has been made for you.

(4) おちゃが、いれてありますから、飲んでくださいね。
Green tea has been made for you, so please enjoy (drink) it.

(5) ここに、名前が書いてあります。
Here is the name (of the owner) (in case it's lost).

### 4. ～ないで（ください）：**Please don't do it.**

The negative form of "te + kudasai" is "nai de kudasai," meaning "Please don't do such and such." "Nai" is in plain negative form, and you can derive it in the following manner.

Formation of the "nai" form:

| Consonant Verbs | Vowel Verbs | Irregular verbs |
|---|---|---|
| 1st base ＋　ない | Stem of the verb ＋　ない | する→　しない |
| 行か　ない | 食べ　ない | |
| 書か　ない | 見　　ない | くる→　こない |
| 立た　ない | 入れ　ない | |
| 読ま　ない | 負け　ない | |
| 話さ　ない | 寝　　ない | |

(1) せんそうに　行かないでください。
(戦争 war)
Please don't go to a war.

(2) まだ、書かないでください。
Please don't write it yet.

(3) ボートの中で、立たないでください。あぶないですよ。
Please don't stand up on the boat. It's dangerous.

（４）　クラスで　まんがを　読まないでください。
Please do not read comic books in class.

（５）　大きい声で、話さないでください。
Please don't talk loud.

（６）　教室では、食べないでください。
Please do not eat in the classroom.

（７）　人のテストを見ないでね。
Please don't look at my test.

（８）　ここに、ごみを　入れないでください。
Please do not put your trash here.

（９）　試合に負けないでね。
(game)
Please win the game (Please don't lose the game).

（１０）　じゅぎょうちゅうに、寝ないでくださいね。
（授業中 during a lecture)
Please do not fall asleep during the lecture.

## 5. Three Types of Adverbs: 〜く、〜に、〜と endings

### 1. く -type adverbs

This type of adverb is made from the adjectives.  Change the final "い" ending to "く."
れい：
あたらしい→　あたらしく、うつくしい→　うつくしく、よい→　よく、かわいい→　かわいく、やさしい→　やさしく、　たのしい→　たのしく、　おいしい→　おいしく、うまい→　うまく

### 2. に -type adverbs

This type of adverb is made from the copula nouns.  Change the final "な" ending to "に."
れい：

きれいな→　きれいに、じょうずな→　じょうずに、　へたな→　へたに、げんきな→　げんきに、親切な→　親切に、　健康な→　健康に、上品な→
(healthy)　　　　　　(elegant)
上品に、下品な→　下品に、エレガントな→　エレガントに、
(crude; unpolished)

### 3．と-type adverbs

This type of adverb is often made from mimesis and onomatopoeias by adding "と" to them, such as クスクスと、クルクルと、ニコニコと、サンサンと、ザーザーと、ドキッと (startled)、ハッと (suddenly realized)、パッと (swiftly)、キャッと (short outcry due to a surprise) etc.

れい：

（１）　それを聞いて、どきっとしました。
　　　　I was startled to hear that.

（２）　お日さまが、サンサンと、降り注いでいます。
　　　　　　　　　　　　　　　　（ふりそそぐ pour down/over）
　　　　The sun is pouring over us.

（３）　雨がザーザーと ふっています。(ザーザーと  heavily.)
　　　　It's raining cats and dogs.

（４）　それを見て、はっとしました。
　　　　I was startled (=taken a back; surprised) to see it.

（５）　子どもたちは、くるくると、池のまわりをまわっています。
　　　　　　　　　　　　　　　　（まわる go around; circulate）
　　　　Children are circulating around the pond repeatedly.

（６）　女の人たちは、クスクスと　笑いました。(わらう laugh)
　　　　The ladies all giggled.

（７）　どろぼうは、おまわりさんを見て、ぱっと、隠れました。
　　　　　　　　　　　　　　　　　　　　　（かくれる hide）
　　　　The thief hid himself quickly at seeing a policeman.

（８）　私は蛙を見て、キャッと　叫びました。(さけぶ scream)
　　　　I screamed at seeing a frog.

# Present State of Being: "te" form of Intransitive Verbs + iru

つく (get turned on)

| ろうそく が ついている | でんきが ついている | テレビが ついている | 火（ひ）が ついている |
|---|---|---|---|
| The candle is lit. | The light is on. | TV is on. | The fire is on. |

きえる (become extinguished)

| ろうそくが きえている | でんきが きえている |
|---|---|
| The candle is extinguished. | The light is off. |

ぬれる (get wet) ↔ かわく (get dry)        こむ (get crowded)

| ぬれている | かわいている | こんでいる |
|---|---|---|

The shirt is wet.        The shirt is dry.    I am thirsty.                The train is crowded.
                                    （のどがかわいている）

おちる (fall)

> りんごがおちている

Apples have fallen and now on the ground.

はいる (enter)

> はいっている

The money is in the wallet.

あく (open) ↔ しまる (close)

> とがあいている

The door is open.

> ハンドバッグがあいている

The purse is open.

> とがしまっている

The door is closed/locked.

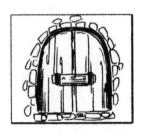

> きんこがしまっている

The safe is closed/locked

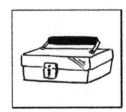

## Present State of Being:
## Description of physical features: overweight or thin, ～ている

| ふとっている | やせている |
|---|---|

## Present status: married, clear, hungry ～ている

| けっこんしている | はれている | おなかがすいている |
|---|---|---|

## Emotions: surprised, down, angry. ～ている

| おどろいている | しょんぼりしている | おこっている |
|---|---|---|

Chapter 10 (D) Exercises

A.  Change the given affirmative verbs into their negative forms (ない form).

(1) Examples for Consonant Verbs:   1<sup>st</sup> base + nai

> 飲む　→　飲まない
> 書く　→　書かない
> 行く　→　行かない

(2) Examples for Vowel Verbs:       V. stem + nai

> あげる→　あげない
> 食べる→　食べない
> 見る　→　見ない

(3) Irregular Verbs

> する　　→　しない、　くる→　こない

[Consonant Verb Group]

| | | |
|---|---|---|
| 1．つくる | 2．あるく | 3．わかる |
| 4．あそぶ | 5．はしる | 6．かう |
| 7．およぐ | 8．はなす | 9．まつ |
| *10．あう | 11．かえす | 12．きく |
| 13．おどる | 14．すむ | 15．のる |

**\*Attention**:  The double vowel ending verbs such as "au, k<u>au</u>, ar<u>au</u>, shim<u>au</u>, <u>iu</u>, etc._" need special attention.  Their first base is "wa," therefore their verb conjugation is "wa-i-u-e-o."  For example, the negative form of "iu" is "i-wa-nai."  Try next verbs:

| | | |
|---|---|---|
| 16. かう | 17. あらう | 18. しまう |

[Vowel Verb Group]

| | | |
|---|---|---|
| 1．おしえる | 2．おりる | 3．いれる |
| 4．かりる | 5．ねる | 6．くれる |
| 7．たすける | 8．またせる | 9．みせる |
| 10．みえる | 11．いる | 12．あびる |
| 13．たべる | 14．みる | 15．にげる |

[Irregular Verbs]

１６．する　　　　　１７．くる

B. Translate into Japanese, using ないでください。
   1. Please don't go.
   2. Please don't look.
   3. Please don't eat.
   4. Please don't drink.
   5. Please don't touch. (to touch さわる)
   6. Please don't say.
   7. Please don't sleep in the classroom.
   8. Please don't run.
   9. Please don't show it.
   10. Please don't play here.

C. Pair-work: Guess what your partner hasn't done before coming to school, using
   ～ないで. In response, s/he can say either「いいえ、ちがいます！」or「はい、
   そうなんです。～ないで、学校へ来ました。」

Example れい：きょう、しゅくだいをしないで、学校へ、きましたね？

Hints:
Without eating breakfast,
Without taking a shower,
Without feeding dogs/cats,
Without combing his/her hair（to comb one's hair かみをとく）,
Without listening to the news,
Without reading a newspaper, etc.

Your sentences:

D. Change the words in the parentheses into phrases using the ～ないで form. Supply
   particles when needed.

Example れい：きょうは、（ともだち、会う）、うちに帰ってきた。
　　　　　　　きょうは、ともだちに会わないで、うちに帰ってきた。

（１）じかんがないので、外で（ごはん、食べる）、帰りましょう。

（２）やさしい本だから、（じしょ、使う）、読むことができました。

（３）そのじしょは、高かったので、（買う）、帰りました。

（４）バスにもタクシーにも(乗る)、歩いて　行きました。

（５）きょうは、（にく、さかな、ちゅうもんする）、サラダにしました。

E. Change the underlined words into appropriate compound verbs, using ～すぎる

れい：ピザを<u>たくさん食べたので</u>、おなかがいっぱいです。
　　　　　　→　　たべすぎたので
　　　　or　　たべすぎて

（１）おさけを<u>たくさん飲んで</u>、気分がわるくなりました。
　　　　　　　　　　　　　　feelings
　　　　　→

（２）きょうは、<u>たくさんうんどうしたので</u>、つかれました。
　　　　　　　　　　（うんどうする to exercise）（つかれる to be tired）
　　　　　→

（３）そのかたは、<u>とてもゆうめいなので</u>、ここにはいらっしゃらないでしょう。
　　　　　→

（４）このシャツは、私には<u>ちいさいので</u>、着ることができません。
　　　　　　　　　　　　　　　→

（５）同じキャットフードを　<u>たくさん買ったので</u>、ねこが食べなくなりました。
　　　　　　　　　　　　　　　→

（６）このケーキは　<u>甘くて</u>、私には、食べることができません。
　　　　　　　　　　→

（７）このイヤリングは、<u>高くて</u>、買うことができません。
　　　　　　　　　　　→

（８）<u>あまりにもひまなので</u>、たいくつです。
　　　　→

　　　　（あまりにも is similar to とても or たいへん, meaning "very," "extremely,"
　　　　or "unbearably"; たいくつ means "bored" or "boring"）

F. Change the underlined words into expressions of conjecture, using そうです。
Example れい：

(Looking up in the sky, you say) たいふうが　<u>来ます</u>。→　たいふうが来そうです。

1. あの子は、泣きます。→

2. このテストは、むずかしいです。→

3. 父は、元気です。→

4. このじしょは、べんりです。→
             convenient

5. あの人は、がけから、落ちます。→
         cliff     to fall

6. このドレスは、高いです。→

7. 山田さんは、ねむいです。→
             sleepy

8. あの学生は、さむいです。→

9. しけんに　失敗します。→
         to fail

10. しけんに　うかります。→
         to pass

11. お金がありません。→お金がないです。→

12. このじしょが、いいです。→よいです。→

13. あたまがいいです。→

14. テストがあります。→

15. このつくえは、　じょうぶです。→

G. Change the sentence structure to "adverb (そうに) + verb"

Example れい : あの人は、さむそうです。立っています。

→　あの人は、さむそうに　立っています。

1. 田中さんは、つまらなそうです。すわっています。
        （つまらない bored）     （すわる to sit）

→

2. こどもたちは、たのしそうです。あそんでいます。
        （たのしい happy）    （あそぶ to play）

→

３．犬<sup>いぬ</sup>は、<u>うれしそうです</u>。<u>待<sup>ま</sup>っています</u>。
　　　　　（うれしい glad）　　　（まつ to wait）

→

４．さとうさんは、<u>さみしそうです</u>。<u>立<sup>た</sup>っています</u>。
　　　　　　　　　（さみしい lonely）　（たつ to stand up）

→

５．平田<sup>ひらた</sup>さんは、<u>いそがしそうです</u>。<u>はたらいています</u>。
　　　　　　　　（いそがしい busy）　（はたらく to work）

H. Translate the following into Japanese phrases, using 〜そうな or 〜そうに.

1. sleepy-looking dog
2. bored-looking student
3. delicious-looking cake
4. busy-looking person
5. lonely-looking person
6. happy-looking dog
7. a difficult-looking test
8. A man is standing looking cold.
9. My friend is busy working.
10. Children are playing happily.

I. Come up with **checklists** for the following events, using 〜てある.

　2. 1. Before a birthday party for your mother:
　(1) Has the house been vacuumed?　（うち、そうじする）
　(2) Are the flowers decorated?　（はな、かざる）
　(3) Has the cake been bought?　（ケーキ、かう）
　(4) Have the windows been opened?　（まど、あける）
　(5) Has the birthday card been written?　（おたんじょうカード、かく）

　2. Before a midterm or final examination:
　(1) Have the vocabulary words been memorized?　（たんご、おぼえる）
　(2) Are all the kanji practiced?　（かんじ、れんしゅうする）
　(3) Is all the homework turned in?　（しゅくだい、だす）
　(4) Has the alarm clock been set?　（めざましどけい、セットする）
　(5) Have pencils and erasers been put in a bag?（えんぴつ、けしごむ、いれる）

J. Pair-work. Practice the dialogue with your pair. After the first practice round, replace the underlined words with provided options 1 through 4.

1. A: へやのそうじは、してありますか。
　 B: いえ、まだ　<u>して</u>ありません。これから　<u>し</u>ます。

A: そうですか。

1. さくぶん、かく
2. ビール、冷<sub>ひ</sub>やす(to cool something)
3. わからないところ、しらべる(to check)
4. あしたのじゅんび(preparation)、する

2. A: お肉<sub>にく</sub>もお魚<sub>さかな</sub>も　買<sub>か</sub>ってありますか。
   B: ええ、買<sub>か</sub ってあります。もう、れいぞうこに　入<sub>い</sub>れてあります。
   A: そうですか。ありがとう。　　　　refrigerator
   B: いいえ。

1. 花<sub>はな</sub>を買<sub>か</sub>う、かびん(vase)に入<sub>い</sub>れる
2. さとうさんに　話<sub>はな</sub>す、電話<sub>でんわ</sub>する
3. 飲<sub>の</sub>み物<sub>もの</sub>を　用意<sub>ようい</sub>する(to prepare)、れいぞうこに　入<sub>い</sub>れる
4. サンドイッチをつくる、おさらに盛<sub>も</sub>る(serve, fill)

K. Pair-work: Ask your partner the following questions.

1. 今<sub>いま</sub>、どこに住<sub>す</sub>んでいますか。

2. 結婚<sub>けっこん</sub>していますか。

3. だれか、日本人<sub>にほんじん</sub>を　知<sub>し</sub>っていますか。

4. おなかが　すいていますか。

5. のどが　かわいていますか。

6. 今日<sub>きょう</sub>の空<sub>そら</sub>は、晴<sub>は</sub>れていますか。

7. さいふの中<sub>なか</sub>に　いくら入<sub>はい</sub>っていますか。

8. 先生<sub>せんせい</sub>は、今<sub>いま</sub>、立<sub>た</sub>っていますか、すわっていますか。

9. 今日<sub>きょう</sub>のばんごはんは、もうできていますか。

10. かぞくの中<sub>なか</sub>で、だれが一番<sub>いちばん</sub>、やせていますか。

L.   Which illustration will best describe the words?  Match them up.

1. うれしそう  2. ねむそう (ねむい sleepy) 3. くやしそう (くやしい regrettable)
4. さむそう 5. あつそう 6. いたそう (いたい painful) 7. かなしそう (かなしい sad)

A. _____    E. _____

B. _____    F. _____

C. _____    G. _____

D. _____

M.  Describe how they look, using ~ soo desu.
  Vocabulary hints: おもしろい、おいしい、さみしい (lonely)、はずかしい (shy)、
食べたい、ひま、げんき

A. _____ .

B. _____ .

C. _____ .

D. _____ .

E. _____ .

F. _____ .

G. _____ .

Chapter 10 (D): Dict-A-Conversation
Respond orally to the following statements and write down your answers. Please answer in <u>complete sentences,</u> writing in hiragana and in kanji where applicable.

1. _____

2. _____

3. _____

4. _____

5. _____

6. _____

7. _____

8. _____

9. _____

10. _____

Chapter 10 (E)   Writing Composition: "A Recent Event"
## 作文を書く：「最近の出来事」

---

### 最近の出来事

　昨日　友だちが　私のアパートに　来ました。そして、私と　二人で　カレーライスを　作りました。

　初めに、マーケットへ　行きました。そこで、にんじん、玉ねぎ、チキン、カレールーを　買いました。私は、カレールーを　初めて見ましたが、それは、スパイスの　かたまりで、チョコレートみたいでした。

　作り方は、かんたんでした。まず、やさいと肉を切りました。それから、おなべで　炒めます。そのあと、水を入れて、よく煮ました。さいごにカレールーを入れて、できあがり。

　ごはんは、少し　かたかったですが、カレーライスは、とても　おいしかったです。それに、新しい日本語の言葉を、習いました。それは、「きつね色」です。

　友だちが、「玉ねぎは、『きつね色』になるまで、炒めてね」と　言いましたが、私には、そのいみが　よく分かりませんでした。「きつね」は、英語でＦｏｘ　です。その　毛の色は、うすい茶色ですから、「きつね色」は、「うす茶色」のことでした。

　友だちは、私のアパートが　たいへん気に入りました。とくに、まどが二つあるのが、いい　と言いました。私のキッチンは　とても小さいですが、りょうりができるのが、うれしいです。それに、レストランへ行くより、けいざいてきです。

　晩ごはんを食べた後で、紅茶にスパイスを入れて飲みました。大変おいしかったです。楽しい一日でした。

Chapter 10 (E)

---

### Composition: A Recent Event

Yesterday, my friend came to my apartment and we prepared curry rice together.

First, we went to the market and bought carrots, onions, chicken, and a box of curry roux. I was introduced to curry roux for the first time. It was a chunk of spices and looked like a chocolate bar.

The cooking process was simple. First, I chopped the vegetables and meat, then sautéed them in a pan. Then I added water to cook it well. Lastly, I put in (a chunk of) curry roux, and then it was done!

The rice was a bit hard, but curry was very good. I even learned a new Japanese vocabulary word. It's "kitsune-iro."

My friend said to me, "Please sauté the onions until they become 'kitsune-iro'." I didn't understand what she meant. "Kitsune" is fox in English. I realized later it meant "light brown," as foxes have light brown coats.

My friend really liked my apartment; she especially liked the two windows. My kitchen is small, but I am happy I can cook now. Besides, it's more economical than going to a restaurant.

After eating supper, we had some black tea with spices. It was delicious. I had a fun day.

---

二人でカレーライスを
つくりました。

たまねぎを、きつね色になる
まで、いためてください。

そのあと、水をいれて、よく煮ます。

Chapter 10 (E)                            Vocabulary List

1. Expressions

「きつね色」は、「うす茶色」のこと　"Fox color" refers to light brown, the color
　　　　　　　　　　　　　　　　　　of a fox's coat.

まどが二つある<u>の</u>が、いい。　　　It's nice to have two windows.

りょうりができる<u>の</u>が　うれしい。　I'm happy to be able to cook.

レストランへ<u>行くより</u>、けいざいてき。It's more economical than going to a restaurant.

<u>食べた後で</u>、紅茶をのみました。　After eating, I had tea.

2. Nouns

（お）なべ　　　　　　　　　　　　　cooking pan

スパイス　　　　　　　　　　　　　　spices

かたまり　　　　　　　　　　　　　　a chunk

　　スパイスのかたまり　　　　　　　"chunk" of spices

つくりかた(作り方)　　　　　　　　how to make

ことば　　　　　　　　　　　　　　word, language

いみ　　　　　　　　　　　　　　　meaning

　　ことばのいみ　　　　　　　　　meaning of a word

きつね　　　　　　　　　　　　　　fox

きつねいろ　　　　　　　　　　　　fox color; light brown

うすちゃいろ（うす茶色）　　　　　light brown

け　　　　　　　　　　　　　　　　hair, fur

けのいろ(毛の色)　　　　　　　　　the color of hair or fur

いちにち(一日)　　　　　　　　　　one day

　　楽しい一日　　　　　　　　　　an enjoyable day

3. Copula Nouns

かんたん　　　　　　　　　　　　　simple, easy

けいざいてき　　　　　　　　　　　economical

4. Adjectives

（かたい）　　　　　　　　　　　　hard, firm

5. Adverbs

そして　　　　　　　　　　　　　　And

はじめに(初めに)/さいしょに/まず　at first

それから　　　　　　　　　　　　　and then, after that

さいごに　　　　　　　　　　　　　at last; in the end; finally

とても　　　　　　　　　　　　　　very (personal overtone)

たいへん（大変）　　　　　　　　　very (formal)

それに　　　　　　　　　　　　　　in addition to it; besides that

---

## Additional Vocabulary from Grammar Notes, Exercises, and Dict-A-Conversation

---

[Nouns]

| | |
|---|---|
| ほこり（誇り） | pride |
| ほこりにおもう | to be proud of |
| さき（先） | ahead; future |
| ひたい | forehead |
| ちゅうかんしけん（中間しけん） | midterm examination |
| たわら | straw bag |
| ひのみやぐら | fire-watch tower |
| こたつ | low, quilt-covered frame with a heat source inside |
| おまわりさん | police officer |
| がりべん（ガリ勉） | cram; grinding |
| イギリスしき（式） | British style |
| ロシアしき（式） | Russian style |
| どくしょ（読書） | reading |
| （すいえい　水泳） | swimming |
| 指揮者（しきしゃ） | conductor |
| コンサート | concert |
| かたつむり | snail |
| いちご | strawberry |
| 数学（すうがく） | Mathematics |

[Adjectives]

| | |
|---|---|
| まるい | round |

[な Adjectives/Copula Nouns]

| | |
|---|---|
| きんべん（勤勉） | diligence; hard work |
| らく（楽） | comfortable; easy |

[Adverbs]

| | |
|---|---|
| ふつう | ordinarily |
| さらに | moreover |
| つぎに | next |
| ふかく | deeply |

[Verbs]

| | |
|---|---|
| はたらく（働く） | to work |
| あむ（編む） | to knit |
| のんびりする/リラックスする | to relax |

| | |
|---|---|
| そつぎょうする | to graduate |
| タバコをすう | to smoke cigarettes |
| ギターをひく | to play a guitar |
| 気が変わる | to change one's mind |
| ～と思う | I think that ~ . |
| お湯を沸かす | to boil water |
| 外食する | to eat out |
| お辞儀をする | to bow |
| ひるねをする | to take a nap |

[Expressions]

| | |
|---|---|
| めとはなのさき（目と鼻の先） | near |
| はながたかい（鼻が高い） | be proud |
| ねこのひたい | narrow |

----------------------Vocabulary from Dict-A-Conversation-------------------------------------

[Nouns]

| | |
|---|---|
| クリームチーズ | cream cheese |
| ハンドミキサー | hand mixer |
| （お）さら | dishes |
| サワークリーム | sour cream |
| 一センチぐらいのあつさ | one-centimeter width |
| オーブン | oven |
| ひとばん（一晩） | one night |
| やきかた（焼き方） | how to bake |
| しんぱい（心配） | worry |

[Verbs]

| | |
|---|---|
| まぜる（混ぜる） | to mix |
| やく（焼く） | to bake |

Chapter 10 (E)                    Grammar and Cultural Notes

## 1. A（というの）は B のことだ

Essentially this expression means A is equal to B, but this pattern is often used when A is an euphemism – one that is enigmatic or puzzling to the speaker. For a foreigner like Monica, "fox color" wasn't readily understandable. Thus, she wrote in her diary,「きつねいろ」（というの）は、「うすちゃいろ」のことでした。So, if you come across with the word「きんべん」, you may ask「きんべん（というの）は、なんのことですか。」And a response you receive may be,「きんべん（というの）は、あなたのことですよ。よくはたらくことです。」("kinben" means 'working hard.')

Examples例:

1) A：「目と鼻の先」（というの）は、なんのことですか。
   B：「目と鼻の先」（というの）は、「すぐ近く」ということです。
                              「すぐ近く」のいみです。

2) A：「鼻が高い」（というの）は、なんのことですか。
   B：「鼻が高い」（というの）は、「ほこりにおもう」ことです。英語で、"I'm proud (of it)." といういみです。

3) A：「ねこのひたい」（というの）は、なんのことですか。
      cat's forehead
   B：「ねこのひたい」は、「せまい」ことです。

4) A：「ちゅうかんしけん」って、なんのことですか。
   B：「ちゅうかんしけん」は、Midterm Examination のことです。

## 2. ねるより たべるほうがいい: Comparative form of a verb

A verb used in the comparative structure is in dictionary form. 食べる、ねる、見る、行く、買う、つくる go with the particles "より" and "ほう." For instance, "I prefer eating to sleeping" in Japanese is 寝るより 食べるほうがいい. Compare this with using the noun form in a comparative. "I like tea better than coffee," コーヒーより お茶のほうが いい。You would need the particle "no" after the noun to form the pattern of "noun no hoo." In Monica's diary, she wrote, レストランへ行くより、けいざいてきです。(Cooking at home) is more economical than going to a restaurant.

Compare the dictionary form verb used with various particles:   （X）is wrong, and （O）is correct.

（ O ）1. 食べるのと、ねるのと、どちらがすきですか。
          Which do you prefer, eating or sleeping?

（　X　）2.　食べるのより、ねるのほうが、すきです。Wrong formation!
I prefer sleeping to eating.

（　O　）3.　食べるより、ねるほうが、すきです。
I prefer sleeping to eating.

（　O　）4.　よるおそく食べるのは、からだによくないです。
Eating late at night is not good for you.

Examples:

（１）セーターを編むのと、買うのと、どちらのほうが、けいざいてきですか。
Which is more economical, knitting a sweater or buying one?

（２）たぶん、編むより、買うほうが、安いでしょう。でも、編むほうが楽しいですよ。
Perhaps buying it is cheaper than knitting, but knitting is more fun.

（３）ふつうは、かんじを書くより、読むほうが　やさしいですね。
Usually, reading kanji is easier than writing kanji.

## 3. V たあと（で）: After doing ~

The plain past tense verb "ta" is used with "ato de" to mean "after doing something, after taking an action." You must use the past tense "ta" form, even if the sentence is not in past tense. It is more logical for the Japanese to think that a subsequent action is taken only after the first action has been completed/finished. Thus, always use the "ta" form with "ato de (after)," regardless of the tense of the main clause. The particle "de" may be dropped. Examine the example sentences:

（１）ごはんを食べたあとで、コーヒーを飲みましょう。
Let's drink a cup of coffee after the meal.

（２）ごはんを食べたあとで、コーヒーを飲みました。
I had a cup of coffee after I ate.

（３）シャワーをあびたあと、のんびりしました。
After taking a shower, I relaxed.

（４）日本語のクラスがおわったあとで、としょかんへ行きました。
I went to the library after Japanese class.

（５）しゅくだいをしたあとで、テニスをしました。
After finishing my homework, I played tennis.

（６）えいがを見たあと、買い物をしませんか。
Won't we go shopping after seeing the movie?

Chapter 10 (E) Exercises

A. Pair-work: Ask your classmate the meaning of the following words and answer them, using the pattern ～ （というの） は、なんのことですか。～ （というの） は、～の ことです。 Use a dictionary if necessary.

1. たわら
2. ひのみやぐら
3. こたつ
4. おまわりさん
5. がりべん

B. Ask your classmate the following questions and checkmark his/her response in the parentheses.

1. りょうりをするのとたべるのと、どちらのほうがすきですか。
    （　　） たべるほうが、すきです。
    （　　） つくるほうが、すきです。

2. かんじをよむのと、かくのと、どちらのほうが、やさしいですか。
    （　　） よむほうが、やさしいです。
    （　　） かくほうが、やさしいです。

3. うみへいくのと、やまへいくのと、どちらのほうが、たのしいですか。
    （　　） うみへいくほうが、たのしいです。
    （　　） やまへいくほうが、たのしいです。

4. しゅくだいをするのと、てすとのべんきょうをするのと、どちらがいいで すか。
    （　　） しゅくだいをするほうが、いいです。
    （　　） テストのべんきょうをするほうが、いいです。

5. くるまをうんてんするのと、バスにのるのと、どちらのほうが、<u>らく</u>です か。　　　　　　　　　　　　　　　　　　　　　　　　　　　　(comfortable)
    （　　） くるまをうんてんするほうが、らくです。
    （　　） バスにのるほうが、らくです。

C. Translate the following into Japanese, using the "A-verb yori B-verb hoo ga ~" pattern.

1. I like sleeping more than eating.


2. It is easier to read kanji than writing.


3. Cooking is more fun than doing homework.

4. Staying at home is more relaxing than going out. (to go out でかける、is relaxing
   リラックスできる or のんびりできる)

D.  Translate into English.
１．わたしは、花子さんがピアノをひいているのを　見ました。

２．かとうさんは、むすこが、タバコをすっているのを、見ました。

３．おとうとさんが、ギターをひいているのが、聞こえました。とても上手で
すね。

４．こうちゃにミルクを入れて飲むのは、イギリス式ですか。

５．こうちゃにジャムを入れて飲むのは、ロシア式ですか。

E. Change "Noun の　あと" to "V た　あと"
例：シャワーのあと→　シャワーをあびたあと

　　1）べんきょうのあと→　べんきょうをしたあと

　　2）しごとのあと→

　　3）デートのあと→

　　4）かいもののあと→

　　5）おふろのあと→

　　6）しょくじのあと→

　　7）えいがのあと→

　　8）読書のあと→
　　　　(reading a book)
　　9）水泳のあと→
　　　　(swimming)

F-1.  Ask your classmates the following questions and fill in the chart with his/her name and answer.  Use the pattern "～のは（なんじ，どこ，なん，etc.）ですか"

1.  What time do you get up? (What time is it that you get up?)
  おきるのは、なんじですか。

2.  What time do you go to bed? (What time is it that you go to bed?)
  ねるのは、なんじですか。

3.  When are you going to graduate?
  そつぎょうするのは、いつですか。

4.  What is the first thing you do after you get up?
  おきたあと、さいしょにするのは、なんですか。
  （or おきて）

5.  Who is the first person you see after getting up in the morning?
  おきたあと、　さいしょに見るのは、だれですか。
  （or おきて）

6.  What is the subject of the next test for you?
  つぎにあるのは、何のテストですか。

|  | 1.おきるのは、なんじですか。 | 2.ねるのは、なんじですか。 | 3.そつぎょうするのは、いつですか。 | 4.おきてさいしょにするのは、なんですか。 | 5.おきてさいしょにみるのは、だれですか。 | 6.つぎにあるのは、なんのテストですか。 |
|---|---|---|---|---|---|---|
| （　　）<br>さん |  |  |  |  |  |  |
| （　　）<br>さん |  |  |  |  |  |  |

F-2.  Report your findings to class, using "S ga V no wa, ...... desu" pattern.  For example, if you asked Mary and Bob, you will report to class as follows:
  （１）メリーさんが、おきるのは、七時です。
  （２）ボブさんが、おきるのは、六時です。

G. 日本語に　ほんやくしなさい。Challenge these translation tasks!

1.　I changed my mind and went to the library (instead).

2.　At first, I thought it was a fox's hair, but it was a dog's hair.

3.　Please go to the market first, and go to Starbucks next.

4.　At first, cut the vegetables please, then boil hot water next, and at last put vegetables into the boiling water.

5.　I like (the fact) that the kitchen is small.

6.　Cooking at home is more economical than going out to eat.

7.　At the end of the concert, I saw the conductor bowed deeply.

8.　I heard Tom was talking to his dog.

9.　I prefer napping to doing homework.

10.　I'm glad I can cook at home.


たんごヘルプ
1．気が変わる change one's mind
2．〜と思う　I think that it is ~
4．お湯を沸かす boil water
6．外へ食べに行く（外食する）
7．コンサート concert、指揮者 conductor、深く deeply、お辞儀をする to bow
9．ひるねをする to nap
10.　"I'm glad" ~ のが　うれしい。

Ch. 10E.  Additional Exercises: Connecting sentences with adverbs 文と文をつなぐ

（１）（　）の中に、てきとうなことばをえらんで、入れなさい。
Fill in the blanks with appropriate adverbs from the box.

A. かんじの「川」のかきかた
1. （　　　）左がわの　たてのせんを　かきます。(vertical line)
2. （　　　）まんなかの　まっすぐのせんを　かきます。(straight line)
3. （　　　）右がわの　たてのせんを　いちばん ながく かきます。

> はじめに、つぎに、　さいごに

B. マヨネーズのつくりかた
1. （　　　）お酢と卵黄を　用意します。(Prepare vinegar and egg-yolk)
2. （　　　）たまごを　よく　まぜます。(mix)
3. （　　　）お酢を　少しずつ　いれて、(little by little)
4. （　　　）よく　まぜます。(さらに moreover)
5. （　　　）白くなったら　できあがりです。

> さいごに、さらに、まず、はじめに、　つぎに

C. インスタントラーメンのつくりかた
1. （　　　）お湯を沸かします。
2. （　　　）カップラーメンのふたを　とります。(remove the lid)
3. （　　　）カップにあついお湯を注いで、ふたをします。(cover)
4. （　　　）三分、待ちます。
5. （　　　）調味料を入れて、できあがりです。
salt, pepper, miso, etc.

> さいごに、そして、それから、はじめに、つぎに

**(2)** つぎの短文を読んで、（　）の中に、てきとうなことばを　入れなさい。
**A.** 「今日のできごと」
1. 今日、友だちと私は　時間がありました。
2. （　　　）えいがを見に行くことに　しました。
3. 私は、ロマンチックなえいがが　見たかったです。
4. （　　　）ともだちは、アクションえいがが　見たいと言いました。
5. 私は、どちらでもよかったので、アクションえいがを見ることにしました。
6. （　　　）は、とてもつまらなかったですが、もう少し見ていると、
7. （　　　）は、少しおもしろくなってきました。

8.（　　　　　）もう少し、見ていると、
9.（　　　　　）は、もっとおもしろくなってきました。
10.（　　　　　）は、もう一度、見たくなりました。

---

さいご、そこで、こんど、でも、さらに、はじめ、つぎに

---

**B. Simple development of your thesis.  Talk about something you like/dislike.**
例1：
私は、（かたつむり）が　すきです。
　　　　　　　　snail
（まるい）の（orところ）が　いいです。
　being round
でも、ひとつだけ、わるいことが　あります。

それは、（私のいちごを食べる）ことです。
　　　　　　　　　　　　　Verb
（Make your 2nd paragraph: ある日、こんなことが　ありました。to continue）

例2：
私は、まんがが　好きです。
たのしいところが　いいです。
でも、ひとつだけ　わるいことが　あります。
それは、しゅくだいのじかんが　なくなることです。
　　　　　（=しゅくだいをするじかん）

例3：
私は、すうがくが　好きです。
シンプルなところが　いいです。
でも、ひとつだけ　わるいことが　あります。
それは、じかんが　かかることです。
それで、ほかのクラスのべんきょうが　できなくなります。

**C.**　Now write your own short paragraph.

私は、＿＿＿＿＿＿＿が　すきです。

＿＿＿＿＿＿＿＿の（ところ）が　いいです。

でも、ひとつだけ、わるいことが　あります。

それは、＿＿＿＿＿＿＿＿＿＿＿＿ことです。

Chapter 10 (E): Dict-A-Conversation
Listen to Chapter 10 (E)'s Dict-A-Conversation on the student CD, and write in the checkmark in either "Truth" or "False" columns, after judging the credibility of each statement.

[Vocabulary Help]:

| | |
|---|---|
| チーズケーキを焼く | to bake a cheesecake |
| やわらかくなるまで | until it becomes soft |
| ハンドミキサーで 混ぜる | to mix with a hand mixer |
| お皿（さら） | a plate |
| サワークリーム | sour cream |
| １センチぐらいの 厚さ | about one centimeter thickness |
| オーブンで 焼く | to bake in oven |
| れいぞうこ | refrigerator |
| 一晩（ひとばん） | one night; overnight |
| 心配だ | I am worried. |

| statements | Truth （ほんとう） | False （うそ） |
|---|---|---|
| 1 | | |
| 2 | | |
| 3 | | |
| 4 | | |
| 5 | | |
| 6 | | |
| 7 | | |
| 8 | | |
| 9 | | |
| 10 | | |

Chapter 10 (E) – (1)

| 文 (a sentence; a design) | ふみ<br>あや<br>ブン | *[文（ふみ）=てがみ a letter]<br>*[目も文な（めもあやな） brilliant; bright colors]<br>文（ぶん） a sentence<br>文章（ぶんしょう） a sentence<br>作文（さくぶん） a composition |
| | | (4)<br>丶　亠　ナ　文 |
| 毛 (wool; hair) | け/げ<br>モウ | 毛（け） hair; wool<br>[髪の毛（かみのけ） hair]<br>羊毛（ようもう） wool<br>毛布（もうふ） blanket |
| | | (4)<br>ノ　二　三　毛 |
| 茶 (tea) | ちゃ<br>サ | お茶（ちゃ） tea<br>[抹茶（まっちゃ） green tea (finely ground tea powder)]<br>[茶道（さどう） tea ceremony]<br>[喫茶店（きっさてん） coffee shop] |
| | | (9)<br>一　十　サ　ヴ　犬　苶　本　茶　茶 |
| 変 (to change; strange) | か（わる）<br>か（える）<br>ヘン | 変わる（かわる） something changes<br>変える（かえる） you change something<br>大変（たいへん） very; an alarming thing<br>[変化（へんか） a change] |
| | | (9)<br>丶　亠　ナ　古　亦　亦　亦　亦　変 |
| 晩 (evening, night) | バン | 晩（ばん） night<br>今晩（こんばん） tonight<br>明晩（みょうばん） tomorrow night<br>昨晩（さくばん） last night<br>晩年（ばんねん） one's later years |
| | | (12)<br>丨　冂　日　日　旷　晘　晘　晩　晩　晩　晩　晩 |

Chapter 10 (E) – (2)

| | | |
|---|---|---|
| 飲<br><br>(to drink) | の（む）<br>イン | 飲む（のむ）to drink<br>飲食（いんしょく）drinking and eating;<br>　　　　　　　　　　　　　dining<br>[飲酒（いんしゅ）drinking liquor] |
| | | (12)<br>ノ 𠆢 𠆢 今 今 今 食 食 食 飲<br>飲 飲 |
| 石<br><br>(stone, rock) | いし<br>セキ | 石（いし）a stone<br>大石（おおいし）a big stone; a surname<br>石油（せきゆ）petroleum |
| | | (5)<br>一 ア ズ 石 石 |
| 度<br><br>(degrees,<br>frequency) | たび<br>ド | その度（たび）に every time<br>今度（こんど）this time, next time<br>三度（さんど）three times<br>百度（ひゃくど）one hundred degrees; one<br>　　　　　　　　　　hundred times<br>[角度（かくど）angle] |
| | | (9)<br>、 亠 广 广 庐 庐 庐 庐 度 |

お茶を飲
む度に
おいしい
なと思う。
ん一杯いか
がです
か。

Kanji Practice for Chapter 10 E
かんじの れんしゅう

1. つぎの ことばを よみなさい。それから、クラスメートに いみを
   ききなさい。 Read the following words to your classmates and ask them for the
   meaning of each word.

   （１）　作文

   （２）　九十度

   （３）　今度

   （４）　今晩

   （５）　石油

   （６）　変人

   （７）　飲食

   （８）　お茶

   （９）　茶色

   （１０）　毛布

2. Write kanji in the box to complete the compound word.

   (1)　composition

   作 □

   (2)　eating & drinking

   □ 食

   (3)　petroleum

   石 □

   (4)　tonight

   今 □

   (5)　strange person

   □ 人

   (6)　this time, last time, next time

   今 □

3. よんでから、よみがなをかいて、えいごでいいなさい。Read first, then write yomigana above each kanji, and translate into English.

    （１）    英語の作文も　日本語の作文も　むずかしいです。

    （２）    今晩は、少し　さむいです。

    （３）    友だちの　かみの毛は、ずいぶん　ながくなりました。

    （４）    今晩は、月が　変に　赤く見えます。

    （５）    お茶を飲んで、おかしを　食べましょう。

    （６）    山の上には、大きな石が、ごろごろたくさんありました。

    （７）    今度は、晩じゃなくて、朝、来て見ましょう。

    （８）    今日は、あついので、三十度も　あります。

4. 日本語にしなさい。Translate into Japanese, writing the underlined words in kanji.

(1) My blanket is made of acrylic fiber (= acryl アクリル).  It's not <u>wool</u>.
        (is made of ~ で　できています)

(2) My <u>hair</u> is <u>black</u> and long.

(3) Let's <u>drink tonight</u>.

(4) The <u>Middle East</u> has more <u>petroleum oil</u>.

# An Arrangement to Meet Someone

Chapter 11A:  Asking for directions
*Expressions*
"When summer comes, it will become hot"  "If you don't study, you'll fail"
"Please go straight on this street"  "Please make a right turn at the corner"
*Kanji practice from Chapter 11A*

Chapter 11B:  Meeting with Ms. Tanaka
*Expressions*
"Go play after you finish your homework"
"What are you going there for?"
"The person gave me the favor of drawing a map"
*Kanji practice from Chapter 11B*

Chapter 11C:  Night view of cherry blossoms
*Expressions*
"May I go home now?"
"You must not smoke here"
"Would you mind doing it for me?"
*Kanji practice from Chapter 11C*

Chapter 11D:  Monica's diary
*Expressions*
"When I was a child, I often climbed trees"
"I washed my hands before the meal"
"He swims like a fish"
"I want to buy it even if it's expensive"
*Kanji practice from Chapter 11D*
*Kanji Bingo Chapter 11BCD*

しだれざくら（枝垂桜）
Shidare-zakura (weeping cherry)

Chapter 11A: Asking for Directions   **679**

Chapter 11    An Arrangement to Meet Someone  まちあわせ

## (A) Asking for directions    道を聞く

モニカ：　　すみません。円山公園は、どちらの方ですか。　　　　　　　　　1

通行人：　　祇園の円山公園ですか。　　　　　　　　　　　　　　　　　　　2

　　　　　　この道は河原町通りですから、この道をまっすぐ行ってください。3

　　　　　　あそこに、信号が見えますね。あの信号で、左に曲がってください。

　　　　　　そうすると、四条通りです。　　　　　　　　　　　　　　　　　5

　　　　　　円山公園は、四条通りの「どんつき」です。　　　　　　　　　　6

モニカ：「どんつき」？　　　　　　　　　　　　　　　　　　　　　　　　7

通行人：　　あ、すんません。「どんつき」は、京都弁ですね。　　　　　　　8
　　　　　　ひょうじゅん語で、「つきあたり」です。　　　　　　　　　　　9

モニカ：　　わかりました。あの信号を左に曲がって、　　　　　　　　　　　10
　　　　　　まっすぐ行くと、あるんですね。　　　　　　　　　　　　　　　11

通行人：　　そうです。歩いて、二十五分ぐらいですよ。　　　　　　　　　　12

モニカ：　　どうも　ありがとうございました。　　　　　　　　　　　　　13

[English translation:]

Monica:　Excuse me.  Which direction is Maruyama Park?
Passerby: (You mean) Maruyama Park in Gion?
　　　　　This street is Kawaramachi-doori.  Please go straight on this street.
　　　　　Can you see the traffic light over there?  Please make a left turn at the traffic
　　　　　light.  Once you do so, you'll be on Shijyoo-doori.
　　　　　Maruyama Park is "dontsuki" of Shijyoo-doori.
Monica:　"Dontsuki"?
Passerby:  Oh, I'm sorry.  "Dontsuki" is a Kyoto dialect.  In standard Japanese, it means
　　　　　"the end of a street."
Monica:　I see.  I (need to) make a left turn at the traffic light, and go straight, right?

Passerby:  That's right.  It'll be about twenty five minutes by foot.
Monica:    Thank you so much.

Chapter 11 (A)  [Vocabulary List]

1. Expressions

そうすると、しじょうどおりです。     If you do so, it'd be Shijyoo Street.

まっすぐ行くと、あるんです。      If you walk straight ahead, it'd be right there.

2. Nouns

| | |
|---|---|
| まちあわせ | arrangement for a meeting |
| みち(道) | street, way |
| とおり(通り) | street |
| まっすぐ | straight |
| しんごう(信号) | traffic lights, signals |
| ひだり(左) | left |
| [additional vocabulary]: | |
| みぎ(右) | right |
| どんつき | end of a street (Kyoto dialect) |
| つきあたり | end of a street |
| きょうとべん(京都弁) | Kyoto dialect |
| ひょうじゅんご(ひょうじゅん語) | standard language |

3. Verbs

| | |
|---|---|
| きく(聞く) | to ask; inquire |
| まがる(曲がる) | to turn |

4. Adverbs

| | |
|---|---|
| まっすぐ（に） | straight |

5. Particles

を                      a particle used with motion verbs to denote the space covered by that motion

Conjunctive Particle

と                      if or when; one of the four particles showing the conditionals

　そうすると、           If you do so,

........................................................................

**Additional Vocabulary from Grammar Notes, Exercises, and Dict-A-Conversation**

........................................................................

[Nouns]

(Ordinal numbers)
Counters for street (blocks)

| | | |
|---|---|---|
| ひとつめ （一つ目） | / いっぽんめ （一本目） | the first |
| ふたつめ （二つ目） | / にほんめ （二本目） | the second |
| みっつめ （三つ目） | / さんぼんめ （三本目） | the third |
| よっつめ （四つ目） | / よんほんめ （四本目） | the fourth |

(Vocabulary for directions/maps)

| | |
|---|---|
| ちず | map |
| かど | corner |
| まがりかど | (turning) corner |
| みぎて／ みぎがわ | on the right hand side |
| ひだりて／ ひだりがわ | on the left hand side |
| むかいがわ、 まえ | across the street, front |
| うら／ （うしろ） | behind, back |
| （となり） | next door |
| （あいだ） | between |
| このちかく | near here, vicinity |
| てまえ | beforehand |
| むこう | beyond |
| まんなか | middle, center |
| ろうか | corridor |
| ほどう | side walk |
| おうだんほどう | pedestrian crossing |
| こうさてん | intersection |
| いっぽんみち | street with no junctions |
| ふみきり | railroad crossing |
| （えき） | train station |
| バスてい | bus stop |
| はし | bridge |
| こうばん | police station |
| じんじゃ | Shinto shrine |
| （お） てら | Buddhist temples |
| （こうえん） | park |
| ちゅうしゃじょう | parking lot |
| びょういん | hospital |

(Various stores/shops)

| | |
|---|---|
| みせ | store |
| くつや | shoe shop |
| はなや | flower shop |
| くだものや | fruit shop |
| (やおや) | green grocer |
| (ほんや) | bookstore |
| カメラや | camera shop |
| (パンや) | bakery |
| にくや | meat shop |
| さかなや | fish market |
| でんきや | electric appliance store |
| くすりや／やっきょく | drugstore, pharmacy |
| ゆうびんきょく | post office |
| えいがかん | movie theatre |
| スーパー | supermarket |
| ぎんこう | bank |

[Adverbs]

| | |
|---|---|
| いっぱい | full |
| ぐるっと（まわる） | (going) round |
| みちなりに | along with the street |

[Verbs]
(Motion verbs)

| | |
|---|---|
| とまる | to stop (intransitive verb) |
| とめる | to stop something (transitive verb) |
| わたる | to cross |
| すぎる | to pass |
| (はしる) | to run |
| (あるく) | to walk |

(Others)

| | |
|---|---|
| こおる | to freeze |
| （めがねを　かける） | to wear (glasses) |
| （れいてんを　とる） | to get zero points |
| （日が）のぼる | to rise (The sun rises.) |
| （日が）しずむ | to sink (The sun sets.) |

Chapter 11(A)                    Grammar and Cultural Notes
             Learning how to ask and understand directions:
What would you do if you got lost in Japan?  You may want to ask a passerby how to get
to your destination, right?  Suppose you want to get to a train station.  How would you
ask it in Japanese? 「ちょっと、すみません。えきは、どこですか。」That's right!
If you could say 「えきは、どちらのほうですか。」, it's even better.  And, if you
could say, 「えきは、どういけば　いいですか。」, that sounds so sophisticated!
What if the kind passerby said, 「えきですか。えきは、このみちをまっすぐ行くと、
ありますよ。」, but you didn't understand what you were told?  The major purpose of
this chapter is for you to understand given instructions in Japanese.  In the statement
given by a passerby, two new expressions are included: One is the " と " conditional
clause, and the other is a new usage of " を " particle.

## 1. と **Conditional : "if," "when, "whenever" in English**

と conditional clause is equivalent to "if~," "when ~ ," or "whenever ~" in English.  と is
always preceded by a non-past tense verb (such as 行く、見る、食べる) or "nai" form
（行かない、見ない、食べない）.  You have learned already another conditional
clause, なら in Chapter 6(B) in a sentence such as あなたなら、（あるいて）二十分
ぐらいでしょう。じてんしゃなら、八分ぐらいです。 Two more conditionals (ば
and たら) will be later introduced.  Each of these four conditionals has its own
characteristics, and how to use each one of them requires experience and practice, though
sometimes they are interchangeable.  Among the four conditionals in Japanese, the と
conditional is often used to state a natural phenomenon, or eternal truth and facts.  In the
と conditional sentence, the relationship between the subordinate clause (conditional
clause) and the main clause is of an inevitable and habitual nature.  For this reason, it is
often used for directions, because directions such as the location of buildings normally
does not fluctuate arbitrarily.

Formation of the " と " conditional sentence:

| Conditional clause | Main clause |
|---|---|
| Dictionary form verb (plain non-past tense) ＋ と | Natural consequence |
| 1. 春になると When spring comes, | あたたかくなります。 it will become nice and warm. |
| 2. 夏になると When summer comes, | あつくなります。 it will become hot. |
| 3. 秋になると When autumn comes, | すずしくなります。 it will become nice and cool. |
| 4. 冬になると When winter comes, | さむくなります。 it will become cold. |
| 5. たくさん　食べると If you eat a lot, | 太ります。 you'll gain weight. |
| 6. 水が　0度になると When the water temperature becomes zero centigrade, | 凍ります。 it will freeze. |
| 7. まっすぐ行くと、If you go straight, | 銀行が　あります。 there will be a bank. |

Formation of the "to" conditional

| Conditional clause | Main clause |
|---|---|
| Negative plain non-past verb（〜ない）+　と | Natural consequence |
| 1. べんきょうしないと If you don't study, | テストで　零点をとりますよ。<br>you'll get zero points on the test. |
| 2. かんじは　書かないと If you don't write kanji, | じょうずに　なりません。<br>you won't improve. |
| 3. めがねを　かけないと If I don't wear eyeglasses, | よく　見えません。I can't see well. |
| 4. うんどうを　しないと If you don't exercise, | 太ります。you'll gain weight. |

## 2. を：**Particle covering space denoted by a motion verb**

In the direction given by a passerby, 「えきは、このみちをまっすぐ行くと、ありますよ。」a new usage of particle を is used. Please note that this particle is used with the verb 行く, which is a motion verb. Motion verbs include verbs such as 歩く、走る、飛ぶ、泳ぐ、渡る, etc. The particle を is used when motion covers an entire span of space. For example, when you walk down a street, you proceed in a linear line without leaving untrodden territory. In other words, you cover the entire stretch from point A to point B on the street. The particle を should be used to address that space, as particle で encompasses the entire perimeter of where action takes place. If you cross a river, use particle を, not で, as the same logic applies, where you're covering linear space from one end to another. Similarly, the idea of "flying in the sky," is expressed with そらを とぶ, and not with
そらで とぶ.

Examples:

（１）このみちを、まっすぐ行ってください。
　　　Please go straight on this street.
（２）川を　泳いで　渡った。(わたる to cross)
　　　I swam across the river.
（３）ろうかを　走らないでください。
　　　Please don't run down the corridor.
（４）橋を　渡ると、右手に　銀行が　あります。
　　　When you cross the bridge, there will be a bank on your right-hand side.
（５）道の真ん中を　歩くと、あぶないですよ。
　　　It's dangerous if you walk in the middle of the street.

### 3. <u>Watch particles with motion verbs!</u>

(1) particle に to show a direction

みぎ <u>に</u> まがる
  turn right

ひだり <u>に</u> まがる
  turn left

あちら <u>に</u> 行く
  go over that direction

東の方に 行く
  go to the East

(2) particle を for the space totally covered by the motion verbs

かど <u>を</u> まがる
  turn the corner

まんなか <u>を</u> あるく
  walk in the middle

はし <u>を</u> わたる
  cross the bridge

ろうか <u>を</u> はしる
  run down the corridor

川 <u>を</u> およぐ
  swim (across) the river

そら <u>を</u> とぶ
  fly in the sky

(3) particle から for a starting point

かど<u>から</u>、2けん目
  second house (building) from the corner

ここ<u>から</u> えきまで
  from here to the station

(4) no particle after numbers

百メートルぐらい (X) 行く
  go about 100 meters

まっすぐ (X) 行く
  go straight

一キロ (X) あるく
  walk 1 kilometer.

千メートル (X) およぐ
  swim 1000 meters

<u>Essential vocabulary for the directions:</u>

| | |
|---|---|
| traffic lights | しんごう |
| street | みち、とおり |
| bridge | はし |
| to cross the bridge | はしを わたる |
| end of a street | つきあたり |

| | |
|---|---|
| right hand side | みぎて |
| left hand side | ひだりて |
| turn right | みぎに まがる |
| turn left | ひだりに まがる |
| go straight | まっすぐ いく |
| go along with the street | みちなりに いく (often used with a curve) |
| across the street, front | むかいがわ、まえ |
| next to it, next door | となり |
| between | あいだ |
| behind, back | うしろ、うら |
| corner | かど |
| vicinity, near here | このちかく、そば |
| fourth house from the corner | かどから よんけんめ |

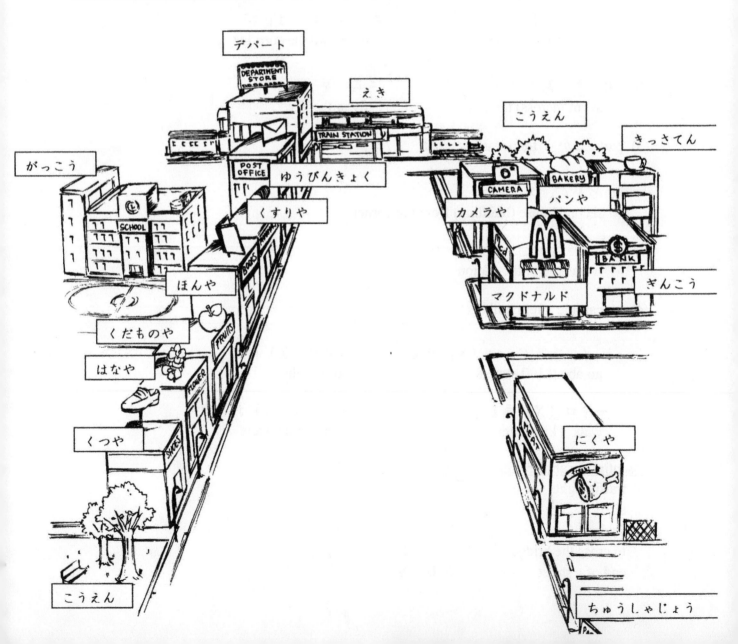

<u>タクシーのうんてんしゅさんに　いいます。</u>

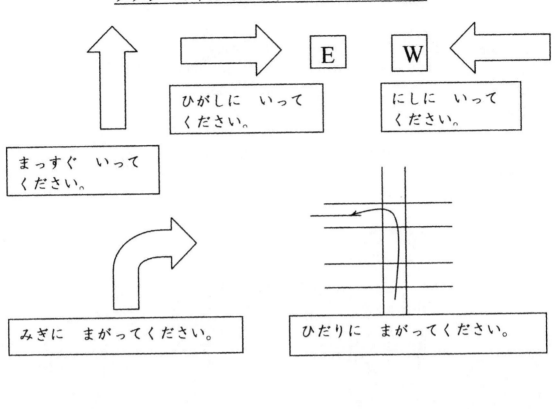

ひがしに　いって
ください。

にしに　いって
ください。

まっすぐ　いって
ください。

みぎに　まがってください。

ひだりに　まがってください。

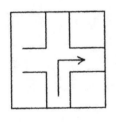

つぎを　　みぎに　まがってください。
（つぎのみちを）

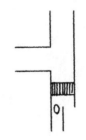

おうだんほどうの　てまえで
とまってください。
（とめてください）

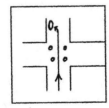

しんごうの　むこうで
とまってください。
（とめてください）

## What's on the map?

A. shoe shop　　　くつや
B. flower shop　　はなや
C. fruit shop　　　くだものや
D. book store　　　ほんや
E. drug store くすりや、やっきょく
F. school　　　　　がっこう
G. post office　　　ゆうびんきょく
H. department store　デパート
I. train station　　えき

J. camera shop　　カメラや
K. bakery　　　　パンや
L. coffee shop　　きっさてん
M. McDonalds　　マクドナルド
N. bank　　　　　ぎんこう
O. meat shop　　　にくや
P. parking lot　　ちゅうしゃじょう
Q & R. park　　　　こうえん

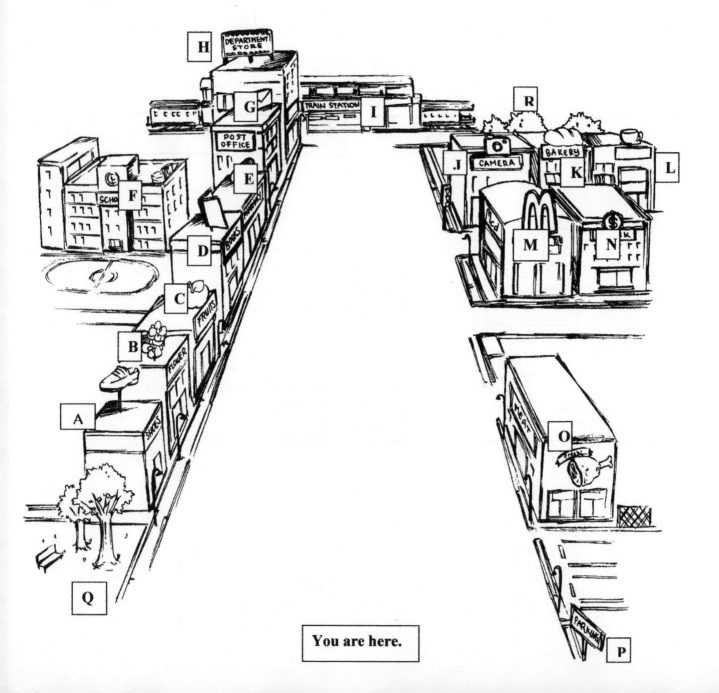

You are here.

Chapter 11(A) Exercises

A. Based on the map, judge whether the following statements are correct or incorrect.  Mark (O) for true and (X) for false.

(1) (    ) えきは、このみちのつきあたりに　あります。

(2) (    ) マクドナルドは、三つ目のみちの、みぎがわのかどにあります。

(3) (    ) こうえんは、ふたつあって、このすぐちかくと、えきのちかくに
あります。

(4) (    ) がっこうは、このみちをまっすぐ行って、みぎにまがると、
あります。

(5) (    ) がっこうは、三つ目のみちをひだりにまがって、すこし行くと、
あります。

(6) (    ) ゆうびんきょくは、にくやの　まえに　あります。

(7) (    ) はなやは、くつやと　くだものやの　あいだにあります。

(8) (    ) ぎんこうは、えきの　すぐまえに　あります。

(9) (    ) きっさてんは、このみちをまっすぐいって、しんごうを　みぎに
まがると　ひだりてに　あります。

(10)(    ) カメラやは、マクドナルドの　むかいがわにあります。

(11)(    ) デパートは、このみちをまっすぐ行くと、みぎてにあります。

(12)(    ) やっきょくは、がっこうの　まえに　あります。

(13)(    ) ちゅうしゃじょうは、めのまえに　あります。こうえんの
むかいがわです。

B. Read the following instructions while keeping an eye on the map on the next page. Figure out which listed place is being described and write its assigned numbers in the brackets.

(1)

A:  マクドナルドは、どこにありますか。

B:  ああ、マックなら　えきから　ちかいですよ。えきをでて、バスていのまえ
のみちを　にしのほうへ、あるきます。すると、いっぽんめのみちのかどに
あります。ゆうびんきょくのむかいがわですよ。

A:  わかりました。どうもありがとう。

＊マクドナルドは、ちずのうえで（　　　　　）です。

(2)

A:  たなかさんのうちは、えきから　どちらのほうですか。

T:  えきから、にしのほうですよ。えきのまえにがっこうがあります。がっこう
とちゅうしゃじょうのあいだのみちを　にしのほうへいくと、こうさてんの
かどに　こうばんがあります。そのとなりが　くつやです。わたしのうちは、
くつやのまえです。かどから、さんげんめです。わかりますか。

A:  だいじょうぶ、わかります。

＊たなかさんのうちは、ちずのうえで（　　　　　）です。

(3)

A:  もしもし、いま　えきまえのちゅうしゃじょうにいるんですが、じんじゃへ
は、どういけば　いいでしょうか。(How should I get there?)

B:  じんじゃは、ちゅうしゃじょうのきたのほうにあります。ちゅうしゃじょう
をでて、みぎにまがって、まっすぐきたにあるくと、みっつめのみちのかど
です。ぎんこうをすぎると、すぐとなりですが、、、。あ、そうそう、じん
じゃのまえに、きっさてんがありますよ。

A:  わかりました。ありがとうございました。

＊じんじゃは、ちずのうえで（　　　　　）です。

(4)

A:  もしもし、びょういんへは、どういけばいいですか。(How should I get there?)

B:  おくるまですか、でんしゃですか。

A:  くるまでいきます。

B:  いま、びょういんのちゅうしゃじょうは、いっぱいですから、えきのまえの
ちゅうしゃじょうに　くるまをとめてください。ちゅうしゃじょうをでて、
みぎにまがると、みぎがわに　がっこうが　みえます。がっこうをすぎて、
そのかどをみぎにまがると、みぎてにくすりやが　あります。びょういんの
いりぐちは、そのむかいがわです。

A:  わかりました。ちゅうしゃじょうをでて、なんぼんめのみちを　みぎにまが
りますか。

B:  にほんめです。

A:  ありがとう。

＊びょういんは、ちずのうえで（　　　　　）です。

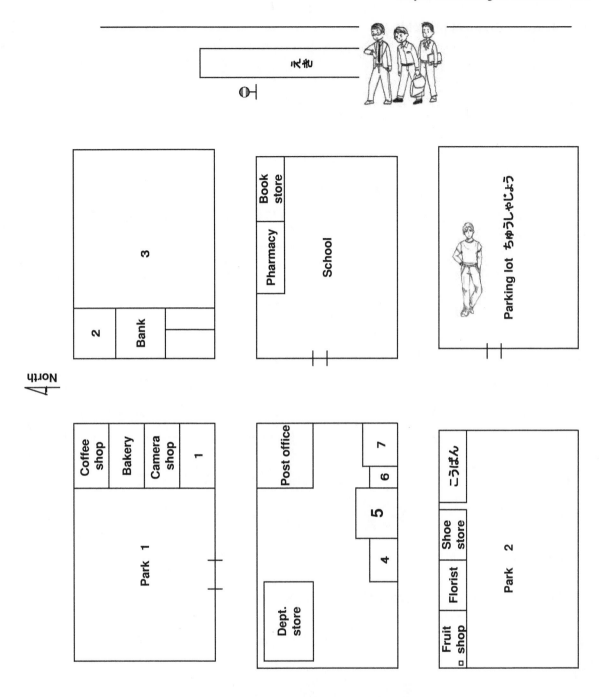

C. Choose the correct particles.

1. みぎ（に、で）まがります。そして、つぎのかど（を、に）ひだり（に、で）まがります。まっすぐいく（と、し）、しんごうが　あります。

2. そのはし（を、で）わたって、みぎ（に、を）いくと、ぎんこうが、あります。

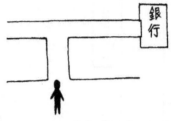

3. このみち（を、で）百メートル（を、に）行くと、川が　ありますから、その川を　わたらないで、その川のまえのみち（を、で）、みちなりに、行ってください。                    along with the street

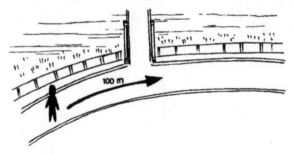

D. Fill in the blanks with appropriate words or sentences.

1. はしを　わたる（　　　）、右がわに、（ゆうびん）ポストが　あります。

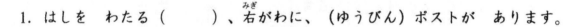

2. この道（　　　）まっすぐ（　　　　）、ぎんこうが　あります。

3. 朝になる（　　　）、東から日がのぼります。そして、夕方になる
（　　　）、西に　日がしずみます。　　　　　　　　　　dusk
The sun sets (literally: sinks) in the west.

4. そのはしの（　　　　　　）に、大きなこうえんが見えます。そのこうえん
の中を、一人で　歩く（　　　）が、大好きです。

5. たくさん食べる（　　　）、太るから、あまり食べないでね。

6. 水が　百度になると（　　　　　）になります。
　　　　100°C

7. 水が　零度になると（　　　　　）になります。
　　　　0°C

8. 大人になると（　　　　　　　　　　　　　　　　　　）。
　adults

9. ビールを飲みすぎると（　　　　　　　　　　　　　　）。

10. 1 に　1を　（　　　）と、2になります。

11. （　　　　　　　　　　　　　　　　　）と、やせます。

12. 毎日たくさんお金をつかうと、（　　　　　　　　　　　　　）。

13. 勉強しないと、（　　　　　　　　　　　　　）。

14. めがねをかけないと、（　　　　　　　　　　　　　　　）。

15. （　　　　　　　　）しないと、太<sub>ふと</sub>ります。

16. 冬<sub>ふゆ</sub>になると、（　　　　　　　　　　　　　　）。

17. （　　　　　　　　　　　）、さくらの花<sub>はな</sub>が　咲<sub>さ</sub>きます。

18. 道<sub>みち</sub>のまん中<sub>なか</sub>（　　　）歩<sub>ある</sub>くと、あぶないですよ。

E. Translate into Japanese, using the kanji appropriately.

1. If you turn right, you'll see the bank. (Do not use "見ます.")

2. When/If you cross the bridge, there's a school on its right.

3. Please go straight on this street for about 50 meters.

4. Please stop in front of the department store.

5. Please stop beyond the traffic light.

6. How do I get to the drugstore?

7. The <u>hospital</u> is across the street from the pharmacy.
   病院（びょういん）

8. The bakery is between a florist and a <u>green-grocer</u>.
   八百屋（やおや）

9. Mrs. Tanaka's house is the fifth house from the corner.

F. Pair or group work: Consult the map and complete the dialogue.

1. (Group A)

A：私<sub>わたし</sub>の家<sub>いえ</sub>にあそびに来<sub>き</sub>てください。

B：ありがとう、でも　どうやって　行<sub>い</sub>けばいいですか。

A：でんしゃの駅<sub>えき</sub>（　　　　）東口<sub>ひがしぐち</sub>で、出<sub>で</sub>ます。そして、右<sub>みぎ</sub>（　　　）ま
がります。くだものやの前<sub>まえ</sub>（　　　）すぎて、まっすぐ行きます。する
と、かどに、ゆうびんきょくが　あります。そのかどを（　　　　）に
まがります。私<sub>わたし</sub>の家<sub>いえ</sub>は、ゆうびんきょくの（　　　　）です。かど
から、二<sub>に</sub>けん目<sub>め</sub>です。

B：じゃ、今日<sub>きょう</sub>の午後<sub>ごご</sub>、うかがいます。

Ａ：待ってます。

Vocabulary help:

| | | | |
|---|---|---|---|
| あそびにくる | to come to visit | ひがしぐち | east exit, east gate |
| くだものや | fruit shop | すぎる | to pass (in front of ~) |
| すると | if/when you do so | ゆうびんきょく | post office |
| かど | corner | にけんめ | the second house/building |
| うかがう | to visit (humble form) | | |

2. (Group B)

Ａ：神社に行きたいんですが、どう行けばいいですか。
Ｂ：神社ですか。駅から近いですよ。駅の西口から出て、まっすぐ西へ行く
　（　　　　）、あります。一本道で　つきあたりですから、すぐわかります。
Ａ：駅を出て、（　　　　）ですね。わかりました。どうもありがとう。

Vocabulary help:

| | | | |
|---|---|---|---|
| じんじゃ | shrine | まっすぐ | straight |
| いっぽんみち | a street with no junctions | つきあたり | end of a street |

3. (Group C)

Ａ：あのう、すみません。銀行へ行きたいんですけど、、、
Ｂ：銀行なら、駅の 東 です。駅からまっすぐ（　　）へ行くと、川に出ま
　す。その橋（　　）わたって、一本目の道を（　　）に 曲がります。
　その道には、（　　　　）がありますから、すぐわかりますよ。銀行は、
　ちょっと歩くと　左手にあります。
Ａ：その通りのなまえは、なんと言うんですか。
　Ｂ：通りのなまえは、わすれましたが、大きい（　　　　）ですから、
　だいじょうぶです。
Ａ：行ってみます。ありがとう。

Vocabulary help:

| | | | |
|---|---|---|---|
| かわ | river | ～にでる | to come to ~ |
| はし | bridge | しんごう | traffic lights |
| とおり | street | わすれました | I forgot |
| だいじょうぶ | It's all right. | こうさてん | an intersection |

4. (Group D)

A：くつ屋は、どこにありますか。

B：くつ屋は、ここから、ちょっと遠いです。駅から（　　　　　）のほう
にありますが、、駅を（　　　　）で　出て、さいしょの道を右に
（　　　　　　）。そうすると、（　　　　　）にびょういんが、見えて
来ます。びょういんの横に　ちいさい道がありますから、その道を
右（　　　）曲がって、みちなりに行くと、まがりかどに三（　　　）
みせが　あります。くつ屋は、花屋と薬屋の（　　　）です。

Vocabulary help:

| | | | |
|---|---|---|---|
| くつや | shoe shop | さいしょ | the first |
| びょういん | hospital | みえてくる | to start showing up |
| みちなりにいく | to go along with the street | みせ | a store |
| まがりかど | a (turning) corner | | |

5. (Group E)

A：お寺は、どちらのほうにありますか。

B：お寺ですか。こうえんのすぐ前にあるんですが、、、

A：こうえんは、知らないんです。

B：だいじょうぶです。そんなに遠くありません。
駅を東口で出て、左にまがってください。すこし行くと、ふみきりが
あります。そのふみきりをわたって、まっすぐ行くと、つきあたりに
（　　　　　）が　あります。そのつきあたりで、右の道を行くと右手
（　　　）お寺が　あります。お寺の入口は、（　　　　　）がわですから、
ぐるっと回ってください。

Vocabulary help:

| | | | |
|---|---|---|---|
| おてら | a temple | ふみきり | railroad crossing |
| いりぐち | an entrance | | |
| ～　がわ | side | ぐるっとまわる | to go around |

**Map to be used for Exercise F. 1 ~ 5**

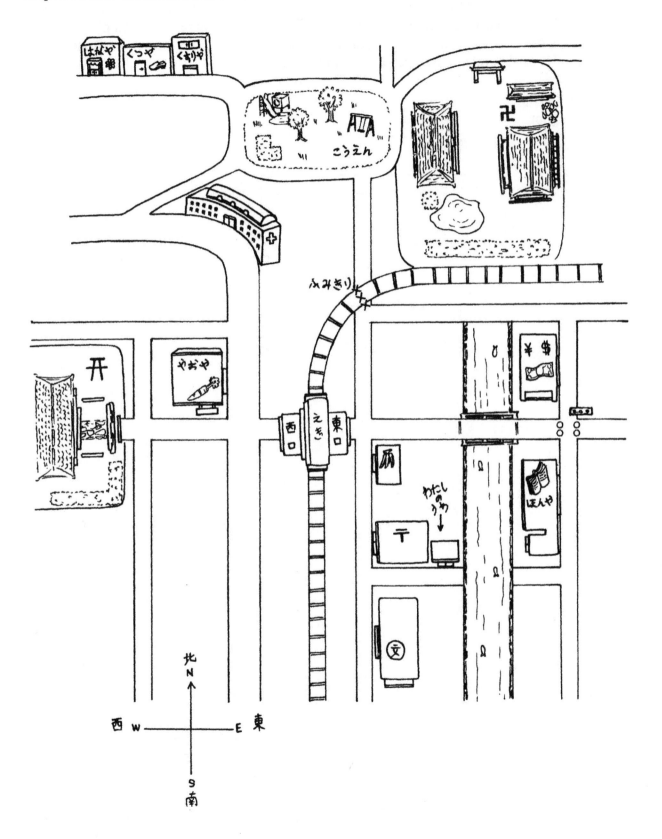

Chapter 11 (A): Dict-A-Conversation

Listen to Chapter 11(A)'s Dict-A-Conversation on the student CD, whiling watching the map. You will hear a direction to each location on the map. Figure out which place that is from the list below and write its alphabets in the answer column. "Soko" or "sono basho" is used to refer to each location in question.

[Vocabulary Help]

parking lot:  ちゅうしゃじょう

bus stop  バス停(てい)

| Directions | |
|---|---|
| 1 | |
| 2 | |
| 3 | |
| 4 | |
| 5 | |

a. デパート
b. くつや
c. ぎんこう
d. くすりや
e. ほんや

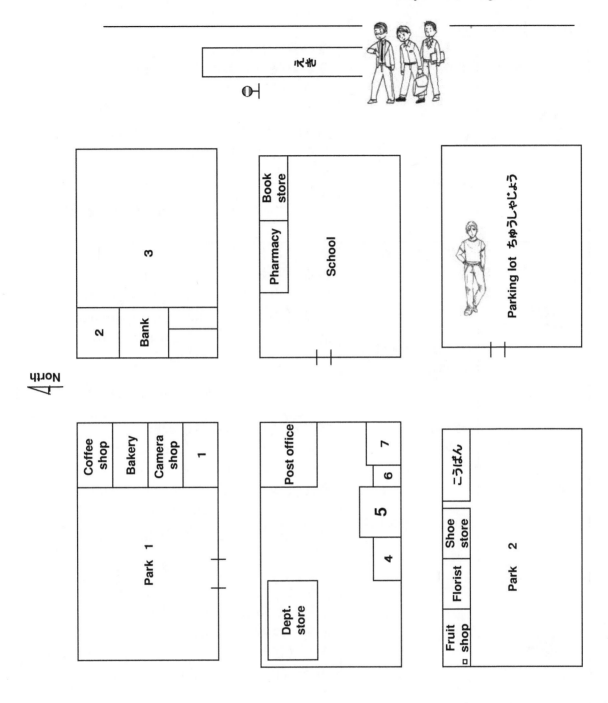

Chapter 11 (A) - (1)

| 道 (a way; street) | みち<br>ドウ<br><br>(a way; street) | 道 （みち） a way; street<br>分かれ道 （わかれみち） a fork in the road<br>[道路 （どうろ） a road]<br>北海道 （ほっかいどう） Hokkaido district<br>[剣道 （けんどう） Japanese fencing]<br>歩道 （ほどう） sidewalk<br>車道 （しゃどう） roadway |
|---|---|---|
| | | (12)<br>丶 ` ⺌ ⺍ 并 首 首 首 首 首 道 道 |
| 通 (to pass through; a street) | とお （り、る）<br>ツウ<br><br>(to pass through; a street) | 通り （とおり） a street<br>通る （とおる） to pass through<br>通行 （つうこう） passing through; traffic<br>交通 （こうつう） traffic; transportation<br>文通 （ぶんつう） correspondence by writing letters |
| | | (10)<br>⺄ ⻊ ⻊ 甬 甬 甬 甬 通 通 |
| 信 (to believe; belief) | （のぶ）<br>シン （じる）<br><br>(to believe; belief) | 信じる （しんじる） to believe<br>自信 （じしん） confidence<br>信用 （しんよう） する to trust<br>通信 （つうしん） communication through electronics<br>*信子 （のぶこ） girl's name |
| | | (9)<br>ノ イ 仁 产 产 佇 佇 信 信 |
| 号 (number; designation; sign) | ゴウ<br><br>(number; designation; sign) | 一号 （いちごう） a number; an issue<br>信号 （しんごう） traffic lights<br>年号 （ねんごう） name of era<br>号外 （ごうがい） an extra edition (of a newspaper)<br>[番号 （ばんごう） serial number] |
| | | (5)<br>丶 ロ ロ 므 号 |
| 左 (left) | ひだり<br>サ<br><br>(left) | 左 （ひだり） left<br>左手 （ひだりて） left hand; left hand side<br>左足 （ひだりあし） left leg<br>[左折 （させつ） a left-turn] |
| | | (5)<br>一 ナ 左 左 左 |

Ch 11 (A) – (2)

| 右 (right) | みぎ ウ | 右 (みぎ) right<br>[右折 (うせつ) a right-turn]<br>左右 (さゆう) right and left |
| | | (5)<br>ノ ナ オ 右 右 |
| 曲 (to turn; a music piece) | ま (がる) キョク | 曲がる (まがる) to turn<br>曲 (きょく) a music piece<br>作曲 (さっきょく) する to compose |
| | | (6)<br>丨 冂 由 曲 曲 曲 |

Kanji Practice for Chapter 11(A)

かんじの　れんしゅう

1. つぎの　ことばを　よみなさい。それから、クラスメートに　いみをきき
なさい。 Read the following words to your classmates and ask them for the meaning
of each word.

(1) 大きな道を　行く

(2) 小さな道を　通る

(3) 見ることは、信じることだ。

(4) あの信号を渡ってください。(渡る [わたる] to cross)

(5) 左に曲がってください。

(6) 右に曲がってください。

(7) 作曲家

(8) 道を渡るときは、左右をよく　見てください。

(9) ヨーロッパの人と　文通してみたいです。

(10) Communication through electricity は、日本語で「通信」と言います。

(11) 人が歩く道を　「歩道」といいます。

2. Write kanji in the box to complete the compound word.

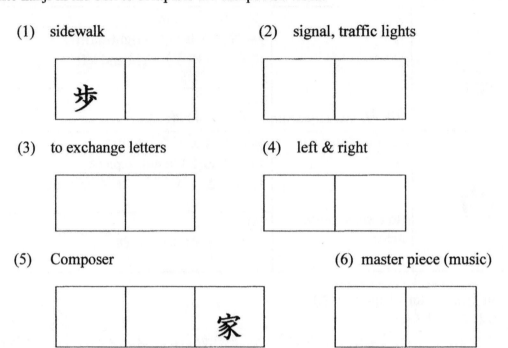

(1)　sidewalk

歩　

(2)　signal, traffic lights

(3)　to exchange letters

(4)　left & right

(5)　Composer

　　家

(6)　master piece (music)

3. よんでから、よみがなをかいて、えいごでいいなさい。Read first, then write yomigana above each kanji, and translate into English.

（１）　この道は、古い道です。

（２）　その道を通って、小学校に行きました。

（３）　信号で　止まってください。

（４）　左に曲がって、まっすぐ行くと、駅が見えます。

（５）　右手に　白い建物が　あります。

（６）　歩道を　歩いてください。

（７）　歩道と車道が、わかれていません。

（８）　道をわたるときは、左右を　見てください。

（９）　信号の手前に、米屋が　あります。

（１０）　道路の真ん中で、立ち止まっては、あぶないですよ。

（１１）　茶道を　ならっています。

（１２）　右手の道を行くと、中学校が　あります。

（１３）　曲を作ることを、作曲と言います。

（１４）　ベートーベンは、有名な作曲家です。

（１５）　モーツァルトは、多くの名曲を作りました。

4.　しつもんにこたえなさい。 **Answer the questions.**

（１）あなたの家の近くにコンビニがありますか。

（２）あなたは、だれのどんな曲が好きですか。

（３）きょうしつを出て、前を見ると、何がありますか。

（４）あなたの家からゆうびんきょくまで、どのぐらいありますか。

（５）きょうしつの戸は、あなたの右にありますか、左にありますか。

（６）今日、きょうしつに入ったとき、先生はどこにいましたか。

（７）「つきあたり」って何ですか。

（８）京都では、「つきあたり」のことを何と言いますか。

（９）「ふみきり」って何ですか。あなたの学校の近くにありますか。

（１０）東京の人は、「ひょうじゅん語」を話しますか。

Chapter 11(B)　　Meeting with Ms. Tanaka　田中さんとのまちあわせ

(On the phone: 電話で)

モニカ：もしもし、田中さん。　　　　　　　　　　　　　　　　　　　　　　1

田中　：はい、田中です。　　　　　　　　　　　　　　　　　　　　　　　2

モニカ：モニカです。すみませんが、少しおくれます。　　　　　　　　　3

田中　：だいじょうぶです。まだ二時半だから、、、　　　　　　　　　4

モニカ：バスを一つ　手前で　おりたので、、　　　　　　　　　　　　5

田中　：道は、分かりますか。　　　　　　　　　　　　　　　　　　　6

モニカ：はい、今　おしえてもらいました。あと十分ほどで　つきます。　7

田中　：しんぱいしないで。じゃね。　　　　　　　　　　　　　　　　8

モニカ：はい。　　　　　　　　　　　　　　　　　　　　　　　　　　9


[English Translation]:  Telephone conversation　電話での会話

Monica:  Hello, Ms. Tanaka?
Tanaka:  Yes, this is she.
Monica:  It's Monica.  I am sorry I am going to be late.
Tanaka:  That's all right.  It's only two thirty.
Monica:  I got off the bus one stop early. (That's why)
Tanaka:  Do you know how to get here?
Monica:  Yes, someone just told me.  I will be there in about ten minutes.
Tanaka:  Don't worry. See you then.
Monica:  Okay.

(In front of Maruyama Park: 円山公園の前で)

| | | |
|---|---|---|
| 田中 : | モニカさん！ | 1 |
| モニカ : | あ、田中さん。よかった。間に合って！ | 2 |
| 田中 : | だいじょうぶ。円山公園の桜は、夜、ライトアップしてからが、 | 3 |
| | きれいだから。今は、まだ明るいでしょう？ | 4 |
| モニカ : | でも、その前に、えいがをみるんでしょう？ | 5 |
| 田中 : | そう。学生は、三本で六百円。安いでしょう？ | 6 |
| | 私は、社会人だから、もう少し高いけれど、、、 | 7 |
| モニカ : | どこで、見るんですか。 | 8 |
| 田中 : | ほら、あそこに　えいがかんが見えるでしょう？ | 9 |
| モニカ : | はい、あの「ぎおん会館」っていうのですか。 | 10 |
| 田中 : | そうそう、今、三時だから、あそこでえいがを見てから、 | 11 |
| | 円山公園の夜桜を　見に行きましょう。 | 12 |

[English translation:] (In front of Maruyama Park)

Tanaka: Monica!
Monica: Ah, Tanaka san. I'm so glad to make it in time.
Tanaka: That's all right. The cherry blossoms of Maruyama Park are beautiful at nights after the light-up. It's still bright, isn't it?
Monica: Yet, aren't we going to see a movie before then?
Tanaka: Yes. The student fare is six hundred yen for three movies. Isn't it reasonable? Since I am (considered) an employed worker, it'd be a bit more expensive for me...
Monica: Where are we going to watch the movies?
Tanaka: Look over there. Can you see the movie theater?
Monica: Yes, you mean that "Gion-Kaikan"?
Tanaka: That's right. It's three o'clock now. After watching the movies, let's go see the night cherry blossoms at Maruyama Park.

## Chapter 11(B)　　　　　　Vocabulary List

### 1. Expressions

| | |
|---|---|
| もしもし | Hello (over the phone). |
| すみませんが、、、 | Excuse me, but… |
| あと十分ほどで　つきます。 | I'll arrive in about ten minutes. |
| しんぱいしないで。 | Don't worry. |
| じゃね。 | Bye (casual). |
| よかった、まにあって。 | Glad I made it. |
| そうそう | That's right. |
| ほら | Look! |
| 〜っていうの | the one called so and so |

### 2. Nouns

| | |
|---|---|
| てまえ(手前) | beforehand |
| 十分ほど | about ten minutes |
| さくら(桜) | cherry blossoms |
| よざくら　(夜桜) | night cherry blossoms |
| よる　(夜) | night |
| ライトアップ | light-up |
| しゃかいじん　(社会人) | working person |
| (えいが) | movie |
| (えいがかん) | movie theatre |

### 3. Adjectives

| | |
|---|---|
| (やすい　安い) | cheap; reasonable |
| (たかい　高い) | expensive |

### 4. Verbs

| | |
|---|---|
| (〜を)おりる | to get off (〜) |
| おりて | "te" form of "oriru" |
| おりた | "ta" form of "oriru" |
| おくれる | to be late; get behind |
| おくれて | "te" form of "okureru" |
| おくれた | "ta" form of "okureru" |
| おしえる | to teach |
| おしえて | "te" form of "oshieru" |
| おしえた | "ta" form of "oshieru" |
| しんぱいする | to worry |
| まにあう | to make it in time |

## Additional Vocabulary from Grammar Notes, Exercises & Kanji sections, and D-A-C

..................................................................................

[Nouns]

| | |
|---|---|
| すな | sand |
| せなか | one's back |
| （びょうき） | illness |
| わすれもの　（忘れ物） | lost property; a thing left behind |
| （おまわりさん） | policeman |
| （へんじ　返事） | reply |
| （こんや　今夜） | tonight |
| よなか（夜中） | the middle of the night |
| やかん（夜間） | during the night |
| しゃかい（社会） | society |
| （かいしゃ　会社） | company |
| かいごう（会合） | meeting |
| こころ（心） | heart |

[Adjectives]

| | |
|---|---|
| （かゆい） | itchy |

[Copula Nouns]

| | |
|---|---|
| やす(安)らか | peaceful |
| あんしん（安心） | peaceful mind |
| （けっこう） | fine; good |

[Verbs]

| | |
|---|---|
| き（気）がつく | to notice |
| と（取）りに行く | to pick up; go get something |
| お（起）こす | to wake up someone (transitive verb) |
| おごる | to treat (by paying) |
| か（掻）く | to scratch |
| なぐさめる | to comfort someone |
| つきあう | to socialize |
| まにあう（間に合う） | to make in time |
| み（見）つける | to find |

Chapter 11(B)                Grammar and Cultural Notes

## 1.〜てから : after doing something

The "te" form verb + "kara" express the meaning of "after doing something" and forms an adverbial phrase. 食べてから means "after eating," and 起きてから means "after getting up."

Examples:

（１）朝ごはんを食べてから、さんぽをしました。
      After eating breakfast, I strolled.

（２）子供が起きてから、いっしょにごはんを食べましょう。
      Let's eat with the kids after they wake up.

（３）学校に来てから、さいふがないのに、気がついた。

                                    (気がつく to notice; realize)
      I realized that I didn't have my wallet after I arrived at school.

（４）しゅくだいをやってから、あそびなさい。
      Go play after you finish your homework.

（５）このえいがをみてから、ちょっとモールの中を歩きませんか。
      Why don't we walk in the (shopping) mall after watching this movie?

## 2. 食べに行く to go eat: go/come/return for the purpose of V-ing

The "masu" form verb + ni + 行く、来る、帰る expresses the idea you are going/coming/returning for the "purpose" of taking action. For example, if your purpose of going to the park is to read a book, in Japanese it'd be こうえんへ、本を読みに行く。
Formation:

| "masu" form (the 2<sup>nd</sup> base of consonant verbs or the stem of vowel verbs) 飲み、読み、つくり、話し 食べ、寝、教え、勉強し | に | + 行く 来る 帰る |
| --- | --- | --- |

Examples例:

（１）そこへ　何をしに、行くんですか。
      What are you going there for?

（２）日本へ、英語をおしえに　行きます。
      I am going to Japan to teach English.

（３）今から、おすしを　食べに行くんですよ。
      We are going to eat o-sushi.

（４）しゅくだいを 取<sup>と</sup>りに、帰<sup>かえ</sup>ってきました。
I came back to pick up my homework.

（５）えいがを みに 行きませんか。
Won't we go to see a movie?

（６）あそびに 来<sup>き</sup>てください。
Please come to visit me.

Remember we learned this expression in Chapter 5?

| |
|---|
| しょくじ <u>に</u> 行<sup>い</sup>きます |
| 来<sup>き</sup>ます |
| 帰<sup>かえ</sup>ります |

"に ni" is used to show a "purpose" in motion verbs (such as "go," "come," and "return") Thus, the above sentence means "I will go/come/return for a meal."

Examples

(1) えいが に 行<sup>い</sup>きませんか。     Won't we go see a movie?

(2) かいもの に 行<sup>い</sup>きました。     I went for shopping.

(3) ドライブ に 行<sup>い</sup>きましょう。    Let's go for a drive.

(4) しごと に 行<sup>い</sup>ってきます。     I'm leaving for work.

Aside from "movie," "shopping," "driving" and "work" as mentioned above, you can add "purpose" to any motion verb by following the below formula.

| |
|---|
| "V-stem" + に ni + motion verb |

For example:

(1) 家<sup>うち</sup>へ 寝<sup>ね</sup>に かえります。am going home to sleep.

(2) ごはんを 食<sup>た</sup>べに 行<sup>い</sup>きます。I am going out to eat.

(3) えいがを 見<sup>み</sup>に 行<sup>い</sup>きました。  I went to see a movie.

(4) かばんを 買<sup>か</sup>いに 行<sup>い</sup>きます。I am going shopping for a bag.

(5) パブへ 飲<sup>の</sup>みに 行<sup>い</sup>きましょう。Let's go to a pub for drinks.

Ask yourself what is the purpose of going to the following places.
つぎのばしょへ なにを しに 行きますか。

(1) えいがかん

(2) プール

(3) としょかん

(4) どうぶつえん a zoo

(5) レストラン

(6) デパート

(7) スーパーマーケット super market

(8) ガソリン・スタンド gas station

(9) えき

(10) びじゅつかん museum

Possible answers:

(1)  えいがを　みに　行きます。

(2)  およぎに　行きます。

(3)  本を　よみに　行きます。（かえしに to return something.、かりに to borrow something）

(4)  どうぶつを　みに　行きます。(どうぶつ animals)

(5)  食べに　行きます。

(6)  スーツケースを　買いに　行きます。

(7)  にくややさいを　買いに　行きます。

(8)  ガソリンを　いれに　行きます。（ガソリンを　入れます to put gasoline）

(9)  ともだちを　むかえに　行きます。（むかえに行きます to pick up）

(10)  えを　みに　行きます。

### 3. ～てもらう: receiving a favor

In Chapter 9, we have learned the verbs of giving and receiving: あげる、もらう、くれる. You can use these verbs with the "te" form verb when the favor is being done. For example, if someone was kind enough to write down directions for you, you can form two sentences using もらう and くれる. When you make yourself (the recipient of a favor) the subject of the sentence, use もらう, and when you make the kind person (the giver of the favor) the subject of the sentence, use くれる. Observe:

1）わたしは、ちずを　かいてもらいました。
   I received the favor of someone drawing me a map.

2）その人は、ちずを　かいてくれました。
   That person gave me the favor of drawing a map.

Formation of giving & receiving in action

| The "te" form verb 書いて、読んで、見て、話して、聞いて | | あげる もらう くれる |
|---|---|---|
| | + | |

Examples:

(1) 私は、今日、小さい子に　本を　読んであげました。

I read a book to a little kid today.

(2) 私は、おまわりさんに、道を教えてもらいました。

A policeman was kind enough to give me directions.

(I received a favor from a policeman who" taught me" directions.)

(3) おまわりさんは、ちずを　かいてくれました。

The policeman drew me a map.

(4) 父が、くるまを　買ってくれました。

My father bought me a car.

(5) おじいさんに、めがねを　さがしてあげました。

I searched for eyeglasses for an old man.

Who did what to whom?  Read the short passage and answer the questions.

次の　短い文を読んで、質問に答えてみましょう。

私は、昨日、知り合いのパーティーに行くところでした。でも、私はその家の住所しか知らないので、地図を見ながら、行きました。道がくねくねと曲がっているので、ちっともその家がわかりません。そこで、人のよさそうなおじさんに、聞きました。そのおじさんは、とても親切に、道を教えてくれましたから、その後、すぐに、知り合いの家に行くことができました。そのおじさんは、私を心配して、いっしょに、その家まで来てくれたんです。知り合いが家の中から出てきて、おじさんにお礼を言ってくれたので、私もうれしかったです。

[Vocabulary Help]

知り合い　　　　acquaintance

くねくね（と）　　zigzags

人がよい　　　　kind-hearted

心配する　　　to worry

お礼を言う　　to say thank-you

質問1　道を教えてくれたのは、だれですか。

質問2　だれが、何を心配したのですか。

質問3　だれが、だれにお礼を言いましたか。

質問4　どうして、私はうれしかったのですか。

## Chapter 11(B) Exercises

### A. Choose the appropriate answers.

1. レストランへ　何をしに行きますか。
   - (　　) ①. 本を読みに
   - (　　) ②. てがみを書きに
   - (　　) ③. 食べに

2. プールへ　何をしに行きますか。
   - (　　) ①. 食べに
   - (　　) ②. 泳ぎに
   - (　　) ③. 寝に

3. としょかんへ、何をしに行きますか。
   - (　　) ①. 本を読みに
   - (　　) ②. 本を返しに
   - (　　) ③. ともだちと会いに
   - (　　) ④. あそびに

4. こうえんへ、何をしに行きますか。
   - (　　) ①. さんぽに
   - (　　) ②. 飲みに
   - (　　) ③. 本を読みに

5. 海へ、何をしに行きますか。
   - (　　) ①. 買いものに
   - (　　) ②. 泳ぎに
   - (　　) ③. 砂とあそびに
     (sand)

### B. Change the verbs to the appropriate form to show "purpose" in motion verbs.
Examples:

(1) ごはんを（食べます）に いき
　　ます。　　　　↓
　　　　　　　たべ

(2) コーヒーを（飲みます）に いき
　　ます。　　　　↓
　　　　　　のみ

1. えいがを（見ます）に 行きます。
2. 先生に（会います）に 来ます。
3. パンを（買います）に 行きます。
4. べんきょうを（します）に 行きます。
5. 友だちが、本を（読みます）に 来ます。
6. 田中さんが（話します）に 来ます。
7. ごはんを（食べます）に うちへ、帰ります。
8. 海へ（泳ぎます）に 行きます。
     ocean     to swim

C. Pair-work: Ask your partner the following questions and write his/her answers on the board.

(1) きっさてんへ、何を のみに 行きますか。
(2) 友だちのうちへ なにを しに 行きますか。
(3) 学校へ 何を しに 来ますか。
(4) 海へ 何を しに 行きますか。
(5) 本屋さんへ 何を しに 行きますか。
(6) 日本へ なにを しに 行きますか。
(7) ビヤガーデンへ 何を しに 行きますか。
(8) 酒屋さんへ、何を 買いに 行きますか。

D. ペアワーク：「Vに行く・くる」の れんしゅう
かいわを かんせいしなさい。(Complete the dialogue.) それから、れんしゅう
しなさい。

(1). Eat out たべにいく

A: もう（　　　　　）を 食べましたか。
B: いいえ、まだですけど。（　　　　　）さんは？
A: 私もまだです。（　　　　）を食べに行きませんか。
B: いいですね。どこが いいですか。
A: （　　　）は（　　　　）が おいしいですよ。
B: じゃ、（　　　　　）へ 行きましょう。

(2). Movie えいが を 見に行く

A: （　　　　）さんは、よく えいがを 見ますか。
B: いいえ、あまり 見ません。えいがは、さいきん たかいんです。
A: えいがのチケットが二まい あるんですけど、いっしょに 見に行きませ
んか。

B: え、ほんとですか。ぜひ。どんなえいがが　いいですか。

A: （　　　　　）さんの　好きなえいがで　いいですよ。

B: 私は、（　　　　　　　　）を　みに行きたいです。

A: じゃ、そうしましょう！

(3).　Shopping かいもの　に　行く

A: おまちどおさま。(Thank you for waiting.)

B: だいじょうぶです。どこへ　行きましょうか。

A: きれいな色の（　　　　　　）を　かいに行きたいんですけど、、、

B: （　　　　　）なら、（　　　　　　　　　　）が　いいですよ。

A: じゃ、（　　　　　　）へ　行きましょう。

B: そのあと、うでどけいを　見に行っても　いいですか。

A: もちろんです。

(4).　To the Ocean 海へ　行く

A: あついですね。プールで　およぎませんか。

B: プールもいいですけど、海へ　行きませんか。

A: そうですね、海へ　およぎに行きましょう。

B: どこの海が　いいですか。

A: （　　　　　　　　　　　　）はどうですか。あそこの海はきれいだから。

B: じゃ、そうしましょう！

E. Change ～てから to たあとで

1．朝、シャワーを　あびてから、コーヒーを　飲みます。
→

2．テレビのニュースをみてから、しゅくだいを　しました。
→

3．しんぶんを　読んでから、でかけました。
→

4．友だちに、「行く」と電話をしてから、サイフがないのに、気がつきました。
→

5．お父さんが、帰ってから、話しましょう。
→

F. あなたは、人に何をしてもらうのが　好きですか。左の（　　）に、チェックをしてください。それからクラスメートに同じしつもんをして、そのこたえを、右の（　　）に、書き入れてください。What do you enjoy people doing for you?  Checkmark the ones you enjoy in the left column, then ask your classmate the same questions and checkmark the right column.

（1）（　）（　）朝、起こしてもらうこと(起こす to wake up someone)

（2）（　）（　）朝ごはんを　つくってもらうこと

（3）（　）（　）学校まで　うんてんしてもらうこと

（4）（　）（　）友だちに　おごってもらうこと　（おごる to treat）

（5）（　）（　）人に、お茶をいれてもらうこと(お茶をいれる to serve tea)

（6）（　）（　）せんたくを　してもらうこと

（7）（　）（　）そうじを　してもらうこと

（8）（　）（　）かゆいときに、せなかを　かいてもらうこと

　　　　　　　(itchy)　　　　(back)　　(掻く to scratch)

（9）（　）（　）悲しいときに、なぐさめてもらうこと

　　　　　　　　　　　　　　　（なぐさめる to comfort）

（10）　（　）（　）病気のときに、ごはんをつくってもらうこと

　　　　　　　(illness)

G. 何をしてあげるのが　好きですか。好きなことに（　√　）を　書いてください。それからクラスメートに同じしつもんをしてください。What do you enjoy doing for others?  Checkmark the ones you enjoy in the left column, then ask your classmate the same questions and checkmark the right column.

1.（　）（　）りょうりをつくってあげること

2.（　）（　）そうじをしてあげること

3.（　）（　）せんたくをしてあげること

4.（　）（　）友だちに　おごってあげること　（おごる to treat）

5.（　）（　）人に、お茶を　いれてあげること　(お茶をいれる to serve tea)

6.（　）（　）しゅくだいを　たすけてあげること

7.（　）（　）かいものに　つきあってあげること

　　　　　　　　　　　（つきあう to accompany）

8.（　）（　）なくしものを　さがしてあげること

　　　　　　lost property　（さがす to search）

9.（　）（　）朝　起こしてあげること

　　　　　　(起こす to wake up someone)

10.（　）（　）小さい子とあそんであげること

H. つぎの人々は、あなたに　どんなことをしてくれます/くれましたか。

（1）　お母さん

（2）　お父さん

（3）　先生

（4）　おまわりさん

（5）　ともだち

I. あなたは、今　だれに　どんなことをしてあげたいですか。

J. しけんに失敗したとき、何と言って、なぐさめてもらいたいです。

K. あなたが病気の時、一番してもらいたいことは、何ですか。

Chapter 11 (B): Dict-A-Conversation （1）
Listen to a short passage in Chapter 11(B)'s Dict-A-Conversation on the student CD, then
choose the statement that matches to what you heard by giving a checkmark.

1. わたしは、きょう　としょかんへ
①(　)　本を　読みに　行きました。
②(　)　本を　返しに　行きました。

2. わたしは、としょかんで
①(　)　いいれきしの本を　見つけました。(見つける to find)
②(　)　いいれきしの本を　見つけることが　できませんでした。

3. わたしは、としょかんで
①(　)　れきしの本を　読みました。
②(　)　日本語のべんきょうを　しました。

4. ともだちは、わたしに
①(　)　モールへ　行ってもらいたいんです。
②(　)　ともだちの家で　あそんでもらいたいんです。

5. わたしは、こんやは、
①(　)　ひまです。
②(　)　いそがしいです。

6. わたしは、ともだちのEメールに
①(　)　へんじ (reply) を　しませんでした。
②(　)　すぐに　へんじ (reply) を　しました。

7. わたしは、こんや、ともだちと
①(　)　モールへ　行くつもりです。
②(　)　モールへ　行かないつもりです。

Ch 11 (B)

| 合<br><br>(to match) | あ（う）<br>ゴウ<br><br><br><br>（to match） | 合う（あう）to match<br>間に合う（まにあう）to make in time<br>[似合う（にあう）looks good]<br>[合格（ごうかく）する to pass an<br>　　　　　　　　　　　　examination]<br>会合（かいごう）meeting<br>[待ち合わせる（まちあわせる）arrange to<br>　　　　　　　　　　　　　　　meet] |
|---|---|---|
| | | (6)<br>ノ　人　△　合　合　合 |
| 安<br><br><br>(comfort; cheap) | やす（らか）<br>やす（い）<br>アン | 安らか（やすらか）comfortable<br>安い（やすい）cheap<br>安心（あんしん）feel reassured; peace of mind<br>安全（あんぜん）safety; security<br>不安（ふあん）uneasiness; anxiety |
| | | (6)<br>丶　丶ˊ　宀　宀　安　安 |
| 高<br><br><br>(high; expensive) | たか（い）<br>コウ | 高い（たかい）high; expensive<br>高田（たかた、たかだ）a surname<br>高山（こうざん）high mountains<br>高名（こうめい）high reputation<br>[高価（こうか）な　expensive] |
| | | (10)<br>丶　亠　宀　产　卢　卢　高　高　高　高 |
| 夜<br><br><br>(night) | よる<br>よ<br>ヤ | 夜（よる）night<br>夜中（よなか）during the night<br>今夜（こんや）tonight<br>夜間（やかん）during the night |
| | | (8)<br>丶　亠　广　疒　疒　夜　夜　夜 |
| 社<br><br><br>(a Shinto shrine, company) | やしろ<br>シャ / ジャ | 神社（じんじゃ）a Shinto shrine<br>会社（かいしゃ）a company<br>社内（しゃない）inside the company<br>社会（しゃかい）society |
| | | (7)<br>丶　ラ　オ　ネ　ネ　社　社 |

## Kanji Practice for Chapter 11(B)
かんじの　れんしゅう

1.つぎの　ことばを　よみなさい。それから、クラスメートに　いみを
ききなさい。Read the following words to your classmates and ask them for the
meaning of each word.

（1）　　Meeting　は、「会合」と言います。

（2）　　「今日の夜」は、「今夜」とも　言います。

（3）　　ねだんが　高い。

（4）　　高校

（5）　　会社

（6）　　社会

（7）　　心（こころ）が安らかなことを「安心（しん）」と言います。

2.Write kanji in the box to complete the compound word.

(1)　high school

| | |
|---|---|
| | |

(2)　comfort; peaceful mind

| | しん<br>心 |
|---|---|
| | |

(3)　company (commercial organization)

| 会 | |
|---|---|
| | |

(4)　society

| | |
|---|---|
| | |

(5)　tonight

| 今 | |
|---|---|
| | |

(6)　meeting

| | 合 |
|---|---|
| | |

3. よんでから、よみがなをかいて、えいごでいいなさい。 **Read first, then write yomigana above each kanji, and translate into English.**

（1）　その色とこの色は、よく合います。

（2）　このTシャツは、安かったので　買いました。

（3）　今夜は、あたたかいです。

（4）　高校の時、よく きっさてんへ　行きました。

（5）　右手に　高いたてものが　見えます。

（6）　今日の夜は、友だちと神社 (shrine)へ　行きます。

（7）　会社の友人と　飲みに　行きます。

（8）　日本社会も　少し　変わってきました。

Chapter 11 (C)    夜桜     Night-View of Cherry Blossoms

(In the Maruyama Park at night)

モニカ ： わあ、すごい、、、桜が こんなに 大きい。                          1

田中 ： この桜が有名な「しだれ桜」です。                              2

モニカ ： 雪みたい。                                              3

田中 ： みごとでしょう？もっと近くに行ってみましょう。                      4

モニカ ： はい、さわっても いいですか。                                5

田中 ： さわっては、いけない、、、みたいよ。ここに立て札がある。              6

モニカ ： 立て札？                                              7

田中 ： サインのことね。『柵の中に入らないでください』、ほらね。          8

モニカ ： デジカメで写真をとって、両親に送りたいんですが。              9

田中 ： 写真をとるのは、だいじょうぶよ。                          10

(To other spectator)

あ、すみません。ちょっと写真をとってくださいませんか。                  11

見物人 ： いいですよ。                                          12

田中 ： このボタンを 押してください。                              13

見物人 ： ぼくのと同じタイプだから、わかりますよ。                  14

いいですか。はい、笑って！ あ、もう少し、後ろに下がってください。で、もうちょっとくっついて、、はい、ポーズ。とりました。

モニカ・田中： どうも　ありがとうございました。 1

見物人 ： いいえ。どういたしまして。 2

[English translation:]  (In the Maruyama Park at night)

Monica:  Wow!  Awesome…cherry tree is so big.

Tanaka:  This cherry tree is a famous "Shidare-Zakura (hanging cherry)."

Monica:  It looks like snow (fall).

Tanaka:  Isn't it splendid?  Let's get closer.

Monica:  May I touch it?

Tanaka:  I'm afraid we can't….it seems.  Here is a "tate-fuda" sign.

Monica:  "Tate-fuda"?

Tanaka:  It's a notice board.  It says, "Please do not enter inside the fence."  See?

Monica:  I want to take photos in my digital camera and send them to my parents…

Tanaka:  It's all right to take photos.

(To other person)  Excuse me.  Will you please take a photo for us?

Spectator:  Sure.

Tanaka:    Please push this button.

Spectator:  I know this camera since it's the same type as mine.  Are you ready?  Smile!
        Ah, please back up a little bit.  So, then get closer to each other…Yes.  Pose.
        It's done.

Monica/Tanaka:  Thank you very much.

Spectator:  You're very welcome.

## Ch11 (C)

しゃしんをとってくださいませんか。

さくらに　さわっても　いいですか。
さわっては　いけないみたいよ。

Chapter 11 (C)                     Grammar and Cultural Notes

## 1. ～てもいい: **giving permission**

The expression "Verb + te mo ii" indicates "permission" and is equivalent to "you may do it" or "It's all right to do so and so" in English.  It can also be used with adjectives, nouns and な adjectives (= copula nouns).

Formation:

| | | |
|---|---|---|
| The "te" form of verbs<br>行って、書いて、見て、<br>吸って、帰って、起きて | + も | いい（です）<br>だいじょうぶ（です）<br>かまいません<br>オーケーです<br>　（all right） |
| The "te" form of adjectives<br>小さくて、大きくて、固くて、<br>冷たくて、せまくて | | |
| Nouns<br>下手、子ども、なん（何）、いつ | + でも | |

Examples for verbs:

（1）もう、帰ってもいいです。
　　　You may go home now.

（2）ここで、タバコを　吸ってもいいですか。
　　　May I smoke here?

（3）このおはしを　使っても　いいですか。
　　　May I use these chopsticks?

（4）今、教室を　出ても　いいですか。
　　　Is it all right if I leave the classroom now?

（5）このお水は　飲んでも　かまいません。
　　　It's all right to drink this water.

Examples for adjectives:

（1）つくえが、小さくても　いいですか。
　　　Is it all right (with you) even if the desk is so small?

（2）字が、きたなくても　だいじょうぶです。
　　　It's all right even if your handwriting is bad.

（３）へやが、せまくても　オーケーです。
No problem.  A small room is fine with me.

（４）コーヒーが　冷<ruby>つめ</ruby>たくても　いいです。
It's all right even if the coffee is cold.

Examples for nouns and な adjectives (copula nouns) :

（１）そのしごとは、日本語が下手<ruby>へた</ruby>でも　できますか。
Can I do that job even if my Japanese isn't good?

（２）火曜日は忙<ruby>いそが</ruby>しいので、水曜日でも　かまいませんか。
Is Wednesday all right (with you) since I am busy on Tuesday?

（３）ペンがないなら、えんぴつでも　いいですよ。
It's all right to write with a pencil if you don't have a pen.

## 2. 〜ては　いけません: **prohibition**

The expression "V/Adj./Nouns + te wa ikenai" expresses "prohibition" and means that "one must not do such and such" or "something must not be so and so" in English.

| The "te" form of verbs<br>行<ruby>い</ruby>って、書<ruby>か</ruby>いて、見<ruby>み</ruby>て、<br>吸<ruby>す</ruby>って、帰<ruby>かえ</ruby>って、起<ruby>お</ruby>きて、遅<ruby>おく</ruby>れて | + は | いけません<br>だめです |
|---|---|---|

Examples:

（１）ここでタバコを　吸<ruby>す</ruby>ってはいけません。
You must not smoke here.

（２）ほかの人のテストを　見<ruby>み</ruby>てはいけません。
You must not look at others' tests.

（３）クラスに　遅<ruby>おく</ruby>れては　だめですよ。(遅<ruby>おく</ruby>れる to be late)
You mustn't be late for class.

（４）教室<ruby>きょうしつ</ruby>で　食<ruby>た</ruby>べては　いけません。
You mustn't eat in the classroom.

（５）髪<ruby>かみ</ruby>（かみ hair）は、長<ruby>なが</ruby>すぎては、だめです。
Your hair must not be too long.

| The "te" form of adjectives<br>小さくて、大きくて、固くて、<br>ちい　　　　おお　　　　かた<br>冷たくて、せまくて、短くて<br>つめ　　　　　　　　みじか | + は | いけません<br>だめです |
|---|---|---|

Examples:

（１）　作文は、あまり短くては、いけません。
　　　　さくぶん　　　　みじか
　　　　Your composition must not be too short.

（２）　コーヒーが　冷たくては、だめです。
　　　　　　　　　　　つめ
　　　　Coffee shouldn't be cold.

（３）　たてものの高さは、あまり高くては、いけません。
　　　　　　　　　たか　　　　　　　たか
　　　　The height of the building must not be too tall.

| Nouns<br>子ども、おとな、下手、なまけも<br>　　　　　　　　へた<br>の (lazy person)、(成績が)F<br>　　　　　　　せいせき | + では | いけません<br>だめです<br>できません |
|---|---|---|

（１）　そのしごとは、こどもでは、だめです。
　　　　That type of work cannot be done by a kid.

（２）　日本語が下手では、日本で　しごとは、できません。
　　　　　　　　　　へた
　　　　You cannot work in Japan unless your Japanese is good.

（３）　なまけものでは、だめですよ。
　　　　You shouldn't be lazy.

## 3. こんなに～ : "this much" ko-so-a-do pattern

"こんなに" expresses degree and follows the "ko-so-a-do" pattern. Therefore, its counterparts include そんなに，あんなに, and どんなに. If you want to describe how big the fish you caught is to your friend, you can spread your arms widely and say "こんなに　大きいさかな　でした." Your friend may say, "わぁ、そんなに　大きいさかなだったんですか." You may reflect on its size again later, saying, "あんなに　大きいさかなは、めずらしいなぁ (It's quite rare to see such a big fish.)"

Examples:

（１）　ねぇ、見てみて。手が、こんなに　赤い。
　　　　　　　　み　　　　て　　　　　　あか
　　　　Look!  My hands are so red (literally: as red as this).

（２）そんなに　赤いのは、めずらしいね。
It's rare to see that kind of red.

（３）こんなにおいしいおちゃは、はじめてです！
It's the first time I've had such delicious tea.

（４）あんなにがんばったけれど、だめだったね。　（がんばる to work hard）
You worked so hard, but it didn't work out.

（５）犬がいなくなって、どんなに　さみしいことでしょう。
(lonely)
I wonder how lonely you feel after losing your dog.

## 4. ～てくださいませんか。Polite request form

In Chapter 6 (D), we learned the polite request form, "~ te kudasai." You can make it politer if you say "~te kudasai masenka."

Examples:
（１）すみませんが、お名前を書いてくださいませんか。
Excuse me, will you please write your name?

（２）ちょっと　すわってくださいませんか。
Will you please sit down for a moment?

（３）あそこで、待っていてくださいませんか。
Would you mind waiting for me over there?

（４）しゃしんを　とってくださいませんか。
Would you be so kind to take our photo?

（５）日本語をおしえてくださいませんか。
Would you please teach me Japanese?

（６）それを英語で言ってくださいませんか。
Will you please say it in English?

Chapter 11 (C) Exercises れんしゅう

A. Change the following phrases to sentences asking for permission.

Examples例：うちに　かえる　→　うちにかえっても　いいですか。
えいがが、ながい→　えいがが　ながくても　いいですか。
英語が下手　→　　英語が下手でも　いいですか。

(Verbs)

1. じしょを　使う→
2. きょうかしょを　見る→
3. えんぴつで　書く→
4. トイレに　行く→
5. 水を　飲む→
6. ラーメンを　食べる→
7. まどを　開ける→
8. まどを　閉める→
9. 英語で　話す→
10. タバコを吸う→

(Adjectives)

11. 字が小さい→
12. 書くのが　遅い(late)→
13. へやが　きたない(dirty)→
14. アパートが　せまい(tight space)→
15. 教室が　やかましい(noisy)→

(Nouns)

16. 子ども　→
17. ひらがな　→
18. 日本語が下手→
19. 明日→
20. 英語　→

B. Change the following phrases to prohibition sentences.

Examples例：うそを　つく→　　うそを　ついては　いけません。
(to lie)　　　　　　(You must not lie.)
スピーチがみじかい　→　スピーチが　みじかくては、いけません。
(speech)

(Verbs)

1．おさけを　飲みすぎる　→
2．ケーキを　食べすぎる　→
3．お金を　使いすぎる　→
4．人のテストを　見る　→
5．としょかんで　話す　→
6．じゅぎょうちゅうに　まんがを　読む　→

(Adjectives)

1．コーヒーが　冷たい　→
2．かみが　ながい　→
3．くつしたが　みじかい　→
4．シャツが　きたない　→
5．教室がやかましい　→

(Nouns)

1．テストが　0点　→
2．ローマ字　(Roman letters) →
3．なまけもの　(a lazy person) →
4．うそつき　( a liar) →
5．あまのじゃく　(a contrarian) →

C. Request the following as politely as you can.
　　Use ～てくださいませんか。

1．しゃしんをとる　→
2．いっしょに　すわる　→
3．日本語で　話す　→
4．話を聞く　→
5．でんわばんごうをおしえる　→
6．せつめいを　読む　→
　　　　　(instruction, explanation)
7．いっしょに　行く　→
8．これを見る　→
9．ペンを貸す　(to loan)　→
10．でんわをする　→

D. Regulations きそく（規則）：社会にはいろいろなきそくが　ありますね。
学校には、学校のきそくがありますし、会社の寮には、寮のきそくがあり
ます。There are many rules in society: a school has its own and a company has its own.

(1) あなたが高校生のとき、学校のきそくには、どんなものがありましたか。
つぎのしつもんをクラスメートにしてみましょう。しつもんには、「はい」
か「いいえ」で、こたえてください。

When you were in high school, what kind of rules did it have? Ask yourself and
your classmates the following questions. Answers can either be "yes" or "no."

| しつもん | わたしの学校 | （　　　）さんの学校 | （　　　）さんの学校 |
|---|---|---|---|
| おけしょうをしても<br>make-up<br>よかったですか。 | | | |
| ピアスをしても<br>よかったですか。 | | | |
| くるまで行っても<br>よかったですか。 | | | |
| オートバイで行っても<br>よかったですか。 | | | |
| じゅぎょう中に、の<br>みものをのんでもよか<br>ったですか。 | | | |
| きょうしつのそうじを<br>しないで、かえっても<br>よかったですか。 | | | |
| いれずみをしても<br>tattoo<br>よかったですか。 | | | |
| 授業中に　かってに<br>(without permission)、<br>となりのクラスへ行っ<br>てもよかったですか。 | | | |

(2)　この学校にはどんな規則がありますか。聞いてみてください。Ask your
classmates if it's permissible to do the following in classroom, using 〜てもいいですか。
教室でしてもいいことに　**O** を、しては　いけないことに **X** を　書きなさい。

1. (　)　おさけを　のむ
2. (　)　じしょを　つかう
3. (　)　まんがを　よむ
4. (　)　コンピューターゲームを　する
5. (　)　わからないことを　先生に　きく
6. (　)　本に　書き込みを　する (write in)
7. (　)　タバコを　すう
8. (　)　ペットを　連れて来る (bring in)
9. (　)　じてんしゃを　持ち込む (bring in)
10.(　)　ピザの出前を　たのむ　(to order food delivery)

(3) つぎのはりがみは、ある会社の寮のきそくです。文を完成しなさい。
　　　　poster　　　　　　　　　　　dormitory rules　　　complete the sentence

```
┌─────────────────────────────────────┐
│            りょうのきそく             │
│                                     │
│  (X) ペットを　かう                   │
│  (X) ロビーで　たばこを　すう         │
│  (X) ロビーで　おさけを　飲む         │
│  (X) 午前 12 時から 6 時までの間、    │
│      ロビーで　テレビをみる           │
│  (X) 自転車を　へやに持ち込む         │
│  (0) 五人までの　ゲストをへやに入れ    │
│      る                             │
│  (0) ロビーで　十人までの　プライベ   │
│      ート・パーティーを　する         │
│  (0) 出前をたのむ (ロビーで受け取る   │
│      なら)                          │
└─────────────────────────────────────┘
```

[Vocabulary Help]
持ち込む（もちこむ）　　to bring in
出前（でまえ）をたのむ　to order (food) delivery
受け取る（うけとる）　　to receive

この会社の寮の規則によると、
　　　　　　　　According to~

（1）ロビーでは、たばこをすって（　　　　　　　　　　　　　　）。
（2）ロビーでは、おさけを（　　　　　　　　　　　　　　　　　）。

（３）真夜中(まよなか)の十二時から、早朝(そうちょう)の六時までの間(あいだ)は、ロビーでテレビを
（　　　　　　　　　　　　　　　　　　　）。

（４）ペットを（　　　　　　　　　　　　　　　）。

（５）自転車(じてんしゃ)を　へやに　持(も)ち込(こ)んで（　　　　　　　　　　）。

（６）五人までなら、ゲストをへやに（　　　　　　　　　）。

（７）十人までなら、ロビーでプライベート・パーティーを
（　　　　　　　　　　　　　　　　　）。

（８）ロビーで受(う)け取(と)るなら、出前(でまえ)を（　　　　　　　　　　）。

E. 日本語で言いなさい。Translation Exercise on "polite request."  Use ～てくださいませんか。

1.  Excuses me.  Will you please tell me how to get to a nearest station?
2.  Would you please <u>loan</u> your pen?
貸(か)す
3.  Will you please <u>step back</u> to the <u>white line</u>?
下(さ)がる　　　白線(はくせん)
4.  Will you please buy my car?
5.  Will you please look at this?
6.  I cannot see well.  Would you please read this newspaper for me?
7.  Would you please wait here for me?  I'll be right back.

F. 日本語で言いなさい。Translation Exercise on "Prohibition" & "Permission": Translate into Japanese.　　Use ～ても　いいです, ～ては　いけません or their equivalents.

1.　Your essay shouldn't be short.
2.　A pair-work may be done with 3 people.
3.　No party should be done on weekdays.
4.　No pets allowed - you shouldn't have a pet in your apartment.
5.　You may drink water, but you shouldn't eat any food in classroom.
6.　You shouldn't put makeup when you go to high school.
7.　Your hair shouldn't be longer than your shoulder.
8.　You shouldn't have a tattoo.
9.　Can it be done by kids?
10.　Is it all right even if my Japanese isn't good?

単語(たんご)ヘルプ：

1. essay 作文、2. pair-work　ペアワーク、3. 週日(しゅうじつ)、4. ペットを飼(か)う、6. お化粧(けしょう)、
7. 髪(かみ)、肩(かた)、8. 刺青(いれずみ)

Chapter 11C: Dict-A-Conversation (1)
Listen to Chapter 11C's DAC on the student CD, and checkmark the request expected of you.

(What's been requested of me?)
1.
(      ) A. To tell my name.
(      ) B. To write my name.
2.
(      ) A. To watch her bag.
(      ) B. To wait here for her.
3.
(      ) A. To take her pictures.
(      ) B. To let her take your pictures.
4.
(      ) A. To make her come back tomorrow.
(      ) B. To come back tomorrow.
5.
(      ) A. To stand up.
(      ) B. To sit down.

Chapter 11C: Dict-A-Conversation (2)
Listen to Chapter 11C's DAC (2) on the student CD.  You are a new employee at Starbucks.  Your manager is going to tell you the "Do's and Don'ts."  Listen carefully to your manager and mark (O) for "Do's" and (X) for "Don'ts."
[Vocabulary Help]
かみ hair, つめ nails, すいどうのみず tap water, けっこう fine; good

1.  (      ) To come in late.
2.  (      ) To smoke.
3.  (      ) To eat in front of the customers.
4.  (      ) To drink alcohol.
5.  (      ) To have long hair かみ.
6.  (      ) To have long nails つめ.
7.  (      ) To serve hot drinks cold.
8.  (      ) To have two days off in a week.
9.  (      ) To close at 10:45 pm.
10. (      ) To eat in the backroom.
11. (      ) To drink water in front of the customers.
12. (      ) To talk for a long time with the customers.
13. (      ) To smile at the customers.
14. (      ) To smile extensively to the customers.
15. (      ) To use tap water extensively.
16. (      ) To make a new order when the first was a mistake.
17. (      ) To add plenty of whipped cream when requested.

Ch 11 (C)

| 雪<br><br>(snow; to snow) | ゆき<br>セツ | 大雪（おおゆき）heavy snow<br>雪女（ゆきおんな）snow woman (in a legend)<br>除雪（じょせつ）removal of snow |
|---|---|---|
| | | (11)<br>一 厂 戸 戸 乐 乑 乑 雨 雪 雪 雪 |
| 立<br><br>(to stand) | た（つ）<br>リツ | 立つ（たつ）to stand<br>立ち上がる to rise; to stand up<br>自立（じりつ）self-support; independence<br>起立（きりつ）する to rise; to stand up |
| | | (5)<br>、 二 十 立 立 |
| 札<br><br>(a card; label)<br>(a bill) | ふだ<br>さつ | 立て札（たてふだ）a notice board<br>お札（おさつ）a bill; paper money<br>千円札（せんえんさつ）a 1000-yen bill |
| | | (5)<br>一 十 才 木 札 |
| 押<br><br>(to press; push) | お（す）<br>オウ | 押す（おす）to press; push<br>押収（おうしゅう）する seize; confiscate;<br>　　　　　　　　　　　　Impound<br>押し合う（おしあう）push one another |
| | | (8)<br>一 十 扌 扌 押 押 押 押 |
| 用<br><br>(an errand;<br>business) | もち（いる）<br>ヨウ | 用（もち）いる to use<br>用（よう）がある to have an errand<br>用事（ようじ）an errand<br>使用（しよう）a use<br>私用（しよう）a private use<br>社用（しゃよう）a company business<br>用件（ようけん）business<br>[急用（きゅうよう）an urgent errand] |
| | | (5)<br>丿 几 月 月 用 |

Kanji Practice for Chapter 11 C

かんじの　れんしゅう

1．つぎの　ことばを　よみなさい。それから、クラスメートに　いみを
ききなさい。Read the following words to your classmates and ask them for the
meaning of each word.

(1)　　A notice board　は、「立札」と言います。

(2)　　足立さんは、お礼を言って、立ち去りました。
　　　　　　　　　　(say thank-you)

(3)　　今日の夜は、雪がふりますよ。

(4)　　ちょっと用事がありますから、これで失礼します。

(5)　　社用で　この近所まで　来ました。

(6)　　このボタンを押すと、コーヒーが　出て来ます。

(7)　　会社に用があって、立ち寄りました。

(8)　　お祭りで、人と人が押し合うのは、楽しい。

2．Write kanji in the box to complete the compound word.

(1)　heavy snow (kun-kun reading)

| 大 | |
|---|---|

(2)　a notice board (kun-kun reading)

| | |
|---|---|

(3)　an errand

| | |
|---|---|

(4)   become independent

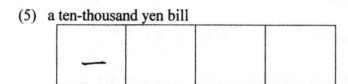

自 |

(5)   a ten-thousand yen bill

一 | | |

3. よんでから、よみがなをかいて、えいごでいいなさい。 Read first, then write yomigana above each kanji, and translate into English.

(1)   その女の人は、雪の中で　立っていました。

(2)   デモ隊は、警察と　押し合いになりました。
　　　(デモ隊 demonstration group) (警察 police)

(3)   今夜は、大雪です。

(4)   立札に、「土足禁止」とありますが、どんないみですか。

(5)   右手のボタンを押してください。

(6)   二十才になって、自立しました。

(7)   用事で　会社を休みました。

(8)   千円札を　二まい　ください。

## Chapter 11 (D)　モニカの日記　Monica's Diary
### Cherry Blossoms at Maruyama Park　円山公園の夜桜

---

四月三日（木曜日）　　晴れ

昨日の夜、田中さんといっしょに、円山公園の桜を見に行った。とてもきれいだった。白い桜が、雪のように　美しかった。

夜の暗やみの中に、ボーッと白い桜が見えた時、「神秘的」と言う日本語を思い出した。なんとなく、「ゆうれい」とか「おばけ」とかのイメージも　ぴったりだった。この桜のあたりに、ゆうれいが出て来ても、あたりまえという気がした。

たくさんの人が　公園の中を　歩いていた。夜の公園が、こんなに　にぎやかなのが、不思議な感じだった。でも、おまわりさんは、いなかった。みんなしずかに、桜を見ていた。

桜が散る前に、ぜひもう一度、見に行きたい。

---

[English translation:]  Monica's Diary

---

April 3rd (Th.)  Nice day

　Last night, I went with Ms. Tanaka to view the cherry blossoms at Maruyama Park.  They were so beautiful.  White cherry blossoms were as beautiful as snow.

　In the darkness of the night where white cherry blossoms modestly surfaced, the Japanese word "mystic" came to mind.  Somehow, I thought the word descriptively suited the images of "ghosts" and "goblins" too.  I won't be surprised if ghosts emerged from behind the cherry blossoms.

　Many people were walking in the park.  I thought it strange that the park was so crowded with people at night.  And there were no policemen.  Everyone was watching cherry blossoms so quietly.

　I would love to admire the cherry blossoms again before the end of the blooming season.

Chapter 11 (D)     Vocabulary List

1. Expressions

| | |
|---|---|
| <ruby>雪<rt>ゆき</rt></ruby>のように　きれいだ。 | It's as beautiful as snow. |
| ボーッと　見える。 | It's faintly visible. |
| ぜひもう一度来たい。 | I really want to come back. |
| あたりまえだ。 | It's only natural; a matter of course. |

2. Nouns

| | |
|---|---|
| にっき　(日記) | diary |
| くらやみ　(暗闇) | darkness |
| ゆうれい | ghost |
| おばけ　(お化け) | ghost (casual) |
| イメージ | image |
| ぴったり | perfect fit |
| (〜の)　あたり | around 〜 ; vicinity |
| あたりまえ | natural, a matter of course |
| たくさん | a lot |
| かんじ　(感じ) | feeling |
| (おまわりさん) | policeman |
| もういちど　(もう一度) | one more time |
| もう + numerals | additional something |
| もうひとつ | additional thing, one more thing |
| もうひとり | additional person, one more person |

3. Copula Nouns

| | |
|---|---|
| しんぴてき　(神秘的) | mysterious, mystic, enigmatic, veil covered |
| ふしぎ　(不思議) | marvelous, strange, miraculous, mysterious |

4. Verbs

| | |
|---|---|
| おもいだす　(思い出す) | to recall |
| でてくる　(出て来る) | to come out |
| (〜という)　きがする　(気がする) | I feel as if 〜 |
| (〜が)　ちる　(散る) | to scatter; (flower petals) fall |

5. Adverbs

| | |
|---|---|
| ボーッと | faintly; unclearly; without focused |
| ぜひ | by all means |

------------------------------------------------------------------------

## Additional Vocabulary from Grammar Notes, Exercises, and Dict-A-Conversation

------------------------------------------------------------------------

[Nouns]

| | |
|---|---|
| ゴルフ | golf |
| アスピリン | aspirin |
| ぶんらく（文楽） | puppet theatre (also Ningyoo-Jyooruri) |
| （え　絵） | picture; drawing |
| そら（空） | sky |
| はな（花） | flowers |
| ダイヤモンド | diamond |
| ほしぞら（星空） | night sky with stars |
| かがみ（鏡） | mirror |
| ひづけ（日付） | date |
| あまのじゃく | contrarian |
| バックミラー | rear-view mirror |
| よやく（予約） | reservation |
| こいびと（恋人） | lover |
| もみじ | maple |
| けしき | scenery |
| にんぎょう（人形） | doll |
| ゆでダコ | boiled octopus |
| しょうがじる | ginger-juice |
| （かぜ　風邪） | cold (illness) |
| ばっちり | perfect (casual term) |

[Copula Nouns]

| | |
|---|---|
| じょうぶ | strong; healthy; sturdy |
| なめらか | smooth |
| へいき（平気） | no bother |

[Adverb]

| | |
|---|---|
| まるで | as if |

[Verbs]

| | |
|---|---|
| チェックする | to check |
| よう（酔う） | to become drunk |
| （は[歯]を）みがく | to brush one's teeth |
| （じしょを）ひく | to look up in the dictionary |
| とまる（泊まる） | to stay overnight |

Chapter 11 (D)            Grammar and Cultural Notes

## 1. <u>Sentence ＋ 時<sup>とき</sup> as a Subordinate Conjunction; "the time when~"</u>

A clause with "toki" equates to "the time when ~" in English. In its sentence, the subject would be marked by the particle "ga," as it is a subordinate clause. The particle に、は、には may be added to "toki" depending on context.

Formation:

| Subordinate Clause | Main Clause |
|---|---|
| (1) Noun ＋ の　とき<br>(2) Adjective　（い）＋　とき<br>(3) Copula Noun な ＋　とき<br>(4) Verb ＋ とき | 本<sup>ほん</sup>を読<sup>よ</sup>みます。<br>　　読<sup>よ</sup>みました。 |

Examples:
(1) Noun ＋ の　とき

１．こどものときは、よく木<sup>き</sup>に登<sup>のぼ</sup>りました。
　　When I was a child, I often climbed trees.

２．学生<sup>がくせい</sup>の時<sup>とき</sup>は、本屋<sup>ほんや</sup>で　アルバイトをしました。
　　When I was a (college) student, I worked part-time at a bookstore.

３．休<sup>やす</sup>みの時<sup>とき</sup>には、たいてい父<sup>ちち</sup>とゴルフをします。
　　When I have a day off, I usually play golf with my father.

(2) Adjective　（い）＋　とき
１．小<sup>ちい</sup>さいときに、よく病気<sup>びょうき</sup>をしました。
　　When I was young, I often got ill.

２．暑<sup>あつ</sup>いときは、氷<sup>こおり</sup>で　あたまを　冷<sup>ひ</sup>やします。
　　When it's hot, I use ice to cool my head.

３．歯<sup>は</sup>が　いたい時<sup>とき</sup>は、アスピリンを飲<sup>の</sup>みます。
　　When I have a toothache, I take aspirin.

(Negative verb form [nai form] is adjectival)
４．あまりお金<sup>かね</sup>がないときは、レストランに行<sup>い</sup>きません。
　　I don't go to restaurants when I don't have a lot of money.

5．しゅくだいができない時は、母が手つだってくれました。

When I couldn't do my homework, my mother helped me.

(3) Copula Noun な ＋ とき

1．ひまなときは、本を読みます。

When I have free time, I read books.

2．祖父が　元気な時は、よく　歌舞伎に連れて行ってくれました。

When my grandfather was well, he often took me to Kabuki.

3．母がじょうぶな時は、よく　りょうりをしていました。

When my mother was healthy, she cooked often.

(4) Verb ＋ とき

1．日本人は、食べる時、「いただきます」と言います。

Japanese say, "Itadakimasu," when they eat.

2．バスに乗るときは、前のほうがいいですよ。

When you get on a bus, sitting in the front seat is better.

3．でんしゃをおりるとき、大前さんに　会いました。

When I was getting off the bus, I met Mr. Omae.

4．日本に行った時、文楽を見ました。

When I went to Japan, I saw the Bunraku puppet theatre.

5．東京タワーにのぼった時、海や山が見えました。

When I climbed Tokyo Tower, I was able to see the ocean and the mountains.

6．タクシーに乗った時、かさを　忘れました。

When I took a taxi, I left my umbrella (forgetting to bring it with me).

## 2. 前 as a Subordinate Conjunction; "the time before~"

"Mae" means "front" or "before," and it works with nouns and verbs to mean "before such and such" or "before doing so and so." With verbs, only the non-past tense would precede "mae." The subject in a "mae" clause is marked by "ga" as it is subordinate. The particle に、は、には may follow "mae" depending on context.

Formation:

| Subordinate Clause | Main Clause |
|---|---|
| (1) Noun + の　まえに<br>(2) Verb (dictionary form) + まえに | きょうかしょを　見ます。 |

(1) Noun + の　まえに

1.  テストの前<sup>まえ</sup>に、もう一度<sup>いちど</sup>、きょうかしょを　読<sup>よ</sup>みます。
    Before the test, I read the textbook one more time.

2.  食事<sup>しょくじ</sup>の前<sup>まえ</sup>に、手<sup>て</sup>を洗<sup>あら</sup>いました。
    I washed my hands before the meal.

3.  しごとの前<sup>まえ</sup>に、お茶<sup>ちゃ</sup>をいっぱい　飲<sup>の</sup>みませんか。
    Won't you have a cup of tea before work?

(2) Verb (dictionary form) + まえに

1.  先生<sup>せんせい</sup>がいらっしゃる前<sup>まえ</sup>に、こくばんを　きれいにしました。
    I cleaned the blackboard before the teacher came.

2.  いつも　寝<sup>ね</sup>る前<sup>まえ</sup>に、本<sup>ほん</sup>を読<sup>よ</sup>みます。
    I always read a book before going to bed.

3.  学校<sup>がっこう</sup>へ行<sup>い</sup>く前<sup>まえ</sup>に、もう一度<sup>いちど</sup>、かばんをチェックします。
    I would check my bag once more before going to school.

### 3.　～のよう **It is like ~**

"Noun + no yoo" is typically used as a simile and is equivalent to "~like (noun)" in English.  Its copula verb ending is "ようだ", copula noun ending "ような," and adverbial form "ように." Sometimes,"まるで (as if)" may precede "~ no yoo" in upping the similarity factor.

Formation:

| Noun の | ようだ（ようです）。 |
|---|---|
| | ような + Noun |
| | ように + Adj., Verb, Adverb |

（１）Noun のようだ

    1．今日は、まるで春のようだ。ほんとうにあたたかい。

      Today is a spring-like day.  It's so nice and warm.

    2．きょうの空は、美しくて、まるで絵のようだ。

      The sky today is as beautiful as a painting.

（２）Noun のような

    1．まゆみさんは、まるで花のような人です。

      Mayumi is a girl as pretty as a flower.

    2．ダイヤモンドのような星空ですね。

      The stars in the sky tonight shimmer like diamonds.

（３）Noun のように

    1．加藤さんは、魚のように、じょうずに泳ぎますね。

      Mr. Kato swims like a fish.

    2．今日の海は、鏡のように、なめらかです。

      Today's ocean appears as smooth as the surface of a mirror.

## 4. ～ても even if ~

The "te" form verb/adj./noun + particle "mo" expresses the idea of "even if" in English. It is similar to the permission form in Chapter 11 (C), except what follows after "te mo" is not as limited.  The adjectival "te" form is "kute," and nominative "te" form is "de."

Formation of the "te mo" form

| "te" form of verbs | て | |
|---|---|---|
| "te" form of adjectives | くて | + も |
| "te" form of nouns/copula nouns | で | |

See examples:

(Verbs)

    （１）ゆうれいが　出て来ても、平気です。

      I don't mind it, even if ghosts appear.

    （２）たくさん飲んでも、酔いません。

      I don't get drunk even if I drink a lot.

（３）そこへ行<ruby>行<rt>い</rt></ruby>っても、だれも　いませんよ。
No one will be there even if you go there.

(Adjectives)

（４）<ruby>高<rt>たか</rt></ruby>くても、<ruby>買<rt>か</rt></ruby>いたいです。
I want to buy it even if it's expensive.

（５）<ruby>安<rt>やす</rt></ruby>くても、わるいものは、<ruby>買<rt>か</rt></ruby>いません。
I won't buy a bad one even if it's cheap.

（６）<ruby>暑<rt>あつ</rt></ruby>くても、スーツを<ruby>着<rt>き</rt></ruby>て<ruby>来<rt>き</rt></ruby>てください。
Please come in a suit even if it's hot.

(Nouns, Copula Nouns)

（７）<ruby>四月<rt>しがつ</rt></ruby>でも、<ruby>今年<rt>ことし</rt></ruby>は、さむいですよ。
Despite it being April, it's cold this year.

（８）ひまでも、しごとが　できない。
Even if I have free time, I cannot accomplish my work.

（９）このもんだいは、かんたんでも、<ruby>分<rt>わ</rt></ruby>からない。
Even if this problem is simple, I still cannot solve it.

（１０）<ruby>下手<rt>へた</rt></ruby>でも、がんばっている。
Even if he is not good at it, he is making an effort.

Chapter 11 (D) Exercises

A.  Change the 〜てから to the 〜まえに form.

Example:

シャワーをあび<u>てから</u>、あさごはんを食べます。

→あさごはんを<u>食べるまえに</u>、シャワーをあびます。

(1)    まんがを読んでから、勉強します。
   →

(2)    ごはんを食べてから、コーヒーを飲みます。
   →

(3)    シャワーをあびてから、デートをします。
   →

(4)    べんきょうしてから、テストをうけます。
   →

(5)    きょうの日付とお天気を書いてから、日記を書きます。
   →

(6)    テレビを見てから、ひるねをします。
   →

(7)    しゅくだいをしてから、おふろに入ります。
   →

B.  Pair-work:  Try to be an "あまのじゃく," a contrarian.  When you are playing the "あまのじゃく" role, start your sentences with "そうですか," with the intonation of ( ⌒↗ ).

Example:

（A）：わたしは、あさごはんを食べてから、しんぶんを読みます。

（B）：そうですか（⌒↗）。わたしは、しんぶんを読んでから、
         あさごはんを食べます。

Hints: variety of activities

はをみがく、かおをあらう、てをあらう、テレビを見る、しゅくだいをする、デートをする、シャワーをあびる、コーヒー(水、おちゃ)を飲む、としょかんに行く、かいものをする、そうじをする、せんたくをする、おふろに入る、ちゃわんをあらう、しょくじをする、えいがをみる、本を読む、お酒を飲む、ねる、おきる、ひるねをする、勉強する、テストをうける、先生と話す、先生に聞く、でんわをする、かみに書く、じしょをひく、へやに入る、戸をあける、戸をしめる、ごはんをつくる、食べる、走る、考える

C. Change 〜のまえに to the "Verb＋まえに" form.

Example例:

　（1）　　しょくじの前に、手を洗いましょう。
　　　　　→しょくじをする前に、手を洗いましょう。

　（2）　　シャワーの前に、はを　みがきました。
　　　　　→シャワーをあびる前に、はを　みがきました。

　（3）　　テストの前に、勉強しました。
　　　　　→テストをうける前に、勉強しました。

　1.　　おふろの前に、テレビをみました。
　　　　→

　2.　　勉強の前に、コーヒーを飲みました。
　　　　→

　3.　　うんどうの前に、水を飲みました。
　　　　exercises
　　　　→

　4.　　水泳の前に、たいそうをしました。
　　　　swimming　　　stretch
　　　　→

　5.　　うんてんの前に、バックミラーを見ました。
　　　　driving　　　　　　　rearview mirror
　　　　→

D. Change "たあとで" to "Verb＋まえに".

　Example例:

　シャワーを浴びたあとで、あさごはんを食べます。
　　　　→ あさごはんを食べる前に、シャワーを浴びます。

1. 朝ごはんを食べたあとで、はをみがきます。
　　　→

2. 勉強したあとで、テレビを見ます。
　　　→

3. 予約をしたあとで、ホテルに泊まります。

→

4．地図を見たあとで、うんてんします。

→

E-1. Team in groups of three or four and take turns asking questions, using 〜ても、
平気ですか、（〜てもだいじょうぶですか）with the goal of finding someone not
bothered by such situations.

Example:

A：あなたのへやに、へびがでてきても　平気ですか。

snake　（出て来る to come out, show up）

B：ぼくは、ちょっと、、へびは、苦手です。

(weak point, a person that is hard to deal with)

C：わたしも、へびは、こわいです。

(scared)

D：ぼくは、へびがでてきても、平気です。

(of no bother)

A：あ！へびだ！


D：きゃあ〜！

Hints:

1．あしたテストがあっても、平気ですか。
2．となりの人が、あなたのテストを見ても、平気ですか。
3．きょうかしょが、高くても、だいじょうぶですか。
4．毎日、雨でも平気ですか。
5．恋人がタバコを吸っても　平気ですか。

E-2. Translate into Japanese. 日本語で言ってみましょう。

1. Are you all right even if the tuition ( 授業料 ) is high?
2. Will you drink milk even if it's old?
3. Will you buy a comic book ( まんが ) even if you don't have money?
4. Will you go to bed early even if you have a test tomorrow?
5. Will you eat bananas even if they are still green?
6. Will you go to a concert even if a typhoon is coming?

F. Fill in the blanks with appropriate words.

1．ダイヤモンドのような（　　　　　　　）ですね。


2．もみじのような（　　　　　　　）ですね。
　　maple leaves

3．（　　　　　　　）のように、やさしい人ですね。

4. （　　　　　　　）のように、<u>こわい</u>ですよ。
　　　　　　　　　　　　　　scary

5. （　　　　　　　）のように、じょうずに泳ぎます。

6. きょうは、あたたかくて、まるで（　　　　　　　）のようですね。

7. （　　　　　　　）のように　かたいパンですね。

8. （　　　　　　　）のように、美しい<u>けしき</u>ですね。
　　　　　　　　　　　　　　　　　　　scenery

9. きょうの<u>海</u>は、<u>なめらか</u>で、（　　　　　　　）のようです。
　　　　　　　　　　smooth

10. （　　　　　　　）のように、美しい人を見ました。

G. Change ～のように to～くて（or ～で）～のようです.
　　Examples:
　　　(1) 花子さんは、お人形<u>のように</u> 色が白いです。
　　　　→ 花子さんは、色が白<u>くて</u>、お人形<u>のようです</u>。

　　　(2) ジョージさんは、日本人<u>のように</u>、日本語が上手です。
　　　　→ ジョージさんは、日本語が上手<u>で</u>、日本人<u>のようです</u>。

1. 私の兄は、<u>きりん</u>のように、せが　高いです。
→　　　　　　giraffe

2. あの人は、魚のように、泳ぎが上手です。
→

3. 田中さんは、私には家族のように、しんせつです。
→

4. ここは、れいぞうこのように、寒いです。
→

5. お酒を飲んで、<u>ゆでダコ</u>のように、顔が赤いです。
→　　　　　　　　boiled octopus

H. Practice on simile （まるで as if）（の）ようです。（の）ような～、
（の）ように: Fill in the blanks with appropriate Japanese words.

1. あなたの彼は、走るのも速くて、力も強くて、やさしくて、まるで

_____ 人ですね。
　　　 like Superman

2. 白雪姫の肌は、_____ 白かった。
　　Snow White's skin　　　　　　　　like snow

3. 白雪姫の髪は、_____ 黒かった。
　　　　　　 hair　　　　　 like ebony　（ebony 黒炭）

4. 白雪姫の唇は、_____ 赤かった。
　　　　　　 lips　　　　 like blood

5. このパンは、固くて、まるで_____です。
　　　　　　 hard　　　　　　 like a rock

6. あの人は、やさしくて、まるで_____です。
　　　　　　　　　　　　　 like an angel/God

7. 田中さんの手は、小さくて、まるで_____手ですね。
　　　　　　　　　　　　　 like a child

_____手ですね。
　　　　　　 like a maple (leaf)

8. あの恐ろしい顔が、まるで_____です。
　　　　　　　　　 like a demon

9. その動物の耳は、長くて細くて、まるで_____です
ね。
　　　　　　　　　　　　 like a rabbit

I. Advanced simile exercises: Choose the right ones from the box to fill in the blanks.

氷（こおり）、亀（かめ）、猫の額（ねこのひたい）、河童（かっぱ）、狸（たぬき）、狐（きつね）、雪、きりん、幽霊（ゆうれい）、紅葉（もみじ）、人形（にんぎょう）、星（ほし）、借りてきた猫（かりてきたねこ）、山

1. ケンさんは、（　　　　）のように、すもうと泳ぎが　うまい。
　　　　　　　　　　　　　　　　　Sumo wrestling

2. あの人は、人をだますのが（　　　　）のように、うまい。
　　　　　　　　　　deceive

3. 犯人は（　　　　）のように、細い目をしている。
　　culprit　　　　　　　　　　thin; narrow

4. 白雪姫の肌は、（　　　　）のように、白い。
　　Snow White's skin

5. 山田さんの手は、（　　　　）のように、かわいい。

6. 山本さんは、（　　　　）のように、かわいらしくて、おとなしい。
　　　　　　　　　　　　　　　adorable

7. あの人の顔は、（　　　　）のように、青白かった。

8. 宿題が（　　　　）のように、ある。

9. あなたの手は、（　　　　）のように、冷たい。

10. 兄は、（　　　　）のように、首が長い。
　　　　　　　　　　　　neck

11. 田中さんは、（　　　　）のようにのろいが、仕事は、完璧だ。
　　　　　　　　　　　　　　slow　　　　　　　perfect

12. 日本のまんがの女の子の目は、（　　　　）のように、輝いている。
　　　　　　　　　　　　　　　　　　　　　shining

13. 私の庭は、（　　　　）のように、狭い。

14. 子供を友人の家に連れて行くと、初めのうちは、（　　　　）の
　　　　　　　　　　take
　　ように、おとなしい。
　　quiet & obedient

Vocabulary Hints: こおり ice, かめ turtle, ねこのひたい a narrow space, かっぱ legendary boy with a plate on his head, たぬき badger, きつね fox, ゆき snow, きりん giraffe, ゆうれい ghost, もみじ maple leaf, にんぎょう a doll, ほし stars, かりてきたねこ a borrowed-cat; timid, やま mountains

J. Answer the following questions, using "Verb (dictionary form) + とき."

1. 日本人は、どんな時、「いただきます」と言いますか。

2. 日本では、どんな時、「いってきます」と言いますか。

3. 日本では、どんな時、「さようなら」と言いますか。

4. 日本人は、どんな時、「おやすみなさい」と言いますか。

K.  Answer the following questions, using "V た form ＋ とき."

1．日本では、どんな時、「おかえりなさい」と言いますか。

2．日本では、どんな時、「ただいま」と言いますか。

3．日本では、どんな時、「ごちそうさま」と言いますか。

4．どんな時、日本語で、「ごめんなさい」と言いますか。

5．どんな時、「はじめまして」と言いますか。

L.  Ask several classmates what they do under the given situations and fill in the chart.

        A：ひまなとき、どうしますか。(何をしますか。)

        B：そうですねぇ、ひまなときは、コンピューターゲームをします。

| | (　　　　) さん | (　　　　) さん | (　　　　) さん |
|---|---|---|---|
| ひまなとき | | | |
| ねむいとき | | | |
| あたまがいたい とき | | | |
| 勉強したくない とき | | | |

M. Pair-work:  Ask your partner what s/he would drink in the following situations.

　　Ask ～時、何を飲みますか。

Selection of drinks

スポーツドリンク、みず、さゆ (hot water)、 おちゃ、 コーヒー、カプチーノ、
ワイン、ウィスキー、コーラ、ぎゅうにゅう（ミルク）、オレンジジュース、
しょうがじる(ginger juice)、レモネード、ココア、　おさけ

1．スポーツをした時、.........................................................................

2．これから　ねる時、.......................................................................

3．おすしを食べる時、.......................................................................

4．スターバックスへ　行った時、....................................................

5．朝、おきた時、............................................................................

6．カレーライスを食べる時、...........................................................

7．ディスコでおどった時、...............................................................
　　　　　　　　（おどる to dance）

8．フランスりょうりの店に入った時、..............................................

9．かぜの時、..................................................................................
　　（When I caught a cold）

１０．はじめてのデートの時、...........................................................

Chapter 11 (D): Dict-A-Conversation    (1)

Try to be a contrarian （あまのじゃく）and defensively respond to the statements
verbally, and write down your answers.  Please answer in <u>complete sentences</u>, writing in
hiragana, katakana, and kanji when possible.

Example:

(You hear):　私は、コーヒーをのんでから、シャワーをあびます。

(You say):　　私は、シャワーをあびてから、コーヒーをのみます。

1. _____
2. _____
3. _____
4. _____
5. _____

Chapter 11 (D): Dict-A-Conversation    (2)
Fill in the missing dialogue to complete the below conversations.  When you hear the chime, verbally ask the appropriate questions before hearing the answers.  Please write in short answers in hiragana, katakana and kanji.

1.  Please ask me if I ate breakfast before I came to school.

———————————————————————————————
いいえ、学校へ来てから、食べました。

2.  Please ask me if I ate at the cafeteria.

———————————————————————————————
いいえ、学校の近くのバーガーキングで　食べました。
いつも、クラスがはじまる前に、朝ごはんを食べるんです。

3.  Please ask if it's all right with me to eat at Burger King every day, using "~ temo daijyoubu desu ka?"

———————————————————————————————
だいじょうぶです。学校から帰ったあと、家でたくさん　やさいを食べますから。

4.  Please ask me if I studied before the test.

———————————————————————————————
もちろん　しました。今日のテストは、ばっちりです！

5.  Please ask me what "bacchiri" means.

———————————————————————————————
「ばっちり」というのは、「かんぺき」とか「パーフェクト」のことです。

6.  Please make the remark that your test will be "bacchiri" also.

———————————————————————————————
がんばってください。

Ch 11 (D) – (1)

| 書 (to write; books) | か（く）<br>ショ | 書く（かく）to write<br>書物（しょもつ）books<br>書道（しょどう）calligraphy |
| | | (10)<br>一 フ ヨ ヨ ヨ 圭 聿 書 書 書 書 |
| 昨 (previous) | サク | 昨日（さくじつ、きのう）yesterday<br>一昨日（いっさくじつ、おととい）the day before yesterday<br>昨夜（さくや）last night<br>昨晩（さくばん）last night |
| | | (9)<br>丨 日 日 日 旷 旷 昨 昨 昨 |
| 美 (beautiful) | うつく（しい）<br>ビ<br>ミ | 美しい（うつくしい）beautiful<br>美人（びじん）a beautiful woman<br>美男子（びなんし）a handsome man |
| | | (9)<br>丶 丷 丷 半 半 美 美 美 美 |
| 暗 (dark) | くら（い）<br>アン | 暗い（くらい）dark<br>[暗闇（くらやみ）darkness]<br>暗黒（あんこく）pitch-dark<br>明暗（めいあん）を分（わ）ける to divide a fate (bright and dark)<br>暗号（あんごう）a secret code<br>暗記（あんき）する to memorize |
| | | (13)<br>丨 日 日 日 日 旷 旷 旷 暗 暗 暗 暗 暗 |
| 思 (to think) | おも（う）<br>シ | 思う（おもう）to think<br>思い出（おもいで）a memory<br>[思考（しこう）thought]<br>[意思（いし）an intention; a wish] |
| | | (9)<br>丨 口 田 田 田 甲 思 思 思 |

Ch 11 (D) – (2)

| 出<br><br>(to go out; leave) | で（る）<br>だ（す）<br>シュツ | 出る（でる）to leave; to appear<br>思い出（おもいで）memory<br>出す（だす）to present; to turn in; to mail<br>思い出す（おもいだす）to recollect<br>外出（がいしゅつ）する to go out<br>出口（でぐち）an exit |
| --- | --- | --- |
| | | (5)<br>　丨 屮 屮 出 出 |
| 神<br><br>(god; deity) | かみ<br>シン<br>ジン | 神（かみ）さま deities; the God<br>神学（しんがく）theology<br>神話（しんわ）myth; mythology<br>神道（しんとう）Shinto<br>神社（じんじゃ）a Shinto shrine<br>女神（めがみ）female deities |
| | | (9)<br>　丶 ラ ネ ネ ネ 初 初 袘 神 |
| 秘<br><br>(secret) | ヒ<br>ピ | 神秘（しんぴ）a mystery<br>[神秘的（しんぴてき）mysterious]<br>[秘密（ひみつ）a secret] |
| | | (10)<br>　丶 二 千 千 手 禾 秒 秘 秘 秘 |
| 音<br><br>(the sound) | おと<br>ね<br>オン | 音（おと）sound<br>音色（ねいろ）tone quality; a tone color<br>音楽（おんがく）music |
| | | (9)<br>　丶 亠 ナ 立 立 产 音 音 音 |
| 読<br><br>(to read) | よ（む）<br>ドク | 読む（よむ）to read<br>読み物（よみもの）reading matter (books etc.)<br>読み方（よみかた）how to read<br>音読（おんどく）read aloud<br>読書（どくしょ）reading books |
| | | (14)<br>　丶 二 亖 亖 亖 言 言 言 訇 訶 詰 読<br>訪 読 |

**Etymology of sheep** 羊    **& beautiful**   美:

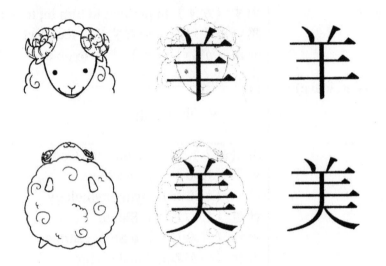

**Etymology of sheep** 羊, **wear** 着, **and** 洋:

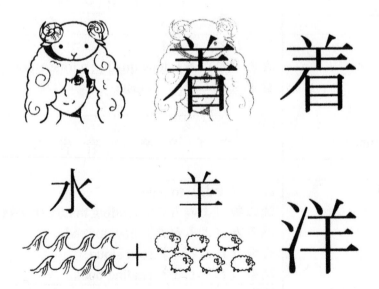

Kanji Practice for Chapter 11 D
かんじの　れんしゅう

1. つぎの　ことばを　よみなさい。それから、クラスメートに　いみを
   ききなさい。 Read the following words to your classmates and ask them for the
   meaning of each word.

   （１）　本を読むのが　好きです。

   （２）　日記を書くのは、楽しいです。

   （３）　本を読む事を　「読書」と言います。

   （４）　昨夜の雪は、美しかったですね。

   （５）　昨日は、外出しませんでした。

   （６）　一昨日のしゅくだいは、大変だったと思います。

   （７）　漢字で書くと、アメリカは「米国」になります。

   （８）　神社は、神道の神さまを祀りますが、お寺は、仏教の仏
   さまを祭ります。(祀ります deify, 祭ります worship)

   （９）　今日は、雨がふっているので、家の中が　暗いです。

   （１０）　ふじ山の「初日の出」は、神秘的です。

   （１１）　音楽を聞くのは、いつも楽しいです。

2. Write kanji in the box to complete the compound word.

   (1)  Shinto shrine

   (2)  music

   音

   (3)  the U.S. in Japanese

   国

   (4)  bright & dark (antonym)

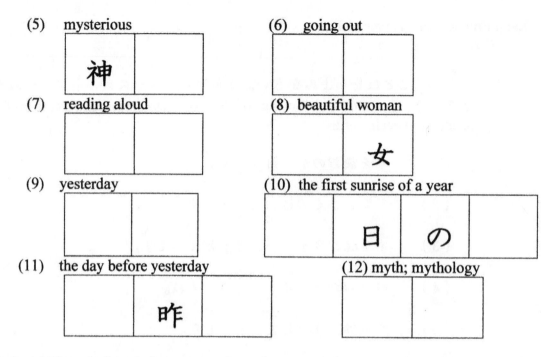

(5)　mysterious
神

(6)　going out

(7)　reading aloud

(8)　beautiful woman
女

(9)　yesterday

(10)　the first sunrise of a year
日　の

(11)　the day before yesterday
昨

(12)　myth; mythology

3. よんでから、よみがなをかいて、えいごでいいなさい。Read first, then write
   yomigana above each kanji, and translate into English.

（１）　昨日は、日本語で　作文を　書きました。

（２）　一昨日の朝の雪は、美しいと思いました。

（３）　神社は、神さまを祀る所です。神秘的な所です。
　　　　　　　　　　　(enshrine)

（４）　秘密があると、暗い気持ちになります。

（５）　声を出して　読むことを、「音読」と言います。

（６）　外出先から、母に　電話を　入れました。

（７）　書道の先生から、毛筆の使い方を　習いました。

（８）　「音を立てる」って、どんないみですか。

Kanji Bingo Sheet (11)  Chapter 11BCD
**Fill in the blanks with the kanji and play Bingo.**
Kanji Ch11B  合う、安らか、高い、夜、社（会、心、校、今）
ヒント：　会合、安心、高校、今夜、会社、社会

| 合 | 会 | 社 |
|---|---|---|
| 安 | 夜 | 高 |
| 心 | 今 | 校 |

| | | |
|---|---|---|
| | | |
| | | |
| | | |

| | | |
|---|---|---|
| | | |
| | | |
| | | |

Kanji Ch11C  雪、立つ、札、押す、用　（大、社、私、女）

| 大 | 雪 | 女 |
|---|---|---|
| 用 | 押 | 札 |
| 社 | 私 | 立 |

| | | |
|---|---|---|
| | | |
| | | |
| | | |

| | | |
|---|---|---|
| | | |
| | | |
| | | |

Kanji Ch11D  書く、昨、美しい、暗い、思う、出る、神、秘める、音、読む
　　　（ショ）　　（ビ）　　（アン）　　　（シュツ）(シン)　　　（オン)(ドク)
ヒント：暗記、秘書、神秘、外出、読書

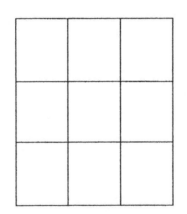

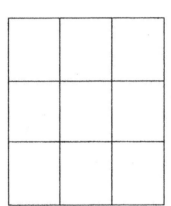

| | | |
|---|---|---|
| | | |
| | | |
| | | |

# A Missing Child

*Expressions*
"While I was getting an ice cream, he disappeared"
"I couldn't eat anything while I was sick"
"He's about one-meter tall, a bit chubby, wearing blue pants and yellow T-shirt"
"He's not wearing a hat"
"He's looking around"

*Kanji practice from Chapter 12*

*Sample composition by a student*

Chapter 12              A Missing Child 迷子

モニカ：どうしたんですか。                                            1

女の子：弟がいないんです。                                            2

モニカ：まあ、それは、大変。弟さんは、何才ぐらいですか。                3

女の子：五才です。ずっといっしょにいたんですが、私がアイスクリームを

　　　　買いに行っている間に、いなくなったんです。                     5

モニカ：私も　いっしょにさがしてあげましょう。                         6

女の子：ありがとうございます。                                        7

モニカ：弟さんの背丈やふくそうについて、おしえてちょうだい。            8

女の子：弟は、背が一メートルぐらいで、ちょっと太っているので、年より

　　　　大きく見えます。今日は、青いズボンをはいて、黄色いTシャツを    10

　　　　着ていました。ぼうしは、かぶっていません。                     11

　　　　白いテニスシューズを　はいています。                           12

モニカ：あ、あの子は？                                                13

女の子：どの子ですか。                                                14

モニカ：あそこで、きょろきょろしてる男の子、、、                       15

女の子：あ！そうです！タケシ〜！！                                    16

タケシ：お姉ちゃん！                                                  17

Chapter 12
[English translation:]

Monica: Is anything wrong?

Girl:     My brother is missing.

Monica: Oh, no.  How old is he?

Girl:     Five years old.  I was with him the entire time; but while I left to get
          some ice cream (for him), he disappeared.

Monica: Let me search for him with you.

Girl:     Thank you so much.

Monica: Please tell me his height and attire (at the time).

Girl:     He's about one-meter tall, and looks big for his age as he's a bit chubby.
          Today, he's wearing blue pants and a yellow T-shirt.  He's not wearing a hat.

Monica: Oh, is that him?

Girl:     Which one?

Monica: That boy who's looking around over there.

Girl:     Ah, yes!  That's him!  Takeshi~~~!!

Takeshi: Big sis!

Chapter 12                     Vocabulary List

1. Expressions
それは、たいへん。（大変）            That's serious.
（ふとっている。太っている）          S/he is fat.
ズボンをはいている。                S/he is wearing pants
Ｔシャツを　き（着）ている。          S/he is wearing a T-shirt.
ぼうしを　かぶっている。             S/he is wearing a hat.
きょろきょろしている。              S/he is looking around.
〜ているあいだに　（間に）          While ~ was doing ~,...

2. Nouns
（たいへん　大変）                 alarming, serious, terrible
せたけ（背丈）/ せ（背）            height
一メートル                     one meter
ふくそう                      clothing
とし（年、歳、年齢）               age
（ズボン）                     pants
（Ｔシャツ）                    T-shirt
ぼうし                       hat; cap
テニスシューズ                  tennis shoes
（おねえちゃん　お姉ちゃん）         big sister (affectionate term)

3. Adjectives
（あおい　青い）                 blue
（きいろい　黄色い）              yellow

4. Verbs
（さがす）/さがして              to search/ "te" form of "sagasu"
（おしえる）/おしえて             to instruct / "te" form of "oshieru"
きる（着る）                   to wear (clothing items over the shoulders)
　　きている                   "te" form of "kiru"
はく                        to wear (items under the waistline)
　　はいている                 "te" form of "haku"
かぶる                       to wear; put on (things over one's head)
　　かぶっている                "te" form of "kaburu"
きょろきょろする                to look around repeatedly

.....................................................................

Additional Vocabulary from Grammar Notes, Exercises, and Dict-A-Conversation

.....................................................................

[Nouns]
ドレス                       dress
ジーンズ                      jeans

| | |
|---|---|
| コンタクトレンズ | contact lenses |
| かわぐつ（革靴） | leather shoes |
| いま（居間） | living room |
| おれい(お礼) | gratitude; thanks |
| うわさばなし | rumors |
| Y－シャツ | dress shirt |
| スニーカー | sneakers |
| ビデオ | video |
| マイク | microphone |
| ひざ | knees |
| サラリーマン | salaried man |
| かがくしゃ（科学者） | scientist |
| プライド | pride |
| けいじ（刑事） | detective |
| もくげきしゃ | witness |
| はんにん（犯人） | criminal |

[Copula Nouns]

| | |
|---|---|
| けんこう | healthy |
| し（死）にそう | feel like dying |
| うちき（内気） | shy |
| あまえんぼう | wheedling child |
| ひっこみじあん | diffident |
| しゃこうてき | sociable |
| おこりんぼう | quick-tempered; hothead |

[Adjectives]

| | |
|---|---|
| がまんづよい | patient |

[Adverbs]

| | |
|---|---|
| わりあい/まあまあ | relatively |

[Verbs]

| | |
|---|---|
| （かさを）さす | to put up an umbrella |
| あやまる | to apologize |
| かんがえる | to contemplate |
| （ひざを）つく | to get on one's knees |
| けいえいする | to run (business) |

Chapter 12                        Grammar and Culture Notes

## 1. あいだ: "while ~" as a Subordinating Conjunction

"あいだ" is an independent noun which means "between" in English. When it is preceded by a phrase or a sentence, it works as a subordinating conjunction and indicates "during the time when ~" or "while ~."

Note 1:

When the subject in the "あいだ" clause is different from the one in the main clause, it is marked by "が." Think of the sentence such as "While <u>my brother</u> was watching a television, <u>I</u> was doing my homework." The subject of "while ~" sentence is "my brother" and the subject of the main clause is "I." So, you mark "my brother" with "ga," as you see in sentence (1) below. If the subject (doer) is one and the same person, you don't have to mention twice for each clause (see the sentence [2] below). Compare:

1)  おとうとが　およいでいるあいだ、私は、しゅくだいをしていました。
    While my brother was swimming, I was doing my homework.

2)  テレビをみているあいだ、私は、母のことを　かんがえていました。
    While watching television, I was thinking of my mother.

Note2:

There is a big difference between "あいだ" and "あいだに," since particle "ni" focuses on the end period of time. The event or action of the main clause takes place <u>throughout</u> the time span described in the "あいだ" phrase or clause. However, the event or action stated in the main clause takes place <u>only at a certain point</u> during the time described in the "あいだに" phrase or clause. The same is true between "まで" and "までに," the former means "until that time period," while the latter means "by (that dead-line)." Compare:

1)  母が、りょうりをする<u>あいだ</u>、私は、本を読んでいました。
    While my mother was cooking, I was reading a book (throughout the time).

2)  母が、りょうりをする<u>あいだに</u>、私は、その本を終わってしまいました。
    While my mother was cooking, I finished reading the book.

Example sentences:

(1) Noun の　あいだ/あいだに

1．びょうきのあいだ（は）、何も　食べることができませんでした。
    I couldn't eat anything while I was sick.

2．休みのあいだ、日本にいました。
    I was in Japan during vacation.

3．休みのあいだに、りょこうするつもりです。
    I intend to travel while I'm on vacation.

4．学生のあいだに、たくさん本を読みたいです。

　　I want to read many books while I am a student.

(2) Adjective + あいだ/あいだに

1．魚が新しいあいだに、すしにしましょう。

　　Let's make sushi while the fish is fresh.

2．若いあいだに、たくさん恋をしなさい。

　　Fall in love a lot while you are young.

3．しごとが　いそがしいあいだは、りょこうが　できない。

　　I cannot travel while I am busy with work.

(3) Copula Noun + な　あいだ/あいだに

1．父が、元気なあいだに、かおを見せに行きたい。

　　I want to come and see my father while he is well.

2．勉強が　大変なあいだは、テレビを見ることはできません。

　　I cannot watch television while I am busy with studying.

3．内気なねこは、とおりがにぎやかなあいだは、外に出てこない。

　　That shy cat won't come out while the street is busy.

(4) Verb + ているあいだ/あいだに

1．雨がふっているあいだ、ずっと家にいた。

　　I was home while it was raining.

2．赤ちゃんがねているあいだに、おせんたくをすませました。

　　I finished laundry while the baby was asleep.

3．電車が止まっているあいだに、お茶を買いました。

　　I bought tea while the train was stopping.

4．車が来ないあいだに、みちを　渡りなさい。

　　Cross the street while no car is coming.

When the verb in the "aida (ni)" clause indicates an action, it is always stated in the form of "~ te iru" whether it refers to the past or non-past event.

## 2. ～ている **for clothing**

We were introduced to such expressions as 知っています (I know) in Chapter 4 (E), and 持っています (I have) in Chapter 8, and おなかがすいています (I'm hungry) in Chapter 10 (D).  They describe the "present state of being.  It is the same idea to describe one's clothing.  We use "te iru" form whether someone is wearing shoes, hat, shirts, pants, watch, a tie, necklace, or a pin on the head. There are three verbs for "wear" depending on where in the body.  Use the following verbs:

For head: かぶる→ 　かぶって

For over one's shoulder (such as a shirt, blouse, coat)" 着る → 　着て
For under the waist line: はく → 　はいて
For belongings such as jewelry, watch, tie, belt, etc: する→ 　して
Use either する or かける（→かけて） for eyeglasses.

Examples:
1.  私は、ドレスを 着ています。　2. まゆみさんは、ブラウスを着ています。
     I'm wearing a dress                         Mayumi's wearing a blouse.

3.  カレンさんは、スカートを 　はいています。
     Karen's wearing a skirt.

4.  ミシェルさんは、ズボンを 　はいています。
     Michelle's wearing pants.

     Tシャツを 　着ています。
     (She's) wearing T-shirt.

5.  ボブさんは、ぼうしを　かぶっています。
         Bob's wearing a T-shirt.
    セーターを　きています。
         (He's) wearing a sweater.

    かとうさんは、シャツとジャケットをきています。
      Mr. Kato's wearing a shirt and jacket.

6.  アンジェラさんは、スカーフを　しています。
                Angela's wearing a scarf

             ベルトをしています。
             She's wearing a belt.

             とけいを　していません。
             She's not wearing a watch.

7.  お父さんは、ネクタイを　しています。
      Ken's wearing a tie.
    スーツを　着ています。
      He's wearing a suit.
    かわぐつを　はいています。
      He's wearing leather shoes.
    めがねを　かけています。
         She's wearing eyeglasses.
    コンタクト（レンズ）を　していません。
         She's not wearing contact lenses.

### 3. 〜ている **for progressive actions**

In this chapter, we are learning another usage of "te iru" form. It describes "on-going actions" such as eating and studying. Its English equivalent is a gerund, "am/is/are + V-ing." However, the Japanese "te iru" form not only expresses "current on-going actions," but also "on-going action in some time span" just like English "present perfect progressive" (have + been+ V-ing) does.

Examples:

1. 母は、今、台所で、ばんごはんを作っています。
   My mother is cooking dinner in the kitchen now.

2. 父は、居間で　コーヒーを飲んでいます。
   My father is drinking his coffee in the living room.

3. 弟は、あそこで、本を読んでいます。
   My younger brother is reading a book over there.

4. 姉は、今、プールで、泳いでいます。
   My big sister is swimming in the pool now.

5. 兄はシャワーを浴びています。
   My big brother is taking shower now.

6. 妹は音楽を　聞いています。
   My younger sister is listening to a music.

7. 私は、もう二年ぐらい　日本語をべんきょうしています。
   I have been studying Japanese for about two years.

8. 高校のとき、フランス語をべんきょうしていました。
   I was studying French when I was in a high school.

お父さんは、背が高いです。　　お母さんは背が低いです。

お父さんは、皮ぐつを
はいています。

お母さんは、サンダルを
はいています。

めがねを　かけています。

時計をしています。

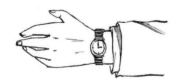

Chapter 12.  Exercises

A. お父さんとお母さんのイラストを見て、意味が通るように（　　）に、言葉を書いてください。Fill in the blanks with suitable words so that each sentence correctly describe Dad and Mom in illustration.

1. お父さんは、（　　　　）が　高いです。

2. お母さんは、背が　（　　　　　）です。

3. お父さんは、時計を　（　　　　　　）います。

4. お父さんもお母さんも、（　　　　）を
   かけています。

5. お母さんは、イヤリングを　して（　　　　　　　）。

6. ブラウスを　着ているのは、（　　　　　）さんです。

7. サンダルを　（　　　　）いるのは、お母さんです。

8. ネクタイを　しているのは、（　　　）さんです。

9. お父さんは、スーツを　（　　　　）います。

10. ネックレスを（　　）いるのは、お母さんです。

11. ベルトを　しているのは、（　　　）さんです。

12. Ｙ－シャツを　（　　　）いるのは、お父さんです。

13. （　　　）を　はいているのは、お父さんです。

14. スカートを　（　　）いるのは、お母さんです。

B. 正しいイラストをえらびなさい。Choose the matching illustrations and fill in the blanks with their alphabets.

1. べんきょうしている　　（　　　）　　2. おしゃべりを　している　（　　　）
3. テレビを　みている　　（　　　）　　4. てがみを　かいている　　（　　　）
5. おんがくを　きいている（　　　）　　6. でんわを　かけている　　（　　　）
7. しんぶんを　よんでいる（　　　）　　8. たべている　　　　　　　（　　　）
9. しゃしんを　とっている（　　　）

Ex. C.  かぞく について： Description of each family member

First, fill in the blanks about your family. Then, ask your classmates about their families.

しつもんのしかた(how to ask)：
1）あなたのかぞくのなかで、（いちばん）　しんせつなのは、だれですか。
2）スポーツが　とくいなのは、だれですか。
3）せがたかいのは、だれですか。

|  | わたしのかぞく | （　　　　　）<br>さんの　かぞく | （　　　　　）<br>さんの　かぞく |
|---|---|---|---|
| しんせつ（な） | 母（はは） |  |  |
| スポーツがとくい<br>（な） | 弟（おとうと） |  |  |
| ねるのがだいすき<br>（な） | 妹（いもうと） |  |  |
| せがたかい | 兄（あに） |  |  |
| せがひくい | 私（わたし） |  |  |
| ふとっている | 母（はは） |  |  |
| やせている | 父（ちち） |  |  |
| けっこんしている | 姉（あね） |  |  |
| およぐのが<br>じょうず（な） | 祖父（そふ） |  |  |
| ガーデニングが<br>すき（な） | 祖母（そぼ） |  |  |

たんごヘルプ(Vocabulary help)：
しんせつ　　　　　　kind to others
とくい　　　　　　　skilled
せがたかい　　　　　tall
せがひくい　　　　　short
ふとっている　　　　chubby; fat
やせている　　　　　skinny
けっこんしている　married

D. Match these people with their given descriptions.

D-1. どのひとですか。
（　　　　）マイラさんは、ギターをひいています。
（　　　　）ボブさんは、ビデオをとっています。
（　　　　）きょうこさんは、きものをきて、いすにすわっています。
（　　　　）キャシーさんは、マイクをもって、たっています。
（　　　　）まりさんは、たって、ワインをのんでいます。
（　　　　）トムさんも、ワインをもって、たっています。

D-2. Look at the illustration in the previous page and fill in the blanks.

１．すわって、ギターを（　　　　　　）ているのは、マイラさんです。
２．きものを、（　　　　　　）て、すわっているのは、きょうこさんです。
３．（　　　　　　）て、ワインを（　　　　）て、マイラさんの（　　　　）にいる
　　のは、まりさんです。
４．マイクを（　　　　　　）て、うたを（　　　　　　）いるのは、
　　キャシーさんです。
５．ひざをついて、ビデオを（　　　　　　　　）いるのは、ボブさんです。
６．ワインを（　　　　　　）て、こしに手をあてて、（　　　　　　　　）いるのは、
　　トムさんです。

### E. Pair-work: Health Check けんこうチェック

Use the chart below to interview your partner to find out how stressful his/her life is.

| | | | | | | |
|---|---|---|---|---|---|---|
| 毎朝あさごはんをたべている | →はい | よくうんどうをしている | →はい | | リラックスしている | |
| ↓<br>いいえ | | ↓<br>いいえ | | いいえ | ↓<br>はい | |
| テストのことをしんぱいしている<br>↓ | →いいえ | アルバイトをしている<br>↓ | →いいえ | | よくおんがくをきいている<br>↓ | |
| はい | | はい | | いいえ | ↓<br>はい | |
| あまりねていない<br>↓ | →いいえ | 毎日ひるごはんをたべている<br>↓ | →いいえ | | まいにちべんきょうをしている | |
| はい | | はい | | いいえ | ↓<br>はい | |
| しゅくだいで死にそう (feel like dying)<br>↓<br>はい<br>↓ | →いいえ<br><br>いいえ | たいていよくねている<br>↓<br>はい<br>↓ | | いいえ | まいばんよくねている<br>↓<br>はい<br>↓ | |
| あまりけんこうじゃない<br>(not very healthy) | | わりあい<br>(まあまあ)<br>けんこう<br>(relatively healthy) | | もんだいあり<br>**(need help)** | とても<br>けんこう<br>(very healthy) | |

### F. Connect each pair of sentence with either "aida" or "aidani."

Examples:

(1) 日本にいた / 京都に二度行った。 →　日本にいるあいだに、
京都に二度行った。

(2) 学校が休みだ / としょかんは、閉まっている。 →　学校が休みのあいだ、
としょかんは、閉まっている。

(3) ひまだ/てがみを書くつもりだ。→ひまなあいだに、てがみを書くつもりだ。

1．セールだ/ デパートは、こんでいる。 →

2．ひこうきにのっていた/ えいがを三つ見た。 →

3．子どもがねている/ 家の中は、しずかだ。 →

4．家の中がしずかだ/ 本を読みたい。 →

5．びょうきだ/ しずかに休みたい。 →

G.  Translate into Japanese.

1. I want to buy a sweater while it's on a sale.

2. The library is quiet during the holidays.

3. My mother left for work while I was asleep.

4. During the winter, no one was at the beach.

5. I have been studying Japanese for one and a half years.

H.  Fill in the blanks with appropriate words.

1. Ｔシャツを（　　　　　　　） いる。
2. ぼうしを（　　　　　　　） いる。
3. くろいくつを（　　　　） いる。
4. ネックレスを（　　　　） いる。
5. ベルトを（　　　　　　　） いる。
6. めがねを（　　　　　　　） いる。
7. きょろきょろ（　　　　） いる。
8. （　　　　） は、一メートルぐらいです。
9. （　　　　） は、十才ぐらいです。
10. 私がかいものをしている（　　　　　　　）、いなくなった。

I. Pair-work:  Ask your partner the following questions.

１．今、どこに住んでいますか。

２．結婚していますか。

３．だれか、日本人を　知っていますか。

４．おなかが　すいていますか。

５．のどが　かわいていますか。

６．今日の空は、晴れていますか。

７．さいふの中に　いくら入っていますか。

８．先生は、今、立っていますか、すわっていますか。

９．今日のばんごはんは、もうできていますか。

１０．かぞくの中で、だれが一番、やせていますか。

Chapter 12 Additional Exercises: Translate into Japanese.

A. 「あいだ」、「あいだに」　のれんしゅう

1. While I wasn't home, a thief entered my house.

2. I did my homework while my teacher was not watching.

3. Please put salt while the soup is still hot.

4. During a holiday, the town was quiet.

5. Please don't talk to me while I'm working.

6. I read a book quietly, while the children had gone to school.

B. 様子をあらわす言い方 (expressing a person's "posture, manner, or appearance")

1. Kato-san, wearing a yellow hat, is talking on the phone over there.

2. Cathy, holding an umbrella, is standing in the rain.

3. Tom, holding a microphone, is singing.

4. A boy is happily eating. (happily = deliciously-looking)

5. Bob, holding his bag in his hand, is walking.

6. Ken, kneeling down on the floor, is video-taping.

7. Sam, sitting in the darkness, is crying.

8. A girl, holding candy in her hand, is looking around.

9. Hanako, wearing a kimono, is standing in front of a house.

Chapter 12 Dict-A-Conversation (1):  Criminal Investigation

Purpose:
Listen to the CD, and help the detective determine which of the four suspects is the culprit.

Situation:
Yesterday, the Bank of Japan in Tokyo was robbed by three men.  The detective has returned from the crime scene and is now investigating the possible suspects.  Look at the four profiles and, after listening to the questions and answers between the detective and the witnesses, locate the culprits.

Vocabulary:
けいじ detective,　もくげきしゃ witness,　はんにん culprit

1.
けいじ　　　　 : ............................................
もくげきしゃ : ............................................
けいじ　　　　 : ............................................
もくげきしゃ : ............................................
けいじ/あなた：じゃ　はんにんは、
　　　　　　　　.................だ！

2.
けいじ　　　　 : ............................................
もくげきしゃ : ............................................
けいじ　　　　 : ............................................
もくげきしゃ : ............................................
けいじ/あなた：じゃ　はんにんは、
　　　　　　　　................. だ！

3.
けいじ　　　　 : ............................................
もくげきしゃ : ............................................
けいじ　　　　 : ............................................
もくげきしゃ : ............................................
けいじ/あなた：じゃ　はんにんは、
　　　　　　　　...............だ！

## Chapter 12 Dict-A-Conversation (2)    Narratives and Answers

おんせんに
（　　　　　　　　　）のは、
カレンさんです。

テレビを
（　　　　　　）
のは、
かとうさんです。

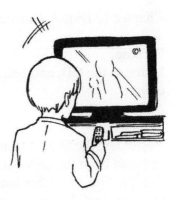

おなかが（　　　　　　）のは、
モニカさんです

ラジオを
（　　　　　　　　　）のは、
ナンシーさんです。

おしゃべりを
（　　　　　　　　　）のは、
（　　　　）さんと、けんたくん
です。

パンを（　　　　　　　　）のは、
けいこさんです。

Chapter 12 Dict-A-Conversation (3)
Listen to the CD and fill in the missing
information.
〜ているのは、だれですか。

Before listening to the CD,
study the illustrations with
people's names.

やまだ　ブラウン　たかし
かとう　スミス　こうじ
トム　しらさわ

Answers:

(1) .........................

(2).........................

(3) .........................

(4).........................

(5) .........................

(6) .........................

(7) .........................

(8) .........................

Chapter 12 – (1)

| | | |
|---|---|---|
| 弟<br><br>(younger brother) | おとうと<br>テイ<br>ダイ | 弟（おとうと）younger brother<br>兄弟（きょうだい）siblings<br>子弟（してい）young people; children |
| | | (7)<br>丶 丶 丷 丷 丷 弟 弟 |
| 姉<br><br>(older sister) | あね<br>シ | 姉（あね）older sister<br>姉妹（しまい）sisters |
| | | (8)<br>く 夕 女 女' 夝 妒 姉 姉 |
| 背<br><br>(the back; height) | せ（い）<br>ハイ | 背（せ、せい）the back; height<br>背中（せなか）the back<br>背信（はいしん）betrayal<br>背後（はいご）a space behind one's back |
| | | (9)<br>一 丬 ヨ 少 北 北 背 背 背 |
| 丈<br><br>(height; length) | たけ<br>ジョウ | 丈（たけ）height; length<br>丈夫（じょうぶ）healthy |
| | | (3)<br>一 ナ 丈 |
| 太<br><br>(thick) | ふと（い）<br>タイ | 太い（ふとい）thick<br>太古（たいこ）ancient times<br>太陽（たいよう）the Sun |
| | | (4)<br>一 ナ 大 太 |

Chapter 12 - (2)

| 青 | あお（い）<br>セイ<br><br><br>（blue; young;<br>unripe） | 青い（あおい）blue; unripe<br>青年（せいねん）young man<br>青春（せいしゅん）youth |
|---|---|---|
| | | (8)<br>一 十 キ キ 主 青 青 青 |
| 黄 | き<br>オウ<br><br><br><br>（yellow） | 黄色（きいろ）yellow<br>黄土（おうど）ocher |
| | | (11)<br>一 十 卅 井 芦 芦 苗 苗 苗 黄 黄 |
| 着 | き（る）<br>つ（く）<br>チャク<br><br><br><br>（to wear; to arrive） | 着る（きる）to wear<br>着く（つく）to arrive<br>一着（いっちゃく）(counter for clothes) one ~<br>着信（ちゃくしん）receipt (of an e-mail)<br>到着（とうちゃく）arrival |
| | | (12)<br>、 ソ ソ ソ ソ 羊 羊 羊 着 着 着 |

Kanji Practice for Chapter 12
かんじの れんしゅう

1. つぎの ことばを よみなさい。それから、クラスメートに いみを
  ききなさい。Read the following words to your classmates and ask them for the
  meaning of each word.

  （1）　弟は、背が高くなった。

  （2）　私たち兄弟は、仲が いい。
  　　　　　　　　　　なか
  　　　　　　　（relationship）

  （3）　姉は、背が低い。
  　　　　　　　　ひく

  （4）　「姉と妹」を、「姉妹」と言う。

  （5）　竹の子の背丈が 伸びて、太くなった。
  　　　たけ　　　　　　の
  　　　（bamboo shoot）　（伸びる to grow taller）

  （6）　信号は、まだ 黄色だ。

  （7）　今日は、黄色いシャツを 着たい。

  （8）　青いジーンズは、ちょっと太めだ。
  　　　　　　　　　　　　　　（a bit wide）

  （9）　青年は、木の下で 本を読んでいた。

  （10）　この虫は、太古の昔 から、生きている。
  　　　　　　　　　　　むかし

  （11）　この机 は、大変 丈夫だ。
  　　　　　　つくえ　　　　　ぶ

  （12）　さむいから、上着を着た。
  　　　　　　　　　うわぎ

2. Write kanji in the box to complete the compound word.

  (1) siblings (brothers)　　　　　　(2) sisters

  ┌─────┬─────┐　　　　　┌─────┬─────┐
  │　　　│　　　│　　　　　│　　　│　　　│
  └─────┴─────┘　　　　　└─────┴─────┘

(3)  the ancient times

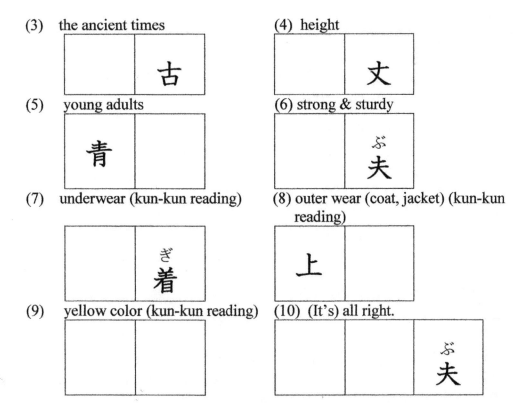

(4)  height

(5)  young adults

(6)  strong & sturdy

(7)  underwear (kun-kun reading)

(8)  outer wear (coat, jacket) (kun-kun reading)

(9)  yellow color (kun-kun reading)

(10)  (It's) all right.

3. よんでから、よみがなをかいて、えいごでいいなさい。 Read first, then write yomigana above each kanji, and translate into English.

（１）　弟は、一年で、背丈が　十センチも　伸びました。
　　　　　　　　　　　　　　　（伸びる to grow taller）

（２）　黄色いTシャツと　青いズボンは、合いますか。

（３）　よく勉強したので、テストは、大丈夫だと思います。

（４）　妹は、最近(recently)　ちょっと太りました。

（５）　下は、赤いスカートをはいて、上は、白いブラウスを着ました。

（６）　日本の信号は、「赤、青、黄」の　三色です。

（７）　姉は背が高いので、いつもズボンをはいています。

学生の作文  Sample composition by a student: 私の兄弟

私のかぞくは　五人かぞくです。私には兄弟が　二人あります。私は、まん中です。

兄は　二十二さいの大学四年生で、せんこうは　けいえいがくです。兄はせが　たかくて　かみが　みじかくて　めが　ほそいです。たいてい　Ｔシャツを　きて　ジーンズを　はいて　めがねを　かけています。そして、スポーツが　できて、あたまも　よくて　しんせつです。バスケットボールとフットッボールと　スノーボードが　だいすきです。しゅうまつ　兄は　アルバイトをします。兄は　かいものも　すきですから　私は　兄と　よく　かいものにいきます。

弟も　兄と同じように、めがねを　かけています。弟は　十四さいで、中学生です。やせていていて　せが　ひくいですが、はながたかくて　かわいいです。弟は　たいてい　ファミこんを　しますから　あまりでかけません。でも私は　ときどき　弟と　こうえんで　バスケットボールを　します。弟は　食べるのがすきじゃないですが、ハンバーガーは、よく食べます。弟は　ときどき本を　よみに　としょかんに　いきます。ハリー　ポターの本が　だいすきです。
私は　たまに　兄と弟と三人で　レストランへ　ごはんを　たべにいきます。兄と弟が　だいすきですから、いっしょにいるのが　たのしいです。

[English translation]
My family consists of 5 people. I have two siblings. I'm the middle child.

My big brother is 22 years old. He's a senior in college. His major is business management. He's tall and has small eyes. Usually, he wears T-shirts, jeans, and glasses. He likes to play sports, is smart, and kind. He really likes football, basketball and snowboarding. On the weekends, he has a part time job. Because he really likes to go shopping, we often go shopping together.

My younger brother also wears glasses like my big brother. He's 14 years old and a middle school student. He's skinny and short, but has a long nose and cute. He usually plays computer games so he rarely goes out. But sometimes, we play basketball at the park. He doesn't like to eat, but he really likes hamburgers. Sometimes, he goes to the library to read books. He really likes Harry Potter books.

Occasionally, my brothers and I go to eat at a restaurant. Since I really like them, it's fun to be with them.

# <u>A Letter to My Japanese Teacher</u>

*Expressions*
"Eyes convey much more than the mouth" (proverb)
"Sad-looking, happy-looking, lonely-looking"

Conjunctions: sorekara, sonoato, sorede, sokode, demo, soshite, nanoni, dakara
Adverbs: umaku, kanarazu, chanto

*Kanji practice from Chapter 13*

日本の文化について、感想を　書く。

**Chapter 13**    日本語の先生へのてがみ    A Letter to My Japanese Teacher

先生、お元気ですか。

　私は日本へ来てから、日本語をたくさん習っていますが、それ以上に、日本の文化について　たくさん勉強しています。

　　昨日は、友だちと　えいがかんへ　行くつもりでした。でも、好きなえいがが　なかったので、食事のあと、二人で　ビデオ屋さんへ　行って、古い日本えいがを　借りました。そのとき、友だちが　侍のえいがを「チャンバラえいが」と呼びました。私は「チャンバラ」のいみが、わかりませんでした。そこで、ともだちに　聞きましたが、かのじょも　うまくせつめいできませんでした。

　えいがをみて、いろいろな　ぎもんが　わきました。昔の日本人は、あまりおしゃべりじゃなかったのでしょうか。ぎもんがあっても、それを口にしません。男も女も　そうです。でも、ちゃんと　分かるのが　ふしぎです。

　えいがの中で、かなしそうな目、うれしそうな目、さみしそうな目などを、見ました。友だちが、『目は、口ほどに、ものを言い』と言いました。その上、「日本人は目で話すのよ。」とも　言いました。どうやって目で話すことができるんでしょう。

　それから、女の人が、必ず　男の人のうしろを歩くのも、変でした。今の日本人は、ちゃんと、並んで歩きます。ところが、今日、道で　女の人が　男の人の二、三歩うしろを、歩いているのを、見ました。ともだちは、それは、あの人たちが、中年のふうふだからと　言いました。

　日本の古いしゅうかんの中には、ちょっと変なものも　ありますね。
　それでは、先生、またお便りいたします。お元気で。

　　　　九月十日

　　　　　　　　　　　　　　　　　　モニカ

Chapter 13
[English translation:] A Letter to My Japanese Teacher in the US

Dear Sensei, how are you?

My Japanese has vastly improved since I came to Japan, and I've learned about the Japanese culture to a much greater extent.

Yesterday, I was thinking of going to a movie theater with my friend, but since I found no movies interesting, my friend and I went to a video shop after dinner and rented an old Japanese movie. My friend called the samurai film a "chanbara movie," but I did not understand what that meant. I asked my friend, but she could not explain it well to me.

After watching the movie, many questions came to my mind. In the long ago past, weren't the Japanese talkative at all? Even when they had questions, they didn't express them in words. It was true with both men and women. The fact they understood each other (without verbalizing much) is a mystery.

In the movie I observed sad eyes, happy eyes, lonely eyes, and more. My friend shared an old Japanese saying, "Eyes can convey more than the mouth," and she said, "the Japanese talk with their eyes." How could anyone talk with their eyes?

I also felt it strange that women always walked behind men (as seen in the movie). Modern Japanese men and women walk alongside each other. But on the street today, I saw a woman walking behind a man by a few steps. My friend explained to me it's because they're a middle-aged couple.

I find some of the Japanese customs a bit odd.

Farewell, sensei. I will write to you again. Please take care.

September Tenth

Monica

Chapter 13                    Vocabulary List

1. Expressions
   「目は、口ほどに　ものを言い」          Eyes convey much more than the
                                          mouth.

2. Nouns
   〜いじょう　（〜以上）                   more than 〜
   ぶんか（文化）                          culture
     日本の文化                            Japanese culture
     日本文化                              Japanese culture
   （えいが）                              movie
   （えいがかん）                          movie theatre
   （ビデオ）                              video
   ビデオや（ビデオ屋）                     video shop
   さむらい（侍）                          warrior; samurai
   チャンバラえいが                        samurai movie
   かのじょ（彼女）                        she
   ぎもん                                  question, doubt
   むかし（昔）                            olden times, long ago past
   に、さんぽ（二、三歩）                    a few steps
   ちゅうねん（中年）                       middle-aged (person)
   ふうふ                                  married couple
   しゅうかん（習慣）                       custom
   たより（便り）                          letter, correspondence

3. Copula Nouns
   かなしそうな                            sad-looking
   うれしそうな                            happy-looking
   さみしそうな                            lonely-looking
   へんな（変な）                          strange, weird
   いろいろな                              various

4. Adjectives
   （かなしい）                            sad
   （うれしい）                            happy; glad
   （さみしい）                            lonely; lonesome

5. Verbs
   かりる（借りる）                        to borrow
   せつめいする（説明する）                 to explain
   （ぎもんが）わく                        have doubts, question
   口にする                                to mention; say

| | |
|---|---|
| ならぶ （並ぶ） | to line up |
| ならんで （並んで） | "te" form of "narabu" |
| おたよりする （お便りする） | to write a letter to someone |
| いたす | humble form of "suru" (do) |

## 6. Adverbs

| | |
|---|---|
| うまく | skillfully; well |
| かならず （必ず） | for sure, definitely |
| ちゃんと | correctly; adequately |

## 7. Conjunctions

| | |
|---|---|
| それいじょうに （それ以上に） | more than that |
| （でも） | but |
| そのとき | on that moment; at that time; then |
| そこで | therefore; because of that; due to that |
| そのうえ （その上） | moreover; on top of it |
| （それから） | after that |
| ところが | however; on the contrary |
| それでは | in that case |

······································································

## Additional Vocabulary from Grammar Notes, Exercises, and Dict-A-Conversation

······································································

**[Nouns]**

| | |
|---|---|
| しゅうまつ （週末） | weekend |
| （おく 奥） | the depths |
| かたち （形） | shape |
| おおよろこび | big joy |
| たいじゅう （体重） | weight |

**[Adverb]**

| | |
|---|---|
| ぐうぜん | by chance; coincidently |

**[Verbs]**

| | |
|---|---|
| かたづける | to tidy up |
| すっきりする | to become clear |
| つれていく | to take someone |

**[Expression]**

| | |
|---|---|
| しかたがない | Nothing can be helped. |

話 の 泉 ： なぜ、チャンバラ？

"Chanbara" means "sword fight"; therefore a samurai movie can be referred to as a "chanbara eiga." The origin of this word is perhaps onomatopoeic. The sound of swords upon contact (or impact) are like "chan chan," and "bara bara" to Japanese ears.

Chapter 13 Grammar and Cultural Notes

## 1. <u>Conjunctions</u>

Conjunctions connect two separate sentences. Unlike が, a coordinating conjunction used at the end of the first sentence like in 私は、日本から来ましたが、ナンさんは、インドから来ました, the conjunction でも is used when the first sentence is not connected to another: 私は、日本から来ました。 If the successive sentence contains "opposing" or "contradicting" content, use でも.

Compare:

(1) 私は、日本から来ました<u>が</u>、ナンさんは、インドから来ました。

(2) 私は、日本から来ました<u>。でも</u>、ナンさんは、インドから来ました。

I came from Japan, but Nunn came from India.

The conjunction そして is used to connect two separate sentences, non-contradicting and consistent in meaning. See the following examples.

(1) 私は、日本から来ました。<u>そして</u>、田中さんも、日本から来ました。

I came from Japan, and Mr. Tanaka also came from Japan.

(2) 私は、朝7時におきました。<u>そして</u>、かおを あらいました。

I woke up at seven o'clock in the morning, and washed my face.

Unlike the particle と that connects two "nouns," そして connects two "sentences."

There are other conjunctions that are used in speech and composition. They will help develop your narrative "logically" and "sequentially." The following are examples:

それから     after that, then

そのあと     after that (similar to それから, but それから has a stronger sense of "sequence," while そのあと emphasizes the idea of "after that.")

それで     consequently, because of that, due to that (それで is similar to だから, but だから merely points to the "reason," while それで expresses a sense of "sequence."

そこで     consequently (similar to それで, but それで is often followed by the sequential statement as situations, feelings, and phenomena, while そこで is followed by actions taken consequently.)

For example:

A: フリーウェイで、くるまがパンクした。(I got a flat tire on a freeway.)

B: <u>それで</u>、どうなったの？ 事故になったの？(Then what happened? Did you get an accident?)

C: そこで、どうしたの？　タイヤを替えたの？(Then what did you do?
Did you change a tire?)

する と　　　as a result of the preceding action/event

Now look at the following narrative and observe how conjunctions help readers understand its logical development.

Topic of Composition: "Christmas-Tree Picking"

私は、週末　かぞくといっしょに、山へ行きました。
Over the weekend I went to the mountains with my family.

そして、クリスマスツリーになりそうな　木をさがしました。
And we looked for a tree to become our Christmas tree.

でも、いい木が、ありません。
But there was no good tree (for that purpose).

そこで、もっと山のおくに　入っていきました。
Therefore, we went deeper into the mountains.

すると、とても形のいい木が　見つかりました。
Doing that, we found a nicely-shaped tree.

私たちは、大喜びで、家に帰りました。
We went back home all excited.

そして、クリスマスツリーに　水をやりました。
And we gave water to the Christmas tree.

それから、クリスマスツリーを　かざりました。
Then we decorated our tree.

そのあと、みんなで、ばんごはんを　食べました。
After that, we all ate dinner.

楽しかったです。
It was a lot of fun.

---

クリスマスツリーをさがして

私は、週末　かぞくといっしょに、山へ行きました。そして、クリスマスツリーになりそうな　木をさがしました。でも、いい木が、ありません。そこで、もっと山のおくに　入っていきました。すると、とても形のいい木が　見つかりました。私たちは、大喜びで、家に帰りました。そして、クリスマスツリーに　水をやりました。それから、クリスマスツリーを　かざりました。そのあと、みんなで、ばんごはんを　食べました。楽しかったです。

Chapter 13   How to use the Adverbs うまく、かならず、ちゃんと

例文：

1. うまく (well)

(1) テストは、うまく　いきました。My tests went well.

(2) うまくいけば、十分で　着きます。
If everything goes well, we'll arrive in ten minutes.

Write your own sentence, using うまく.

------------------------------------------------------------------------------------------------

2. かならず (for sure)

(1) かならず　もう一度、ここに　来ます。I'll for sure return here.

(2) かならず　テストで　百点を　取るつもりだ！
I'm determined to get a hundred percent (points) on the test.

(3) 田中さんは、十時になると、かならず　外へ　出ます。何をしているんでしょう？
Mr. Tanaka always goes out at 10 o'clock.  I wonder what he's doing.

Write your own sentence, using かならず.

------------------------------------------------------------------------------------------------

3. ちゃんと (appropriately; as expected)

(1) ちゃんと　しなさい。Act appropriately.

(2) ちゃんと　服を　たたみなさい。Fold up your clothes neatly.

(3) 人の言うことを、ちゃんと　聞いていますか。
Are you listening to me as you are expected to do?

(4) ほらね、ちゃんと　時間に間に合ったでしょう？See?  We made in time as I said.

Write your own sentence, using ちゃんと.

------------------------------------------------------------------------------------------------

Chapter 13: Conjunctions でも、そして、だから、そこで、（それ）なのに

キャシーは、背が高い。｜でも｜　やせてはいない。
　　　　　　　　　　　｜そして｜やせている。
　　　　　　　　　　　｜なのに｜縦のストライプの服を　着ている。
　　　　　　　　　　　　　　　　clothing with vertical stripes
　　　　　　　　　　　｜だから｜いつも背中を丸くしている。
　　　　　　　　　　　　　　　　　　　rounds her back
　　　　　　　　　　　｜そこで｜背が高く見えないような工夫をしている。
　　　　　　　　　　　　　　　　　　making an effort not to look tall
　　　　　　　　　　　　　　例えば
　　　　　　　　　　　　　　（1）ヒールをはかない。
　　　　　　　　　　　　　　（2）縦のストライプの柄を着ない
　　　　　　　　　　　　　　　　　not to wear the patterns of vertical stripes
　　　　　　　　　　　　　　（3）背の低い人と　いっしょに歩かない。

ボブは　目が悪い。｜でも｜　メガネを　かけていない。
　　　　　　　　　　　　　　それを　かくしている。
　　　　　　　　　　　　　　　　　is hiding
　　　　　　　　　｜そして｜耳も悪い。
　　　　　　　　　｜なのに｜コンピューター・ゲームばかりしている。
　　　　　　　　　　　　　　playing nothing but a computer game
　　　　　　　　　｜だから｜いつも目を細くしている。is always squinting
　　　　　　　　　｜そこで｜教室では、一番前に座る。

Complete the sentences:

トムは　頭がいい。｜でも｜

　　　　　　　　　｜そして｜

　　　　　　　　　｜なのに｜

　　　　　　　　　｜だから｜

　　　　　　　　　｜そこで｜

Chapter 13 Exercises
A. Pair-work:
 (1) Read the following passage to your partner and have him/her fill in
    the blanks in English.

今日の朝、私は、７時におきました。そして、水をいっぱい飲みました。そ
れから、７時はんごろ　シャワーをあびて、そのあと、八時ごろに、朝ごはんを
食べました。九時に家を出て、九時四十五分に　学校につきました。化学のクラ
スは、十時に始まって、十二時に終わりました。そのあと、ともだちとカフェテ
リアで　おひるごはんを食べました。

　　　　　　………. woke up

　　　7:30　　……………………

　　　　　　………. ate breakfast

　　　9:00　　……………………

　　　　　　………. arrived at school

　　　10:00　　……………………

　　　　　　………. Chemistry class ended

　　　After that, ………………………

 (2) Listen to your partner who will read the passage in the next page for you, and fill in
    the blanks in English.

　　　　　　…………. returned to school

　　　2:00-4:00 ………………………..

　　　　　　…………. returned home

　　　6:00　　………………………….

　　　　　　…………. studied Japanese

　　　After that, ………………………

　　　11:00　　……………………...

今日は、おひるごはんを食べてから、ともだちとこうえんをさんぽしました。学校へ帰ったのは、もう2時ごろでした。それで、れきしのクラスへは、行きませんでした。でも、としょかんで、れきしの勉強をしました。4時ごろ、としょかんを出て、家に帰りました。家に帰ったのは、5時ごろでした。すぐ、夕食をつくって食べて、6時からテレビを見ました。それから、7時から9時まで、日本語の勉強をして、そのあと、音楽をきいて、11時ごろ　ねました。

B. Fill in the blanks with the appropriate conjunctions from the list.

そして、それから、そのあと、そこで、だから、でも

1. 今日の朝は、おなかがすいていませんでした。（　　　　　）朝ごはんは
   食べませんでした。

2. 朝、五時におきました。（　　　　　）たいそうを　しました。（　　　　　）
   朝ごはんをつくって、食べました。

3. 今日、雨がふっていました。（　　　　　）家にいたかったです。
   （　　　　　）、クラスがあるので、学校へ行きました。

4. 家に帰って、ばんごはんを食べました。（　　　　　）、しゅくだいをし
   ました。（　　　　　）テレビを見て、ねました。

5. きのう学校を休みました。（　　　　　）ともだちに電話で、しゅくだい
   のことを　聞きました。

6. 朝、学校へいつものように来ました。（　　　　　）、だれもいません。
   今日は、お休みだったのです。

C. Fill in the blanks with the appropriate adverbs from the list.

| うまく、かならず、ちゃんと、とても、あまり、ぜんぜん |
|---|

1．犬<sub>いぬ</sub>が死<sub>し</sub>んで、（　　　　　）かなしい。
2．勉強<sub>べんきょう</sub>したから、しけんは、（　　　　　）（　　　　　）いくはずだ。
3．へやを、（　　　　　）かたづけた(かたづける tidy up)。
4．朝<sub>あさ</sub>ごはんを食<sub>た</sub>べたのが、おそかったから、まだ（　　　　　）おなかがすい
ていない。
5．今日<sub>きょう</sub>のテストは、（　　　　　）だめだった。しかたがない。勉強<sub>べんきょう</sub>しなかっ
たから。　　　　　　　　　　　　　　　　(Nothing can be done.)

D. Use your common sense to choose between inserting 以上（いじょう）or 以下（い
か）in the blanks.

1．テストは、９０点<sub>てん</sub>（　　　　　　　）が　Aです。
2．あなたのテストが、５９点<sub>てん</sub>（　　　　　）のときは、Fになります。
3．背<sub>せ</sub>がふつうで、体重<sub>たいじゅう</sub>が、４５キロ（　　　　　）の人は、やせすぎです。
　　height　　　　　　weight
4．背<sub>せ</sub>がふつうで、体重<sub>たいじゅう</sub>が、１００キロ（　　　　　）の人は、ふとりすぎです。
5．コーヒーを一日<sub>いちにち</sub>に　十杯<sub>じゅっぱい</sub>（　　　　　）飲<sub>の</sub>むんですか。それは飲<sub>の</sub>みすぎです。
6．今年<sub>ことし</sub>は、タバコを一日<sub>いちにち</sub>に　十本<sub>じゅっぽん</sub>（　　　　　）に　したいです。

E. Ask your classmates the following questions.
1．一日<sub>いちにち</sub>に　何時間<sub>なんじかん</sub>ぐらい　ねますか。

　　a.五時間以上<sub>ごじかんいじょう</sub>、六時間以下<sub>ろくじかんいか</sub>
　　b.六時間以上<sub>ろくじかんいじょう</sub>、七時間以下<sub>しちじかんいか</sub>
　　c.七時間以上<sub>しちじかんいじょう</sub>

2．一日<sub>いちにち</sub>に　何時間<sub>なんじかん</sub>ぐらい　勉強<sub>べんきょう</sub>しますか。
　　a.一時間以下<sub>いちじかんいか</sub>
　　b.一時間以上<sub>いちじかんいじょう</sub>、二時間以下<sub>にじかんいか</sub>
　　c.二時間以上<sub>にじかんいじょう</sub>、三時間以下<sub>さんじかんいか</sub>
　　d.三時間以上<sub>さんじかんいじょう</sub>、四時間以下<sub>よじかんいか</sub>
　　e.四時間以上<sub>よじかんいじょう</sub>

3. 一日に、何杯ぐらい 水を飲みますか。
   a. 一杯以上、三杯以下
   b. 三杯以上、五杯以下
   c. 五杯以上

4. 一週間に 何杯ぐらい お酒を飲みますか。
   a. おさけは、まったく 飲みません。
   b. 一杯以上、三杯以下
   c. 三杯以上、五杯以下
   d. 五杯以上

5. 一週間に 何日ぐらい うんどうをしますか。
   a. ぜんぜん うんどうしません。
   b. 一日以上、三日以下
   c. 三日以上、五日以下
   d. 五日以上

F. Define the following proverbs （ことわざ）. Are there similar expressions in English?

1. 便りのないのは よい便り

2. 石の上にも三年

3. 猿も木から落ちる

4. 井の中の 蛙 大海を知らず

5. 弘法も筆の 誤り

G. Pair or group work:
(1) Find the matching vocabulary entry from the list and write them down.

1. culture .................................

2. custom .................................

3. correspondence, letter .................................

4. married couple .................................

5. middle-aged person .................................

6. warrior .................................

7. warrior movie .................................

8. olden times .................................

9. she .................................

10. a few steps .................................

11. doubt, question .................................

12. movie theatre .................................

13. to mention .................................

14. to line up .................................
    (to stand side by side)
15. skillfully .................................

16. definitely, for sure .................................

17. correctly, adequately .................................

18. sad .................................

19. glad, happy .................................

20. lonely .................................

21. to explain .................................

22. to borrow .................................

かのじょ、さむらい、チャンバラえいが（じだいげき）、かなしい、
うれしい、さみしい、ぶんか、しゅうかん、えいがかん、ぎもん、ふうふ、
ちゅうねん、たより、にさんぽ、かりる、くちにする、ならぶ、うまく、
かならず、ちゃんと，せつめいする、むかし

(2) Use at least two vocabulary words from the list and make as many sentences as you can.

Examples:

かのじょは、日本の文化を　うまく　せつめいした。

中年のふうふは、にさんぽ　歩いて、止まった。

........................................................................

........................................................................

........................................................................

........................................................................

........................................................................

........................................................................

........................................................................

H. Have you ever felt differences in customs 習慣の違い? From a micro view, we have differences from one household to another; and from a macro perspective, from one country to another. Discuss your experiences and observations with your group.

I. Reading comprehension practice: つぎの<ruby>文<rt>ぶん</rt></ruby>を<ruby>読<rt>よ</rt></ruby>んで、しつもんに<ruby>答<rt>こた</rt></ruby>えなさい。
Choose either A [hiragana version] or B [kanji version]. The content is the same.
A ： [hiragana version]

　わたしは、きのうあたまがいたくて、つかれていたので、はやくうちにかえって、やすみました。でも、そのうち　めもいたくなってきたので、びょういんへいきました。<u>ところが</u>、びょういんは、もうしまっていました。びょういんのうしろに、くすりやが　あるはずなので、いってみましたが、<u>そこも</u>　しまっていました。わたしは、<u>なきたいようなきもちになりました</u>。<u>そこへ</u>、ぐうぜん、ともだちのたかたさんが、きて、わたしを　たかたさんのうちのちかくの　おいしゃさんに　つれていってくれました。<u>そこで</u>、おくすりをもらって、うちにかえりました。きょうのあさ、あたまも　めも　すっきりしていました。

B ： [kanji version]

　私は、きのう頭が痛くて、疲れていたので、早く家に帰って、休みました。でも、そのうち目も痛くなってきたので、病院へ行きました。<u>ところが</u>、病院は、もう閉まっていました。病院の後ろに、薬屋が　あるはずなので、行ってみましたが、<u>そこも</u>　閉まっていました。私は、<u>泣きたいような気持ちになりました</u>。<u>そこへ</u>、ぐうぜん、ともだちの高田さんが来て、私を、高田さんの家の近くのお医者さんに　連れて行ってくれました。<u>そこで</u>、お薬をもらって、家に帰りました。今日の朝、頭も目も　すっきりしていました。

[Vocabulary help]:

| | |
|---|---|
| あたま | head |
| いたい | painful |
| つかれている | to be tired |
| やすむ | to rest |
| いたくなってくる | start hurting |
| びょういん | a hospital |
| しまっている | closed |
| くすりや | drugstore, pharmacy |
| なきたい | want to cry |
| なきたいようなきもちになる | |
| | to feel like crying |
| ぐうぜん | by chance |
| （お）いしゃ（さん） | |
| | A medical doctor, clinic |
| つれていく | to take someone |
| （お）くすり | medicine |
| すっきりする | to become clear |

つぎのしつもんにこたえなさい。

1. この人は、きのう　どうして　はやく　うちへ　かえったのですか。
   Answer with a structure 「Sentence ＋ からです。」 "It's because S+V."
   Use a casual form ending in a sentence before からです。

2. この人は、びょういんと　くすりやがちかいことをしっていました。それ
   が、わかる文をさがして、かきだしなさい。
   Write out the sentence that supports the fact.

3. 「ところが」とおなじいみのことばを、みつけて、かきだしなさい。
   Write down the word that has the same meaning as ところが.

4. どうして、なきたいような　きもちに　なったのですか。
   Answer with a structure 「Sentence ＋ からです。」 "It's because S+V."
   Use a casual form ending in a sentence before からです。

5. この人は、たかたさんのうちへ　いきましたか。

6. この人は、どこで　おくすりを　もらいましたか。

7. きょうのあさの　きぶんは、どうでしたか。

8. 「そこも」、「そこへ」、「そこで」　と三回、「そこ」　がでてきます
   が、それぞれ何を　さしていますか。(At what does each one of them point?)

Hints: "Soko" not only refers to a previously mentioned place or location, but it can
also refer to a previously mentioned situation.

Chapter 13: Dict-A-Conversation  (1) (2) (3) (4)
Listen to each passage in the Chapter 13 Dict-A-Conversation on the student CD, and fill in the blanks with the words you hear.

（１）
きのうは、がっこうを　やすみました。（　　　　　　　）からです。
（　　　　）、ともだちに　でんわをして、（　　　　　　　）のことを　き
きました。（　　　　　）そのともだちも、びょうきで、がっこうをやすんで
いたのです。わたしたちは、せんせいに、（　　　　　　）をかいて、きくこ
とにしました。せんせいに、しゅくだいを　おしえて（　　　　　　）から、
きゅうにきぶんが　よくなったので、わたしは、しゅくだいをする
（　　　　　）、テレビで、えいがをみました。そのえいがは、
（　　　　　　　）えいがでした。とてもおもしろかった（　　　　　　）、
ハッと　きがついたときは、（　　　　　）じゅうにじに　なっていました。
（　　　　　　）しゅくだいをしたので、（　　　　　　　）ときは、もうい
ちじはんでした。これからは、しゅくだいをした（　　　　　　）、テレビを
みるつもりです。

（２）
きょうのすうがくのクラスは、（　　　　　　）むずかしかった。
（　　　　　　）わからなかった。でも、となりのボブは、すずしい
（　　　　　）をしていたなぁ、、、きょうの（　　　　　）は、
（　　　　　）がんばってべんきょうする！テレビをみる（　　　　　）、きょ
うかしょを（　　　　　　　）、いちじかんは、べんきょうする
（　　　　　　）だ。そして、こんどの（　　　　）では、
（　　　　　　）ひゃくてんを（　　　　　　）つもりだ。

（３）
きのうのテストは、（　　　　　　）できた。ともだちが、うちにきてコンピ
ューターゲームをして（　　　　　　）も、ぼくは、（　　　　　　）べ
んきょうしていたから。いいてんを（　　　　　　）、いいきぶんだなぁ～！

（４）
そのひとは、あかいくつを（　　　　　　）、しろいドレスを
（　　　　　）んですか。ぼうしは、（　　　　　　　）いませんでしたか。
かぶっていた？なにいろのぼうしでしたか？は？あかいぼうしを
（　　　　　　）。わかりました。そのひとは、まゆみさんです。

Chapter 13

| | | |
|---|---|---|
| 屋 (roof; store[suffix]) | や<br>オク | 本屋 （ほんや） a bookstore<br>屋根 （やね） roof<br>家屋 （かおく） a house; building<br>屋上 （おくじょう） the housetop; roof<br>屋外 （おくがい） outside of a house<br>屋内 （おくない） inside of a house<br>屋号 （やごう） general term for store's name |
| | | (9)<br>ァ ヮ 尸 尸 屋 屋 屋 屋 屋 |
| 聞 (to hear) | き （く）<br>き （こえる）<br>ブン<br>（モン） | 聞く （きく） to hear; listen<br>聞こえる （きこえる） being audible; can hear<br>新聞 （しんぶん） a newspaper |
| | | (14)<br>丨 冂 冋 冋 冋 門 門 門 門 門 閂 閅<br>聞 聞 |
| 話 (to talk; speech) | はな （す）<br>ワ | 話す （はなす） to talk; speak; tell<br>会話 （かいわ） conversation<br>手話 （しゅわ） sign language |
| | | (13)<br>、 ニ 二 言 言 言 言 言 訂 訂 話<br>話 |
| 化 (to change; disguise) | ば （ける）<br>カ<br>ケ | 化ける （ばける） to change; disguise<br>化学 （かがく） chemistry<br>変化 （へんか） change<br>化石 （かせき） fossil<br>[化粧 （けしょう） make-up] |
| | | (4)<br>ノ イ 仁 化 |
| 昔 (long time ago) | むかし<br>セキ | 昔 （むかし） long time ago<br>昔々 （むかしむかし） once upon a time<br>昔話 （むかしばなし） a folktale<br>昔日 （せきじつ） long time ago |
| | | (8)<br>一 十 艹 昔 昔 昔 昔 昔 |
| 侍 (a warrior) | さむらい<br>はべ （る）<br>ジ | 侍 （さむらい） a warrior<br>[侍る （はべる） wait on a person]<br>侍女 （じじょ） a lady-in-waiting |
| | | (8)<br>ノ イ 仁 仕 什 侍 侍 侍 |

## Kanji Practice for Chapter 13
かんじの　れんしゅう

1. つぎの　ことばを　よみなさい。それから、クラスメートに　いみを
   ききなさい。Read the following words and sentences to your classmates and
   ask them for their meanings.

   （１）　本屋

   （２）　友だちと話をする。

   （３）　英語で　会話をした。

   （４）　昔話と文学

   （５）　テストのことを、先生に　聞いた。

   （６）　店の名前を「屋号」と言う。この店の屋号は、「すずや」だ。
   
   （７）　家の中を「屋内」、家の外を「屋外」とも言う。

   （８）　一昔前、デパートの屋上は、たいていビアガーデンか、
   　　　　ゆうえんちだった。　　　　　　　　　　　　（a beer garden）
   　　（amusement park）

   （９）　お化けの話は　好きですか。

   （１０）　化学のクラスは、おもしろい。

   （１１）　日本文化を、習いたい。

   （１２）　生き物は、毎分　変化している。

   （１３）　毎日、新聞を読むのが、楽しみだ。

   （１４）　新しい上着を着た。

   （１５）　"The Seven Samurai" を日本語で言うと、「七人の侍」になる。

kanji in the box to complete the compound word.

(1) Culture

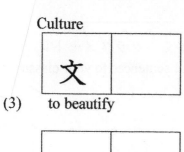

(2) literature

(3) to beautify

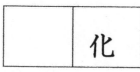

(4) newspaper

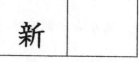

(5) conversation

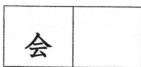

(6) book stores (on-kun reading)

(7) folk tales (kun-kun reading)

(8) the roof; the housetop

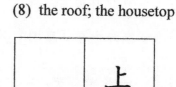

(9) inside of a house

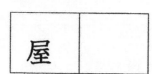

(10) the sign language (hand-talk)

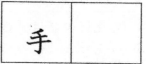

3. 日本語で　こたえなさい。Answer the following questions in complete sentences using the given kanji.

（１）　　八百屋で、どんな物を　売っていますか。

（２）　　侍って、どんな人ですか。

（３）　　日本文化のどんなことを、知っていますか。

（４）　アメリカのデパートの屋上にもゆうえんちやビアガーデンが
ありますか。　　　　　　　　　(amusement park, a beer garden)

（５）　化学のクラスは、好きですか。

（６）　今、どこかから、工事の音が、聞こえますか。
　　　　　　　　　　　　　(construction)

（７）　日本語の会話を、五分ぐらいできますか。

（８）　「昔々、ある所に」を　英語で　言ってください。

（９）　「大昔」って、何年ぐらい前だと　思いますか。

（１０）　昔話を　一つ、話してください。

（１１）　日本のお化けの話を　知っていますか。それは、どんな
お話ですか。

（１２）　生物と化学と　どちらの方が、おもしろいと思いますか。
それは、どうしてですか。

（１３）　あなたには、高校の時から、どんな変化がありましたか。

*Expressions*
"I worked from morning to night for the sake
"I'm going to Japan to study Japanese"
"Due to the snow, the school is closed"
"I think tomorrow is a clear day"
"I heard that we have no test tomorrow"
"Ms. Tanaka is gentle and easy to talk to"
"This pen is hard to write with"
"You look prettier when you put your hair up"

*Learn vocabulary for part of the human body*
*Kanji practice from Chapter 14*
*What is the most popular surname in the US?*

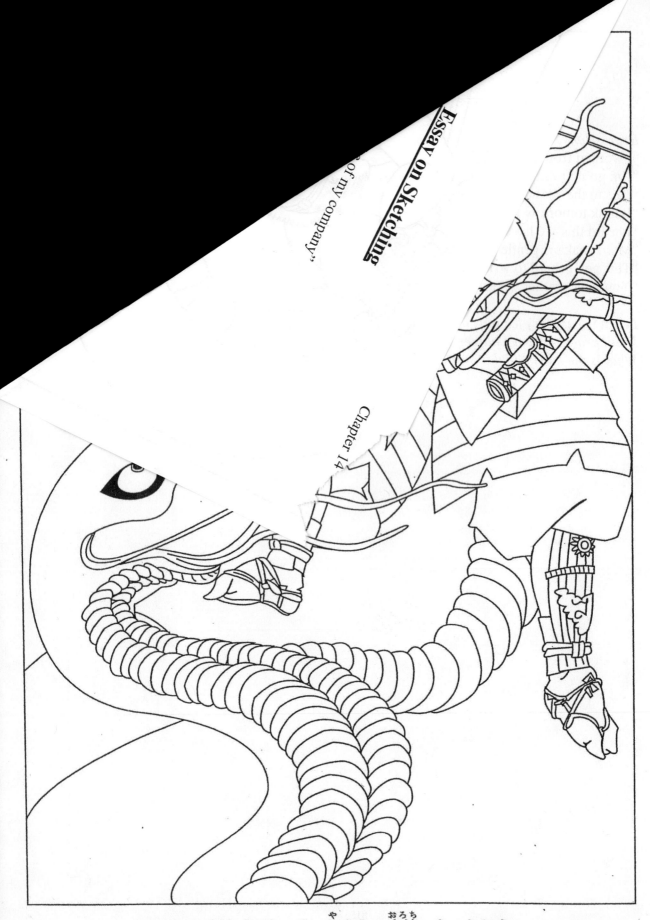

日本の神話「スサノオ、八またの大蛇」を　たおす。

## Chapter 14   Essay on Sketching   　描写についてのエッセー

### 人物描写

　美術のクラスで、「人物描写」をした。人物描写は、むずかしい。人を描くのは、木や花を描くより、もっとむずかしい。動物を描くのと、人間を描くのと、どちらのほうが、むずかしいだろう。どちらもむずかしいが、人を描くほうが、ずっとむずかしいと思う。

　例えば、人の顔を描く時、はじめに目をうまく描いても、その後、まゆ毛を描くと、ぜんぜんちがう人になる。

　鼻は、あんがいかんたんだ。でも日本人の鼻は低いので、かえって描きにくい。西洋人の高い鼻の方が　描きやすい。

　それに比べて、口は、描きにくい。口の端をちょっと上げても、ちがう顔になる。反対に、ちょっと下げると、怒った顔になる。

　しわを描くのは、注意が要る。ひたいのしわは、不きげんに見える。口元のしわは、ちょっと上げると　うれしそうに見えるけれども、下がって長くなると　年よりに見える。モナリザのほほえみは、たしかに神秘的だ。

　耳の形にも　いろいろある。人によって　ずいぶんちがう。ひたいと目、鼻、口と、耳のバランスをとるのは、むずかしい。でも、顔の中では、一番描きやすい。

　来週は、このクラスで　人の体全体を描くと聞いた。人間の筋肉を描くなんて、私には　とうていできない。

　レオナルド・ダヴィンチは、天才だと思う。でも、天才でも　たくさん練習したはずだ。私も　もっとうまくなるために、これから　デッサンの練習に励むつもりだ。

Chapter 14
[English translation:]  Essay on Sketching

### Portrait

I did a portrait (lit: personal sketch) in art class.  It was hard.  Portraying people is by far harder than sketching trees and flowers.  I wonder which is harder: sketching animals or people?  Both are equally difficult, but portraying people is much harder, I think.

For instance: When sketching people, even if you think you've drawn eyes perfectly, it's only after adding eyebrows that would enhance and complete the final look.

Unexpectedly, portraying a nose is easier.  But Japanese noses are usually small, making illustration difficult.  A westerner's distinctive nose is easier to draw.

Compared to noses, mouths are harder to sketch.  Different impressions (lit: faces) are created simply by raising the edges of a mouth.  Conversely, you easily portray an angry face by lowering its edges.

Drawing wrinkles require a lot of detailed attention.  Adding wrinkles on a forehead makes a face look displeased.  Sketching wrinkles around the mouth might depict a smiling countenance, while making lines longer in a downward fashion might add ... Mona Lisa's smile is certainly mysterious.

There exists many ear shapes.  They vary from one person to another.  Drawing ears, however, is the simplest (of facial features).

I heard in this class next week we're sketching the whole anatomy of a person .  To me, it seems totally impossible to draw human muscles.

I think Leonardo da Vinci is a genius.  But even a genius must have had a lot of practice.  I intend to practice more (preliminary, basic sketching) from now on.

Chapter 14                Vocabulary List

1. Expressions
|  |  |
|---|---|
| 〜とおもう　（と思う） | I think that 〜 |
| 〜ときく　（と聞く） | I hear that 〜 |
| かきやすい　（描きやすい） | easy to draw |
| かきにくい　（描きにくい） | difficult to draw |
| ふきげんにみえる　（不きげんに見える） | looks unhappy; appears in a bad mood |
| としよりにみえる　（年よりに見える） | looks old |
| バランスをとるのは、むずかしい。 | It's hard to keep balance |
|  | (See Chapter 10[A]'s grammar notes) |
| 〜なんて…！ | such a (terrible) thing as 〜！ |

2. Nouns
|  |  |
|---|---|
| びょうしゃ　（描写） | sketch; description |
| エッセー | essay |
| びじゅつ　（美術） | arts |
| クラス | class |
| じんぶつ　（人物） | people, character |
| 　　じんぶつびょうしゃ（人物描写） | description of people, sketch of people |
| ひと　（人） | person, people |
| にんげん　（人間） | human beings |
| はな　（花） | flower |
| はな　（鼻） | nose |
| どうぶつ　（動物） | animal |
| まゆ | eyebrow |
| 　　まゆげ　（まゆ毛） | eyebrow |
| くちのはし　（口の端） | the edges of a mouth |
| かお　（顔） | face |
| しわ | wrinkle |
| ちゅうい　（注意） | caution |
| ひたい | forehead |
| くちもと　（口元） | mouth, and around the mouth |
| としより　（年より） | the old |
| モナリザ | Mona Lisa |
| ほほえみ | smile |
| みみ　（耳） | ears |
| かたち　（形） | shape |
| いろいろ | variety; many |
| バランス | balance |
| らいしゅう　（来週） | next week |
| からだ　（体） | body |

| | |
|---|---|
| ぜんたい　（全体） | the whole |
| きんにく　（筋肉） | muscles |
| レオナルド・ダヴィンチ | Leonardo da Vinci |
| てんさい　（天才） | a genius |
| れんしゅう　（練習） | practice |
| デッサン | sketching |

### 3. Copula Nouns

| | |
|---|---|
| ふきげん（な）　（不きげんな） | unhappy, in a bad mood |
| かんたん（な） | simple; easy |

### 4. Adjectives

| | |
|---|---|
| むずかしい | difficult |
| 〜やすい | easy to (do~) |
| 　　かきやすい | easy to write |
| 〜にくい | difficult to (do~) |
| 　　かきにくい | difficult to write |

### 5. Verbs

| | |
|---|---|
| おもう　（思う） | to think; consider |
| びょうしゃする　（描写する） | to describe, to draw |
| かく　（描く） | to draw |
| ちがう | to differ |
| くらべる　（比べる） | to compare |
| あげる　（上げる） | to lift up; raise |
| さげる　（下げる） | to lower |
| おこる　（怒る） | to be angry |
| 　　おこった　（怒った） | is angry |
| いる　（要る） | to need |
| 　　ちゅういが　いる　（注意が要る） | attention/caution is needed |
| ひとによる | to depend on a person |
| 　　人によって | depending on a person |
| バランスをとる | to balance |
| 〜と　きく　（聞く） | thus (I) hear ~ |
| 　　と　きいた　（聞いた） | thus (I) heard ~ |
| れんしゅうする　（練習する） | to practice |
| はげむ　（励む） | to make an effort; to work hard |

### 6. Adverbs

| | |
|---|---|
| もっと | more |
| ずっと | by far |
| ぜんぜん〜ない | not at all |

| | |
|---|---|
| あんがい | unexpectedly |
| かえって | rather; on the contrary |
| たしかに | for sure; definitely; certainly |
| とうてい（〜ない） | no chance for ~; no way to (do ~) |

7. Conjunctions

| | |
|---|---|
| たとえば　（例えば） | for example |
| そのご　（その後） | after that |
| それにくらべて　（それに比べて） | in comparison with ~; on the contrary |

Chapter 14                          Grammar and Cultural Notes

**1. ために for the sake of (showing purpose) or because of (showing cause/reason)**
"Tame" is a noun that indicates a purpose, benefit, reason or cause.  It is equivalent to
"on account of ~," "for the benefit of ~," "for the sake of ~," "in order to ~," or "because
of ~."

Formation for the non-past tense:

| Noun | の | |
|---|---|---|
| Copula Noun | な | ために |
| Adjective Plain | い | |
| Verb Plain form 行く、見る etc | | |

Formation for the past tense:

| Noun | だった | |
|---|---|---|
| Copula Noun | だった | |
| Adjective Plain | かった | ために |
| Verb Plain form | Ｖた | |

Examples:
[For the sake/purpose of ~]
（１）日本へ行くために、お金を貯金しています。
I'm saving money to go to Japan.

（２）お母さんのために、マーケットへ行きました。
I went to the market for my mother.

（３）会社のために、朝から晩まで 働きました。
I worked from morning to night for the sake of my company.

（４）日本語の勉強のために、日本へ行きます。
I'm going to Japan to study Japanese.

[Because of ~, due to ~]
"Tame no/ni" expresses cause or reason when the main clause describes a non-
controllable situation, or when the "tame no/ni" clause is in the past tense (where
something unchangeable has already happened).  In these cases, "tame no/ni" would
never express purpose.

（１）雪のために、学校は休校になりました。
Due to the snow, the school is closed.

（２）事故のために、電車が、おくれます。
Due to the accident, the train will be late.

（３）字が下手なために、はずかしい思いをしました。
Because my handwriting is poor, I have often felt embarrassed.

（４）私は、父が死んだために、大学院へ行くのをあきらめた。
Because my father passed away, I gave up going to graduate school.

（５）親が甘かったために、子供がだめになりました。
Because the parents were too lenient, the children were spoiled.

**2.** ～と思う **"I think ~"** A quotation sentence that shares the same pattern as "～と言う" we saw in earlier chapters. Variations of "～と思う" include "～と考える (I contemplate ~)" and "～と信じる (I believe ~). "

[Caution]

1) When the subject in a main clause is in the third person, ～と思う、～と考える、and ～と信じる take the form of "te + iru.," such as with ～と思っている、～と考えている、～と信じている, respectively.

2) This form, "te + iru," also shows duration of time for the first person subject. For example, "I have been thinking of going to Japan for a long time" would be わたしは、ずっと日本に行きたいと思っています/ or 思っていました。

Formation:
[Non-past tense]

| | |
|---|---|
| あしたは、晴れ だ (Noun +だ ) | |
| あしたは、天気が　いい(Adj.い ) | と　思います。 |
| あしたは、晴れる (Verb-plain form) | |

[Past tense]

| | |
|---|---|
| きのうは、晴れ だった (Noun +だった ) | |
| きのうは、天気がよかった　 (Adj.かった ) | と　思います。 |
| きのうは、晴れた (た form) | |

Examples:

1. あしたは、雨だと思います。
I think it will rain tomorrow.

だれだと思いますか。 → Noun だと思います。

(1)       (2)       (3)       (4)

2．あしたは、お天気がよくないと思います。
I don't think we have nice weather tomorrow.

3．こどもたちは、あした雨がふると思っています。
Children believe it will rain tomorrow.

4．きのうのさくらは、きれいだったと思います。
I think the cherry blossoms yesterday were beautiful.

5．きのうお天気になって、よかったと思います。
I'm glad it turned out to be a nice day yesterday.

6．ともだちは、もう学校へ行ったと思います。
I believe my friend has already gone to school.

7．こどもたちは、サンタクロースがいると信じています。
Kids believe in Santa Clause.

8．もうだめだと思いましたが、助けが来て、助かりました。
I thought I'd be doomed, but I was rescued when help arrived.

9．だれも来ないと思って、寝ていたら、ともだちが来ました。
I was asleep, thinking no one would come, but a friend of mine came.

10．長い間、人に助けを求めるのは、はずかしいと考えていましたが、そうではないことが、分かりました。
For a long time, I thought it to be a shame to seek for help, but I realized that was not true.

### 3. 〜と聞く ”I heard that~”

The particle "と" is preceded by a quotation sentence, just like with "〜と言う."

Examples:
1. ないとうさんは、あした日本へ帰ると聞きましたが、本当ですか。
   I heard that Mr. Naito would go back to Japan tomorrow; but is it true?

2. あすクラスでテストがあると聞いたんですが、本当なんですか。
   I heard that we have a test in class tomorrow; but is it true?

3. ともだちから、テストは、ないと聞きました。
   I heard that we have no test tomorrow.

4. ラジオで、きょうの午後、雨がふると　聞きました。
   I heard on the radio it would rain this afternoon.

5. エリザベスさんから、キャロルさんは、パーティに来ないと聞いた。
   I heard from Elizabeth that Carol wouldn't come to the party.

### 4. 〜やすい "easy to do~" and 〜にくい "difficult to do~"

"Masu-form Verb + yasui" is equivalent to "something is easy to do" in English and its conjugation is the same as that of adjectives (because it ends with "i").
Formation of "~ やすい "and "~ にくい":

| "masu" form Verb | 2nd base of Consonant Verbs 飲み、書き、使い、分かり、話し、持ち | + やすい。 |
| | Stem of Vowel Verbs/Irregular verbs 食べ、見、寝、教え、着、し、来 | or + にくい。 |

Examples of "〜やすい"
1. 田中さんは、やさしくて、話しやすい。
   Ms. Tanaka is gentle and easy to talk to.

2. これは、先にぎざぎざがあって、おそばでも、食べやすいおはしです。
   These chopsticks are corrugated at the ends, so it's even easy to eat buckwheat noodles.

3. もっと見やすい席に　行きましょう。
   Let's go to seats that would allow us a better view (lit: make it easier to see).

4．書きやすいペンが　ありますか。

Do you have a pen that is easy to write?

5．うすくて、飲みやすいコップが　ほしいんですが。

I would like to have a glass (tumbler; Portuguese origin "kop") that's easy to drink with.

6．このへやは、しずかで、勉強しやすいです。

This room is quiet and easy to study in.

Examples of "～にくい"

1．山田さんは、こわい顔をしているので、話しにくい。

Mr. Yamada looks angry, so it's (likely) hard to talk to him.

2．このおはしは、先がつるつるなので、おそばは、食べにくいです。

These chopsticks are slippery at the ends, making it difficult to eat buckwheat noodles.

3．この席からは、スクリーンが見にくいですよ。もっと前に行きましょう。

It's hard to see the (movie) screen from this seat.  Let's move up.

4．このペンは、書きにくいです。

This pen is hard to write with.

5．このコップは、厚くて、持ちにくいです。

This glass is thick and hard to handle.

6．かとうさんとは、先日けんかをしたので、彼のパーティーには　ちょっと行きにくい。

I fought with Mr. Kato the other day, so it's a bit hard to go to his party.

Conjugation of やすい:

|  | Casual/Plain form | Formal/Polite form |
|---|---|---|
| Non-past tense | わかりやす-い | わかりやすいです |
| Negative-non-past | わかりやす-くない | わかりやすくありません |
| Past tense | わかりやす-かった | わかりやすかったです |
| Negative-past | わかりやす-くなかった | わかりやすくありませんでした |

Conjugation of にくい:

| | Casual/Plain form | Formal/Polite form |
|---|---|---|
| Non-past tense | 食べにくい | 食べにくいです |
| Negative-non-past | 食べにくくない | 食べにくくありません |
| Past tense | 食べにくかった | 食べにくかったです |
| Negative-past | 食べにくくなかった | 食べにくくありませんでした |

## 5. ～に見える **looks** ~

"Noun/Copula Noun + ni mieru" is often used to describe the way things are perceived by people. Its English equivalent is "It looks (strange, pretty, angry, etc.), or It looks like ~." In the diary entry in Chapter 14, you saw the following expressions:

ひたいのしわは、<u>ふきげんに見える</u>。 The wrinkles on your forehead make you look unhappy/discontent.

<u>としよりに見える</u>。 You look like an old person.

Observe also:

1) きれいに見える。 (You) look prettier.
   髪の毛を上げたほうが、きれいに見えますよ。 You look prettier when you put your hair up.

2) 元気に見える。　 (You) look healthy.
   自転車にのっていると、元気に見える。　You look more energetic when you are riding a bicycle.

3) 上手に見える　 (It) looks skillful.
   きちんと書くと、字が上手に見えます。　Your handwriting looks better when you write more neatly.

The equivalent of "Noun/Copula Noun + ni mieru" is "Adjecive-ku + mieru."

うつくしい ＋ 見える → うつくしく 見える (looks beautiful)
わかい ＋ 見える → わかく 見える (looks young)
きたない ＋ 見える → きたなく 見える (looks dirty)

1) このくつをはくと、背が高く見えます。 When I put on these shoes, I look taller.

2) このねこは、若く見えますが、もう十才です。 This cat looks young, but she's already ten years old.

3) へやにものがたくさんあると、きたなく見えるので、かたづけなさい
   When the room is cluttered, it looks dirty. Please tidy up.

## Chapter 14 Exercises

A. (1) Add "～やすい" (easy to do ~)

    1. 食べる

    2. 見る

    3. 教える

    4. 着る

    5. 信じる(to believe)

    6. やせる (to lose weight)

    7. 倒れる (to fall)

    8. なる

    9. 働く(to work)

   10. 書く

   11. 読む

   12. はく(to wear shoes)

   13. 話す

   14. 太る (to gain weight)

   15. なおる (to heal)

(2) Add "～にくい" (difficult to do~) to the following verbs.

    1. 汚れる (to become dirty)

    2. 落ちる (to come off, fall, drop)

    3. 開ける (to open something)

    4. ぬれる (to get wet)

    5. 閉める (to close something)

    6. 入れる (to insert)

    7. 出る (to leave)

    8. 行く

    9. 持つ (to have, hold)

   10. 歩く

   11. かぶる (to wear something on the head)

   12. 乗る (to ride)

   13. 入る (to enter)

   14. 走る

   15. 止まる (to stop)

B. Ask your classmates the following questions and record the results using はい、〜や すいです or いいえ、〜やすくありません。〜にくいです。

| | (          )さん | (          )さん | (          )さん |
|---|---|---|---|
| そのペンは、書き やすいですか。 | | | |
| そのくつは、はき やすいですか。 | | | |
| あなたは、信じや すいですか。 | | | |
| お父さんは、話し やすいですか。 | | | |
| 先生の話は、わ かりやすいです か。 | | | |

C. Pair-work: Ask the following questions, then have your partner ask you.

1. ステーキを食べる時、おはしとナイフとフォークでは、どちらのほうが、 食べやすいと思いますか。

2. 走るとき、サンダルとハイヒールとでは、どちらのほうが、走りにくい と思いますか。

3. うそをつくとき、お母さんとお父さんでは、どちらのほうに、うそをつ
   to lie
   きにくいですか。

4. しずかに、勉強したいとき、としょかんと自分のへやでは、どちらのほ うが、勉強しやすいですか。

D. Choose the right words from the box below to fit in each sentence.

1. 字が小さくて、（                              ）。
   letters, characters, handwriting

2. このきかいは、（                              ）ので、だれも使いません。
   machine

3. このえんぴつは、やわらかくて、（                              ）。

4. (　　　　　　　　　）りょうりを　おしえてください。

5. (　　　　　　　　　）ズボンを　買<sup>か</sup>いたいです。

6. (　　　　　　　　　）セーターを　編<sup>あ</sup>みました。
　　　　　　　　　　　　　　　　　knitted

7. (　　　　　　　　　）ぼうしなので、好<sup>す</sup>きです。

8. 先生<sup>せんせい</sup>の説明<sup>せつめい</sup>が、(　　　　　　　　　）ので、すぐ答<sup>こた</sup>えが出<sup>で</sup>ました。
　　　　　　　　　　　　　　　　　　　　　　　came up with answers

9. うすくて (　　　　　　　　　） コップが　いいです。

10. すすきださんは、いつも　むずかしい顔<sup>かお</sup>をしていて、
　　　　　　　　　　　　　　looks sullen/displeased
　　(　　　　　　　　　）人<sup>ひと</sup>ですよ。

---

つくりやすい、話<sup>はな</sup>しにくい、分<sup>わ</sup>かりやすい、読<sup>よ</sup>みにくい、書<sup>か</sup>きやすい、飲<sup>の</sup>みやすい、着<sup>き</sup>やすい、はきやすい、かぶりやすい、使<sup>つか</sup>いにくい

---

E. Pair-work: Ask each other the following questions and report to class, using と言<sup>い</sup>いました、と信<sup>しん</sup>じています、or と聞<sup>き</sup>きました。
Example:
A: そのセーターは、洗<sup>あら</sup>いやすいですか。
　　　　　　　　　easy to wash
B: このセーターですか。ええ、洗<sup>あら</sup>いやすいです。
(You report to class now)
A: Bさんは、セーターは、洗<sup>あら</sup>いやすいと言<sup>い</sup>いました。
　Or

　わたしは、Bさんから、セーターは、洗<sup>あら</sup>いやすいと聞<sup>き</sup>きました。

1. あなたのくつは、はきやすいですか。

2. あなたのペンは、書<sup>か</sup>きやすいですか。

3. 大<sup>おお</sup>きいビタミンざいは、飲<sup>の</sup>みやすいですか。
　　vitamin tablets

4. 小さい字のじしょは、読みにくいですか。

5. としょかんは、行きやすいですか。

6. 市役所までの道は、分かりやすいですか。
   the way to the City Hall

7. すうがくの先生は、質問しやすいですか。

F. Pair or group work: Ask the following questions to each other, answering true or false.

1. あしたテストがあると聞いたんですが、本当ですか。

2. 先生が、日本へ帰ると聞いたんですが、本当ですか。

3. 来週、アメリカの大統領が、この大学に来ると聞いたんですが、本当なんですか。

4. 今週の金曜日は、クラスがないと聞いたんですが、本当ですか。

G. Ask the following questions to your classmates and report your findings to class.

1. 世界には、いつか 終わりが来ますか。[Use 〜と信じています]

2. テレビは、子供によくないですか。[Use 〜と考えています]

3. サンタクロースは、いますか。[Use either 〜と信じています or 思っています]

H. Translate into Japanese, using the best one among 〜と言う、と思う、と信じる、と考える、and と聞く.

1. I said, "Please be quiet."
2. I think Bob is right.
3. Many people believe television is no good for children.
4. Young children believe that Santa Clause really exits.
5. I heard on the news that a famous movie star is coming from Paris.

I. Group work: Make recommendations to each other, asking the rest of the group what they think of your idea. Use "…..と、……(〜に , or 〜く)見えますよ。"

Examples:

(1)

Ａ：Ｂさん、髪を上に上げると、もっときれいに　見えますよ。

　　みんなも、そう、思いませんか。

Ｃ，Ｄ、Ｅ：私も、そう思います。


(2)

Ｂ：Ｃさん、めがねをかけると、もっとインテリ(intelligent)に　見えますよ。

　　みなさん、そう思うでしょう？

Ａ：私は、そう思いません。めがねをかけると「がり勉」(nerdy) に見えると

　　思います。

Ｄ：ぼくは、めがねをかけると、もっとハンサムに見えると思います。

　　：賛成(agreed) !

(3)

Ｃ：Ｄさん、そのぼうしをとると、もっとあたまがよさそうに見えますよ。

　　みんなも、そう思うでしょ？

Ａ：私もそう思います。

Ｂ：私は、そう思いません。ぼうしをかぶると、クールに見えると思います。

　　Ｄさんは、どう思いますか。

Ｄ：ぼくは、ぼうしをかぶると、かっこよく(cool)見えると思っています。


Possible vocabulary to use:

おとなっぽく、わかく、元気そうに、あたまがよさそうに、お金持ちに、
grown-up-like

みりょくてきに、おとなしく、ひまそうに、
attractive　　　　　　　　obediently


J. Pair or group work:  Guessing Game.  Pictures 1 through 5 show a snapshot of an object, and 6 through 10 a shadow of someone doing something.  Ask your partner(s) what the objects are or what the person is doing, using the plain form + と思います.

Example 1:

Ａ：このえは、なんだと思いますか。

Ｂ：「くぎ」(a nail)だと思います。Ａさんは、なんだと思いますか。

Ａ：私は、これは、えんぴつの底(bottom)だと　思います。

Ｂ：あ〜なるほど！

1.

2.

3.

4.

5.

Example 2:

Ａ：このえでは、<u>なにをしている</u>と思いますか。

Ｂ：さあ、ちょっとわかりません。あ！わかった！
　　しんぶんを読んでいると思います。

6.

7.

8.

9.

10.

K. Pair-work: Guessing Game. Conceal the affirmative/negative chart below with a piece of paper and guess whether the following verbs are affirmative or negative.

For example, ask your partner, "飲むと思いますか、飲まないと思いますか," or 食べると思いますか、食べないと思いますか, and vice versa. The person with the most correct guesses wins the game.

| Verbs | Affirmative | Negative |
|---|---|---|
| のむ | | のまない |
| みる | みる | |
| する | | しない |
| つくる | | つくらない |
| くる | | こない |
| まがる | まがる | |
| とまる | とまる | |
| ねる | | ねない |
| おきる | おきる | |
| かく | | かかない |
| 着る（きる） | きる | |
| かぶる | かぶる | |
| はく | | はかない |
| なる | | ならない |

Continue the game with Adjectives:

Example: 大きいと思いますか、大きくないと思いますか。

| Adjectives | Affirmative | Negative |
|---|---|---|
| たかい | | たかくない |
| やすい | やすい | |
| あぶない | | あぶなくない |
| あつい | | あつくない |
| さむい | | さむくない |
| うつくしい | うつくしい | |
| いそがしい | いそがしい | |
| はやい | | はやくない |
| おそい | おそい | |
| すずしい | | すずしくない |
| おいしい | おいしい | |
| いたい | いたい | |
| たのしい | | たのしくない |
| うらやましい | | うらやましくない |

Continue the game with Nouns and Copula Nouns:

Example: <u>すてき</u>だと思いますか、<u>すてき</u>じゃないと思いますか。
wonderful

| Adjectives | Affirmative | Negative |
|---|---|---|
| げんき | | げんきじゃない |
| ひま | ひまだ | |
| きれい | | きれいじゃない |
| ゆうめい | | ゆうめいじゃない |
| しずか | しずかだ | |
| ざんねん | ざんねんだ | |
| すき | | すきじゃない |
| きらい | きらいだ | |
| しんせつ | | しんせつじゃない |
| にぎやか | にぎやかだ | |
| しあわせ happy | しあわせだ | |
| いたずら mischievous | | いたずらじゃない |
| ハンサム | ハンサムだ | |
| りっぱ | | りっぱじゃない |

L. Add と思います to the end of each sentence.  Make sure the preceding sentence ends in a casual form.

Example: すべての花は、美しいです。　→ すべての花は、美し<u>いと思います</u>。

あれは、けいこさんです。　→あれは、けいこさん<u>だと思います</u>。

おかしが　あります。　　→　おかしが<u>あると思います</u>。

1. きょうは、お天気がいいです。

2. あしたは、雨です。

3. 田中さんは、午後に　来ます。

4. ないとうさんは、朝は、来ません。

5. キャシーさんは、やさしい人です。

6. バラの花は、きれいです。
rose

7. この橋は、美しい形をしています。
bridge　　　　shape

8. トムさんの時計は、セイコーです。

9. あしたは、晴れます。(become clear/nice day)

10. あしたは、曇ります(become cloudy)。

M．そう思います。 Or, そうじゃないと思います。(そうは、思いません。)
Choose whether you agree or not the following comments. If you agree, mark (O), if not, mark (X). Ask your classmates each question and write their answers in each column. Begin your sentence with "日本では."

| 日本では | 私 | （　）さん | （　）さん | （　）さん |
|---|---|---|---|---|
| 1．数字の4が好きです。 | | | | |
| 2．若い女の人のほうが男の人より、たばこを吸います。 | | | | |
| 3．人が死んだ時、顔に白い布をかけます。 | | | | |
| 4．たいていの人は、朝おふろに入ります。 | | | | |
| 5．デパートで虫を売っています。 | | | | |
| 6．おみやげを買うのは、習慣です。 | | | | |
| 7．自販機で、タバコを買うことができます。 | | | | |
| 8．自販機で、お酒を買うことができます。 | | | | |
| 9．パンがおいしいです。 | | | | |
| 10．タクシー運転手は、白い手袋をしています。 | | | | |
| 11．信号は、赤、青、黄色の三色です。 | | | | |

N. Connect left and right columns with ために

1. バスに間に合う           学校をあきらめた。
2. 旅行する                電車が　遅れた。
3. 試験に受かる             走った。
4. 事故があった             お金を貯金している。
5. 父が死んだ               勉強している。

Vocabulary help:

---

間に合う to make in time    旅行する to travel    試験に受かる to pass an examination
事故 accident   死ぬ to die  あきらめる to give up   遅れる to be late
貯金する to save money

---

O.

(1) Choose from the list with whom (だれのために) you do the following.

1. だいどころで　おてつだいをする
2. さんぽする
3. 新聞を読んであげる
4. アイスクリームを買ってあげる
5. しゅくだいを　おしえてあげる

---

目がわるいおじいさん、犬、お母さん、ともだち、　妹

---

(2) Choose from the list for what (なんのために) you do the following.

1. 勉強する
2. お金を貯金(save)する
3. しごとをする
4. 本を読む
5. 運動(exercises)をする

---

結婚、旅行、将来(future)、生活(life, living)、知識(knowledge), 健康(health)

---

P.  Answer the following questions based on your truth.

1. あなたは、なんのために、日本語をならっていますか。

2. あなたは、会社のために働きますか、それとも、家族のために働きますか。
   company        to work

3. あなたのお母さんは、あなたのために、どんなことをしてくれましたか。

4. あなたのお父さんは、あなたのために、どんなことをしてくれましたか。

5. 刑務所は、なんのためにあると思いますか。
   prison

6. 「天は、人の上に人をつくらず、人の下に人をつくらず」と言うことばを知っていますか。(つくらず= つくらない, don't make)

Q.  Additional questions.

1. あなたのまわりに だれか、「モナリザのほほえみ」の人がいますか。

2. 「はながいい(花がいい)」と「はながいい(鼻がいい)」のおとのちがいを
                                                    difference
   上手に、言うことができますか。

3. 「ひと」と「にんげん」の間に、どんないみのちがいがあると思いますか。

4. 人のからだの中で、さいごまで、成長するのは、どこですか。
                    till its end      to grow

5. 「目と鼻の先」と言うことばを 知っていますか。どんないみですか。

Chapter 14: Essay on Sketching **839**

6. 「ねこのひたい」と言うことばを　知っていますか。どんないみですか。

7. わたしたちは、笑うとき、くちのはしを上げますか、下げますか。

8. あなたは、犬も笑うと思いますか。

9. あなたは、顔にしわが　ありますか。どこに一番多くありますか。

10.「口もと」と言うことばを習いました。では、「目のあたり」を何と言います
    か。

11.「口先（くちさき）で笑う」と言うことばがあります。これは、いいこと
    でしょうか、わるいことでしょうか。

12. 犬にも「まゆ（げ）」があると思いますか。

13. あなたの「まゆ（げ）」は、どんな形ですか。半月のかたちをしていま
    　　　　　　　　　　　　　　　　　　　　half moon

    すか。それとも、三日月の形ですか。
    　　　　　　crescent moon

14. 背の高さを「身長」と言います。体の重さを「体重」と言います。で
    は、体の調子を　なんと言うと思いますか。

15. ミケランジェロは、天才だと思いますか。あなたは、だれか天才を知っ
    ていますか。

## Learn the Vocabulary for Parts of the Human Body

**A)  General terms**

1. Body　からだ　2. Head　あたま　3. Hands　て　　4. Legs/Feet　あし　5. Face　かお

**B) Detailed terms**

1.  Head & face　　あたま　と　　かお

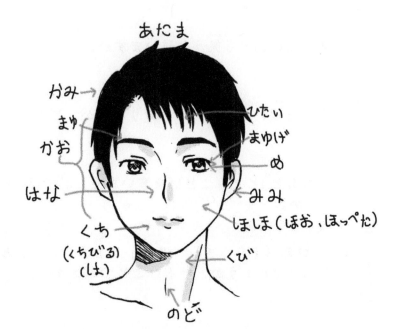

  A. hair　　　　　かみ
  B. ears　　　　　みみ
  C. forehead　　ひたい
  D. eyes　　　　　め
  E. eyebrows　まゆ
  F. eyelashes　まつげ
  G. nose　　　　はな
  H. mouth　　　くち
  I.　lips　　　　くちびる
  J. cheeks　　　ほお（ほほ、ほっぺた）
  K. neck　　　　くび
  L. throat　　　のど
  M. teeth　　　は

2.  Upper body

  A. chest/breast　　むね
  B. shoulders　　　かた
  C. back　　　　　せなか
  D. arms　　　　　うで
  E. hands　　　　て
  F. fingers　　　　ゆび
      a. thumb　　　　おやゆび　b. forefinger ひとさしゆび　c. middle finger なかゆび
      d. ring finger　くすりゆび e. pinky　こゆび
  G. nails　　　　　つめ

3.  Lower body

  A. waist　ウエスト　B. lower abdomen　　おなか　C. hips こし D. buttocks おしり
  E. legs/feet　あし　　F. knees　ひざ　G. toes つまさき（ゆび）

4.  Additional Vocabulary

  A. wrinkles　しわ　　　　　　　　　E. height　せ、しんちょう
  B. muscles　きんにく　　　　　　　F. weight　たいじゅう
  C. stomach　い
  D. lower intestines　　ちょう、はら

Chapter 14 Dict-A-Conversation
Where does it hurt?  Fill in the blanks with the appropriate letters.

1. (          ) 2. (          ) 3. (          ) 4. (          ) 5. (          )
6. (          ) 7. (          ) 8. (          ) 9. (          ) 10. (          )

Ch 14 – (1)

| 花 (flowers) | はな<br>カ<br><br><br><br><br>(flowers) | 花（はな）flowers<br>花々（はなばな）many flowers<br>花屋（はなや）a florist<br>押し花（おしばな）a pressed flower<br>雪月花（せつげっか）scenes of the four<br>seasons<br>[花瓶（かびん）a vase] |
|---|---|---|
| | | (7)<br>一 十 卄 艹 艼 花 花 |
| 動 (to move) | うご（く）<br>うご（かす）<br>ドウ<br><br><br>(to move) | 動く（うごく）to move<br>動かす（うごかす）to move something<br>動物（どうぶつ）animals<br>動作（どうさ）movement |
| | | (11)<br>一 二 千 斤 斤 盲 重 重 重 動 動 |
| 鼻 (the nose) | はな<br>ビ<br><br><br><br>(the nose) | 鼻（はな）the nose<br>小鼻（こばな）the wings of the nose<br>耳鼻科（じびか）ear-nose-throat doctor |
| | | (14)<br>丶 丆 宀 宀 自 自 自 皀 皀 鼻<br>畠 畠 皇 鼻 |
| 低 (low) | ひく（い）<br>テイ<br><br><br>(low) | 低い（ひくい）low<br>低下（ていか）a fall; drop<br>高低（こうてい）height; a pitch<br>低学年（ていがくねん）lower graders |
| | | (7)<br>ノ イ 亻 仃 仾 低 低 |
| 怒 (anger; to get angry) | おこ（る）<br>いか（り）<br>ド<br>ヌ<br><br>(anger; to get angry) | 怒る（おこる）to get angry<br>怒り（いかり）anger<br>怒号（どごう）howl (with rage)<br>[憤怒（ふんぬ）indignation] |
| | | (9)<br>く タ 女 如 奴 奴 怒 怒 怒 |

Ch 14 – (2)

| 天 (the sky; the heavens) | あま テン | 天の川（あまのがわ）the Milky way <br> 天気（てんき）weather <br> 天女（てんにょ）celestial women <br> 雨天（うてん）rainy weather |
|---|---|---|
| | | (4) <br> 一 二 チ 天 |
| 耳 (ears) | みみ ジ | 早耳（はやみみ）(a person) with quick hearing <br> 内耳（ないじ）the inner ear <br> 外耳（がいじ）the external ear <br> [耳鼻科（じびか）の医者 a nose, ear and throat doctor（耳鼻咽喉科じびいんこうか） |
| | | (6) <br> 一 丁 下 下 王 耳 |
| 形 (a shape) | かたち ケイ ギョウ | 形（かたち）a shape; a form <br> 三角形（さんかくけい）a triangle <br> 四角形（しかくけい）a square <br> 人形（にんぎょう）a doll |
| | | (7) <br> 一 二 チ 开 形 形 形 |
| 週 (week) | シュウ | 今週（こんしゅう）this week <br> 先週（せんしゅう）last week <br> 来週（らいしゅう）next week <br> 週末（しゅうまつ）weekend |
| | | (11) <br> ノ 几 月 门 冋 冃 周 周 `周 週 週 |
| 番 (a number; order; to look after) | バン | 番号（ばんごう）a number <br> 一番（いちばん）number one <br> 留守番（るすばん）watching over a house (while the family is out) |
| | | (12) <br> 一 丷 ㅜ 立 平 平 釆 釆 番 番 番 |

## Kanji Practice for Chapter 14
かんじの　れんしゅう

1. つぎの　ことばを　よみなさい。それから、クラスメートに　いみを
   ききなさい。Read the following words to your classmates and ask them for the
   meaning of each word.

（１）　いいお天気

（２）　私の犬は、耳の形がよい。

（３）　中学の時、週番で、花の手入れ(care)をした。

（４）　「天は人の上に人を作らず、人の下に人を作らず」
          (作らず "zu" is the negative form verb and it's the same as "nai")

（５）　犬が鼻をピクピク動かすときは、本当(とう)に　かわいい。
          (ピクピク動かす to wiggle)

（６）　人間と動物は、友だちでありたい。

（７）　晴天の日に、低い山に　のぼった。

（８）　私のねこは、怒ると、しっぽが　太くなる。

（９）　電(でん)話番号は、626 の 585 の 7975 です。

（１０）　人々は、たいてい　ひなまつり(Doll Festival)の一ヶ月ぐらい
              前に、箱(はこ)から　人形を出してかざる(display)。

（１１）　今週は、晴天の日より、雨天の日が　多かった。

（１２）　天井で　小さな生き物が　動いている。

（１３）　小学校では、高学年と低学年のせいとが、いっしょにあそぶ。
                          (pupils)

（１４）　右の耳がいたくて、耳鼻科(か)へ　行った。

（１５）　先週、花屋で　きれいな花を　買った。

2. 四角の中にことばを入れて完成しなさい。 Write kanji in the box to complete the compound word.

(1) animals

| | |
|---|---|
| | |

(2) weekly duty

| | 番 |
|---|---|
| | |

(3) florist; flower shop

| | |
|---|---|
| | |

(4) clear sky

| 晴 | |
|---|---|
| | |

(5) a doll

| 人 | |
|---|---|
| | |

(6) this week

| 今 | |
|---|---|
| | |

(7) high & low (antonyms)

| | |
|---|---|
| | |

(8) a roar (in anger); howl (with rage)

| | 号 |
|---|---|
| | |

(9) a rainy day

| | |
|---|---|
| | |

3. 日本語で　こたえなさい。 Answer the following questions in complete sentences using the given kanji.

（１）　花屋で、どんな花を　売っていますか。
　　　　チューリップ？カーネーション？ばら？ゆり？

（２）　あなたの耳は、いい形だと　思いますか。

（３）　あなたの鼻の形は、お母さんに似ています(resemble)か、
　　　　お父さんに似ていますか、それともどちらにも似ていませんか。
　　　　　　　　　　　　　(Or, resembles neither one of them)

（４）　犬が　あなたの言うことを聞かないとき、怒りますか。それとも、
やさしく、もう一度、おしえますか。


（５）　動物が、好きですか。


（６）　今週と先週では、どちらの方が、いい週でしたか。


（７）　お休みの日は、晴天と　雨天と、どちらの方が、いいですか。


（８）　「ひな人形」を　見た事がありますか。


（９）　あなたは、きょうだいの中で、何番目ですか。


（１０）今日は大変晴れて、よいお天気でした。日記には、何と書きますか。
日記の中で使うみじかい言葉です。


（１１）昨日は、雨でした。日記には、何と書きますか。


（１２）動物の中で、低体温の動物がいますね。どんな動物がそうだと
思いますか。　(体温　body temperature)

**What is the most popular surname in the U.S.?**
アメリカで一番、多い 「姓」は、何だと思いますか。


あなたの姓は、何と言いますか。「姓」は、「苗字」とも言います。日本で一番多い姓は、「佐藤」です。そして、「鈴木」、「高橋」、「田中」と続きます。(2012 年)


アメリカで一番多い「姓」は、つぎのうち、どれだと思いますか。一番から、二番、三番、四番、そして五番まで、順番(order)をつけてください。

Which surname do you think is most popular in the U.S.?  Please number them in ascending order from 1 to 5 in the blanks.
(       ) ジョンソン
(       ) ブラウン
(       ) スミス
(       ) ジョーンズ
(       ) ウィリアムズ

答えは、一番が、スミス、二番がジョンソン、三番が、ウィリアムズ、四番と五番が 同じ数で、ブラウンとジョーンズでした。

|   | Surnames |
|---|---|
| 1 | スミス |
| 2 | ジョンソン |
| 3 | ウィリアムズ |
| 4 & 5 | ブラウンとジョーンズ |

あなたは、正解(correct answer)でしたか。
ヒスパニック系(Hispanic descent) の名前では、「ガルシア」が十八番に入りました。


(2012 年の国勢調査による)
　(According to the year 2012 national census,)

読むれんしゅう Reading practice

と

作文の手引き Compositions guide

[読むれんしゅう **1**]

<u>モニカのゆめ</u>

　あるばん、モニカは、ゆめをみました。ゆめの中で、モニカは、森の中を歩いていました。川に出ると、カエルがいっぴき、泣いています。モニカはふしぎに思って、聞きました。

　　　「かえるさん、どうしたの？」

カエルは、

　　　「目がいたくて、いたくて、たまらないんだ。」

と言いました。
モニカは、カエルをかわいそうに思って、ハンカチを水で　ぬらして、カエルの目をふいてやりました。カエルは、

　　　「ああ、すっかりよくなった。ありがとう。おれいに『まほうのマント』
　　　　をあげるね。」

と言い、モニカに『まほうのマント』をくれました。

　さらに、どんどん森の中を歩いていくと、こんどは、沼に出ました。沼のほとりに、小人がいて、シクシク泣いています。モニカは、聞きました。

　　　「こびとさん、どうしたの？」

すると、小人は、悲しそうに、こう言いました。

　　　「ぼくは、さむくて、さむくて、たまらないんだ。」

モニカは、小人をかわいそうに思って、『まほうのマント』をやりました。

　　　「ああ、あたたかい。ありがとう。おれいに『まほうのつえ』をあげる
　　　　ね。」

と、言って、モニカに『まほうのつえ』をくれました。

さらに、もっと森のおくに入っていくと、今度は、みずうみに出ました。みずうみのほとりに、おじいさんが、いて、おじいさんは、とてもかなしそうに、石の上にすわっていました。モニカは、聞きました。

「おじいさん、どうしたんですか。どこか、わるいのですか。」

すると、おじいさんは、こう言いました。

「わしは、こしがいたくて、いたくて、歩くことができないんじゃ。」

モニカは、おじいさんを　きのどくに思って、こう言いました。

「それじゃ、おじいさんにこの『まほうのつえ』をあげましょう。」

おじいさんは、『まほうのつえ』を持つと、すぐに立ち上がり、こう言いました。

「ありがとう。これで歩くことができる。わしは、おれいがしたいのだが、なにかほしいものが　あるかね？」

モニカは、答えました。
「おじいさん、私には何もほしいものは、ありません。」

そこで、モニカは、目がさめました。なんだか、とてもいい気分の朝でした。

[Vocabulary help]:

| | |
|---|---|
| ゆめをみる | to dream, to have a dream |
| もりのなかをあるく | to walk in the forest |
| かわにでる | to come to the river |
| カエル | a frog |
| ないている（泣いている） | is crying |
| たまらない | unbearable |
| かわいそう | feel sorry; pity |
| ぬらす | to wet something |
| （目を）ふく | to wipe off |
| すっかり | completely |
| おれい | a reward |

| おれいに | as a token of one's thankfulness |
| まほうのマント | a  magic mantle; a cloak |
| さらに | furthermore |
| どんどん | (go ahead) rapidly |
| ぬま | a marsh; a swamp |
| ぬまのほとり | close by; near |
| こびと | a dwarf |
| シクシク（なく） | to sob; to weep |
| まほうのつえ | a magic cane |
| おく | the inner part |
|     もりのおく | deep in the forest |
| みずうみ | a lake |
| どこかわるい | something is wrong |
| こしがいたい | one's hip is hurting |
| きのどくにおもう | to feel pity |
| たちあがる | to stand up |
| めがさめる | to wake up |
| なんだか | somehow |

Answer the following questions in Japanese. つぎの質問に 答えなさい。

1.    ゆめの中で、モニカは、どこにいましたか。

2.    一番はじめに会ったのは、だれでしたか。

3.    なぜ（どうして）モニカは、かわいそうに思ったのですか。

4.    モニカは、何をしてあげたのですか。

5.    おれいに、モニカがもらったのは、何ですか。

6.    二番目に会ったのは、だれでしたか。

7.    なぜ、モニカは、かわいそうに思ったのですか。

8.    モニカは、何をしてあげたのですか。

9.    おれいに、モニカがもらったのは、何ですか。

10. 三番目に会ったのは、だれでしたか。

11. なぜ、モニカは、きのどくに思ったのですか。

12. モニカは、何をしてあげましたか。

13. このひとが、お礼をしたいと言った時、モニカは、何と
こたえましたか。

14. モニカは、朝おきた時、どんな気持ちがしましたか。

[読むれんしゅう **2**]

モニカの四つの宝物：人生で一番だいじなものは？

　モニカは、ある日、洞窟の中で　たくさんの宝物を　見つけました。そこには、小人の番人がいて、モニカにこう言いました。

　「好きなものを　四つだけ、持って行っても　いいよ。」

そこで、モニカはいろいろ　考えたあと、つぎの四つの宝物をえらびました。「まほうの　のみ」、「まほうの仮面」、「まほうのゆびわ」、そして、「まほうのつぼ」です。

　でも、帰り道に　悪魔が　モニカのおくりものを　うばいに来て、こう　言いました。

　「宝物を　よこせ。そうしないと、命がないぞ。」

命が助かるためには、おくりものを、渡さなければなりません。モニカは、「まほうのつぼ」を　渡しました。こうして一番目の悪魔は、「まほうのつぼ」をもらって、喜んで、帰って行きました。

　でも、すぐに、二番目の悪魔が　やって来て、

　「宝物を　よこせ。そうしないと、命がないぞ。」と言いました。

モニカは、「まほうの仮面」を　渡しました。

　すると、そのあとに、三番目の悪魔が　やってきて、

　「宝物を　よこせ。そうしないと、命がないぞ。」と言いました。

モニカは、「まほうの　ゆびわ」と「まほうの　のみ」を　よく見比べてから、「まほうの　ゆびわ」を　渡しました。三番目の悪魔も　宝物をもらって、喜んで帰っていきました。

　もうすぐ、家です。もう悪魔は　やってきませんでした。モニカの手に　残ったのは、「まほうの　のみ」でした。モニカは、幸せでした。

........................................................................................

[Vocabulary help]

| | | | |
|---|---|---|---|
| どうくつ | cave | たからもの | treasures |
| みつける | to find | こびと | midget |
| ばんにん | a guard | もっていく | to bring |
| 〜てもいい | you may do so | えらぶ | to choose |
| まほう | magic | のみ | chisel |
| かめん | mask | ゆびわ | ring |
| つぼ | pot | かえりみち | on the way home |

| | | | |
|---|---|---|---|
| あくま | demon | おくりもの | gift |
| うばう | to rob | うばいにくる | to come to rob |
| よこせ | Give it to me! | いのち | life |
| たすかる | save | わたす | to hand something |
| わたさなければならない _must to hand in_ | | よろこんで | happily |
| やってくる | come along | みくらべる | compare by looking |
| のこる | to remain | しあわせ | happiness |

••••••••••••••••••••••••••••••••••••••••••••••••••••••••••••••••••••••••••••••••••••

1. モニカは、一番目のあくまに、何を　わたしましたか。

2. つぎに、二番目のあくまに、何を　わたしましたか。

3. そして、三番目のあくまに、何を　わたしましたか。

## 解説 (Commentary)

　三人の悪魔は、去り、モニカの命は助かりました。モニカは、みっつのたからものをなくしましたが、自分にとって、命のつぎに、何が一番たいせつか、
なくす _to lose_ 　　　　　　　　next to life 　　　　　　precious
分かったのです。それは、モニカが　あくまに　じゅんばんにわたしたもので、
分かります。　　　　　　　　　　　　　　　　　　in order

　まず、まほうのつぼは、「お金」です。モニカにとって、お金は、あまりだいじ
　　　　　　　　　　　　　　　　　　for Monica
では、ありませんでした。

　つぎに、「まほうの仮面」は、「プライド」(pride)です。モニカにとって、プライドは、お金より、たいせつですが、ほかのふたつほど、だいじではありませんでした。　　　　　　　　　　(It's) not as important as the other two.

　つぎに、モニカは、「まほうのゆびわ」をわたしました。「まほうのゆびわ」は、「愛」(love)です。モニカにとって、「愛」は、「プライド」より、「お金」より、たいせつでした。

　でも、モニカが　さいごまで、わたしたくなかったものが、あります。それ
は　　　　　　something she did not want to hand in till end
「まほうの　のみ」でした。「まほうののみ」は、「向上心」です。モニカにと
　　　　　　　　　　　　　　　　　desire to improve oneself
って、よっつの中で、一番たいせつなものは、「向上心」だったのです。あなたなら、どうしますか。

[English Translation]

Four Treasures of Monica: What's most important in your life?

One day, Monica found a lot of treasures in a cave. There was a midget who was watching the treasures, and he said the following to her:
"You may take four treasures with you, only four though."
Then Monica, after contemplating deeply, chose the next four treasures; magic chisel, magic mask, magic ring and magic pot.
On the way her home, however, a demon appeared before her and demanded a treasure or her life. She gave up on her magic pot and handed it to him. The demon joyfully left her alone.
(As she walks toward her home), next demon appeared. He demanded her life or a treasure. She gave up on her magic mask and handed it to him. The second demon joyfully left her alone.
(When she was close to her home), the third demon appeared. He also demanded her life or a treasure. She looked at both magic ring and magic chisel to compare, and decided to give up on her magic ring and handed it to him. The third demon joyfully left her alone.
It's almost her home. No more demons appeared before her. She looked at what's left in her hand: It was a chisel. Monica was happy.

1. What did Monica hand in to the first demon?
2. What did Monica hand in to the second demon?
3. What did Monica hand in to the third demon?

[Commentary]

Three demons left Monica unharmed and her life was spared. Though Monica lost three precious treasures, she realized next to life what's most important for her. That was revealed by the order in which she had given to the three demons.

First of all, the magic pot means "money." It was the least important to her.

Secondly, the magic mask indicates "pride." It was more important than money to her, but not as important as the other two.

Thirdly, Monica gave her magic ring. It indicates "love." It was more important than money and pride to her, but not as important as the last treasure.

What Monica wanted to keep most, among four, was the magic chisel. The magic chisel represents "desire for self-improvement." It was her "wish to become a better person" that Monica didn't want to give up most strongly. What would you do (if you were Monica)?

Chapter 14 Reading Practice 2: Monica's Decision. 人生で一番大事なものは、何か。

作文の手引き〔てび〕 How to write a composition in Japanese?

Write a short composition about your "recent event さいきんのできごと."

[Brainstorming]
1．さいきん　なにか　<u>とくべつなことが</u>　ありましたか。それは、どんな
　　　　　　　　　　 a special event/thing/happening
　　ことでしたか。あなたにとって、初〔はじ〕めてのことでしたか。

2．それは、どこで　ありましたか。

3．そのとき、だれかと　いっしょに　いましたか。

4．それは、いいことでしたか、わるいことでしたか、<u>めずらしいことでし</u>
　　　　　　　　　　　　　　　　　　　　　　　　　　　　　　　 rare
　　たか。　　うれしいことでしたか、それとも、かなしいことでしたか。

5．それは、<u>どうして　おこりましたか。</u>
　　　　　　 How did it occur?  What caused it?

6．あなたは、それが <u>もういちど、おこってほしいですか。</u>
　　　　　　　　　　　 Do you want it to happen again?

7．そのあと、<u>あなたのかんがえかたに</u>、<u>へんか</u>がありましたか。
　　　　　　 your way of thinking　　　　 change

**<u>Sample composition 1</u>** (1~7 correspond to the brainstorming above)

1．一週間前〔いっしゅうかんまえ〕、<u>山火事〔やまかじ〕</u>がありました。たくさん<u>森〔もり〕</u>や<u>家〔いえ〕</u>が　<u>焼〔や〕けました。</u>
　　　　　　　　　mountain fire　　　　　 forest　　やける to be burnt
　　山火事〔やまかじ〕は、時々〔ときどき〕ありますが、近〔ちか〕くで見〔み〕たのは初〔はじ〕めてです。

2．サンディエゴで　ありました。
3．ともだちといっしょでした。
4．わるいことです。そして、かなしいことです。たくさんの人が家を <u>失〔うしな〕い</u>、<u>動物〔どうぶつ〕</u>
　　　　　　　　　　　　　　　　　　　　　　　 うしなう to lose　　 animals
　　が <u>死〔し〕にました。</u>
　　　 しぬ to die
5．タバコの「ポイ捨て〔す〕」が、<u>原因〔げんいん〕</u>です。(It's caused by cigarette littering.)
　　　　　　　　　　　　　　 a cause
6．もう<u>二度と〔にど〕</u>おこってほし<u>くありません。</u>　(二度と〔にど〕～ない never again)

7. 前は、山火事について、ぜんぜん、かんがえたことがありませんでした
   I have never thought of

   が、今は、もっとみんなに、気をつけてほしいと 言いたいです。
   気をつける to be careful


[Put1〜7 together まとめ] → 作文

---

　一週間前、私は、ともだちといっしょに、サンディエゴへ行きましたが、そこで、山火事を見ました。たくさんの家が焼け、森も焼けました。動物もたくさん死にました。とてもかなしいできごとです。山火事は、時々ありますが、こんなに近くで見たのは初めてでした。

　この火事の原因は、タバコの「ポイ捨て」です。一人の人の不注意が、大きな不幸の原因になりました。こんなことは、もう二度とおこってほしくありません。いままで、山火事について、かんがえたことは、ありませんでしたが、今は、もっとみんなに、気をつけてほしいと 言いたいです。

---

[Vocabulary list from Composition 1]

[Nouns]

| | |
|---|---|
| かんがえかた（考え方） | way of thinking |
| へんか（変化） | change |
| やまかじ（山火事） | mountain fire |
| もり（森） | forest |
| どうぶつ（動物） | animals |
| ポイすて | cigarette littering |
| げんいん（原因） | cause |
| できごと | incident; event |
| ふちゅうい（不注意） | carelessness |
| しょうぼうしゃ | fire engine |

[な Adjectives/Copula Nouns]

| | |
|---|---|
| とくべつ（特別） | special |
| ふこう（不幸） | misery; misfortune; unhappy |

[Adverbs]

| | |
|---|---|
| もういちど | one more time |
| たぶん | perhaps |

[Verbs]

| | |
|---|---|
| おこる（起こる） | to occur |
| やける（焼ける） | to burn; be burnt |
| うしなう（失う） | to lose |
| しぬ（死ぬ） | to die |
| きをつける | to be careful |

## Sample composition 2

1．先週の土曜日に、走り高跳びの大会(high-jump competition)がありました。私は、選手(a representative player)ですから、試合(games)は、初めてではありませんが、大きな大会に出たのは、初めてです。

2．私の大学です。

3．ほかの選手(other players)と　いっしょにいました。

4．はじめは、わるいことのように見えました。でも後で、うれしいことに変わりました。

5．友だちが　励ましてくれたおかげです。(はげます to encourage)

6．もちろん、もう一度、おこってほしいです。

7．今まで、走り高跳びは、孤独な(lonely)スポーツだと思っていました。一人でがんばるだけだと　思っていました。でも、今は、チームのみなといっしょにできるスポーツだと信じています(I believe)。

[Put 1～7 together]→ 作文

---

　　先週の土曜日に、私の大学で走り高跳びの大会がありました。私は、選手ですから、試合は、初めてではありませんが、大きな大会は、初めてでした。それで、すっかりあがってしまい、いつもは、跳ぶことの出来る高さでも、つぎつぎに失敗してしまいました。

　きんちょうして、足が震えて、力が入らないのです。もうだめだと思ったとき、同じチームの仲間が、じっとぼくを見つめていました。その目は、「がんばるんだ。きみなら、ぜったいできるよ。」と言っていました。

　それを見て、なぜか　ぼくは落ち着いて、目の前のバーを見ることができました。そして走り出し、地面を強く蹴って、高く跳んだのです。そのときワーッという、みんなの歓声が　聞こえました。

　ぼくは、りっぱに跳んだんです。これは、仲間が　励ましてくれたおかげです。

　これまで、走り高跳びは、孤独なスポーツだと思っていました。一人でがんばるだけだと　思っていました。でも、今は、チームのみなといっしょにできるスポーツだと信じています。

---

[Vocabulary list from Composition 2]:

1st paragraph:

| | |
|---|---|
| あがる | to get stage fright; get nervous (すっかり completely) |
| いつもは跳ぶことの出来る高さ | the height that I can normally clear (= jump) |
| つぎつぎに | one after another |
| 失敗する | to fail |

2nd paragraph:

| | |
|---|---|
| きんちょうする | to become nervous; get flustered |
| 足が震える | the legs become trembled |
| 力が入らない | cannot put the strength |
| なかま | teammates; friends |
| じっと見つめる | to gaze intently |

3rd paragraph:

| | |
|---|---|
| おちつく | to calm down |
| 走り出す | to dash |
| 地面を蹴る | to kick the ground hard |

4th paragraph:

| | |
|---|---|
| 歓声 | a shout of joy |
| はげます | to cheer |
| こどくな | lonely |

あなたの作文をここに 書きましょう。

```




```

# APPENDICES

# Appendix A: Sentence Endings (Predicate Types Patterns)

| Predicate | | Formal-Polite | Informal-Plain |
|---|---|---|---|
| 1. Noun ------- | Non-past--- ( Affirmative | [Noun]  desu | [Noun]  da |
| | ( Negative | [Noun]  jya arimasen | [Noun]  jya nai |
| | Past------ ( Affirmative | [Noun]  deshita | [Noun]  datta |
| | ( Negative | [Noun]  jya arimasen deshita | [Noun]  jya nakatta |
| II. Adjective -- | Non-past--- ( Affirmative | [Adj. Stem]  - i desu | [Adj. Stem]  - i |
| | ( Negative | [Adj. Stem]  - ku nai desu <br> - ku arimasen | [Adj. Stem]  - ku nai |
| | Past------ ( Affirmative | [Adj. Stem]  - katta desu | [Adj. Stem]  - katta |
| | ( Negative | [Adj. Stem]  - ku nakatta desu <br> - ku arimasen deshita | [Adj. Stem]  - ku nakatta |
| III. Verb ------ | Non-past--- ( Affirmative | [Masu Form]  - masu | [Dictionary Form] |
| | ( Negative | [Masu Form]  - masen | [Nai Form]  - nai |
| | Past------ ( Affirmative | [Masu Form]  - mashita | [Ta form] |
| | ( Negative | [Masu Form]  - masen deshita | [Nai Form]  - nakatta |

# Appendix B: The Origins of Kanji

<u>Chapter 1</u>

1. 一

It illustrates an index finger, showing the number "one."

2. 二

It depicts two fingers, the middle and index, showing "two."

3. 三

It illustrates three fingers – the middle, index and ring – showing "three."

4. 四

It shows four fingers with the thumb held in, indicating "four."

5. 五

It depicts three fingers (on one hand) pointing horizontally and two fingers (on the other hand) pointing vertically, shaping "five."

6. 六

Illustrating one thumb sticking upright and the other fingers held in, shaping "six."

7. 七

It derived from the number "six"; but with the index finger protruding, making "seven."

8. 八

With the index finger and thumb pointing down, and the rest of fingers held in, making "eight."

9. 九

Include an elbow while shaping the number "seven" would bring forth "nine."

10. 十

It illustrates two arms coming together to form a cross.

11. 月

It depicts a crescent moon partially covered by the clouds.

12. 日

It illustrates the shape of the Sun.

13. 本

The bottom of a tree: synonym to the source of knowledge (a book)

14. 円

Originally the round shape of the seashell was the origin of the coins.

Chapter 2 A

15. 大

It illustrates a man standing with legs far apart and arms stretched out.

16. 学

The bottom portion is a "child" and the top portion is his/her decorated hat, ready to go to school to "learn."

17. 生

A new sprout is coming out of the ground

18. 何

Left radical is a person and the right portion is illustrating a person tilting his head to ask a question "what is it?"

19. 白

It illustrates the half moon in your thumb (which is white).

20. 私

Represent the grain for personal use. Left radical means "rice" and the right is the shape of one's elbow (as if showing this rice is mine!)

21. 犬

It illustrates a dog with its tail up.

Chapter 2 B

22. 年

It illustrates the ripening grain.

23. 語

Left radical means "to say" and the top right gives the sound of "go," while the bottom-right illustrates the mouth through which the language is spoken.

24. 田

It illustrates a rice field.

25. 山

It illustrates the mountains.

26. 来

It illustrates rye (plant + grain + leaves).

## Chapter 3 B

27. 百

Indicating a hundred thumbnail (one [一] + white nail skin [白] → a great number; all; hundred)

28. 小

It illustrates a child.

29. 中

A needle is penetrating an object right in the middle.

## Chapter 3 C

30. 千

It illustrates the multiplication of ten by many tens.

31. 万

It illustrates many weeds floating on the water.

32. 水

It depicts the stream of the water.

33. 女

It illustrates a kneeling woman.

34. 色

It illustrates a person with a stick (which make it stands out to recognize the differences → colors)

35. 入

Waves go into a cave.

## Chapter 4 A

36. 先

A person who goes ahead (i.e., a person + his toe + his legs); a tip-end (of a pencil) ; ahead of this position.

37. 人

A man is standing with his legs apart.

38. 今

A sundial (i.e., a person -- dial watcher + hand of dial + shadow made by the sundial indicating time)

39. 上

It illustrates the upper half of an object.

40. 下

It illustrates the lower half of an object.

Chapter 4 B

41. 回

Two circles illustrate the rotation.

42. 分

A sword (刀 かたな) can cut and divide.

43. 言

A person is saying what he thinks.   心 ＋ 口

44. 口

It illustrates the square shape of mouth.

45. 同

Illustrating similar goods stored in a warehouse.

Chapter 4 C

46. 食

Top portion is a man 人 and the bottom is the roots 根: consumption of roots.

47. 気

A rice cooker is letting out steam.   氣 ( 米 is rice)
It means "air, steam, atmosphere, mood, etc."

48. 好

A mother 女 loves her child 子.

49. 方

It depicts a plow.

<u>Chapter 4 D</u>

50. 父

A father is holding a hatchet (ie, ax [斧]; a tribal head's symbol of power).

51. 母

It illustrates a kneeling mother with breasts to nurse.

52. 近

It depicts a tree ax 斧 on its right and a footage of distance on its left, indicating proximity when you hear the sound of an ax chopping wood → near.

53. 子

It illustrates a baby or a child.

54. 兄

It depicts a mouth 口 on top and legs in the bottom, indicating a person capable of instructing the younger with words (or a big brother has always a big moth?).

55. 妹

It depicts a young woman 女 not yet of age 未 (未だ this kanji means "not yet").

56. 目

It depicts the eye, tilted 90 degrees [  ] → [目].

<u>Chapter 4 E</u>

57. 毎

It represents the idea that everyone [人] has a mother 母.

58. 時

It shows an ancient temple （寺） and a sundial （日）.The temple bells told people what time it was.

59. 半

It shows a half and the kanji illustrates the action of cutting in half.

60. 行

Roads.  The left radical shows people's procession and the right portion indicates the streets.

61. 知

Information was obtained by a letter attached to an arrow. (arrow 矢 + mouth 口 [report; letter, words of mouth]

Chapter 5

62.  曜

The left radical is the sun 日, which is high in the sky.  The top-right portion [ヨヨ] came from the feather 羽 and the bottom-right is a bird, making the right portion together a "bird flying"). Combining all parts together makes the meaning of this kanji "bright sunlight" and ultimately "days of the week."

63.  火

It depicts the flames.

64.  木

It illustrates a tree.

65.  金

It depicts men working in a goldmine for gold.

66.  土

It depicts sprout appearing on the earth's surface.

67.  川

It depicts a river.

68.  古

It depicts oral [口] tradition transcending many generations [十].  When the same things are said ten times, it gets old.

69.  男

It depicts a man showcasing strength 力 in the rice field 田.

70.  会

Showing people coming together to dine.

71.  午

It depicts the movement of a pestle, pounding grain up
and down between morning and afternoon → Noon

72.  前

Showing the severance of a man's head from his body with a sword (neck 首  + flesh
肉/月 + sword 刀)

73.  後

The left indicates half of the a crossroad;
the top right, a bundle of thread
(illustrating a painstaking process), and the bottom right,
a foot in a backwards direction →
and all together this kanji represents delay,
backwardness, or falling behind.

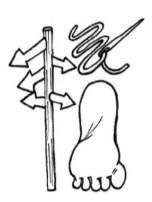

Chapter 6 A

74.  家

It illustrates a housed pig (豚) (under a roof).

75.  遠

It indicates traveling a long way. (Right: 土 [land → road] + 口 [place] + 人 + 人, Left:
traveling). The radical on the left always means "traveling."

76.  新

A standing 立 tree 木  is cut with a hatchet 斧.
A new surface is new and fresh.

77.  車

A cart from top down: wheel, body, and axle.

78. 自

Showing one pointing to oneself (目 eye → face)

Chapter 6 B

79. 見

It depicts a combination of a standing person [人] looking (目) at something.

80. 歩

It depicts few (少) footprints (止).

81. 買

Buying goods in a basket ([四] indicated by the top portion) with money (= seashells 貝 ).

82. 広

The top-left portion is a radical to show a warehouse and the inside shows the emptiness of space within a bent arm (ム).

83. 明

Where the brightness of the sun 日 and moon 月 combines

84. 南

The lighting of a fire (flames [ ソ ] + chimney [十] + house [ left-top-right enclosure]) to heat a room (makes the house as warm as the direction of the South)

85. 東

The sun 日 rising behind a tree 木

86. 朝

The sun 日 rises from the horizon while the moon 月 still remains in the western sky.

87. 光

A man with a torch

88. 西

It depicts a bird returning to the nest when the sun sets in the west.

89.  北

Representing the shape of two people seated back to back (as people tend to turn to the south for warmth)

Chapter 6 C

90.  井

It depicts a well, viewed from the top.

91.  多

It illustrates many evenings (夕 ).

92.  寺

It depicts the government office (土: place, 手: work) transformed into temples.

93.  有

It depicts meat 肉/月 placed on a hand 手.

94.  名

It illustrates a person calling [口] out his name in the evening [夕] to identify himself.

95.  持

Representing the maintenance of a temple (手 hand→ maintain, 寺 temple).

96.  内

It shows one entering a house (人 person, [enclosure] house).

97.  外

A fortuneteller practicing divination (卜: bamboo divining sticks) under a full moon (夕: evening)

98.  少

Representing few (derived from 小).

Chapter 6 D

99.  池

It shows water [水] and a snake [right portion] in a pond.

100.  魚

A fish tilted ninety degrees.

101.  英

Beautiful flowers (the top radical showing "plant" and the bottom 央 meaning "a center"→ prominent; outstanding).

102.  苦

A bitter-tasting plant (the top radical showing "plant" and the bottom portion 古 indicating "old age" → staleness → bitterness).

103.  手

It illustrates the shape of a hand.

104.  赤

It depicts an earthenware kiln (the top portion 土 meaning "earth" and the bottom portion indicating "fire" or a "burn").

105.  黒

Representing black soot in a chimney (the top [里] indicating a "chimney" and the bottom four dots being "soot")

106.  才

Showing a sprout and its roots (where the horizontal line [一] indicates the earth and the last two strokes the sprout and its roots)

107.  若

Illustrating the harvesting of young tea leaves (with the top radical meaning "plant" and the bottom portion 右 meaning "right hand" for picking).

108.  足
A person's leg

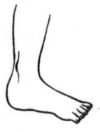

Chapter 7

109.  住

A resident of a house (with the left radical meaning a "person" and the right portion meaning a "master")

110.  和

Stored rice (with the left radical meaning "rice/grain," and the right portion 口 an "opening" → "storehouse," and together it means "harmony, peace, unity")

111.　洋

Illustrating the vastness of the ocean, and how it resembles a large flock of sheep (with the left radical [氵] meaning water, and the right 羊 "sheep").

112.　甘

It depicts something sweet in the mouth.

113.　間

It depicts the sun 日 shining between the slats of a gate 門.

114.　事

Representing clerical work (hand [一] + bamboo plate/paper [口] + hands [ヨ] + writing brush [vertical line]).

115.　戸

It depicts a person [人] under a roof [一].

116.　所

It shows a construction site (戸 door/house + hatchet 斤) → a sight, scene; place.

Chapter 8

117.　力

It shows a man flexing his biceps.

118.　薬

Medicinal plants (with the top radical meaning "plant" and the bottom portion 楽 to "relieve" or "enjoy").

119.　虫

It depicts the picture of a coiled snake.

120.　助

It depicts things piled up (with the left side) are assisted by others' strengths 力.

121.　強

The right side representing a beetle and the left, 弓, strength.

122.　楽

Representing a string instrument being played (with the four strokes on the top right and left indicating strings; [白] representing a fingernail; [木] on the bottom showing that the instrument is made of wood).

Chapter 9 ABC

123.  雨

It illustrates the raindrops under the clouds.

124.  困

It illustrates an enclosed tree (木) that cannot grow.

125.  駅

It shows a train station where horses (馬) are measured (尺) and changed.

126.  帰

A married woman returns to her maiden home. The left side indicates footprints and the right, wife (婦).

127.  記

It depicts a person 己 taking dictation (言).

128.  晴

It depicts the shining sun 日 and blue sky 青.

129.  返

It depicts the action of turning around (反) and proceeding (行).

130.  海

All (毎) living creatures came from the sea (water radical 水).

Chapter 10 A

131.  校

A social club (木 showing a wooden building and 交 meaning socialize).

132.  玉

A king with a jeweled crown (with marbles strung together; and a dot added to distinguish it from 王, king).

133.  肉

It depicts a piece of meat.

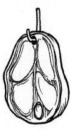

134. 米

It depicts stalks and rice.

135. 友

It illustrates the idea of lending a hand to another.

Chapter 10 B

136. 物

Domestic animals (牛 on the left representing cattle and on the right, a pig 豚) → indicating various things.

137. 牛

It represents the head of a bull.

138. 初

Showing the first step in sewing kimono (the left radical is 衣 [clothes], and the 刀 on the right represents a knife).

139. 辛

A tattoo or acupuncture (with the top portion 立 meaning to "stand" and bottom 十 meaning "needle"). Together, the character means "painful."

Chapter 10 C

140. 切

Cutting wood ([七] on the left meaning "wood" and 刀 on the right a sword)

141. 油

Oil made from seeds (由 showing the image of seeds hanging on a twig) and fluid like water 水.

142. 煮

Burning at the stake (i.e., a person 者 condemned to death by fire [the bottom four dots], 火).

143. 止

It depicts a footprint.

144.   炊

A steam from cooking (left: fire 火, right: steam emanating 欠; 吹く).

145.   作

A person making a house (i.e., person イ/人+ half-done a house [on the right])

Chapter 10 E

146.   文

Showing a person's back being tattooed with patterns.

147.   毛

It illustrates a feather.

148.   茶

Representing the picking of tea leaves (showing tea leaves [草], tea picker [人], tea plant [木] ).

149.   変

(1) It depicts a curing stammering (Originally the top is made of [糸+言+糸]; thread 糸, speak 言, and the bottom is made of a person [丿, 人] + hand [又]).

(2) A bundle of thread and a nail (the top portion + a backward foot 丿+又) → Things do not turn as the way they normally do → unusual; strange; odd).

150.   晩

(1) Releasing [免] from day [日] work → the end of all things → night

(2) The sun [日] setting and spotting a rabbit [         in the moon.

→ 免]

151.   飲

It shows consuming [食] a drink by "opening the mouth" [欠].

152.   石

It depicts stones [口] at the bottom of a cliff [top-left radical].

153.   度

(1) Throwing firewood into a heating stove (house [top-left radical] + stove [top of inside portion] + hand [又]) → degree or temperature).

(2) Measuring the size of a house [top-left radical] by hand [手] many times [top of inside portion = twenty times] → indicating degree/angle.

<u>Chapter 11 A</u>

154.  道
People heading down a road (neck 首 + going [left radical]).

155.  通
It depicts opening the pasture gate, letting cattle out (hand [マ, 手], fence [用], going [left radical]).

156.  信
It depicts belief in what a person イ/人 says 言.

157.  号
It depicts a man shouting (i.e., person 人 [the bottom portion] and [口] roar/mouth) at a tiger 虎. (Original kanji is [号+虎]).

158.  左
It depicts a tool in the left hand ([  the left hand viewed from the side] + a tool 工).

159.  右
(1) It depicts hailing (口) with one's right hand.
(2) It depicts eating (口)) with a right hand.

160.  曲
(1) A round bamboo basket.
(2) Shou (笙), a Japanese reed instrument.

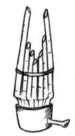

<u>Chapter 11 B</u>

161.  合
It indicates that people come to an agreement (i.e., people [人] discussing [口] a matter [一]).

162.  安
It depicts a woman 女 in a house [家] → comfort; feeling at ease; peaceful.

163.  高
A tall building (chimney [ 、] + roof [亠] + window [口] + house + entrance [口]).

164. 夜

A man returning to his house at night (house [top portion] + person [人] + evening [夕] + enter [入]).

165. 社

It depicts a local guardian deity (revelation ネ、示→ god, land 土→ rural community).

## Chapter 11 C

166. 雪

It depicts he shoveling of snow (rain 雨→ precipitation → snow, hand 手 → shoveling [ヨ]).

167. 立

It depicts a person standing.

168. 札

A person is praying on her/his knees (prayers written on wood 木+ a kneeled person [                    ]).

169. 押

It depicts the back of a hand (i.e., hand [手] + the back of the hand 甲).

170. 用

It means the stacked boards with nails holding them together → "to use" 用いる.

## Chapter 11 D

171. 書

Five fingers all engaged with a brush pen, expressing thought through it (five horizontal lines + a vertical line indicating a brush pen + mouth [口]+ tongue [一]→ saying 日).

172. 昨

A house was made only half-a-way (day 日+ make [作] → a house only half-made "yesterday").

173.  美

In ancient Chinese culture a large sheep was synonym to beauty（large 大 + sheep 羊 → beauty 美.

174.  暗

Indicating silence after closing the gates (gate 門→ 日 + sound 音).

175.  思

It depicts the brain and the heart (skull 口 + brain 田, heart 心).

176.  出

It depicts sprout appearing from the earth (earth 土 + birth 生).

177.  神

It depicts the revelation of a god (god 示 + 申 revelation).

178.  秘

(1) Concealing and storing precious grains (grains [left radical] + fence/divide 必).
(2) Praying to a god secretly in one's mind (god [示] + 心).

179.  音

It depicts the sound formed by mouth (stand up 立→ produce, mouth 口 + tongue 一).

180.  読

Street peddlers calling out to sell (call/say 言 + sell 売).

Chapter 12

181.  弟

Representing the stringing of a bow (tie around [ソ], bow 弓, string [丿] → younger brother's faithful service to his older).

182.  姉

It depicts a working girl (an older sister) in the market (woman 女 + market 市).

183.  背

Showing one's back turned to another (turn back on another 北 + body [月→ 肉 person]).

184. 丈

Showing ten times the length of a person's arm (ten [十] + measurement [diagonal line丶, 尺 shaku) 30.3 cm]).

185. 太

Showing hugeness (big 大 + emphasis [ 、]).

186. 青

A growing sprout from a seed (to appear 出 + to grow 生, seed [月←円 ground/seed])

187. 黄

The color of the "rice field," being "twenty" times more "yellow" than the fire (twenty [廿], rice field 田).

188. 着

It depicts wearing a woolen hood (sheep 羊→ wool, eye 目→ head).


Chapter 13

189. 屋

(1) A house (door 戸 + room 至/室).
(2) A person sleeping under a roof (person 人 + a bird comes and stays).

190. 聞

It depicts listening carefully near a gate (gate 門 + ears/hear 耳).

191. 話

Speaking (say 言 + tongue 舌).

192. 化

A man standing and a man sitting → indicating transformation (person イ/人 + person sitting ヒ )

193. 昔

Many accumulated days (accumulate → [廿] + days 日).

194. 侍

The Imperial guards (A man who guards イ/人 government office 寺).

<u>Chapter 14</u>

195.  花
A transformed plant (plant + changing form 化).

196.  動
It means that one uses strength in moving a heavy object (heavy 重 + strength 力).

197.  鼻
It depicts the profile of a nose (oneself 自, nostrils 田, lips 一, breathing ノ).

198.  低
It depicts a person with a lower ranking (person イ/人, family/clan 氏, lower 一).

199.  怒
It shows a slave's resentment (slave 奴 + heart 心→ resentment).

200.  天
It illustrates a person looking at the sky (person 大/人 + sky [一]).

201.  耳
It depicts a profile of the ear.

202.  形
A square shape and the contour of hair decor (square [井→开], hair decor [ ↝→ 彡→彡 ]).

203.  週
A period/cycle of time (going [辶] + cycle 周).

204.  番
Representing the taking of turns watching rice grow after its seeds are planted (hand ノ, 手, rice 米, rice field 田).

## Appendix C: Japanese-English Glossary

| Roma-ji | Kana (Kanji) | English |
|---|---|---|
| aamondo | アーモンド | almond |
| abiru | （シャワーを）あびる | to take a shower |
| abunai | あぶない | dangerous |
| abura | あぶら　（油） | oil, cooking oil |
| achira | あちら | over that way, over that side (far for both) |
| ageru | あげる | to give |
| ageru | あげる　（上げる） | to lift up; raise |
| aida | あいだ（間） | between |
| aidani | あいだにに | while: during the time period |
| aidea | アイデア | idea |
| airon | アイロン | iron (as in ironing) |
| aisatsu | あいさつ | greetings |
| aisatsu suru | あいさつする | to greet |
| aisu | アイス | iced coffee |
| aisukuriimu | アイスクリーム | ice cream |
| aji | あじ | taste |
| ajia-kei | アジア系 | Asian decent |
| ajimi suru | あじみ　（味見）（を）する | to try taste |
| akachan | あかちゃん | baby |
| akai | あかい | red |
| akarui | あか（明）るい | bright |
| akeru | あける（開ける） | to open (t.v.) |
| aki | あき | fall, autumn |
| akirameru | あきらめる | to give up |
| aku | あく（開く） | to open (i.v.) |
| akuma | あくま | devil |
| amaenboo | あまえんぼう | indulgent child |
| amai | あまい　（甘い） | sweet |
| amaku suru | あまくする | to sweeten |
| amakuchi | あまくち　（甘口） | sweet side, not spicy |
| amanojyaku | あまのじゃく | contrarian |
| amari~ nai | あまり～ない | not very (much) |
| amarinimo | あまりにも | unbearably; extremely |
| ame | あめ（雨） | rain |
| ame | あめ（飴） | candy |
| ame ga furu | あめがふる | to rain |
| Amerika | アメリカ | America |
| amu | あむ（編む） | to knit |
| anata | あなた | you |
| ane-oneesan | あね--おねえさん | older sister (casual)/(formal) |
| angai | あんがい | unexpectedly |
| ani | あに | older brother |
| anime | アニメ | anime (animation) |
| ani-oniisan | あに--おにいさん | older brother (casual)/(formal) |
| an'na | あんな | such ~ as that |
| ano | あの | that (noun modifier) |
| ano-hito-tachi | あのひとたち | they |
| anone | あのね | May I say something? |

| Roma-ji | Kana (Kanji) | English |
|---|---|---|
| Anoo | あのう | An expression showing hesitance |
| an-pan | あんパン | bread with sweet red beans |
| anshin | あんしん（安心） | peace of mind |
| anzen | あんぜん | safe |
| aoi | あおい　（青い） | blue |
| apaato | アパート | apartment |
| ara | あら | Oh (feminine expression of faint surprise) |
| arau | あらう（洗う） | to wash |
| are | あれ | that one over there |
| ari | あり | ant |
| arigatoo | ありがとう | Thank you. |
| arimasu | あります | to exist ("masu" form of "aru") |
| aru | ある | to exist (for inanimate subject) |
| aru tokoro | あるところ | somewhere |
| arubaito | アルバイト | part-time job; side job |
| aruku | ある（歩）く | to walk |
| asa | あさ（朝） | morning |
| asa-gohan | あさごはん | breakfast |
| asa-neboo | あさねぼう | late riser |
| asatte | あさって | the day after tomorrow |
| ashi | あし | legs/feet |
| ashita | あした | tomorrow |
| asobu | あそぶ | to play |
| asoko | あそこ | over there |
| asu | あす | tomorrow |
| asupirin | アスピリン | aspirin |
| atama | あたま | head |
| atarashii | あたら（新）しい | new |
| atari | あたり | around ~ ; vicinity |
| atarimae | あたりまえ | natural, a matter of course |
| atatakai | あたたかい | nice and warm |
| ato | あと | the rest, remaining |
| atsui | あつい | hot |
| au | あう（合う） | to match |
| au | あう（会う） | to meet |
| ayamaru | あやまる | to apologize |
| bacchiri | ばっちり | perfect (casual term) |
| bakku-miraa | バックミラー | rear-view mirror |
| ban | ばん（晩） | evening |
| ban | ばん（番） | ordinal numbers |
| banana | バナナ | banana |
| bando | バンド | (music) band |
| ban-gohan | ばんごはん | dinner |
| baransu | バランス | balance |
| baransu wo toru | バランスをとる | to balance |
| basho/tokoro | ばしょ/ところ | place (specific/ broad sense) |

## Appendix C: Japanese-English Glossary

| Roma-ji | Kana (Kanji) | English |
|---|---|---|
| basu | バス | bus |
| basuketto booru | バスケットボール | basketball |
| basu-tei | バスてい | bus stop |
| beddo | べっど（ベッド） | bed |
| benkyoo | べんきょう | study |
| benkyoo suru | べんきょうする | to study |
| benri | べんり | convenient |
| beruto | べると（ベルト） | belt |
| Betonamu-go | ベトナムご | Vietnamese |
| bideo | ビデオ | video |
| bideo ya | ビデオや （ビデオ屋） | video shop |
| bifuteki | ビフテキ | beef steak |
| biifu | ビーフ | beef |
| bijyutsu | びじゅつ | arts |
| bijyutsukan | びじゅつかん | museum |
| boku | ぼく | male form of "I" |
| booru-pen | ぼうるぺん（ボールペン） | ballpoint pen |
| booshi | ぼうし | hat; cap |
| booto | ボート | boat |
| boottsu to | ボーッと | faintly |
| botan | ボタン | button |
| budoo | ぶどう | grapes |
| bukabuka | ブカブカ | clothing that is too big |
| Bunraku | ぶんらく（文楽） | puppet theatre (also Ningyoo-Jyooruri) |
| bunboogu | ぶんぼうぐ | stationary |
| bungaku | ぶんがく | Literature |
| bunka | ぶんか（文化） | culture |
| burausu | ぶらうす（ブラウス） | blouse |
| burokkori | ブロッコリ | broccoli |
| Bushido | ぶしどう | the way of warriors |
| buta | ぶた | pig |
| butaniku | ぶたにく （豚肉） | pork |
| butsuri | ぶつり | Physics; short form of "butsuri-gaku" |
| byooin | びょういん | hospital |
| byooki | びょうき | illness |
| byoosha | びょうしゃ(描写) | sketch; description |
| chaahan | チャーハン | fried rice |
| chairoi | ちゃいろい | brown |
| chanbara eiga | チャンバラえいが | samurai movie |
| chanto | ちゃんと | correctly; adequately |
| chekku suru | チェックする | to check |
| chichi | ちち | father (humble form, my father) |
| chigau | ちがう | to be different |
| chiisai | ちいさい | small |
| chiizu | チーズ | cheese |
| chiizu-baagaa | チーズバーガー | cheeseburger |
| chiizu-keeki | チーズケーキ | cheesecake |
| chika | ちか | underground |
| chikaku | ちか（近）く | vicinity, nearby |

| Roma-ji | Kana (Kanji) | English |
|---|---|---|
| chikamichi | ちかみち | shortcut |
| chikatetsu | ちかてつ | subway |
| chiketto/ ken | チケット/けん | ticket |
| chikin | チキン | chicken |
| chikin-raisu | チキンライス | chicken rice (fried rice with chicken) |
| chikoku suru | ちこくする | to become late |
| chirachira | ちらちら（チラチラ） | fluttering through air |
| chirashi-zushi | ちらしずし | rice with vinegar topped with egg, seafood |
| chiru | ちる （散る） | to scatter; (flower petals) fall |
| chishiki | ちしき（知識） | knowledge |
| chizu | ちず | map |
| chokin | ちょきん | savings |
| chokin suru | ちょきん（貯金）する | to save |
| chokoreeto | チョコレート | chocolate |
| choodo | ちょうど | exactly |
| choodo ii | ちょうどいい | just fine |
| chooku | チョーク | chalk |
| chotto | ちょっと | little (a little) |
| chuu | ちゅう （中） | medium size |
| chuugakkoo | ちゅうがっこう | junior high school |
| chuugoku-go | ちゅうごくご | Chinese |
| chuu-gukusei | ちゅうがくせい | junior high school students |
| chuuhai | ちゅうハイ | Scotch liquor with water |
| chuui | ちゅうい （注意） | caution |
| chuui ga iru | ちゅういが　いる( 注意が要る) | attention/caution is needed |
| chuukan-shiken | ちゅうかんしけん （中間しけん） | midterm examination |
| chuukosha | ちゅうこしゃ（中古車） | used car |
| chuumon | ちゅうもん | an order |
| chuumon suru | ちゅうもんする | to order |
| chuunen | ちゅうねん （中年) | middle-aged (person) |
| chuurippu | チューリップ | tulip |
| chuusha | ちゅうしゃ | parking |
| chuusha-jyoo | ちゅうしゃじょう | parking lot |
| da | だ | casual form of "desu" |
| dai | だい （大） | big size |
| daidokoro yoohin | だいどころようひん | kitchen utensils |
| daigaku | だいがく | college, university |
| daigakusei | だいがくせい | college student |
| daiji | だいじ | valuable, important |
| daijyoobu | だいじょうぶ(大丈夫) | all right, no problem |
| daikon | だいこん | daikon radish |
| daishoo | だいしょう （大小） | size (big & small) |

## Appendix C: Japanese-English Glossary

| Roma-ji | Kana (Kanji) | English | Roma-ji | Kana (Kanji) | English |
|---------|--------------|---------|---------|--------------|---------|
| daisuki | だいすき（大好き）（な） | most favorite | dondon | どんどん | one after another; spontaneously |
| daiyamondo | ダイヤモンド | diamond | dontsuki | どんつき | dead end (Kyoto dialect) |
| dakara | だから | therefore, for that reason | doo | どう | how |
| dake | だけ | only | Doo itashi mashtie | どういたしまして | you're welcome. |
| dame | だめ | no good | Doo yatte ? | どうやって | how? |
| dare | だれ | who | doobutsu | どうぶつ（動物） | animal |
| dareka | だれか | someone | doobutsu-en | どうぶつえん | zoo |
| darooka | だろうか | I wonder if～ | dooshite | どうして | Why? |
| dasu | だす（出す） | to turn in; to mail; to take out | doraibu | ドライブ | drive |
| de | で | at or in (location of actions) | dore | どれ | which one (among many) |
| de | で | by means of | doresu | ドレス | dress |
| de | で | particle to show limit | doroboo | どろぼう | thief |
| deeto | デート | date | doro-doro | ドロドロ | muddy, thick |
| deeto suru | デートする | to date | doru | ドル | dollar |
| deguchi | でぐち | exit | do-yoobi | どようび | Saturday |
| de-iri | でいり | coming in and out | e | え | picture; drawing |
| deji-kame | デジカメ | digital camera | e wo kaku | （えを）かく | to draw a picture |
| dekakeru | でかける | to go out | edo-jidai | えどじだい | the Edo Period (A.D. 1603～1865) |
| dekiagari | できあがり | It's done～! | eiga | えいが | movie |
| dekigoto | できごと | incident; event | eigakan | えいがかん | movie theatre |
| dekiru | できる | to be able to do | ei-go | えいご | English |
| dekiru | できる | to finish; accomplish | eki | えき | train station |
| demae | でまえ（出前） | food delivery | enjinia | エンジニア | engineer |
| demo | でも | but; however | enpitsu | えんぴつ | pencil |
| demo | でも（Noun でも） | or something like that | erabu | えらぶ | to choose |
| denka seihin | でんかせいひん | electric appliances | erebeetaa | エレベーター | elevator |
| denki ya | でんきや | electric appliance store | esa | えさ | pet food; bait |
| densha | でんしゃ | street car | essei | エッセー | essay |
| dentoo | でんとう（電灯） | lamp; light | esukareetaa | エスカレーター | escalator |
| denwa | でんわ | telephone | fasshon | ファッション | fashion |
| denwa (wo) suru | でんわ（を）する | to make a telephone call | fooku | フォーク | folk |
| denwa bangoo | でんわばんごう | telephone number | fuben | ふべん | inconvenient |
| depaato | デパート | department store | fuchuui | ふちゅうい（不注意） | carelessness |
| deru | でる（出る） | to exit; to leave | fudoosan ya | ふどうさんや | realtor |
| dessan | デッサン | sketching | fujin-fuku | ふじんふく | women's clothing |
| desu | です | to be (copula verb) | fukazake | ふかざけ | excessive drinking |
| detekuru | でてくる（出て来る） | to come out | fukigen (na) | ふきげん（な）（不きげんな） | unhappy, in a bad mood |
| dezain | デザイン | design | fukoo | ふこう（不幸） | misery; misfortune; unhappy |
| disuko | ディスコ | disco | fuku | ふく | to wipe |
| do | ど | degrees | fukuro | ふくろ | sack; bag |
| dochiragawa | どちらがわ | which side | fukusoo | ふくそう | clothing |
| doggufuudo | ドッグフード | dog food | fumikiri | ふみきり | railroad crossing |
| dokitto suru | ドキッとする | to get startled | fun/pun | ふん/ぷん | minutes (time counter) |
| doko | どこ | where | fune | ふね | ship, boat |
| dokushin | どくしん | single; unmarried | fura-dansu | フラダンス | hula dance |
| dokusho | どくしょ（読書） | reading | furaido poteto | フライドポテト | French fries |
| don'na | どんな | What kind of ? | furaito | フライト | flight |
| donata | どなた | (= dareだれ): who | | | |

# Appendix C: Japanese-English Glossary

| Roma-ji | Kana (Kanji) | English |
|---|---|---|
| Furansu-go | フランスご | French |
| furii-uei | フリーウェイ | freeway |
| furimasu | ふります | rain (snow) Ame ga furimasu. (It rains.) |
| furo | （お）ふろ | (hot) bath |
| furu | ふる（降る） | to fall; to snow or rain |
| furueru | ふるえる | to shake; tremble |
| furui | ふるい(古い) | old |
| fushigi | ふしぎ（不思議） | marvelous, strange, miraculous, mysterious |
| fushinsetsu | ふしんせつ | unkind |
| futari | ふたり | two people |
| futatsu | ふたつ | two (general counter for small items) |
| futoi | ふとい | thick |
| futoru | ふとる（太る） | to gain weight |
| futsuu | ふつう | usually, ordinarily |
| futtobooru | フットボール | football |
| fuufu | ふうふ | married couple |
| fuusoku | ふうそく（風速） | wind velocity (speed) |
| fuyu | ふゆ | winter |
| ga | が | but or although |
| gaikokugo | がいこくご | foreign languages |
| gake | がけ | cliff |
| gakka | がっか | academic subjects |
| gakki | がっき | musical instruments |
| gakkoo | がっこう | school |
| gakuchoo | がくちょう | university president |
| gakunen | がくねん | school year |
| gakusei | がくせい | student |
| gakusei-ka | がくせいか | student office |
| gamanzuyoi | がまんづよい | patient |
| gamu | がむ（ガム） | gum |
| gan | ガン（がん） | cancer |
| ganbaru | がんばる | to work hard |
| gariben | がりべん（ガリ勉） | cram; grinding |
| gashan | ガシャン | crack! (noise) |
| gengo-gaku | げんごがく | Linguistics |
| gen'in | げんいん（原因） | cause |
| genki | げんき | healthy; energetic |
| geshuku | げしゅく | boarding house |
| gesuto | ゲスト | guest |
| getsu-yoobi | げつようび | Monday |
| gimon | ぎもん | question, doubt |
| ginkoo | ぎんこう | bank |
| gitarisuto | ギタリスト | guitarist |
| gizagiza | ぎざぎざ | corrugation |
| goboo | ごぼう | burdock root |
| Gobusata shiteimasu | ごぶさたしています。 | Excuse me (for long absence) |
| gochagocha | ごちゃごちゃ | cluttered |
| gochisoo | ごちそう | feast |
| gochisoo sama (deshita) | ごちそうさま（でした） | thank you for the meal |

| Roma-ji | Kana (Kanji) | English |
|---|---|---|
| go-chuumon | ごちゅうもん | polite form of "chuumon" |
| gogaku | ごがく（語学） | languages |
| go-gatsu | ごがつ（五月） | May |
| gogo | ごご | P.M. afternoon |
| gohan | ごはん | meal, cooked rice |
| gohan wo tsukuru | ごはんをつくる | to cook |
| gokugoku | ゴクゴク | gulping liquid |
| gomen | ごめん | I'm sorry (casual form) |
| gomen kudasai | ごめんください。 | excuse me (used as greeting) |
| gomen'nasai | ごめんなさい | I'm sorry. |
| gomi-bako | ごみばこ | trash bin |
| go-riyaku | ごりやく | benefit |
| goro (gurai) | ごろ（ぐらい） | about, around |
| gorufu | ゴルフ | golf |
| go-shujin | ごしゅじん | husband (polite form) |
| go-shuugi | ごしゅうぎ | gratuity |
| Gozaimasu | ございます | polite form of "arimasu" |
| gozen | ごぜん | A.M., morning |
| gozen-chuu | ごぜんちゅう | during the morning (hours) |
| guramu | グラム | gram |
| gurutto (mawaru) | ぐるっと（まわる） | (going) round |
| guuzen | ぐうぜん | by chance; coincidently |
| gyooza | ぎょうざ | dumpling |
| gyuuniku | ぎゅうにく（牛肉） | beef |
| gyuunyuu | ぎゅうにゅう | milk |
| ha | は（葉） | leaf |
| ha | は（歯） | teeth |
| ha-burashi | はブラシ | tooth brush |
| hachi-gatsu | はちがつ（八月） | August |
| hachi-ue | はちうえ | potted plants |
| hagaki | はがき | post card |
| hagemu | はげむ（励む） | to make an effort; to work hard |
| haha | はは | mother (humble form) |
| hai | はい | Yes |
| hairu | はいる（入る） | to enter ~ (~ ni hairu) |
| hajimaru | はじまる | to begin |
| hajime | はじめ（初め） | the beginning, first |
| hajime ni | はじめに | at first |
| Hajimemashite | はじめまして | Pleased to meet you. |
| hako | はこ | box |
| haku | はく | to wear (items below waistline such as pants, skirt) |
| hamachi | はまち | yellow tail |
| ha-migaki | はみがき | tooth paste |
| hamu | ハム | ham |

## Appendix C: Japanese-English Glossary

| Roma-ji | Kana (Kanji) | English |
|---|---|---|
| han | はん | half-hour; thirty minutes |
| hana | はな （鼻） | nose |
| hana | はな （花） | flower |
| hana ya | はなや | flower shop |
| hanabi | はなび（花火） | firework |
| hanasu | はなす（話す） | to speak, talk |
| hanbaagaa | ハンバーガー | hamburger |
| hando-mikisaa | ハンドミキサー | hand mixer |
| hankachi | はんかち（ハンカチ） | handkerchief |
| han'nin | はんにん（犯人） | criminal |
| hansamu | ハンサム | handsome |
| hanzai | はんざい | crime |
| harahara | はらはら（ハラハラ） | light, thin objects, or liquid of a dewy |
| hareru | はれる （晴れる） | to become a nice day |
| harigami | はりがみ | poster |
| harikeen | ハリケーン | hurricane |
| haru | はる | spring |
| hashi | はし（橋） | bridge |
| hashi (o-hashi) | （お）はし | chopsticks |
| hashiru | はしる（走る） | to run |
| hata | はた | flag |
| hataraku | はたらく | to work |
| hatsuon | はつおん（発音） | pronunciation |
| hayai | はやい | early |
| hayakuchi-kotoba | はやくちことば | tongue twister |
| hayaoki | はやおき | early bird |
| hazu (da) | はず（だ） | to be expected (supposed) to ~ |
| hazukashii | はずかしい | shy; embarrassed |
| hebi | へび | snake |
| Hee | へえ | Hmm!, Wow! |
| heiki | へいき（平気） | no bother; nonchalant |
| hen na | へんな （変な） | strange, weird |
| henji | へんじ （返事） | reply |
| henka | へんか（変化） | change |
| herikoputaa | ヘリコプター | helicopter |
| heta | へた（下手） | poor, unskilled |
| heya | へや | room |
| hi | ひ （火） | fire |
| hidari | ひだり（左） | left |
| hidarite | ひだりて（左手） | on the left hand side |
| hidoi | ひどい | terrible |
| higashi | ひがし（東） | East |
| hikidashi | ひきだし | drawer |
| hikkomijian | ひっこみじあん | diffident |
| hikooki | ひこうき | airplane |
| hiku | ひく（弾く） | to play (music instruments) |
| hima | ひま | free (time) |
| himawari | ひまわり | sunflower |
| himojii | ひもじい | starving |
| hinomiyagura | ひのみやぐら | fire-watch tower |
| hiroi | ひろ（広）い | spacious |
| hiru | ひる | daytime |
| hiru-gohan | ひるごはん | lunch |
| hirune | ひるね | nap |
| hitai | ひたい | forehead |
| hito | ひと （人） | person, people |
| hito hako | ひとはこ （一箱） | counter for boxes |
| hito ni yoru | ひとによる | to depend on a person |
| hitoban | ひとばん（一晩） | one night |
| hitomae | ひとまえ （人前） | in public |
| hitori | ひとり | one person, alone |
| hitori dake | ひとりだけ | only one person |
| hitori-bun | ひとりぶん | one serving (for one person) |
| hitoride | ひとりで | alone |
| hitori-k-ko | ひとりっこ | single child (a single child) |
| hitosashiyubi | ひとさしゆび | index finger |
| hitotsu | ひとつ（一つ） | one (general counter for small objects) |
| hitotsu zutsu | ひとつずつ | one by one |
| hitotsume | ひとつめ（一つ目） | first (the first) |
| hitsuji | ひつじ | sheep |
| hitsuyoo | ひつよう（必要） | necessary |
| hiyasu | ひやす（冷やす） | to cool |
| hiyoko | ひよこ | chick |
| hiza | ひざ | knees |
| hiza wo tsuku | ひざをつく | to get on one's knees |
| hizuke | ひづけ（日付） | date |
| hodoo | ほどう | sidewalk |
| hoho/hoo, hoppeta | ほほ（ほお、ほっぺた） | cheeks |
| hohoemi | ほほえみ | smile |
| hoka | ほか | other |
| hokori | ほこり | dust |
| hokusei | ほくせい（北西） | Northwest |
| hokutoo | ほくとう（北東） | Northeast |
| hon | ほん | book |
| hon ya | ほんや | bookstore |
| hon'nori | ほんのり | slightly |
| hontate | ほんたて | bookshelf |
| honto(o) | ほんと（う） | true |
| hoo (~ no hoo) | ほう（～のほう） | side of |
| hoorensoo | ほうれんそう | spinach |
| hooseki | ほうせき | jewelry |
| hora | ほら | Look! |
| hoshii | ほしい | is desired; is wanted |
| hoshizora | ほしぞら（星空） | night sky with stars |
| hotate sarada | ほたてサラダ | scallop salad |
| hotto | ホット | hot coffee |
| hyakuten | ひゃくてん | one hundred points |
| hyoojyungo | ひょうじゅんご（ひょうじゅん語） | standard language |
| ichi nichi | いちにち（一日） | one day |

## Appendix C: Japanese-English Glossary

| Roma-ji | Kana (Kanji) | English |
|---|---|---|
| ichi-ban | いちばん | number one; best (or most) |
| ichiban-shita | いちばんした | the lowest; the youngest |
| ichiban-ue | いちばんうえ | the highest; the oldest |
| ichido | いちど （一度） | once, one time |
| ichi-gatsu | いちがつ（一月） | January |
| ichijiku | いちじく | figs |
| ichi-nen-sei | いちねんせい | freshman, first-year student |
| ichi-nichi-jyuu | いちにちじゅう | all-day long |
| igirisu-shiki | イギリスしき（式） | British style |
| ii | いい | good |
| iie ( or ie) | いいえ （いえ） | no |
| ijyoo | いじょう （〜以上） | more than ~ |
| ika | いか | squid |
| ikimono | いきもの | living things |
| ikiru | いきる | to live |
| ikkai | いっかい | once |
| ikko | いっこ （一個） | counter for non-flat, small items |
| iku | いく （行く） | to go |
| Ikura desu ka. | いくらですか。 | How much is it? |
| ima | いま | now |
| imasu | います | to exist (for animate things) |
| imeeji | イメージ | image |
| imi | いみ | meaning |
| imooto | いもうと | younger sister |
| interi | インテリ | intelligent |
| inu | いぬ | dog |
| ippai | いっぱい | full |
| ippon | いっぽん （一本） | counter for long items |
| ipponme | いっぽんめ（一本目） | the first |
| irasshai mase | いらっしゃいませ | may I help you? |
| irassharu | いらっしゃる | to go, come, & stay in a polite form |
| irasuto | イラスト | illustration |
| ireru | いれる （入れる） | to insert, put in |
| ireru | いれる （煎れる） | to make (as in tea or coffee) |
| ireru | いれる | to turn on (like a switch) |
| irezumi | いれずみ | tattoo |
| iriguchi | いりぐち | entrance |
| iro | いろ | color |
| iroiro | いろいろ | variety; many |
| iru | いる （居る） | to exist (for animate subject) |
| iru | いる （要る） | to need |
| isha | （お）いしゃ（さん） | medical doctor |
| ishi | いし （石） | stone; rock |
| isogu | いそぐ | to hurry |
| isoide | いそいで | in a hurry |
| issho ni | いっしょに | together |
| isu | いす | chair |
| itadakimasu | いただきます | I humbly receive this |
| itadaku | いただく | to receive (humble form) |
| itai | いたい | painful |
| itameru | いためる（炒める） | to stir-fry |
| Itari(y)a-go | イタリアご | Italian |
| itasu | いたす | to do (humble form) |
| itazura | いたずら | mischievous |
| itoko | いとこ | cousin |
| itsu | いつ | when |
| itsuka | いつか | some time |
| itsumo | いつも | always |
| itsutsu | いつつ | five |
| itte (i)rasshai | いって（い）らっしゃい | greeting to see someone off |
| itte kimasu | いってきます | I'm leaving |
| iu | いう （言う） | to say |
| iya | いや | dislikable; unpleasant |
| ji | じ （字） | letters; characters; handwriting |
| ji | じ （時） | o'clock (time counter) |
| jibun | じぶん（自分） | oneself |
| jidoosha | じどうしゃ（自動車） | car; automobile |
| jihanki | じはんき(自販機) | vending machine |
| jiinzu | ジーンズ | jeans |
| jikan | じかん(時間) | time (hours of duration) |
| jiko | じこ （事故） | accident |
| jikoshookai suru | じこしょうかい（を）する | to introduce oneself |
| jimu | ジム | gym |
| jimusho | じむしょ | office |
| jinbutsu | じんぶつ （人物） | people, character |
| jinbutsu-byoosha | じんぶつびょうしゃ(人物描写) | description of people, sketch of people |
| jinjya | じんじゃ | Shinto shrine |
| jisho | じしょ | dictionary |
| jitensha | じてんしゃ | bicycle |
| jitsuwa | じつは | To tell you the truth |
| jogingu | ジョギング | jogging |
| jya | じゃ | in that case, then |
| jya mata | じゃ また | see you later |
| jyagaimo | じゃがいも | potato |
| jyamu | ジャム | jam |
| jyanai | じゃない | casual form of ではありません |
| jyanpu suru | ジャンプする | to jump |
| jyazu | ジャズ | jazz |
| jyoobu | じょうぶ | strong; healthy; sturdy |
| jyoodan | じょうだん | joke |

## Appendix C: Japanese-English Glossary

| Roma-ji | Kana (Kanji) | English |
|---|---|---|
| jyooge | じょうげ（上下） | top and bottom (high and low) |
| jyoozu | じょうず（上手） | good, skilled |
| jyoshi | じょし | girls |
| jyugyoo | じゅぎょう | lecture |
| jyugyoo ni deru | じゅぎょうにでる | to attend a class |
| jyugyoochuu | じゅぎょうちゅう | during the class |
| jyunban | じゅんばん（順番） | order |
| jyunbi | じゅんび | preparation |
| jyuu-gatsu | じゅうがつ（十月） | October |
| jyuu-ichi-gatsu | じゅういちがつ（十一月） | November |
| jyuu-ni-gatsu | じゅうにがつ（十二月） | December |
| jyuusho | じゅうしょ | address |
| ka | か | question (particle marking a question) |
| kaaten | かあてん（カーテン） | curtain |
| kaban | かばん | bag; briefcase |
| kabe | かべ | wall |
| kabin | かびん | flower vase |
| kabocha | かぼちゃ | Japanese squash |
| kabuki | かぶき | Kabuki theater |
| kaburu | かぶる | to wear; put on (on the head) |
| kado | かど | corner |
| kaeru | かえる（帰る） | to go home; to return |
| kaeru | かえる（蛙） | frog |
| kaesu | かえす（返す） | to return something |
| kaette | かえって | rather; on the contrary |
| kafeteria | カフェテリア | cafeteria |
| kagaku | かがく（化学） | Chemistry |
| kagakusha | かがくしゃ（科学者） | scientist |
| kagami | かがみ | mirror |
| kagu | かぐ | furniture |
| kai | （〜）かい（階） | counter for floors of a bldg. |
| kai | （〜）かい・(回) | times; frequency |
| kaidan | かいだん（階段） | stairs |
| kaigoo | かいごう（会合） | meeting |
| kaimasu | かいます | buy |
| kaimono | かいもの | shopping |
| kaisha | かいしゃ（会社） | company |
| kaishain | かいしゃいん/サラリーマン | company employee |
| kaji | かじ（火事） | fire |
| kakaru | かかる（おかねがかかる） | to cost |
| kakaru | かかる（じかんがかかる） | to take (time) |
| kakaru | かかる（かぎがかかる） | to lock |
| kakeru | （メガネ）をかける | to wear (glasses) |

| Roma-ji | Kana (Kanji) | English |
|---|---|---|
| kakeru | かける | to hang |
| kaki-goori | かきごおり | shaved ice |
| kakkoyoku | かっこよく | cool |
| kaku | かく（描く） | to draw |
| kaku | かく（掻く） | to scratch |
| kaku | かく（書く） | to write |
| kame | かめ | turtle |
| kamera ya | カメラや | camera shop |
| kami | かみ（紙） | paper |
| kami | かみ（髪） | hair |
| kami wo toku | かみをとく | to comb |
| kana? | 〜かな？ | I wonder? |
| kanarazu | かならず（必ず） | for sure, definitely |
| kanari | かなり | quite |
| kanashii | かなしい | sad |
| kandenchi | かんでんち | batteries |
| kangaekata | かんがえかた（考え方） | way of thinking |
| kangaeru | かんがえる（考える） | to think; contemplate |
| kangaruu | カンガルー | kangaroo |
| kanji | かんじ（感じ） | feeling |
| kanjiru | かんじる | to feel |
| kankan (ni) | かんかん（に） | blazing sun, or extreme anger |
| kankoku-go | かんこくご | Korean |
| kanojyo | かのじょ（彼女） | she; girlfriend |
| kantan | かんたん | easy; simple |
| kao | かお（顔） | face |
| kapuchiino | カプチーノ | cappuccino |
| kara | から | conjunctive particle "because" |
| kara | から | from |
| karada | からだ（体） | body |
| karai | からい（辛い） | spicy (taste); salty |
| karakuchi | からくち（辛口） | spicy (taste) |
| kare | かれ | he, boyfriend |
| karee-raisu | カレーライス | curry rice (curry on rice) |
| karera | かれら | they |
| kariru | かりる（借りる） | to borrow |
| kasa | かさ | umbrella |
| kashikomari mashita | かしこまりました | understood (humble form) |
| kashu | かしゅ（歌手） | singer |
| kasu | かす（貸す） | to loan |
| kata | かた（方） | person; politer than "hito" |
| kata | かた（肩） | shoulders |
| katachi | かたち（形） | shape |
| katai | かたい（固い） | hard, firm |
| katamari | かたまり | chunk |
| kataru | かたる（語る） | to narrate |
| katazukeru | かたづける | to tidy up |
| kau | か（買）う | to buy |

## Appendix C: Japanese-English Glossary

| Roma-ji | Kana (Kanji) | English |
|---|---|---|
| kawa | かわ（川） | rivers |
| kawagutsu | かわぐつ | leather shoes |
| kawaii | かわいい | cute |
| kawaku | かわく/ かわいている | to become dry or thirsty |
| kawaru | かわる（変わる） | to undergo a change |
| ka-yoobi | かようび | Tuesday |
| kayui | かゆい | itchy |
| kazaru | かざる | to decorate |
| kaze | かぜ | a cold |
| kaze wo hiku | かぜをひく | to catch a cold |
| kazegusuri | かぜぐすり | cold medicine |
| kazoku | かぞく | family |
| ke | け（毛） | hair, fur |
| ke no iro | けのいろ（毛の色） | the color of hair or fur |
| kedo | けど | though, but… |
| keeki | ケーキ | cake |
| kehoo; (o) kehoo | （お）けしょう | make-up |
| kei | ～けい　（系） | system; course |
| keidai | けいだい（境内） | temple yard |
| keiei susru | けいえいする | to run (business) |
| keiji | けいじ（刑事） | detective |
| keimusho | けいむしょ | prison |
| keitaidenwa | けいたいでんわ | cell phone |
| keiyakusho | けいやくしょ | contract |
| keizai(-gaku) | けいざい（がく） | Economics |
| keizaiteki | けいざいてき | economical |
| kekkon | けっこん | marriage |
| kekkoo | けっこう | fairy well, the same as かなり |
| kekkoo desu | けっこうです | No thank you ~. |
| ken | （～）けん（軒） | counter for houses/buildings |
| kenka | けんか | fight; quarrel |
| kenkoo | けんこう | healthy |
| kenkyuu | けんきゅう | research |
| keshigomu | けしごむ | eraser |
| keshiki | けしき | scenery |
| keshoohin | けしょうひん | cosmetics |
| kesu | けす | to erase |
| ki | き（木） | tree |
| ki ga suru | き（気）がする | to feel like |
| ki ga tsuku | き（気）がつく | to notice |
| ki wo tsukeru | きをつける（気をつける） | to be careful |
| kicchin | キッチン（だいどころ） | kitchen |
| kieru | きえる（消える） | to extinguish; disappear |
| kii-horudaa | きいほるだあ（キーホルダー） | key holder |
| kiiroi | きいろい（黄色い） | yellow |
| kiken | きけん | dangerous |
| kikoeru | きこえる | to be audible |
| kiku | きく（聞く） | to ask; inquire |

| Roma-ji | Kana (Kanji) | English |
|---|---|---|
| kiku | きく（聞く） | to listen |
| kimi | きみ | you (male or casual form) |
| kimochi | きもち（気持ち） | feelings |
| kimono | きもの | Japanese kimono |
| kin | きん | gold |
| kinben | きんべん（勤勉） | diligence; hard work |
| kingyo | きんぎょ | gold fish |
| kiniiru | きにいる（気に入る） | to like |
| kin'iro | きんいろ（金色） | gold (golden color) |
| kinjyo no hito | きんじょのひと | neighbor |
| kin'niku | きんにく（筋肉） | muscles |
| kinoo | きのう | yesterday |
| kinu | きぬ | silk |
| kin-yoobi | きんようび | Friday |
| kirei (na) | きれい（な） | pretty, clean |
| kirimasu | きります（切ります） | cut |
| kirin | きりん | giraffe |
| kiru | きる（切る） | to cut |
| kiru | きる（着る） | to wear (over the shoulders like a shirt) |
| kisetsu | きせつ | season |
| kisoku | きそく | rules; regulations |
| kissaten | きっさてん | coffee shop |
| kitanai | きたない | dirty |
| kitsune | きつね | fox |
| kitsune iro | きつねいろ | fox color; light brown |
| kitte | きって | stamps |
| kitto | きっと | surely, certainly, probably |
| koara | コアラ | koala |
| kochira | こちら | this way, this side (close to the speaker) |
| kochira-sama | こちらさま | this person (polite form) |
| kodomo | こども | child, children |
| koi | こい（鯉） | carp (koi/fish) |
| koibito | こいびと（恋人） | lover |
| koko | ここ | here (this place) |
| kokonotsu | ここのつ | nine |
| kokoro | こころ（心） | heart |
| kokuban | こくばん | blackboard |
| kokuban-keshi | こくばんけし | blackboard eraser |
| komaru | こまる（困る） | to be troubled |
| komatta koto | こまったこと | something that troubles you |
| kome | こめ（米） | rice |
| komono | こもの | small items; accessory |
| komu | こむ/こんでいる | to become crowded |
| Kon'nichiwa | こんにちは | Good afternoon. Hello. |
| Konbanwa | こんばんは | Good evening. |
| konbini | コンビニ | convenience store |

## Appendix C: Japanese-English Glossary

| Roma-ji | Kana (Kanji) | English |
|---|---|---|
| kondo | こんど | this time; last time |
| kongakki | こんがっき | this semester |
| kon-getsu | こんげつ | this month |
| kono | この | this (noun modifier) |
| kono chikaku | このちかく | near here, vicinity |
| konohen | このへん | this neighborhood |
| konpyuutaa | こんぴゅうたあ（コンピューター） | computer |
| konpyuutaa saiensu | コンピューターサイエンス | Computer Science |
| konsaato | コンサート | concert |
| konshuu | こんしゅう | this week |
| kontakuto-renzu | コンタクトレンズ | contact lenses |
| kon'ya | こんや　（今夜） | tonight |
| kon-yaku | こんやく | marriage engagement |
| kon'yaku suru | こんやくする | to get engaged |
| kooban | こうばん | police station |
| koocha | こうちゃ | red tea; black tea |
| kooen | こうえん（公園） | park |
| koogaku | こうがく　（工学） | Engineering |
| koogaku-bu | こうがくぶ | Engineering Department |
| koohii | コーヒー | coffee |
| kookoo | こうこう | high school |
| koora | コーラ | Coke |
| koori | こおり　（氷） | ice |
| kooru | こおる（凍る） | to freeze |
| koosaten | こうさてん | intersection |
| koppu | コップ | tumbler (Portuguese origin "kop") |
| kore | これ | this one (near the speaker) |
| kore-gurai | これぐらい | this much; about this size |
| korekara | これから | now, from now on |
| koshi | こし | hips |
| kotae | こたえ | answer |
| kotatsu | こたつ | quilt frame (with heater inside) |
| koto | こと | thing (abstract thing(s)) |
| koto ga dekiru | ことができる | to be able to ~, can do ~ |
| kotoba | ことば | word, language |
| kotori | ことり | small bird |
| kotoshi | ことし（今年） | this year |
| kowai | こわい | scared; scary |
| koyubi | こゆび | little finger; pinkie |
| kozukai | こづかい　（おこづかい） | allowance |
| kubi | くび | neck |
| kuchi moto | くちもと　（口元） | mouth, and around the mouth |
| kuchi ni suru | くち（口）にする | to mention; say |

| Roma-ji | Kana (Kanji) | English |
|---|---|---|
| kuchi no hashi | くちのはし　（口の端） | the edges of a mouth |
| kuchibiru | くちびる | lips |
| kudamono | くだもの | fruits |
| kudamono ya | くだものや | fruit shop |
| kudasai | ください | Please give me. |
| ku-gatsu | くがつ（九月） | September |
| kugi | くぎ | nail |
| kujira | くじら | whale |
| kumori | くもり | cloudy |
| kuni | くに | country |
| kuraberu | くらべる(比べる) | to compare |
| kurabu | クラブ | club activities at school |
| kurai | くらい（暗い） | dark |
| kurasu | クラス | class, lecture, classroom |
| kurayami | くらやみ(暗やみ) | darkness |
| kureru | くれる | to give (me/my in-group) |
| kuri | くり | chestnut |
| kuriimu | クリーム | cream (also for milk) |
| kurisumasu | クリスマス | Christmas |
| kuro | くろ | black (noun form) |
| kuroi | くろい | black (adjectival form) |
| kuroo | くろう | effort |
| kuru | くる（来る） | to come |
| kuru-kuru | くるくる | onomatopoeia for going around |
| kuruma | くるま | car |
| kurushii | くるしい | suffering |
| kusukusu | くすくす（クスクス） | laughter (low, stifled) |
| kusuri | くすり(薬) | medicine |
| kusuriya | くすりや | drugstore, pharmacy |
| kusuriyubi | くすりゆび | ring finger |
| kutsu | くつ | shoes |
| kutsu ya | くつや | shoe shop |
| kutsushita | くつした | socks |
| kuttsuku | くっつく | to adhere; get closer (casual form) |
| kuuki | くうき | air |
| kuuraa | クーラー | air conditioner |
| kuyashii | くやしい | regrettable; vexing |
| kyabetsu | キャベツ | cabbage |
| kyanpasu | キャンパス | campus |
| kyonen | きょねん | last year |
| kyoo | きょう | today |
| kyoodai | きょうだい | siblings |
| kyooiku-gaku | きょういくがく | Education |
| kyoojyuu | きょうじゅう（今日中） | within today |
| kyookasho | きょうかしょ | textbook |
| kyooshitsu | きょうしつ | classroom |

## Appendix C: Japanese-English Glossary

| Roma-ji | Kana (Kanji) | English |
|---|---|---|
| kyoro-kyoro suru | きょろきょろする | to look around repeatedly |
| Kyooto | きょうと | Kyoto, ancient capital of Japan |
| Kyooto-ben | きょうとべん（京都弁) | Kyoto dialect |
| kyuukoo | きゅうこう （休校) | school being closed |
| kyuuri | きゅうり | cucumber |
| kyuuto | キュート | cute |
| maa maa | まあまあ | so so |
| machi | まち | town |
| machi awase | まちあわせ | arrangement for a meeting |
| machigaeru | まちがえる | to make a mistake |
| mada | まだ | yet, still |
| made | まで | up to, until, as far as |
| mado | まど | window |
| mae | まえ | front |
| magarikado | まがりかど | corner (turning corner) |
| magaru | まがる（曲がる) | to turn |
| maguro | まぐろ | tuna fish |
| maido | まいど | every time |
| maiku | マイク | microphone |
| mainichi | まいにち | everyday |
| mairu | まいる | to come humbly |
| manabu | まなぶ | to learn |
| manga | まんが | comic books |
| maniau | まにあう （間に合う) | to make it in time |
| man'naka | まんなか | middle, center |
| man'nen hitsu | まんねんひつ | fountain pen |
| manzoku | まんぞく | satisfaction |
| marude | まるで | as if |
| massugu (ni) | まっすぐ （に) | straight |
| mata | また | again |
| mataseru | またせる | to make someone wait |
| matsu | まつ （待つ) | to wait |
| matsuge | まつげ | eye lashes |
| mayonaka | まよなか （真夜中) | midnight |
| mayu (ge) | まゆ(げ) （まゆ毛) | eyebrow |
| mazeru | まぜる （混ぜる) | to mix |
| mazushii | まずしい | poor |
| me | め （目) | eye(s) |
| me (~ me) | ～ め （目) | ordinal numbers |
| me ga sameru | めがさめる | to wake up |
| meeru wo suru | メールをする | to email |
| meetoru | メートル | meter (unit) |
| megane | めがね | eye glasses |
| megusuri | めぐすり （目薬) | eye drop |
| mendoo | めんどう | troublesome |
| mezamashi-dokei | めざましどけい | alarm clock |
| mezurashii | めずらしい | rare |
| michi | みち （道) | street, way |
| michi no ikikata | みちの行きかた | how to get there |

| Roma-ji | Kana (Kanji) | English |
|---|---|---|
| michinari (ni) | みちなり （に) | along with the street |
| midori | みどり | green |
| mieru | み （見) える | to be visible |
| migaku | みがく | to polish; brush |
| migi | みぎ(右) | right |
| migite | みぎて | on the right-hand side |
| migoto | みごと （見事) | splendid |
| miito soosu | ミートソース | spaghetti with meat sauce |
| mikan | みかん | tangerine |
| mikkusu sando | ミックスサンド | mixed sandwich |
| mimi | みみ | ears |
| mimizuku | みみずく | horned owl |
| min'na | みんな | everyone |
| minami | みなみ （南) | South |
| minami-gawa | みなみ （南) がわ | south side |
| Minami-za | みなみざ | Kabuki theater in Kyoto |
| miru | みる （見る) | to see, look, watch |
| mirugai | みるがい | giant clam |
| miruku | ミルク | milk |
| miruku sheeku | ミルクシェーク | milk shake |
| miryokuteki ni | みりょくてきに | attractive |
| mise | みせ | store |
| misoshiru | みそしる | miso soup |
| mitaini | みたいに | adverbial form of "mitai" (seems like) |
| mitaini mieru | みたいにみえる （見える) | looks like~, seems like ~ |
| mitarashi-dango | みたらしだんご | small rice ball on a stick |
| mitsu | みつ （蜜) | honey |
| mitsukeru | みつける （見つける) | to find |
| mittsu | みっつ | three |
| mizu | みず （水) | water |
| mo | も | also |
| mo | も | for emphasis, as many as ~ |
| mochikomu | もちこむ （持ち込む) | to bring in |
| mochiron | もちろん | certainly, of course |
| modoru | もどる | to return |
| mogumogu | もぐもぐ | chew without opening mouth widely |
| mokugekisha | もくげきしゃ | witness |
| moku-yoobi | もくようび | Thursday |
| momen; men | （も) めん | cotton |
| momiji | もみじ | maple |
| Monariza | モナリザ | Mona Lisa |
| mono | もの | things (material things) |
| monogatari | ものがたり | story; narrative |
| moo hitori | もうひとり | additional person, one more person |
| moo hitotsu | もうひとつ | additional thing, one more thing |

## Appendix C: Japanese-English Glossary

| Roma-ji | Kana (Kanji) | English |
|---|---|---|
| moo ichido | もういちど （もう一度） | one more time |
| moo nai | もう～ない | no longer exist |
| moo sukoshi | もうすこし | little more |
| mooru | モール | shopping mall |
| moosugu | もうすぐ | pretty soon |
| morau | もらう | to receive (when Subject is receiver) |
| mori | もり （森） | forest |
| moru | もる （おさらにもる） | to dish up; heap; serve; fill |
| motomeru | もとめる （求める） | to seek |
| motsu | もつ （持つ） | to hold, have |
| mottei iru | もっている（持っている） | to have, own |
| motto | もっと | more |
| mukaigawa (mae) | むかいがわ （まえ） | front, across the street |
| mukashi | むかし （昔） | olden times, long time ago |
| mukoo | むこう | beyond |
| mukuchi | むくち （無口） | not talkative; quiet |
| mune | むね | chest |
| murasaki | むらさき | purple |
| muri | むり | impossible |
| mushi | むし（虫） | bugs, insects |
| musuko | むすこ | son |
| muttsu | むっつ | six |
| muzukashii | むずかしい | hard, difficult |
| myooji | みょうじ （苗字） | sir name |
| na(a) | な （あ） | sentence final particle (speaker's murmur) |
| nabe | なべ | cooking pan |
| nagai | ながい | long |
| nagame | ながめ | view, scenery |
| nagashi | ながし | kitchen sink |
| nagusameru | なぐさめる | to comfort |
| nai | ない | nonexistent; negative of "aru" |
| naifu | ナイフ | knife |
| naisho | ないしょ | secret |
| naka | なか （中） | in, inside |
| naka | なか （仲） | relationship |
| nakayoku | なかよく | friendly; harmoniously |
| nakayubi | なかゆび | middle finger |
| nakimushi | なきむし | crybaby |
| naku | なく （泣く） | to cry |
| naku | なく （鳴く） | to sing, chirp, bark |
| nama | なま （生） | raw |
| namae | なまえ | name |
| nameraka | なめらか | smooth |
| nan (= nani) | なん （なに） | what |
| nan de? | なんで | in what way? How? |
| nan kai | なんかい | how many times |
| nanatsu | ななつ | seven |
| nan-ban | なんばん | what number? |

| Roma-ji | Kana (Kanji) | English |
|---|---|---|
| nan-gatsu nan-nichi | なんがつなんにち | What day and month is it? |
| nani-go | なにご | what language? |
| nanika | なにか | something, anything |
| nan-ji goro | なんじごろ | around what time |
| nan-nen-sei | なんねんせい | what year (in school) student |
| nansei | なんせい （南西） | Southwest |
| nante...! | なんて～！ | such a thing like that! |
| nantoo | なんとう （南東） | Southeast |
| nan'yoobi | なんようび | What day of the week? |
| naoru | なおる | to heel |
| naporitan | ナポリタン | spaghetti with tomato sauce |
| nara | なら （N.なら） | if it is ~, |
| narabu | ならぶ （並ぶ） | to line up |
| narau | ならう （習う） | to learn |
| naru | なる （～になる） | to become ~ |
| naruhodo | なるほど | I see. |
| nasaru | なさる | to do (polite form) |
| nashi | なし | Japanese pear |
| natsu | なつ | summer |
| nattoo | なっとう | fermented soybeans |
| ne | ね | isn't it? (a tag question) |
| neboo | ねぼう | late riser |
| neko | ねこ | cat |
| nekutai | ねくたい （ネクタイ） | necktie |
| nemui | ねむい | sleepy |
| nen | ねん （年） | years (~ years) |
| neru | ねる | to go to bed, sleep |
| nezumi | ねずみ | mouse |
| ni | に | at (showing specific time) |
| ni ~ san po | に、さんぽ （二、三歩） | few steps |
| ni naru | なる （～になる） | to become |
| ni shimasu | ～にします | to decide on ~ |
| nichi-yoobi | にちようび | Sunday |
| nigai | にがい | bitter |
| nigate | にがて （苦手） | weak point; not good at |
| ni-gatsu | にがつ （二月） | February |
| nigeru | にげる | to run away; escape |
| nigiru | にぎる | to grab; grip |
| Nihon | にほん | Japan |
| nihon-en | にほんえん （日本円） | Japanese currency |
| nihon-go | にほんご | Japanese language |
| nikki | にっき （日記） | diary |
| nikkoo | にっこう （日光） | sunshine, sunlight |
| nikoniko | にこにこ | smile happily and warmly |
| niku | にく （肉） | meat |
| nikui (~ nikui) | ～にくい | difficult to (do~) |
| nimotsu | にもつ | luggage |

## Appendix C: Japanese-English Glossary

| Roma-ji | Kana (Kanji) | English |
|---|---|---|
| nin-bun | にんぶん（〜人分） | servings (a counter) |
| ni-nen-sei | にねんせい | second-year student, sophomore |
| ningen | にんげん（人間） | human beings |
| ningyoo | にんぎょう（人形） | doll |
| ninjin | にんじん | carrots |
| ninki | にんき（人気） | popularity |
| niru | にる（煮る） | to cook in a sauce or soup |
| nishibi | にしび（西日） | afternoon sun from the West |
| niwa | にわ | yard; garden |
| niyaniya | にやにや（ニヤニヤ） | smile (blissful) |
| no | の | modifier; connect two nouns |
| no koto | 〜のこと | about 〜 |
| nobiru | のびる（伸びる） | to stretch; to grow |
| noboru | のぼる | to rise (e.g., the Sun) |
| node | ので | because |
| nokku shimashita | ノックしました | knocked |
| nokoru | のこる（残る） | to remain |
| nomimono | のみもの | drinks |
| nomu | のむ（飲む） | to drink |
| nonbiri suru | のんびりする/リラックスする | to relax |
| nooto | ノート | notebook |
| nori | のり | seaweed |
| noru | のる | to ride; get on〜 (〜ni noru)) |
| nugu | ぬぐ | to remove; take off |
| nuno | ぬの（布） | cloth |
| nurasu | ぬらす | to wet something (t.v.) |
| nureru | ぬれる | to get wet (i.v.) |
| nyuu-gaku | にゅうがく | entrance to school |
| nyuuyooku | ニューヨーク | New York |
| obaasan | おばあさん | old woman, grandma |
| obake | おばけ（お化け） | ghost (casual) |
| oba-obasan | おば--おばさん | aunt (casual)(formal) |
| o-bentoo | （お）べんとう | boxed lunch |
| obi | おび | sash |
| ocha | おちゃ | green tea |
| ochiru | おちる（落ちる） | to fall |
| odoru | おどる（踊る） | to dance |
| ofisu | オフィス | office |
| ofuro | おふろ | bath |
| o-futari-sama | おふたりさま | polite form for "two people" |
| ogoru | おごる | to treat someone |
| Ohayoo | おはよう | Good morning. (Casual) |
| Ohayoo gozaimasu | おはようございます | Good morning. (Formal) |
| o-hi-sama | おひさま（お日さま） | the sun, sunshine |
| O-hisashiburi desu | おひさしぶりです | It's been a while since I last saw you. |
| o-ire-shimasu | おいれします | I shall put it in (humble form) |
| oishii | おいしい | tasty |
| oishisoo | おいしそう | delicious (It looks delicious) |
| ojiisan | おじいさん | old man, grandpa |
| ojisan (oji) | おじさん（おじ） | uncle (formal) (casual) |
| Ojyama shimashita | おじゃましました | Sorry to have bothered you. |
| okaasan | おかあさん | mother (respect form) |
| Okaeri (nasai) | おかえり（なさい） | Welcome home. |
| okaeshi | おかえし | return, change (also called "o-tsuri") |
| Okage sama de | おかげさまで | Thank you for your concern. |
| okami-san | おかみさん | wife; madam |
| okane | おかね | money |
| okanemochi | おかねもち | rich |
| o-kashi | おかし | snacks |
| okazu | おかず | dishes to go with the rice |
| okiru | おきる（起きる） | to get up |
| okome | おこめ（米） | raw rice |
| okorinboo | おこりんぼう | quick-tempered; hothead |
| okoru | おこる（怒る） | to be angry |
| okoru | おこる（起こる） | to take place; to happen |
| okosan | おこさん | child (polite form) |
| okosu | おこす（起こす） | to wake up someone |
| oku | おく（奥） | the depths |
| okujyoo | おくじょう | top floor; roof |
| okureru | おくれる | to be late; get behind |
| okuru | おくる（送る） | to send |
| okusan | おくさん（奥さん） | wife (polite form) |
| Omachi kudasai | おまちください | Please wait. |
| o-mamori | おまもり | (good luck) charm |
| Omatase shimashita | おまたせしました | Thank you for waiting. |
| omawari san | おまわりさん | policeman |
| omiai | おみあい | match-making |
| omizu | おみず | polite form of "mizu" |
| omocha | おもちゃ | toy |
| omoidasu | おもいだす（思い出す） | to recall |
| omoshiroi | おもしろい | interesting; fun |
| omou | おもう（思う） | to think; consider |
| omuraisu | オムライス | fried rice covered by omelet |
| omuretsu | オムレツ | omelet |
| on'na-mono | おんなもの | things for women |
| onaji | おなじ（同じ） | same |
| onaka | おなか | stomach; abdomen |
| onaka ga suku | おなかがすく | to become hungry |

## Appendix C: Japanese-English Glossary

| Roma-ji | Kana (Kanji) | English | Roma-ji | Kana (Kanji) | English |
|---|---|---|---|---|---|
| ondo | おんど | temperature | otonappoku | おとなっぽく | grown-up-like |
| oneechan | おねえちゃん（お姉ちゃん） | big sister (affectionate term) | otonashii | おとなしい | docile; quiet |
| | | | otona-yoo | おとなよう | for adult |
| onegai suru | おねがいする | to do me a favor | otoosan | おとうさん | father (respect form) |
| ongaku | おんがく | Music | otooto-otooto san | おとうと― おとうとさん | younger brother (casual) (formal) |
| oni | おに　（鬼） | ogre; demon | | | |
| onigiri | おにぎり | rice ball | otsuri | おつり | (the) change |
| onigiri bentoo | おにぎりべんとう | boxed lunch with rice balls | owari | おわり | end |
| | | | owaru | おわる（終わる） | to end |
| oobun | オーブン | oven | Oyasumi (nasai) | おやすみ（なさい） | Good night |
| oodan-hodoo | おうだんほどう | pedestrian crossing | oyayubi | おやゆび | thumb |
| ooi | おおい | more (in quantity) | oyogu | およぐ（泳ぐ） | to swim |
| ookami | おおかみ | wolf | paatii | パーティー | party |
| ookii | おおきい | big, large | pabu | パブ | pub |
| ookisa | おおきさ　（大きさ） | size | pai | パイ | pie |
| | | | pairotto | パイロット | pilot |
| oosaji | おおさじ | one tablespoon | pan | パン | bread |
| ootobai | オートバイ | motorcycle | pan ya | パンや | bakery |
| ooya | おおや（大家） | landlord | panda | パンダ | Giant Panda |
| ooyorokobi | おおよろこび | big joy | pari | パリ | Paris |
| orei | おれい | gratitude; thanks | pasadena | パサデナ | Pasadena |
| orenji | おれんじ（オレンジ） | orange | pasu suru | パスする | to pass the ball |
| | | | pen | ペン | pen |
| origami no orikata | おりがみのおりかた | how to fold origami-paper | pengin | ペンギン | penguin |
| | | | pepushi | ペプシ | Pepsi |
| oriru (~ wo oriru) | おりる　（～をおりる） | to get off~ | petto | ペット | pet |
| | | | piasu | ピアス | pierced earrings |
| oru | おる | to fold | pittari | ぴったり | perfect fit |
| orugooru | オルゴール | music box | poisute | ポイすて | cigarette littering |
| osake | おさけ | liquor; Japanese rice wine | pokapoka | ぽかぽか（ポカポカ） | nice warm weather |
| osara | （お）さら | dishes | pooku | ポーク | pork |
| o-sechi (ryoori) | おせち | New Year dishes | poriesuteru | ぽりえすてる（ポリエステル） | polyester |
| o-seji | おせじ | flattery | | | |
| oshaberi suru | おしゃべり（を）する | to chat | posutaa | ぽすたあ（ポスター） | poster |
| oshieru | おしえる (教える) | to teach; instruct | pun (fun) | ぷん（ふん） | minutes |
| oshiire | おしいれ | closet | puraido | プライド | pride |
| oshinagaki | おしながき | menu | puree | プレー | a play |
| oshiraseshimasu | おしらせします | I'll let you know | purezento | プレゼント | present |
| oshiri | おしり | buttocks | puro | プロ | pro (professional) |
| osoi | おそい | late | puuru | プール | swimming pool |
| osu | おす　（押す） | to press | pyuupyuu | ピューピュー | wing sound (shrill) |
| osushi-ya san | おすしやさん | sushi restaurant | raamen | ラーメン | Chinese noodles in soup |
| otaku | おたく | fanatic | | | |
| otamajyakushi | おたまじゃくし | tadpole | rabo | ラボ | lab |
| otanjyookaado | おたんじょうカード | birthday card | rai-getsu | らいげつ | next month |
| | | | rainen | らいねん | next year |
| otayori suru | おたよりする（お便りする） | to write a letter to someone | rainichi | らいにち | coming to Japan |
| | | | raion | ライオン | lion |
| otearai | おてあらい | bathroom | raishuu | らいしゅう (来週) | next week |
| otera | （お）てら | Buddhist temples | raito appu | ライトアップ | light-up |
| otetsudai | おてつだい | help; assistance | rakuda | らくだ | camel |
| oto | おと（音） | sound; noise | reeyon | れえよん（レーヨン） | rayon |
| otoko no hito | おとこのひと | male (person) | | | |
| otona | おとな | adult | | | |

## Appendix C: Japanese-English Glossary

| Roma-ji | Kana (Kanji) | English |
|---|---|---|
| reiten | れいてん | zero points |
| reizouko | れいぞうこ | refrigerator |
| remon skasshu | レモンスカッシュ | lemonade |
| renkyuu | れんきゅう | consecutive holidays |
| renraku | れんらく | contact |
| renshuu | れんしゅう（練習） | practice |
| renshuu suru | れんしゅうする（練習する） | to practice |
| reshipi | レシピ | recipe |
| resutoran | レストラン | restaurant |
| retasu | レタス | lettuce |
| rikuesuto | リクエスト | request |
| ringo | りんご | apple |
| rippa (na) | りっぱ（な） | magnificent |
| risaachi | リサーチ（けんきゅう） | research |
| robii | ロビー | lobby |
| rokku | ロック | rock |
| rokku guruupu | ロックグループ | rock group |
| roku-gatsu | ろくがつ（六月） | June |
| rooka | ろうか | corridor |
| Rosanjerusu | ロサンジェルス | Los Angeles |
| Roshi(y)a-go | ロシアご | Russian |
| roshia-shiki | ロシアしき（式） | Russian style |
| Rosu | ロス | Los Angeles |
| rusu | るす（留守） | being not home |
| ryokoo | りょこう | trip |
| ryoo | りょう（寮） | dormitory |
| ryoo | りょう（量） | amount |
| ryoori | りょうり | cooking |
| ryoori suru | りょうりする | to cook |
| ryooshin | りょうしん（両親） | parents (polite form is "go-ryooshin") |
| ryuu-gakusei | りゅうがくせい | foreign exchange students |
| Saa | さあ | Let's, or I wonder |
| saafin | サーフィン | surfing |
| sabaku | さばく | desert |
| sagaru | さがる（下がる） | to step back |
| sagasu | さがす（探す） | to search |
| sageru | さげる（下げる） | to lower |
| sai | さい（才） | years old (~ years old) |
| saifu | さいふ | wallet |
| saigoni | さいごに | at last; in the end; finally |
| saikin | さいきん | recently |
| saikoo | さいこう（最高） | best |
| sain | サイン | post (a post) |
| sain | サイン | signature |
| saisho | さいしょ | first |
| saizu | サイズ | size |
| sakadachi | さかだち | standing on the head |
| sakan | さかん | prosperous, flourished |
| sakana | さかな（魚） | fish |
| sakana ya | さかなや | fish market |
| saka-ya | さかや | liquor shop |
| sake | さけ | salmon |
| saki | さき（先） | ahead; future |
| sakkaa | サッカー | soccer |
| saku | さく（柵） | fence |
| sakubun | さくぶん（作文） | composition |
| sakura | さくら（桜） | cherry blossoms |
| samishii | さみしい | lonely; lonesome |
| samui | さむい | cold |
| samurai | さむらい（侍） | warrior; samurai |
| sandoicchi | サンドイッチ | sandwich |
| sangaidate | さんがいだて | three-story building |
| san-gatsu | さんがつ（三月） | March |
| san-kai-sei | さんかいせい | the same as "san-nen-sei," junior |
| sanma | さんま | mackerel |
| sanpo | さんぽ | stroll, walking |
| sanpo (wo) suru | さんぽ（を）する | to stroll |
| sansan | サンサン | the way the sun shines |
| sansei | さんせい（賛成） | agreement |
| sanshoku | さんしょく（三色） | three colors |
| sarada | サラダ | salad |
| sarariiman | サラリーマン | salaried man |
| saru | さる（去る） | to leave |
| saru | さる（猿） | monkey |
| sashiageru | さしあげる | to give humbly |
| sashimi | さしみ | raw fish |
| sasu | （かさを）さす | to put up an umbrella |
| satoo | さとう | sugar |
| sawaa-kuriimu | サワークリーム | sour cream |
| sawaru | さわる | to touch |
| Sayoonara | さようなら | Good bye. (to your equal) |
| se | せ（背） | height |
| seeru | セール | sale |
| sei | せい（姓） | sir name |
| seibutsu(-gaku) | せいぶつ（がく） | Biology |
| seijinshiki | せいじんしき | ceremony for coming of age |
| seikai | せいかい（正解） | correct answer |
| seikatsu | せいかつ（生活） | life, lifestyle |
| seiki | せいき（世紀） | century |
| seinoo | せいのう | performance |
| seiseki | せいせき | grades |
| sekai | せかい | world |
| seki | せき（席） | seat |
| sekken | せっけん | soap |
| sekushii | セクシー | sexy |
| semai | せまい | small/narrow-spaced |
| semi | せみ | cicada |
| senaka | せなか | back (one's back) |
| senchi (meetoru) | センチ（メートル） | centimeter |
| sen-getsu | せんげつ | last month |
| senjitsu | せんじつ | the other day |

# Appendix C: Japanese-English Glossary

| Roma-ji | Kana (Kanji) | English |
|---|---|---|
| senkoo | せんこう | major |
| sensei | せんせい | teacher, professor, doctor |
| sen-shuu | せんしゅう | last week |
| sensoo | せんそう | war |
| sentaku | せんたく | laundry |
| sentaku suru | せんたくする | to do laundry |
| sentakumono | せんたくもの | laundry |
| sento | セント | cent |
| sentoo | せんとう（銭湯） | public bath |
| setake | せたけ（背丈） | height |
| setsumei | せつめい | explanation |
| setsumei suru | せつめいする（説明する） | to explain |
| setto suru | セットする | to set |
| shaberu | しゃべる（しゃべります） | to chat |
| shakai | しゃかい（社会） | society |
| shakaijin | しゃかいじん（社会人） | working person |
| shakooteki | しゃこうてき | sociable |
| shashin | しゃしん（写真） | photograph |
| shatsu | しゃつ（シャツ） | shirt |
| shawaa | しゃわあ（シャワー） | shower |
| shawaa wo abiru | シャワーをあびる | to take a shower |
| sheikusupia | シェイクスピア | Shakespeare |
| shi | し | and what's more |
| shiai | しあい | games; match |
| shiawase | しあわせ | happy |
| shibai | しばい | play (a play) |
| shichi-gatsu | しちがつ（七月） | July |
| shidare zakura | しだれざくら（しだれ桜） | weeping cherry blossoms |
| shi-gatsu | しがつ（四月） | April |
| shigoto | しごと | job, work |
| shii-shii | シーシー（ＣＣ） | cubic centimeter, milliliter |
| shika | しか | deer |
| shikakui | しかくい | square |
| shiken | しけん | examination |
| shiki | しき | four seasons |
| shiku/hiku | しく／ひく | to make or spread (like a futon) |
| shikushiku | しくしく（シクシク） | To sob softly and continuously |
| shimaru | しまる（閉まる） | to close (i.v.) |
| shimeru | しめる（閉める） | to close (t.v.) |
| shinayaka | しなやか | supple |
| shinbun | しんぶん | newspaper |
| shingoo | しんごう（信号） | traffic lights, signals |
| shinisoo | し（死）にそう | feel like dying |
| shinjiru | しんじる（信じる） | to believe |
| shin-kan-sen | しんかんせん | bullet train |
| shinpai | しんぱい | worry |
| shinpai suru | しんぱいする | to worry |
| shinpiteki | しんぴてき（神秘的） | mysterious, mystic, enigmatic |
| shinsetsu | しんせつ | kindness |
| shinsha | しんしゃ（新車） | new car |
| shinshi-fuku | しんしふく | men's wear |
| shinu | しぬ（死ぬ） | to die |
| shio | しお | salt |
| shio-karai | しおからい | salty |
| shippai suru | しっぱいする | to fail |
| shiraberu | しらべる | to check; investigate |
| shiriai | しりあい | acquaintance |
| shiriaru | シリアル | cereal |
| shiroi | しろい（白い） | white |
| shishi | しし（獅子） | lion |
| shita | した | under; below |
| shita kara ni-ban-me | したからにばんめ | second lowest; second youngest |
| shitoshito | しとしと（シトシト） | rain falling lightly |
| shitsumon | しつもん | question |
| shitsurei suru | しつれい（失礼）する | to excuse oneself; to be rude |
| shitteiru | し（知）っている | to know |
| shiwa | しわ | wrinkle |
| shizuka (na) | しずか（な） | quiet |
| shizukani | しずかに | quietly |
| shizumu | （日が）しずむ | to sink (The sun sets.) |
| shocchuu | しょっちゅう | all the time |
| shokki | しょっき | tableware |
| shokuhin | しょくひん | food |
| shokuji | しょくじ（食事） | meal |
| shonbori sursu | ションボリする | to be downhearted |
| shoo | しょう（小） | small size |
| shoo shoo | しょうしょう | little (a little) |
| shooboosha | しょうぼうしゃ | fire engine |
| shoogajiru | しょうがじる | ginger-juice |
| shoogakkoo | しょうがっこう | elementary school |
| shoo-gakusei | しょうがくせい | elementary school students |
| shoogo | しょうご | noon |
| shoohi-zei | しょうひぜい | sales tax |
| shoojikini | しょうじきに | honestly |
| shoorai | しょうらい | in the future |
| shufu | しゅふ | homemaker; housewife |
| shukudai | しゅくだい | homework |
| shuto | しゅと | capital |
| shuukan | しゅうかん（習慣） | custom |
| shuumatsu | しゅうまつ | weekend |
| shuuto wo kimeru | シュートを きめる | to sink a shot |
| soba | そば | nearby |
| soba | そば | buckwheat noodle |
| sobo-obaasan | そぼ--おばあさん | grandmother (casual)/(formal) |

## Appendix C: Japanese-English Glossary

| Roma-ji | Kana (Kanji) | English | Roma-ji | Kana (Kanji) | English |
|---------|--------------|---------|---------|--------------|---------|
| sochira | そちら | that way, that side (close to the listener) | sukiyaki | すきやき | beef & vegetables cooked in shallow pan |
| sofu-ojiisan | そふ‐‐おじいさん | grandfather (casual)/(formal) | sukkiri suru | すっきりする | to become clear |
| soko | そこ | there (near the listener) | sukoshi | すこし | little (more formal than "chotto) |
| soko | そこ（底） | bottom | sukunai | すくない | fewer |
| sokode | そこで | therefore; because of that; due to that | sukuriin | スクリーン | screen |
| | | | sumi | すみ | in-corner |
| sono | その | that (noun modifier) | sumimasen | すみません | I'm sorry (more formal); excuse me |
| sono ta | そのた | others | | | |
| sono ue | そのうえ（その上） | moreover; on top of it | sumu | すむ（住む） | to live |
| | | | suna | すな | sand |
| sonogo | そのご（その後） | after that | suniikaa | スニーカー | sneakers |
| sonotoki | そのとき | on that moment; at that time; then | sunooboodo | スノーボード | snowboard |
| | | | sunookeru | スノーケル | snorkeling |
| soo | そう | the same as English "so" | supageti | スパゲティ | spaghetti |
| | | | supaisu | スパイス | spices |
| soo shimashoo | そうしましょう | Let's do that | Supein-go | スペインご | Spanish language |
| soo suru to | そうすると | if you do so | supiido unten | スピードうんてん | speeding |
| sooji | そうじ | cleaning | supootsu | スポーツ | sports |
| soosu | ソース | sauce | suppai | すっぱい | sour |
| sora | そら（空） | sky | supuun | スプーン | spoon |
| sore | それ | that one (near the listener) | suru | する | to do |
| | | | sushi (o-sushi) | （お）すし | cooked and vinegard rice |
| sore de | それで | because of that, due to that | | | |
| sore ni kurabete | それにくらべて | in comparison with ~; on the contrary | sutaa | スター | stars; celebrity |
| | | | sutando | すたんど（スタンド） | electric stand |
| soredewa | それでは | then, in that case (formal) | | | |
| sorejya chotto | それじゃ、ちょっと | that won't do | suteeki | ステーキ | steak |
| | | | suteru | すてる（捨てる） | to throw away; to discard |
| sorekara | それから | and then, after that | | | |
| soreni | それに | in addition to it; besides that | sutoroo | ストロー | straw |
| | | | suu | すう（吸う） | to inhale |
| soshite | そして | And | suugaku | すうがく | Mathematics |
| soto | そと | outside | suuji | すうじ（数字） | numbers |
| sotsugyoo suru | そつぎょうする | to graduate | suupaa | スーパー | supermarket |
| soyosoyo | そよそよ（ソヨソヨ） | breeze (soft) | suwaru | すわる（座る） | to sit |
| | | | suzushii | すずしい | nice and cool |
| subarashii | すばらしい | wonderful | tabako | たばこ | tobacco |
| sugiru | すぎる（過ぎる） | to go beyond; exceed | tabako wo suu | （タバコを）すう | to smoke |
| sugoku | すごく | casual form "very," awesome | tabemono | たべもの | food |
| | | | taberu | たべる（食べる） | to eat |
| suicchi | スイッチ | switch | tabi | たび | socks cloven at the big toe |
| suiden | すいでん | rice paddy | | | |
| suidoo | すいどう | faucet | tabun | たぶん | perhaps |
| suiei | すいえい | swimming | tachiyoru | たちよる | to stop by |
| suihanki | すいはんき（炊飯器） | rice cooker | tadaima | ただいま | I'm home |
| | | | tai | たい | sea bream |
| suika | すいか | watermelon | Tai-go | タイご | Thai language |
| sui-yoobi | すいようび | Wednesday | taihen | たいへん（大変） | hard work, alarming, terrible (noun) |
| sukaato | すかあと（スカート） | skirt | | | |
| | | | taihen | たいへん（大変） | very (formal) (adverb) |
| suki | すき | likable; pleasing; favorable | taijyuu | たいじゅう（体重） | weight |
| | | | taiko | たいこ | drum |
| sukii | スキー | ski | taikutsu | たいくつ | boring |

## Appendix C: Japanese-English Glossary

| Roma-ji | Kana (Kanji) | English | Roma-ji | Kana (Kanji) | English |
|---|---|---|---|---|---|
| taipu | タイプ | type | tetsudau | てつだう | to help |
| taitei | たいてい | usually | tii-shatsu | Tシャツ | T-shirt |
| takai | たかい　（高い） | expensive | to | と | and (to connect two nouns) |
| takigi | たきぎ | firewood | | | |
| takusan | たくさん | many, a lot | to | と | if or when |
| takushii | タクシー | taxi | to | と | with (someone) |
| tamago | たまご | egg | to/doa | と/ドア | door |
| tama-negi | たまねぎ（玉ねぎ） | onions | tobi-ishi | とびいし | stepping-stone |
| tana | たな | shelf | tobu | とぶ | to fly; jump |
| tanbo | たんぼ | rice field | todana | とだな | cabinet |
| tango | たんご | vocabulary | toho | とほ | walking |
| tanomu | たのむ | to ask for a favor | toho de, aruite | とほで、あるいて | via walking |
| tanoshii | たのしい | enjoyable; fun | toire | トイレ | toilet, bathroom |
| tanoshimi | たのしみ | pleasure; something to look forward to | tokage | とかげ | lizard |
| | | | tokei | とけい | clock |
| tansu | たんす | chest | tokidoki | ときどき | sometimes |
| tanuki | たぬき | raccoon | tokoro | ところ | place |
| tanuki-udon | たぬきうどん | udon soup with tempura batter bits | tokoroga | ところが | however; on the contrary |
| taoreru | たおれる | to fall (i.v.) | tokoya | とこや | barber shop |
| tashika | たしか | if I'm not mistaken | tokubetsu | とくべつ（特別） | special |
| tashikani | たしかに | for sure; definitely; certainly | tokui | とくい | strong point; good at |
| | | | tomaru | とまる（止まる） | to stop (i.v.) |
| tasu | たす（足す） | to add | tomaru | とまる（泊まる） | to stay over night |
| tasukaru | たすかる（助かる） | to be rescued, saved | tomato | トマト | tomato |
| tataku | たたく | to hit; beat | tomeru | とめる（止める） | to stop (t.v.) |
| tatefuda | たてふだ（立て札） | notice/bulletin board | tomodachi | ともだち | friend |
| tatemono | たてもの | building | tonari | となり | next (to the same group) |
| tatoeba | たとえば（例えば） | for example | | | |
| tatsu | たつ（立つ） | to stand up | tonkatsu | とんかつ | pork cutlet |
| tawara | たわら | straw bag | too | とお | ten |
| tayori | たより　（便り） | letter, correspondence | tooi | とお（遠）い | far |
| te | て | hand(s) | tooku | とおく（遠く） | place that is far |
| tebukuro | てぶくろ | gloves | Tookyoo | とうきょう | Tokyo |
| teeburu | てえぶる（テーブル） | table | toomorokoshi | とうもろこし | corn |
| | | | toori | とおり（通り） | street |
| teepu | テープ | tape | tooru | とおる（通る） | to pass through |
| tegami | てがみ | letters | tootei | とうてい（～ない） | no chance for ~; no way to (do ~) |
| teido | ていど | degree | | | |
| teinei | ていねい | politeness | tora | とら | tiger |
| teineini | ていねいに | politely; carefully; thoroughly | torakku no unten | トラックのうんてん | driving a track |
| teishoku | ていしょく | assorted meal | tori | とり | bird |
| temae | てまえ（手前） | beforehand | tori ni iku | と（取）りに行く | to pick up; go get something |
| ten | てん | dot; point; spot | | | |
| tenisu shuuzu | テニスシューズ | tennis shoes | tori-nanban | とりなんばん | buckwheat noodles with chicken |
| tenpura | てんぷら | deep-fried vegetables and seafood | | | |
| | | | toriniku | とりにく（とり肉） | chicken |
| tenpura soba | てんぷらそば | buckwheat noodles with tempura | torobi | とろび（とろ火） | low heat |
| | | | toro-toro | トロトロ | thick and syrupy |
| tensai | てんさい（天才） | genius | toru | とる（しゃしんを撮る） | to take a picture |
| tenshi | てんし（天使） | angel | | | |
| tera | てら（寺） | Buddhist temple | toru | とる（取る） | to get; receive |
| terebi | テレビ | television | toshi | とし（年） | age |
| tesuto | テスト | test | toshi wo toru | とし（年）をとる | to age |

# Appendix C: Japanese-English Glossary

| Roma-ji | Kana (Kanji) | English |
|---|---|---|
| toshiyori | としより（年より） | the old |
| toshokan | としょかん | library |
| totemo | とても | very (personal overtone) |
| tottemo | とっても | very (informal "totemo") |
| tsugi ni | つぎに | next |
| tsukareru | つかれる（疲れる） | to become tired |
| tsukeru | つける（点ける） | to turn on; to light |
| tsuki | つき | the moon |
| tsukiatari | つきあたり | dead end |
| tsukiau | つきあう | to accompany; to date |
| tsukimi udon | つきみうどん | udon noodles served with egg |
| tsuku | つ（着）く | to arrive |
| tsuku | つく（点く） | to be lit or turned on |
| tsukue | つくえ | desk |
| tsukuri kata | つくりかた（作り方） | how to make |
| tsukuru | つくる（作る） | to make |
| tsumaranai | つまらない | boring; uninteresting |
| tsumasaki | つまさき | toe |
| tsume | つめ | nails |
| tsumetai | つめたい | cold (by touch) |
| tsumori (da) | つもり（だ） | to intend to ~ |
| tsurete iku | つれていく | to take someone |
| tsurutsuru | つるつる | slippery |
| tsuyoi | つよい | strong |
| tsuzuku | つづく | to continue |
| tte | って | short form of "to (iu no wa)" quotation |
| U~n | う～ん | Well let me think. |
| ubau | うばう | to rob; steal |
| uchi | うち | house, home |
| uchiki | うちき（内気） | shy |
| ude | うで | arms |
| udon | うどん | thick flour noodles |
| udon-ya-san | うどんやさん | noodle shop |
| ue | うえ | above; top; on |
| ueitoresu | ウエートレス | waitress |
| uesuto | ウエスト | waist |
| ukagau | うかがう（伺う） | to visit (humble form) |
| ukaru | うかる（受かる） | to pass the examination |
| ukeru | うける | to receive |
| uketoru | うけとる（受け取る） | to receive |
| uma | うま | horse |
| umai | うまい | skillful |
| umaku | うまく | skillfully; well |
| umareru | うまれる | to be born |
| ume-boshi | うめぼし | soured pickled plum |
| umi | うみ | sea; ocean |
| Un | うん | casual expression of "Yes" |
| unagi | うなぎ | Japanese eel |
| uni | うに | sea urchin eggs |
| unmei | うんめい（運命） | fate |
| unten | うんてん | drive |
| unten suru | うんてんする | to drive |
| untenshu | うんてんしゅ（運転手） | driver |
| ura | うら | back, backyard |
| urayamashii | うらやましい | envious |
| ureshii | うれしい | happy, glad (I am happy, glad) |
| uriba | うりば | (selling) section |
| usagi | うさぎ | rabbit |
| ushi | うし | cow |
| ushinau | うしなう（失う） | to lose |
| ushiro | うしろ（後ろ） | behind, back |
| uso | うそ | a lie |
| uso wo tsuku | うそをつく | to lie |
| usu chairo | うすちゃいろ（うす茶色） | light brown |
| uta | うた（歌） | song |
| utsukushii | うつくしい | beautiful |
| Uwaa | うわあ | Wow! |
| uwaan | うわ～ん | cry (loud like child) |
| uwasa-banashi | うわさばなし | rumors |
| wa | わ | sentence final used by women |
| wa | は | topic marker |
| wai-shatsu | Ｙ－シャツ | dress shirt |
| wakai | わかい（若い） | young |
| wakaru | わかる（分かる） | to understand |
| wakasu | わかす | to boil the hot-bath water |
| wakeru | わける（分ける） | to share; to split |
| waku | わく | to gush (spring) out |
| walking | とほ | toho |
| wani | わに | crocodile |
| wan-wan | ワンワン | onomatopoeia of a dog's bark |
| warai sugiru | わらいすぎる | to smile/laugh excessively |
| warau | わらう（笑う） | to smile, laugh |
| wariai/maamaa | わりあい/まあまあ | relatively |
| washoku | わしょく（和食） | Japanese food |
| wasuremono | わすれもの（忘れ物） | lost property; a thing left behind |
| wasureru | わすれる（忘れる） | to forget |
| wataru | わたる | to cross |
| watashi | わたし | I |
| watasu | わたす | to hand over |
| wo | を | particle used after a direct object |
| yakamashii | やかましい | noisy |
| yakan | やかん（夜間） | during the night |
| yakeru | やける | to be burnt |
| yakikata | やきかた（焼き方） | bake (how to) |

## Appendix C: Japanese-English Glossary

| Roma-ji | Kana (Kanji) | English | Roma-ji | Kana (Kanji) | English |
|---------|--------------|---------|---------|--------------|---------|
| yakitori | やきとり | chicken roasted | yuuenchi | ゆうえんち | amusement park |
| yakkyoku | やっきょく | drugstore, pharmacy | yuugata | ゆうがた | dusk |
| yaku | やく（焼く） | to bake | yuumei (na) | ゆうめい（な） | famous |
| yakyuu | やきゅう | baseball | yuurei | ゆうれい | ghost |
| yama | やま（山） | mountains | yuu-utsu | ゆううつ | depressed; melancholic |
| yameru | やめる | to quit | zairyoo | ざいりょう | ingredient |
| yaoya | やおや | green grocer | zaru soba | ざるそば | buckwheat noodle soup |
| yaru | やる | to do (casual form of "suru") | zasshi | ざっし | magazine |
| yaru | やる | to give, feed (to someone lower) | zehi | ぜひ | by all means |
| yasai | やさい | vegetables | zenbu | ぜんぶ | everything |
| yaseru | やせる | to lose weight | zentai | ぜんたい（全体） | the whole |
| yasui | やすい（安い） | cheap; reasonable | zenzen | ぜんぜん | never (used with negative) |
| yasui (~ yasui) | ～やすい | easy to (do~) | zou | ぞう | elephant |
| yasumi | （お）やすみ | holiday; absent; rest | zubon | ズボン | pants |
| yasumu | やすむ（休む） | to rest; to be absent | zuibun | ずいぶん | very, extremely |
| yasuraka | （やす）安らか | peaceful | zutsu | ずつ | each |
| yattsu | やっつ | eight | zutto | ずっと | by far |
| yawarakai | やわらかい | soft | zutto | ずっと | throughout the time |
| yo | よ | sentence final used for affirmation | | | |
| yobu | よぶ | to invite; call | | | |
| yogoreru | よごれる | to become dirty | | | |
| yoko | よこ | next (to the different group) | | | |
| yoku | よく | often | | | |
| yokunai | よくない | no good | | | |
| yomu | よむ | to read | | | |
| yonaka | よなか（夜中） | middle of the night; midnight | | | |
| yooi (jyunbi) suru | よういする（＝じゅんびする） | to prepare | | | |
| yooki | ようき | happy-go-lucky | | | |
| yooshoku | ようしょく（洋食） | Western food | | | |
| yori | より | than (~ than) | | | |
| yoroshii | よろしい | good (polite/formal form) | | | |
| yoru | よる（夜） | night | | | |
| yosan | よさん | budget | | | |
| yottsu | よっつ | four | | | |
| you | よう（酔う） | to become drunk | | | |
| yoyaku | よやく（予約） | reservation | | | |
| yozakura | よざくら（夜桜） | night cherry blossoms | | | |
| yu | ゆ（湯） | water (hot) | | | |
| yubi | ゆび | finger/toe | | | |
| yudedako | ゆでダコ | boiled octopus | | | |
| yuka | ゆか | floor | | | |
| yukai | ゆかい | pleasing; fun | | | |
| yuki | ゆき（雪） | snow | | | |
| yukidaruma | ゆきだるま | snowman | | | |
| yukisugiru | 行き過ぎる | to pass; go too far | | | |
| yukkuri | ゆっくり | slowly | | | |
| yurusu | ゆるす（ゆるして） | to forgive | | | |
| yuubinkyoku | ゆうびんきょく | post office | | | |

## Appendix D: English-Japanese Glossary (verbs)

| English | Roma-ji | Kana (Kanji) |
|---|---|---|
| to add | tasu | たす（足す） |
| to adhere; get closer (casual form) | kuttsuku | くっつく |
| to age | toshi wo toru | とし（年）をとる |
| to apologize | ayamaru | あやまる |
| to arrive | tsuku | つ（着）く |
| to ask for a favor | tanomu | たのむ |
| to ask; inquire | kiku | きく（聞く） |
| to attend a class | jyugyoo ni deru | じゅぎょうにでる |
| to bake | yaku | やく（焼く） |
| to balance | baransu wo toru | バランスをとる |
| to be (copula verb) | desu | です |
| to be able to ~, can do ~ | koto ga dekiru | ことができる |
| to be able to do | dekiru | できる |
| to be angry | okoru | おこる（怒る） |
| to be audible | kikoeru | きこえる |
| to be born | umareru | うまれる |
| to be burnt | yakeru | やける |
| to be careful | ki wo tsukeru | きをつける（気をつける） |
| to be different | chigau | ちがう |
| to be expected (supposed) to ~ | hazu (da) | はず（だ） |
| to be late; get behind | okureru | おくれる |
| to be lit or turned on | tsuku | つく（点く） |
| to be rescued, saved | tasukaru | たすかる(助かる) |
| to be troubled | komaru | こまる（困る） |
| to be visible | mieru | み（見）える |
| to become | (ni) naru | なる（～になる） |
| to become crowded | komu | こむ/ こんでいる |
| to become dirty | yogoreru | よごれる |
| to become drunk | you | よう（酔う） |
| to become dry or thirsty | kawaku | かわく/ かわいている |
| to become hungry | onaka ga suku | おなかがすく |
| to become late | chikoku suru | ちこくする |
| to become tired | tsukareru | つかれる(疲れる) |
| to begin | hajimaru | はじまる |
| to believe | shinjiru | しんじる（信じる） |
| to boil the hot-bath water | wakasu | わかす |
| to borrow | kariru | かりる（借りる） |
| to bring in | mochikomu | もちこむ（持ち込む） |
| to buy | kau | か（買）う |
| to catch a cold | kaze wo hiku | かぜをひく |
| to chat | oshaberi suru | おしゃべり（を）する |
| to chat | shaberu | しゃべる（しゃべります） |
| to check | chekku suru | チェックする |
| to check; investigate | shiraberu | しらべる |
| to choose | erabu | えらぶ |
| to close (i.v.) | shimaru | しまる（閉まる） |
| to close (t.v.) | shimeru | しめる（閉める） |

| English | Roma-ji | Kana (Kanji) |
|---|---|---|
| to comb | kami wo toku | かみをとく |
| to come | kuru | くる（来る） |
| to come humbly | mairu | まいる |
| to come out | detekuru | でてくる （出て来る） |
| to comfort | nagusameru | なぐさめる |
| to compare | kuraberu | くらべる(比べる) |
| to continue | tsuzuku | つづく |
| to cook | gohan wo tsukuru | ごはんをつくる |
| to cook | ryoori suru | りょうりする |
| to cook in a sauce or soup | niru | にる（煮る） |
| to cool | hiyasu | ひやす（冷やす） |
| to cost | kakaru | かかる（おかねがかかる） |
| to cross | wataru | わたる |
| to cry | naku | なく（泣く） |
| to cut | kiru | きる（切る） |
| to dance | odoru | おどる（踊る） |
| to date | deeto suru | デートする |
| to decide on ~ | ni shimasu | ～にします |
| to decorate | kazaru | かざる |
| to depend on a person | hito ni yoru | ひとによる |
| to die | shinu | しぬ（死ぬ） |
| to dish up; heap; serve; fill | moru | もる（おさらにもる） |
| to do | suru | する |
| to do (casual form of "suru") | yaru | やる |
| to do (humble form) | itasu | いたす |
| to do (polite form) | nasaru | なさる |
| to do laundry | sentaku suru | せんたくする |
| to do me a favor | onegai suru | おねがいする |
| to draw | kaku | かく（描く） |
| to drink | nomu | のむ（飲む） |
| to drive | unten suru | うんてんする |
| to eat | taberu | たべる（食べる） |
| to email | meeru wo suru | メールをする |
| to end | owaru | おわる（終わる） |
| to enter ~ (~ ni hairu) | hairu | はいる（入る） |
| to erase | kesu | けす |
| to excuse oneself; to be rude | shitsurei suru | しつれい（失礼）する |
| to exist (for animate subject) | iru | いる（居る） |
| to exist (for inanimate subject) | aru | ある |
| to exit; to leave | deru | でる（出る） |
| to explain | setsumei suru | せつめいする（説明する） |
| to extinguish; disappear | kieru | きえる（消える） |
| to fail | shippai suru | しっぱいする |
| to fall | ochiru | おちる（落ちる） |
| to fall (i.v.) | taoreru | たおれる |
| to fall; to snow or rain | furu | ふる（降る） |

## Appendix D: English-Japanese Glossary (verbs)

| English | Roma-ji | Kana (Kanji) | English | Roma-ji | Kana (Kanji) |
|---|---|---|---|---|---|
| to feel | kanjiru | かんじる | to leave | saru | さる（去る） |
| to feel like | ki ga suru | き（気）がする | to lie | uso wo tsuku | うそをつく |
| to find | mitsukeru | みつける（見つける） | to lift up; raise | ageru | あげる（上げる） |
| to finish; accomplish | dekiru | できる | to like | kiniiru | きにいる（気に入る） |
| to fly; jump | tobu | とぶ | to line up | narabu | ならぶ（並ぶ） |
| to fold | oru | おる | to listen | kiku | きく（聞く） |
| to forget | wasureru | わすれる（忘れる） | to live | ikiru | いきる |
| to forgive | yurusu | ゆるす（ゆるして） | to live | sumu | すむ（住む） |
| to freeze | kooru | こおる（凍る） | to loan | kasu | かす（貸す） |
| to gain weight | futoru | ふとる（太る） | to lock | kakaru | かかる（かぎがかかる） |
| to get engaged | kon'yaku suru | こんやくする | to look around repeatedly | kyoro-kyoro suru | きょろきょろする |
| to get off ~ | oriru (~ wo oriru) | おりる（〜をおりる） | to lose | ushinau | うしなう（失う） |
| to get startled | dokitto suru | ドキッとする | to lose weight | yaseru | やせる |
| to get up | okiru | おきる（起きる） | to lower | sageru | さげる（下げる） |
| to get wet (i.v.) | nureru | ぬれる | to make | tsukuru | つくる（作る） |
| to get; receive | toru | とる（取る） | to make (as in tea or coffee) | ireru | いれる（煎れる） |
| to give | ageru | あげる |  |  |  |
| to give (me/my in-group) | kureru | くれる | to make a mistake | machigaeru | まちがえる |
| to give humbly | sashiageru | さしあげる | to make an effort; to work hard | hagemu | はげむ（励む） |
| to give up | akirameru | あきらめる |  |  |  |
| to give, feed (to someone lower) | yaru | やる | to make it in time | maniau | まにあう（間に合う） |
| to go | iku | いく（行く） | to make or spread (like a futon) | shiku/hiku | しく／ひく |
| to go beyond; exceed | sugiru | すぎる（過ぎる） |  |  |  |
| to go home; to return | kaeru | かえる（帰る） | to make someone wait | mataseru | またせる |
| to go out | dekakeru | でかける | to match | au | あう（合う） |
| to go to bed, sleep | neru | ねる | to meet | au | あう（会う） |
| to go, come, & stay in a polite form | irassharu | いらっしゃる | to mention; say | kuchi ni suru | くち（口）にする |
|  |  |  | to mix | mazeru | まぜる（混ぜる） |
| to grab; grip | nigiru | にぎる | to narrate | kataru | かたる（語る） |
| to graduate | sotsugyoo suru | そつぎょうする | to need | iru | いる（要る） |
| to greet | aisatsu suru | あいさつする | to notice | ki ga tsuku | き（気）がつく |
| to gush (spring) out | waku | わく | to open (i.v.) | aku | あく（開く） |
| to hand over | watasu | わたす | to open (t.v.) | akeru | あける（開ける） |
| to hang | kakeru | かける | to order | chuumon suru | ちゅうもんする |
| to have, own | mottei iru | もっている（持っている） | to pass the ball | pasu suru | パスする |
|  |  |  | to pass the examination | ukaru | うかる（受かる） |
| to heel | naoru | なおる |  |  |  |
| to help | tetsudau | てつだう | to pass through | tooru | とおる（通る） |
| to hit; beat | tataku | たたく | to pass; go too far | yukisugiru | 行き過ぎる |
| to hold, have | motsu | もつ（持つ） | to pick up; go get something | tori ni iku | と（取）りに行く |
| to hurry | isogu | いそぐ |  |  |  |
| to inhale | suu | すう（吸う） | to play | asobu | あそぶ |
| to insert, put in | ireru | いれる（入れる） | to play (music instruments) | hiku | ひく（弾く） |
| to intend to ~ | tsumori (da) | つもり（だ） |  |  |  |
| to introduce oneself | jikoshookai suru | じこしょうかい（を）する | to polish; brush | migaku | みがく |
|  |  |  | to practice | renshuu suru | れんしゅうする（練習する） |
| to invite; call | yobu | よぶ |  |  |  |
| to jump | jyanpu suru | ジャンプする | to prepare | yooi (jyunbi) suru | よういする（＝じゅんびする） |
| to knit | amu | あむ（編む） |  |  |  |
| to know | shitteiru | し（知）っている | to press | osu | おす（押す） |
| to learn | manabu | まなぶ | to put up an umbrella | sasu | （かさを）さす |
| to learn | narau | ならう（習う） | to quit | yameru | やめる |

## Appendix D: English-Japanese Glossary (verbs)

| English | Roma-ji | Kana (Kanji) |
|---|---|---|
| to rain | ame ga furu | あめがふる |
| to read | yomu | よむ |
| to recall | omoidasu | おもいだす　（思い出す） |
| to receive | ukeru | うける |
| to receive | uketoru | うけとる（受け取る） |
| to receive (humble form) | itadaku | いただく |
| to receive (when Subject is receiver) | morau | もらう |
| to relax | nonbiri suru | のんびりする/リラックスする |
| to remain | nokoru | のこる（残る） |
| to remove; take off | nugu | ぬぐ |
| to rest; to be absent | yasumu | やすむ（休む） |
| to return | modoru | もどる |
| to return something | kaesu | かえす（返す） |
| to ride; get on~ (~ni noru)) | noru | のる |
| to rise (e.g., the Sun) | noboru | のぼる |
| to rob; steal | ubau | うばう |
| to run | hashiru | はしる（走る） |
| to run (business) | keiei susru | けいえいする |
| to run away; escape | nigeru | にげる |
| to save | chokin suru | ちょきん(貯金)する |
| to say | iu | いう（言う） |
| to scatter; (flower petals) fall | chiru | ちる　（散る） |
| to scratch | kaku | かく（掻く） |
| to search | sagasu | さがす（探す） |
| to see, look, watch | miru | みる（見る） |
| to seek | motomeru | もとめる（求める） |
| to send | okuru | おくる（送る） |
| to set | setto suru | セットする |
| to shake; tremble | furueru | ふるえる |
| to share; to split | wakeru | わける（分ける） |
| to sing, chirp, bark | naku | なく（鳴く） |
| to sink (The sun sets.) | shizumu | （日が）しずむ |
| to sink a shot | shuuto wo kimeru | シュートを　きめる |
| to sit | suwaru | すわる（座る） |
| to smile, laugh | warau | わらう　（笑う） |
| to smile/laugh excessively | warai sugiru | わらいすぎる |
| to smoke | tabako wo suu | （タバコを）すう |
| to sob softly and continuously | shikushiku | しくしく（シクシク）なく |
| to speak, talk | hanasu | はなす（話す） |
| to stand up | tatsu | たつ（立つ） |
| to stay over night | tomaru | とまる（泊まる） |
| to step back | sagaru | さがる　（下がる） |
| to stir-fry | itameru | いためる(炒める) |
| to stop (i.v.) | tomaru | とまる（止まる） |
| to stop (t.v.) | tomeru | とめる（止める） |
| to stop by | tachiyoru | たちよる |

| English | Roma-ji | Kana (Kanji) |
|---|---|---|
| to stretch; to grow | nobiru | のびる（伸びる） |
| to stroll | sanpo (wo) suru | さんぽ（を）する |
| to study | benkyoo suru | べんきょうする |
| to sweeten | amaku suru | あまくする |
| to swim | oyogu | およぐ（泳ぐ） |
| to take (time) | kakaru | かかる（じかんがかかる） |
| to take a picture | toru | とる（しゃしんを撮る） |
| to take a shower | abiru | （シャワーを）あびる |
| to take a shower | shawaa wo abiru | シャワーをあびる |
| to take place; to happen | okoru | おこる（起こる） |
| to take someone | tsurete iku | つれていく |
| to teach; instruct | oshieru | おしえる (教える) |
| to think; consider | omou | おもう（思う） |
| to think; contemplate | kangaeru | かんがえる（考える） |
| to throw away; to discard | suteru | すてる（捨てる） |
| to tidy up | katazukeru | かたづける |
| to touch | sawaru | さわる |
| to treat someone | ogoru | おごる |
| to try taste | ajimi suru | あじみ　（味見）（を）する |
| to turn | magaru | まがる（曲がる） |
| to turn in; to mail; to take out | dasu | だす（出す） |
| to turn on (like a switch) | ireru | いれる |
| to turn on; to light | tsukeru | つける（点ける） |
| to undergo a change | kawaru | かわる（変わる） |
| to understand | wakaru | わかる（分かる） |
| to visit (humble form) | ukagau | うかがう（伺う） |
| to wait | matsu | まつ（待つ） |
| to wake up | me ga sameru | めがさめる |
| to wake up someone | okosu | おこす（起こす） |
| to walk | aruku | ある（歩）く |
| to wash | arau | あらう（洗う） |
| to wear (glasses) | kakeru | （メガネ）をかける |
| to wear (items below waistline such as pants, skirt) | haku | はく |
| to wear (over the shoulders like a shirt) | kiru | きる(着る) |
| to wear; put on (on the head) | kaburu | かぶる |
| to wet something (t.v.) | nurasu | ぬらす |
| to wipe | fuku | ふく |
| to work | hataraku | はたらく |
| to work hard | ganbaru | がんばる |
| to worry | shinpai suru | しんぱいする |
| to write | kaku | かく　（書く） |
| to write a letter to someone | otayori suru | おたよりする（お便りする） |

## Appendix D: English-Japanese Glossary (non-verbs)

| English | Roma-ji | Kana (Kanji) | English | Roma-ji | Kana (Kanji) |
|---|---|---|---|---|---|
| A.M. , morning | gozen | ごぜん | around ~ ; vicinity | atari | あたり |
| about ~ | no koto | ～のこと | around what time | nan-ji goro | なんじごろ |
| about, around | goro (gurai) | ごろ（ぐらい） | arrangement for a meeting | machi awase | まちあわせ |
| above; top; on | ue | うえ | | | |
| academic subjects | gakka | がっか | arts | bijyutsu | びじゅつ |
| accident | jiko | じこ（事故） | as if | marude | まるで |
| acquaintance | shiriai | しりあい | Asian decent | ajia-kei | アジア系 |
| additional person, one more person | moo hitori | もうひとり | aspirin | asupirin | アスピリン |
| | | | assorted meal | teishoku | ていしょく |
| additional thing, one more thing | moo hitotsu | もうひとつ | at (showing specific time) | ni | に |
| address | jyuusho | じゅうしょ | at first | hajime ni | はじめに |
| adult | otona | おとな | at last; in the end; finally | saigoni | さいごに |
| after that | sonogo | そのご（その後） | | | |
| afternoon sun from the West | nishibi | にしび（西日） | at or in (location of actions) | de | で |
| again | mata | また | attention/caution is needed | chuui ga iru | ちゅういが　いる(注意が要る) |
| age | toshi | とし（年） | | | |
| agreement | sansei | さんせい（賛成） | attractive | miryokuteki ni | みりょくてきに |
| ahead; future | saki | さき（先） | August | hachi-gatsu | はちがつ（八月） |
| air | kuuki | くうき | aunt (casual)(formal) | oba-obasan | おば--おばさん |
| air conditioner | kuuraa | クーラー | baby | akachan | あかちゃん |
| airplane | hikooki | ひこうき | back (one's back) | senaka | せなか |
| alarm clock | mezamashi-dokei | めざましどけい | back, backyard | ura | うら |
| all right, no problem | daijyoobu | だいじょうぶ(大丈夫) | bag; briefcase | kaban | かばん |
| | | | bake (how to) | yakikata | やきかた（焼き方） |
| all the time | shocchuu | しょっちゅう | bakery | pan ya | パンや |
| all-day long | ichi-nichi-jyuu | いちにちじゅう | balance | baransu | バランス |
| allowance | kozukai | こづかい（おこづかい） | ballpoint pen | booru-pen | ぼうるぺん（ボールペン） |
| almond | aamondo | アーモンド | banana | banana | バナナ |
| alone | hitoride | ・ひとりで | (music) band | bando | バンド |
| along with the street | michinari (ni) | みちなり（に） | bank | ginkoo | ぎんこう |
| also | mo | も | barber shop | tokoya | とこや |
| always | itsumo | いつも | baseball | yakyuu | やきゅう |
| America | Amerika | アメリカ | basketball | basuketto booru | バスケットボール |
| amount | ryoo | りょう（量） | bath | ofuro | おふろ |
| amusement park | yuuenchi | ゆうえんち | bathroom | otearai | おてあらい |
| An expression showing hesitance | Anoo | あのう | batteries | kandenchi | かんでんち |
| | | | beautiful | utsukushii | うつくしい |
| an order | chuumon | ちゅうもん | because | node | ので |
| And | soshite | そして | because of that, due to that | sore de | それで |
| and (to connect two nouns) | to | と | | | |
| | | | bed | beddo | べっど（ベッド） |
| and then, after that | sorekara | それから | beef | biifu | ビーフ |
| and what's more | shi | し | beef | gyuuniku | ぎゅうにく（牛肉） |
| angel | tenshi | てんし（天使） | beef & vegetables cooked in shallow pan | sukiyaki | すきやき |
| animal | doobutsu | どうぶつ（動物） | | | |
| anime (animation) | anime | アニメ | beef steak | bifuteki | ビフテキ |
| answer | kotae | こたえ | beforehand | temae | てまえ(手前) |
| ant | ari | あり | the beginning, first | hajime | はじめ（初め） |
| apartment | apaato | アパート | behind, back | ushiro | うしろ（後ろ） |
| apple | ringo | りんご | being not home | rusu | るす（留守） |
| April | shi-gatsu | しがつ（四月） | belt | beruto | べると（ベルト） |
| arms | ude | うで | benefit | go-riyaku | ごりやく |

## Appendix D: English-Japanese Glossary (non-verbs)

| English | Roma-ji | Kana (Kanji) |
|---|---|---|
| best | saikoo | さいこう（最高） |
| between | aida | あいだ（間） |
| beyond | mukoo | むこう |
| bicycle | jitensha | じてんしゃ |
| big joy | ooyorokobi | おおよろこび |
| big sister (affectionate term) | oneechan | おねえちゃん（お姉ちゃん） |
| big size | dai | だい（大） |
| big, large | ookii | おおきい |
| Biology | seibutsu(-gaku) | せいぶつ（がく） |
| bird | tori | とり |
| birthday card | otanjyookaado | おたんじょうカード |
| bitter | nigai | にがい |
| black (adjectival form) | kuroi | くろい |
| black (noun form) | kuro | くろ |
| blackboard | kokuban | こくばん |
| blackboard eraser | kokuban-keshi | こくばんけし |
| blazing sun, or extreme anger | kankan (ni) | かんかん（に） |
| blouse | burausu | ぶらうす（ブラウス） |
| blue | aoi | あおい（青い） |
| boarding house | geshuku | げしゅく |
| boat | booto | ボート |
| body | karada | からだ（体） |
| boiled octopus | yudedako | ゆでダコ |
| book | hon | ほん |
| bookshelf | hontate | ほんたて |
| bookstore | hon ya | ほんや |
| boring | taikutsu | たいくつ |
| boring; uninteresting | tsumaranai | ・つまらない |
| bottom | soko | そこ（底） |
| box | hako | はこ |
| boxed lunch | o-bentoo | （お）べんとう |
| boxed lunch with rice balls | onigiri bentoo | おにぎりべんとう |
| bread | pan | パン |
| bread with sweet red beans | an-pan | あんパン |
| breakfast | asa-gohan | あさごはん |
| breeze (soft) | soyosoyo | そよそよ（ソヨソヨ） |
| bridge | hashi | はし（橋） |
| bright | akarui | あか（明）るい |
| British style | igirisu-shiki | イギリスしき（式） |
| broccoli | burokkori | ブロッコリ |
| brown | chairoi | ちゃいろい |
| buckwheat noodle | soba | そば |
| buckwheat noodle soup | zaru soba | ざるそば |
| buckwheat noodles with chicken | tori-nanban | とりなんばん |
| buckwheat noodles with tempura | tenpura soba | てんぷらそば |

| English | Roma-ji | Kana (Kanji) |
|---|---|---|
| Buddhist temple | tera | てら（寺） |
| Buddhist temples | otera | （お）てら |
| budget | yosan | よさん |
| bugs, insects | mushi | むし（虫） |
| building | tatemono | たてもの |
| bullet train | shin-kan-sen | しんかんせん |
| burdock root | goboo | ごぼう |
| bus | basu | バス |
| bus stop | basu-tei | バスてい |
| but or although | ga | が |
| but; however | demo | でも |
| buttocks | oshiri | おしり |
| button | botan | ボタン |
| buy | kaimasu | かいます |
| by all means | zehi | ぜひ |
| by chance; coincidently | guuzen | ぐうぜん |
| by far | zutto | ずっと |
| by means of | de | で |
| cabbage | kyabetsu | キャベツ |
| cabinet | todana | とだな |
| cafeteria | kafeteria | カフェテリア |
| cake | keeki | ケーキ |
| camel | rakuda | らくだ |
| camera shop | kamera ya | カメラや |
| campus | kyanpasu | キャンパス |
| cancer | gan | ガン（がん） |
| candy | ame | あめ（飴） |
| capital | shuto | しゅと |
| cappuccino | kapuchiino | カプチーノ |
| car | kuruma | くるま |
| car; automobile | jidoosha | じどうしゃ（自動車） |
| carelessness | fuchuui | ふちゅうい（不注意） |
| carp (koi/fish) | koi | こい（鯉） |
| carrots | ninjin | にんじん |
| casual expression of "Yes" | Un | うん |
| casual form "very," awesome | sugoku | すごく |
| casual form of "desu" | da | だ |
| casual form of ではありません | jyanai | じゃない |
| cat | neko | ねこ |
| cause | gen'in | げんいん（原因） |
| caution | chuui | ちゅうい（注意） |
| cell phone | keitaidenwa | けいたいでんわ |
| cent | sento | セント |
| centimeter | senchi (meetoru) | センチ（メートル） |
| century | seiki | せいき（世紀） |
| cereal | shiriaru | シリアル |
| ceremony for coming of age | seijinshiki | せいじんしき |
| certainly, of course | mochiron | もちろん |

## Appendix D: English-Japanese Glossary (non-verbs)

| English | Roma-ji | Kana (Kanji) |
|---|---|---|
| chair | isu | いす |
| chalk | chooku | チョーク |
| change | henka | へんか（変化） |
| (the) change | otsuri | おつり |
| cheap; reasonable | yasui | やすい（安い） |
| cheeks | hoho/hoo, hoppeta | ほほ（ほお、ほっぺた） |
| cheese | chiizu | チーズ |
| cheeseburger | chiizu-baagaa | チーズバーガー |
| cheesecake | chiizu-keeki | チーズケーキ |
| Chemistry | kagaku | かがく（化学） |
| cherry blossoms | sakura | さくら（桜） |
| chest | mune | むね |
| chest | tansu | たんす |
| chestnut | kuri | くり |
| chew without opening mouth widely | mogumogu | もぐもぐ |
| chick | hiyoko | ひよこ |
| chicken | chikin | チキン |
| chicken | toriniku | とりにく（とり肉） |
| chicken rice (fried rice with chicken) | chikin-raisu | チキンライス |
| chicken roasted | yakitori | やきとり |
| child (polite form) | okosan | おこさん |
| child, children | kodomo | こども |
| Chinese | chuugoku-go | ちゅうごくご |
| Chinese noodles in soup | raamen | ラーメン |
| chocolate | chokoreeto | チョコレート |
| chopsticks | hashi (o-hashi) | （お）はし |
| Christmas | kurisumasu | クリスマス |
| chunk | katamari | かたまり |
| cicada | semi | せみ |
| cigarette littering | poisute | ポイすて |
| class, lecture, classroom | kurasu | クラス |
| classroom | kyooshitsu | きょうしつ |
| cleaning | sooji | そうじ |
| cliff | gake | がけ |
| clock | tokei | とけい |
| closet | oshiire | おしいれ |
| cloth | nuno | ぬの（布） |
| clothing | fukusoo | ふくそう |
| clothing that is too big | bukabuka | ブカブカ |
| cloudy | kumori | くもり |
| club activities at school | kurabu | クラブ |
| cluttered | gochagocha | ごちゃごちゃ |
| coffee | koohii | コーヒー |
| coffee shop | kissaten | きっさてん |
| Coke | koora | コーラ |
| a cold | kaze | かぜ |
| cold | samui | さむい |
| cold (by touch) | tsumetai | つめたい |
| cold medicine | kazegusuri | かぜぐすり |
| college student | daigakusei | だいがくせい |
| college, university | daigaku | だいがく |
| color | iro | いろ |
| comic books | manga | まんが |
| coming in and out | de-iri | でいり |
| coming to Japan | rainichi | らいにち |
| company | kaisha | かいしゃ（会社） |
| company employee | kaishain | かいしゃいん/サラリーマン |
| composition | sakubun | さくぶん（作文） |
| computer | konpyuutaa | こんぴゅうたあ（コンピューター） |
| Computer Science | konpyuutaa saiensu | コンピューターサイエンス |
| concert | konsaato | コンサート |
| conjunctive particle "because" | kara | から |
| consecutive holidays | renkyuu | れんきゅう |
| contact | renraku | れんらく |
| contact lenses | kontakuto-renzu | コンタクトレンズ |
| contract | keiyakusho | けいやくしょ |
| contrarian | amanojyaku | あまのじゃく |
| convenience store | konbini | コンビニ |
| convenient | benri | べんり |
| cooked and vinegard rice | sushi (o-sushi) | （お）すし |
| cooking | ryoori | りょうり |
| cooking pan | nabe | なべ |
| cool | kakkoyoku | かっこよく |
| corn | toomorokoshi | とうもろこし |
| corner | kado | かど |
| corner (turning corner) | magarikado | まがりかど |
| correct answer | seikai | せいかい（正解） |
| correctly; adequately | chanto | ちゃんと |
| corridor | rooka | ろうか |
| corrugation | gizagiza | ぎざぎざ |
| cosmetics | keshoohin | けしょうひん |
| cotton | momen; men | （も）めん |
| counter for boxes | hito hako | ひとはこ（一箱） |
| counter for floors of a bldg. | kai | （〜）かい（階） |
| counter for houses/buildings | ken | （〜）けん（軒） |
| counter for long items | ippon | いっぽん（一本） |
| counter for non-flat, small items | ikko | いっこ（一個） |
| country | kuni | くに |
| cousin | itoko | いとこ |
| cow | ushi | うし |
| crack! (noise) | gashan | ガシャン |
| cram; grinding | gariben | がりべん（ガリ勉） |
| cream (also for milk) | kuriimu | クリーム |
| crime | hanzai | はんざい |
| criminal | han'nin | はんにん（犯人） |

## Appendix D: English-Japanese Glossary (non-verbs)

| English | Roma-ji | Kana (Kanji) |
|---|---|---|
| crocodile | wani | わに |
| cry (loud like child) | uwaan | うわ～ん |
| crybaby | nakimushi | なきむし |
| cubic centimeter, milliliter | shii-shii | シーシー（ＣＣ） |
| cucumber | kyuuri | きゅうり |
| culture | bunka | ぶんか（文化） |
| curry rice (curry on rice) | karee-raisu | カレーライス |
| curtain | kaaten | かあてん（カーテン） |
| custom | shuukan | しゅうかん（習慣） |
| cut | kirimasu | きります（切ります） |
| cute | kawaii | かわいい |
| cute | kyuuto | キュート |
| daikon radish | daikon | だいこん |
| dangerous | abunai | あぶない |
| dangerous | kiken | きけん |
| dark | kurai | くらい（暗い） |
| darkness | kurayami | くらやみ（暗やみ） |
| date | deeto | デート |
| date | hizuke | ひづけ（日付） |
| daytime | hiru | ひる |
| dead end | tsukiatari | つきあたり |
| dead end (Kyoto dialect) | dontsuki | どんつき |
| December | jyuu-ni-gatsu | じゅうにがつ（十二月） |
| deep-fried vegetables and seafood | tenpura | てんぷら |
| deer | shika | しか |
| degree | teido | ていど |
| degrees | do | ど |
| delicious | oishii | おいしい |
| department store | depaato | デパート |
| depressed; melancholy | yuu-utsu | ゆううつ |
| description of people, sketch of people | jinbutsu-byoosha | じんぶつびょうしゃ(人物描写) |
| desert | sabaku | さばく |
| design | dezain | デザイン |
| desk | tsukue | つくえ |
| detective | keiji | けいじ（刑事） |
| devil | akuma | あくま |
| diamond | daiyamondo | ダイヤモンド |
| diary | nikki | にっき（日記） |
| dictionary | jisho | じしょ |
| difficult to (do~) | nikui (~ nikui) | ～にくい |
| diffident | hikkomijian | ひっこみじあん |
| digital camera | deji-kame | デジカメ |
| diligence; hard work | kinben | きんべん（勤勉） |
| dinner | ban-gohan | ばんごはん |
| dirty | kitanai | きたない |
| disco | disuko | ディスコ |
| dishes | osara | （お）さら |

| English | Roma-ji | Kana (Kanji) |
|---|---|---|
| dishes to go with the rice | okazu | おかず |
| dislikable; unpleasant | iya | いや |
| docile; quiet | otonashii | おとなしい |
| dog | inu | いぬ |
| dog food | doggufuudo | ドッグフード |
| doll | ningyoo | にんぎょう (人形) |
| dollar | doru | ドル |
| door | to/doa | と/ドア |
| dormitory | ryoo | りょう（寮） |
| dot; point; spot | ten | てん |
| drawer | hikidashi | ひきだし |
| dress | doresu | ドレス |
| dress shirt | wai-shatsu | Ｙ－シャツ |
| drinks | nomimono | のみもの |
| drive | doraibu | ドライブ |
| drive | unten | うんてん |
| driver | untenshu | うんてんしゅ（運転手） |
| driving a track | torakku no unten | トラックのうんてん |
| drugstore, pharmacy | kusuriya | くすりや |
| drugstore, pharmacy | yakkyoku | やっきょく |
| drum | taiko | たいこ |
| dumpling | gyooza | ぎょうざ |
| during the class | jyugyoochuu | じゅぎょうちゅう |
| during the morning (hours) | gozen-chuu | ごぜんちゅう |
| during the night | yakan | やかん（夜間） |
| dusk | yuugata | ゆうがた |
| dust | hokori | ほこり |
| each | zutsu | ずつ |
| early | hayai | はやい |
| early bird | hayaoki | はやおき |
| ears | mimi | みみ |
| East | higashi | ひがし（東） |
| easy to (do~) | yasui (~ yasui) | ～やすい |
| easy; simple | kantan | かんたん |
| economical | keizaiteki | けいざいてき |
| Economics | keizai(-gaku) | けいざい（がく） |
| Education | kyooiku-gaku | きょういくがく |
| effort | kuroo | くろう |
| egg | tamago | たまご |
| eight | yattsu | やっつ |
| electric appliance store | denki ya | でんきや |
| electric appliances | denka seihin | でんかせいひん |
| electric stand | sutando | すたんど（スタンド） |
| elementary school | shoogakkoo | しょうがっこう |
| elementary school students | shoo-gakusei | しょうがくせい |
| elephant | zou | ぞう |
| elevator | erebeetaa | エレベーター |
| end | owari | おわり |
| engineer | enjinia | エンジニア |

## Appendix D: English-Japanese Glossary (non-verbs)

| English | Roma-ji | Kana (Kanji) |
|---|---|---|
| Engineering | koogaku | こうがく　　（工学） |
| Engineering Department | koogaku-bu | こうがくぶ |
| English | ei-go | えいご |
| enjoyable; fun | tanoshii | たのしい |
| entrance | iriguchi | いりぐち |
| entrance to school | nyuu-gaku | にゅうがく |
| envious | urayamashii | うらやましい |
| eraser | keshigomu | けしごむ |
| escalator | esukareetaa | エスカレーター |
| essay | essei | エッセー |
| evening | ban | ばん　（晩） |
| every time | maido | まいど |
| everyday | mainichi | まいにち |
| everyone | min'na | みんな |
| everything | zenbu | ぜんぶ |
| exactly | choodo | ちょうど |
| examination | shiken | しけん |
| excessive drinking | fukazake | ふかざけ |
| Excuse me (for long absence) | Gobusata shiteimasu | ごぶさたしています。 |
| excuse me (used as greeting) | gomen kudasai | ごめんください。 |
| exit | deguchi | でぐち |
| expensive | takai | たかい　（高い） |
| explanation | setsumei | せつめい |
| eye drop | megusuri | めぐすり　（目薬） |
| eye glasses | megane | めがね |
| eye lashes | matsuge | まつげ |
| eye(s) | me | め　（目） |
| eyebrow | mayu (ge) | まゆ(げ)　（まゆ毛) |
| face | kao | かお　（顔） |
| faintly | boottsu to | ボーッと |
| fairy well, the same as | kekkoo | けっこう/かなり |
| fall, autumn | aki | あき |
| family | kazoku | かぞく |
| famous | yuumei (na) | ゆうめい　（な) |
| fanatic | otaku | おたく |
| far | tooi | とお　（遠）　い |
| fashion | fasshon | ファッション |
| fate | unmei | うんめい　（運命） |
| father (humble form, my father) | chichi | ちち |
| father (respect form) | otoosan | おとうさん |
| faucet | suidoo | すいどう |
| feast | gochisoo | ごちそう |
| February | ni-gatsu | にがつ　（二月） |
| feel like dying | shinisoo | し　（死）　にそう |
| feeling | kanji | かんじ　（感じ） |
| feelings | kimochi | きもち　（気持ち） |
| fence | saku | さく　（柵） |
| fermented soybeans | nattoo | なっとう |
| ～ steps | ni ～ san po | に、さんぽ　（二、三歩) |

| English | Roma-ji | Kana (Kanji) |
|---|---|---|
| fewer | sukunai | すくない |
| fight; quarrel | kenka | けんか |
| figs | ichijiku | いちじく |
| finger/toe | yubi | ゆび |
| fire | hi | ひ　（火） |
| fire | kaji | かじ（火事） |
| fire engine | shooboosha | しょうぼうしゃ |
| fire-watch tower | hinomiyagura | ひのみやぐら |
| firewood | takigi | たきぎ |
| firework | hanabi | はなび　（花火） |
| first | saisho | さいしょ |
| first (the first) | hitotsume | ひとつめ　（一つ目） |
| fish | sakana | さかな（魚) |
| fish market | sakana ya | さかなや |
| five | itsutsu | いつつ |
| flag | hata | はた |
| flattery | o-seji | おせじ |
| flight | furaito | フライト |
| floor | yuka | ゆか |
| flower | hana | はな　（花) |
| flower shop | hana ya | はなや |
| flower vase | kabin | かびん |
| fluttering through air | chirachira | ちらちら　（チラチラ) |
| folk | fooku | フォーク |
| food | shokuhin | しょくひん |
| food | tabemono | たべもの |
| food delivery | demae | でまえ　（出前） |
| football | futtobooru | フットボール |
| for adult | otona-yoo | おとなよう |
| for emphasis, as many as ～ | mo | も |
| for example | tatoeba | たとえば（例えば) |
| for sure, definitely | kanarazu | かならず　（必ず） |
| for sure; definitely; certainly | tashikani | たしかに |
| forehead | hitai | ひたい |
| foreign exchange students | ryuu-gakusei | りゅうがくせい |
| foreign languages | gaikokugo | がいこくご |
| forest | mori | もり　（森） |
| fountain pen | man'nen hitsu | まんねんひつ |
| four | yottsu | よっつ |
| four seasons | shiki | しき |
| fox | kitsune | きつね |
| fox color; light brown | kitsune iro | きつねいろ |
| free (time) | hima | ひま |
| freeway | furii-uei | フリーウェイ |
| French | Furansu-go | フランスご |
| French fries | furaido poteto | フライドポテト |
| freshman, first-year student | ichi-nen-sei | いちねんせい |
| Friday | kin-yoobi | きんようび |
| fried rice | chaahan | チャーハン |

### Appendix D: English-Japanese Glossary (non-verbs)

| English | Roma-ji | Kana (Kanji) | English | Roma-ji | Kana (Kanji) |
|---|---|---|---|---|---|
| fried rice covered by omelet | omuraisu | オムライス | greeting to see someone off | itte (i)rasshai | いって（い）らっしゃい |
| friend | tomodachi | ともだち | greetings | aisatsu | あいさつ |
| friendly; harmoniously | nakayoku | なかよく | grown-up-like | otonappoku | おとなっぽく |
| frog | kaeru | かえる（蛙） | guest | gesuto | ゲスト |
| from | kara | から | guitarist | gitarisuto | ギタリスト |
| front | mae | まえ | gulping liquid | gokugoku | ゴクゴク |
| front, across the street | mukaigawa (mae) | むかいがわ（まえ） | gum | gamu | がむ（ガム） |
| fruit shop | kudamono ya | くだものや | gym | jimu | ジム |
| fruits | kudamono | くだもの | hair | kami | かみ（髪） |
| full | ippai | いっぱい | hair, fur | ke | け（毛） |
| furniture | kagu | かぐ | half-hour; thirty minutes | han | はん |
| games; match | shiai | しあい | ham | hamu | ハム |
| genius | tensai | てんさい（天才） | hamburger | hanbaagaa | ハンバーガー |
| ghost | yuurei | ゆうれい | hand mixer | hando-mikisaa | ハンドミキサー |
| ghost (casual) | obake | おばけ（お化け） | hand(s) | te | て |
| giant clam | mirugai | みるがい | handkerchief | hankachi | はんかち（ハンカチ） |
| Giant Panda | panda | パンダ | | | |
| ginger-juice | shoogajiru | しょうがじる | handsome | hansamu | ハンサム |
| giraffe | kirin | きりん | happy | shiawase | しあわせ |
| girls | jyoshi | じょし | happy, glad (I am happy, glad) | ureshii | うれしい |
| (going) round | gurutto (mawaru) | ぐるっと（まわる） | | | |
| gloves | tebukuro | てぶくろ | happy-go-lucky | yooki | ようき |
| gold | kin | きん | hard work, alarming, terrible (noun) | taihen | たいへん（大変） |
| gold (golden color) | kin'iro | きんいろ（金色） | | | |
| gold fish | kingyo | きんぎょ | hard, difficult | muzukashii | むずかしい |
| golf | gorufu | ゴルフ | hard, firm | katai | かたい（固い） |
| good | ii | いい | hat; cap | booshi | ぼうし |
| good (polite/formal form) | yoroshii | よろしい | he, boyfriend | kare | かれ |
| | | | head | atama | あたま |
| Good afternoon. Hello. | Kon'nichiwa | こんにちは | healthy | kenkoo | けんこう |
| | | | healthy; energetic | genki | げんき |
| Good bye. (to your equal) | Sayoonara | さようなら | heart | kokoro | こころ（心） |
| | | | height | se | せ（背） |
| Good evening. | Konbanwa | こんばんは | height | setake | せたけ（背丈） |
| (good luck) charm | o-mamori | おまもり | helicopter | herikoputaa | ヘリコプター |
| Good morning. (Casual) | Ohayoo | おはよう | help; assistance | otetsudai | おてつだい |
| | | | here (this place) | koko | ここ |
| Good morning. (Formal) | Ohayoo gozaimasu | おはようございます | high school | kookoo | こうこう |
| Good night | Oyasumi (nasai) | おやすみ（なさい） | hips | koshi | こし |
| good, skilled | jyoozu | じょうず（上手） | Hmm!, Wow! | Hee | へえ |
| grades | seiseki | せいせき | holiday; absent; rest | yasumi | （お）やすみ |
| gram | guramu | グラム | homemaker; housewife | shufu | しゅふ |
| grandfather (casual)/(formal) | sofu-ojiisan | そふ―おじいさん | homework | shukudai | しゅくだい |
| | | | honestly | shoojikini | しょうじきに |
| grandmother (casual)/(formal) | sobo-obaasan | そぼ―おばあさん | honey | mitsu | みつ（蜜） |
| | | | horned owl | mimizuku | みみずく |
| grapes | budoo | ぶどう | horse | uma | うま |
| gratitude; thanks | orei | おれい | hospital | byooin | びょういん |
| gratuity | go-shuugi | ごしゅうぎ | hot | atsui | あつい |
| green | midori | みどり | hot coffee | hotto | ホット |
| green grocer | yaoya | やおや | house, home | uchi | うち |
| green tea | ocha | おちゃ | how | doo | どう |

## Appendix D: English-Japanese Glossary (non-verbs)

| English | Roma-ji | Kana (Kanji) | English | Roma-ji | Kana (Kanji) |
|---|---|---|---|---|---|
| how many times | nan kai | なんかい | ingredient | zairyoo | ざいりょう |
| How much is it? | Ikura desu ka. | いくらですか。 | intelligent | interi | インテリ |
| how to fold origami-paper | origami no orikata | おりがみのおりかた | interesting; fun | omoshiroi | おもしろい |
| how to get there | michi no ikikata | みちの行きかた | intersection | koosaten | こうさてん |
| how to make | tsukuri kata | つくりかた (作り方) | iron (as in ironing) | airon | アイロン |
| how? | Doo yatte ? | どうやって | is desired; is wanted | hoshii | ほしい |
| however; on the contrary | tokoroga | ところが | isn't it? (a tag question) | ne | ね |
| hula dance | fura-dansu | フラダンス | It's been a while since I last saw you. | O-hisashiburi desu | おひさしぶりです |
| human beings | ningen | にんげん （人間） | It's done~! | dekiagari | できあがり |
| hurricane | harikeen | ハリケーン | Italian | Itari(y)a-go | イタリアご |
| husband (polite form) | go-shujin | ごしゅじん | itchy | kayui | かゆい |
| I | watashi | わたし | jam | jyamu | ジャム |
| I humbly receive this | itadakimasu | いただきます | January | ichi-gatsu | いちがつ （一月） |
| I see. | naruhodo | なるほど | Japan | Nihon | にほん |
| I shall put it in (humble form) | o-ire-shimasu | おいれします | Japanese currency | nihon-en | にほんえん（日本円） |
| I wonder if ~ | darooka | だろうか | Japanese eel | unagi | うなぎ |
| I wonder? | kana? | ～かな？ | Japanese food | washoku | わしょく（和食） |
| I'm home | tadaima | ただいま | Japanese kimono | kimono | きもの |
| I'm leaving | itte kimasu | いってきます | Japanese language | nihon-go | にほんご |
| I'm sorry (more formal); excuse me | sumimasen | すみません | Japanese pear | nashi | なし |
| I'm sorry. | gomen'nasai | ごめんなさい | Japanese squash | kabocha | かぼちゃ |
| ice | koori | こおり （氷） | jazz | jyazu | ジャズ |
| ice cream | aisukuriimu | アイスクリーム | jeans | jiinzu | ジーンズ |
| iced coffee | aisu | アイス | jewelry | hooseki | ほうせき |
| idea | aidea | アイデア | job, work | shigoto | しごと |
| if I'm not mistaken | tashika | たしか | jogging | jogingu | ジョギング |
| if it is ~, | nara | なら (N.なら) | joke | jyoodan | じょうだん |
| if or when | to | と | July | shichi-gatsu | しちがつ （七月） |
| if you do so | soo suru to | そうすると | June | roku-gatsu | ろくがつ （六月） |
| I'll let you know | oshiraseshimasu | おしらせします | junior high school | chuugakkoo | ちゅうがっこう |
| illness | byooki | びょうき | junior high school students | chuu-gukusei | ちゅうがくせい |
| illustration | irasuto | イラスト | just fine | choodo ii | ちょうどいい |
| I'm sorry (casual form) | gomen | ごめん | Kabuki theater | kabuki | かぶき |
| image | imeeji | イメージ | Kabuki theater in Kyoto | Minami-za | みなみざ |
| impossible | muri | むり | kangaroo | kangaruu | カンガルー |
| in a hurry | isoide | いそいで | key holder | kii-horudaa | きいほるだあ （キーホルダー） |
| in addition to it; besides that | soreni | それに | kindness | shinsetsu | しんせつ |
| in comparison with ~; on the contrary | sore ni kurabete | それにくらべて | kitchen | kicchin | キッチン（だいどころ） |
| in public | hitomae | ひとまえ （人前） | kitchen sink | nagashi | ながし |
| in that case, then | jya | じゃ | kitchen utensils | daidokoro yoohin | だいどころようひん |
| in the future | shoorai | しょうらい | knees | hiza | ひざ |
| in what way? How? | nan de? | なんで | knife | naifu | ナイフ |
| in, inside | naka | なか （中） | knocked | nokku shimashita | ノックしました |
| incident; event | dekigoto | できごと | knowledge | chishiki | ちしき （知識） |
| inconvenient | fuben | ふべん | koala | koara | コアラ |
| in-corner | sumi | すみ | Korean | kankoku-go | かんこくご |
| index finger | hitosashiyubi | ひとさしゆび | Kyoto dialect | Kyooto-ben | きょうとべん（京都弁） |
| t child | amaenboo | あまえんぼう | | | |

## Appendix D: English-Japanese Glossary (non-verbs)

| English | Roma-ji | Kana (Kanji) |
|---|---|---|
| Kyoto, ancient capital of Japan | Kyooto | きょうと |
| lab | rabo | ラボ |
| lamp; light | dentoo | でんとう（電灯） |
| landlord | ooya | おおや（大家） |
| languages | gogaku | ごがく（語学） |
| last month | sen-getsu | せんげつ |
| last week | sen-shuu | せんしゅう |
| last year | kyonen | きょねん |
| late | osoi | おそい |
| late riser | asa-neboo | あさねぼう |
| late riser | neboo | ねぼう |
| laughter (low, stifled) | kusukusu | くすくす（クスクス） |
| laundry | sentaku | せんたく |
| laundry | sentakumono | せんたくもの |
| leaf | ha | は（葉） |
| leather shoes | kawagutsu | かわぐつ |
| lecture | jyugyoo | じゅぎょう |
| left | hidari | ひだり（左） |
| legs/feet | ashi | あし |
| lemonade | remon skasshu | レモンスカッシュ |
| Let's do that | soo shimashoo | そうしましょう |
| Let's, or I wonder | Saa | さあ |
| letter, correspondence | tayori | たより（便り） |
| letters | tegami | てがみ |
| letters; characters; handwriting | ji | じ（字） |
| lettuce | retasu | レタス |
| library | toshokan | としょかん |
| a lie | uso | うそ |
| life, lifestyle | seikatsu | せいかつ（生活） |
| light brown | usu chairo | うすちゃいろ（うす茶色） |
| light, thin objects, or liquid of a dewy | harahara | はらはら（ハラハラ） |
| light-up | raito appu | ライトアップ |
| likable; pleasing; favorable | suki | すき |
| Linguistics | gengo-gaku | げんごがく |
| lion | raion | ライオン |
| lion | shishi | しし（獅子） |
| lips | kuchibiru | くちびる |
| liquor shop | saka-ya | さかや |
| liquor; Japanese rice wine | osake | おさけ |
| Literature | bungaku | ぶんがく |
| little (a little) | chotto | ちょっと |
| little (a little) | shoo shoo | しょうしょう |
| little (more formal than "chotto) | sukoshi | すこし |
| little finger; pinkie | koyubi | こゆび |
| little more | moo sukoshi | もうすこし |
| living things | ikimono | いきもの |
| lizard | tokage | とかげ |

| English | Roma-ji | Kana (Kanji) |
|---|---|---|
| lobby | robii | ロビー |
| lonely; lonesome | samishii | さみしい |
| long | nagai | ながい |
| Look! | hora | ほら |
| looks like~, seems like ~ | mitaini mieru | みたいに みえる（見える） |
| Los Angeles | Rosanjerusu | ロサンジェルス |
| Los Angeles | Rosu | ロス |
| lost property; a thing left behind | wasuremono | わすれもの（忘れ物） |
| lover | koibito | こいびと（恋人） |
| low heat | torobi | とろび（とろ火） |
| luggage | nimotsu | にもつ |
| lunch | hiru-gohan | ひるごはん |
| mackerel | sanma | さんま |
| magazine | zasshi | ざっし |
| magnificent | rippa (na) | りっぱ（な） |
| major | senkoo | せんこう |
| make-up | kehoo; (o) kehoo | （お）けしょう |
| male (person) | otoko no hito | おとこのひと |
| male form of "I" | boku | ぼく |
| many, a lot | takusan | たくさん |
| map | chizu | ちず |
| maple | momiji | もみじ |
| March | san-gatsu | さんがつ（三月） |
| marriage | kekkon | けっこん |
| marriage engagement | kon-yaku | こんやく |
| married couple | fuufu | ふうふ |
| marvelous, strange, miraculous, mysterious | fushigi | ふしぎ（不思議） |
| match-making | omiai | おみあい |
| Mathematics | suugaku | すうがく |
| May | go-gatsu | ごがつ（五月） |
| may I help you? | irasshai mase | いらっしゃいませ |
| May I say something? | anone | あのね |
| meal | shokuji | しょくじ（食事） |
| meal, cooked rice | gohan | ごはん |
| meaning | imi | いみ |
| meat | niku | にく（肉） |
| medical doctor | isha | （お）いしゃ（さん） |
| medicine | kusuri | くすり（薬） |
| medium size | chuu | ちゅう（中） |
| meeting | kaigoo | かいごう（会合） |
| men's wear | shinshi-fuku | しんしふく |
| menu | oshinagaki | おしながき |
| meter (unit) | meetoru | メートル |
| microphone | maiku | マイク |
| middle finger | nakayubi | なかゆび |
| middle of the night; midnight | yonaka | よなか（夜中） |
| middle, center | man'naka | まんなか |
| middle-aged (person) | chuunen | ちゅうねん（中年） |
| midnight | mayonaka | まよなか（真夜中） |

## Appendix D: English-Japanese Glossary (non-verbs)

| English | Roma-ji | Kana (Kanji) |
|---|---|---|
| midterm examination | chuukan-shiken | ちゅうかんしけん（中間しけん） |
| milk | gyuunyuu | ぎゅうにゅう |
| milk | miruku | ミルク |
| milk shake | miruku sheeku | ミルクシェーク |
| minutes | pun (fun) | ぷん（ふん） |
| minutes (time counter) | fun/pun | ふん／ぷん |
| mirror | kagami | かがみ |
| mischievous | itazura | いたずら |
| misery; misfortune; unhappy | fukoo | ふこう（不幸） |
| miso soup | misoshiru | みそしる |
| mixed sandwich | mikkusu sando | ミックスサンド |
| modifier; connect two nouns | no | の |
| Mona Lisa | Monariza | モナリザ |
| Monday | getsu-yoobi | げつようび |
| money | okane | おかね |
| monkey | saru | さる（猿） |
| moon | tsuki | つき |
| more | motto | もっと |
| more (in quantity) | ooi | おおい |
| more than ~ | ijyoo | いじょう（～以上） |
| moreover; on top of it | sono ue | そのうえ（その上） |
| morning | asa | あさ（朝） |
| most favorite | daisuki | だいすき（大好き）（な） |
| mother (humble form) | haha | はは |
| mother (respect form) | okaasan | おかあさん |
| motorcycle | ootobai | オートバイ |
| mountains | yama | やま（山） |
| mouse | nezumi | ねずみ |
| mouth, and around the mouth | kuchi moto | くちもと（口元） |
| movie | eiga | えいが |
| movie theatre | eigakan | えいがかん |
| muddy, thick | doro-doro | ドロドロ |
| muscles | kin'niku | きんにく（筋肉） |
| museum | bijyutsukan | びじゅつかん |
| Music | ongaku | おんがく |
| music box | orugooru | オルゴール |
| musical instruments | gakki | がっき |
| mysterious, mystic, enigmatic | shinpiteki | しんぴてき（神秘的） |
| nail | kugi | くぎ |
| nails | tsume | つめ |
| name | namae | なまえ |
| nap | hirune | ひるね |
| natural, a matter of course | atarimae | あたりまえ |
| near here, vicinity | kono chikaku | このちかく |
| nearby | soba | そば |
| ...ssary | hitsuyoo | ひつよう（必要） |

| English | Roma-ji | Kana (Kanji) |
|---|---|---|
| neck | kubi | くび |
| necktie | nekutai | ねくたい（ネクタイ） |
| neighbor | kinjyo no hito | きんじょのひと |
| never (used with negative) | zenzen | ぜんぜん |
| new | atarashii | あたら（新）しい |
| new car | shinsha | しんしゃ（新車） |
| New Year dishes | o-sechi (ryoori) | おせち |
| New York | nyuuyooku | ニューヨーク |
| newspaper | shinbun | しんぶん |
| next | tsugi ni | つぎに |
| next (to the different group) | yoko | よこ |
| next (to the same group) | tonari | となり |
| next month | rai-getsu | らいげつ |
| next week | raishuu | らいしゅう（来週） |
| next year | rainen | らいねん |
| nice and cool | suzushii | すずしい |
| nice and warm | atatakai | あたたかい |
| nice warm weather | pokapoka | ぽかぽか（ポカポカ） |
| night | yoru | よる（夜） |
| night cherry blossoms | yozakura | よざくら（夜桜） |
| night sky with stars | hoshizora | ほしぞら（星空） |
| nine | kokonotsu | ここのつ |
| no | iie ( or ie) | いいえ（いえ） |
| no bother; nonchalant | heiki | へいき（平気） |
| no chance for ~; no way to (do ~) | tootei | とうてい（～ない） |
| no good | dame | だめ |
| no good | yokunai | よくない |
| no longer exist | moo nai | もう～ない |
| No thank you ~. | kekkoo desu | けっこうです |
| noisy | yakamashii | やかましい |
| nonexistent; negative of "aru" | nai | ない |
| noodle shop | udon-ya-san | うどんやさん |
| noon | shoogo | しょうご |
| Northeast | hokutoo | ほくとう（北東） |
| Northwest | hokusei | ほくせい（北西） |
| nose | hana | はな（鼻） |
| not talkative; quiet | mukuchi | むくち（無口） |
| not very (much) | amari~ nai | あまり～ない |
| notebook | nooto | ノート |
| notice/bulletin board | tatefuda | たてふだ（立て札） |
| November | jyuu-ichi-gatsu | じゅういちがつ（十一月） |
| now | ima | いま |
| now, from now on | korekara | これから |
| number one; best (or most) | ichi-ban | いちばん |
| numbers | suuji | すうじ（数字） |
| o'clock (time counter) | ji | じ（時） |

**Appendix D: English-Japanese Glossary (non-verbs)**

| English | Roma-ji | Kana (Kanji) |
|---|---|---|
| October | jyuu-gatsu | じゅうがつ（十月） |
| office | jimusho | じむしょ |
| office | ofisu | オフィス |
| often | yoku | よく |
| ogre; demon | oni | おに　（鬼） |
| Oh (feminine expression of faint surprise) | ara | あら |
| oil, cooking oil | abura | あぶら　（油） |
| old | furui | ふるい(古い) |
| old person | toshiyori | としより（年より） |
| old man, grandpa | ojiisan | おじいさん |
| old woman, grandma | obaasan | おばあさん |
| olden times, long time ago | mukashi | むかし　（昔） |
| older brother | ani | あに |
| older brother (casual)/(formal) | ani-oniisan | あに--おにいさん |
| older sister (casual)/(formal) | ane-oneesan | あね--おねえさん |
| omelet | omuretsu | オムレツ |
| on that moment; at that time; then | sonotoki | そのとき |
| on the left hand side | hidarite | ひだりて（左手） |
| on the right hand side | migite | みぎて |
| once | ikkai | いっかい |
| once, one time | ichido | いちど　（一度） |
| one (general counter for small objects) | hitotsu | ひとつ（一つ） |
| one after another; spontaneously | dondon | どんどん |
| one by one | hitotsu zutsu | ひとつずつ |
| one day | ichi nichi | いちにち(一日) |
| one hundred points | hyakuten | ひゃくてん |
| one more time | moo ichido | もういちど　（もう一度） |
| one night | hitoban | ひとばん　（一晩） |
| one person, alone | hitori | ひとり |
| one serving (for one person) | hitori-bun | ひとりぶん |
| one tablespoon | oosaji | おおさじ |
| oneself | jibun | じぶん（自分） |
| onions | tama-negi | たまねぎ（玉ねぎ） |
| only | dake | だけ |
| only one person | hitori dake | ひとりだけ |
| onomatopoeia for going around | kuru-kuru | くるくる |
| onomatopoeia of a dog's bark | wan-wan | ワンワン |
| or something like that | demo | でも　（Noun でも） |
| orange | orenji | おれんじ（オレンジ） |
| order | jyunban | じゅんばん　（順番） |
| ordinal numbers | ban | ばん　（番） |
| ordinal numbers | me (~ me) | ～　め（目） |
| other | hoka | ほか |
| others | sono ta | そのた |
| outside | soto | そと |
| oven | oobun | オーブン |
| over that way, over that side (far for both) | achira | あちら |
| over there | asoko | あそこ |
| P.M.  afternoon | gogo | ごご |
| painful | itai | いたい |
| pants | zubon | ズボン |
| paper | kami | かみ（紙） |
| parents (polite form is "go-ryooshin") | ryooshin | りょうしん(両親) |
| Paris | pari | パリ |
| park | kooen | こうえん　（公園） |
| parking | chuusha | ちゅうしゃ |
| parking lot | chuusha-jyoo | ちゅうしゃじょう |
| particle to show limit | de | で |
| particle used after a direct object | wo | を |
| part-time job; side job | arubaito | アルバイト |
| party | paatii | パーティー |
| Pasadena | pasadena | パサデナ |
| patient | gamanzuyoi | がまんづよい |
| peace of mind | anshin | あんしん　（安心） |
| peaceful | yasuraka | （やす）安らか |
| pedestrian crossing | oodan-hodoo | おうだんほどう |
| pen | pen | ペン |
| pencil | enpitsu | えんぴつ |
| penguin | pengin | ペンギン |
| people, character | jinbutsu | じんぶつ　（人物） |
| Pepsi | pepushi | ペプシ |
| perfect (casual term) | bacchiri | ばっちり |
| perfect fit | pittari | ぴったり |
| performance | seinoo | せいのう |
| perhaps | tabun | たぶん |
| person, people | hito | ひと　（人） |
| person; politer than "hito" | kata | かた　（方） |
| pet | petto | ペット |
| pet food; bait | esa | えさ |
| photograph | shashin | しゃしん　（写真） |
| Physics; short form of "butsuri-gaku" | butsuri | ぶつり |
| picture; drawing | e | え |
| pie | pai | パイ |
| pierced earrings | piasu | ピアス |
| pig | buta | ぶた |
| pilot | pairotto | パイロット |
| place | tokoro | ところ |
| place (specific/ broad sense) | basho/tokoro | ばしょ/ところ |
| place that is far | tooku | とおく　（遠く） |
| play (a play) | shibai | しばい |

## Appendix D: English-Japanese Glossary (non-verbs)

| English | Roma-ji | Kana (Kanji) |
|---|---|---|
| Please give me. | kudasai | ください |
| Please wait. | Omachi kudasai | おまちください |
| Pleased to meet you. | Hajimemashite | はじめまして |
| pleasing; fun | yukai | ゆかい |
| pleasure; something to look forward to | tanoshimi | たのしみ |
| police station | kooban | こうばん |
| policeman | omawari san | おまわりさん |
| politely; carefully; thoroughly | teineini | ていねいに |
| politeness | teinei | ていねい |
| polyester | poriesuteru | ぼりえすてる（ポリエステル） |
| poor | mazushii | まずしい |
| poor, unskilled | heta | へた（下手） |
| popularity | ninki | にんき（人気） |
| pork | butaniku | ぶたにく　（豚肉） |
| pork | pooku | ポーク |
| pork cutlet | tonkatsu | とんかつ |
| post (a post) | sain | サイン |
| post card | hagaki | はがき |
| post office | yuubinkyoku | ゆうびんきょく |
| poster | harigami | はりがみ |
| poster | posutaa | ぼすたあ（ポスター） |
| potato | jyagaimo | じゃがいも |
| potted plants | hachi-ue | はちうえ |
| practice | renshuu | れんしゅう（練習） |
| preparation | jyunbi | じゅんび |
| present | purezento | プレゼント |
| pretty soon | moosugu | もうすぐ |
| pretty, clean | kirei (na) | きれい（な）・ |
| pride | puraido | プライド |
| prison | keimusho | けいむしょ |
| pro (professional) | puro | プロ |
| pronunciation | hatsuon | はつおん（発音） |
| prosperous, flourished | sakan | さかん |
| pub | pabu | パブ |
| public bath | sentoo | せんとう（銭湯） |
| puppet theatre (also Ningyoo-Jyooruri) | Bunraku | ぶんらく（文楽） |
| purple | murasaki | むらさき |
| question | shitsumon | しつもん |
| question (particle marking a question) | ka | か |
| question, doubt | gimon | ぎもん |
| quick-tempered; hothead | okorinboo | おこりんぼう |
| quiet | shizuka (na) | しずか（な） |
| quietly | shizukani | しずかに |
| quilt frame (with heater inside) | kotatsu | こたつ |
| quite | kanari | かなり |
| ...bit | usagi | うさぎ |
| | tanuki | たぬき |

| English | Roma-ji | Kana (Kanji) |
|---|---|---|
| railroad crossing | fumikiri | ふみきり |
| rain | ame | あめ（雨） |
| rain (snow) Ame ga furimasu. (It rains.) | furimasu | ふります |
| rain falling lightly | shitoshito | しとしと（シトシト） |
| rare | mezurashii | めずらしい |
| rather; on the contrary | kaette | かえって |
| raw | nama | なま（生） |
| raw fish | sashimi | さしみ |
| raw rice | okome | おこめ（米） |
| rayon | reeyon | れえよん（レーヨン） |
| reading | dokusho | どくしょ（読書） |
| realtor | fudoosan ya | ふどうさんや |
| rear-view mirror | bakku-miraa | バックミラー |
| recently | saikin | さいきん |
| recipe | reshipi | レシピ |
| red | akai | あかい |
| red tea; black tea | koocha | こうちゃ |
| refrigerator | reizouko | れいぞうこ |
| regrettable; vexing | kuyashii | くやしい |
| relationship | naka | なか　（仲） |
| relatively | wariai/maamaa | わりあい/まあまあ |
| reply | henji | へんじ　（返事） |
| request | rikuesuto | リクエスト |
| research | kenkyuu | けんきゅう |
| research | risaachi | リサーチ（けんきゅう） |
| reservation | yoyaku | よやく（予約） |
| restaurant | resutoran | レストラン |
| return, change (also called "o-tsuri") | okaeshi | おかえし |
| rice | kome | こめ　（米） |
| rice ball | onigiri | おにぎり |
| rice cooker | suihanki | すいはんき（炊飯器） |
| rice field | tanbo | たんぼ |
| rice paddy | suiden | すいでん |
| rice with vinegar topped with egg, seafood | chirashi-zushi | ちらしずし |
| rich | okanemochi | おかねもち |
| right | migi | みぎ(右) |
| ring finger | kusuriyubi | くすりゆび |
| rivers | kawa | かわ（川） |
| rock | rokku | ロック |
| rock group | rokku guruupu | ロックグループ |
| room | heya | へや |
| rules; regulations | kisoku | きそく |
| rumors | uwasa-banashi | うわさばなし |
| Russian | Roshi(y)a-go | ロシアご |
| Russian style | roshia-shiki | ロシアしき　（式） |
| sack; bag | fukuro | ふくろ |
| sad | kanashii | かなしい |

## Appendix D: English-Japanese Glossary (non-verbs)

| English | Roma-ji | Kana (Kanji) |
|---|---|---|
| safe | anzen | あんぜん |
| salad | sarada | サラダ |
| salaried man | sarariiman | サラリーマン |
| sale | seeru | セール |
| sales tax | shoohi-zei | しょうひぜい |
| salmon | sake | さけ |
| salt | shio | しお |
| salty | shio-karai | しおからい |
| same | onaji | おなじ（同じ） |
| samurai movie | chanbara eiga | チャンバラえいが |
| sand | suna | すな |
| sandwich | sandoicchi | サンドイッチ |
| sash | obi | おび |
| satisfaction | manzoku | まんぞく |
| Saturday | do-yoobi | どようび |
| sauce | soosu | ソース |
| savings | chokin | ちょきん |
| scallop salad | hotate sarada | ほたてサラダ |
| scared; scary | kowai | こわい |
| scenery | keshiki | けしき |
| school | gakkoo | がっこう |
| school being closed | kyuukoo | きゅうこう（休校） |
| school year | gakunen | がくねん |
| scientist | kagakusha | かがくしゃ（科学者） |
| Scotch liquor with water | chuuhai | ちゅうハイ |
| screen | sukuriin | スクリーン |
| sea bream | tai | たい |
| sea urchin eggs | uni | うに |
| sea; ocean | umi | うみ |
| season | kisetsu | きせつ |
| seat | seki | せき（席） |
| seaweed | nori | のり |
| second lowest; second youngest | shita kara ni-ban-me | したからにばんめ |
| second-year student, sophomore | ni-nen-sei | にねんせい |
| secret | naisho | ないしょ |
| see you later | jya mata | じゃ また |
| seems like (adverbial form of "mitai") | mitaini | みたいに |
| sentence final particle (speaker's murmur) | na(a) | な（あ） |
| sentence final used by women | wa | わ |
| sentence final used for affirmation | yo | よ |
| September | ku-gatsu | くがつ（九月） |
| servings (a counter) | nin-bun | にんぶん（～人分） |
| seven | nanatsu | ななつ |
| sexy | sekushii | セクシー |
| Shakespeare | sheikusupia | シェイクスピア |
| shape | katachi | かたち（形） |
| shaved ice | kaki-goori | かきごおり |
| she; girlfriend | kanojyo | かのじょ（彼女） |
| sheep | hitsuji | ひつじ |
| shelf | tana | たな |
| Shinto shrine | jinjya | じんじゃ |
| ship, boat | fune | ふね |
| shirt | shatsu | しゃつ（シャツ） |
| shoe shop | kutsu ya | くつや |
| shoes | kutsu | くつ |
| shopping | kaimono | かいもの |
| shopping mall | mooru | モール |
| short form of "to (iu no wa)" quotation | tte | って |
| shortcut | chikamichi | ちかみち |
| shoulders | kata | かた（肩） |
| shower | shawaa | しゃわあ（シャワー） |
| shy | uchiki | うちき（内気） |
| shy; embarrassed | hazukashii | はずかしい |
| siblings | kyoodai | きょうだい |
| side of | hoo (~ no hoo) | ほう（～のほう） |
| sidewalk | hodoo | ほどう |
| signature | sain | サイン |
| silk | kinu | きぬ |
| singer | kashu | かしゅ（歌手） |
| single child (a single child) | hitori-k-ko | ひとりっこ |
| single; unmarried | dokushin | どくしん |
| sir name | myooji | みょうじ（苗字） |
| sir name | sei | せい（姓） |
| six | muttsu | むっつ |
| size | ookisa | おおきさ（大きさ） |
| size | saizu | サイズ |
| size (big & small) | daishoo | だいしょう（大小） |
| sketch; description | byoosha | びょうしゃ（描写） |
| sketching | dessan | デッサン |
| ski | sukii | スキー |
| skillful | umai | うまい |
| skillfully; well | umaku | うまく |
| skirt | sukaato | すかあと（スカート） |
| sky | sora | そら（空） |
| sleepy | nemui | ねむい |
| slightly | hon'nori | ほんのり |
| slippery | tsurutsuru | つるつる |
| slowly | yukkuri | ゆっくり |
| small | chiisai | ちいさい |
| small bird | kotori | ことり |
| small items; accessory | komono | こもの |
| small rice ball on a stick | mitarashi-dango | みたらしだんご |
| small size | shoo | しょう（小） |
| small/narrow-spaced | semai | せまい |
| smile | hohoemi | ほほえみ |

## Appendix D: English-Japanese Glossary (non-verbs)

| English | Roma-ji | Kana (Kanji) | English | Roma-ji | Kana (Kanji) |
|---|---|---|---|---|---|
| ...sful) | niyaniya | にやにや (ニヤニヤ) | spoon | supuun | スプーン |
| | | | sports | supootsu | スポーツ |
| smile happily and warmly | nikoniko | にこにこ | spring | haru | はる |
| | | | square | shikakui | しかくい |
| smooth | nameraka | なめらか | squid | ika | いか |
| snacks | o-kashi | おかし | stairs | kaidan | かいだん (階段) |
| snake | hebi | へび | stamps | kitte | きって |
| sneakers | suniikaa | スニーカー | standard language | hyoojyungo | ひょうじゅんご (ひょうじゅん語) |
| snorkeling | sunookeru | スノーケル | | | |
| snow | yuki | ゆき (雪) | standing on the head | sakadachi | さかだち |
| snowboard | sunooboodo | スノーボード | stars; celebrity | sutaa | スター |
| snowman | yukidaruma | ゆきだるま | starving | himojii | ひもじい |
| so | soo | そう | stationary | bunboogu | ぶんぼうぐ |
| so so | maa maa | まあまあ | steak | suteeki | ステーキ |
| soap | sekken | せっけん | stepping-stone | tobi-ishi | とびいし |
| soccer | sakkaa | サッカー | stomach; abdomen | onaka | おなか |
| sociable | shakooteki | しゃこうてき | stone; rock | ishi | いし (石) |
| society | shakai | しゃかい (社会) | store | mise | みせ |
| socks | kutsushita | くつした | story; narrative | monogatari | ものがたり |
| socks cloven at the big toe | tabi | たび | straight | massugu (ni) | まっすぐ (に) |
| | | | strange, weird | hen na | へんな (変な) |
| soft | yawarakai | やわらかい | straw | sutoroo | ストロー |
| some time | itsuka | いつか | straw bag | tawara | たわら |
| someone | dareka | だれか | street | toori | とおり (通り) |
| something that troubles you | komatta koto | こまったこと | street car | densha | でんしゃ |
| | | | street, way | michi | みち (道) |
| something, anything | nanika | なにか | stroll, walking | sanpo | さんぽ |
| sometimes | tokidoki | ときどき | strong | tsuyoi | つよい |
| somewhere | aru tokoro | あるところ | strong point; good at | tokui | とくい |
| son | musuko | むすこ | strong; healthy; sturdy | jyoobu | じょうぶ |
| song | uta | うた (歌) | student | gakusei | がくせい |
| Sorry to have bothered you. | Ojyama shimashita | おじゃましました | student office | gakusei-ka | がくせいか |
| | | | study | benkyoo | べんきょう |
| sound; noise | oto | おと (音) | subway | chikatetsu | ちかてつ |
| sour | suppai | すっぱい | such ~ as that | an'na | あんな |
| sour cream | sawaa-kuriimu | サワークリーム | such a thing like that! | nante...! | なんて～！ |
| soured pickled plum | ume-boshi | うめぼし | suffering | kurushii | くるしい |
| South | minami | みなみ (南) | sugar | satoo | さとう |
| south side | minami-gawa | みなみ (南) がわ | summer | natsu | なつ |
| Southeast | nantoo | なんとう (南東) | Sunday | nichi-yoobi | にちようび |
| Southwest | nansei | なんせい (南西) | sunflower | himawari | ひまわり |
| spacious | hiroi | ひろ (広) い | sun, sunshine | o-hi-sama | おひさま (お日さま) |
| spaghetti | supageti | スパゲティ | | | |
| spaghetti with meat sauce | miito soosu | ミートソース | sunshine, sunlight | nikkoo | にっこう (日光) |
| | | | supermarket | suupaa | スーパー |
| spaghetti with tomato sauce | naporitan | ナポリタン | supple | shinayaka | しなやか |
| | | | surely, certainly, probably | kitto | きっと |
| Spanish language | Supein-go | スペインご | | | |
| special | tokubetsu | とくべつ (特別) | surfing | saafin | サーフィン |
| speeding | supiido unten | スピードうんてん | sushi restaurant | osushi-ya san | おすしやさん |
| spices | supaisu | スパイス | sweet | amai | あまい (甘い) |
| spicy (taste) | karakuchi | からくち (辛口) | sweet side, not spicy | amakuchi | あまくち (甘口) |
| spicy (taste); salty | karai | からい (辛い) | swimming | suiei | すいえい |
| | hoorensoo | ほうれんそう | swimming pool | puuru | プール |
| | migoto | みごと (見事) | | | |

## Appendix D: English-Japanese Glossary (non-verbs)

| English | Roma-ji | Kana (Kanji) |
|---|---|---|
| switch | suicchi | スイッチ |
| system; course | kei | 〜けい　（系） |
| table | teeburu | てえぶる（テーブル） |
| tableware | shokki | しょっき |
| tadpole | otamajyakushi | おたまじゃくし |
| tangerine | mikan | みかん |
| tape | teepu | テープ |
| taste | aji | あじ |
| tasty | oishii | おいしい |
| tattoo | irezumi | いれずみ |
| taxi | takushii | タクシー |
| teacher, professor, doctor | sensei | せんせい |
| teeth | ha | は（歯） |
| telephone | denwa | でんわ |
| telephone number | denwa bangoo | でんわばんごう |
| television | terebi | テレビ |
| temperature | ondo | おんど |
| temple yard | keidai | けいだい（境内） |
| ten | too | とお |
| tennis shoes | tenisu shuuzu | テニスシューズ |
| terrible | hidoi | ひどい |
| test | tesuto | テスト |
| textbook | kyookasho | きょうかしょ |
| Thai language | Tai-go | タイご |
| than (~ than) | yori | より |
| thank you for the meal | gochisoo sama (deshita) | ごちそうさま（でした） |
| Thank you for waiting. | Omatase shimashita | おまたせしました |
| Thank you for your concern. | Okage sama de | おかげさまで |
| Thank you. | arigatoo | ありがとう |
| that (noun modifier) | ano | あの |
| that (noun modifier) | sono | その |
| that one (near the listener) | sore | それ |
| that one over there | are | あれ |
| that way, that side (close to the listener) | sochira | そちら |
| that won't do | sorejya chotto | それじゃ、ちょっと |
| then, in that case (formal) | soredewa | それでは |
| there (near the listener) | soko | そこ |
| therefore, for that reason | dakara | だから |
| therefore; because of that; due to that | sokode | そこで |
| they | ano-hito-tachi | あのひとたち |
| they | karera | かれら |
| thick | futoi | ふとい |
| thick and syrupy | toro-toro | トロトロ |

| English | Roma-ji | Kana (Kanji) |
|---|---|---|
| thick flour noodles | udon | うどん |
| thief | doroboo | どろぼう |
| thing (abstract thing(s)) | koto | こと |
| things (material things) | mono | もの |
| things for women | on'na-mono | おんなもの |
| this (noun modifier) | kono | この |
| this month | kon-getsu | こんげつ |
| this much; about this size | kore-gurai | これぐらい |
| this neighborhood | konohen | このへん |
| this one (near the speaker) | kore | これ |
| this person (polite form) | kochira-sama | こちらさま |
| this semester | kongakki | こんがっき |
| this time; last time | kondo | こんど |
| this way, this side (close to the speaker) | kochira | こちら |
| this week | konshuu | こんしゅう |
| this year | kotoshi | ことし（今年） |
| though, but... | kedo | けど |
| three | mittsu | みっつ |
| three colors | sanshoku | さんしょく（三色） |
| three-story building | sangaidate | さんがいだて |
| throughout the time | zutto | ずっと |
| thumb | oyayubi | おやゆび |
| Thursday | moku-yoobi | もくようび |
| ticket | chiketto/ ken | チケット/けん |
| tiger | tora | とら |
| time (hours of duration) | jikan | じかん(時間) |
| times; frequency | kai | （〜）かい（回） |
| tobacco | tabako | たばこ |
| today | kyoo | きょう |
| toe | tsumasaki | つまさき |
| together | issho ni | いっしょに |
| toho walking | toho | とほ |
| toilet, bathroom | toire | トイレ |
| Tokyo | Tookyoo | とうきょう |
| tomato | tomato | トマト |
| tomorrow | ashita | あした |
| tomorrow | asu | あす |
| tongue twister | hayakuchi-kotoba | はやくちことば |
| tonight | kon'ya | こんや　（今夜） |
| tooth brush | ha-burashi | はブラシ |
| tooth paste | ha-migaki | はみがき |
| top and bottom (high and low) | jyooge | じょうげ（上下） |
| top floor; roof | okujyoo | おくじょう |
| topic marker | wa | は |
| town | machi | まち |
| toy | omocha | おもちゃ |
| traffic lights, signals | shingoo | しんごう(信号) |

# Appendix D: English-Japanese Glossary (non-verbs)

| | Roma-ji | Kana (Kanji) | English | Roma-ji | Kana (Kanji) |
|---|---|---|---|---|---|
| | eki | えき | vocabulary | tango | たんご |
| | gomi-bako | ごみばこ | waist | uesuto | ウエスト |
| tree | ki | き（木） | waitress | ueitoresu | ウエートレス |
| trip | ryokoo | りょこう | walking | toho | とほ |
| troublesome | mendoo | めんどう | wall | kabe | かべ |
| true | honto(o) | ほんと（う） | wallet | saifu | さいふ |
| T-shirt | tii-shatsu | Tシャツ | war | sensoo | せんそう |
| Tuesday | ka-yoobi | かようび | warrior; samurai | samurai | さむらい（侍） |
| tulip | chuurippu | チューリップ | water | mizu | みず（水） |
| tumbler (Portuguese origin "kop") | koppu | コップ | water (hot) | yu | ゆ（湯） |
| | | | watermelon | suika | すいか |
| tuna fish | maguro | まぐろ | way of thinking | kangaekata | かんがえかた（考え方） |
| turtle | kame | かめ | | | |
| two (general counter for small items) | futatsu | ふたつ | weak point; not good at | nigate | にがて（苦手） |
| two people | futari | ふたり | Wednesday | sui-yoobi | すいようび |
| type | taipu | タイプ | weekend | shuumatsu | しゅうまつ |
| udon noodles served with egg | tsukimi udon | つきみうどん | weeping cherry blossoms | shidare zakura | しだれざくら（しだれ桜） |
| udon soup with tempura batter bits | tanuki-udon | たぬきうどん | weight | taijyuu | たいじゅう（体重） |
| | | | Welcome home. | Okaeri (nasai) | おかえり（なさい） |
| umbrella | kasa | かさ | Well let me think. | U~n | う～ん |
| unbearably; extremely | amarinimo | あまりにも | Western food | yooshoku | ようしょく（洋食） |
| uncle formal (casual) | ojisan (oji) | おじさん（おじ） | whale | kujira | くじら |
| under; below | shita | した | what | nan (= nani) | なん（なに） |
| underground | chika | ちか | What day and month is it? | nan-gatsu nan-nichi | なんがつなんにち |
| understood (humble form) | kashikomari mashita | かしこまりました | | | |
| | | | What day of the week? | nan'yoobi | なんようび |
| unexpectedly | angai | あんがい | What kind of ? | don'na | どんな |
| unhappy, in a bad mood | fukigen (na) | ふきげん（な）（不きげんな） | what language? | nani-go | なにご |
| | | | what number? | nan-ban | なんばん |
| university president | gakuchoo | がくちょう | what year (in school) student | nan-nen-sei | なんねんせい |
| unkind | fushinsetsu | ふしんせつ | | | |
| up to, until, as far as | made | まで | when | itsu | いつ |
| used car | chuukosha | ちゅうこしゃ（中古車） | where | doko | どこ |
| | | | which one (among many) | dore | どれ |
| usually | taitei | たいてい | | | |
| usually, ordinarily | futsuu | ふつう | which side | dochiragawa | どちらがわ |
| valuable, important | daiji | だいじ | while: during the time period | aidani | あいだに |
| variety; many | iroiro | いろいろ | | | |
| vegetables | yasai | やさい | white | shiroi | しろい（白い） |
| vending machine | jihanki | じはんき(自販機) | who | dare | だれ |
| very (formal) (adverb) | taihen | たいへん（大変） | (= dareだれ): who | donata | どなた |
| very (informal "totemo") | tottemo | とっても | Why? | dooshite | どうして |
| | | | wife (polite form) | okusan | おくさん（奥さん） |
| very (personal overtone) | totemo | とても | wife; madam | okami-san | おかみさん |
| | | | wind velocity (speed) | fuusoku | ふうそく(風速) |
| very, extremely | zuibun | ずいぶん | window | mado | まど |
| via walking | toho de, aruite | とほで、あるいて | wing sound (shrill) | pyuupyuu | ピューピュー |
| vicinity, nearby | chikaku | ちか（近）く | winter | fuyu | ふゆ |
| video | bideo | ビデオ | with (someone) | to | と |
| video shop | bideo ya | ビデオや（ビデオ屋) | within today | kyoojyuu | きょうじゅう（今日中） |
| | | | | | |
| mese | Betonamu-go | ベトナムご | witness | mokugekisha | もくげきしゃ |
| y | nagame | ながめ | wolf | ookami | おおかみ |

## Appendix D: English-Japanese Glossary (non-verbs)

| English | Roma-ji | Kana (Kanji) |
|---|---|---|
| women's clothing | fujin-fuku | ふじんふく |
| wonderful | subarashii | すばらしい |
| word, language | kotoba | ことば |
| working person | shakaijin | しゃかいじん （社会人） |
| world | sekai | せかい |
| worry | shinpai | しんぱい |
| Wow! | Uwaa | うわあ |
| wrinkle | shiwa | しわ |
| yard; garden | niwa | にわ |
| years (~ years) | nen | ねん （年） |
| years old (~ years old) | sai | さい （才） |
| yellow | kiiroi | きいろい(黄色い) |
| yellow tail | hamachi | はまち |
| Yes | hai | はい |
| yesterday | kinoo | きのう |
| yet, still | mada | まだ |
| you | anata | あなた |
| you (male or casual form) | kimi | きみ |
| You're welcome. | Doo itashi mashtie | どういたしまして |
| young | wakai | わかい （若い） |
| younger brother (casual)(formal) | otooto-otooto san | おとうと― おとうとさん |
| younger sister | imooto | いもうと |
| zero points | reiten | れいてん |
| zoo | doobutsu-en | どうぶつえん |

## Appendix E: Particles

### Challenging particles へ、に、で、を、は、が

へ

The particle "e" indicates the direction of motion verbs (e.g., go, come, and return). Its English equivalent is "toward" or "to" and is usually interchangeable with the particle "ni."

1. うちへ　かえります。（帰る＝to return, go home）
2. そとへ　でました。(外＝outside、出る＝to come out, leave)
3. 学校へ　もどりましょう。(戻る＝to return, go back to where you were before)
4. あっちのほうへ、行きましょうか。Shall we go to that direction?

に

(1) The particle "ni" indicates the destination of a motion verb.
All the sentences above demonstrating the use of particle "e" can be replaced by "ni."

However, "ni" implies the actions take place in a given location as well. For example, in the sentence「えいがに　行きませんか。」, "movie" does not merely determine "destination." It also implies you will "watch" a movie, once you get to the theater. Likewise, in the sentence「大学に　入りました。」, there is implication beyond the action of just "entering" college. And similarly, 「おふろに　入ります。」 implies the action of taking a hot bath, beyond immersing oneself in a bathtub.

(2) The particle "ni" marks the purpose of a motion verb (typically the verb "to go"). Think about the purpose of visiting a department store: "shopping." How about a restaurant? "To eat." The particle "ni" is used with such concepts as "shopping," "dining," "studying," "traveling," "sightseeing," "observing" (and many more Chinese compound nouns) to indicate the purpose of going to a destination.

1. デパートへ　買い物に　行きます。( I go to a department store to shop / for the purpose of shopping.)
2. レストランへ　食事に　行きませんか。(Won't you go to a restaurant to eat?)
3. 図書館へ、勉強に　行きました。(I went to a library to study.)
4. ヨーロッパへ、旅行に　行きます。(I'm going to Europe to tour.)

Additional information: The particle "ni" indicates the purpose of the verb in the form of "V-stem + ni," along with a motion verb.

1．映画を見に、行きましょう。(Let's go see a movie.)

2．ごはんを食べに、行きませんか。(Shall we go eat?)

3．本を買いに 来ました。(I came to buy a book.)

4．友だちの家に、遊びに 来ました。(I came to my friend's house for fun.)

5．川へ、泳ぎに 行きました。(I went to a river for swimming.)

6．海へ、つりに 行きます。(I will go to an ocean for fishing.)

(3) The particle "ni" marks a specific point in time. Its English equivalent is "at," "in," or "on." Note that the particle "ni" is not needed for vague periods of time when you cannot pinpoint them as specific, like "today," "tomorrow," "yesterday," "this year," "next week," "last month," or "all day." By the same token, the words that indicate a specific duration of time (such as "one hour") do not take the particle "ni."

1．毎朝、五時に 起きます。(I get up at five o'clock every morning.)

2．毎年、六月に 日本へ 行きます。(I go to Japan in June every year.)

3．私は、1980年に 生まれました。(I was born in 1980.)

Compare:

4．きのう、パーティーが ありました。(There was a party yesterday.)

5．今年は、暑いですよ。(It will be hot this year.)

6．夕方、一時間ぐらい、ジョギングを しました。(I jogged for about one hour in the early evening.)

(4) The particle "ni" marks an indirect object. English sentence pattern of S + V + O + O (i.e., Tom taught me English) is S + O + O + V in Japanese.

(A direct object is marked by particle "を wo.")

1．ブラウンさんは、学生に 英語を 教えます。(Mr. Brown teaches English to students.)

2．母は、私に りんごを くれました。(My mother gave me an apple.)

3．私に その本を 見せてください。(Please show me that book.)

4．田中さんに、電話を かけましたか。(Did you call Mr. Tanaka?)

(5) The particle "ni" marks the location of existence.

    1．ここに、おいしいりんごが、あります。(Here is a delicious apple.)

    2．あそこに、大<sub>おお</sub>きい犬<sub>いぬ</sub>が　います。(There is a big dog over there.)

    3．私<sub>わたし</sub>の家<sub>いえ</sub>に、プールが　あります。(I have a swimming pool at my house.)

    4．デパートの前<sub>まえ</sub>に、おおぜいの人<sub>ひと</sub>が、いました。(There were many people in front of the department store.)

There are a few more functions of "ni," in so that it marks the agent of the action, expressed through passive, causative and causative passive verbs.  They will be learned later.

## で

(1) The particle "de" marks the **place** where an action or event occurs.  Its English equivalent is "in" or "at."

    1．夕食<sub>ゆうしょく</sub>は、家<sub>いえ</sub>で　食<sub>た</sub>べます。(I eat dinner at home.)

    2．喫茶店<sub>きっさてん</sub>で、コーヒーを　飲<sub>の</sub>みました。(I drank coffee at a coffee shop.)

    3．図書館<sub>としょかん</sub>で、勉強<sub>べんきょう</sub>します。(I study in the library.)

    4．ラボで、テープを　聞<sub>き</sub>きます。(I listen to the tapes in the language laboratory.)

(2) The particle "de" marks the **means** or **instrument** of doing something. Its English equivalent is "by," "with," "in," and so on.

    1．日本語<sub>にほんご</sub>で　話<sub>はな</sub>してください。(Please speak in Japanese.)

    2．ペンで、書<sub>か</sub>きました。(I wrote with a pen.)

    3．東京<sub>とうきょう</sub>まで　飛行機<sub>ひこうき</sub>で、行<sub>い</sub>きました。(I went to Tokyo by airplane.)

    4．船<sub>ふね</sub>で、その島<sub>しま</sub>へ、行<sub>い</sub>きました。(I went to that island by ship.)

    5．タクシーで　来<sub>き</sub>てください。(Please come by taxi.)

    6．すきやきは、おはしで、食<sub>た</sub>べます。(I eat sukiyaki with chopsticks.)

(3) The particle "de" indicates cause. Its English equivalent is "because of," or "due to."

    1．雨<sub>あめ</sub>で、道路<sub>どうろ</sub>が　見<sub>み</sub>えません。(I cannot see the road because of the rain.)

    2．風<sub>かぜ</sub>で、木<sub>き</sub>が　倒<sub>たお</sub>れました。(Trees were knocked down by the wind.)

３．地震で、フリーウェイが、壊れました。(Freeways were destroyed by the earthquake.)

４．仕事で、日本へ行きます。(I will go to Japan on business.)

５．風邪で、学校を　休みました。(I was absent from school due to a cold.)

(4) The particle "de" indicates a required time or quantity. Its English equivalent is "within," "in" or "with."

１．あと一年で、大学を　卒業します。(I will graduate from college in a year.)

２．この車は、二万ドルでは　買えません。(You cannot buy this car with $20,000.)

３．一週間で、プロジェクトを完成しました。(I finished this project in a week.)

４．来週で、今学期は、終わります。(This semester will end next week.)

(5) The particle "de" indicates boundary. For example, in a superlative sentence such as "Mt. Fuji is the highest mountain," you must delineate the extent to which you are comparing height -- whether just in Japan, or in all of Asia, or in the world. The particle "de" has a function of showing boundary.

１．日本で、一番高い山は、富士山です。(The tallest mountain in Japan is Mt. Fuji.)

２．アメリカで、一番長い川は、ミシシッピ川です。(The longest river in the U.S. is the Mississippi River.)

３．このクラスで、一番よくできる人は、だれですか。(Who is the smartest student in this class?)

４．家族で　一番おしゃべりなのは、私です。(It is I who is the chatterbox in the family.)

を

(1) The particle "wo" marks the preceding word or phrase as a direct object in the sentence.

１．それを　ください。(Please give that to me.)

２．コーヒーを　飲みました。(I drank coffee.)

３．朝ごはんを　食べました。(I ate breakfast.)

４．おもしろい映画を　見ました。(I watched an interesting movie.)

５．日本語を勉強しています。(I am studying Japanese.)

(2) The particle "wo" marks a place of departure, or a place in where motion goes through when used with a motion verb.

1. 毎日、七時に　家を　出ます。(I leave home everyday at seven o'clock.)

2. 電車は、駅を　出ました。(The train left the station.)

3. 私は、ＵＳＣを　出ました。(I graduated from USC.)

4. 電車を　降りて、歩きました。(I got off the train and walked.)

5. この道を　通りましょう。(Let's go through this street.)

6. この道を　歩きましょう。(Let's walk this street.)

7. この道を　行きましょう。(Let's take this street.)

8. あの角を　曲がってください。(Please turn at that corner.)

9. 橋を　渡りました。(I crossed the bridge.)

10. 川を　渡りました。(I crossed the river.)

11. 飛行機は、空を　飛びます。(Airplanes fly in the sky.)

# は

(1) The particle "wa" marks the topic of a sentence. Its English equivalent is close to "speaking of which." A word or phrase preceding "wa" would be "old information" or "shared information" already mentioned previously or is obvious through situation, context, or universally accepted facts. A topic of a sentence can be anything; e.g., location, people, things, time, etc.

1. わたしは、学生です。(I am a student.)

2. この本は、いい本です。(This book is a good book.)

3. それは、何の本ですか。(What subject is that book?)

4. 朝ごはんは、もう食べましたか。(Did you eat breakfast already?)

5. あしたは、いいお天気でしょうか。(Will tomorrow be a nice day, I wonder.)

(2) The particle "wa" also marks contrast and comparison; that is, a word or phrase marked by "wa" is contrasted or compared with something else, even if the object of comparison is not mentioned. The contrastive element is obvious in negative sentences.

1. コーヒーは、すきじゃありませんが、おちゃは、すきです。
   (I don't like coffee, but I like tea.)

2. 京都へは、行きましたが、神戸へは、行きませんでした。

(I went to Kyoto, but not Kobe.)

3. いつもは、電車で行きますが、今日は、歩いて行きました。

(I usually go by train, but today I walked.)

4.「コーヒーを　どうぞ。」(Please have a cup of coffee.)

「すみません。私は、コーヒーは、飲まないんです。」(I'm sorry, I don't drink coffee.)

5. 今日は、勉強は、したくない。のんびりしたい。(I don't want to study today. (Instead) I want to relax.

(3) In interrogative question sentences, the particle "wa" always precedes the interrogative pronouns.

1. テストは、<u>いつ</u>ですか。(When is the test?)

2. おいしいケーキは、<u>どれ</u>ですか。(Which cake is a delicious one?)

3. あの人は、<u>だれ</u>ですか。(Who is that person?)

4. うちは、<u>どこ</u>ですか。(Where is your home?)

5. 田中さんは、<u>どの人</u>ですか。(Which person is Mrs. Tanaka?)

が

(1) The particle "ga" marks the subject of a sentence. The word or phrase that precedes "ga" is new information. It has the effect of demonstrating the speaker's "personal," "subjective," or "immediate" feelings. Words preceding the particle "wa" convey more "objective" or "impersonal" feelings.

1. あ、鳥が鳴いています。(Oh, a bird is singing!)

2. 足が　いたい。(My feet hurt.)

3. あの人は、目が　きれいですね。(She has beautiful eyes.)

4. むこうから　友だちが　来ます。(My friend is approaching.)

5. 祖父は、耳が　悪い。(My grandfather has bad ears / suffers from hard of hearing.)

(2) In the interrogative question sentences, the particle "ga" is always preceded by interrogative pronouns.

1. <u>だれ</u>が　田中さんですか。(Who is Miss Tanaka?)

2. <u>何</u>が　おいしかったですか。(What tasted good?)

3. <u>どの人</u>が、来ますか。(Which person / who is coming?)

4. <u>どこ</u>が、いいですか。(Where is a good place to go?)

5. テストは、<u>いつ</u>が、いいですか。(When is a good time for a test?)

(3) Some predicates take "ga" instead of "wo" for direct objects. They are:

要る(need), 欲しい(want), したい(want to), 見える(can see, visible), 聞こえる(can hear / is audible), 分かる (understandable), できる(can do), 好き(likable), 嫌い (dislikable)

1. お金が要ります。(I need money.)
2. 家が欲しい。(I want a house.)
3. その映画が　見たい。(I want to see that movie.)
4. 富士山が　見えます。(I can see Mt. Fuji.)
5. きれいな　音楽が　聞こえます。(I can hear beautiful music.)
6. 日本語が　分かります。(I understand Japanese.)
7. 英語が　できます。(I know English.)
8. お茶が　好きです。(I like [green] tea.)
9. コーヒーが　嫌いです。(I don't like coffee.)

(4) The subject in a subordinate clause is marked by "ga," when different from the subject of the main clause.

1. 友だちが来ましたから、（私は）いっしょに　テレビをみました。
(Since my friend came, I watched television with him.)
2. 弟が　生まれたとき、母は、３０歳でした。
(When my brother was born, my mother was thirty years old.)
3. 私がその赤ちゃんを見たら　（赤ちゃんは）　泣きました。
(When I looked at the baby, she started crying.)
4. 戸が　開くと、知らない人が、入ってきました。
(When the door opened, someone unknown came in.)

In a relative clause, the subject is marked by "ga."

5. 母が買った時計は、とてもいい時計です。(The watch my mother bought was a very good one.)
6. 私が見た映画は、「さよなら」です。(The movie I saw was "Sayonara.")
7. あの人は、昨日　父が話していた人です。(He is the man with whom my father was speaking yesterday.)
8. これは、去年　私が、買ったハンカチです。(This is the handkerchief I bought last year.)